THE *New* POPULAR
HISTORY
OF THE WORLD
IN TWO VOLUMES

Editorial Advisers

THE *New* POPULAR
HISTORY OF THE WORLD

The Story of Mankind
from Earliest Times to the Present Day

———————

WALLACE E. CALDWELL
Prof. of History, University of North Carolina

EDWARD H. MERRILL
Co-author of "History of the American Way"

Maps by
ERWIN RAISZ
Institute of Geographical Exploration, Harvard University

with an Introduction by LOWELL THOMAS

———————

VOLUME TWO

PUBLISHED BY

THE GREYSTONE PRESS

100 SIXTH AVENUE, NEW YORK 13, N. Y.

Acknowledgments

For many of the illustrations which appear at the end of each chapter, the Publishers make grateful acknowledgment to Mr. Clark Kinnaird, King Features Syndicate, and Prof. Wallace E. Caldwell; also, to Prof. Carl Pegg, for his textual contributions to Chapters 37 and 38.

Library of Congress
Catalog Card Number: 54-12130

Lithographed in the U.S.A. by W. S. Konecky Associates

CONTENTS- - - - - - - - - - - - - - - - - VOLUME TWO

PAGE

CONTENTS------------------VOLUME TWO

PAGE

MAPS IN VOLUME TWO

FIGHTING ON THE BARRICADES

The early 1830's saw many parts of Europe in open rebellion against oppression by reactionary governments. To satisfy their national aspiration the Belgians fought for separation from the Netherlands, and Belgium became a constitutional monarchy in August 1830. Popular uprisings in the Papal States aimed at the formation of an Italian nation, however, were unsuccessful for many years. In Germany, the rulers of Brunswick, Saxony, and other principalities were forced either to resign or to grant more liberal constitutions.

The last of the Bourbon kings of France was overthrown in a series of riots which broke out when the king, Charles X, tried to revive absolutist rule. Spurred by the influential *bourgeoisie,* the French people rose against the king's "four ordinances," which threatened their hard-won civil liberties.

JULY REVOLUTION IN PARIS, 1830

PART VII

The Impact of Political Ideas on Life in Later Modern Times

Two sets of political ideas were prevalent in the minds of men in 1815, the conservative and the liberal. The conservatives wished to restore the absolute monarchies and to repress all ideas of democracy or even of moderate constitutional government.

The liberals derived their concept of government from the ideas of the French Revolution. They fought for constitutional government, for even more democracy, for the equality of all men before the law, and for democratic nationalism in a peaceful fraternity of nations.

In 1815 the conservatives were in power in all the countries of Europe. From 1815 to 1848 the liberals struggled against the conservatives for power and leadership. In the early struggles the liberals won some victories over the conservatives, but in 1848 the conservatives triumphed over the liberals.

From 1848 to 1871 forceful leaders took over the governments of four nations on the Continent. Louis Napoleon overthrew the Second French Republic and established the Second Empire. Cavour and his associates united the Italian people and established the Kingdom of Italy. Bismarck, aided chiefly by von Moltke and von Roon, established the German Empire. Emperor Francis Joseph and Francis Deak changed the Austrian Empire into the Dual Monarchy of Austria-Hungary.

From 1871-1914, the peoples of some countries strengthened democracy, but in others the conservatives succeeded in strengthening autocracy. Great Britain moved steadily toward more democracy. The French overthrew the Second Empire and established the Third French Republic. Italy continued to be a constitutional monarchy. The government of the new German Empire became autocratic and the government of Russia continued autocratic. The Balkan nations secured their independence from Turkey and became constitutional monarchies in theory but autocracies in practice.

During the nineteenth century the Spanish and Portuguese colonies in the New World won their political independence and began their long struggles for more and more democracy.

426

CHAPTER 21

Liberalism Against Conservatism in Europe
(1815-1848)

In 1815 the conservatives led by Metternich of Austria were in power in all the countries of Europe. They were determined to keep their power and leadership by stamping out, if possible, the ideas of the French Revolution. They feared that these ideas might spread and lead to new revolutions which would endanger their power and leadership and disrupt the peace of Europe.

The ideas of the French Revolution were not to be easily suppressed. The armies of the Revolution and of Napoleon had spread the watchwords—Liberty, Equality, and Fraternity—to many peoples throughout Europe. Some of the soldiers in the armies of occupation in France at the close of the Napoleonic Wars were influenced by the democratic effects of the French Revolution. As a result largely of French influences, liberal movements sprang up in every country in Europe. The leaders of the liberals presented programs for political, economic, and humanitarian reforms. Revolutions which broke out in many countries in 1830 were in part successful. The liberal movement reached its climax in 1848. In that year the liberals won some victories, but, in general, the conservatives triumphed.

• • •

Prince Metternich of Austria, the leader of the Conservatives, stated their policies. He was a very wealthy and highly educated nobleman and extremely proud. He was vain enough to think that he was called upon to

preserve absolute monarchy by suppressing legislative bodies, free discussions, liberal education, and by stamping out all revolutions before they could get well under way. At the end of his life he was still convinced that he had never made a mistake. As the leader and spokesman of the conservatives, he was so influential that the years 1815-1848 are often called the Era of Metternich.

In the Austrian Empire he censored all intellectual life. He sponsored laws which forbade the importation into the Austrian Empire of books of a liberal character, such as those which described the government of the United States. Only textbooks which supported the conservative regime were prescribed by the government. Its spies listened to professors' lectures and made lists of all the books they took out of libraries, and turned these lists over to the government. Students had to go to church and to confession, and they were forbidden to discuss political and religious questions in public meetings. No Austrian could travel legally to another country without the permission of the government.

In the German states university students formed secret societies to promote liberalism and German nationalism. In October, 1817, on the three hundredth anniversary of the publication of Luther's theses they held a meeting at Wartburg, where Luther had lived, known as the Wartburg Festival. Here after listening to fiery speeches about liberty, they burned the books, pamphlets, and papers of conservative authors. This demonstration alarmed the conservatives and helped Metternich to get the Diet of the German Confederation to pass the Carlsbad Decrees (1819). They extended to schools and universities in the German states the censorship of education which Metternich had already clamped down upon Austrian schools and universities.

Fear of revolution, which might lead to the overthrow of the conservatives in any country in Europe, led Metternich to oppose war and to favor international co-operation to preserve peace. This co-operation he called the Concert of Europe. He proposed that the leaders of the chief European nations meet in conference from time to time to adjust international disputes that might lead to war. He proposed that when a revolution broke out in any country the leaders should hold a conference. If the conference agreed, then one or more nations who were members of the Concert were to suppress the revolution.

To put the Concert of Europe into practice, Metternich persuaded Russia, Prussia, Austria, and Great Britain to form the Quadruple Alliance (1815). In 1818 France joined them. This alliance held conferences and intervened in Italy and Spain to suppress revolutions. However, the Quadruple Alliance became confused in the minds of many people with a very different organization, the Holy Alliance, which was started by Tsar Alexander I of Russia. At first it included Russia, Prussia, and Austria. The monarchs of these three countries pledged themselves to govern according to the principles of the Christian religion and before long nearly all the countries of Europe joined it. Though the Holy Alliance actually did nothing, many people in every country blamed it for the acts of repression committed by the Quadruple Alliance and so the Holy Alliance became to liberals a symbol of Metternich's policy.

The liberals made vigorous and widespread use of the ideals of the French Revolution. They wrote pamphlets and books and made speeches in which they interpreted the basic ideals of the French Revolution to the peoples of Europe. They said that these ideals—Liberty, Equality, and Fraternity—would meet the needs of the new generation. The chief exponents of nineteenth century liberalism were two Englishmen, Jeremy Bentham and John Stuart Mill.

The liberals presented their program for political reform. They interpreted Liberty, the first ideal of the French Revolution, to mean that all men should be free. This meant that serfdom and slavery should be abolished wherever they existed, that men should be free to express themselves in speech and in writing, and to worship God according to the dictates of their own consciences. The liberals believed also that all men should be equal before the law. To protect personal liberty and equality before the law, they said that the powers of rulers should be limited by constitutions. They believed these constitutions should contain provisions for the election of members to legislative bodies and also the guarantees of liberty and equality and others contained in the American Bill of Rights. At first many of the liberals were not wholly democratic because they believed that only property owners should be allowed to vote. Gradually, however, liberals came to believe in universal manhood suffrage, and later on in suffrage for women.

The liberals presented their program for economic reform. Freedom for the individual meant to the liberal also freedom to work as he chose. In the beginning of their agitation for reform, the liberals opposed any and all government restrictions such as tariffs and regulation of hours of work, wages, and prices. The arguments for the freedom of business from control were based on a theory

Bettmann Archive

JEREMY BENTHAM. Many political and legal reforms in Great Britain resulted in part from the ideas set forth by this English political philosopher in his many publications.

called *laissez faire* (let things alone). The theory was based largely on the ideas contained in the *Wealth of Nations* (1776) by Adam Smith.

The liberals argued that economic laws governed business and they should be permitted to operate free from any kind of interference. Jeremy Bentham said that if everyone is allowed to seek his own profit, then the greatest good will be brought to the greatest number. The capitalist who makes money will invest some of his money to expand his business and some in new enterprises to make more money, and thereby he will furnish work for more workers. He will regulate hours and conditions of labor to secure the best returns on his investment. The worker who sells his labor will get the best return in wages that he can from his employers. Wages, said the liberals, depend upon the law of supply and demand.

One famous English writer, Malthus, in his *Essay on Population* (1789) said that wages would always remain at the level which would permit a worker to earn only a bare living because of competition among workers. As a result of these theories of the liberals, unions and strikes were forbidden by law in Great Britain and France, as they were thought to be unwarranted attempts to interfere with economic laws and with the property rights of employers.

When later experience had proved that *laissez faire* did not work for the good of all, many liberals gradually came to the belief that a certain amount of governmental regulation of economic activities was necessary to protect the interests of all concerned.

The liberals presented their program for humanitarian reforms. The liberals interpreted Fraternity, the third ideal of the French Revolution, to mean that all men are brothers and should help and protect one another. Therefore, it was the duty of more fortunate men to relieve the distress of their less fortunate brothers. To this end they founded private charitable organizations. They endeavored to lessen the harshness of criminal laws and to improve conditions in prisons and in houses for the poor. The anti-slavery movement in Great Britain and the United States grew out of these humanitarian beliefs.

The liberals' campaign for public education was both political and humanitarian. If men were to be given the right to vote, it was necessary that they should be well enough educated to vote with some understanding of public issues. If men were to become skillful workers and to live happily, it was equally necessary that they should be educated.

The missionary movement was a part of the movement for humanitarian reforms. In this movement liberals and conservatives united. For centuries devoted Catholic missionaries had been engaged in spreading Christianity. In the first quarter of the nineteenth century the Catholic missionary movement was carried on more vigorously. Although Protestant missionaries had done some missionary work before 1800, the Protestant missionary movement as an organized movement began at about that time. Most Protestant denominations established boards of foreign missions which sent devoted men and women, many of them doctors, to foreign lands as missionaries. The Catholic and Protestant missionary movements have gained in strength until their efforts have affected the whole world. The accomplishments of these missionaries, priests, preachers, teachers, and doctors who have devoted their lives to the service of the ideals of the missionary movement have been of untold value to the people to whom they ministered. Many missionaries have lost their lives in so doing but a rich harvest has been reaped from their work in the improvement of the conditions of the people with whom and for whom they worked. In the Second World War the lives of many soldiers were saved by people of distant lands among whom these missionaries had worked.

The liberals presented their program for nationalism and internationalism. Fraternity, the third ideal of the French Revolution, the liberals interpreted to mean nationalism also. They defined a nation as a group of people having a common inheritance, a common tradition, a common government, and generally a common language. They believed that the people of each nation had qualities and abilities of their own which should be developed freely for the good of all the peoples. They looked forward to a community of nations working together in peace. Alfred Lord Tennyson, poet laureate of Victorian England, expressed the same idea in these words:

Till the war-drum throbb'd no longer, and the battle-flags were furl'd.
In the Parliament of man, the Federation of the world.

The struggle of the liberals for political independence failed in Northern Italy, Naples, and Spain. Although in 1815 the forces of the conservatives were everywhere in control, the liberal movement soon began to make headway. In 1820 a revolution against autocratic rule broke out in Spain, in Naples which was ruled by a Spanish Bourbon, and in 1821 in Northern Italy which was a part of the Austrian Empire. Under the leadership of Metternich, congresses of all the leading European nations were held for the purpose of making plans to suppress these revolutions as required by his doctrine of intervention. In consequence, Austria suppressed the revolutions in Naples and Northern Italy and France restored the autocratic power of the king in Spain.

The liberal struggle for political independence was successful in the Spanish colonies in America. After a number of revolutions in the Spanish colonies in the Americas, most of them succeeded by 1823 in establishing their political independence. When King Ferdinand of Spain asked the European powers to help restore the Spanish colonies to Spain, the United States (1823) issued the Monroe Doctrine. In it President Monroe warned the European powers that the Western Hemisphere was no longer open to colonization by any of them and that any attempt to interfere with existing governments in the New World would be regarded by the United States as an unfriendly act. When the British, who were building up a profitable trade with the new Latin American republics, now freed from Spanish mercantilism, indicated that they would support the Monroe Doctrine with their fleet, King Ferdinand's proposal for intervention was dropped.,

Bettmann Archive

In this lithograph Honoré Daumier, a famous French caricaturist, pictured the fate of French citizens who opposed Louis Philippe. Daumier himself was imprisoned for six months for caricaturing the king.

The struggle of the liberals in Greece succeeded. For more than three centuries the Turks had ruled the Greeks autocratically. In 1821 they revolted to secure their freedom. After they had been defeated in the first battles, Great Britain, Russia, and France entered the war against the Turks. Liberals in the United States contributed money to aid the Greek cause and Henry Clay, an American statesman, applauded the Greeks. In 1829, after eight years of war, the Turks acknowledged the independence of Greece.

The struggle of the liberals in France succeeded in large part. In 1830 liberal revolts, beginning with an uprising in France, swept over Europe. Louis XVIII, who became king of France for the second time after the Congress of Vienna (1814), ruled with a fair amount of moderation because his powers were limited by the Charter of 1814. His brother, Charles X, who succeeded him (1824) was an out and out political reactionary and autocrat. He wanted to restore the estates and the privileges that the nobles had lost in the French Revolution, and also the absolute power of the king. In July, 1830, he issued three decrees (the July Ordinances) which rigidly controlled the press, dissolved

the Chamber of Deputies, and reduced the number of voters from an already small number, considering the population, to 25,000. In that way, he believed that the July Ordinances would result in the election of candidates favorable to his autocratic program. The opponents of his program led a revolt in Paris (1830), known as the July Revolution, and Charles X, who saw the handwriting on the wall, fled to England in great haste. Instead of establishing a republic, however, the revolutionists, under the leadership of Lafayette, named Louis Philippe, Duke of Orleans, to be king of the French. The years of his reign are called the July Monarchy.

The July Revolution in Paris stimulated the revolutionary spirit in Belgium. In August, 1830, Belgian patriots revolted and Belgian workingmen, after violent fighting, forced the Dutch troops to evacuate Brussels and set up a provisional government which declared Belgium independent of the Kingdom of the Netherlands. In 1831 Great Britain, Russia, Prussia, and Austria signed a treaty in which they recognized the independence of Belgium and promised to respect its neutrality. The Germans violated this treaty (1914) when their armies invaded Belgium.

The struggle of the liberals in Great Britain and the United States resulted in many reforms. In Great Britain the liberals in Parliament passed the Reform Bill of 1832 which granted more people the right to vote and was in effect a peaceful revolution which brought great changes to the government of Great Britain.

The wave of liberalism in Europe reached across the Atlantic Ocean to the United States. In 1828, Andrew Jackson, a man of the people, was elected president. Liberals in some state legislatures succeeded in passing many reform measures, including universal manhood suffrage, public education, and prison reform.

Bitter controversy over slavery resulted in the American Civil War. After the War of 1812 Americans turned their backs on Europe and energetically began the tremendous development of their own country. A wave of westward migration carried thousands of settlers into the Louisiana Purchase territory acquired from France by Jefferson in 1803, and the settlement of Florida, purchased from Spain in 1819, was begun.

From 1815 to 1825 the spirit of nationalism developed. Evidences of this nationalism were the protective tariff of 1816, the chartering of the Second United States Bank, the building of the National Road, the Monroe Doctrine, and the decisions of the Supreme Court under Chief Justice John Marshall. After 1825 a bitter sectionalism arose out of geographical and economic differences between the agricultural South and the commercial and industrial North. The North finally won the support of the West.

During the 1830's William Lloyd Garrison and other abolitionists demanded an end to slavery as they thought it was morally wrong. During the 1840's the question of the extension of slavery into the newly acquired territories in the West became a burning issue in politics. In 1845 Texas, which had acquired its independence from Mexico in 1836, was annexed as a slave state. In 1846 the Oregon country was acquired from Great Britain. In the Mexican War (1846-48), the United States gained the vast Mexican Cession.

During the 1850's further compromise over the problem of the extension of slavery into the territories became impossible. The new Republican party (1854) opposed the extension of slavery into the territories while the southern Democrats claimed slaveholders had a constitutional right to take their slaves into them. After the North elected Abraham Lincoln President in 1860, eleven slave states seceded from the Union, formed the Confederate States of America, and the nation was plunged into the Civil War.

After four years of bloody conflict, the South, unable to secure the military aid it expected from Great Britain, bowed to the North's superior manpower and economic resources and Lee surrendered to Grant at Appomattox on April 9, 1865. Although Lincoln was assassinated on the eve of final victory, his supreme purpose, the preservation of the Union, had been accomplished. The Thirteenth Amendment (1865) confirmed his Emancipation Proclamation.

The struggle of the liberals in the revolution of 1848 in France failed. The revolutions of 1848, like those of 1830, began in France. Louis Philippe, in the first years of his reign as a constitutional monarch, advocated a fairly liberal program. His best known minister was Thiers, a liberal and an historian, who was a great admirer of the French Revolution and Napoleon. Thiers' most celebrated act was to bring the body of Napoleon from St. Helena to Paris, to be laid in a great tomb under the golden dome of the chapel in the Hotel des Invalides, a hospital for disabled soldiers. Guizot, also an historian and prime minister (1840-1848), was a conservative who believed in a high property qualification for voters. He held that the poor should acquire property before being granted the right to vote. He was faced with many new problems which came to France as a result of the spread of the Industrial Revolution to France, especially the problems of the workers in the factories and growing cities.

French liberals gave much attention to the way to bring the new industries under the control of government and to improve the conditions of the workers. Many other Frenchmen still believed in the principles of *laissez faire*. One group, including Saint-Simon and Fourier, advocated Utopian Socialism after Sir Thomas More's *Utopia,* an

English book (published in the sixteenth century) which described an ideal society.

Fourier proposed the establishment of small communities each of which would own land and factories where all would work and share equally in the profits. So fervently did Fourier believe in his own proposal that he went home every day at noon to see whether a rich man had come to finance one or more of these communities. The rich man never came, but numerous communities of this kind were formed in the United States, including Brook Farm near Boston and the Oneida Community in central New York. The phrases often quoted today: "From each according to his abilities and to each according to his needs" and "production for use not for profit" were stated by these early socialists. Louis Blanc, another French socialist, declared that every man had a right to employment and proposed that the government should establish workshops in whose management and profits the workers should share.

Guizot, the prime minister, opposed all reforms and even attempted to stop the liberals from discussing reforms of any kind. These attempts caused so much unrest that in February, 1848, the workers revolted and set up barricades in the streets of Paris. When Louis Philippe saw that the revolutionists had control of the city of Paris, he abdicated in favor of his son. The republicans and socialists quarreled with each other. The revolutionists proclaimed a republic and the nephew of Napoleon Bonaparte, Louis Napoleon, who posed as a liberal, was elected president of the Second French Republic. On December 2, 1852, the anniversary of the coronation of Napoleon I, Louis Napoleon declared himself Napoleon III, Emperor of the French. Once again in France, liberalism had failed.

Revolutions in 1848 in other countries in Europe failed. The February revolution in Paris in 1848 was the spark that touched off a number of revolutionary explosions in other countries. Riots broke out in Vienna and (March 14, 1848) Metternich fled to London. Hungarians, under the leadership of Louis Kossuth, established a self-governing state within the Austrian Empire. Bohemia did likewise. While uprisings were taking place in Berlin, the king of Prussia promised the people a liberal constitution. Revolutionary movements took place in most of the small German states, in Denmark, and in the Netherlands. Revolutions broke out in almost all the Italian states. The people of Milan and of Venice rose up and drove the Austrians out of their cities. Charles Albert, king of Sardinia, granted his people a liberal constitution, declared war on Austria, and tried to drive the Austrians out of Italy. He received detachments of troops from the other Italian states. Hopes were high for a unification of Italy under liberal leadership. At the high point of liberal success the leaders of the liberals in the German states persuaded the Diet of the German Confederation to call a German national assembly to draw up a liberal federal constitution for Germany. This assembly met at Frankfort in May, 1848.

In spite of these successes, the liberals failed almost everywhere. Most of them were of the middle class and they failed to get or to hold the support of the laboring classes and the peasants. They wasted time quarreling among themselves about abstract ideas on government and constitutional promises. The conservatives, with the assistance, in most cases, of the army, quickly regained control in the countries in which revolutions had broken out.

An Austrian army restored order in Bohemia. Another defeated the Italians under Charles Albert, suppressed the revolts in Lombardy and Venetia, and restored the rulers of the other Italian states to their full power. A reactionary government supported by military force secured control of Vienna. The new Hungarian state, weakened by internal quarrels between the Magyars and the Croats, was crushed by a Russian army that came to the aid of Austria. Kossuth, the revolutionary leader in Hungary, fled to Turkey, then he went to England and later to the United States where he was received as a great patriot. He spent his last years in exile in Italy.

The king of Prussia granted his people a constitution, but it placed most of the power in the hands of the wealthier citizens. Austria helped most of the other German rulers to put down the liberal movements in their states. The Frankfort Assembly tried to make the king of Prussia emperor of Germany. He refused the title partly because it was accompanied by a liberal constitution and partly because he was aware of the opposition of Austria. The Frankfort Assembly thus failed completely. Many German liberals fled to the United States.

But liberalism did not suffer a complete defeat. Sardinia kept its liberal constitution. Switzerland which had been affected by the liberal movement emerged as a democratic federal republic. The people of Denmark and the Netherlands kept the gains which they had made. Nevertheless, it seemed to the world as if liberalism had failed in 1848.

SUMMARY

The years 1815-1848 witnessed a struggle between liberals and conservatives for leadership in Europe. In 1815 the conservatives, led by Metternich of Austria, were in control in all the countries of Europe. He proposed the Concert of Europe and promoted the Quadruple Alliance both of which were designed to crush revolutionary movements in any country in Europe. In the Austrian Empire he suppressed liberal books and liberal teachings in schools and universities. After a demonstration by liberal German students at the Wartburg Festival (1817) had alarmed the conservatives, he influenced the Diet of the German Confederation to pass the Carlsbad Decrees which outlawed all liberalism in German education.

The ideas of the liberals were based on the principles of the French Revolution. They believed that all men should be free and equal before the law. They advocated constitutions limiting the power of rulers and providing for the election of legislative bodies. They believed in the principle of laissez faire, that business should be free from government restrictions and that all men should be free to work as they chose. They worked for humanitarian reforms and for the promotion of public education. The missionary movement was a part of the movement for humanitarian reform in which both liberals and conservatives united. The liberals believed in nationalism and at the same time in a community of nations working together in peace.

The first attempts of the liberals to secure political power failed when revolutions in Spain, Northern Italy, and Naples were suppressed. They won victories in the Spanish colonies in America and also in Greece, France, Great Britain, and the United States. Elsewhere the conservative forces were victorious.

The revolution of 1830 in France resulted in the establishment of the middle-class monarchy of Louis Philippe. From 1830-1840 his prime minister was Thiers, a liberal historian, who was a great admirer of the French Revolution and Napoleon. He was succeeded by Guizot (1840-1848), also an historian, but a conservative. The spread of the Industrial Revolution in France during this period led to much discussion of the problems it caused. Some men favored Utopian Socialism. Louis Blanc advocated a form of state socialism. Guizot's attempts to suppress all discussion of reform brought on the revolution of 1848.

This started as a liberal movement and resulted in the overthrow of Louis Philippe and the establishment of the Second French Republic. Louis Napoleon, however, was elected president and soon transformed the republic into the Second Empire.

The revolution in France was followed by liberal outbreaks in Austria, Hungary, Bohemia, Prussia, many smaller German states, Denmark, the Netherlands, and the Italian states. The revolts were put down in most countries. After the failure of the liberals in the revolutions of 1848, powerful leaders rose to leadership in France, Italy, and Germany.

EVENTS THAT TOOK PLACE AT ABOUT THE SAME TIME

1815

Holy Alliance and Quadruple Alliance formed, 1815.	Metternich (1773-1859) leading figure in European politics, 1815-1848.
Wartburg Festival, 1817.	Carlsbad Decrees, 1819.
Revolutions in Northern Italy and Greece, 1821	Revolutions in Spain and Naples, 1820.
Greek independence recognized by Turkey, 1829.	Congress of Troppau, 1820.
	Congress of Verona, 1822.
Belgian Revolution, 1830.	Monroe Doctrine proclaimed, 1823.
Independence of Belgium recognized by leading powers, 1831.	July Ordinances—July Revolution in France, 1830.
Guizot (1787-1874), French historian and statesman.	Louis Philippe king, 1830-1848.
Growth of Utopian Socialism of St. Simon and Fourier accompanied the rapid industrialization of France.	Thiers (1797-1877) French historian and statesman opposed to Guizot.
	Body of Napoleon brought back from St. Helena to Paris, 1840.
Revolutions in Austrian Empire, Italian, and German states, 1848.	Revolution of 1848 in France. Second French Republic created. Louis Napoleon elected president.

NEW HARMONY EXPERIMENT. Above, the School of Industry, New Harmony, Indiana, part of an early Socialist colony.

ROBERT OWEN. Right, the British reformer who established New Harmony and inspired, by his economic theories, other experiments in community planning.

REVOLUTION OF 1848 IN FRANCE. Above, street crowds before the Hotel de Ville in Paris, at the proclamation of the Second Republic.

PRINCE METTERNICH. The old order in Europe was skillfully restored by Metternich at the Congress of Vienna.

PRESIDENT MONROE. A new order for the Western Hemisphere was instituted by Monroe with his Doctrine closing the Americas to European colonization.

PRESIDENT JACKSON. Election of "Old Hickory" brought a new popular power to Washington.

Nationalism and Forceful Political Leaders in Europe (1848-1871)

From 1848 to 1871 forceful political leaders in France, Italy, Germany, and the Austrian Empire sponsored great changes intended to benefit their countries.

In France, Louis Napoleon revived the Napoleonic tradition, overthrew the Second Republic, and established the Second Empire. He tried to strengthen France and to increase its pride and prestige. His defeat in the Franco-Prussian War ended the Second Empire. Its successor was the Third French Republic.

In Italy, Cavour, the prime minister; Garibaldi, a colorful warrior; and Victor Emmanuel II, a wise king, united the Italian people and established the kingdom of Italy, a constitutional and hereditary monarchy.

In Germany, the skillful political leadership of Bismarck, aided by the military leadership of von Moltke and von Roon, united all the German states except Austria and established the German Empire. In the Austrian Empire the emperor, Francis Joseph, and the Hungarian leader, Francis Deak, by their intelligent and conservative handling of its problems established the Dual Monarchy of Austria-Hungary.

• • •

Louis Napoleon overthrew the Second Republic and established the Second Empire. He was the son of Napoleon's brother Louis, whom Napoleon had made king of Holland before annexing it to France. In his adventurous life he had taken part in unsuccessful revolutionary uprisings in Italy, and twice he had tried, but unsuccessfully, to overthrow the monarchy of Louis Philippe. After the second of these attempts, he was imprisoned in the fortress of Ham from which he escaped to England. He wrote a book on Napoleonic ideas in which he had glorified his uncle and another one, *The Abolition of Poverty,* in which he set forth his own ideas for the improvement of the condition of tne poor. When the revolution of 1848 broke out, he left England and returned to France where he was one of the candidates for president of the Second French Republic. The traditions of the great days of the Napoleonic Empire were still strong in France; the evil side had been forgotten. When an old Frenchman was asked why he had voted for Louis Napoleon in 1848, he replied, "Should I not vote for this gentleman? I, whose nose was frozen at Moscow." The 7,000,000 Frenchmen who voted for him elected him president of the Second French Republic for a four-year term.

While president, Louis Napoleon courted the favor of all the people—workers, radicals, and conservatives alike. By taking advantage of a bitter controversy (1850) in the Legislative Assembly over universal manhood suffrage, he made himself appear to be the champion of universal manhood suffrage. After the Assembly had, at his suggestion, passed a law depriving many people of the

EMPEROR NAPOLEON III. Louis Napoleon Bonaparte, the nephew of Napoleon Bonaparte, was President of the Second French Republic and Emperor of the Second Empire.

right to vote, he posed as the champion of universal manhood suffrage by attacking it for depriving many men of the right to vote.

In December, 1851, a year before his term of office expired, he requested the Legislative Assembly to repeal the provision in the constitution which made a president ineligible for re-election. After the Assembly refused his request, Louis Napoleon used his power over the army and the police to carry out a *coup d'état*. He had some of his opponents arrested, dissolved the Legislative Assembly, and seized printing presses and the postal and telegraph systems. About three weeks after his *coup d'état,* the voters of France in a plebiscite (7,500,000 to 640,000) authorized Louis Napoleon to draw up a new constitu-

tion. It provided that he should be president for ten years. On November 21, 1852, another plebiscite was held in which the voters voted to end the Second French Republic and to make France a hereditary empire with Louis Napoleon as emperor. On December 2, 1852, the anniversary of the coronation of Napoleon Bonaparte, Louis Napoleon was proclaimed Napoleon III, Emperor of the French. The period of his rule is known as the Second Empire.

The Second Empire (1852-1870) had a brief blaze of glory. The Second Empire during its first years contributed greatly to French national pride. The Industrial Revolution was now in full swing. Many railroads were being built and new industries were being developed. Rising prices for agricultural products needed by workers in industries brought prosperity to the peasants. Louis Napoleon carried out an extensive program of public works. Paris was rebuilt, streets were widened, and new boulevards built. All this construction provided work for the poor. An imperial court, presided over by the beautiful and charming Empress Eugenie, was established. The styles in dress and furniture in vogue during the Second Empire were copied in many parts of the world.

For a time Napoleon III's foreign policies proved to be successful both at home and abroad. In 1853 the sultan of Turkey, acting on advice from Great Britain and France, refused the Tsar's demand that he be permitted to protect Greek Catholics throughout the Turkish Empire. After the Tsar's armies invaded Turkish territory, Turkey declared (1853) war on Russia. The Russians seemed to be winning the war and Constantinople was threatened. This brought the British into the war. Louis Napoleon entered the war because he had a personal grudge against the Tsar and also a desire to compensate for the national humiliation caused by the Russian invasion of France (1814-1815). Great Britain and France sent their war fleets and troops into the Black Sea to take the naval base of Sevastopol which the Russians needed for any future attack on Constantinople.

This war is known as the Crimean War (1854-1856) because most of the fighting took place near Sevastopol in the Crimean peninsula. After a siege of eleven months, a murderous land assault captured Sevastopol at the sacrifice of about half a million men, many of whom died from food poisoning and lack of sanitary and hospital care. Under the direction of Florence Nightingale, women nurses were placed in British army hospitals. They greatly reduced the mortality rate among British soldiers by the use of up-to-date methods of sanitation and hygiene. France and Great Britain defeated Russia and peace was made at the Congress of Paris (1856). In the Treaty of Paris (1856) the Black Sea was neutralized. War vessels were prohibited, but merchant vessels were free to enter it. The Danube River was to be open to the navigation of the ships of all countries. The treaty was very humilating to Russia. The Congress of Paris brought great glory to the emperor because he was host to the many distinguished statesmen and diplomats whom he welcomed and entertained. He presided at the sessions of the Congress.

Louis Napoleon gained the favor of the French imperialists by completing the annexation of Algeria (1857) begun by Louis Philippe and by gaining a foothold in Indo-China (1858). As in the time of Napoleon Bonaparte, France again enjoyed great prestige as the greatest military power in Europe.

The Second Empire ended in complete disaster. In the latter part of his reign, Louis Napoleon's foreign policy involved him in serious troubles at home and in war abroad. To help the cause of Italian unity and to gain land for France and prestige for himself, he

Bettmann Archive

FLORENCE NIGHTINGALE SUPERVISING THE HOSPITAL AT SCUTARI, TURKEY, DURING THE CRIMEAN WAR.

aided the kingdom of Sardinia in a war against Austria. Because his intervention met with the opposition of the Pope, he made himself unpopular with Catholics at home. To offset this unpopularity, he promised to help Catholic Poland in its effort to gain its independence from Russia. This promise offended Russia and Prussia. When Prussia objected and threatened war, he withdrew his promise and thereby earned the censure of both liberals and Catholics in France.

To increase his power and prestige abroad, he tried to make Archduke Maximilian (brother of Francis Joseph of Austria) emperor of Mexico. However, when the United States, freed from the burden of the War Between the States, called Napoleon's attention to the Monroe Doctrine and threatened to send troops into Mexico, Louis Napoleon withdrew his support of Maximilian. After Maximilian had been captured and shot by the Mexicans, the imperialists at home and also the Austrians blamed Louis Napoleon for his death.

In an effort to regain his domestic popularity he allowed France in 1870 to be drawn into a war with Prussia. The French army was decisively defeated at Sedan (1870), Napoleon III was captured and imprisoned by the Germans, and deposed by the provisional government of France that had been

Bettmann Archive

FIRST MEETING OF GARIBALDI AND MAZ-
ZINI. Garibaldi (on the left) was a picturesque man;
Mazzini an eloquent orator.

set up after his capture. When released from
prison, he went to England where he died.
The Second Empire had begun in a blaze of
glory, but it ended in complete disaster for
the French people.

**A divided Italy was under the control
of a number of rulers.** To understand conditions in Italy when its leaders began their
work of unification, we must go back to the
Congress of Vienna. It had restored all of the
old rulers in Italy that had been deposed
during the era of the French Revolution and
Napoleon. It restored the king of Sardinia to
the kingdom of Sardinia (Piedmont, Northwestern Italy, and the island of Sardinia).
His capital was Turin in Piedmont. It ceded
the Italian provinces of Lombardy and
Venetia to Austria. It restored the rulers of
the small duchies in Central Italy. It returned

to the Pope the Papal States stretching from
Rome to the Adriatic. It restored the reactionary and oppressive rule of a branch of the
Bourbons to the kingdom of the Two Sicilies
which consisted of the southern part of Italy
and the island of Sicily.

In spite of these restorations, some of
which the people did not want, the spirit of
Italian nationalism that had been fostered by
the French Revolution and by Napoleon, who
had established a kingdom of Italy, helped to
keep alive the idea of a united Italy in the
minds of Italian patriots. One of these was
Mazzini.

**Mazzini (1805-1872) tried to establish
a republic.** After the Congress of Vienna,
the small states in Italy were ruled chiefly by
Austrians who were under the control of
Metternich. As he urged them to suppress all
liberals and liberal ideas, they tried to do
away with all the liberalism of the French
Revolution and Napoleon. Police and spies
ferreted out liberals, who were forbidden to
read liberal books or write or talk on liberal
subjects.

The persecution of liberals led to the formation of secret societies. One of these was
the Carbonari (charcoal burners). In 1820
the members of the Carbonari were spreading
liberal ideas far and wide and working for
the development of unity. They took part in
the revolution (1820) which Austria, acting
as the agent of the Concert of Europe,
crushed with much bloodshed.

In 1831 Mazzini, a liberal who had been
put in prison and later on exiled, founded,
while in France, a new society, Young Italy,
which former members of the Carbonari
joined. In a few years probably 60,000 young
Italian liberals were members. They went
amongst the Italian people almost with the
zeal of missionaries. With religious fervor
they tried to arouse enthusiasm for the liberation and unification of Italy. The purpose

of Young Italy was to unify the states of Italy under a republican form of government.

Mazzini was a great idealist who consecrated his life to the cause of liberalism and international peace. He spent most of his life in exile in London where he wrote many pamphlets and letters to further the causes in which he believed. He carried on a voluminous correspondence with the leaders of Young Italy and stirred up many minor uprisings. He was a fiery and eloquent orator who was able to arouse the emotions of his hearers.

His ideas on the unification of Italy met with opposition among Italian liberals who were not agreed on the form of government of a united Italy. One group of Italian patriots was in favor of a federal state under the presidency of the Pope. Another and more powerful group was in favor of a constitutional monarchy under the liberal king of Sardinia. This lack of unity among Italian patriots made the unification of Italy impossible at this time.

In 1848, the year of many revolutions in Europe, Charles Albert, king of Sardinia, granted a constitution to his subjects. His army took part in the revolution of 1848 in Italy against the rule of Austria, but the Austrians defeated it. Because he had granted a constitution to Sardinia and attempted to oust Austria from Italy, many Italians looked upon him as the leader of a movement for Italian unity, but after his army was defeated by Austria he abdicated in favor of his liberal son, Victor Emmanuel II.

In 1849 Mazzini established a republic in the city of Rome, but it was shortly overthrown by a French army. The republican movement was discredited, the Pope was offended and turned against Italian unity, and most advocates of Italian unity turned to Victor Emmanuel II, the king of Sardinia, for leadership.

Victor Emmanuel II (1820-1878) and Cavour (1810-1861) strengthened the kingdom of Sardinia. Victor Emmanuel II was a sincere and honest king, and Count Cavour, his prime minister, was one of the great statesmen of Europe. In early life Cavour, who had been educated as an army engineer, retired from the army (1831) and devoted himself to the management of his family estate and to scientific farming. Meanwhile he became interested in building factories, mills, railways, and even operating steamships on Lake Maggiore. He was now one of the Italian patriots who advocated the development of Italian unity under the king of Sardinia. His interest in the development of Italian unity led him to found (1847) *Il Risorgimento* (The Resurrection), a newspaper devoted to that cause. He had persuaded (1848) Charles Albert, king of Sardinia, to give Sardinia a liberal constitution.

After the failure of the revolution of 1848 against Austria, Cavour entered the cabinet under Victor Emmanuel II and soon became his prime minister. He built railroads, promoted industries, encouraged trade, and strengthened the Sardinian army. He took the kingdom of Sardinia into the Crimean War (1855). A victory which the small Sardinian army won caused an outburst of patriotic enthusiasm in the kingdom. But Cavour's main purpose in entering the war was to gain a seat at the peace conference where he would have an opportunity to present the cause of Italian unity to the statesmen of Europe. This he did in a stirring speech at the Congress of Paris (1856). It helped to arouse public opinion in Europe for Italy and against Austria. His eloquence and the great ability he showed as a diplomat helped him to win the sympathy of Great Britain and the friendship of Louis Napoleon.

Shortly after the Congress of Paris, Cavour and Louis Napoleon made a secret treaty

Unification of Italy

In contrast to the great kingdoms of Europe, Italy was still a patchwork of small duchies, kingdoms, and the Papal States. It was united under the leadership of Cavour and Garibaldi and the king of Sardinia became king of Italy. The new unified kingdom of Italy became in time one of the great European powers.

(1858) against Austria, which bound Louis Napoleon to assist the kingdom of Sardinia in a war against Austria if Austria attacked Sardinia. In return for this assistance (if given) Sardinia was to cede the provinces of Savoy and Nice, which were largely French in population, to France. Cavour's problem was to get Austria to declare war on Sardinia because if it did public opinion would be on his side and make more certain the aid promised by Louis Napoleon. This he accomplished by skillful diplomatic tactics that caused Austria to make the outrageous demand that Sardinia disband its army, and when Sardinia refused Austria declared war (1859). Although Napoleon came to Sardinia's aid, he did not completely fulfill his

agreements. After two unusually bloody battles, Cavour signed a treaty of peace with Austria in which Austria ceded the Austrian province of Lombardy to Sardinia, but kept the province of Venetia. The kingdom of Sardinia ceded Savoy and Nice to France.

This partial victory of Sardinia led to successful revolts in the duchies in Central Italy and in one of the Papal States. The revolutionists drove their rulers out and then by plebiscites voted to join the kingdom of Sardinia, now well on its way to becoming the kingdom of Italy. A spectacular episode completed the process.

Garibaldi (1807-1882) and his Red Shirts conquered the kingdom of the Two Sicilies. The achievements of Garibaldi and his supporters in their efforts to conquer the kingdom of the Two Sicilies were spectacular and picturesque. Garibaldi was a devoted follower of Mazzini. As a member of Young Italy he had engaged in uprisings and had been driven into exile. He went to South America where he engaged in local uprisings against rulers of the new republics. He returned wearing a red shirt to take part in the republican movement (1848-1849) only to flee again, this time to New York. In 1859 he went to Genoa to work again for Italian unity. Because Mazzini favored a republican form of government for Italy, he could not be won over to the unification of Italy under the kingdom of Sardinia, but Garibaldi and many of his supporters, who wanted above all the unity of Italy were won over to the side of Cavour and his supporters.

In 1860 with a reckless band of volunteers (Red Shirts) and with the private but not public support of Cavour, Garibaldi sailed from Genoa for Sicily where he landed his Red Shirts under the protection of British warships. The Sicilians rallied to his support. In a very skillful and dramatic maneuver his motley army crossed the Straits of Messina into Italy. The army of the king of the Two Sicilies melted away before Garibaldi's army and the king fled into exile. After a Sardinian army that had come down from the north had joined forces with Garibaldi, they captured Naples.

Victor Emmanuel II established the Kingdom of Italy (1861). Garibaldi might have become the dictator of a new republic, but in the interest of Italian unity he handed over his conquests to Victor Emmanuel II who established the Kingdom of Italy with himself as king. Rome, garrisoned by French troops since 1849, was governed by the Pope and the province of Venetia in Northern Italy was still under the reactionary rule of Austria.

Cavour died from overwork (1861) but his task was accomplished. He died saying, "Italy is made." An American historian said of him, "In his ability to get as many as possible, even against their will, to fight under his banner, he has had no equal save Abraham Lincoln."

In 1866 Prussia, abetted by Louis Napoleon, made a military alliance with Italy in which Italy agreed to join Prussia within three months with Venetia as a reward if war broke out between Austria and Prussia. In 1866 Austria declared war on Prussia. In the Austro-Prussian War which followed Italy fought on the side of Prussia and gained Venetia (1866). In 1870 after the French government had withdrawn the French garrison from Rome to take part in the Franco-Prussian War, the forces of the Kingdom of Italy entered Rome and it was made the capital of a united Italy. After the end of the First World War, the Paris Peace Conference (1919) ceded Trieste at the head of the Adriatic and the province of Trentino, a part of the Tyrol, to Italy, and thus the unification of Italy was complete after 100 years of agitation and struggle.

In Germany strong leaders unified the German states into the German Empire. To understand the background on which these leaders built, we must remember that the Holy Roman Empire of the German Nation had failed to unite the German states into a nation. In 1648 they numbered more than 300, all poverty stricken and desolated by the ravages of the Thirty Years' War. In the 100 years that followed, two powerful German states, Austria and Prussia, rose to power. Prussia had become a strong state through the efforts of Frederick William, the Great Elector, and Frederick the Great. Austria, the chief rival of Prussia, had become a strong state through the efforts of the Hapsburg dynasty.

In 1848 Austria itself was very small in area. The location of its capital, Vienna, on the Danube helped to make it a city of great commercial importance. Its Hapsburg emperor was also king of Bohemia and Hungary and ruler of Lombardy and Venetia in Northeastern Italy. The vast extent of the non-Germanic possessions of the Hapsburgs made them unacceptable to the other German states as rulers, but even so they occupied a dominant position among them. Because the Hapsburgs were very likely to lose this dominant position if the German states united, they opposed their unification and feared the formation of a strong German nation.

In the German states, as in Italy, the French Revolution and the work of Napoleon aroused desires for democracy and national unity. Napoleon abolished a great number of the smaller German states and formed some of them into the Kingdom of Westphalia and the Confederation of the Rhine. The Congress of Vienna at the close of the Napoleonic Wars did not restore independence to all of them. Instead it established a German Confederation of thirty-eight states dominated by Austria.

Bettmann Archive

COUNT HELMUTH VON MOLTKE. As head of the Prussian General Staff he planned the strategy used in the three wars that brought about the unification of Germany.

German liberals tried to unite the German states. They struggled valiantly to bring about reforms and to unite the German states into a nation, but without success. After the failure of the Frankfort Assembly (1849), many of the liberal leaders fled to the United States where some of them, notably Carl Schurz, played an important part in history. German unification was accomplished after 1849 by the conservatives under the leadership of a strong man, Otto von Bismarck (1815-1898).

Bismarck believed the German states should be united under Prussian leadership. In 1862 Otto von Bismarck became prime minister of Prussia. He had already had a varied career. As a youth and university student he was known for his escapades and his fondness for dueling. As he grew to manhood he settled down, married, and became

deeply religious and an extreme reactionary. He believed in the divine right of kings, was devoted to Prussia, and opposed uniting the German states. He bitterly opposed the Frankfort Assembly. After its dissolution, he entered the service of the king of Prussia as a member of the Diet of the German Confederation. There he learned that Austria feared Prussia and was determined to keep it in a subordinate position. His experiences converted him to a program of German unification under Prussian leadership with Austria excluded. Visits to Great Britain and France, a term as ambassador to Russia (1856-1861) and to France (1861) gave him considerable knowledge of political conditions in Europe. In 1862 King William I called him home from France to deal with a crisis in the Prussian government.

During the revolution of 1848, the king of Prussia had granted the people a constitution. It provided for a parliament elected by popular vote, but under a three-class voting system which was supposed to give the majority to wealthy citizens. In spite of this system, the liberals elected to parliament were in the majority. They opposed an increase in the size of the army and refused to vote money to run the government until their wishes were recognized. Bismarck had a strong belief in the greatness of Prussia and in Prussian leadership of the Germans and also supreme confidence in himself as leader of Prussia. He brushed aside the protests of the liberals and raised money without its being voted.

In his first speech he said, "Not through fine speeches and majority resolutions will the questions of the hour be decided . . . but by Blood and Iron." William I, king of Prussia, gave Bismarck loyal, even eager support, and so did von Roon, minister of war, and von Moltke, the ablest general of the times. Bismarck was wise enough to make full use

Germany, like Italy, was also a patchwork of small kingdoms and duchies, among which Austria and Prussia fought for supremacy. After Austria was defeated (1866) and the war against France was won (1871), the German states were united into an empire under the Prussian king. It became a strong military power, whose boundless ambition later on helped launch the First World War.

of the enthusiasm for German nationalism that had been developed by the liberals. Unity of language, the centuries-old tradition of German military glory which went back even to the days of Caesar, and pride in the great works of German literature, particularly the writings of Goethe and Schiller, were the great sources of German nationalism. By this time nearly all Germans desired some form of unity among the German states.

Prussia was the largest of the German states. It had a glorious military tradition, particularly in the wars of Frederick the Great. Queen Louise had been a leader in liberating the Germans from the control of Napoleon. In 1833 Prussia established the Zollverein (tariff union) that joined all the German states except Austria in economic unity. A group of intellectual leaders headed by the historian Treitschke at the University of Berlin lectured to students on the historic right of Prussia to lead the German states.

PARIS DURING THE FRANCO-PRUSSIAN WAR. Citizens standing in line in front of a butcher shop to receive daily ration of meat.

Making skillful use of all these factors and others, Bismarck tried hard to make German unification under Prussian leadership acceptable to the other German states.

The chief obstacles to German unity were: the small states feared the power of Prussia; Catholic states of the south—Bavaria, Württemberg, and Baden—distrusted Lutheran Prussia; and Austria was very hostile to any movement that would tend to destroy its dominant power among the German states.

Bismarck's threefold program for the unification of the German states was a success. He proposed to expel Austria from the German Confederation; to annex many small states to Prussia; and to combine the remaining states into a strong union with William I, king of Prussia, as emperor. He carried out his program by a shrewd combination of diplomacy and war. After picking a quarrel

with Denmark over the possession of two duchies (Schleswig and Holstein), he persuaded Austria to join in the war which followed. Easily victorious in that war, he stirred up trouble with Austria over the division of the spoils. As a result, Austria declared war on Prussia in 1866. Bismarck persuaded Great Britain and France to remain neutral and made a military alliance with the new kingdom of Italy. Most of the smaller German states joined with Austria. The Austrians were defeated at Königgrätz (1866) and in seven weeks Prussia had won the war. The military skill of von Moltke had given Prussia a quick victory.

By the Peace of Prague at the end of the war, Bismarck annexed Hanover, Schleswig-Holstein, and other states to Prussia. Austria was forced to cede Venetia to Italy. These annexations united the original territories of

Prussia with those small territories it had gained on the Rhine by earlier wars and by the Congress of Vienna (1815). Now Prussia reached from Russia on the east to France on the west. It was by far the largest and most powerful of the German states. Bismarck also united the north German states including Prussia into a North German Confederation under the presidency of the king of Prussia; Austria and the south German states were excluded from the Confederation.

In 1870 the Spanish throne was vacant and Prince Leopold of Hohenzollern accepted it. Most Frenchmen thought that the national security of France would be endangered by having a Hohenzollern on the throne of Spain. Louis Napoleon sent the French ambassador to visit the Prussian king at Ems to ask Leopold to withdraw his acceptance. The king refused, but sent a secret messenger to tell Leopold what had happened. On July 12, 1870, Prince Leopold withdrew his acceptance. Napoleon III then made the mistake of asking William to promise that he would not allow a Hohenzollern prince to become a candidate again. When the French ambassador presented this request, the king politely refused. The king reported his interview to Bismarck in Berlin in a telegram, known as the Ems Dispatch.

By making some changes in the king's telegram when he gave it to the press, Bismarck made it appear that King William had insulted the French ambassador. France rose in wrath at this "red rag to the Gallic bull" and declared war in 1870. The North German Confederation and the south German states joined Prussia in the war against France. The careful military preparation of von Roon and the ability of General von Moltke gave Prussia a very great advantage in the war known as the Franco-Prussian War (1870-1871). Napoleon III was decisively defeated at Sedan and Paris surrendered after a bitter siege.

Bettmann Archive

BISMARCK, THIERS, AND JULES FAVRE DISCUSSING THE SURRENDER OF PARIS TO THE GERMANS.

The siege was made famous by the use of carrier pigeons for sending messages in and out of the city, and by the use of balloons for observation and transport.

After the German victory over France, the south German states that had been excluded from the North German Confederation by the Peace of Prague agreed to join with the North German Confederation in the creation of the German Empire. The only German state outside of the German Empire was Austria. In the great Hall of Mirrors in the palace of Louis XIV at Versailles on January 18, 1871, Bismarck read the imperial decrees proclaiming William IV of Prussia, Emperor William I of the German Empire. The Hohenzollern dynasty had at last succeeded in uniting the German states.

In May, 1871, Bismarck and Thiers, head of the French provisional government, met in the palace at Versailles to negotiate terms of peace. King William and von Moltke insisted that Bismarck demand that France cede Alsace, most of Lorraine, and the city of Belfort to Germany and also pay a huge indemnity. Bismarck did not want to demand the cession of so much of Lorraine because it contained so many French inhabitants. He said, "I do not like so many Frenchmen in our house against their will." Thiers was bitterly opposed to ceding so much territory to the German Empire. At a tense point in the heated negotiations, he said, "These negotiations are nothing but a sham. Make war then! Ravage our provinces, burn, slaughter! . . . We will fight you to our last breath. We may be defeated, but at least we will not be dishonored." Bismarck was somewhat alarmed at Thiers' attitude and he feared also that other European powers who were disturbed by Prussia's astounding victory might intervene. Consequently, he gave up the demand for the cession of Belfort. The terms of peace were then agreed upon at Versailles and the French and Germans signed the treaty of peace at Frankfort (May 10, 1871). By this treaty the French provinces of Alsace and most of Lorraine were ceded to the German Empire. France agreed to pay an indemnity of $1,000,-000,000 and to pay the expenses of a German army of occupation until the indemnity was paid.

The Austrian Empire was changed into the constitutional monarchy of Austria-Hungary. In 1848 Emperor Francis Joseph who was head of the Hapsburg dynasty lived in his capital in Vienna. He was a sickly young man who succeeded to the throne of the Austrian Empire in 1848. He was not expected to live long and many thought that when he died the Austrian Empire would fall apart. To the great surprise of all, he proved to be an able leader and lived until 1916. He ruled Germans in Austria, Italians in Lombardy and Venetia, Magyars in Hungary, Poles in Galicia, Czechs in Bohemia, Serbs and Croats in Croatia, and also other groups of Slavs in the German states and Italy. His power and influence were great.

From 1859 to 1867 he saw his power in Italy destroyed by the wars with Italy and the founding of the kingdom of Italy and his power in the German states stripped from him by the war with Prussia which led to the formation of the North German Confederation. What was more he saw that his power within his own country was beginning to grow weaker. Consequently, he had to come to terms with his own subjects, many of whom were greatly discontented with his autocratic rule.

In 1848 an upsurge of nationalism had caused revolts in the kingdoms of Bohemia and Hungary, which he suppressed. The kingdom of Bohemia was abolished, Bohemia was annexed to Austria, and Austria made efforts to stamp out Czech nationalism. The kingdom of Hungary, however, was so strong that Austria could not abolish it. Under the leadership of Francis Deak, a strong and able Magyar, Hungary continued to struggle for its independence.

Francis Joseph met the first test of his strength as emperor in the struggle with Deak, the Magyar leader. After long continued negotiations they reached an agreement called the Compromise of 1867. By it the Austrian Empire was changed into the Dual Monarchy of Austria-Hungary in which powers formerly wielded by Austria alone were divided between the Germans in Austria and the Magyars in Hungary. Austria contained Poles, Czechs, Slovenes, and Italians in addition to the Germans who were the most numerous racial group. Over the Austrian part of the Dual Monarchy Francis Joseph was emperor. He was also king of Hungary, which contained a Magyar majority and also Slovaks, Rumanians, Ruthenians, and other minority groups.

Under the Compromise of 1867 each monarchy had its own parliament and cabinet. The Dual Monarchy had ministers of war, foreign affairs, and finance in common. The parliament of the Dual Monarchy consisted of two national houses, one composed of the representatives from Austria, the other from Hungary. The Compromise of 1867 made the Magyars loyal subjects of the emperor, but it ignored the national aspiration of the racial minorities in the Dual Monarchy. The persistent desire of these minorities for freedom, particularly of the Slavs, became an important cause of the First World War.

SUMMARY

A number of forceful political leaders contributed to the growth of nationalism in Europe. Louis Napoleon, elected president of the Second French Republic, overthrew the republic and made himself Emperor of the Second Empire. His policies stimulated French national pride. He endeavored to please all elements of the population. By his policies, industry, agriculture, internal communications, and trade improved and the French empire in Africa and the Far East was enlarged. He increased French prestige by taking part in the Crimean War and by aiding the Italians to expel the Austrians from Lombardy. His later foreign policies were a failure. His venture in Mexico collapsed; he failed to carry out his promises to the Poles; he allowed France to be drawn into war with Prussia. The Prussian armies defeated his armies and the Germans captured and imprisoned him. The Second Empire came to an inglorious end in military defeat in the Franco-Prussian War.

Victor Emmanuel II, Cavour, and Garibaldi unified Italy. Cavour was the leading figure in the development of Italian unity. He strengthened the kingdom of Sardinia and secured the aid of Louis Napoleon in expelling Austria from Lombardy. Most of the states in central Italy voted in plebiscites to join Sardinia. Garibaldi and his Red Shirts liberated the kingdom of the Two Sicilies (Sicily and Southern Italy) from the rule of their Bourbon king. He turned all the lands he had captured over to Victor Emmanuel II who became the first king of the new kingdom of Italy. The kingdom of Italy gained the province of Venetia in 1866, the city of Rome in 1870, and Trieste and the province of Trentino in 1919.

Bismarck brought about the unification of the German states by a policy of Blood and Iron. He was ably supported by King William I and the militarists, headed by von Roon and von Moltke. He secured land for Prussia by a war with Denmark (1864). After defeating Austria in the Austro-Prussian War (1866) he annexed enough of the German states to Prussia so that it extended from Russia to France. He organized the North German Confederation with Prussia at the head. He brought on a war with France in which the Confederation and the south German states joined. German victory in this war resulted in the formation of the German Empire. The unification of all the German states under Prussian leadership had been accomplished and Germany soon became a very powerful country.

Francis Joseph, emperor of Austria, contrary to expectation, became an able leader. He worked out an agreement with Francis Deak, Magyar leader, which brought peace to his empire. By this agreement, known as the Compromise of 1867, Austria and Hungary were constituted as separate kingdoms. Together they formed the Dual Monarchy. They were united in allegiance to the emperor and by a joint parliament and common ministers of war, foreign affairs, and finance. Although this arrangement satisfied the Austrians and Hungarians, the dissatisfied minorities in the Dual Monarchy looked forward to the day when they could gain their freedom.

EVENTS THAT TOOK PLACE AT ABOUT THE SAME TIME

FRANCE	ITALY	GERMANY AND AUSTRIA
Revolution of 1848. Louis Napoleon elected president of Second French Republic. Louis Napoleon's *coup d'état,* 1851. Louis Napoleon elected emperor, 1852. Second Empire, 1852-1870. France in Crimean War, 1854-1856. Congress of Paris, 1856.	Revolution of 1848. Sardinia granted a constitution by its king, 1848. Victor Emmanuel became king of Sardinia, 1848. Cavour (1810-1861) appointed prime minister of Sardinia, 1852. Sardinia entered Crimean War, 1855.	Revolution of 1848. Frankfort Assembly, 1848-1849.
Louis Napoleon and Cavour made secret agreement against Austria, 1858.		
France entered Austro-Sardinian War, 1859. France obtained Nice and Savoy, 1860. Louis Napoleon's Mexican expedition began, 1861.	Austro-Sardinian War, 1859. Sardinia annexed Lombardy. Parma, Modena, Tuscany, Romagna voted to join kingdom of Sardinia, 1860. Sicily and Naples conquered by Garibaldi, 1860. Kingdom of Italy proclaimed, 1861.	Von Roon appointed minister of war in Prussia; von Moltke chief of staff, 1859. Bismarck appointed prime minister of Prussia, 1862. Schleswig-Holstein War, 1864.
Louis Napoleon withdrew his troops from Mexico on demand of United States, 1866. Franco-Prussian War, 1870-1871. Louis Napoleon captured at Sedan. Third Republic proclaimed, 1870. Treaty of Frankfort, 1871.	Italy entered Austro-Prussian War, 1866. Venetia annexed. Kingdom of Italy seized Rome which became capital of Italy, 1870.	Austro-Prussian War, 1866. North German Confederation formed, 1867. Dual Monarchy Austria-Hungary created by Compromise of 1867. Franco-Prussian War, 1870-1871. Proclamation of the German Empire, 1871.

LOUIS NAPOLEON AND BISMARCK. Victor and vanquished after the battle of Sedan, which ended the Franco-Prussian war of 1870. (*Top*.)

MAXIMILIAN IN MEXICO. The last days of the ill-fated Emperor, from a photograph taken only a few days before his execution.

FRANCIS JOSEPH OF AUSTRIA. The King-Emperor reigned for sixty-eight years. (*Right*.)

ABRAHAM LINCOLN. This photograph of the Civil War President was made in Washington a short time before Lincoln's assassination.

ROBERT E. LEE. The Confederate general at his home in Virginia. (*Top right.*)

BENITO JUAREZ. His revolution had United States support and, as President of Mexico, Juarez based his policies on those of Lincoln. (*Right.*)

CHAPTER 23

Democracy and Autocracy in Europe (1871-1914)

The struggles for power between the liberals and the conservatives in each of the major European nations between 1815 and 1848 continued throughout the rest of the nineteenth century. The outcome was different in each nation. Great Britain continued to grow steadily in democracy even when its leaders were conservative. France, after its disastrous bid for glory under the Second Empire, joined the democratic group by establishing the Third Republic. After its unification, Italy became a constitutional monarchy which leaned toward democracy.

Germany, Russia, and the Balkan countries made up the autocratic group. Although William I of the German Empire and Bismarck appeared to foster democratic government, nearly all power rested in their hands. In Russia the Tsar kept his autocratic power unimpaired throughout the nineteenth century. The Balkan countries secured their freedom from Turkey. Though they had constitutions and parliaments, they were for the most part under the autocratic control of monarchs.

• • •

Nationalism and the tradition of democracy were already strong in Great Britain. British nationalism had been forged in the fires of the medieval wars and molded into form in the stirring time of Queen Elizabeth. In the long struggle with Napoleon, nationalism provided Great Britain with a tenacity which would not admit defeat.

A strong tradition of parliamentary rule had been established by the seventeenth century struggle between the Stuart kings and Parliament which ended in victory for the latter. Yet closer examination shows that in 1815 the British government was not really democratic. It was rather a constitutional monarchy in which wealthy aristocrats and merchants wielded nearly all power. Since then the British government has become more democratic because the right to vote has been granted to more British subjects and the powers of the House of Commons have been increased.

The government was not democratic in 1815 because Parliament represented only a part of the English people. It consisted of two houses. The House of Lords was composed of nobles who inherited membership in it and bishops of the Anglican Church, who were appointed by the king, and so it was in no way responsive to the will of the people. The House of Commons was composed of representatives from the ancient counties and towns, but it too failed to represent all the people. There were two major reasons for this failure. Few had the right to vote. In 1815 less than half a million out of 6,000,000 men possessed that right. In addition, Catholics and dissenters (Protestants who were not members of the Anglican Church) were forbidden by law to hold office. With the shifting of population from Southern to Northern and Central England as a result of the Industrial Revolution, Liver-

The Metropolitan Museum of Art

THE HOUSE OF LORDS. The Lord Chancellor is presiding; the Government peers sit on the benches to his right, the Opposition peers to his left.

pool, Manchester, Sheffield, and other towns had become large cities. None of these was represented (1815) in Parliament. Many of the old towns had decreased in size and some had no population at all. Yet each of these continued to elect two representatives to the House of Commons. In some of them (rotten boroughs) the few voters were easily bribed or controlled by the ruling class. In others, the aristocrat who owned the land had the appointment of the representatives in his pocket, so to speak, and so these boroughs were called "pocket boroughs." Thus it was possible with a little planning for a few great landowners to control the majority of the seats in the House of Commons.

The Reform Bill of 1832 admitted the middle class to a share in government. The Tory party, made up for the most part of conservative landowners, was perfectly satisfied with the system of representation as it was. They were opposed to changes which

might lead toward democracy which they feared. The Duke of Wellington, victor of Waterloo, declared that the British parliamentary system of government was the best that could ever be devised. The Whig leaders, whose interests were chiefly in commerce, favored minor reforms.

At about the time of the American Revolution Englishmen began to propose political reforms. But the violence and bloodshed that accompanied the French Revolution frightened even the Whigs, and all movement toward reform died out until after Waterloo. Then the reform movement began again. By this time some of the leading industrial capitalists were in the Whig party. It contained also a group of men called radicals, who were intellectual liberals and believers in democracy, small business men, working people, Protestant dissenters, and Catholics. The dissenters and Catholics could vote, but they could not hold office or sit in Parliament till the Catholic Emancipation Act was passed in 1829. The leaders of the reform movement carried on an active agitation until Lord Grey, leader of the Whigs, took up their cause.

The Whig party won a victory in the election of 1831 and a Reform Bill was passed by the House of Commons in 1832. When the Bill was first voted on in the House of Lords it was rejected. Public opinion was so incensed that threats of revolution were heard. To prevent serious trouble, Lord Grey advised the king to create enough new Whig peers (nobles) to pass the Bill. To avoid this increase in its membership, the House of Lords gave in and passed the Bill.

The Reform Bill of 1832 (1) abolished the smaller boroughs, (2) gave the industrial cities in the north of England the right to elect members of the House of Commons, (3) gave the vote to all men of property, chiefly small businessmen and professional men in the cities and small landowners in the country. In 1828 and 1829 the dissenters and Catholics were granted the right to hold public office. In 1858 Jews were also given the right to hold public office.

The method by which the Reform Bill of 1832 was forced through Parliament by Lord Grey made the House of Commons supreme over the House of Lords. Henceforth, whenever the House of Commons had strong popular support for its measures, the House of Lords could be compelled to yield. From this time on, the Cabinet definitely represented the party which had a majority in the House of Commons and the king had to appoint his ministers from this party. Following these reforms the political parties became known as the Conservative and the Liberal.

The wave of middle class liberalism which passed the Reform Bill made itself felt also in many other phases of British life. In 1833 as a result of the agitation led by William Wilberforce (1759-1833), the

Bettmann Archive

ANTI-CORN LAW LEAGUE. English people demonstrating against the Corn Laws which were repealed in 1846 after the campaign conducted by Cobden and Bright.

British Parliament passed an act that abolished slavery in the colonies and compensated slave-holders in the sum of about $100,000,-000. A uniformed and regular police force was established. This was a step of the greatest importance because public order was to be maintained by civilian methods. The criminal laws were lightened by the abolition of the death penalty for about 100 crimes, including such offenses as stealing a fish and damaging Westminster Bridge. Government aid was extended to education, but fully-supported state schools were not established until after the First World War. Laws were passed limiting hours of labor and plac-

JOHN BRIGHT. This British statesman, orator, and textile manufacturer eloquently demanded the repeal of the Corn Laws. He was a great admirer of Lincoln and defended the North to Englishmen during the War Between the States.

ing restrictions on the employment of women and children in factories and mines.

Perhaps the most significant result of the growth in power of the urban middle class was the repeal of the Corn Laws. These measures, passed in 1815, placed tariffs on the importation of grain and so increased the price at which farmers sold their grain. The great landowners leased lands to farmers. By keeping up the price of grain, the Corn Laws enabled the farmers to pay high rents to the landlords. This great advantage to landowners caused hardship to laboring men who had to pay a higher price for bread, and to their employers who were thereby forced to pay higher wages. After much public and political discussion for the repeal of the Corn Laws, in which John Bright played a leading part, the Conservative leader, Robert Peel, yielded and brought about their repeal in 1846. The industrial interests had won a great victory over the agricultural interests. Great Britain remained a free trade country until after the First World War.

The Chartists presented a program of complete democracy. Some radicals were not satisfied with what had been accomplished by the Reform Bill of 1832. They and workingmen who had not yet received the vote started a movement to make more reforms. They drew up the People's Charter (1838) and the movement took on the name Chartist. Their program consisted of: (1) universal manhood suffrage, (2) yearly elections of members to the House of Commons, (3) electoral districts equal in population, (4) vote by ballot, (5) removal of all property-owning requirements for members of the House of Commons, (6) payment of its members so that anyone could afford to serve.

The people of Great Britain were not ready for a program so forward looking. The Chartist leaders could not agree and after a brief revival of Chartism, while the Revolution of 1848 was going on in France, the movement collapsed. When the House of Commons voted salaries ($2000 yearly) for its members (1911), all but the second of the Chartist reforms had become law.

Leaders in both political parties promoted and strengthened democracy. Party politics made the chief contributions to the next reform measures. In 1867 Disraeli (1804-1881), the Conservative leader, in an attempt to prove to the people that his party would do more for them than the Liberals, secured the passage of a Reform Bill doubling the number of voters by granting the right to vote to the workingmen in the industrial cities. The Liberal leader Gladstone (1809-1898), not to be outdone by the Conservatives, advocated more reforms. A law providing for the secret ballot was passed in 1872. By the Reform Bill of 1884 the vote was extended to workers in the country and in the following year Great Britain was divided into electoral districts according to population. The requirement that members of Parliament should own property had already been removed in 1858. Thus the program of the Chartists was carried on by both Conservatives and Liberals even though the movement itself had collapsed.

The Liberal leader during this era was William Ewart Gladstone. Wealthy, well-educated, and deeply religious, he first gained renown as a student of the Bible and of Homer. Starting his career as a Conservative, he became the outstanding exponent of the liberal ideas of popular government and free trade. He became the champion of Home Rule for Ireland. He refused a peerage that he might remain a leader in the House of Commons.

Gladstone's great rival was Disraeli, a highly cultivated man and a novelist. The power of his intellect and his personality enabled him to become the leader of the Conservative party. In spite of his reform measure of 1867, he is thought by many to have distrusted the people. His major interest and the one to which he devoted his attention and energies was the expansion of the British Empire. In 1876 Disraeli engineered the passage of an act of Parliament which declared Queen Victoria to be Empress of India.

Queen Victoria (1837-1901) had the longest reign of any monarch in English history. She was respected for her courage, strength of character, and the tact with which she recognized the limitations of the crown and yielded to the steadily increasing power of British ministries. She came to be regarded above all as a symbol of imperial unity. Her reign was a period of vast industrial expansion and increasing material prosperity.

Bettmann Archive

QUEEN VICTORIA. Her reign (1837-1901) was the longest in English history. Probably Queen Victoria was more highly respected by the British people than any other monarch.

It was celebrated also for its many great writers, artists, and scientists and on the whole, her people were prosperous and happy. It is little wonder that she became the much-loved symbol and center of British patriotism.

In the early years of the twentieth century the Liberal Prime Minister, Campbell-Bannerman, and his Chancellor of the Exchequer, Lloyd George, launched a new attack on the social problems that had arisen out of the Industrial Revolution in Great Britain. They secured the passage of a Workmen's Compensation Act (1906) and an Old Age Pension Act (1908). A National Insurance Act was passed (1911) after the death of Campbell-Bannerman and while Asquith was Prime Minister.

To pay the cost of these acts and to provide funds for naval expansion made necessary by the activities of Germany, more taxes were necessary. In 1909 Lloyd George in his budget aimed to shift the tax burden

The British Isles

Orkney Is.
Scapa Flow

Inverness

Aberdeen

SCOTLAND

Iona
Dundee
Stirling
Edinburgh
Glasgow
Berwick

NORTH
SEA

Tyne R.
Newcastle

Londonderry
NORTHERN
IRELAND
Belfast
Carlisle
Durham
CUMBERL'D

I. of Man
Lancaster
York
Blackburn
Leeds
Hull
Humber R.
Galway
Dublin
Liverpool
Manchester
Sheffield
Chester
Stoke
Lincoln
Nottingham
Lynn
Norwich
Limerick
ENGLAND
Yarmouth
Shannon
Airport
Waterford
WALES
Birmingham
Leicester
Coventry
Warwick
Cambridge
Cobh
(Queenstown)
Hereford
Stratford
St.Albans
Gloucester
Oxford
London
Thames R.
Swansea
Cardiff
Bristol
Reading
Croydon
Canterbury
Dover
Dunkirk
Bath
Winchester
Calais
Salisbury
Southampton
Hastings
Brighton
Portsmouth
Exeter
Weymouth
Plymouth
Falmouth

EIRE

Irish Sea

Shannon R.

English Channel

Dieppe
Cherbourg
Le Havre
Rouen
Caen

0   100 Miles

Industrial centers
Historic towns
Coal mines

The people on these islands have wielded a great influence on the shaping of the modern world.
They developed an enormous, far-flung, overseas empire built on sea power.

DEMOCRACY AND AUTOCRACY IN EUROPE

from producers to possessors of wealth. He proposed an income tax, an inheritance tax, taxes on unearned income (dividends on stocks and bonds), heavy taxes on monopolies, liquor licenses, a tax on the increase in land values resulting from growth of population or industrial development, a tax on land not under cultivation, especially parks and game preserves, and a tax on mining royalties. Lloyd George's budget was more than a tax measure; it was a measure intended to make the rich pay more of the costs of the social reforms which he had carried through Parliament. The tax on idle land was intended to encourage its use for agricultural purposes.

The Budget of 1909 became law in 1910 but the determined opposition to it by the House of Lords led to the Parliament Act of 1911. This Act provided (1) that all money bills would become law one month after passage by the House of Commons with or without the consent of the House of Lords; (2) That all other measures if rejected by the Lords would become laws after they had been passed in three successive sessions of the Commons, provided that two years had elapsed since their first introduction.

The British government has a democratic basis. The British Constitution is not a written document like the American. It consists of a number of documents including the Great Charter of 1215, the Petition of Right, the Bill of Rights, the Reform Bills, and the Parliament Act of 1911, reinforced by many age-old customs and traditions which are even stronger than laws. It can be amended at will simply by vote of Parliament.

Under the Constitution the office of king is hereditary. He is the head of the nation and the Anglican Church. He has large property holdings and Commons provides him with an income of about $3,000,000 a year, hardly enough to fulfill his obligations and maintain his position. He has very little power as king, but his influence is great. To the peoples of Great Britain and the Empire he is a symbol of unity and the object of their loyalty.

The members of the House of Commons are elected by the voters and in 1911 the Commons for the first time voted a salary of about $2000 for its members. The duration of Parliament is five years; but the Commons may be dissolved at any time and a new election to the Commons ordered by the Prime Minister. A member need not be a resident of the electoral district that he represents. Important party members are nominated by their parties in districts where there is a safe majority for that party. The leading member of the majority party must be designated Prime Minister by the king. In turn he appoints other members of his party to offices in the Cabinet. Since they are all members of Parliament, they participate in debates and guide its deliberations. The Prime Minister and his cabinet are called His Majesty's Government. Any one of them can introduce a measure into Parliament. The minority party, His Majesty's Opposition, criticizes and attacks the measures introduced by the Cabinet. If the Cabinet is unable to get a majority vote of the Commons on one of its measures, it must by custom resign or dissolve Parliament. Then either the leaders of the Opposition become the Government and form a Cabinet, or, as more often happens, a new election is ordered so that the measure on which the Government has been defeated may be submitted to the voters. If in the election the Government wins a majority in Commons, it is returned to power; but if not, the Opposition which is now in the majority forms a new government.

The Cabinet does much more than initiate legislation. It supervises the administration of all acts passed by Parliament. Its members are

BARRICADE FIGHTING DURING THE UPRIS-
ING OF THE PARIS COMMUNE, 1871. For two
months the Communards and the army fought desperately in the streets of Paris.

heads of the departments of the government
and makers of policies. Under them is a
great host of secretaries and assistants known
as the Civil Service. Many of the members of
the civil service are university graduates and
certain positions in the service are much
sought for. They remain in office, independent of changing ministries. The British Civil
Service is noted for its ability, honesty, and
integrity.

The dependence of the Cabinet on the
Commons gives the voters a chance through
their representatives to exercise immediate
influence on the government. The pressure of
public opinion may force a change of government policy or the dismissal of an unpopular
or unskillful member of the Cabinet at any
time while Parliament is in session. The British government is democratic because it is
subject to the will of the voters.

**The Third French Republic was born of
the adversity which came out of the
Franco-Prussian War.** Immediately after his
army had been defeated at Sedan, Louis Napoleon, a prisoner of the Germans, was deposed by the provisional government that had
just been established in Paris. An armistice
with Germany enabled the French to elect a
National Assembly which was to decide

whether to continue the war or make final
terms of peace with Germany. The National
Assembly governed France from 1871-1875.
It made terms of peace with Germany and
drew up a new constitution for France. Before it drew up a constitution, however, it had
to deal with two other problems, the restoration of order in Paris and the renewal of
French military power.

**The National Assembly crushed the re-
volt of the Paris Commune.** Radical republicans in Paris were both disappointed and
alarmed after it had fallen to the Germans
in 1871. They were humiliated by the terms
of peace accepted by the National Assembly
and disturbed because a majority of the members of this assembly were monarchists. The
Parisians had suffered terribly while the Germans besieged the city for four months. They
thought this suffering would have been in
vain if the National Assembly set up a monarchy. Considerable unemployment added
fuel to the flames of their discontent.

During the siege of Paris, the city had
been defended and protected by the National
Guard which included many workingmen
who believed in a republic. It still had in its
possession arms, even cannons. The National
Assembly in session at Versailles stopped the
pay of the National Guard, ordered it to give
up its arms, and sent regular army troops to
see that its orders were enforced. A government for the city of Paris (the Paris Commune) was organized to direct the resistance
of the people against the National Assembly.
The bloody conflict which resulted was really
a civil war between the forces of the city of
Paris and regular army troops. Ferocious
fighting took place in the streets, buildings
were burned, hostages murdered, captives
shot, and thousands of people killed. Both
sides were guilty of extreme cruelty. The
Communards, supporters of the Commune,
were hopelessly outnumbered by the troops

of the regular army and their revolt was crushed. The National Assembly had triumphed. Its ruthlessness in victory, however, had weakened the position of those who wished to restore monarchy. The terrible punishment visited upon the Communards also weakened the cause of radicalism for many years.

The National Assembly took immediate steps to renew French military power The Assembly passed (1872) a law establishing compulsory military service for all able-bodied Frenchmen, at first for five, later for two years. France was again striving to become a great military power. Other nations on the Continent soon introduced conscription. The French people bought enough bonds so that the entire billion dollar indemnity imposed by the Germans was paid (1873) and thus secured the withdrawal of the German army of occupation.

The National Assembly voted for a republican form of government. Meanwhile the members of the National Assembly had been discussing the form of the future French government. Some members of the Assembly wanted to establish a republic, but the majority of them favored a return to monarchy. The monarchists, however, were not in agreement. Some were in favor of a descendant of the old Bourbon kings. Others favored an Orleanist, a grandson of Louis Philippe. Still others favored a member of the Bonaparte family. The republicans in the Assembly profited from this disunity. "A republic," Thiers, a member of the Assembly, said, "is the government which divides us least." In 1875 the National Assembly passed a series of laws which established the government of the Third Republic. However, the monarchists continued their efforts to restore a monarchy throughout the sixty-five years of the life of the Third Republic. Their activities helped cause its downfall in 1940.

The government established by the laws of 1875 was democratic. They provided for a parliament composed of two houses, a Chamber of Deputies and a Senate. The Chamber of Deputies (1914) had 602 members elected for a four-year term from districts by universal manhood suffrage. No law could be passed without the consent of the Chamber of Deputies and all tax bills had to be initiated by it. Two hundred twenty-five members of the Senate were chosen for a term of nine years by electoral assemblies in the Departments, the administrative divisions of France. The other seventy-five were elected for life by the National Assembly (later by the Senate). In 1884 life membership was discontinued. The president was elected for a term of seven years by the Chamber of Deputies and the Senate sitting together in a National Assembly. Because all of a president's acts had to be countersigned by a member of the Cabinet, his position was one of influence rather than of power, resembling in a way the position of the king in Great Britain.

The executive and administrative powers were in the hands of a Cabinet, which was responsible to parliament. For premier, the president appointed the political leader who possessed the support of a majority of the Chamber of Deputies. The premier appointed the rest of the cabinet. The cabinet system, though similar in appearance to the British, was actually quite different. This difference was due to the many political parties in France. Some of these parties represented varieties of political opinion, others represented different elements in the population.

A Royalist party, a Catholic party, a Radical-Socialist party, and a Socialist party were the most prominent. For years the party that had the greatest numbers in the Chamber of Deputies was the Radical-Socialist party. It was actually neither radical nor socialist as its members represented the middle class.

International News

CAPTAIN ALFRED DREYFUS. He was imprisoned for five years in the French penal colony on Devil's Island, French Guiana. In 1906 he was acquitted of treason, granted the Legion of Honor, and raised to the rank of major. His victory proved the strength of the Third Republic.

Because there were so many parties, no one party was ever in the majority in the Chamber of Deputies. As a result, a Cabinet represented a coalition of parties. A minor disagreement among the parties might therefore break the coalition, destroy the majority, and cause the defeat of the Cabinet. In case of a defeat, one or more of the ministers, usually including the premier, would be forced to resign. A new coalition would be formed and a new premier appointed. Because some of the same parties helped form both coalitions some ministers remained in office under two coalitions, thus providing a continuous element in the French Cabinet amid its frequent changes. Nevertheless, these changes sometimes prevented vigorous or consistent action when the government faced serious problems.

The majority of the French people upheld and sustained the Third Republic. Frenchmen who favored monarchy continued their efforts to restore the monarchy even after the laws of 1875 had established the government of the Third Republic. The National Assembly elected (1873) Marshal MacMahon president. He was a descendant of an Irish family who went with James II into exile in France. During the Franco-Prussian War he was forced to surrender a French army of 81,000 men at the battle of Sedan. He was a monarchist who derived his support largely from army officers and Catholics. The republicans were afraid that he was planning to re-establish the monarchy. When in the elections of 1877 and 1879 the people elected a majority of republicans to the Chamber of Deputies and the Senate, MacMahon resigned. The Republic had weathered its first crisis.

A second attempt to overthrow the Republic was made by the monarchists when they supported General Boulanger in his attempt to secure (1888) the passage of laws which would make the president of France a dictator. The general, however, summoned by the Senate to appear before it to stand trial for treason, fled to Belgium where he committed suicide. The majority of the people of France demonstrated their loyalty to the Third French Republic by electing again (1889) a republican majority to the Chamber of Deputies and the Senate and once more in 1893. This election of 1889 averted the second crisis.

The Dreyfus Case provided a severe test of the strength of the Third Republic. In 1894 Captain Alfred Dreyfus, an Alsatian Jew, was accused of selling military secrets to Germany. Although he protested his innocence, he was convicted by a military court and sentenced to life imprisonment on Devil's Island off the coast of French Guiana. His case was reopened in 1896 when his supporters offered proof that the documents on which he was convicted had been forged. For four years violent controversy raged over his innocence or guilt. Many army officers were determined to uphold the verdict of the military court. Some of the French newspapers indulged in anti-Semitic tirades. In general, conservatives, many of whom were monarchists, supported the conviction of Dreyfus. Emile Zola, a great novelist, was the chief spokesman for the liberals who supported the Republic and defended the innocence of Dreyfus. Thus the case became a test of the strength of the Third Republic. The facts discovered by the supporters of Dreyfus seemed to prove that his conservative enemies—monarchists, army officers, and clericals—were using his case to destroy the Republic. In 1899 he was pardoned by the president of France. In 1906 the highest court of appeal set aside the verdict of the military court. Dreyfus was then restored to the army and raised to the rank of major. This victory of the republican supporters of Dreyfus proved for the third time the strength of the Third French Republic.

The Third Republic separated the church from the state. The attitude of Catholics in these three crises caused leading republicans to think that the Church itself was an enemy of the Third Republic. These republicans, who were opposed to the influence of the Church in government, were called anti-clericals. Their first point of attack on the Church was in the field of education.

Napoleon had planned the establishment of a non-sectarian system of public schools supported by the nation, but his plans had never been completely carried out. As a result, most of the elementary schools in France in 1880 were Church schools in which the teaching was done by men and women belonging to religious orders. As the republican leaders were convinced that education was a basic necessity in a democratic state, they feared the influence which the teachers in Church schools had over the minds of the children. In 1881 and 1882, to help overcome this influence, Jules Ferry, minister of education, succeeded in securing the passage of laws which made primary education free and compulsory in a system of public schools in which the teachers were appointed and paid by the government. Church schools, however, were allowed to continue. In 1901 the Law of Associations forbade the existence of religious orders without the consent of the government. A law passed in 1904 provided that all teaching by religious orders should cease in ten years.

Ever since the agreement between Napoleon and the Pope (the Concordat of 1801), the government had paid the salaries and had some control over the appointment of Catholic priests, Protestant ministers, and rabbis. By the Separation Act of 1905 the government withdrew its financial support from churches and gave up its right of control over these appointments. Henceforth church and state were separated and all churches became private institutions much as they are in the United States.

The Third French Republic promoted the material prosperity of the people. Many measures were taken by the French government to aid the farmers who comprised a majority of the people. A ministry of agriculture was created (1881) and agricultural schools were founded. Financial aid was given to farmers to promote the production of grapes, silk, and flax. Agriculture was protected from foreign competition by a tariff act passed in 1892. These measures increased the prosperity of the French peasantry, long the great strength of France.

Industry and commerce also were helped by the government. Tariffs encouraged the production of metals and the building of factories. More highways, canals, and railroads were built. Jules Ferry, while premier, entered upon a policy of colonial expansion in Asia and Africa to provide a supply of raw materials and a market for French goods.

Along with the promotion of agriculture, industry, and commerce, measures were taken to protect the welfare of the workers. In 1884 labor unions that heretofore had been unlawful were legalized. In the following years, laws were passed regulating the hours and conditions of labor and the employment of women and children. In 1910 an Old Age Insurance Act provided compulsory insurance for all wage earners. In 1914 France was again strong, prosperous, and united.

The government of Italy was a constitutional monarchy modeled after the British monarchy. After the kingdom of Italy had been established, it adopted the constitution that Charles Albert had given Sardinia (1848). It was liberal rather than democratic. The monarch was retained with influence rather than power and the parliament was composed of two houses. The Senate consisted of princes of the royal family who held office by inheritance and of Italians who had achieved prominence in the various fields of human activity. The latter were appointed by the king and served for life. The members of the Chamber of Deputies were elected. At first, literacy and property tests kept the large number of Italians who were illiterate and poor from voting. In 1912 parliament passed a law establishing universal manhood suffrage. The Cabinet represented a majority in the Chamber of Deputies. As in France, there were many parties and so a Cabinet represented a coalition.

The government faced many difficult problems. The first of these was how to bind the people together in national unity. The reason for disunity was that Italy had so long been divided into city-states and duchies that loyalty to local communities was stronger than loyalty to the new kingdom of Italy. This problem was made more difficult by the great differences between Northern and Southern Italy. Northern Italy was more advanced economically and so was more prosperous, and besides the people were better educated. Southern Italy had lived long under the oppressive rule of despotic kings. Most of the people were poor and illiterate, and the region needed roads and schools badly. While the prosperous North paid most of the taxes, more of the tax money was spent in Southern Italy than in Northern Italy. Although the government did much to remove the causes of disunity, the problem of national unity is not yet solved.

The attitude of the Pope toward the kingdom of Italy tended to increase disunity among the Italian people. For many centuries before 1871, the Pope had controlled Rome and the Papal States in Central Italy. After the Pope had lost the Papal States during the unification of Italy, the Italian government attempted to make peace with the Pope by passing the Law of Papal Guarantees (1871). This law recognized the Pope as an independent monarch ruling over parts of Rome, most important of which was an area of thirty-two acres which contained the Church of St. Peter and the Vatican, the palace of the Pope. To compensate the Pope for the loss of the Papal States, he was voted an annual payment of about $650,000. The Pope, however, refused to accept either the Law of Papal Guarantees or the annual payment, shut himself up voluntarily as the "prisoner of the Vatican" and forbade Catholics to take part in the Italian government. Some obeyed and others did not, thus increasing the disunity. From 1871 until 1929, when Mussolini came to terms with the

Pope, no Pope ever set foot outside the grounds of the Vatican.

The most difficult of all the Italian problems was how to relieve the poverty of the people. It caused many thousands to emigrate every year, especially to the New World. To help relieve the poverty of the people, the government took many measures. It encouraged an increase in the cultivation of olive trees, grape vines, and mulberry trees (for silkworms). It encouraged the terracing of hillsides and the draining of swamps. It helped to promote industrial development by encouraging the manufacture of steel and also the manufacture of silk and cotton textiles. It encouraged the use of water power to generate electric power because coal was scarce. The government aided the development of a fine merchant marine. To promote national unity and at the same time to secure markets for Italian goods, the Italian government embarked on a policy of colonial expansion chiefly in North Africa, a faint memory of the glorious days of the Roman Empire centuries before.

The German Empire (1871) was a federation. It consisted of kingdoms, duchies, principalities, and free cities. Each state maintained its own government and each had a share in the government of the empire even though the empire was really controlled by Prussia, the greatest kingdom. At the head of the German Empire was the emperor who was also king of Prussia. The parliament was composed of two houses, the Reichstag and the Bundesrat. The constitution of the German Empire provided that members of the Reichstag were to be elected by universal manhood suffrage. This body had the right to vote on all questions submitted to it; but the superior power of the Bundesrat and the cabinet, who decided what should be submitted, reduced it actually to the status of a debating society. The Bundesrat was made up of delegates appointed by the heads of the states. It was undemocratic because its members were not elected. In the Bundesrat, Prussian influence prevailed. The Bundesrat controlled all legislation. The Chancellor and the cabinet under him were responsible not to the majority of the Reichstag but only to the emperor.

The imperial government had many and extensive powers, including control over foreign affairs, the army and the navy, finance, and interstate relations, and it also exercised power in criminal and civil law. The states had much less control over their internal affairs than the states in our country. The concentration of power in the hands of the Emperor and the Chancellor made any German claim that their government was democratic a mockery.

Bismarck conducted a campaign against the Catholic Church to promote German nationalism. Bismarck's program after the Franco-Prussian War was intended to increase German nationalism. The Catholic states of South Germany, which wanted more local rights, seemed to him to be the chief enemies of nationalism. To overcome them, Bismarck began an attack on the Catholic Church which was grandly called the "fight for civilization" (*Kulturkampf*). This term was coined by Rudolf Virchow, a celebrated scientist. The Jesuits were expelled from the empire. In Prussia, Catholic seminaries were closely supervised by the government and the use of the German language was made compulsory in religious instruction. No one except a German educated in a German university was permitted to hold an office in the Catholic Church. The movement ended in complete failure and in 1878 Bismarck gave up the struggle against the Catholic Church. In fact he even turned to the Catholics for support against the Social Democrats, the new enemy of his regime.

KARL MARX. He was the father of modern socialism and his *Das Kapital* has been translated into most of the languages of the world.

The Social Democrats were followers of Karl Marx (1818-1883). He was the son of well-to-do Jewish parents in Germany who became Christians when Marx was a child. He studied law, history, and philosophy at the universities of Bonn, Berlin, and Jena, obtaining the degree of doctor of philosophy from Jena in 1841. He desired to become a university professor, but because of his radical opinions, the leaders of the Prussian government kept him from obtaining a teaching position. When the government suppressed a radical newspaper that Marx was editing, he went into voluntary exile in Paris. Here the French government also suppressed his newspaper. Marx then went to Brussels from which he returned to Paris in 1848 and played a part in the revolution that overthrew Louis Philippe. In the same year he returned to Germany where revolution had broken out. He was exiled. He then found an asylum in London where he lived from 1849 until his death in 1883. Here he eked out a bare existence for himself and family chiefly by journalistic work and translating books. For a time he was a foreign correspondent for the *New York Tribune*. Much of his time was spent in the library of the British Museum in London where he read widely, studied much, thought deeply, and wrote a great deal.

From his studies he worked out a theory of society which has had great influence ever since. Marx expressed his ideas in many works of which two are most important, *The Communist Manifesto,* written in collaboration with his friend Friedrich Engels, and *Das Kapital,* which he wrote himself. Both of these works have been translated into almost every language in the world and so their influence has been world-wide. Marx's ideas may be considered in four steps. (1) He believed in the economic interpretation of history. This interpretation meant that the desire for food, clothing, shelter, and money, gives men the motives for nearly everything they do. (2) From the economic interpretation of history, he worked out his theory of the class struggle. According to this theory there has always been a struggle between classes, between the "haves" and the "have nots." Indeed, he held that such a struggle is unavoidable. He said that the struggle which lay directly ahead was that between capital and labor. (3) The belief that this struggle must come was based on his theory of "surplus value." According to this theory all value was produced by labor. Iron ore, as long as it stays in the ground, is valueless; but after it has been taken out, worked over, and made into fine steel it has value. This value, he said, is the product of the labor of the working class. Of all this value created by labor, the laboring class gets barely enough to live on. The rest or surplus value is taken by the capitalist class. (4) This theory of surplus value led Marx to predict the final destruction of the capitalist system. He held that the capitalists will continue to take surplus value until capital becomes concentrated in a few hands; the middle class will have disappeared; and the burden of the working class will have become unbearable. When this time comes, he reasoned, the working class will rise up, overthrow the capitalist class and seize the capital. Society (the workers) will then own all the means of production and each worker will receive full value for his work.

These theories of Karl Marx had a wide effect even beyond his followers who called themselves *socialists*. Many historians have accepted without reservation the economic interpretation of history and some of them have even made it more far-reaching than Marx had. Many men who called themselves socialists accepted his theory of surplus value and also his belief that society should own all the means of production without agreeing that revolution was necessary. For example, a group of Englishmen, including George Bernard Shaw, H. G. Wells, and the Webbs, believed that reforms could be brought about gradually by constitutional means. They called themselves Fabian Socialists after Fabius, the Roman general, who tried to defeat Hannibal by wearing him down instead of beating him in battle. Others became Marxian Socialists; that is, they agreed with everything Marx had written. They believed in and worked for revolution and the dictatorship of the proletariat. Today Marxian Socialists are called Communists.

Bismarck battled with the Social Democrats. The Social Democrats in Germany, like the Fabians in England, wanted to bring socialism about gradually. They formed a political party (1875) and before long they elected members to the Reichstag. The Social Democratic party seemed dangerous to Bismarck. Accordingly (1878), an Anti-Socialist Law was passed which attempted to suppress the Social Democratic party. Its meetings were forbidden, its publications were suppressed, and some of its members were imprisoned; and then Bismarck turned around and did what they wanted done. He secured the passage of laws that regulated hours and conditions of labor, that provided insurance against industrial accidents and sickness, and that provided old age pensions. In 1911 an Imperial Insurance Code increased the benefits of insurance to workers. Germany thus became under Bismarck a pioneer in social legislation. France and Great Britain passed similar laws later on and Congress and the state legislatures in the United States still later.

In spite of Bismarck's attempt to suppress the Social Democratic party, its membership grew rapidly. The Anti-Socialist Law of 1878 which had been renewed at intervals was not renewed (1890). Bismarck favored its renewal, but the emperor didn't. At the time of the outbreak of the First World War in 1914, the Social Democratic party had more than 100 members in the Reichstag and was the largest political party in Germany.

Under William II Germany developed rapidly. In 1888 William II became King of Prussia and Emperor of the German Empire. Almost at once he differed from the Iron Chancellor over his policy toward the socialists and over his policy toward Russia, and demanded (1890) his resignation.

The rapid and widespread development of the Industrial Revolution in Germany enabled it to take great strides toward wealth and power. The German universities were generously supported and research was promoted in all branches of learning but espe-

The Metropolitan Museum of Art

DROPPING THE PILOT. This very famous political cartoon by Sir John Tenniel was published in the British magazine *Punch.* The Kaiser watches Bismarck leave the German ship of state after they disagreed on policies.

cially in science. Largely as a result of research in chemistry the making of dyes became a German monopoly. Likewise, research in metals helped to increase greatly the output and the variety of the products produced by the German steel industry. At the famous Krupp works in Essen scientists were in charge of huge physical and chemical laboratories that were equipped with the latest scientific instruments. Tariff protection and government subsidies assisted in the development of many kinds of industries. Great ships were built and German goods were carried to markets in all parts of the world. Furthermore, the Germans began a program of colonial expansion in Africa and the Far East to secure markets and to add to the glory of Germany. Universal compulsory military service for able-bodied Germans had already been established by Bismarck and a large and powerful army developed under the German General Staff. Early in his reign William II took steps to create a modern navy for Germany and to embark on empire building.

The rise of Germany to the position of a great industrial, military, and naval power from 1871 to 1914 was one of the most striking developments of modern times.

The Tsarist regime continued with but little change. The autocratic government and policies established by Peter the Great and Catherine continued throughout the nineteenth century with but little change. The Tsars through their ministers controlled both church and state. A number of open-minded nobles had imbibed the ideas of the French Revolution while serving (1814-1815) in the Russian army of occupation in Paris. They advocated the end of autocracy, serfdom, and privilege. In the early part of his reign Alexander I (1801-1825) looked upon their aspirations with some favor. After 1820 and largely under the influence of Metternich, he turned against these liberals. In December, 1825 they rose up against Alexander's successor, Nicholas I (1825-1855). The Tsar easily suppressed this uprising, but these Decembrists came to be regarded as the first defenders of freedom in Russia. Nicholas I endeavored to suppress all liberalism in Russia. His officials censored all domestic and foreign books. They exercised rigid control over education lest liberal ideas should be taught. The secret police watched all persons suspected of liberalism and even opened their letters.

Nicholas I suppressed the Polish revolt.
Alexander I had given Russian Poland a liberal constitution (1815). The Poles, however, desired independence and revolted (1830). Nicholas I defeated the revolutionists (1831), revoked the constitution, closed the Polish universities, and endeavored to make Russians out of the Poles by making Russian the official language and requiring it to be taught in the schools. Polish patriotism, however, did not die.

Alexander II (1855-1881) freed the serfs. He had liberal views. His greatest reform was the Edict of Emancipation (1861). It was a two-fold reform. Forty million serfs were given their freedom. The government bought about one half the land owned by landowners and paid them for it promptly. The land taken from the landowners was not given the newly freed peasants, but to the village *(mir)* in which they lived. The *mir* then allotted land to each peasant according to the size of his family. Because the sizes of families change, the land was to be reallotted every few years to insure fair treatment. To compensate the government for the money it had paid landowners, the peasants were required to make yearly payments over a period of forty-nine years for their land.

Neither the landowner nor the peasant was completely satisfied with this reform. The landowner had lost half his land, and all his serf labor. The peasant complained that the land allotted to him was not enough to enable him to make a decent living and that the annual payments were greater than he could pay. Above all, most peasants thought that the soil on which they and their ancestors had toiled for centuries should belong to them. As the population increased, the land hunger of the peasants became more acute, and it was a major cause of the revolution (1917), as we shall see.

Between 1892 and 1903 the Industrial Rev-

Sovfoto

LEO TOLSTOY IN 1910. This is one of the last portraits of the great novelist who wrote *Anna Karenina, War and Peace,* and many other works.

olution began in Russia and many railroads were built under the leadership of Count Witte and largely with money borrowed from France. Russia continued, nevertheless, to be chiefly agricultural and its rivers continued to be its chief means of transportation.

The educated class of Russia produced great thinkers and writers including Turgenev and Tolstoy. From the educated class came also some who worked for reform and others who plotted against the government of the Tsars. After 1903 a small group of Marxian Socialists (Bolsheviks) demanded a complete overthrow of the political and economic system. The vast power of the government and the tireless activities of the secret police caused many revolutionists to flee from the country, while others were sent to Siberia.

A revolt which broke out in 1905 after Russia's defeat in a war with Japan was mercilessly suppressed. The Tsar, however, allowed the establishment and election of a parliament called the Duma. This concession was a hollow victory for the reformers as they soon discovered that the Duma had no real power.

In the nineteenth century the very size of Russia and its potential military power made it a source of alarm to European statesmen. Finland had been acquired (1809) from Sweden by a successful war. The Congress of Vienna in 1815 had confirmed Russia's large slice of Poland obtained in the fourth partition of Poland. The Russians continued the development of the resources of Siberia and annexed Turkestan. Russia's desire for an ice-free port in the south was one of the causes of the Crimean War (1854-1856) and the war between Russia and Turkey (1877-1878). The leading European nations, however, did not want Russia to get possession of Constantinople.

The Turks conquered the Balkan Peninsula. The Balkan Peninsula derives its name from the Balkan Mountains which run from the Adriatic to the Black Sea. On the north the Danube valley separates the Balkan Mountains from the Carpathian Mountains. To the south they are prolonged into the highlands of Greece. From Greece to the Black Sea lies the narrow coastal plain of Macedonia and Thrace.

The Balkan Peninsula was once a part of the Roman Empire and later a part of the Byzantine Empire. In the later days of Rome and during the early Middle Ages, it was invaded by Goths, Huns, Magyars, Serbs, Bulgars, and other peoples. Some moved farther westward; others remained and blended in greater or less degree with the descendants of the Roman provincials. After the Roman Empire in the West had collapsed, the Byzantine Empire at Constantinople engaged in fierce wars with the invaders, and the invaders fought among themselves. In 1453 after the fall of Constantinople, the Turks brought the whole peninsula into their empire.

Many different nationalities lived in the Balkans. Although most of the people were Slavs, they differed in speech, in tradition, and in religion. Most were Greek Orthodox, some were Roman Catholics, and some were followers of Mohammed. Each nationality clung fiercely to its own language, religion, and traditions. Memories of ancient wars which were kept alive from generation to generation aroused hatred of one for the other. These nationalities were not, however, in well-defined areas but were hopelessly intermingled in the same area. Even neighboring villages sometimes spoke different languages. The only element of unity among them for years was hatred of the Turks who had oppressed them for about 500 years.

The Balkan nations won their independence from Turkey. Gradually the tide of Turkish power in the Balkans ebbed as corruption and inefficiency weakened the government in Constantinople. With the aid of the Hapsburgs of Austria, Hungary freed itself from Turkey (1699) and afterwards became a part of the Hapsburg Empire. In 1867 it became a partner with the Austrians in the Dual Monarchy.

Greece gained its independence in 1829. The peasants of Montenegro and Serbia asserted their independence and declared war on Turkey in 1876. Russia joined them and Turkey was defeated in 1878. The Treaty of San Stefano, which ended this war, was revised by the powers of Europe in the Congress of Berlin (1878). By the settlement agreed upon at this Congress, the independence of Montenegro, Serbia, and Rumania was recognized. Bosnia and Herzegovina were placed under Austrian supervision. Although Bulgaria was set up as a separate nation, it had to recognize Turkish overlordship until a revolution in 1908 abolished Turkish control. Turkey still owned Macedonia, Thrace, and Constantinople, and thus remained a constant threat to the small Balkan nations.

For a long time quarrels among the Balkan nations prevented action against the common enemy which still possessed a part of the Balkans. Finally, in 1912, under the leadership of Venizelos, a Greek statesman, they combined and waged a successful war on Turkey. Violent disagreements over the spoils caused a second war in 1913 in which Greece, Serbia, and Rumania united against Bulgaria. At the end of these wars, Greece secured Macedonia, and Bulgaria was ceded a part of the Thracian coast. Albania on the Adriatic was established as an independent nation. Turkey in Europe was confined to a small strip of territory north of Constantinople and the Dardanelles.

The Balkan nations were monarchies. The Balkan Peninsula was thus divided among several small nations who distrusted one another; each contained minority groups differing in language, religion, and tradition. Each was governed by a constitutional monarch and a parliament. The government of Greece became a fairly liberal monarchy. The government of Rumania was modeled on the Prussian government which gave the monarch and the upper class control of the government. The kingdom of Serbia had a constitution, but its history was marred by the rivalry of two families for the throne which at times resulted in assassinations of royalty and civil wars. Bulgaria had a constitution, but in practice its government was autocratic. The problems of the Balkan nations were made more difficult by the intrigues of the great European powers, as we shall see.

The Balkans in 1870, 1878, 1913.

SUMMARY

Great Britain in 1832 made the first of a number of reforms which gave the government a firmer democratic foundation. The Reform Bill of 1832 increased the number of voters and gave representation in the House of Commons to the industrial cities of Northern England. The Liberals abolished slavery in the colonies, reformed the penal code, and passed laws which regulated the labor of women and children in factories and mines. The Chartist movement set forth a six-point program for reform in Great Britain; all but one of these reforms were secured by 1911. The Reform Bills of 1867 and 1884 granted more workingmen the right to vote. The Parliament Act of 1911 made the House of Commons supreme over the House of Lords. The British constitution is not a written constitution, but a number of laws and traditions. It places supreme legislative power in the hands of a democratically elected House of Commons. The House of Lords can retard but not prevent the passage of legislation. The formation of policies, the direction of legislation, and the administration of the government are in the hands of a Cabinet which represents the majority party in the House of Commons and is responsible to the Commons.

The Third French Republic was established by a National Assembly which was elected after the defeat (1871) of France by Prussia. This Assembly put down the revolt of the Paris Commune, raised money to pay the reparations to Germany, and adopted universal military conscription. It passed a number of acts (1875) which established the government of the Third Republic. Under the Third French Republic, France was governed by a president and a cabinet responsible to parliament, which consisted of a Senate and a Chamber of Deputies. Because of many parties in France, the Cabinet represented a coalition of parties rather than a single party. As these coalitions often broke up, governments (cabinets) changed often. These frequent changes in cabinets prevented vigorous and consistent action when needed.

The Third French Republic weathered many crises. It separated church and state, supported public education, and passed social legislation.

After the unification of Italy its government became a constitutional monarchy modeled on that of Great Britain. It was ruled by a king, a responsible cabinet, and a parliament of two houses. As in France, many parties were the cause of cabinets that represented coalitions. Italy had many problems including the poverty of southern Italians, the disagreement of the government and the Popes over the seizure of Rome, and the lack of raw materials needed in industry.

The government of the German Empire was autocratic. The Kaiser ruled through his Chancellor, whom he appointed. The Bundesrat represented the rulers of the German states. It had legislative power. The Reichstag which was elected to represent the people had little power. Each of the states had its own government and most of them were autocratic. Bismarck carried on the *Kulturkampf* against the Catholic Church and later on he endeavored to suppress the Social Democrats. German industry and foreign trade developed rapidly. German universities gained international fame. German scientific research was very productive. The German army and navy were greatly strengthened and Germany started (1883) empire-building.

The government of Russia continued to be autocratic. A liberal movement (1825) was suppressed and a revolt in Poland (1830-1831) was put down. Alexander II freed the serfs (1861), but his land reforms left both the great landowners and the peasants dissatisfied. In the last quarter of the nineteenth century the Industrial Revolution began and railways were built under the leadership (1892-1903) of Count Witte. An attempt to overthrow the government (1905) failed, but the Tsar allowed the establishment of a Duma and the election of its members; however, it had very little, if any, power.

During the nineteenth century and early part of the twentieth the Balkan nations won independence from Turkey.

EVENTS THAT TOOK PLACE AT ABOUT THE SAME TIME
1830

Reign of Queen Victoria, 1837-1901.	English Reform Bill, 1832.
Thiers, 1797-1877.	People's Charter drawn up, 1838.
Disraeli, 1804-1881.	
Louis Napoleon, 1808-1873.	
Gladstone, 1809-1898.	
Cavour, 1810-1861.	
Bismarck, 1815-1898.	
Marx, 1818-1883.	
	Repeal of the Corn Laws, 1846.
Revolutions of 1848 in France, Italy, Germany, and Austria.	End of Chartist movement in England.
	Crimean War, 1854-1856.
	Congress of Paris, 1856.
Austro-Sardinian War, 1859.	
Kingdom of Italy proclaimed, 1861.	Edict of Emancipation in Russia, 1861.
	Schleswig-Holstein War, 1864.
	Austro-Prussian War, 1866.
Compromise of 1867 (Austria-Hungary)	English Reform Bill, 1867.
Franco-Prussian War, 1870-1871.	German Empire proclaimed, 1871.
Third French Republic, 1870.	Unification of Italy completed, 1871.
Paris Commune, 1871.	*Kulturkampf*, 1871-1883.
Russo-Turkish War, 1877-1878.	Bismarck's Anti-Socialist Law, 1878.
Congress of Berlin, 1878.	
Ferry Laws in France, 1881-1882.	
	Bismarck's Insurance Laws, 1883-1889.
	English Reform Bill, 1884.
Boulanger Affair in France, 1886-1889.	
	William II became emperor of Germany, 1888.
	Bismarck dismissed, 1890.
	Industrialization of Russia developed under Count Witte, 1892-1903. Railroads built.
Dreyfus Case, 1894-1906.	
Law of Associations in France, 1901.	
Separation of church and state in France, 1905.	Russo-Japanese War, 1904-1905.
	Russian Revolution, 1905.
	Lloyd George Budget, 1909.
German Imperial Insurance Code, 1911.	Balkan Wars, 1912-1913.

Outbreak of the First World War, 1914.

1914

BENJAMIN DISRAELI. England's accomplished Conservative Prime Minister was novelist as well as statesman. After acquiring control of the Suez Canal for England, he made Queen Victoria, in 1876, Empress of India as well.

G. B. S. AT WORK. Bernard Shaw, at left, typing in an out-of-doors workshop at his home in Welwyn, Herts, England.

POMP AND CIRCUMSTANCE, LONDON: This photograph of the King and Queen in the state coach after the opening of Parliament in 1937 illustrates the English blend of representative government with royal pageantry.

BUILDING THE TRANS-SIBERIAN RAILWAY. An old print shows the road which developed Russian trade with China and Japan.

ALEXANDER II. As Czar, he abolished serfdom but repressed liberal thought.

RUSSO - JAPANESE WAR. Japanese troops are seen occupying trenches in the war which ended in 1905 with a Japanese victory that was welcomed by Western powers.

CHAPTER 24

Imperialism, Nationalism, and Democracy in Latin America

The part of the Americas south of the United States is usually called Latin America because its different peoples speak Spanish, Portuguese, or French, languages derived from Latin.

The Spaniards discovered, explored, conquered, and settled the larger part of Latin America, and the Portuguese established a colony in Brazil. After a long period under the rule of their respective mother countries, the colonies won their freedom. Since they gained their political independence, the Latin American countries have faced many political, economic, and social problems. In spite of dictatorships, they seem to be tending toward a more democratic government. Latin American countries have produced famous historians, poets, novelists, artists, and musicians. Their peoples are making an effort to understand and solve their problems. A cause of war among them has been disputes over boundaries, but these are fairly well settled now. Even before the coming of the Second World War the Latin American republics joined in making plans for hemispheric defense.

• • •

Latin America is a land of great geographic contrasts. Latin America is the name given to all the lands in the Western Hemisphere south of the Rio Grande, with the exception of British Honduras, the British West Indies, and British and Dutch Guianas. The total area of Latin America (about 8,500,000 square miles) is almost three times that of the United States, but its population (155,-000,000) is just a little larger than that of our country.

In general the people are not as rich and life is not so highly industrialized and urbanized as in the United States; the peoples are highly artistic and northern visitors find Latin American ways of living interesting and its architecture unusual. The successors of Columbus found a well developed Indian culture in some places and although Spanish conquerors uprooted this old culture wherever they could, much of it still survives, especially in dress, in music and dances, and in festivals. The culture of Latin America reflects the blending of the Indian cultures and Spanish culture and also Indian cultures and Portuguese culture.

Cabral, a Portuguese admiral, in 1500 started to sail from Lisbon around Africa to the East Indies. To avoid the calms off the west coast of Africa and to find favoring winds, he sailed so far westward that he landed on the eastern coast of South America. There he hoisted the flag of Portugal, claimed it for his country, and started its Portuguese occupation. These winds (trade winds) bring moisture and fertility to tropical Latin America. When the low clouds of the trade wind belt pass over moderately high mountains, their temperature is lowered enough to produce rain. The rain falls on the eastern side of the mountains, but there is not any rainfall on their western sides. The eastern slopes of the Andes are unbearably humid to white men. Even on small islands, for example Trinidad and Barbados, there is a wet side on the east and a dry side on the west.

Only Chile and Argentina are in the belt of prevailing westerlies in the Southern Hemisphere; our country is in the belt of prevailing westerlies in the Northern Hemisphere. The high barrier of the Andes makes Southern Chile a very wet and Southern Argentina a very dry country. As the basin of the Amazon lies in the equatorial belt of calms (a region of very heavy rainfall), it contains the largest rain forest in the world, a dense green forest of very tall trees sparsely inhabited by some of the most backward tribes in the world.

The backbone of Latin America is the Andes—a long chain of mountains. It consists in most places of a double chain of mountains with a high plateau between them. On this plateau rise some of the highest volcanoes of the world, the snow-capped summits of which are visible from the monument where the equator crosses the Ecuadorean highway. On this high plateau people enjoy an almost eternal spring and here was developed the great Incan civilization and on it are located nine of the capital cities of the twenty republics of Latin America. This inter-mountain plateau is wide in Mexico and Bolivia and almost absent in Panama and Southern Chile. In the two latter places are the lowest gaps in the Andean chain, the Panama Canal and the Strait of Magellan. Elsewhere the Andean passes are usually very high.

Most of Eastern Brazil is a rolling upland called the Brazilian Highlands and the same kind of uplands north of the Amazon is called the Guiana Highlands. Some ranges in these highlands rise from 6000 to 9000 feet, but most of the uplands are below 3000 feet. Most of this upland is covered by an open, sparse forest with much grass and scrub; the river bottoms are covered with thick forests. The rains fall in summer and the winters are dry.

Between the Andes and the uplands in Brazil and Guiana is a lowland, much like the Central Plains in the United States. In the north this plain is drained by the Orinoco. Here roam many cattle hidden in places by the tall grass that grows on the plain. Farther south, the Amazon lowland is covered by a tropical rain forest. The Amazon carries more water than any other river in the world, and its many tributaries are the main arteries of travel in the Amazon basin. Still farther south the forest opens up in the palm-shaded Gran Chaco of the Paraguay River basin. South of this area the trees get sparser and sparser. The wheat-corn-alfalfa fields of the pampas remind one of Illinois and Iowa. Farther south the plains are bleak and dry but enough grass grows to graze millions of sheep.

Most of the United States is in the North Temperate Zone, but most of Latin America is in the Torrid Zone. Latin Americans provide us with many of our tropical products and in winter some of our fruits and vegetables. We buy sugar, coffee, cocoa, rubber, bananas, pineapples, chicle, mahogany, quebracho (ax breaker) from them, and we sell them automobiles, radios, refrigerators, railway equipment, machetes, and many other kinds of our manufactured goods. Trading ships ply both ways laden with heavy cargoes. Argentina, however, produces wheat, beef, and mutton as we do; thus her foreign trade is directed more to Europe where there is a market for her surpluses.

Latin America has more than its share of the world's minerals. The United States needs the copper, nitrates, and iron it obtains from Chile, the tin and silver from Bolivia, the copper and vanadium from Peru, the mica and quartz crystals and manganese from Brazil, and the manganese from Cuba. A chief source of bauxite for aluminum is in the Guianas. Venezuelan petroleum oiled the war machine of Great Britain. Brazil has mountains of iron ore and is now developing its own steel industry.

The cultures developed by the Indians before the coming of white men differed greatly. They included those of the highly civilized Mayas, Aztecs, and Incans and those of barbaric tribes. These peoples differed in methods of agriculture and industry, in the arts, in religion, and in warlike disposition. The Mayas, Aztecs, and Incans lived in communities; the Indians in northeastern South America and in other places were nomads.

The Mayas are noted for their cultural development. In the far distant past, Indian farmers lived in what we call the Yucatan Peninsula. About 1000 B.C. other Indians called Mayas invaded the peninsula and conquered and enslaved the Indian farmers. The Mayas were a gifted people who developed a brilliant culture that lasted 1500 years. They built cities and stone palaces; they worked with copper, gold, and silver, and they melted these metals and poured them into molds. They drew wires and made gold leaf; they invented a system of writing and a system of numbers that used twenty as its basis. Scholars have only recently learned to decipher about one third of the writings of their learned men. About 580 B.C. the Mayas had worked out a calendar more accurate than any used in Europe before Pope Gregory revised the Julian Calendar (1582) and named the revision the *Gregorian Calendar.* Their culture attained its highest development about 400 to 600 A.D. Then for reasons entirely unknown today, they abandoned

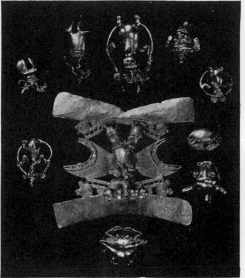

American Museum of Natural History
GOLD FIGURES FROM COSTA RICA.

their cities and migrated to the northern part of the peninsula where their descendants are still farmers.

Toltecs took over the Mayan civilization and the Aztecs overthrew the Toltec Empire. Soon after their migration the Mayas were conquered by another Indian tribe (Toltecs) from the central plateau of what is now Mexico. After conquering the Mayas, they adopted much of Mayan culture, including their writing. The Toltec Empire lasted until about 1450 when it, in turn, was overthrown by the Aztecs, whose ruler was Montezuma when the Spaniards landed in Mexico. The highly civilized Aztecs possessed a well organized and well governed empire. They engaged in agriculture, industry, and trade. A Spaniard declared that Aztec physicians were superior to physicians in Europe at the time of the conquest of the Aztecs by Cortés. The Aztecs were a warlike people who sacrificed human beings to their warrior gods. Heavy taxes and demands for victims for the sacrifices made many of the

INCANS CONSECRATING A VESSEL TO THE SUN WHICH THEY WORSHIPED.

subjects of the Aztec ruler discontented and ripe for revolt when Cortés landed.

Incans developed a highly socialistic form of government. The Indian tribes of Central America engaged in agriculture and commerce and used metals, but they were not as highly civilized as the Aztecs. About 1100 an energetic people (Incans) established their control over large numbers of peasant farmers in Peru. The Incan Empire, about 1230 miles long, contained what is today all of Peru and a part of Ecuador, Bolivia, and Chile. It contained perhaps 3,000,000 inhabitants. The word *Inca* was the title of the ruler. At the head of the government was the Inca, believed by his people to be a descendant of the sun god. His empire consisted of provinces. Within a province the basic social and economic unit consisted of ten families.

The Incans built good roads and bridges to bind the provinces of the empire together. Over them armies marched and the Inca's messengers, who carried the official post, ran in relays; storehouses and inns were erected at convenient places. A governmental system, which might be described as state socialism, regulated and supervised every detail of human life.

State planning regulated the lives of everyone, except the privileged. In the In-

can Empire the state planned, regulated, ordered, and enforced with very strict laws the lives of the masses of the people from birth to death, including their actions, work, social status, homes, marriages, and even the training of their children. Everyone, except those of royal blood and the members of the priesthood, was a mere cog in the machine of the empire; every individual was numbered, a unit tagged like all the others which made up nearly all of the population of the empire.

At birth the place of the child when it grew to maturity was ordained by the state. When five years of age every child, whether male or female, was taken over by the government, reared, and trained for the work and position to which its entire life was to be devoted.

When a man reached the age of twenty-four he was forced to marry; the age limit

A CUP FROM NAZCA, PERU.

of a spinster was eighteen years. Fathers and mothers hadn't any say as to the future of their children. That was ordained by the all-powerful state.

If spinners were needed, girls were trained for that work. If soldiers were needed, boys were trained to be soldiers. If farm workers were needed in a given locality, farm workers not needed in another locality were transferred to the locality where they were needed and there they were compelled to stay.

Persons of royal blood and the members of the priesthood were privileged. All the others were equal, socially and in worldly goods. Each of them contributed in an equal degree to the support of the government, the army, the community, the priesthood, and religion.

In this rigorous and inflexible state plan-

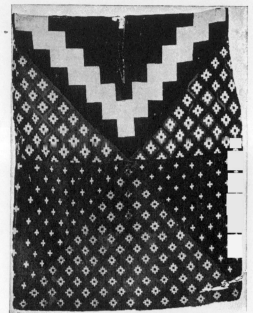

AN INCAN PONCHO FROM THE ISLAND OF TITICACA, BOLIVIA. Note the geometric design on this useful garment.

ning, life was pleasant for rulers, nobles, and priests, all of whom grew rich in gold, silver, and precious stones at the expense of those who did not belong to the privileged classes.

Skilled artisans made metalware, jewelry, and gold and silver models of plants and flowers "some just beginning to sprout, others half-grown, others having reached maturity." Other craftsmen cut, polished, and set amethysts, emeralds, and other precious stones. Ample supplies of foodstuffs, pottery, leather, and metal goods were produced. The llama was domesticated, its flesh was eaten, and its wool used to make garments.

The Indians who lived on the plateaus of Central America, in Colombia, and on the great plains and in the river valleys of South America were hunters, fishermen, and farmers. Those who lived in settlements learned some of the arts of civilization; others were restless and barbaric wanderers.

AN INCAN WATER VESSEL, SHOWING A SEATED FIGURE CARRYING COCOA LEAVES.

American Museum of Natural History

POTTERY OF THE EARLY CHIMU PERIOD, PERU. A warrior in full regalia is depicted on the vessel at the left. The central piece is a "portrait" jar. The vessel at the right shows a hand to hand combat between mythical beings.

The Spanish conquered the Indians in the islands of the West Indies. The land was easily conquered and occupied. The Spanish government set up the House of Trade (1503) whose business it was to see that loyal Spaniards and devout Catholics settled there not only as seekers of gold and silver, but also as farmers, carpenters, masons, and other craftsmen. The government supplied the farmers with horses, cows, goats, sheep, seeds, plants, and farm implements. Soon for the first time in America these farmers were raising wheat, rice, sugar cane, oranges, lemons, and olives. Indians were forced to work as slaves or under a form of forced labor in mines and on farms. The supply of Indian labor proved insufficient, and the conditions of work and white men's diseases that brought death to many decreased the labor supply still further. The shortage was supplied by the introduction of Negro slaves from Africa. The Indians of the West Indies died out; Negroes took their places.

The story of the conquest of the rest of Latin America is very different from that of the West Indies.

Cortés conquered the Aztecs. In 1519 Cortés sailed from Santiago in Cuba in eleven boats with 400 Spaniards, 200 Indians, and thirty-two horses. He landed at what is now Vera Cruz and marched to the Aztec capital (Tenochtitlan), the site of Mexico City. An ancient Indian tradition said that the descendant of a ruler whom they had once rejected would some day return as a god and rule over them. Many Indians, including the Aztec emperor, Montezuma, believed that Cortés and his soldiers were the agents of this god and therefore supernatural beings.

Many Indian subjects of Montezuma joined with the Spaniards to escape from his oppressive rule. Cortés asked Montezuma for an interview. Montezuma refused the request and tried to bribe him to depart. Conferences that lasted several months resulted in Montezuma swearing loyalty to Charles V King of Spain. After Cortés had forced Montezuma to permit him to use a pagan temple for Christian worship, this use of the temple caused the people to revolt against both Montezuma and Cortés because they thought the temple had been violated. In the revolt Montezuma was killed and the Spaniards were driven from the capital in 1520. The next year Cortés returned with reinforce

American Museum of Natural History

CAST OF POTTERY DISH WITH MODELED HUMAN FIGURE FROM THE VALLEY OF NAZCA, PERU.

American Museum of Natural History

INCAN VESSELS WITH RIBBON HANDLES. Left to right: Peru; Island of Titicaca, Bolivia; Island of Titicaca, Bolivia; Cuzco, Peru.

ments and captured the capital, but the Aztec treasure of which Cortés had heard was not to be found. When the successor of Montezuma was tortured, he said that it had been thrown into a nearby lake. The Spanish found little gold in the lake or in the city. The supposed Aztec treasure was never found, but Mexico had been won for the Spanish king. It remained a Spanish possession for about 300 years and during that time it proved to be a rich source of gold and silver, especially for Spain.

Pizarro conquered the part of the Incan Empire known today as Peru. In 1531 Pizarro sailed from Panama on three ships with 180 soldiers and twenty-seven horses for Guayaquil. A civil war which had taken place just before the arrival of Pizarro made his conquest easy. As the Incan emperor, like Montezuma, believed the Spaniards to be supernatural beings, he decided to confer with Pizarro. But to be on the safe side he raised an army of 40,000 soldiers for his protection. After the pagan emperor (Atahualpa) had refused to accept the Christian religion and to agree to Spanish rule, Pizarro ordered his soldiers to fire on the Incans. Thousands of them were killed, the rest fled, and the Inca was captured without the loss

of a single Spaniard. To secure his release from prison, the Inca offered to fill a large room once with gold and a smaller room twice with silver. Pizarro accepted the offer. After dividing the gold and silver (more than $5,000,000) among his soldiers, Pizarro had the Inca killed on trumped up charges and then proceeded to the conquest of the Inca's empire and the accumulation of more loot. Like Mexico, Peru remained a possession of Spain for about 300 years and

American Museum of Natural History

CEREMONIAL URN, PERU. The main figure represents Viracocha, the Creator God worshiped in pre-Incan times in Peru.

Bettmann Archive

SPANIARDS DESTROYING AZTEC IDOLS.

during this time it, too, proved to be a rich source of gold and silver.

Other Spanish conquerors helped to build the Spanish colonial empire in America. The conquests by Cortés and Pizarro were followed by the conquests of other regions. The conquests of the settled communities of Indians in Central America and in northern South America were comparatively easy. A Spaniard with an army of 166 men conquered the Indians of Colombia. The Indians of Chile, however, continued to fight first against the Spaniards, and afterwards against the Chilean government until as late as 1881. Many of the nomadic Indians of Venezuela and Argentina fled into the interior rather than submit to Spanish rule; those who did not flee were annihilated by the Spaniards.

Most of the Spanish conquerors were looking for gold. In their search for riches, glory, and power the Spaniards endured untold hardships. Although they fought with one another, they won in less than a century a colonial empire for Spain unsurpassed at that time in extent and riches.

The conversion of most pagan Indians in Latin America to Catholicism was a great achievement. Missionaries accompanied or followed close behind the conquerors to convert the Indians. They were clergy-men who had been carefully selected from the members of different religious orders. They were appointed by the king or his agents and were given considerable freedom outside the performance of their religious work. After a region had been conquered, missions were established to convert the Indians to Catholicism and to lift them from barbarism to civilization. The missionary had full control of the land and of the Indians who lived in the mission village. Under his direction the men worked the fields and tended the flocks while the women spun or wove. Discipline was severe. The Indians were whipped if they did not obey the missionary. To keep them from running away, a wall was built around the mission and the gates were locked at night. The Indians received a share of the foodstuffs and tobacco they raised and their clothing was made from cloth woven by the women. Indians in the vicinity of a mission who had accepted the missionary's teachings were also placed under his control. Gifts of food, clothing, and trinkets were often used to attract Indians to a mission where they attended church services and received religious instruction.

A mission guard of four or five soldiers was generally able to keep order not only in the mission but also in the Indian villages outside of the mission.

When a mission was established it was expected to last ten years, but some lasted a century or more. The missionaries succeeded in bringing many Indians within the folds of the church, but they were less successful in their efforts to lift the Indians from barbarism to civilization.

Spanish settlers followed in the wake of missionaries. As in the West Indies, they had to be loyal Spaniards and devout Catholics who were skilled farmers, artisans, and merchants. In areas where the Indians were already farmers or worked in mines, the task of the Spanish settlers consisted chiefly in supervising their work.

During the years of the conquests many Indians were made slaves; some slaves were taken to Spain where they served their Spanish masters. Because ill-treatment of the Indians under slavery was reducing their numbers at an alarming rate, the Spanish government forbade Indian slavery in the New Laws of 1542. Then it resorted to other means to force Indians to work. The most common of these was the *encomienda* (trusteeship), an old system that was reformed by the New Laws. Under *encomienda* the government gave a Spanish settler a tract of land and entrusted him with the Indians already on that land or other Indians assigned to him. In return for their forced labor the settler assumed the responsibility of caring for, teaching, and converting the Indians. They were required to work under his direction, and they were not free to leave the settler's land. If he mistreated them or failed to carry out his trust, the government might deprive him of his land. Another means to obtain forced labor was employed in mining districts where able-bodied Indians were chosen by lot to work for forty days in the year for pay. In the areas where the Indians fled or were wiped out, Spanish settlements resembled those that developed in the French and English colonies in North America.

Bishops and priests accompanied the settlers. In the early days of colonization few Spanish women migrated to the colonies. Consequently military men and settlers married Indian women. Settlers established towns at places advantageous for trade. As many of these towns grew into cities, most of the people lived in cities.

Five social classes developed in the Spanish colonies. The highest class was composed of men and women who had been born in

The Metropolitan Museum of Art

THE LAKE AND CITY OF MEXICO. Three years after the City of Mexico was destroyed by the Spaniards, this first printed plan of the city was published, as some Spaniard remembered it and sketched or described it for the illustrator.

Spain and who had come to the colonies as settlers or were sent to the colonies to govern them. The officeholders in the highest class were for the most part nobles. Social distinctions existed among landowners, merchants, and artisans. All of them looked down on all Spaniards who had been born in the colonies even if these Spaniards were wealthier than they.

The second class was composed of the upper class Spaniards (creoles) born in America. Creoles who were the descendants of the conquerors considered themselves higher than the other creoles. Most creoles owned plantations or mines or businesses; others were managers of properties owned by others. Many who prospered financially built houses that had patios (courts) much like those in Spain. They introduced the styles, manners, and customs which were popular in Spain. In time they came to dislike the members of the highest class and to look down on the members of the three classes below them.

The third class was composed of mestizos, offspring of Spanish men and Indian women. Able and intelligent mestizos acquired wealth and even rose to high positions in business. However, they seldom gained social recognition from the two classes above them. Most of the mestizos were poor.

The fourth class was composed of Indians. The safeguards of the system of trusteeship did not prevent Spanish masters from treating many of the Indians cruelly. The chief protectors of the Indians were the clergy. The greatest indictment of Spanish cruelty toward the Indians was written in 1552 by Bartolomé de Las Casas, a Dominican friar, who later became a bishop. Most modern students of the history of these times in Latin America think that the cruelty of the Spaniards has been exaggerated. The government tried to protect the Indians from abuses and nearly always the self-interest of the Indians' masters induced many of them to treat their Indian laborers humanely.

The fifth class was composed of Negroes, mulattoes (part white, part black) and zambos (part black, part Indian). Before 1532 Portuguese slave traders brought most of the Negro slaves to Latin America. They were brought to the West Indies, to Brazil, and to a lesser extent to Venezuela.

The highest of these five social classes despised all the classes below it; each of the other classes hated the class or classes above it and all but the lowest class looked down on the class or classes below it.

The Spanish government regulated the activities of the colonists. The king of Spain maintained complete control over his colonies everywhere. The king and his advisers drew up the regulations for farming, commerce, and industry in the colonies. They were administered by the House of Trade founded in 1503. To advise and assist the king in the government of the colonies, he established (1511) the Council of the Indies. Under the king's direction this council appointed colonial officials and established colonial courts. The Council decided all military questions; it issued laws for the colonies; and it decided appeals from the colonial courts. After more than 170 years of colonial experience (1682) the Council compiled a code of laws known as the Law of the Indies. This Code is considered by many to be the greatest achievement in colonial law in all history.

The highest government official in Spanish America was a viceroy, personal representative of the king in an area called a viceroyalty.

The viceroyalties were divided into areas under captains-general and presidents. Socially the captain-general outranked the president. Therefore he, instead of a president, would be assigned to an area of great military or political importance. These areas were subdivided into provinces under governors. Each viceroy was also governor of the province in which his capital was situated and its captain-general or president. The captain-general or the president was also governor of a province not ruled by a viceroy. No rigid system of officials existed. The powers and duties of the officials were not the same in all districts. The Spanish adapted their form of government to the local military, political, or social situation. In the eighteenth century the king and Council instituted a system of royal representatives called intendants. They desired and intended to make this system uniform throughout the empire. Nevertheless, in practice they gave each intendant powers and duties different if need be from every other to suit the local conditions he encountered.

The king sent a viceroy to Mexico City (1529) to rule the Spanish empire in America. A second viceroyalty was established

(1542) at Lima. It comprised all the Spanish possessions in South America except Venezuela, which remained under the viceroy of Mexico City. In 1717 a third viceroyalty was set up in Bogota; it comprised all northern South America, including Venezuela, and in 1776, the year of the Declaration of Independence, the Plata region was taken away from the viceroyalty of Lima and placed under its own viceroy.

The Spanish empire in America was also divided into eleven districts, each under a court *(audiencia)* that administered colonial laws issued by the Council of the Indies and decided cases brought before it. Local government was in the hands of a town organization *(cabildo)*.

All officials and courts in a viceroyalty were under the supervision of the viceroy. Nevertheless, the captains-general, the presidents of the provinces, and the judges of the courts were appointed by the Council of the Indies and were usually directly responsible to it. The powers and duties of the different courts varied greatly. Some of them were strong enough to disregard orders issued by the viceroy over them. In a viceroyalty difficulties of travel and primitive means of communication made actual control by a viceroy almost impossible. Centralization of authority and uniform government existed in theory but not in practice.

The colonists did not take any part in government. Consequently, they did not get any training in democratic government such as the English colonists did. However, they were sometimes called upon to express their opinions to town organizations.

The House of Trade, acting under orders of the king and the Council of the Indies, regulated the production of precious metals, foodstuffs, and other raw materials so as to produce them in quantities needed in Spain. Though the Council allowed colonists

The Metropolitan Museum of Art

CITY OF ACAPULCO ON THE PACIFIC COAST OF MEXICO. It was the only port in New Spain which was permitted to trade with the East, chiefly the Philippines, a Spanish possession. The first galleon sailed in 1565; the last in 1815.

to manufacture textiles, leather goods, and pottery to satisfy their local needs, it forbade them to sell these goods elsewhere. All goods had to be shipped to or brought from Spain in Spanish ships. For some years all commerce was carried on through cities in the Spanish colonies specified by the House of Trade.

The Spanish government through its House of Trade made a greater effort to enforce the mercantile theory of trade than the government of any other nation that had a colonial empire. Even here, however, the system was not rigid. From the very beginning the House of Trade gave favored individuals or companies of foreign nations the right to trade. But in spite of all its efforts to enforce strictly the mercantile theory, English, Dutch, and French merchants carried on an active smuggling trade in manufactured goods and raw materials with many of the Spanish colonies. Corrupt officials in the colonies found it financially profitable to permit this illegal trade.

The Spanish culture transplanted into the Spanish colonial empire in America was modified by Indian culture. Many of the

Ewing Galloway

Caracas, capital of Venezuela, is over 3000 feet high up on one of the slopes of the Andes. This view shows the University of Caracas, a very modern and up-to-date institution of learning.

settlements became prosperous enough for town governments to support schools for boys. Both churchmen and laymen established schools for the education of boys chiefly in religion, but also in arithmetic and in reading and writing Latin and Spanish. The mission schools taught Indian boys arithmetic, reading, writing, religion, and sometimes gave instruction in trades and crafts. As early as 1535 a printing press was set up in Mexico City. In 1551 a charter was granted for the founding of a university in Mexico City and in the same year a charter was granted for another to be founded in Lima, Peru, almost a hundred years before the founding of the first college in the English colonies. In 1558 a university was chartered in Santo Domingo. The chief purpose of these universities was to educate men to be priests, lawyers, and physicians. The lan-

guage used in the universities was Latin, as it was in the European universities at that time.

Writers in the Spanish colonies began to produce a native literature. Garcilaso de la Vega, son of a Spanish army captain and an Incan princess, wrote *Royal Commentaries,* a fascinating account of the history and customs of the Incans. One of Cortés' captains, Bernal Diaz del Castillo, wrote a *True History of the Conquest of New Spain.* Ercilla, a Spanish soldier in Chile, composed an epic poem based upon the wars between the Spaniards and the Indians.

The Spaniards who settled in the colonies transplanted the Spanish language, the Catholic religion, and Spanish social customs into New Spain. In time, a distinctive colonial culture developed to which the Indians made contributions, particularly in art and music.

The bright colors which the Indians used in their arts and crafts were used by artists in paintings and mosaics both in homes and in churches. Musical rhythms used by the Indians in their songs were used by musicians in the dance music of the colonists. Many beautiful churches and monasteries were built. The bright colors of native costumes and of tropical flowers used by the colonists in their clothing gave charm and even brilliance to religious festivals and processions.

The Spanish developed a colonial empire in America which was fairly prosperous and on the whole well administered. It contributed more than $2,000,000,000 worth of gold and silver to Spain in addition to many valuable products of forest and farm.

The Spanish colonies in New Spain finally won their political independence. Many factors combined to bring Spanish control in Latin America to an end between 1800 and 1825. Some of them were: (1) Social and political discontent which was general in most colonies of the Spanish colonial empire. It was more deep-seated in some colonies than in others. The poor whites, mixed breeds, and Indians who had been oppressed became rebellious. Creoles resented the attitude of social superiority of the Spanish officials. Moreover, they were conscious of their latent power, and consequently they desired a share in government. The practice of the mercantile theory was a constant cause of their discontent.

(2) The desire for liberty. Educated Spanish Americans had read books written by liberal European intellectuals. They knew also that the English colonists in North America had revolted, won their independence, and set up a republican form of government (1776), and that the French people had revolted against Louis XVI (1789) and established the First French Republic.

(3) Weakening Spanish rule. From 1808-1814 Spain was ruled by Louis Bonaparte, brother of Napoleon Bonaparte. The Spanish Americans who refused to recognize him as the rightful king of Spain began revolutionary movements by setting up governments which made reforms to correct the abuses of which they had complained to Spain. In 1814, after the Congress of Vienna had restored Ferdinand VII to the throne of Spain, he refused to agree to these reforms. Thereupon the movement for independence in the Spanish colonies gained greater headway. Local revolts occurred in many parts of New Spain and spread to other places as soon as leaders in them were able to unify and organize the local revolutionists.

As early as 1783 the first great revolutionist, Francisco de Miranda, who was a wealthy Venezuelan creole, began to agitate for independence. For years he endeavored unsuccessfully to interest the governments of the United States, Great Britain, and France in helping the Spanish colonies obtain their independence. He found little support even in his own country, and a revolutionary expedition which he led in Venezuela (1806) was a complete failure. His work, however, had great influence on the leaders of the later revolutionary movements some of whom had helped Miranda.

The revolutionists in the northern part of South America were led by Simon Bolivar (1783-1830), who was born of a wealthy family in Caracas, Venezuela. While he stood as a youth on a hill in Rome (1803) and looked down on the remains of its ancient glories, he took an oath that he would free his homeland from Spain. In 1811 he took part in a revolutionary uprising in Caracas; Miranda commanded the army and Bolivar was one of his lieutenants. After Miranda's revolutionary army was defeated in 1812, he surrendered to the Spanish. Bolivar and his supporters were so angered by this act that

Ewing Galloway

LIMA THE BEAUTIFUL. The cathedral viewed through the Plaza del Armas. The cathedral
was built in 1758 on the site of an earlier one destroyed by earthquake.

they threw Miranda in prison. The Spanish, contrary to the terms of surrender, took him to Spain where he was kept in prison until his death in 1830.

After the Caracas uprising had been suppressed, Bolivar went to what is now Colombia where he organized an army, and declared war to the death against the Spaniards in northern South America. In 1813 he led his army to Venezuela. During eight years of fighting, in which he suffered many defeats and won many victories over the Spanish forces, he finally forced the Spanish government to recognize the independence of both Venezuela and Colombia (1821). In 1822 he went to Guayaquil to liberate Ecuador.

While these revolutionary movements were going on in the north, others had begun and spread in the south. The first of these led to the establishment of an independent government in Buenos Aires, Argentina, on May 25, 1810, which Argentinians celebrate today as Independence Day. The armies of the new government won some victories but could not defeat the Spanish army that was strongly based in the highlands (now Peru) near the Pacific. The failures of the Argentine armies led to the rise of a leader, José de San Martín (1778-1850), who was a military genius. He organized an army of 5000 soldiers and led it (1817) through a 12,000 foot pass in the Chilean Andes. It has been said that this was a more difficult feat than the crossing of the Alps by Napoleon's armies.

In Chile he gained support from a Chilean army led by Bernardo O'Higgins, son of a Chilean woman and an Irish immigrant who had amassed great wealth and had even been viceroy in Lima. O'Higgins is called the "George Washington of Chile." The combined armies of Argentina and Chile were successful in driving the Spanish army out of Chile. After Chile had been proclaimed independent (1818), San Martín sailed with an army of Argentinians and Chileans to help free Peru from Spanish rule. They were transported in warships commanded by Thomas Cochrane, a former British naval officer who had come (1818) to aid the revolutionists in South America and was now in the employ of the Chilean government. In 1821, San Martín's army occupied Lima without bloodshed and the independence of Peru was proclaimed, but the Spanish armies in the highlands of upper Peru (now Peru) that had fought off the Argentinian armies were yet to be defeated.

In the summer of 1822 San Martín went to Guayaquil to confer with Bolivar. The two men differed in temperament, and besides each had his own plan for the future of the new independent countries. Bolivar favored federal republics for the new countries, each under a strong president. San Martín preferred monarchies, each under a king to be chosen from one of the royal families of Europe. Although they did not agree on the form of government for the new countries, they did agree to continue the revolutionary movement until Spain recognized the political independence of all her Spanish colonies in Latin America. No one knows just what was said at the conference, but soon after, San Martín retired from the command of his army, and in 1824 went to Europe where he

lived until his death in 1850. Bolivar led his forces, strengthened by San Martín's army, to victory over the Spanish armies in southeastern Peru and Bolivia and completed their liberation.

The long and courageous struggle of Bolivar against heavy odds and his final victory have caused him to be called the Great Liberator. The English translation of a Spanish inscription on a monument erected to his memory in Cartagena, Colombia, is:

> Bolivar, favorite of fortune,
> Disdained its attraction,
> Consecrated his repose and all his life to his
> fatherland:
> Intrepid soldier,
> Expert leader, victor of a hundred battles,
> He freed his country, gave her laws,
> And submitted himself to them.

Revolts in Mexico and in the colonies in Central America overthrew Spanish rule. By 1822 six Spanish colonies had declared their independence: Mexico (which at that time included Central America), Great Colombia, Peru, Chile, Argentina, and Paraguay. Bolivia declared its independence in 1825. By 1826 Spain had lost all of its colonial empire in the New World except islands in the West Indies.

In 1839 Central America which was under the leadership of the Central American Confederation broke up into the republics of Costa Rica, Nicaragua, Honduras, and El Salvador. Present Uruguay, which was claimed by both Argentina and Brazil, was set up, with the aid of Great Britain, as an independent republic in 1828. Great Colombia, as a confederation, dissolved in 1830, and three separate states evolved from it, Venezuela, Ecuador, and New Granada, later (1861) called Colombia.

The United States recognized Mexico, Great Colombia, Peru, Chile, and Argentina as independent nations in 1822, and in 1823 issued the Monroe Doctrine. Paraguay, following an isolationist program, did not seek for or receive recognition until 1852. Great Britain began its recognition of the new republics in 1825 and France in 1830.

In the Spanish-American War (1898), the United States invaded and captured Cuba and Puerto Rico. This war ended with the Treaty of Paris in which Spain recognized the political independence of Cuba and ceded Puerto Rico to the United States. The Spanish colonial empire in America had come to an end about four hundred years after the first voyage of Columbus.

Brazil, a Portuguese colony, gained its independence. When Admiral Cabral went back to Portugal he took a load of red dyewood and from the name of this wood (*brazil*) the country supposedly got its name. Fortunately for Portugal the land which Cabral discovered lay east of the Papal Line of Demarcation. The Portuguese were slow in colonizing their new possession because of their much greater interest in their new discoveries in the East Indies. The first settlements in Brazil were trading posts along the Atlantic coast, established chiefly for the trade in dyewood.

The first settlers met with the fierce opposition of Indians, many of whom were cannibals. Their opposition died down to some extent when the Indians learned the usefulness of the tools they obtained from the Portuguese. To encourage more settlements, the Portuguese government (1533) offered to grant fifteen strips of land 150 miles wide on the coast and extending inland to the Papal Line of Demarcation to Portuguese who would make settlements in these land grants. The fifteen men who accepted grants transported many thousands of settlers to Brazil who engaged in agriculture, especially in the production of sugar cane, cocoa, and cotton.

With the growth of agriculture the scarcity of farm workers led to the enslavement of Indians. Most Indians resisted bitterly; others fled into the interior. To supply the need for more labor on the plantations, Portuguese traders who had been selling Negroes into slavery to the Spaniards in the West Indies brought to Brazil many Negroes from Angola, a Portuguese colony in West Africa. The presence of Negroes, mulattoes, and zambos created a difficult racial problem for Brazil.

After settlements had been made along the coast, the next step was the exploration and settlement of the interior. The leaders in this movement were Portuguese-Indian cattle raisers (Paulistas) who lived in Sao Paulo. They went into the interior to get Indian slaves. They thought it was their patriotic duty to win and hold for Portugal the vast interior of Brazil. Because the perils in the interior, chiefly hostile Indians, were so great, each Paulista made his will, confessed his sins, and attended Mass before departing. Sometimes all the members of expeditions were wiped out by the Indians. After the danger from the Indians had been removed, Paulistas settled in the interior, taking with them their families, household goods, tools, and domestic animals. They were the real pioneers of Brazil.

As early as 1560 Paulistas discovered gold in small amounts near the site of present-day Rio de Janeiro. After they had discovered richer deposits farther inland (1695), a gold rush from the coast took place. In 1728 a priest who had seen diamonds in the rough in the East Indies found that "pebbles" gold miners were using as counters in a card game were diamonds. The exportation of gold, diamonds, and sugar brought wealth to the owners of the mines and the plantations.

In 1549 the Portuguese government unified all the settlements into a colony and ap-

LATIN AMERICA
— important railways
— Panamerican highway
▭ Tropical rainforest

0 ————— 1000
Miles

For about 300 years Latin America was under the rule of the Spanish kings, except for Brazil, which was Portuguese, and a few small colonies of other European powers. Inspired by the American War of Independence, the Spanish colonies revolted against the mother country and by 1825 all had won their independence. Instead of forming a single great empire, however, the former Spanish colonies became sovereign countries, jealously guarding their independence and even waging war against each other over boundaries.

pointed a captain-general to rule it. He founded Bahia (1549) as the capital of Brazil, and it continued to be the capital during most of the colonial era. For a long time commerce between Portugal and Brazil was managed by companies to which the Portuguese government had given the right to trade in certain ports. The Portuguese government permitted Jews and Protestants to become colonists and many did. In general, the social classes in Brazil corresponded to those in the Spanish colonies. The friction between these classes was complicated by large numbers of Negroes and zambos.

When Napoleon attacked Portugal (1807), the Portuguese royal family, led by Prince John, who was ruling Portugal in place of his mother who was insane, fled from Lisbon to Bahia. Here he established a government in exile which was theoretically the center of the government of Portugal and thereby the importance of Brazil was increased. On the death of his mother (1816) John succeeded to the throne of Portugal as John VI. In 1821 he returned to Lisbon where a revolution threatened to overthrow the government of Portugal. When John returned to Lisbon, he left his son Pedro behind to govern Brazil. In 1822 when the Portuguese government attempted to restore Brazil to its former colonial status, the radical party persuaded Pedro to lead a movement for Brazilian independence. A bloodless revolution and an easy victory were followed by the establishment of a monarchy with Pedro I as emperor and with a relatively liberal constitution. The monarchy in Brazil was to last until 1889.

Independence thrust grave problems on the new republics. One of these was the problem of government. The leaders of the revolutions had spent much time discussing the form of government for each of the new countries. San Martín favored a monarchy

under a member of a European royal family for each of the new countries. Bolivar preferred a republic under a president with ample executive powers. Neither idea was acceptable to the majority of people, especially to the creoles who desired a more liberal form of government. In the end, leaders in most of the new countries drew up constitutions modeled on that of the United States, with one important difference. Most of them did not grant religious liberty. They recognized the Catholic Church as the state church and refused to permit any other religion to hold public services.

Experience with these constitutions showed that they did not work because social, economic, and cultural conditions in these new countries were vastly different from those in the United States.

The transition from a colony to a politically independent country raised very difficult problems. All of these countries except Brazil had the wounds of a long and cruel war to heal; some had to satisfy military groups, often ready to settle political issues by force of arms; all had to adapt colonial institutions and policies to institutions and policies suitable to an independent country. All had to solve financial problems caused by borrowing or the failure to borrow money.

In their new liberties, the new countries had to choose between federalism and centralization in establishing their new governments. They had to decide to what extent and how quickly they should give up governmental policies in effect when they were colonies. The consideration of these and other issues and problems led to varieties of opinions. Most of the new countries were to experience a period of disorder and chaos, of revolutions and political experimentation. Such disorders and unrest, as has been customary in history under much the same conditions, led to dictatorships. In the midst of these turbulent experiences—often called "the Middle Ages of Latin America"—citizens took readily to politics, and formed parties or factions which differed in shades of opinion from extreme liberalism to extreme conservatism.

Dictatorship became the accepted form of government in each of the Spanish-speaking republics. These dictatorships arose from many causes and they have differed greatly from one time to another in the same country and also from one country to another. One cause of dictatorships was the real need to maintain public order and political unity after independence had been won. A general who had commanded an army during a revolution and had helped to liberate a country often took advantage of the social confusion and political disunity in it to make himself its ruler. He was called a *caudillo,* a Spanish word for leader. It has been translated dictator. A dictatorship did not necessarily end, however, after public order had been restored. In all of these countries antagonistic political factions, particularly among the educated, objected to dictators. If one faction could find a leader who had enough supporters, it might and often did succeed in driving the dictator out of the country. Thereupon its leader would become dictator and announce that the revolution was for the benefit of the people.

Military leaders who had exercised arbitrary power over armies generally carried over into civil life the idea that they had, when in office, the right to exercise the same power over civilians that they had exercised over armies. Therefore nearly all of them were unwilling, when elected to office, to submit to the will of the majority and to the law itself.

Not all dictators have been military men, particularly in recent years. Some were able politicians who secured their election by political intrigues, personal favors, and many

kinds of influence. Once in power they endeavored to maintain themselves by controlling elections and by supporting an army to suppress any and all opposition that seemed to imperil their power.

Some of the dictatorships were short-lived. Mexico had fifty-eight dictators between 1824 and 1878. But some dictatorships have been longer-lived. In Mexico Diaz was dictator from 1899 to 1908, and in Venezuela Gomez from 1908 to 1935. After the death of Gomez, the people whom he had ruled so cruelly celebrated his death with wild rejoicing. They hunted down and killed as many of his supporters as they could find. They looted and burned his palatial properties.

Some dictators were able patriotic men who served well the interests of their countries. They respected civil rights and personal liberty. Some dictators promoted the welfare of the poor, supported education, and advanced the economic interest of their countries. Others were self-seeking adventurers who did little for their countries but much for themselves. Some treated their political opponents cruelly, silencing all public criticism of themselves and even all public discussion of political problems. They tried to make it appear that they recognized the need for constitutions by talking much about them even though they did not abide by them. Some rewrote the constitutions of their countries to serve personal interests. In general the everyday lives of the great mass of the people were but little affected by a change in dictators.

Some of the new republics have had stable governments during most of their history. Chile was ruled for many years by a succession of able presidents, each of whom served ten years. In recent years it has emerged as a moderately liberal democracy after suffering political and financial disorders.

Argentina, after experiencing a period of

political disunity and public disorder, achieved unity and order by 1860. The constitution adopted in 1853 is still in force. Since 1928 Argentina has encountered many political and economic difficulties arising from the false liberalism of President Irigoyen, the rise to great political power of military leaders and conservatives, and the fascist sympathies, and as many believe cooperation of its revolutionary governments with the Axis powers during the Second World War.

Mexico has moved steadily towards democracy since 1917. Among the smaller republics, Costa Rica is noted for its democratic government and educational institutions and Uruguay for its social legislation.

The new republics have faced continuing economic problems. Throughout the nineteenth century, foreign capitalists secured concessions from governments to build railroads, to develop plantations and oil fields, and to operate mines. Many of these concessions were necessary for the development of the natural resources of the republics. Not all capitalists exploited the Latin Americans. Sometimes, however, they could secure these concessions only by bribing government officials. It has been charged that certain foreign companies have financed revolutions to oust a competitor and thereby gain its concession. Foreign traders, particularly English, bought wheat, grain, coffee, rubber, cocoa, and other raw materials produced in these countries and sold them manufactured goods. Soon after the establishment of the German Empire (1871) the Germans began to trade and to seek concessions. In this they were very successful. Between the two World Wars, the Japanese increased the sum of their total exports and imports in Latin America from $5,000,000 to $80,000,000.

The growth of international trade has been both beneficial and harmful to the countries of Latin America. On the beneficial side it helped raise the standard of living by making it possible for the Latin Americans to purchase in other countries the kinds of goods they need but which are not manufactured in their own countries. Manufacturers of goods in foreign countries have established branches in the principal cities of Latin America. They employ Latin Americans in many different capacities. Others work on the railroads built with foreign capital; still others work on the fruit plantations and in the mines. In these and other ways foreign capitalists have helped the growth of an enterprising and wealthy middle class.

On the harmful side growth of international trade involved Latin American governments in financial difficulties. With foreigners in control of banks, railroads, other means of transportation, and industries requiring heavy machinery, the chief enterprise under the control of natives was agriculture and not all of that. Of course very many Latin Americans worked in banks, for railroads, and in industries. Foreign ownership all too often meant absentee control and the sending of dividends on investments to foreign countries. Conditions in world markets and the interests of foreign investors strengthened the tendency to concentrate on one crop such as sugar in Cuba, bananas in Central America, and coffee in Brazil. The price of these products in the world market determined the prosperity of their producers. Brazil had a flourishing rubber industry in the Amazon basin during the nineteenth century, but it was crushed and the rubber gatherers were reduced to dire poverty when Malayan and East Indian rubber sold at a lower price in the world market.

The new countries and the cities of Latin America made their economic and financial situation worse by their financial policies. Many of them borrowed large sums from

reign bankers to make modern improve-
ents. Some of this money was spent wisely
ut much of it was squandered recklessly.
Vhen, as often happened, borrowers were
nable to pay even the interest, often high,
n these loans, foreign investors appealed
 their governments to protect their invest-
ents. The foreign governments often threat-
ed to intervene and sometimes did to pro-
ct the interests of their citizens. This led to
urther difficulties and to strained relations
tween the governments involved. Mex-
o attempted to free its mineral wealth from
reign ownership when it adopted (1917)
constitution that denied foreigners the right
 the oil produced on lands owned by them.
or the greater part corporations and citizens
 the United States and Great Britain were
ost affected. After many and long continued
plomatic discussions Mexico agreed (1942)
 pay the owners of these lands for their
ghts.

During the twentieth century the republics
 Latin America became more prosperous as
e demand for their products increased, par-
cularly in the countries of Western Europe.
exico produced petroleum, silver, copper,
d henequen (a material used in making
pes and bags); Cuba, chiefly sugar, tobacco,
d minerals; and the republics of Central
merica, chiefly bananas and coffee. Vene-
ela became one of the chief sources of
troleum. Colombia produced petroleum,
nanas, and coffee; Peru, petroleum, copper,
nadium, sugar, and cotton. One fourth of
e world's supply of tin comes from Bolivia.
ile became a leading exporter of nitrates
d copper. Brazil specialized in fine woods,
ffee, and cotton; Uruguay in live-stock
oducts. The sale of Argentina's grain, meat,
d wool, needed in Great Britain and con-
ental Europe, has given it the greatest per
pita wealth of any of the countries in Latin
nerica.

Since the First World War the protection
afforded industry by tariffs passed by the republics has helped their industries to expand
greatly. Manufacturing plants for the process-
ing of ores and the refining of raw sugar and
crude oil have been built near the sources of
raw materials. Many factories have been
erected, particularly those which make consumer goods including textiles, shoes, and
glassware. Air transport has made travel and
the carrying of goods much easier and quick-
er. Though many of these industries belong
to or have been financed in part by foreigners,
they have helped to increase the prosperity of
the native peoples.

Economic development has led to a rapid
growth of cities and to the rise of a well-to-
do middle class and a large laboring class.
Though merchants and artisans were among
the first settlers, they had little if any political
power. The army and the landowners possessed almost complete political power. More
recently the middle class has taken an active
interest in politics, and still more recently the
large laboring class has begun to discover the
political power of its numbers. Peron in Argentina (1946), waged a campaign for the
election to the presidency by appealing to the
laboring class. Social legislation regulating
the hours and conditions of labor, particularly
for women and children, is now in effect.
Some Latin American countries have enacted
labor laws which would be considered "advanced" in comparison with those of the
United States. Mexico has broken up many
great estates and distributed the land to the
landless, and this work is continuing.

**In many Latin American republics the
Catholic Church has been separated from
the state.** In Colombia it has been the state
church from the beginning. It is supported by
the state and it maintains control over all
education and charitable works. In Brazil it
was separated from the state in 1890 and in

Chile in 1925. Other countries which have separated church and state are Mexico, Cuba, Panama, Honduras, El Salvador, Guatemala, Ecuador, and Uruguay. In these countries it occupies a position much like its position in the United States.

In recent times the Catholic Church in Mexico has been involved in trouble with the government. The constitution of 1917 separated the Church from the state, forbade the Church to own property, and limited the number of clergy. For a time these provisions were not strictly enforced. In 1926 a stricter enforcement of them led to open conflict between the Mexican government and the leaders of the Church. The government seized all church property, closed all church schools, and forbade members of religious orders to conduct schools. The struggle continued for ten years after which the Church was allowed to regain some of its former privileges, but the struggle still continues. In Venezuela, the Church is an established one, but it is without any political power.

The peoples of these new republics have made contributions to literature and the arts. The increased attendance in public schools in all of them and in parochial schools in some has increased the number of persons who can read and write. In Mexico special efforts are now being made to wipe out illiteracy. Attendance at universities has also increased and many universities offer modern courses in the sciences and the social studies.

The awakening of cultural interests among more people than heretofore has stimulated writers, scientists, painters, historians, and musicians. Latin Americans have always made use of literary and artistic sources in their own past and recently their interest in their Spanish and Portuguese heritage has intensified. Historians, including Medina of Chile, who employed the methods and techniques of sound historical research, have written ex-

cellent histories of their countries. Active an productive academies of history exist in man countries. Those of Cuba, Venezuela, an Colombia are especially significant. In th study of law and international law, Lati American scholars and statesmen have w worldwide renown.

A large number of literary journals publi essays and poetry. Many novels depict Indi life, the picturesque Gauchos (cowboys the pampas), and the heroes of revolutiona days. A Chilean poetess, best known by h pen name, Gabriela Mistral, received the N bel Prize for literature (1945). Artists usi the same themes as the novelists have do excellent work. Their use of bright colo often in startling combinations, reminds o of the use of colors by Indian artists. In A gentina De Quiro's painting of the Gauch and in Mexico the murals of Orozco a Rivera are excellent examples of the wo of these Latin American artists. The combi tion of Indian themes and modern music m be noted in the works of music compose who have made use of Indian melodies a also of Indian musical instruments to produ the effects they desire.

The republics of Latin America work for continental solidarity. Any hopes unity among the new countries, whi Bolivar and other liberators may have ha were soon shattered. At the conclusion the wars of independence, it was appare to the leaders of the new republics that pol ical unity among them was impossible a that even a small number of large confe eracies was impracticable. Indeed, as we ha seen, Venezuela and Ecuador broke aw from Great Colombia. The Central Americ Federation broke away from Mexico and th separated into the several Central Americ republics. Disagreements over boundary li between the new republics followed; so of them resulted in war. One of these d agreements led to the War of the Pacific (1879-1884) between Chile on the one side and Bolivia and Peru on the other. A long-continued boundary dispute between Chile and Peru over the ownership of Tacna and Arica was settled by negotiation in 1929. After many years of argument, Bolivia and Paraguay went to war (1932) over the ownership of the Gran Chaco. In 1935 Argentina, Brazil, Peru, and Uruguay persuaded the warring countries to make a truce and negotiate a peaceful settlement of their long disputed ownership.

In spite of these difficulties and others, the Latin American republics have held many congresses to promote continental solidarity. Bolivar called the first Congress at Panama in 1826. It accomplished little. Other congresses were held in succeeding years at which proposals were made for a league of the Latin American states. A conference at Lima (1847) was inspired in part by a fear of the United States that had been aroused by the Mexican War. The attempt of Napoleon III of France to make Maximilian of Austria emperor of Mexico led to the calling of another congress at Lima in 1864. These and other congresses drew up treaties which were never ratified by the republics that took part in the congresses. Nevertheless they did keep alive Bolivar's ideal of continental solidarity.

The United States and the Latin American republics formed the Pan American Union. In 1881, James G. Blaine, Secretary of State of the United States, issued an invitation to the Latin American republics to send delegates to a congress to be held in Washington "for the purpose of considering and discussing the methods of preventing war between the nations of America." He hoped to promote peace in the Western Hemisphere and to increase trade between the United States and the countries to the south. This conference did not meet because Blaine re-signed as Secretary of State following the death of President Garfield. The idea survived, however, and when Blaine became Secretary of State again, a conference was held (1889) with Blaine presiding over the opening session. At this conference the International Union of American Republics was formed. Its headquarters were to be in Washington, D. C. Meetings of the Union have been held about every five years. When the meetings were held in Washington, the delegates were usually diplomatic representatives of the Latin American republics in Washington, and the Secretary of State of the United States presided. At a meeting held in Buenos Aires (1910) the title of the organization was changed to the Pan American Union. Its chief purposes are to promote the peaceful settlement of disputes among its members, to increase trade among them, and to promote better understanding.

In 1915 the secretaries of foreign relations of Argentina, Brazil, and Chile signed a treaty providing that all disputes between them should be settled by diplomatic means or by arbitration. Though this treaty was not ratified, the three nations, known from the initial letters of their names as the ABC powers, continued for some time to work in harmony and thereby they exercised great influence in Latin American affairs.

American intervention caused the Latin American republics to fear the United States. During the first part of the twentieth century, the United States assumed headship among the American republics. This meant that the United States claimed the right to intervene in the affairs of Latin American republics, whenever necessary, to restore order, to settle boundary disputes, to protect foreign and American investments, or to reorganize the finances of a Latin American republic. Our quick recognition of Panama when that little republic declared its independence of Colombia was based on the claim of the United States to national interest in the digging of the Panama Canal. At the same time the idea of headship led the United States to promote health programs, sanitation, and the extension of American cultural influences.

The close connection between our policy toward Latin American countries and the financial investments of citizens of the United States in them led to the use of the phrase, "dollar diplomacy." One result of dollar diplomacy was the development of a bitter resentment against the United States among the peoples of the Latin American republics who feared and distrusted the "Colossus of the North." In an effort to counteract these fears, Elihu Root, Secretary of State, stated in Rio de Janeiro (1906) that the United States believed in the independence of every republic in the Americas.

The Good Neighbor Policy was designed to promote friendship between the United States and the Latin American republics. The Good Neighbor Policy was begun by President Herbert C. Hoover and continued by President Franklin D. Roosevelt and his Secretary of State, Cordell Hull. It has done much to cement friendship between the United States and its neighbors to the south and to allay fear of the "Colossus of the North."

The Good Neighbor Policy has never been stated officially. Dean W. W. Pierson of the University of North Carolina has summed it up under eight points, four of which are: (1) no armed intervention by any American republic in another; (2) a respect for the territorial integrity of every American republic by every other; (3) the recognition of the right of every American republic to determine for itself its own form of government; and (4) the settlement of disputes among the American republics by peaceful means.

At Montevideo (1933) Cordell Hull, Secretary of State, said that no American nation had the right to intervene in the internal affairs of another. This pronouncement was later approved by the United States Senate. In 1936, President Roosevelt, while addressing a conference at Buenos Aires, said that the twenty-one American republics should stand together in the defense of the Western Hemisphere. The Lima Declaration of American Principles (1938) declared that these republics would defend the Western Hemisphere and work together for universal peace. In case of danger they would consult and take the best measures they could to protect and defend one another.

In spite of all the difficulties in the way, the Latin American republics have gradually learned to act together and also with the United States. In other words, they believe in continental solidarity. In the Second World War they acted together to provide a common defense for all of the republics in the Western Hemisphere.

The United States and the Latin American republics reached important decisions at conferences during the Second World War. The outbreak of the Second World War in Europe (September, 1939) led to a conference in Panama City of delegates from each of the twenty Latin American republics and the United States. The conference set up an Inter-American Neutrality Committee which was to sit in Rio de Janeiro as long as the war lasted. Its task was to keep the American republics out of the war. The Panama conference also established a Finance and Economic Advisory Committee to help solve the problems which had arisen out of the effects of the Second World War upon the international trade and international unity of the American republics. The conference adopted the Declaration of Panama which stated that the warships of the powers at war could not come closer than 300 miles to the shores of the Americas, with the exception of Canada. The Declaration said that no hostile act should be committed in this zone by a warring power. The delegates agreed to hold another meeting within a year.

The next conference took place in Havana (July, 1940) shortly after the Germans had conquered the Netherlands and France. Because the delegates feared that Germany might try to seize the French and Dutch possessions in the Western Hemisphere, the conference adopted the Act of Havana. This Act stated that the American republics acting together had the right to take over and administer the affairs of any European possession in the Americas if it was threatened by a European power. Because bauxite from Dutch Guiana was so vital to the American aluminum industry, the United States occupied Dutch Guiana (1941) after making an agreement with the Netherlands and Brazil. After the United States entered the Second World War, a conference of foreign ministers held in Rio de Janeiro (January, 1942) made further plans for the defense of the Western Hemisphere.

The next development of the idea of hemispheric defense was reached at the Inter-American Conference on Problems of War and Peace held in the old castle of Chapultepec in Mexico City, February 25 to March 8, 1945. The Act of Chapultepec declared the equality of all American states. It provided that any act of aggression either by a non-American power or by an American republic against any American republic would be regarded by all as an act of aggression and would give rise to immediate action by all other American republics to repel the aggressor. The Conference called for Inter-American Conferences at four-year intervals and for meetings from time to time of the ministers of foreign affairs and the Secretary of State of the United States. The Conference reorganized the Pan-American Union and provided for an expansion of its activities.

An Inter-American Conference in Brazil drafted the Treaty of Rio de Janeiro. In August, 1947, representatives from the United States and eighteen other American republics held a conference in Brazil, about forty miles from Rio de Janeiro. The purpose of the conference was to draft a treaty binding the republics to take united action against aggression. After nearly two weeks of discussion, the conference approved the Treaty of Rio de Janeiro which becomes effective when ratified by two thirds of the nations that signed it. This treaty provides that (1) any armed attack against an American nation—whether from within or without the Western Hemisphere—shall be considered an attack against all American nations; (2) on request of the attacked nation or nations individual American nations shall take such action against the aggressor as they deem advisable until they decide what action shall be taken together; (3) collective action against the aggressor shall continue until the Security Council of the United Nations decides what measures should be taken to maintain international peace and security. The Treaty of Rio de Janeiro is the strongest tie reached by American nations for defense.

In addition to these conferences on political and economic affairs, over 200 technical conferences have been held dealing with education, music, agriculture, travel, science, and other subjects of common interest. Exchanges of professors and students among universities and colleges in the twenty-one American republics have also aided in promoting international good will.

While each of the American republics has retained its full independence, all have learned to work together for peace and progress without any loss of sovereignty.

SUMMARY

The geographic area now called Latin America was inhabited originally by Indian tribes. A few had a high degree of civilization; some were agricultural; the rest were savages. The Spaniards conquered and settled the largest part of the area. They endeavored to Christianize and civilize the Indians. At the same time, they made many of the Indians work for them. The royal government of Spain developed a complex system of government for the many parts of its colonial empire. Its code of laws, the Law of the Indies, was a monumental achievement in colonial law. The people in the Spanish colonies developed a distinctive culture which was a blend of Spanish and Indian culture. During the first quarter of the nineteenth century, they won their independence from Spain. Bolivar and San Martín were their most celebrated leaders in the heroic struggles for independence.

The Portuguese discovered and settled Brazil. The first settlements were along the Atlantic coast. The Paulistas opened up the interior where the discovery of gold and diamonds contributed greatly to the growth and prosperity of Brazil. The people in Brazil developed a culture which was a blend of Indian and Portuguese culture. It became independent of Portugal when the son of the king of Portugal proclaimed himself emperor of Brazil (1822). It became a republic in 1889.

Independence brought serious political, economic, and international problems which helped to contribute to instability in governments. Most of the republics were ruled at one time or another by dictators. Some dictators were able and patriotic men; most were self-seeking adventurers. The Latin American states are moving toward more and more stable democracies.

Lack of capital at home, a tendency to a one-crop system, and exploitation by foreign capitalists were the chief sources of economic problems. Most of the republics suffered greatly from debts. The development of agriculture, cattle raising, mining, industry, and air transportation have increased prosperity and thereby helped to contribute to the solution of their economic problems.

Most Latin Americans are Catholics. At first the Roman Catholic Church was the established church and had charge of education and charity. It has been disestablished in recent years in many of the republics.

The Latin American republics have made many cultural advances. Their historians and other scholars have made noteworthy studies. Their poets, essayists, novelists, artists, and musicians have produced many fine works which have a distinctly Latin American flavor

In spite of great difficulties and wars due chiefly to local rivalries, the Latin American republics have taken many steps toward continental solidarity by holding conferences to discuss their common problems. The United States took the lead in forming the International Union of American Republics, now called the Pan American Union.

About 1900 when the United States assumed a leadership in the Americas, it claimed the right to intervene in the internal affairs of the smaller states. After the Good Neighbor Policy had been put into effect, the United States gave up its claim to intervention. Since then a series of conferences held in the spirit of the Good Neighbor Policy has laid plans for defense of the Western Hemisphere. The Act of Chapultepec (1945) declared the equality of all American republics and provided for their joint action in any needed defense of any part of the Western Hemisphere. The Treaty of Rio de Janeiro is a formal agreement to carry out the Act of Chapultepec. The American republics have learned to work together.

SUMMARY OF PART VII

From 1815-1914 the forces of liberalism and autocracy have waged constant warfare. In 1815 autocratic conservatism under the leadership of Metternich was in control. Nevertheless, valiant liberals deriving their inspiration from the ideals of the French Revolution offered the world a program of political, economic, and humanitarian reform. They gained signal victories on the Continent in 1830 and in Great Britain in 1832. The second great movement of liberalism in 1848, after temporary successes, was almost everywhere suppressed. Strong leaders took the place of liberal groups in the affairs of Europe. As a result of their work France again became a Napoleonic empire, Italy was united into a nation, and Germany into an empire.

During the period 1871-1914 the lines became more clearly drawn. Great Britain moved steadily toward a more democratic form of government. The Third French Republic, succeeding the defeated empire, weathered many crises and seemed to be firmly entrenched in the hearts of the French people in spite of political difficulties. Italy became and remained a constitutional monarchy beset by many problems. Germany, however, while paying lip service to democracy in its popularly elected Reichstag, was strongly autocratic. Under the leadership of Bismarck and later of William II it endeavored to suppress all forces that seemed to weaken the autocratic power of its rulers. Nevertheless, it made great advances in science, industry, and commerce. Though one Russian Tsar freed the serfs and another allowed the election of a Duma, the government remained an absolute autocracy. In the meantime the Balkan peoples secured their independence from Turkey and entered upon their troubled careers as nations.

In the New World the Latin American republics secured their independence and began their struggle toward democracy, political and cultural maturity, and continental solidarity.

In spite of difficult obstacles on the continent of Europe liberal democracy seemed everywhere to be advancing, so much so that one distinguished American historian declared that the growth of democracy and of free consent were laws of history.

EVENTS THAT TOOK PLACE AT ABOUT THE SAME TIME
1490

	Columbus discovered America, 1492.
Line of Demarcation, 1493.	
	Cabral reached Brazil, 1500.
Negro slavery introduced into Santo Domingo, 1501.	
	Spanish House of Trade founded, 1503.
	Conquest of Mexico by Cortés, 1519-1521.
Viceroyalty of New Spain established, 1529.	
Pizarro's conquest of Peru, 1531-1533.	
	Printing press set up in Mexico City, 1535.
Viceroyalty of Peru established, 1542.	
Universities of Mexico City and Lima founded, 1551.	
	Gold discovered in Brazil, 1560.
	Law of the Indies compiled, 1680.

EVENTS THAT TOOK PLACE AT ABOUT THE SAME TIME (Cónt.)

Viceroyalty of New Granada established, 1717.	
	Diamonds discovered in Brazil, 1728.
Miranda, 1756-1816.	
	Viceroyalty of La Plata established, 1776.
San Martín, 1778-1816.	
Bolivar, 1783-1830.	
Miranda led revolt in Venezuela, 1806.	
	Venezuela, Paraguay, Ecuador proclaimed independence, 1811.
Argentina proclaimed independence, 1816.	
	Mexico and Peru proclaimed independence, 1821.
Brazil proclaimed independence, 1822.	
	Monroe Doctrine, 1823.
Bolivia proclaimed independence, 1825.	
	Uruguay proclaimed independence, 1828.
War between Mexico and the United States, 1846-1848.	
International Union of American Republics founded, 1889 (Pan American Union).	Second American Congress, Lima, 1847.
	Brazil became a republic, 1889.
	Spanish-American War, 1898.
Seventh Pan-American Conference at Montevideo, 1933.	Cuba independent, 1898.
	Lima Declaration, 1938.
	Declaration of Panama, 1939.
Gabriela Mistral, a Chilean poetess, won Nobel Prize, 1945.	Act of Havana, 1940.
	Act of Chapultepec, 1945.
	Treaty of Petropolis, 1947.

THREE GENERALS Gen. John J. Pershing with Mexican generals Obregon, at left, and Pancho Villa, center. Photographed at the International Bridge, El Paso, Texas, in September, 1914.

Tenochtitlan.

PREHISTORIC PALACE. Zapotec Indians beside the ruins of the palace at Mitla, in Mexico. Note the variety of design shown in the elaborate stone carvings. (*Top.*)

AZTEC CALENDAR STONE. As important as the Rosetta stone in the interpretation of Egyptian culture, this monolith discovered in Mexico City contains the clue to the accurate astronomy of the Aztecs. (*Above.*)

Courtesy American Museum of Natural History

CORTEZ WITH MONTEZUMA. From a drawing by Tlaxcalan Indians.

SIMON BOLIVAR. Called "The Liberator," Bolivar worked to free Venezuela, Colombia and Ecuador.

JOSE DE SAN MARTIN, above, helped free Argentina, Chile and Peru.

Courtesy Grace Lin

OLDER THAN THE INCAS. Carved monoliths at Tiahuanaco, in Bolivia, are believed to be nearly 3000 years old.

PART VIII
Imperialism in Modern Times

Modern imperialism arose out of the Industrial Revolution. It began in the second half of the nineteenth century. It developed from the search for markets where raw materials could be bought, finished products of factories at home could be sold, and surplus capital invested. Humanitarian motives contributed to its growth. It affected most of the inhabited areas of the world; Central and South America became new fields for investors, manufacturers, and merchants. "Darkest Africa" was explored and divided among the leading European nations; India, China, and the islands of the seven seas were subjected to imperialism. Japan, seeing the advantages to be gained by imperialism, became imperialistic. In each of these lands the peoples were affected by the culture of one or more of the leading European nations, and not always entirely to their advantage. Imperialistic rivalries among the great nations brought on costly wars which reached their climax in the two World Wars.

The motives for modern imperialism were primarily economic. Among them, three are basic. (1) Modern industry requires a tremendous amount of raw materials, particularly raw cotton and crude rubber which are not produced in Europe, and also metals and oil which are produced in Europe, but not in quantities sufficient to meet the demands. (2) Modern manufacturers produce a great deal more than they can sell at home and therefore they need markets abroad for their surplus goods. (3) Profits from manufactures lead to the accumulation of surplus capital not needed in business at home, but which must be invested to avoid an economic loss. Large areas in South America, Africa, and Asia provided opportunities for the exercise of these three motives; for in them were to be found large supplies of raw materials, ample markets, and a need for capital to develop natural resources and transportation.

The first step in imperialism was economic penetration of foreign lands. Concessions (permissions to do business granted foreign capitalists by native governments) were obtained. Large sums of money were invested in lands, oil wells, mines, railroads, and other businesses. Backward regions were opened up to trade and European goods sold to their peoples. Unfortunately economic

507

penetration did not prove to be sufficient. Natives were often indifferent to the opportunities offered them to toil for low wages and to purchase European goods at high prices. Native governments, after noting the effects of imperialism, sometimes withdrew concessions, confiscated foreign investments, and failed to pay their obligations to imperialistic nations.

The second step in economic imperialism was the establishment of political control. This was in part the result of a desire to protect economic interests and in part the product of an intense nationalism which had developed in European countries and expressed itself in a desire for colonies. Each nation wanted to be self-sufficient and so to control its sources of raw materials, to protect its manufactures by high tariffs on imports, and to have a monopoly of the chief markets where its goods were to be sold. National pride caused each country to wish to transact its business in its own money and under its own flag. These desires could be fulfilled only by political control.

Some European nations had more people than they could support and as a result some of them left their homes for foreign lands. If they went to America they were lost to the mother country as soldiers and as buyers of goods. So these nations felt they must have colonies where their people might go and live under the flag of the mother country. To protect their colonists and their overseas trade, they insisted that they must have naval bases and coaling stations along the routes of trade where they could maintain fleets and supply merchant vessels. Imperialism became a matter of national pride.

Some imperialists were influenced by humanitarian motives. Many people were sincerely convinced that imperialism was beneficial, even necessary for peoples in conquered lands. They talked of the "white man's burden," the duty of the white man to carry his ways of life, his knowledge, and medical skill to "backward races." They pointed out that imperial rule helped to prevent local wars, to wipe out superstitious practices, to stamp out tropical diseases, and to bring the blessings of Christian civilization.

Many benefits were carried to the people of the conquered lands. Unfortunately some imperialists were willing to take advantage of the motives, deeds, and even the misfortunes of devoted missionaries and humanitarians. The murder of two German Catholic missionaries by the Chinese was used by the German government as an excuse for forcing China to grant concessions to Germany, including a ninety-nine year lease of an important part of the Shantung peninsula.

CHAPTER 25

The Partition of Africa and Its Effects

European imperialists found full scope for their ambitions in Africa. During the Commercial Revolution European nations made settlements along its western, southern, and eastern coasts. During the nineteenth century the countries in Northern Africa were conquered or taken under protection by European powers. By 1914 nearly every part of the continent was under the control of one or the other of the European powers.

• • •

Africa was called the "Dark Continent." Although Africa has played a part in human history from its very beginning, only within the last hundred years has its interior been explored by Europeans. Indeed until the last quarter of the nineteenth century so little was known about the greater part of the interior of Africa that many called it the Dark Continent. The geography of Africa was a primary cause for this lack of knowledge.

The northern coastlands from the Atlantic Ocean on the west to the Red Sea on the east bordered on the Mediterranean Sea. These lands must be excluded from our general statement about the Dark Continent for they had had their share, often an important one, in history. South of the northern coastlands lies the Sahara, a desert 3000 miles in length from the Atlantic to the Red Sea and 1000 miles in width from north to south. The desert and the rest of Africa to the south is a vast plateau surrounded by a narrow coastal plain.

Abundant rainfall in the equatorial regions and on the mountains in the eastern part of the plateau furnishes water for the Nile, the Niger, the Congo, and the Zambesi. These rivers run through deep gorges and over cataracts and great falls on their way to the sea. These obstructions helped to prevent European explorers, who knew well the coasts of Africa after the voyages of Vasco da Gama and others, from exploring its interior.

When explorers did ascend the plateau, they found dense jungles and rain forests in equatorial Africa and trackless grasslands to the south. These parts of Africa were inhabited by tribes of blacks, each of which had its own tribal customs and laws.

Some of these were known in ancient times, for the Egyptians fought their way south of the cataracts of the Nile and bought ivory, wood, incense, and slaves from the Nubians. In later times the western coastlands of North Africa were controlled by the Carthaginians, later still by the Romans, and still later by the Vandals. During the Middle Ages (647) the Berbers who lived there were conquered and converted by the Mohammedans and their country made a part of the great Arabic Empire. Since then most of the inhabitants of Northern Africa have been Mohammedans. In 1815 the states along the coast of North Africa, except for Morocco, which was independent, owed allegiance to the Sultan of Turkey, who had succeeded to the power of the caliphs of Bagdad. Actually, the rulers of Algeria and Tunisia were free

CAPE POINT. Southernmost point of Africa where the Indian and Atlantic Oceans meet.

from Turkish control, but Tripoli, Libya, and Egypt were still a part of the Turkish Empire.

On the west coast of Africa, where once traders had gone in search of slaves, the small free state of Liberia was established soon after 1820 by Negroes from the United States. Portugal still owned Angola on the west coast and Mozambique on the east coast. At the southern tip of the continent was Cape Colony founded by the Portuguese, captured from them by the Dutch, and taken from the Dutch (1806) by the British whose possession of it was ratified by the Congress of Vienna. Most of its peoples were Boers (a people of Dutch and French origin).

The states in Northern Africa were the first victims of modern European imperialism. From the fifteenth into the nineteenth century, pirates from North African coasts plundered ships, enslaved their crews, and exacted tribute from Great Britain, France, and many other countries. After the United States became independent, these corsairs attacked American merchant vessels and made their crews galley slaves. After the war of 1812, Stephen Decatur, in charge of an American fleet, captured two Algerian pirate ships and compelled the rulers of Algiers,

Tunis, and Tripoli to sign treaties that abolished all tribute, made them pay indemnities, and release all Christian prisoners. France and Great Britain also took vigorous action and, after the French seized Algeria (1830), piracy in the Mediterranean which had lasted for thousands of years came to an end.

In 1830 French armies sent by Louis Philippe began the conquest of Algeria and after seventeen years it became a French colony. The conquest was completed by Louis Napoleon. In 1881 Jules Ferry, the premier of France, seized Tunis and made it a protectorate of France. About 200,000 French and Italians migrated into Tunis and Algeria, and in the latter the best farming lands were soon owned by the French. Italy secured Tripoli and Libya (1912) after she had won a short war with Turkey for their possession.

Morocco, long the cause of international crises in Europe, was divided by Great Britain, France, and Spain (1911-1917) into three protectorates: the French zone, the Spanish zone, and the international zone which contains the seaport of Tangier. This city was placed under the control of Great Britain, France, and Spain.

Egypt became a center of British imperialism. Great Britain's interest in Egypt arose in part from money lent to its ruler, the khedive, and also from a desire to control the Suez Canal, an important link in the sea route to India. In 1863 Ismail "the spendthrift" became khedive of Egypt. To modernize his country he borrowed money, mostly from the English, to build railroads, primary schools, lighthouses, to install telegraph systems, and to improve harbors, especially the one at Alexandria. He invested $80,000,000 in the Suez Canal. A great deal of the money he borrowed was spent on his own pleasures and extravagances. The Egyptians could not pay enough taxes to pay the interest. To satisfy his creditors, Ismail (1875) sold his interest in the Suez Canal Company to the British government for about $20,000,000. This canal is a part of the shortest and best route to India, and therefore it is of vital importance to the safety and prosperity of the British Empire. The route through the Mediterranean and the Suez Canal is called the "lifeline of the British Empire."

In 1882 the British found it necessary to step in and establish a protectorate to straighten out Egyptian finances, to protect the lives and property of Europeans living in Egypt, and to stand guard over the canal. In general, conditions in Egypt were improved under British guidance, but even so, many Egyptian nationalists were opposed to the British protectorate, especially to the stationing of British troops in Egypt to protect the canal.

In 1914 Great Britain proclaimed Egypt independent of Turkey, but under British protection. After the First World War Great Britain ended (1922) the protectorate and Egypt became an independent nation under a king, prime minister, and parliament. English troops, however, remained on the eastern borders of Egypt to guard the Suez Canal. During the Second World War Egypt remained neutral, although it was in danger of invasion from the west by Italian and German armies. At the same time it was an important base for British armies, which at last drove back the invaders from the west. In July, 1954, the British signed an agreement to withdraw all troops from Egypt.

The expeditions of Livingstone and Stanley awakened widespread interest in equatorial Africa. Gradually many explorers and scientists penetrated the region south of the Sahara, discovered the sources and courses of its rivers, and made maps of the region. Missionaries carried their messages to the natives, and right after the missionary came adventurous traders. One of these mission-

Bettmann Archive

THE SUEZ CANAL, KEY TO INDIA. Cartoon of Disraeli commemorating the acquisition of principal interest in the *Société de Suez,* the company that owned the Suez Canal.

aries was David Livingstone (1813-1873), a Scotsman, who carried on extensive explorations in the region around Lake Tanganyika. As Livingstone had not been heard from for three years, Charles Gordon Bennett, owner of the *New York Herald,* sent Henry M. Stanley, a reporter on his paper, to find him, which he did in 1871. The expeditions of Stanley attracted widespread attention to equatorial Africa. Stanley, who was tremendously impressed by the natural resources of equatorial Africa, endeavored to interest Europeans in exploiting them. Finally he gained the ear of King Leopold of Belgium.

King Leopold of Belgium acquired riches in equatorial Africa. In 1876 Leopold summoned an international geographic confer-

International News

David Livingstone (1813-1873) was a Scottish missionary and explorer whose travels and writings increased geographical knowledge of the Dark Continent. The insert is Henry M. Stanley.

ence composed of scientists, geographers, explorers, and statesmen to meet in Brussels. As a result of the conference, "The International Association for the Exploration and Civilization of Africa" was formed. This Association became a commercial company owned and controlled mainly by King Leopold and Belgian capitalists. The French were already established in the Congo, but at a conference of European powers in Berlin (1885) Leopold's claim to the upper Congo was recognized and the territory acquired by Leopold was given the name of Congo Free State. From this area Leopold expected to draw great riches in rubber and ivory. The natives saw no need to work for white men and so to secure profits for the Association its managers developed a system of forced labor. From 1890 to 1900 Leopold's profits

from rubber alone were over $15,000,000.

When word of this system reached Europe, particularly Great Britain, criticisms and investigation of it led to great reforms. The name Congo Free State (1908) was changed to the Belgian Congo which was to be a colony governed by a Belgian colonial government under an improved system of administration. It improved health conditions, educational opportunities, and living and working conditions of the natives. The industries were turned over to Belgian companies under the careful regulation of the Belgian colonial government. Conditions of life and work became much better than they had been.

Other European nations acquired possessions in equatorial Africa. Although Leopold took the lead by exploiting the upper Congo, other European nations were not far behind. The French had already founded Dakar (1857) in Senegal on the western coast of Africa. During the 1880's and 1890's Frenchmen explored the Sahara, and the French government sent detachments of the Foreign Legion to control the desert tribes. Other Frenchmen established French power in the Niger valley, on the northern bank of the Congo River, and in a region in the interior called the Sudan, and laid claim to a part of it which was called the French Sudan. Germany also, coming in late, acquired small areas in West Africa known as the Kamerun, Togoland, and German Southwest Africa.

The British army went up the Nile into the Sudan, where after hard fighting against the natives, the British gained control of a region which proved to be a good place to grow cotton. As the British expanded their influence and power southward in the Sudan, they came into collision at Fashoda on the White Nile, 450 miles south of Khartoum (1898) with the French. They had come into the Sudan from the west where France now controls a vast area called French

RHODES MEMORIAL, RONDEBOSCH, CAPETOWN.

West Africa. The French government yielded to British demands and by agreement with Britain (1899) gave up all claim to territory in the Sudan. After Egypt became an independent nation (1922), Great Britain recognized its rights to a share in the Sudan and so it was called the Anglo-Egyptian Sudan.

Rhodes, the empire builder, extended British power in South Africa. Meanwhile, the British at Cape Colony had been active in Southern Africa. In the story of British activities in Africa the name of Cecil Rhodes looms large. The Dutch in Cape Colony (Boers) disliked British rule so much that they trekked northward (1835) and founded two small republics, Orange Free State and the Transvaal. In 1867 diamonds were found in Orange Free State, and in 1886 gold was discovered in the Transvaal. The result, of course, was a rush of prospectors, miners, and many other kinds of people that flock to new mining operations.

In 1870 Cecil Rhodes, a young Englishman, was working with his brother trying to raise cotton in Cape Colony. He acquired a claim in the diamond fields, gradually bought up other claims, and eventually formed a company which secured a monopoly of the diamond fields. Not satisfied with that, he acquired another company which owned gold mines in the Transvaal. A great believer in the "white man's burden," he devoted much of his wealth to help increase the size and power of the British Empire. Bechuanaland was occupied by the British and then a fertile and gold-bearing land to the north was taken by treaty from the natives and called Rhodesia. Rhodes was marching from the Cape toward Cairo.

Difficulties and disagreements between the

PAUL KRUGER. His political convictions and military power held Britain's might at bay for three years.

Boers and the British caused the Boer War, 1899-1902. The Boers were led by Paul Kruger. The British won, but after they had won, the Liberal government now in power negotiated (1902) a treaty of peace with the Boers. The Boer language was to be used in schools and courts and the Orange Free State and the Transvaal were to be given self-government as soon as possible. The British government agreed to pay $15,000,-000 for the farms it had destroyed. In 1909 the British government agreed to the union of Cape Colony, Natal, Orange Free State, and the Transvaal into the Union of South Africa.

Four European nations divided East Africa. British possessions in South Africa and their power in Egypt caused them to plan a Cape to Cairo railroad. Before it could be built, they would have to secure control of the regions through which it would pass. Accordingly, the British took over an area called Kenya (British East Africa). Germany interfered with British plans for a Cape to Cairo railroad by seizing Tanganyika (German East Africa) which the Paris Peace Conference mandated to the British at the end of the First World War. But the railroad was never completed, although it was built north from Capetown to the Zambesi River and south from Cairo up the Nile and for a considerable distance in the Anglo-Egyptian Sudan. Probably air transportation will keep it from ever being completed.

France and Italy were also active in seizing lands along the east coast of Africa. During the 1880's France established a protectorate over the great island of Madagascar off the east coast of Africa and took over (1862) the northern part of Somaliland, a barren coastal area in the easternmost part of Africa and called it French Somaliland. The British occupied (1884) a part of Somaliland and called it British Somaliland. It lies between French Somaliland on the north and Italian Somaliland on the south. The Italians seized Eritrea (1882-1890) on the west shore of the Red Sea and the southern part of Somaliland, which they called Italian Somaliland. These possessions were not of much use to the Italians unless they could conquer Abyssinia (Ethiopia), which had good agricultural land and rich natural resources. When the Italian army marched inland in an effort to conquer Abyssinia they were decisively defeated at Adowa (1896), a defeat the Italians did not forget.

Thus was Africa parceled out among Great Britain, France, Spain, Italy, Belgium, and Germany. In 1914 only Abyssinia and Liberia were independent. The European powers controlled all the rest of Africa by direct

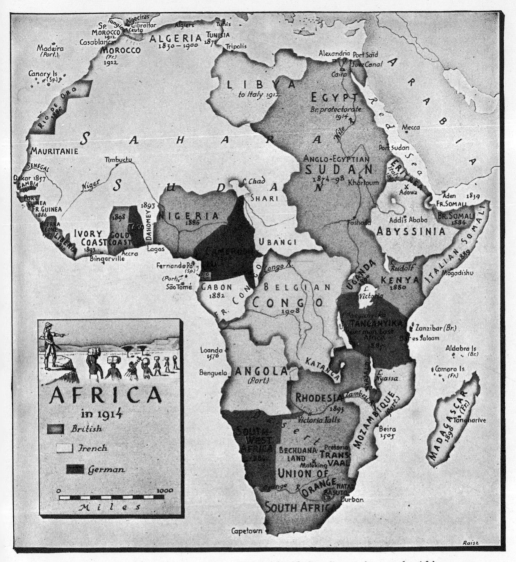

In the seventeenth century European powers erected fortified trading stations on the African coast, from which they exported slaves, gold, ivory, and many other products. In the second half of the nineteenth century the race for inland possessions started and by 1914 all Africa had been partitioned among European powers with the sole exception of Abyssinia and Liberia.

ownership or under the guise of protectorates. Except along the northern coast and in the extreme south the climate was not suitable for European colonists. Consequently, the nations tried to extract profits by making the natives work to produce gold, diamonds, rubber, ivory, cocoa, wool, leather, cotton, tin, copper, palm oil, and other raw materials needed by the nations that had parceled out Africa.

SUMMARY

In 1815 most of the coastlands of Northern Africa belonged to the Turkish Empire. Great Britain, France, and Portugal had small colonies along the other coasts of Africa. Little was known of the interior.

The countries in North Africa were the first victims of modern European imperialism. The French took possession of Tunis and Algeria; the Italians took Tripoli and Libya. Morocco, long the cause of serious international disputes in Europe, was internationalized by Great Britain, France, and Spain (1911-1912) into three protectorates, the French zone, the Spanish zone, and the International Tangier zone. The city of Tangier was placed under the control of an international commission.

The British bought enough stock in the company that built the Suez Canal to obtain control of it and established a protectorate over Egypt to protect their lifeline to India. Great Britain granted Egypt its independence (1922) after the First World War. It was an important British military base during the Second World War. Recently the British Government has announced its intention to withdraw all of its troops from Egypt.

Equatorial Africa was explored by Livingstone and Stanley. King Leopold of Belgium controlled the Congo Free State and drew great wealth from it. It is now called Belgian Congo and its administration after much criticism was greatly improved. The French secured control of part of equatorial Africa. From Egypt the British penetrated the Sudan. Germany occupied lands on the southwest coast and also on the east coast.

The British extended their interests northward from Cape Colony in Southern Africa. Cecil Rhodes took an important part in this expansion. Quarrels with the Boers led to the Boer War (1899-1902). After British victory, the Union of South Africa evolved and became a part of the British Empire.

Great Britain, Italy, Germany, France, and Portugal occupied lands on the east coast of Africa.

EVENTS THAT TOOK PLACE AT ABOUT THE SAME TIME

1814

	Congress of Vienna awarded Cape Colony to Great Britain, 1815.
Liberia founded as a colony for freed American Negro slaves, 1822.	
	French began conquest of Algeria, 1830.
Trek of Boers northward from Cape Colony, 1835-1837.	
French founded Dakar, 1857.	
	Laborers from India first imported into South Africa.
	Ismail became khedive of Egypt, 1863.
Diamonds discovered in Orange Free State, 1867.	Suez Canal opened, 1869.
Stanley found Livingstone, 1871.	

EVENTS THAT TOOK PLACE AT ABOUT THE SAME TIME (Cont.)

	Ismail sold his shares in Suez Canal to Great Britain, 1875.
Brussels conference on Africa, 1876.	
France seized Tunis, 1881.	
	Great Britain established a protectorate over Egypt, 1882.
	Italians took over Eritrea, 1882-1890.
Berlin conference on Africa recognized Leopold's claim to Upper Congo, 1885.	
Gold discovered in the Transvaal, 1886.	
	Italians defeated at Adowa, 1896.
	British and French armed forces met at Fashoda, 1898.
	France renounced claims to Upper Nile, 1899.
Boer War, 1899-1902.	
British Parliament approved formation of Union of South Africa, 1909.	Belgian Parliament took over government of Congo Free State from king, 1908.
	Italy obtained Libya and Tripoli from Turkey after Tripolitan War, 1912.

WATER IN THE DESERT. North African tribesmen getting water from a canal dug by French engineers in the desert of Tafilalet. (Photograph from French Press and Information Service.)

CECIL RHODES, left, founded the Rhodes scholarships with imme wealth drawn from the gold and diamond mines of South Africa.

A KAFFIR KRAAL. Below, native Africans in a stockaded, that roofed village.

BOER COMMANDOS. Daring raiders were called commando troops in the Boer War, which lasted from 1899 until 1902.

BOER WAR BATTLE. Right, the Boers defeated British troops at Colenso.

CHAPTER 26

The Impact of Imperialism on China and Japan

The history of China began in the Old Stone Age and continued through the New Stone Age, and on to the present. The discoveries and inventions of early men listed in the first chapter of this book were made also by the Chinese. They learned to use fire, to make tools, to tame wild animals, to build houses, to farm, to spin, to weave and to dye, to make pottery, to use wheeled carts, to dig canals, to make boats, and to work metals. They developed their own form of writing from pictures.

The Chinese produced great religious teachers, artists, and literary men. They developed dynasties and like other nations felt the might of conquerors.

Despite the business relations of the Chinese in early times with peoples in the Near East and Southern Europe, China was not much influenced by western civilization until the nineteenth century when modern imperialism forced China to open its ports and to begin its modernization. Imperialism brought some benefits to China and in turn the Western world derived some benefits from China. But out of imperialism arose serious political and economic problems which the Chinese have not yet solved.

Japan also has had a long history, but not as long as the Chinese. It, too, was opened up to the Western world in the nineteenth century by modern imperialism. The reaction of the Japanese to imperialism was very different from the Chinese reaction. They profited by the lessons they learned from the West by using them to their own advantage. Japan was rapidly modernized and industrialized and soon became imperialistic itself.

• • •

China is a land of vast extent and enormous population. China has a greater land area than the United States, and approximately 450,000,000 people, or about one fourth of the world's population. Geographically China is a land of river valleys separated by mountains and hills. In these valleys most of the people live. The Tibetan ranges on the west and the Mongolian upland on the northwest form a natural boundary. On the east, China's coast line on the Yellow and China Seas is about 3000 miles in length. For many centuries geographic conditions helped to keep China isolated. The mountains and desert on the west made communication with the countries of the Near East and Europe difficult. The wide reaches of the Indian and Pacific Oceans helped to keep China isolated from Western Europe until after the discovery of the all-water routes to the East during the Commercial Revolution.

Chinese civilization developed principally in three river basins. They are the basin and delta of the Huang Ho (Yellow River), the basin of the Yangtze River, and the basin of the Sikiang (West River) in Southern China. The Yellow River is about 2700 miles long and is sometimes called

Bettmann Archive

PRIMITIVE PLOW AS USED BY A CHINESE PEASANT.

"China's sorrow" because for many centuries it has overflowed its banks, changed its course, and caused great destruction of property and loss of life. The earliest center of Chinese civilization was in this valley, frequently called the North China Plain. Here the climate is more severe than in the south and the rainfall is light and some years fails almost entirely during the growing season. The people, who are larger in stature than those in the south, eat millet and wheat instead of rice, the chief food elsewhere in China.

The basin of the Yangtze and its tributaries is the largest of the three river basins. The Yangtze River, about 3200 miles in length and navigable for 1500 miles, is China's greatest artery of inland trade and transportation. Its valley is the richest and most populous of China's geographic divisions. The people in this area profit from the fertile soil, temperate climate, and ample rainfall. They raise excellent crops of rice, cotton, tea, silk,

and a wide range of vegetables. On the Yangtze River are situated some of China's largest cities, Shanghai, Nanking, Hankow, and Chungking.

The basin of the Sikiang (West River) is smaller than those of the Yellow and the Yangtze; the river is navigable for a considerable distance. Here the climate is semitropical, the rainfall abundant, and rice is the major crop. Furthermore, the people are different in race, language, stature, and temperament from the northern Chinese, from whom they are separated by mountains.

Most Chinese are farmers. China was well-fitted by nature to become the seat of a great agricultural civilization. A glance at the map will reveal that almost all of China lies in the North Temperate Zone. In South China the long growing season permits the raising of as many as three crops in a year while in North China it is possible to grow two crops in many areas. The monsoons sweeping up from the South Pacific in the spring and summer provide sufficient rainfall except in the north where droughts sometimes occur. The fertile soil in the river valleys provides a sound basis for farming.

About three fourths of the total population of China are engaged in farming. Rice is the chief crop in South China; wheat, millet, barley, oats, buckwheat, kaoliang, and other cereals are the chief crops in North China. Likewise in North China, and espo cially in Manchuria, huge crops of soy beans are grown. Many uses have been found for them, ranging from food for humans to oil for industrial processes. One of the most striking facts about Chinese agriculture is the wide variety of plants that are grown. They include all kinds of vegetables, fruits, cereals, and root crops grown in the United States.

One notable difference, however, between our agriculture and theirs is the slight dependence of the Chinese on meat, dairy, and other animal products. Those which they have are derived largely from pigs, chickens, ducks, and geese. Lack of pasturage and the necessity of feeding a large population from the produce of small farms helps to explain the reason for the diet of Chinese. Farm animals are used chiefly as work animals, the water buffalo in South China, and the donkey, horse, mule, and ox in North China. Irrigation is widespread owing to the dry climate in the north and to the demands of rice cultivation in the south. Farms are small, most of the work is done by hand, and the farmer, although unscientific in our sense, possesses a high degree of practical skill in raising crops.

China lacks some vital mineral resources. Heavy industry today is especially dependent on certain basic minerals, and China is not richly endowed with many of them. The coal resources of China are considerable, but it is deficient in iron, copper, sulfur, and petroleum. Lead, zinc, manganese, gold, and silver are produced in small amounts while in the

Bettmann Archive

IRRIGATION METHODS IN CHINA. Chain pump operated by coolies.

production of tungsten and antimony China dominates the world market, and besides it possesses large reserves of tin ore.

The Chinese have had a long history. Chinese legends tell stories of "divine kings" who ruled the land in the beginning. Archaeology has proved that men of the Old Stone Age lived there. Chinese civilization, therefore, has a longer story of continuous growth than any other civilization, with the possible exception of the civilizations of Egypt, India, Mesopotamia, and Central Asia. In a land where people have lived in the same place for generation after generation without knowing what is going on in other places, they tend to reverence what has been done in the place where they live, and thus Chinese reverence the past.

In the course of many centuries different dynasties ruled China. The Shang dynasty (about 1766-1122 B.C.) is the first for which we have historical records. It rose to power on the North China Plain. The Chou dynasty (1122-249 B.C.) followed the Shang and it was in this period that the influential Chinese philosophers and teachers, Lao Tze and Confucius, lived.

The Chou dynasty came to an end (249 B.C.) and a strong ruler, Shih Huang Ti (246-210 B.C.), succeeded to the throne. He was one of the great political geniuses of Chinese history. He established his power over all China and divided it into thirty-six provinces, each ruled by officials appointed by him and responsible to him. He established a uniform system of weights and measures. To defend his empire from the nomadic tribes of the north, he began the construction of the Great Wall of China stretching from the sea over 1500 miles inland along the northern frontier. Succeeding emperors continued to strengthen it until it became a wall thirty feet thick with turrets, towers, and arched gateways. Still standing, it is a great monument to the industry and pacifism of the Chinese people.

During the Han dynasty (206 B.C.-220 A.D.) great developments took place in China. One of these was the invention of paper. To the Chinese this period was a sort of golden age and it so influenced them that they came to speak of themselves as the "sons of Han." The boundaries of the empire were extended; communication by rivers and roads was improved; social and economic conditions were made better; and for the first time persons seeking official positions were given examinations in Chinese classics.

Foreign invaders established their rule over China. For many centuries the Chinese were troubled by the invasions of northern peoples. In the early years of the thirteenth century the Mongols, people from the north under the leadership of Genghis Khan, began their almost world-wide conquests. Genghis in Chinese means "perfect warrior" and this name was correctly applied to him for he was one of the ablest military commanders of all time. The conquests of Genghis Khan and his successors resulted in the establishment of the largest empire known to history. It stretched from the Pacific coast of China westward to Hungary and Poland in Eastern Europe.

Kublai Khan (1259-1294), the grandson of Genghis, became a famous Chinese emperor. In 1280 he founded the Mongol (Yuan) dynasty and to his court came the Venetian merchant and traveler, Marco Polo. The Venetian was surprised by what he saw. Relays of horses carried imperial couriers over well-policed roads along which post houses and inns had been built at convenient intervals. The walls of the capital city were fifty feet high and twenty feet thick. Inside the walls an imperial palace had been erected. It was surrounded by a park sixteen miles in circumference that was dotted with pools and gardens. The outer walls of the palace were covered with tiles of many colors; the inner walls with gold and silver embellished with pictures of dragons, knights, and idols. The streets of the city were broad and clean in great contrast to those of Europe with which Marco Polo was familiar.

The Ming dynasty (1368-1644) displaced the Yuan dynasty. During the Ming dynasty Europeans first came to China by sea and Francis Xavier established a Christian mission in China (1549). The Ming dynasty is famous for the exquisite embroidery which its artisans produced and for its beautiful pottery, very highly prized today by art collectors. The Ming dynasty came to an end (1644) when another foreign people, Manchus from the northeast, conquered the Chinese. They made the Chinese wear their hair in a single pigtail as a mark of their subjection to their Manchu conquerors. Their rule continued until it was overthrown by the Chinese revolution of 1911.

China gave birth to two great religions, Taoism and Confucianism. The founding of Taoism (from *Tao,* meaning the Way, or Way of Life) has been ascribed to Lao Tze, who is supposed to have been a Chinese philosopher of the sixth century B.C. So little is known about him that some think he may not have lived. Taoism is a very old Chinese philosophy of life. It taught its believers to cast aside worldly pleasures, honors, and glory and to be content with their lot. Later on Taoism came to be a religion of spirits and ancestor worship far removed from the original simple teachings. A priesthood arose, shrines and temples were erected, and an elaborate system composed of magic, charms, and spells was developed.

Confucius (551-479 B.C.) is China's greatest philosopher. Though born of a poor family, he secured an education and acquired such fame as a teacher that he was appointed to a position in the government. He rose to become minister in a Chinese state called Lu. After some years in the public service, Confucius became disgusted with the conduct of his ruler, resigned his position, and spent the rest of his life in study and teaching.

The teachings of Confucius are found in the Confucian Classics, the *Four Books* and *Five Canons*. He taught that men should worship their ancestors and adhere to the traditional ways of doing things. He drew up rules of conduct to govern the different relationships of life. The relationships for which he made these rules were five in number: ruler to minister, father to son, husband to wife, brother to brother, and friend to friend.

Five hundred years before Christ he formulated a Chinese Golden Rule when he said, "Do not do unto others what you do not want others to do unto you." His writings are still widely read and often quoted in China.

A Chinese diplomat and biographer has said that the core of Confucian political philosophy is contained in these words:

The men of old, when they wished their virtues to shine throughout the land, first had to govern their states well. To govern

Chicago Natural History Museum

CONFUCIUS. He laid great stress upon the practice of filial piety, by which he meant respect for and obedience to parents.

their states well, they first had to establish harmony in their families. To establish harmony in their families, they first had to discipline themselves. To discipline themselves, they first had to set their minds in order. To set their minds in order, they first had to make their purpose sincere. To make their purpose sincere, they first had to extend their knowledge to the utmost. Such knowledge is acquired through a careful investigation of things. For with things investigated knowledge becomes complete. With knowledge complete the purpose becomes sincere. With the purpose sincere the mind is set in order. With the mind set in order there is real self-discipline. With real self-discipline the family achieves harmony. With harmony in the family the state becomes well governed. With the state well governed there is peace throughout the land.

Confucianism played a part in making the Chinese conservative and satisfied with ways and manners that had, lasted over two thousand years.

Many Chinese accepted a third great religion. Buddhism was brought to China from India in the first century A.D., either by Chinese envoys to India when they returned home or by Indian Buddhist missionaries to China, or both. No one knows exactly which. Buddhism did not contradict the teaching of Taoism or Confucianism nor did it forbid ancestor worship. The Chinese adopted it readily and it spread rapidly throughout China in the dark days that followed the Han dynasty. By 300 A.D. most Chinese were Buddhists.

Buddhism appealed especially to the poor and unlettered who could not comprehend the scholarly teachings of Confucius. It taught that life was suffering, that suffering was caused by desire, and that one must overcome desire to gain peace and happiness. It taught mercy and patience and kindness to all. These were teachings which the poor and unlettered could understand and which appealed also to many of the rich and educated.

The ritual of sacrifices and prayers and the artistic elements in Buddhism also appealed to the Chinese. The desires of Chinese for representations of Buddha led to the painting of pictures and the carving of reliefs and statues of Buddha. In doing so Chinese artists departed from the severity shown in Buddhas portrayed by artists in India. Chinese artists gave grace, vitality, and charm to their representations of Buddha, many of which are very beautiful.

The worship of Buddha also influenced architecture. By order of emperors hundreds of Buddhist temples were built, often high up on the mountain sides. In them priests lived and meditated, and to them worshipers made pilgrimages. Buddhists erected pagodas in which to put religious relics, which the Chinese thought brought good luck to the people around them. Many of these relics are very beautiful.

The family and the village were the basic institutions of Chinese society. The great stress which Confucius placed on the family helped to make it a basic unit in Chinese society. We are accustomed to think that a family consists of the father, mother, and unmarried children, but the Chinese family was quite different. It included not only the husband, wife, and unmarried children, but also the married sons, their wives and children and even others dependent on the family.

The father was the head of the family; he made decisions on all questions affecting the lives of its members, and he was personally responsible to the village for their conduct. He arranged the marriages of his sons and daughters, decided what work his sons should perform, and his consent had to be obtained before any son could leave home. When the father died, it was the duty of his sons to see that the rites of ancestor worship were properly performed. Thus a great premium was placed upon having a son, and if no son was born, the father might take another wife or adopt a son. The wife also had authority, especially if she were a grandmother or a mother of sons. In many Chinese villages family government was the only government the villagers knew. The family educated and employed its members, and it was the center of religious life. Loyalty to family is even today a striking characteristic of Chinese life.

Although most Chinese were farmers, they did not live on their farms as American farmers do but in villages from which they went out to work their farms. The village was a self-sufficient economic unit. The farmers produced the food, and artisans who worked in the home or in small shops made the goods needed by the villagers. Industry was in the handicraft stage and its workers were organized into guilds somewhat like those in Europe in the Middle Ages. The government of the village was largely in the hands of a council of village elders who decided disputes on principles found in the Confucian classics.

Chinese society rested on the cornerstones of the family and the village. Few Chinese ever left their villages and their immediate surroundings. Owing to the separation of the people in the provinces by mountains, differences in dialect, tradition, and custom developed slowly in the course of centuries, but even so the written language of the classics and a quite general belief in the same religion (Confucianism) provided a bond that helped unite all Chinese.

The officials of the empire were chosen by competitive examinations based on the Confucian Classics. This system gave China learned men to rule, but it did not furnish progressive officials trained for specialized tasks. This method of selecting officials coupled with the low salaries paid them led to inefficiency and corruption in government. Progress almost stopped, yet the Chinese regarded themselves as the most civilized people in the world.

Europeans began to trade with China. Chinese commercial relations with the Near East and Europe, though not extensive, were very old. Both the Greeks and the Romans prized highly Chinese silk. In the seventh century Christians had been allowed to settle in China and to teach their doctrines, and in the thirteenth century a medieval Pope sent a mission to the leader of the Mongols.

Of far greater significance in awakening European interest in China were Marco Polo's accounts of his travels in that land. Merchants and Catholic missionaries followed in his train. The Portuguese, the first Europeans to reach China after the discovery of the sea route to the Far East, established themselves at Macao in the second quarter of the sixteenth century. They were followed by Spanish, Dutch, French, and English explorers and merchants.

Along with these traders came Christian missionaries. The Jesuits especially were given a cordial welcome. Jesuits, in addition to preaching Christianity, taught the Chinese the sciences, corrected their calendar, and showed them how to make cannon. Later on, however, quarrels among missionaries, and between them and the Chinese, caused an emperor to expel many of them. Brutal acts of traders led the emperor of the time to confine trading between Chinese and Europeans to one district in the city of Canton. Here, under fixed regulations, Western goods could be exchanged for Chinese goods under the supervision of Chinese merchants who were chosen by the government. The *Empress of China* was the first American ship to sail to the Far East to engage in commerce with Chinese merchants in Canton in 1784. Before long many other American ships followed and as a result the China trade laid the foundation of many American fortunes.

Traders and missionaries believed that they were bringing the Chinese the benefits of Western civilization, but the Chinese took a different view. It was forcibly and effectively expressed by the following message sent by the emperor to George III of England.

. . . our ceremonies and laws differ so completely from your own that, even if your envoy were able to acquire the rudiments of our civilization, you could not possibly transport our manners and customs to your alien soil. . . . As your ambassador can see for himself, we possess all things. I set no value on objects strange or ingenious, and have no use for your country's manufactures.

If one were to judge from the activities of the British that followed the arrival of this message, they were not deeply impressed by it.

British guns during the Opium War opened China's doors to businessmen. British merchants and traders were not satisfied with the commercial arrangements at Canton and besides they resented the emperor's attitude toward them and their goods. Friction resulted and finally war broke out between China and Great Britain. Since an attempt by the Chinese emperor to prevent British merchants from bringing opium from India into China was a cause of this conflict, it is called the Opium War (1839-1842). It is also called the First Anglo-Chinese War. The real purpose of the British was to force China to open wide her ports to trade. In the fighting that followed, the guns used by the British proved so effective that the Chinese asked for peace which led to the signing of treaties.

The signing of the Treaties of Nanking (1842-1843) was a turning point in the relations of China with the nations of the West. Their chief terms were: (1) five treaty ports were opened to British trade and residence; (2) the island of Hong Kong was ceded to the British; and (3) the British were to be granted most-favored nation treatment. Most-favored nation treatment meant that any privilege granted by China in the future to any other nation would have to be granted automatically to Great Britain.

A treaty with the United States (1844) gave its citizens the same rights that had been granted to British subjects and also established the principle of extraterritoriality. This meant that American citizens accused of crimes in China would have the right to be tried in American courts set up in China. The same privilege was also granted to the British. Treaties of the same kind were made with France, Belgium, and Sweden. The guns of imperialism had broken down the isolation of a great empire.

Defeat in the Second Anglo-Chinese War forced the Chinese to grant foreigners more privileges. The execution of a French missionary and Chinese interference with a ship flying the British flag were the immediate causes of joint British-French action in the Second Anglo-Chinese War (1856-1860). When the smoke of this unequal contest had blown away, China's resistance to the political and commercial demands of the West had been completely broken down. Defeated in war by the "foreign devils" and terribly weakened by a widespread uprising at home, known as the Taiping Rebellion (1850-1864), the Manchu government had to surrender to Western demands and to grant foreigners these privileges: (1) to travel in the interior of China, (2) to conduct missionary work, (3) to have diplomats in the capital at Peking, (4) to carry on trade in ten more ports, and (5) to set and to collect the tariff on goods entering any one of them.

The Western powers exploited China. Between 1860 and 1899, not satisfied with the gains already won, Great Britain, Russia, France, Germany, and Japan wrung more gains for themselves and their countrymen from the helpless Manchus. Colonies, naval bases, concessions, and extraterritorial settlements (areas governed directly by foreign powers) were obtained. Foreign businessmen got the right to build railroads, open mines, buy and sell goods, and lend money at high rates of interest. Indeed, by 1899 it looked as though China, like Africa, was going to be divided among the great powers.

However, two events at the opening of the twentieth century halted the "slicing of the Chinese melon." (1) The United States, through its Secretary of State, John Hay, announced (1899) the Open Door Policy. This policy stated that the United States would strive to preserve the political independence of China and to keep its trade open to all nations on equal terms. (2) An uprising known as the Boxer Rebellion broke out in 1900. Rebel Chinese organized a "Society of Heavenly Fists" (called "Boxers" by Europeans) and started an uprising to drive all foreigners out of China. Their favorite motto was "Protect the country, destroy the foreigner." The Empress Dowager, Tzu Hsi, gave her support to the movement by ordering all foreigners to be killed. European powers, the United States, and also Japan sent armed forces which subdued the Boxers and then they forced China to pay an indemnity. The United States used a part of its share of the indemnity to pay for the education of Chinese students in American universities, a policy adopted by other powers. Chinese resistance to Western civilization was broken down and the government itself began reforms which included the introduction of many Western ways.

The Revolution of 1911 overthrew the Manchu dynasty. The Manchu dynasty's reforms went neither fast enough nor far enough to satisfy its opponents, composed chiefly of students who had been educated in universities in the United States and Europe and the new middle business class. The opponents of the Manchu dynasty were ably led by a remarkable man, Dr. Sun Yat Sen (1866-1925), physician, traveler, writer, and revolutionist. Revolution broke out in the fall of 1911 and in 1912 the youthful emperor abdicated, thus bringing to an end the Manchu dynasty that had ruled since 1644. A Chinese Republic was established and Sun Yat Sen

International News

Sun Yat Sen (1866-1925), physician, revolutionist, and statesman, was the first president of the Republic of China and founder of the Kuomintang.

became the first provisional president of the Republic.

The Kuomintang attempted to unify the provinces of China. In 1893 Chinese nationalists organized a secret society which in time was to evolve into the Kuomintang. Chinese intellectuals and businessmen led by Dr. Sun Yat Sen planned (1911) the Chinese Republic based upon Three Principles announced by Sun Yat Sen. They were Nationalism, Democracy, and the Peoples' Livelihood, and they became the platform for the new party called the Kuomintang. Although Sun Yat Sen and his supporters had drawn up a constitution and established a republic, they failed to get control of all of China. In an effort to strengthen and to unite the new republic, Sun resigned the office of president in favor of Yuan Shih Kai, the most powerful of the generals of the Chinese army.

Yuan disregarded the constitution, tried to suppress the Kuomintang, and even to make himself emperor. After his death (1916), his successor established a government in Peking which was recognized by a number of foreign powers including the United States.

Lawlessness followed the death of Yuan Shih Kai and the next year (1917) Sun Yat Sen and the Kuomintang established a republic in Canton, but it, too, was not able to gain control over much of China.

The rest of China was governed by provincial governors known as warlords. They plundered their own provinces and fought with one another to see which of them would become strong enough to control all of China. The Chinese were badly disunited.

In 1923, to gain strength for the unification of China by the Kuomintang, Sun Yat Sen, head of the Canton Republic, made an agreement with the Soviet Union known as the Canton-Moscow Entente which admitted Chinese Communists to the Kuomintang. Thereupon the Soviet Union sent political and military advisers to the Canton government and helped Sun Yat Sen to train an army which was to be used to unify China. In 1925 Sun Yat Sen died. One of his supporters, Chiang Kai-shek, who succeeded him, soon proved himself to be an able general. Under his command, the armies of the Kuomintang won a series of victories which led to the capture of Nanking (1927) and of Peking (1928). Chiang made Nanking the capital of China. Peking was renamed Peiping (Northern Peace). The new nationalist government headed by Chiang was recognized by most of the great powers. In 1928, after Chiang Kai-shek had been made president of the Chinese Republic, he began to exercise dictatorial powers. He inaugurated a vigorous campaign to educate the Chinese and to modernize and strengthen their backward agriculture and industries.

A break between the Kuomintang, Chiang's party, and the Chinese Communists prevented the unification of China. In 1927 Chiang changed the policy of the Kuomintang to meet the desires of the conservative members of his party. They had convinced him that China would fare better under the leadership of its landowners, bankers, and businessmen, and in alliance with the capitalist nations, than under the leadership of its Communists and in alliance with the Soviet Union. In the same year he married Mei-ling, a member of the Soong family, China's most successful bankers. He ordered all Communists expelled from the Kuomintang, dismissed his Russian advisers, and engaged German generals to train his army. In spite of vigorous military campaigns, his efforts to defeat the Communists, who in the meantime had formed an army, failed. They set up a government, raised more armies, and after a celebrated "long march" of 6000 miles from Hunan into Shensi province defended themselves successfully against Chiang's attacks. Warlords likewise defied his authority.

China learned much from the West after it was opened to trade. Foreign missionary organizations sent Christian missionaries to China. They founded schools in which Chinese students were taught much as students are in our schools. They helped to build hospitals for the care of the sick. Chinese teachers, doctors, scientists, engineers, businessmen, and government administrators were educated in schools established in China and also in universities in the United States and Europe. Quite significant also was the coming of the Industrial Revolution to China with the machine production of goods in factories and improved methods of transportation and communication. The constitution of the Chinese republic contains provisions based upon the political experiences of nations in the West. Many indeed were gifts of the West to China.

The West has learned much from China. In ancient times Chinese merchants carried silk overland by the "Silk Road" to Greek and Roman merchants. The Romans thought it was "combed from trees." Toward the close of the sixth century A.D. missionaries smuggled the eggs of silkworms from China to Constantinople, and soon after the silk industry that developed near there was made a state monopoly. From Constantinople the silk industry spread to other parts of Europe, especially to Italy, France, and Germany.

Many other products were carried overland or by sea routes to Europe. From the Chinese we have learned to make porcelain ware (chinaware), paper and gunpowder, and to use the mariner's compass. In the seventeenth century, Europeans acquired such a taste for Chinese tea that it became an important article of trade and still is. Directly, or by way of the Arabs, we have obtained the lemon, orange, and grapefruit, the peony, chrysanthemum, and azalea. More recently tung oil and the soy bean, amazing for the variety of its uses, have been imported from China. Firecrackers, playing cards, dominoes, and kites, all of them Chinese inventions, have given pleasure to thousands of people in the Western world for many years.

Japan is an island empire. While China was being exploited by Western imperialists, Japan profited from the lessons it was learning from the West. Japan lies off the east coast of Asia. It consists of a chain of more than 4000 islands, subject to violent earthquakes that cause widespread destruction. It is thought that in very ancient times two major racial groups came to these islands, one from Asia and another from the islands to the south. The first was Mongolian, relatives of the Chinese. The second was Malaysian. The blend of Mongols and Malaysians made the Japanese people to a considerable extent different from the Chinese.

If the islands of Japan were placed off the eastern coast of North America, they would extend from Greenland to Cuba. Their total land area is a little more than 158,000 square miles, about that of the State of California; and their population is about 78,000,000. The climate ranges from sub-arctic to sub-tropical, but most of the country is in the North Temperate Zone. The summer monsoons provide ample rainfall. However, destructive storms called typhoons often strike the southern coasts. Only about 15 per cent of the land can be cultivated because much of the country is mountainous. Rice is the principal crop, raw silk and tea are secondary. Rice and a plentiful supply of fish enable the Japanese to be almost self-sufficient in food.

The sea has played an important role in Japanese history. It has been one of two chief sources of food for the people. The sea and the straits that separate Japan from Asia were narrow enough to make trade easy and to permit the Japanese to borrow what they desired from the culture of their Chinese neighbors. On the other hand, the waters made invasion of Japan difficult, and besides they have protected it sufficiently from the effects of Chinese influences so that it has been able to develop a distinctive culture. In modern times the good harbors which are to be found on the long coast line have helped Japan to become a great maritime and naval power.

Japan lacks many basic raw materials. After the Japanese adopted industrialization as a national policy, they soon discovered that they lacked many basic raw materials necessary for industrialization. Copper is the only metal whose supply is adequate. Coal exists in considerable amounts, but it is poor in quality. Iron deposits are very inadequate, there is little petroleum, little gold and silver, and all rubber and cotton have to be imported. Japan's lack of cotton was serious in view of its rapidly developing textile industry. Its lack of the basic raw materials needed by industries helps to explain Japan's aggressive foreign policy which led to imperialism.

Japan was ruled by feudal nobles. For many years Japanese were taught that the founder of their country and its first emperor was Jimmu Tenno, descended from the Sun Goddess, who was sent (660 B.C.) to rule them. Actually the chief of the most powerful warlike clan became its ruler and took the title of emperor about the beginning of the Christian era. Ancestor worship and the written language of the Chinese were borrowed in early times from China. About the middle of the sixth century A.D., missionaries brought Buddhism from China to Japan.

In the twelfth century an era of feudalism began which was not overthrown until after Japan's doors were opened to the West by Commodore Matthew C. Perry in the middle of the nineteenth century. The landed estates became feudal domains governed by lords *(daimyo)* who were protected by a warrior class *(samurai)*. The lords were supported by peasants who tilled the fields and were not allowed to leave the estates. The head of the feudal system after 1192 was a *shogun,* a military dictator from the dominant feudal family. The office of emperor was not abolished, but the emperor was shorn of his power and forced to live in retirement.

Kublai Khan, Mongolian emperor of China, prepared for a great invasion (1281) of Japan. The Japanese checked this invasion of their soil by the construction of walls along the shore and by attacking the ships of the invaders. After several weeks of violent combat, Kublai Khan's fleet was scattered and some of his ships destroyed by a typhoon. This storm the Japanese called *Kamikaze* (Divine Wind), a word that became well known to Americans in the closing months of the Second World War because the Japa-nese called their suicide bombers Kamikazes.

Japan expelled foreigners. Europeans went to Japan, as to China, in the sixteenth century. For a time Portuguese, Spanish, Dutch, and English missionaries and traders were allowed in Japan. Eventually the religious and commercial rivalries of these Europeans offended the Japanese and besides they feared that their country might be dominated by them. Drastic action resulted. Christianity was prohibited, churches were destroyed, twenty-six missionaries were crucified, and Japanese Christians were confined in cages in sight of food until they starved to death. In 1640 sixty-one Portuguese were beheaded and their ship burned. The Dutch, the only foreigners allowed to stay, were confined to one port and permitted to send out but one ship a year. At the same time Japanese were forbidden to leave their country. These conditions lasted for a little more than 200 years.

Commodore Perry opened Japan to trade. American trade with China grew rapidly in the first half of the nineteenth century and the whaling industry took American ships into Pacific waters near Japan. Shipwrecked sailors who reached Japanese shores were brutally treated. This ill-treatment, the desire to obtain fresh supplies of provisions and fuel, and the hope of a profitable trade, like that with China, influenced the United States to send Commodore Perry and a fleet to Japan to secure trading ports. His admirable diplomacy coupled with a display of United States naval power made his mission successful.

In 1854 Perry secured from the shogun a commercial treaty which opened two ports to limited trade, provided for the purchase of supplies by the United States, promised fair treatment of shipwrecked sailors, and granted the United States most-favored nation treatment. In 1858 Townsend Harris negotiated another treaty which granted extrater-

Bettmann Archive

PERRY MEETING THE IMPERIAL COMMISSIONERS AT YOKOHAMA. By skillful diplomacy he was able to get the Japanese to agree to most of his requests.

ritoriality and religious freedom, opened more ports, permitted the United States government to set the tariff on American goods shipped to Japanese merchants, and provided that each country would be represented in the other by an ambassador. Japan soon made treaties of the same kind with other Western powers. Japan was now open to the West and soon events of great importance to Japan and to the world took place.

The Japanese adopted many Western practices. The Japanese did not allow their country to be exploited as China had and besides they succeeded by 1899 in getting foreign powers to surrender special treaty rights. From the beginning of their relations with the Western world the Japanese were very receptive to Western ideas and consequently a great transformation soon took place in Japan. The office of Shogunate was abolished (1867) and the emperor, who had been forced into retirement, was brought to Tokyo and restored to high place in the government. Shintoism, the ancient Japanese religion of the worship of the Sun Goddess and the spirits of nature, was revived and made the state religion. One of its chief teachings was the worship of the emperor as a god. Feudalism was abolished (1871) and a new constitution was proclaimed (1889) which contained the provision that the power of the emperor was absolute. The constitution provided also for a cabinet and a parliament of two houses.

Japan was remade with extraordinary rapidity. Able young men were sent abroad to secure a Western education. A public school system was founded and by 1878 one and a half million pupils were in the public schools. Railways were built and telegraph systems were installed. Textile factories and steel mills were built. Shipyards began the con-

Bettmann Archive

OPENING OF THE FIRST JAPANESE PARLIAMENT TO BE HELD UNDER THE TERMS OF JAPAN'S FIRST CONSTITUTION, NOVEMBER 29, 1890.

struction of many ships which later on made the Japanese merchant marine the third in the world. In 1872 military service was made compulsory. A modern army was created and trained by French and German officers. A great fleet was built with British advice. These changes and others made it possible for Japan to become imperialistic.

Japan embarked on an imperialistic program. Japan seized the Ryukyu islands (1874), annexed the Kurile islands (1875) by agreement with Russia, seized the Bonins (1878), and the Volcanoes (1891). Another step on the road to empire building was taken (1894-1895) in the Chino-Japanese War which arose over the control of Korea, a little kingdom lying between the two countries, but politically dependent on China.

Although the Chinese fleet was modern, it was hopelessly inefficient through corruption, and consequently it fell an easy victim to the Japanese.

After driving the Chinese armies out of Korea, the Japanese penetrated Southern Manchuria and captured a number of places including the naval base at Port Arthur on Liaotung Peninsula. They also captured Weihaiwei on Shantung Peninsula. Soon after the Chinese sued for peace.

In the treaty that ended the war, China (1) recognized the independence of Korea, (2) ceded the Liaotung Peninsula in Southern Manchuria, the island of Formosa, and the Pescadores, off the east coast of China, to Japan, (3) agreed to pay an indemnity of $57,000,000, (4) opened four more treaty ports to Japanese trade, and (5) entered into a new commercial treaty with Japan.

Japan's gains in Manchuria caused Germany, Russia, and France to "advise" Japan to return the Liaotung Peninsula to China, on the ground that its occupation would menace the independence of Korea and be a threat to Peking. This "advice" was a thinly veiled threat which the Japanese thought they had not the strength to resist, and so they agreed

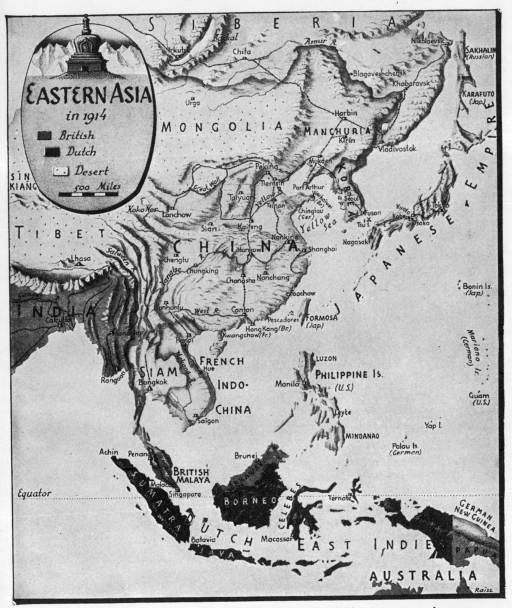

China, isolated for centuries from the rest of the world, gradually lost its power to the extent that only the rivalries of the great powers kept it alive as an independent country.

on condition that the Chinese indemnity be increased. Thereupon the three powers "advised" China to agree to pay an additional indemnity of $24,000,000, and it agreed.

Japan did not forget its humiliation and bided its time. The war had shown how weak China was, and its partition among the great powers of Europe was threatened.

France, Great Britain, Germany, and Russia wrung concessions from a weakened China. Russia (aided by French bankers), Great Britain, and Germany eagerly loaned China money to pay her indemnity to Japan. Customs, the salt tax, and a tax on internal trade in part of the Yangtze Valley were given in security for the loans.

At the request of France, China agreed to change its southwest boundary, giving some territory presumably to Annam, but really to France. It opened three more treaty ports to French trade, and agreed to give French manufacturers and engineers prior rights in three southern provinces in any mining operations and railroad construction (1896-1899), and (1898) a ninety-nine year lease on Kwangchow situated on a bay adjacent to the southernmost of these provinces.

Great Britain, not to be behind France in securing concessions, persuaded China with French approval to change its southwest boundary line along British possessions giving Britain more territory, to open up the West River to British trade in ports on that river, and to grant other commercial advantages to Britain.

Kaiser Wilhelm who had embarked (1895) on empire building seized Kiaochow Bay on the south coast of Shantung, exacted a heavy indemnity for the murder (November, 1897) of two German missionaries, and obtained a ninety-nine year lease (1898) to the Bay of Kiaochow and adjacent islands. The lease included the right to build two railways and the promise that if foreign assistance were needed, German capital, personnel, and materials would be given priority. Soon Germany built a modern port at Tsingtao on Kiaochow Bay.

Within a few days after Germany had obtained its lease at Kiaochow, China granted Russia (1898) a twenty-five year lease on the part of Liaotung Peninsula that it had got back from Japan. On it were Dairen, which Russia developed into a great distributing center for Manchuria, and Port Arthur at which Russia built a strong naval base. The lease included the right to build a railroad connecting the Chinese Eastern Railway, planned in 1896, with Dairen and Port Arthur.

These events spurred Great Britain to obtain (1898) a lease on Weihaiwei for as long as Russia should remain in Port Arthur, and in the same year a ninety-nine year lease on the Kowloon Peninsula on the China mainland opposite Hong Kong.

Russia's expansion in Manchuria and Korea brought her into conflict with Japan. In 1896 China and Russia had formed a secret alliance against Japan. It included a provision for a railroad to be built across Northern Manchuria, to be known as the Chinese Eastern Railway, but in reality it was to be a branch of the Russian-Siberian Railroad to shorten the distance from the west to the east. In addition, Russia was to furnish the funds to build railways, if any, north of the Great Wall.

In the late nineties, Russia was making great strides into Manchuria, a sparsely settled land of vast natural resources. Its lease on the Liaotung Peninsula and the railroads it was building gave it a firm foothold in Manchuria, which was only a part of the vast Russian expansion in Asia which had been going on for centuries. The Boxer uprisings in Southern Manchuria furnished a reason and an opportunity to send thousands of troops to restore order.

Russia's ambitions extended into Korea, where they came into conflict with the Japanese. Japanese and those Koreans who were pro-Japanese killed the queen, because they thought she was an obstacle to Japan's plans in Korea. In a Russo-Japanese agreement (1898) Russia promised not to interfere with

Bettmann Archive

SHELLED FROM THREE POINTS. The destruction of a Russian battery by the concentrated fire of the Japanese during the fighting in Manchuria at the time of the Russo-Japanese War.

Japanese and Korean commercial and industrial relations which Japan was developing rapidly.

Russia was now strong in Northern Korea along the Manchurian border and in spite of the Russo-Japanese agreement the ambitions of the Japanese and the Russians in Korea and elsewhere brought them into frequent conflicts.

And now Great Britain took a hand. Russian expansion had been opposed by Great Britain for years. It had fought the Crimean War to prevent Russia from advancing southward to gain a warm water port. In the last half of the nineteenth century, the British felt that Russian expansion east of the Caspian and the railroads that it had built in that region were threats to India from the northwest. Now the Russian southward penetration into Manchuria seemed to endanger the vast financial and territorial interests of Great

Britain in the Far East. To both Japan and Great Britain, Russia seemed to be a menace.

To meet this menace the Anglo-Japanese Alliance was signed (January, 1902) for five years. The Kaiser was asked to sign by Britain, but he refused. The pact contained many provisions, of course, but only one that concerns us greatly. Each signer agreed to help the other if the one who was engaged in war was attacked by an allied power or powers of its enemy. Japan's victory in its war against China had won the support of the greatest naval power and one of the mighty powers of the West.

Japan's victories in the Russo-Japanese War (1904-1905) raised it to the rank of a great power. At this time Great Britain and the United States were trying to get Russia to remove its troops from Manchuria and to prevent any increase in its privileges there. Russia was making more demands on China, and both Japan and Great Britain were trying to keep China from granting them. Apparently the Japanese were ready to make concessions to Russia to reach an agreement. They proposed to draw a line across Korea, Russia to have a sphere of influence north of it and Japan south. Russia delayed action.

Japan (February 8, 1904) severed diplomatic relations with Russia and the very next day attacked and defeated a Russian fleet off Port Arthur without a declaration of war. The war that followed was chiefly in Manchuria and the seas adjacent. Japan's industrial power, its military tradition, and its westernized armies were a great advantage to it. Japan soon gained control of the Sea of Japan and so could ship men and war supplies wherever needed. Russia's source of supply was far away, and the one-track Trans-Siberian Railroad could not bring enough soldiers and war supplies quickly enough.

Japan captured Dairen and also Port Arthur after a bitterly contested siege. The remnant of the Russian fleet that had been trapped in Port Arthur was destroyed, and the Russian army although it fought stubbornly was pushed northward into Manchuria.

The Russian Baltic fleet had to sail around the Cape of Good Hope, as it could not use the Suez Canal because the Anglo-Japanese Alliance forbade it. It was almost destroyed (May 27 and May 28, 1905) when it reached the Sea of Japan.

Japan's resources were now almost exhausted and revolutionists at home were threatening the Tsar's regime: so both were ready to negotiate a peace at the suggestion of President Theodore Roosevelt. The treaty was signed in Portsmouth, New Hampshire. As Japan was the victor, the terms were somewhat favorable to her, but Russia obtained concessions.

The terms of the treaty which most affected the future were these:

(1) Russia and Japan agreed to evacuate Manchuria (except for Russia's leasehold on the Liaotung Peninsula) which was to go to Japan if China consented. In December, 1905, China agreed to the transfer of Russia's leasehold to Japan.

(2) Russia and Japan agreed they had no territorial or other concessions which impaired the sovereignty of China.

(3) Russia and Japan promised not to obstruct any Chinese plans that would open Manchuria to the trade of all nations.

(4) Russia agreed to cede the southern half of Sakhalin Island to Japan and to grant Japan fishing rights along her coasts in the Japan, Okhotsk, and Behring Seas.

(5) Russia agreed to recognize Japan's special interest in Korea, which Japan annexed in 1910.

As a result of Japan's victories in the Russo-Japanese War, leaders in other countries recognized that Japan was now a first-class power. Japan's prestige in the Far East was greatly increased because Japan was the first nation in the East to win a war against a Western power.

SUMMARY

Modern economic and political imperialism has greatly influenced both China and Japan. China's civilization developed principally in three river valleys and consequently most of its people are farmers. Since about 1766 B.C. China has been ruled by many dynasties. Two of these, the Mongol and the Manchu, were founded by foreign conquerors of China. The Manchu dynasty was overthrown (1911) by a revolution.

The people of China and the peoples of the Western world engaged in trade for many centuries. During the eighteenth century Chinese emperors, however, placed restrictions on Europeans and Americans who wished to trade in China. Two wars between China and Great Britain in the nineteenth century resulted in forcing China to open up her ports to trade and her country to exploitation by the great powers. The Boxer Rebellion (1900), an attempt to force the expulsion of foreigners from China, was put down by armies sent to China by the United States and European powers that were affected by the rebellion.

Many Chinese who studied in universities in Europe and in higher institutions of learning in the United States, upon their return home helped to introduce Western ways. In 1911 a group of Chinese intellectuals and businessmen led by Dr. Sun Yat Sen overthrew the Manchu dynasty (1912) and established the Chinese Republic.

It experienced grave difficulties. After Dr. Sun Yat Sen resigned, Yuan Shih Kai became president of the government at Peking which was recognized by the great powers. After his death, many warlords fought in the provinces for power in China and thus created great disunity in China. The Kuomintang, led by Sun Yat Sen, endeavored to unite China. It sought and received assistance from the Soviet Union. Chiang Kai-shek succeeded Dr. Sun (1925) as China's leader.

He ended the agreement that Dr. Sun Yat Sen had made with the Soviet Union.

Japan is an island empire. Most of its people are farmers, fishermen, and factory workers. For many centuries, however, Japan was ruled by feudal nobles supported by a warrior class. After admitting Europeans to Japan in the sixteenth century, the Japanese stopped nearly all trade with the outside world. For the next 200 years Japan lived entirely to itself.

Commodore Perry negotiated a treaty with Japan which opened Japan to a limited trade, but soon a greater trade was permitted with the United States and other maritime nations. The Japanese learned Western ways and adopted Western practices rapidly. Soon Japan became an important commercial and industrial nation, the feudal nobles lost their power, the emperor became again the ruler, and the Japanese drew up a constitution based largely on the constitution of Bavaria in Germany.

After the industrialization of Japan, its needs far raw materials and markets caused Japan to adopt a policy of imperialism. The Japanese defeated the Chinese in war (1895) and secured Chinese territory. They defeated the Russians (1905) and greatly increased their power in the Far East. Their later ventures in imperialism brought them into the Second World War.

EVENTS THAT TOOK PLACE AT ABOUT THE SAME TIME

CHINA	1828	JAPAN
Opium War, 1839-1842; Treaties of Nanking, 1842-1843.		
Treaty between United States and China, 1844.		
Taiping Rebellion, 1850-1864.		
Second Anglo-Chinese War, 1856-1860.		
		Commodore Perry opened Japan, 1854.
		Townsend Harris made treaty with Japan, 1858.
Dr. Sun Yat Sen, 1866-1925.		
		Shogunate abolished, 1867.
		Feudalism abolished, 1871.

EVENTS THAT TOOK PLACE AT ABOUT THE SAME TIME (Cont.)

	Compulsory military service begun, 1872.
	Ryukyu Islands seized, 1874; Kurile Island annexed by agreement with Russia, 1875; Bonin Islands seized, 1878.
	Emperor proclaimed constitution, 1889.

Chino-Japanese War, 1894-1895; China ceded Formosa and the Pescadores to Japan.

Russia, Great Britain, France, and Germany wrung concessions from China, 1896-1898.	
United States announced Open Door Policy, 1899.	
Boxer Rebellion, 1900.	
	Anglo-Japanese Alliance formed, 1902.
	Russo-Japanese War, 1904-1905; Treaty of Portsmouth, 1905.
	Annexed Korea, 1910.
Revolution of 1911; Republic of China founded 1912.	
Canton Republic founded, 1917.	
Canton-Moscow Entente, 1923.	
Sun Yat Sen died, 1925; Chiang Kai-shek became head of Kuomintang.	
Kuomintang armies captured Peking, 1928.	

Chinese peasants resist seizure of their grain. From a woodcut.

JAPANESE PRINT, below, shows a famous Japanese beauty of the 18th century reading from a manuscript.

the Spencer Collection in the New York Public Library

PERRY'S LANDING AS SEEN BY A JAPANESE ARTIST. Paintings on a silk scroll show, at top of page, Perry's ship; below it, the landing of troops. Notice the Japanese version of the American flag, carried behind the drummer and ahead of the fixed bayonets.

JAPANESE FAMILY. The print at the right, by the 18th century artist Kiyonaga, shows a happy domestic scene.

THEODORE ROOSEVELT. Top, left, T. R. in the uniform of the Rough Riders, the regiment he recruited for the Spanish war.

PHILIPPINE SOLDIERS. Upper right, followers of Aguinaldo who fought, first, against Spain, then against the United States as a new participant in the struggle for power.

THE BOXER REBELLION PUT DOWN, 1900. Chinese watch the march past of foreign guns and broad-brimmed army hats.

THE "SOONG SISTERS" and Chiang Kai-shek. Mme. Chiang is at the left of the Generalissimo. At his right, the widow of Sun Yat Sen; the other sister is Mme. Kung.

BUDDHA OF THE WEI DYNASTY. As Christianity spread over Europe, Buddhist teaching went from India to China, Japan.

CHAPTER 27

The Development of Far-Flung Empires

~~~~~~

One of the most striking facts of modern history is the establishment of colonial empires by European countries in many parts of the world. The Spanish, the Portuguese, the Dutch, the British, and the French empires were established during the Commercial Revolution of the sixteenth and seventeenth centuries. The greater part of the old French empire (Canada and Louisiana) and the greater part of the old British colonial empire (the thirteen colonies) were lost during the second half of the eighteenth century—the former by British conquest, the latter by colonial revolt. The British and the French added to their empires during the nineteenth century. The German and the Italian empires were not established until after these countries had completed their unification in 1871.

In 1914 the British Empire, the largest of the empires, consisted of dominions, crown colonies, protectorates, and India. The dominions were Canada, Newfoundland, Australia, New Zealand, and the Union of South Africa. In 1921 Ireland became a dominion and in 1949 an independent republic. In 1947 India was divided into two dominions, India and Pakistan. Newfoundland became a crown colony (1934) and a province of the Dominion of Canada (1949).

• • •

The British wrested Canada from the French (1689-1763). The British gained possession of a large part of the French empire in America by four intercolonial wars (1689-1763). In the Treaty of Utrecht (1713), which ended Queen Anne's War, France ceded Nova Scotia, Newfoundland, and the lands around Hudson Bay (Rupertsland) to Great Britain. Governors appointed by the British crown ruled all these British possessions except Rupertsland, which was ruled by the Hudson's Bay Company and its officials. In the Treaty of Paris (1763) France ceded to Great Britain all its claims to territory east of the Mississippi and to the lands south of the Ohio River, as well as to those north of it. To provide for the government of the American lands acquired in 1763, Parliament passed the Quebec Act (1774). This act gave power over this vast territory (except Prince Edward Island which became a separate province) to a royal governor who lived in Quebec. However, the act gave the French the right to continue to use the French language and to use French civil law in their courts. The act also confirmed all the privileges the Roman Catholic Church had enjoyed under French rule in New France.

The American Revolution led to many changes in Canada. The colonists attempted to take Canada from Great Britain but they failed, though the peace treaty that ended the Revolution ceded to the United States all lands between the Great Lakes and the Ohio River, which had been included in Canada by the Quebec Act. After the Revolutionary War the migration from the United States made an important change in Canada. About 40,000 Loyalists (Tories) fled from the United States to British possessions in North America. So many settled in Nova

THE PARLIAMENT BUILDINGS AT OTTAWA,
ONTARIO

Scotia that the province was divided into two parts. The northwestern part was called New Brunswick. Many other Tories settled along the St. Lawrence west of Quebec. There they were joined by settlers from Great Britain.

The government established by the Quebec Act, designed for the French, did not satisfy the desires of the English settlers for self-government. To meet their desires, the British Parliament passed the Constitutional Act (1791) which divided Canada into two provinces, Upper and Lower Canada, with the Ottawa River as the dividing line. Upper Canada was mostly British and Lower Canada was mostly French. Each had its own royal governor and council and an elective assembly; the latter body helped to meet their desires for more self-government.

In the War of 1812 the United States tried again to take Canada, but without success, partly because the Canadians were loyal to Great Britain.

The people both in Upper Canada and Lower Canada wanted more self-government than they had under the Constitutional Act of 1791. The French were led by an able lawyer-politician, Louis Joseph Papineau (1786-1871). While speaker of the Assembly of Lower Canada he had tried to secure consti-

tutional reforms. When his attempts failed, he led a revolt (1837) to establish a French republic in North America. In the same year, William Lyon MacKenzie, by agreement with Papineau, led a revolt to secure constitutional reforms in Upper Canada. The British easily suppressed both revolts because only small minorities of the population were in favor of the insurgents in either province. Papineau fled first to the United States and from there to France. He returned to Canada under a proclamation (1847) of amnesty (pardon for political offenses), re-entered politics, and continued to agitate against Great Britain until his death. MacKenzie likewise fled to the United States and he, too, returned to Canada under the same proclamation.

The Dominion of Canada developed gradually after Lord Durham's Report. In 1838 the British made Lord Durham, a prominent British liberal, Governor General and Lord High Commissioner of Canada with vast powers. His activities in Canada displeased many politicians in England because they thought he was too liberal, but the main club used against him was that he had banished to Bermuda many leaders of the late revolt. While he was in Canada, he made a personal investigation of conditions in many parts of the country. On his return to Great Britain he laid before Parliament his *Report on the Affairs of British North America.* This report is considered one of the greatest state papers in the English language. Although its recommendations were not followed immediately, it laid the foundation of the future policy of Great Britain towards its dominions.

Lord Durham recommended that Upper and Lower Canada be reunited and that Canada be allowed to govern itself by an elected parliament and a ministry or cabinet responsible to its parliament. A governor general appointed by the king of Great Britain should represent the British crown (a king or queen)

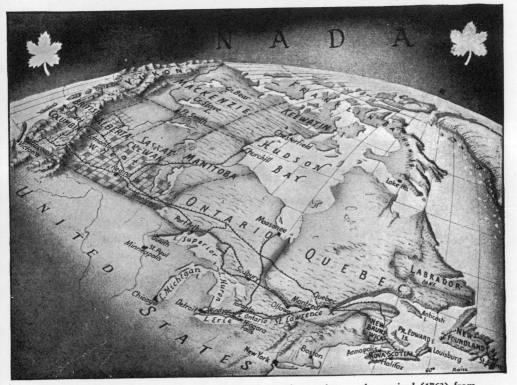

During the American Revolution, Canada, which had been only recently acquired (1763) from France, remained loyal to the English king. Westward expansion went parallel with that in the United States. Near the close of the nineteenth century the population had spread into the great wheat region of Manitoba and Saskatchewan and into the beautiful mountains of Alberta and British Columbia. The boundary between the United States and Canada is the longest unfortified boundary in the world.

and occupy in Canada the same position of influence without political power which the king held in Great Britain.

In 1840 Parliament passed an Act of Union which united Upper and Lower Canada and established a Canadian Parliament in which both were equally represented. Canada became in effect self-governing when Lord Elgin (1849), the Governor General, recognized that the Canadian Parliament was supreme in domestic affairs.

Soon thereafter Canada became a dominion. A conference was held at Quebec (1864) attended by representatives from Canada, New Brunswick, Nova Scotia, and Prince Edward Island. This conference adopted a plan of federation which with slight changes was passed by the British Parliament as the British North America Act (1867). Ontario (Upper Canada), Quebec (Lower Canada), and the provinces of Nova Scotia and New Brunswick were united into the Dominion of Canada. On July 1, 1867, a date since observed as Dominion Day, the Dominion of Canada became self-governing. Four new provinces were later admitted to the Dominion, as Canadians and others migrated to western parts of the Dominion. In 1873 Prince Edward Island joined the Dominion. Newfoundland continued to be a self-gov-

The National Film Board

Growing in fifty years from a hamlet built around a sawmill to a city with a population of more than 275,000, Vancouver has become an important city on Canada's west coast. It is one of the busiest ports in the Dominion.

erning colony, but unable to cope with its economic problems it became (1934) a crown colony. In 1948 it voted to join Canada and in 1949 became a province of Canada.

Canada today consists of ten provinces; each has its own provincial parliament. The Dominion Parliament consists of the House of Commons and the Senate and sits in Ottawa, the capital of the Dominion. The government of Canada as a whole is directed by a cabinet representing the majority party in the House of Commons. Canada has been fortunate in having four very able prime ministers: Sir John Macdonald, leader of the Conservative party (1867-1873 and 1878-1891); Sir Wilfred Laurier, leader of the Liberal party (1896-1911); Sir Robert Borden, a Conservative who played a very important part in imperial affairs during and right after the First World War; and Mackenzie King, a Liberal, who has served off and on since 1921. His part in the Second World War and in the events that followed have won for him a high place in the history of Canada.

The great western expansion took place during the prime ministership of Macdonald.

Chiefly because of his leadership and influence, the Canadian Pacific Railway Company was formed (1879). After the Canadian Pacific Railroad was built from the Atlantic to the Pacific (1885), it aided greatly in the settlement and development of Manitoba, Saskatchewan, British Columbia, and Alberta, and stimulated industries in Eastern Canada. Today in addition to its railroads, it owns and operates many steamships on the Great Lakes, the Atlantic, and Pacific. Macdonald's leadership led to the passage of tariffs intended to aid the development of Canadian industries.

Laurier, a French Canadian, was responsible for the policy of Imperial Preference (1897) by which the tariff on goods imported into Canada from Great Britain was 33⅓ per cent less than the tariff on the same kind of goods imported from places outside Great Britain. His Minister of the Interior, Mr. Clifford Sifton, by making the government-owned lands in the west more attractive to settlement, drew settlers from Great Britain, continental Europe, and even the United States. The policies of Mackenzie King have strengthened Canada and at the same time brought about close relations between the United States and Canada.

Canada has grown in population and wealth since it has become a dominion. Its population is over 13,500,000. Its railroads have been extended. Its celebrated Northwest Mounted Police, established in 1873, have kept order and protected settlers in its western and northern portions. Airplane travel has begun to make available the great resources of metal and furs of its northern areas. It exports wheat, wood products, paper, meat, fish, nickel, and gold. Canadians have shown their loyalty to the British crown by their splendid support of Great Britain in both World Wars. Ever since the War of 1812 Canada and the United States have remained on such good terms that the boundary between them is unfortified. Both the United States and Canada are justly proud of this manifestation of friendly relations.

Australia was known to early European explorers. The French, Spanish, and Dutch all claim to have discovered it. The Dutch were the first to explore the coast. Tasman (1642), who sailed from Batavia, explored the coast of the island now named for him, Tasmania. He hoisted the Dutch flag and

Karsh

PRIME MINISTER W. L. MACKENZIE KING.

took possession of the land for the government of the Netherlands. Tales of giants in the interior seem to have frightened his sailors and the Dutch failed to sustain their claim to ownership by occupation.

The great voyage (1769-1770) of Captain James Cook of the Royal Navy was undertaken primarily for astronomical purposes. He sighted and explored the eastern coast of Australia and claimed it for Great Britain. He made two other voyages of exploration (1772, 1777).

The British settled and developed Australia. The British found Australia inhabited by primitive brown peoples. They were hunters and fishermen with no agriculture and no domestic animals. They were skilled trailers of men and animals. They made tools and weapons of chipped and polished stone like those of the New Stone Age. They worshiped the powers which they believed lived in mate-

SHEEP MUSTERED FOR SHEARING, QUEENSLAND. Australia's sheep produce more than 1,000,-000,000 pounds of wool annually; more than nine-tenths of it is exported.

A VIEW OF A STEEL PLANT AT NEWCASTLE, NEW SOUTH WALES. The plant is one of the largest and most modern in the world, producing high quality steel at low cost.

The first British settlement (1788) in Australia was a convict colony at Port Jackson. Many of the convicts from Great Britain were guilty of very minor offenses and many were debtors who could not pay their debts. Free settlers soon followed. Some were sent out by stock companies whose stockholders hoped to profit from the labors of these settlers. The colony at Port Jackson developed into the colony of New South Wales.

Sheep were introduced into Australia from England (1803) and soon most of the settlers took to sheep-raising for wool and meat. In 1852 the Australians sheared 45,000,000 pounds of wool. The discovery of gold by a miner from California (1851) caused a rush to the gold fields in Southeastern Australia and a marked increase in population. For a time (1852) 2000 people a week landed in Melbourne. Coal was discovered and mined; industries were developed in the cities and

rial objects, in nature, and in people. They offered no serious objection to British exploration and settlement of Australia. Many times they assisted the British explorers of the interior of Australia.

CATTLE BEING DRIVEN FROM QUEENSLAND INTO NEW SOUTH WALES. Cattle are driven for hundreds of miles over stock routes which are the only "roads" in many parts of inland Australia.

**ONE OF THE MAIN BUILDINGS OF SYDNEY UNIVERSITY, LOCATED IN SYD-
NEY, CAPITAL OF NEW SOUTH WALES, AUSTRALIA**

agriculture in the rural areas. The population of Australia today is more than 7,000,000. As the population in other parts of Australia increased, four other colonies were set up in this order: Western Australia, South Australia, Victoria, and Queensland. The north central part is called Northern Territory. The sixth colony was Tasmania (the island of Tasmania), south of Australia.

The colonies of Australia developed the idea of federation. The colonies of Australia developed independently, chiefly because of the great distances between the settled parts of them. By 1860 all but one (Western Australia) were self-governing. The people of South Australia developed a secret ballot (1856) which became known as the Australian ballot; it is used extensively in Great Britain and the United States. All of the Australian states (1894-1908) granted women the right to vote on the same terms as men.

Some of the people in each of the Australian colonies recognized as early as the middle of the nineteenth century that if they were to form a federation, the federation could regulate trade, railways, postage, coinage, and other interests common to all of them. For many years the only step taken to bring federation about was the establishment by the British Parliament of a Federal Council for Australia with very limited powers. After several conferences and much discussion, representatives of the colonies in a convention held in 1897-1898 drew up a federal constitution which all six colonies voted to accept.

When the constitution was ratified by the British Parliament in 1900, the Commonwealth of Australia was established as a self-governing dominion within the British Empire. The government of the Commonwealth consists of a Governor General appointed by

This Coat-of-Arms was granted (1912) by the British Government to Australia. The shield, bordered with ermine, contains the badges of the six provinces.

the British crown; a Senate, consisting of six members from each state elected by the voters; and a House of Representatives, in which the number of representatives from a state depends upon its population. The Prime Minister and his cabinet represent the majority party in the House of Representatives. The government of the Commonwealth controls transportation, postal and telegraphic services, currency and finance, copyrights and patents, immigration, coinage, marriage and divorce, and the settlement of industrial disputes. Each state has its own parliament and cabinet and controls its own affairs.

The government of the Commonwealth of Australia has been democratic and liberal. The Labor party, which first entered politics in 1891, has become the largest party. An Arbitration Act passed in 1904 and strengthened in 1926 provides ways to settle industrial disputes. An Old Age Pension Act of 1908 helps to take care of the aged poor.

Australia is to a large extent pastoral and agricultural. It exports wool, mutton, wheat, and butter, chiefly to Great Britain. Its production of gold and other metals has fallen off during the twentieth century. Its industries produce almost entirely for home markets.

Australian troops fought valiantly for Great Britain in the First World War. In the first part of the Second World War they took part in the African and Greek campaigns and in Malaya, but they were recalled for the defense of Australia against Japan. When the Americans and British began their drives northward against the Japanese, they fought under British command in the Malay peninsula and later on under General MacArthur in New Guinea and Borneo.

The Dominion of New Zealand is noted for its social legislation. New Zealand consists of two large and many small islands. It was annexed by Great Britain (1840) and became a dominion in 1907. Sheep-raising, farming, gold mining, and many industries have attracted settlers and made it prosperous. New Zealand has become famous for

The Right Honorable William Morris Hughes, leader of the United Australia party in the Federal Parliament, was Prime Minister of Australia during the First World War and one of the signers of the Peace Treaty at Versailles.

laws intended to promote the welfare of its people. All railroads, telegraph and telephone lines, and all insurance companies are government-owned and operated. Legislation regulating conditions and hours of labor is strictly enforced and arbitration of labor disputes is compulsory. An Old Age Pension Act provides for the aged poor. The government of New Zealand introduced woman suffrage (1893) long before the nations of the Western world. About 50,000 Maoris, the original inhabitants of New Zealand, still survive. New Zealanders and Maoris fought side by side with Australian troops in both the First and Second World Wars. In New Zealand Maoris have been cabinet ministers.

The Union of South Africa was established after the Boer War. In 1908 representatives from Cape Colony, Natal, Orange Free State, and Transvaal met and drew up a constitution for the Union of South Africa. As in the other Dominions, the king was to be the head and was to be represented by a Governor General. Parliament was to consist of two houses. The Senate was to be composed of eight members from each state and eight additional members appointed by the Governor General. The House of Assembly was to be composed of about 150 members, popularly elected. The English and Dutch languages were established as official languages. The constitution was approved by the British Parliament and went into effect May 31, 1910.

The Boers were in the majority in the Union of South Africa and General Botha, the Boer leader in the Boer War, became the first prime minister. Although a minority opposed aid to Great Britain in both World Wars, the majority led first by General Botha and later by General Smuts rallied to the support of the British.

General Jan Christian Smuts became a world statesman. Born in Cape Colony

LT. GEN. SIR THOMAS BLAMEY, FAMOUS AUSTRALIAN SOLDIER OF THE FIRST AND SECOND WORLD WARS. He commanded the allied forces in New Guinea under General MacArthur during the war against Japan.

(1870) and educated at Cambridge University in England, he took the side of the Boers, his fellow countrymen, in their quarrel with the British. He took part in the Boer War and in the peace conference he worked for compromise between the Boers and the British. After the war he joined his former chief, General Botha, in loyalty to British rule of the South African provinces and in racial conciliation in South Africa. He was a leader in the establishment of the Union of South Africa and one of the delegates at the convention (1908) which drew up the act creating it. He supported Great Britain loyally during the First World War, commanding forces which helped drive the Germans out of East Africa. In 1917 he became a member of the Imperial War Conference in London. He played a prominent part in the making of the peace and in the establishment of the

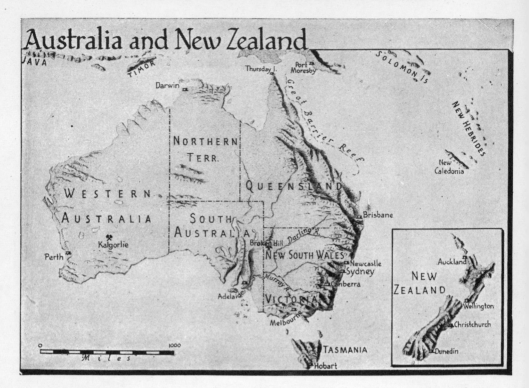

Australia is the only inhabited continent which is all south of the equator and has no land connection with any other continent. New Zealand, a British neighbor of Australia, is one of the most socially advanced countries south of the equator.

League of Nations. The substance of his memorandum on the League was used to a great extent when the Covenant of the League was written. He was the first spokesman and the leader in the establishment of the British Commonwealth of Nations. He has continued to take part in South African policies and in imperial affairs. He played a prominent part in the Second World War and in the establishment of the United Nations.

The Union of South Africa has faced difficult problems arising from nationality and race. Despite the fact that the Boer generals, Botha and Smuts, became leaders of the Union, many Boers refused to be reconciled to the British in the Union. They pursued a nationalistic policy calling at times for in-

dependence of South Africa under Boer rule. In 1915 a few Boers revolted against the government. This revolt was put down, but not before it had stirred up slumbering hatreds and jealousies. In 1924 General Hertzog won the election over Smuts and became prime minister on a nationalist platform. He did not advocate independence, but he did insist upon and did secure the use of the two languages, English and Afrikander, on an equal basis. Many Boers opposed South African entrance into the Second World War and the measure severing relations with Germany (1939) was passed by a very narrow margin.

The problem of the natives caused great difficulties. In spite of the efforts of humanitarians and liberals, most whites were de-

A GENERAL VIEW OF THE UNION HOUSES OF PARLIAMENT AT CAPETOWN.
Although the Union's Legislature meets at Capetown, Pretoria is the Union's capital and seat of administration.

termined to keep the Union in their control even though the native blacks outnumbered the whites nearly four to one. The natives are banned from most skilled occupations. They do the rough work in mines; skilled miners are all white. Most blacks are compelled to live in special areas or to carry passes or other means of identification at all times. Their right to acquire land is restricted. Since 1936 they have elected a representative council to advise the government of the Union in affairs that concern them. The natives of Cape Colony who once had the vote were given the right to elect three officials descended from Europeans to represent them in the national law-making body.

Another difficulty has arisen from the presence of more than 100,000 Indians. Originally brought to South Africa to work on the plantations, they have remained, chiefly in Natal, where they work on the tea plantations. They receive low wages and are refused political rights. Mahatma Gandhi began his career as an agitator in South Africa where he tried to improve the conditions of the Indians in Natal. Though promises of education and rights have been made and though efforts have been made to send them back to India, the problem remains. The unsolved problem of the native blacks and Indians has been brought before the United Nations by their supporters.

Commissioner Street is the principal street in Johannesburg, a city of more than 500,000 inhabitants and the center of the mining industry.

Great Britain and the Dominions formed the British Commonwealth of Nations. Even before the First World War the Dominions in the British Empire had become almost self-governing. After the fighting was over and before the Paris Peace Conference was held, they were invited to send representatives to take part in it because of the splendid and loyal part the Dominions played in the war. They signed the treaties and joined the League of Nations. In 1926 an Imperial Conference (composed of delegates from the Dominions and British delegates) was held in London. It declared each Dominion a political equal of Great Britain and, like it, united in loyalty to the British crown and also a member of the family of nations called the British Commonwealth of Nations. To give effect to this declaration after it had been accepted by each Dominion, the Statute of Westminster was passed by the British Parliament in 1931. Although Great Britain and the Dominions co-operate by giving preference to one another's goods and by frequent exchanges of views on common interests, the Dominions are not subject to any British laws. They do not even have to go to the assistance of the mother country in time of war. However, in 1939 all Dominions went to the aid of Great Britain.

Ireland has had a troubled history. After the First World War the Irish Free State, established in 1922, became one of the self-governing Dominions of the British Empire. Tradition tells of many wars fought by the kings of the ancient Celtic tribes, who once inhabited Ireland. The stories of these kings and of the ancient Celtic capital of Tara inspired a lovely lament by the Irish poet, Thomas Moore (1780-1852):

The harp that once through Tara's halls,
　　The soul of music shed,
Now hangs as mute on Tara's walls
　　As if the soul were fled.
So sleeps the pride of former days,
　　So glory's thrill is o'er,
And hearts that once beat high for praise
　　Now feel that pulse no more!

No more to chiefs and ladies bright
　　The harp of Tara swells,
The cord alone that breaks at night
　　Its tale of ruin tells.
Thus Freedom now so seldom wakes,
　　The only throb she gives
Is when some heart indignant breaks,
　　To show that she still lives.

The ancient Irish were converted to Christianity by Patrick, a Briton, who went to Ireland (432) as a missionary. The Irish became devout Catholics. Missionaries from Ireland converted some of the Angles and Saxons in Northern England and some of the German tribes east of the Rhine. The Irish monastic schools, noted for their brilliant national culture, became celebrated centers of learning and of writing, and Irish scholars taught in the schools established by Charlemagne in

UNIVERSITY OF WITWATERSRAND, TRANSVAAL, UNION OF SOUTH AFRICA.
Students from all parts of Africa are enrolled in it and this view shows some of the girl under-
graduates on one of the spacious lawns with the main block of buildings done in classical style
in the background.

the eighth and ninth centuries at Aachen and elsewhere in his empire.

Although Ireland was little affected by the earlier Germanic invasions of Britain, it suffered greatly in the ninth and tenth centuries from the raids and invasions of the Northmen who were at the same time ravaging parts of the continent.

Henry II (1154-1189), king of England, established his rule over a small part of Ireland known as "the Pale." The authority of the English kings was not extended effectively throughout Ireland until modern times. The Irish Catholics revolted against Queen Elizabeth and were put down with great cruelty. James I, who settled large numbers of Scotch Presbyterians in Ulster, made that province a Protestant stronghold. Many Irish who had supported Charles I were crushed and deprived of their lands by Cromwell who gave them to Englishmen. The conquest of Ireland was completed by William III after he had won the Battle of the Boyne (1690) which the Irish fought in support of the dethroned King James II.

In the course of these conflicts much of the land had been confiscated and given to Englishmen. The Irish had thereby become tenants on what had been their own farms. The property of the Catholic Church was transferred to the Church of England and the Irish were taxed to support a state church (Anglican) to which they did not belong and which they did not respect. The English, after overpowering the Irish people, granted them a parliament but, as Catholics did not have the right to vote or hold office, the members of parliament represented only a few Protes-

GLADSTONE'S FIRST HOME RULE BILL, 1886.
The eloquent Prime Minister is shown here in the
House of Commons urging the passage of the bill
which was defeated because members of his own Liberal
party joined the Conservatives in voting it down.

tants and English landowners. By the Act of
Union (1801) Ireland became a part of the
United Kingdom of Great Britain and Ireland. The parliament in Ireland was abolished, the Protestants of Ireland elected representatives to the House of Commons, and
sent four spiritual lords and twenty-eight
temporal peers to the House of Lords.

**Irish patriots waged a long struggle for
Home Rule.** Agitation for the political freedom of Ireland was started by Thomas Emmet (1798) and renewed after the Act of
Union by his brother Robert Emmet. This
young enthusiast for freedom planned an
uprising (1803) which he hoped would be
helped by the expected Napoleonic invasion
of England. The uprising collapsed miser-
ably and Emmet was tried and executed for
treason.

The failure of the potato crop (1845-
1846) caused famine in Ireland. The population of Ireland which had been rapidly increasing was now about 8,000,000. Ireland
had had no Industrial Revolution; the chief
food was potatoes. When the crop failed,
hundreds of thousands starved. Still more fled
to Great Britain, Australia, Canada, and
above all to the United States. Insurrections
broke out in 1846 and again in 1867. After

the failure of these revolts, the Irish leaders
carried their demands to the British House of
Commons. There they developed a three-fold
reform program: (1) religious reform, (2)
land reform, and (3) Home Rule.

Part of the religious reform had already
been accomplished. The British Parliament
granted Catholics the right to hold office in
1829. In 1869 it discontinued the taxes which
the Irish had been paying for the support of
the Anglican Church in Ireland.

Land reform was put into effect by the
Acts of 1870, 1881, and 1903. The Land Act
of 1870 did not accomplish much and agitation for land reform continued in Ireland.
The Act of 1881 aimed to correct the defects
of the Act of 1870 and to meet the Irish demand for fair rent, fixity of tenure, and free
sale. It pleased neither landlords or tenants.
By the Act of 1903 the British government
provided funds from which Irish farmers
could borrow money at low rates of interest
to purchase land whether tenanted or not. In
1932 the Irish Free State paid 10,000,000
pounds to the British government to wipe
out the debts of all Irish farmers who had
borrowed money to purchase land under the
terms of the Act of 1903.

Home Rule for Ireland proved to be a
most difficult problem to solve. Ulster, in
Northern Ireland, was Protestant and prosperous. Its wealth was obtained largely from
the linen and shipping industries in Belfast.
The Protestants of Ulster feared that they
would suffer under Catholic rule if Home
Rule were granted and that they would be
heavily taxed to support the less prosperous
southern part of Ireland. Many Englishmen,
both Conservative and Liberal, within and
outside Parliament, were opposed to Home
Rule. For many years the ablest leader of the
Irish group in the House of Commons was a
Protestant Irishman, Charles Stewart Parnell.
Gladstone, the British prime minister, intro-

duced two Home Rule Bills, one in 1886, the other in 1893. Both were defeated. When at last a Home Rule Bill became law (1914) the men of Ulster were armed to resist its enforcement by the British government and civil war seemed imminent. The outbreak of the First World War at that time kept the bill from being put into effect by the British government.

Though many Irishmen were loyal to the British Empire in the First World War— many worked in munitions plants and many volunteered to serve in the armed forces—a great majority of the Irish wanted Ireland to be independent. In 1906 a group of Irish leaders had organized a society called *Sinn Fein* (we ourselves). It planned the establishment of an Irish Republic and the revival of the Gaelic (ancient Celtic) language and literature. The leaders of *Sinn Fein* conspired with Germany and fomented an unsuccessful revolt in 1916 during the First World War. After the end of the war the Irish Republican party, whose object was to make Ireland an independent republic, formed an illegal government and tried to ignore the legal government of Ireland. Bitter fighting followed between the Irish Republicans and the British, and many atrocities were committed, particularly by the British police called the Black and Tans. After much political and social disorder and many conferences, a compromise agreement was reached in 1921 by the establishment of the Irish Free State as a self-governing dominion within the British Empire. Ulster, which was not included in the Irish Free State, had its own parliament and its own ministry and representation in the British Parliament. The Irish who wanted political independence were not yet satisfied.

In 1933, under the leadership of De Valera, the oath of allegiance to the King of England was abolished by an act of the parliament of the Irish Free State. In 1937 the Irish Free State drew up a new constitution in which the name Irish Free State was changed to Eire and in which Eire was proclaimed independent of Great Britain, but this independence did not involve the formal separation of Eire from the British Commonwealth of Nations. At the outbreak of the Second World War Eire proclaimed its neutrality, which it maintained throughout the war. Eire's neutrality was not violated by the British government even though it meant that Great Britain could not use bases in Western Ireland which it had ceded to Eire. In 1949 Eire became the Republic of Ireland and completely independent of Great Britain.

The British Empire has many crown colonies and protectorates. The crown colonies are ruled by representatives of the crown. The people in some crown colonies take part in the government of the colony; in others they do not. In some British protectorates there are native rulers; in others British officials rule the peoples directly, although the territory has not been formally annexed. Some of the British protectorates are on the routes of world trade, others are in lands where raw materials are produced or where there are markets for British manufactures. In the Western Hemisphere, Great Britain still owns many islands in the Caribbean Sea, British Honduras in Central America, and British Guiana in South America. Britain's possessions in the Mediterranean—Gibraltar, Malta, and Cyprus, and her control of the Suez Canal—make secure the Mediterranean route to India and the Far East, often called the lifeline of the British Empire.

British East Africa (now known as Kenya), Rhodesia, and possessions on the western coast of Africa give Britain access to the riches of the interior of that continent. British Somaliland in Eastern Africa and just across from it Aden in Arabia guard the southern approaches to the Red Sea. The Anglo-Russian Convention (1907) gave Great Britain a sphere of influence in South Persia, which helped Great Britain to protect the northwestern frontier of India. The island of Ceylon off the southeast coast of India, and Burma (until 1948) across the bay of Bengal on the mainland of Asia, are other rich possessions in Asia. Great rubber plantations and very rich tin mines in the Malay peninsula have increased the prosperity of Great Britain. Great Britain founded Singapore (1819) and developed it into a huge naval base which gave Great Britain control over the Strait of Malacca, a sea passage connecting the Indian Ocean and the Pacific. Hong Kong, off the China coast, became a British naval base and a huge commercial and financial center for trade with Southern and Eastern China. Great Britain owns many islands of strategic and economic value in the South Pacific.

A complex civilization has developed in India. India is a vast triangular peninsula in the southern part of Asia. In the northern part the Himalayan Mountains, the highest in the world, shut India off from the populous parts of the rest of the continent. South of the foothills of the Himalayas is a great plain stretching east and west across India which is watered by three great river systems that have their sources in the Himalayas. These river systems are the Indus in the west, the Ganges and the Brahmaputra in the east. South of the great plain is a mountainous plateau surrounded by a narrow coastal plain. Surrounding India on the west, east, and south is the sea which has helped to keep India apart from the rest of the world. Consequently, India was influenced but little by other peoples until the age of discovery and exploration which began in the fifteenth century.

India is about three fifths the size of the United States. Most of its 400,000,000 inhabitants live in or near the three great river valleys. They are among the most thickly populated regions of the earth. More than 200 people live on every square mile of good farming land and more than 2,000 in the irrigated areas. In India about 75 per cent of the people live on small farms which raise the same crops year after year; in other words, they do not practice crop rotation. The 6,000,-000 farms in the United States produce twice as much as the 40,000,000 farms in India. Consequently, the average income from a farm in the United States is more than thirteen times the average income from a farm in India. Eleven principal languages and hundreds of dialects are spoken. Only the educated speak English; 90 per cent cannot read or write any language. Hinduism is the religion of about 300,000,000 of the people and about 90,000,000 are Mohammedans. Four of the other eight religions number their members in the millions. About 60,000,000 Indians are pariahs who are denied all social rights. Hence, many of them have been converted to Christianity and Mohammedanism.

Hinduism was brought to India by Indo-European (Aryan) invaders. In early times India was inhabited by a dark skinned folk (Dravidians) who seemed to have developed a high degree of culture in the Indus valley in Western India. They may have traded with the Sumerians in the valley of the Euphrates. Shortly after 2500 B.C., the Indus valley was invaded by Indo-Europeans from the northwest. The Indo-Europeans spoke Sanskrit, a language akin to Latin and Greek. The invaders (Aryans) made themselves masters of the Dravidians, settled down in the Indus valley, and later on began to push their way to the south and east, but not as far as Southern India. To what extent Aryans intermarried with Dravidians is not known. Probably the upper classes of the Aryans did not intermarry, but the lower classes mingled with the older inhabitants. Though the Aryans do not

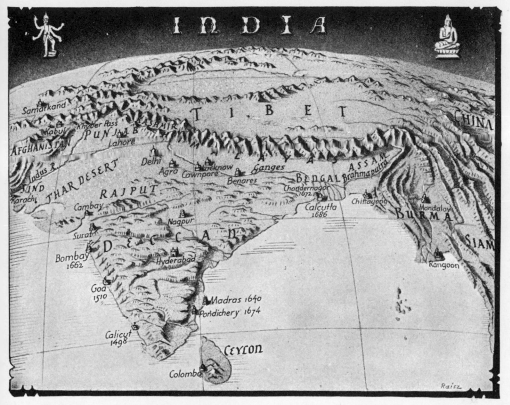

The highest mountain ranges and the deepest gorges in the world isolate India from the rest of Asia. The Air Age will help to break down this isolation.

seem to have entered Southern India, their religious ideas spread there and took hold on the peoples. In Northern India the Aryans formed many small states which fought one another. They possessed a great book, the *Veda,* which contained religious teachings. Scholars (Brahmans), who studied the *Veda,* taught its religious teachings to their followers. The religion they taught was Hinduism.

There are many sects within Hinduism. The more enlightened and philosophical Hindu believe in a single God. Most Hindus worship many gods, believe cows are sacred animals, and that rivers are sacred also. They believe in the transmigration of souls, that is, when a person dies his soul enters the body

of a newborn child or even the body of an animal and, after the death of that person or animal, its soul goes to the body of another person or animal. Consequently, devout Hindus will not kill even a fly. They are vegetarians, lest by eating meat they become cannibals. Hindus also accept without reservation the caste system which has developed in India as a part of the teaching of Hinduism.

The caste system of the Hindus affects all phases of life in India. Castes arose out of the ancient divisions among the people. The Brahmans, who studied and interpreted the *Veda,* were looked up to by the rest of the people and thereby became the highest

Bettmann Archive

AN INDIAN OIL MILL CALLED KOLHU TURNED BY AN OX. In the high stone mortar there is a club in a slanting position to which the crank is attached. A child who is driving the ox goes around with him on a seat.

class. Below them in order were the nobles (warriors), the farmers, and the serfs. Gradually each of these four classes became an hereditary caste which means that a son belongs to the same caste as his father and that he has to follow his father's occupation. These four castes are now subdivided into more than 7000, even a caste of thieves. One who has been expelled from his caste, or one who has no caste by birth, is known as an untouchable, a pariah, and such a person is in a hopeless and pitiable condition. There are almost 60,000,000 untouchables in India.

The caste system is one of the chief obstacles to the improvement of conditions in modern India because a person may not rise into a higher caste than the one into which he was born. Hinduism teaches that anyone born into a lower caste or an untouchable is being punished for the sins committed in his past life. If such a person is calmly resigned to his fate and lives rightly, he will be elevated in caste in his next life. This resignation to fate tends to make the members of the lower castes and the untouchables submissive to the terrible economic and social conditions under which they live. However, the machine age is helping to undermine the caste system. In factories, on trains, in commercial establishments, schools, universities, and political parties, persons belonging to different castes are thrown together more than formerly.

Buddhism was native to India. About 500 B.C. Sidhatta Gautama was born the son of a prince. He grew up in wealth and luxury and married happily. Meditating about the evils of the world led him to abandon his wife, his children, and his wealth and to wander about India as a beggar in search of truth. After many years of wandering and meditation, he found what he thought was truth. He taught what he thought was the truth to many people and gathered many disciples who called him Buddha, Enlightened One. The heart of his teaching is that by right belief, right living, and right thinking man can attain Nirvana (perfect peace).

Two hundred years after Buddha's death Asoka (273-242 B.C.), a great emperor, ruled India. He spread the doctrines of Buddhism all over India. In the first century A.D. Buddhist doctrines spread to China where they were accepted by many people; and from China they were carried to Japan where for many centuries they have had and still have a wide influence. In India Hinduism triumphed and today the number of Buddhists is only about 200,000.

Mohammedanism was brought to India by Mongol invaders. In 1398-1399 the religious and racial problems of India were complicated still more after a great conqueror, Tamerlane (1336-1405), invaded India and set up an extensive empire. His successors (Moguls) continued as emperors for centuries until 1858, though they had little power after they were defeated by a Persian invader in 1739. The Mongols introduced their religion, Mohammedanism, and today about 90,000,000 Indians are of that faith. A lovely memorial of the Mogul Empire is the beautiful shrine Taj Mahal, built in

Northern India by Emperor Jahan (1627-1658) as a tomb for his favorite wife.

India became part of the British Empire.
The history of India in modern times begins with the Commercial Revolution in the fifteenth and sixteenth centuries when the Portuguese established the first trading posts in India. Soon the Dutch, the French, and the English established their trading posts. In wars for the control of trade in India the English won, chiefly through the efforts of Robert Clive who was an employee of the British East India Company. For a time the British possessions in India were ruled by the British East India Company under the supervision of a member of the British cabinet. Native discontent with this rule finally resulted in an outbreak called the Sepoy Mutiny (1857). In part it was caused by the desire of the Indians for independence. Its immediate cause, however, was religious. The British East India Company issued cartridges greased with the fat of cows and pigs for use by its native troops called sepoys. This act offended the Hindus, who believed cows to be sacred, and the Mohammedans, who believed pigs to be unclean. The mutiny was put down with great severity with the aid of large numbers of British soldiers sent over by the British government. After the mutiny the British Parliament decided that the government of its Indian empire should be taken away from the British East India Company. The Company was dissolved (1858) and the British Parliament placed India under the supervision of the Secretary of State for India who was made a member of the British cabinet. On January 1, 1877, Queen Victoria was proclaimed Empress of India at a great celebration held in Delhi.

Until quite recently India has been divided politically into native states whose 93,000,000 people are ruled by native princes and British provinces whose 290,000,000 people

The Metropolitan Museum of Art
TAMERLANE RECEIVING TURKISH PRISONERS.

were governed by a direct central administration at Delhi, strategically located between the Ganges and the Indus lowlands. Seven successive cities have occupied this location. In the seventeenth century Delhi was the capital of the Moguls; it was adorned with magnificent buildings.

The head of the government of British India (about three fifths of all India) was a viceroy appointed by the crown. He appointed a council to advise him and also governors of the nine provinces into which British India was divided. A staff of civil and military officials carried on the work of the government. About three fifths of India, 562 states, were governed by native princes who were autocrats. Some of these were enormously wealthy and all clung tenaciously to

Lindsley F. Hall

THE TAJ MAHAL AT AGRA, INDIA. The tomb is of pure white marble. It is decorated with openwork carvings and inlays of semiprecious stones.

their powers as rulers. They maintained close relations with the government of British India. At their courts there was usually a British resident as adviser, and their foreign relations were carefully controlled by the British. Not counting soldiers, only about 100,000 inhabitants of India were British.

British businessmen obtained great wealth from India. For many years after the British established their power in India, Indians produced and sold to British merchants jute, wheat, cotton, tea, rice, and other foodstuffs in great abundance. In return for these products, Indians bought cotton goods, iron and steel products, and other manufactures from British manufacturers. The construction of railroads, of iron and steel mills (particularly near Calcutta, to take advantage of

the huge iron ore deposits in that region) and of cotton mills (chiefly near Bombay which make much of the white cotton cloth ing used by Indians) furnished opportunitie for British capitalists to make investments. A very large part of the wealth of the British Empire was in India.

The peoples of many countries have helped the peoples of India. Missionaries of many Christian faiths have gone to India in large numbers where they have established schools and hospitals and have done much to improve conditions, particularly among the untouchables. Schools and universities have been established by the British, though not in sufficient numbers to provide an education for all those who need it. Certain superstitious practices have been forbidden and health and public sanitation measures have been carried out.

Indian leaders have tried to win political independence. The age-long and unchanging ways of Indians led them to resist changes in their ways of living, and quarrels among religious groups have made India a difficult country to rule. Late in the nineteenth century Indian nationalists began an "India for the Indians" movement. It increased the difficulties which the British faced in governing India. Hindus and Moslems agreed that India should be free, but they disagreed on what the new government should be. The native princes, who would lose much of their power if India became independent, were hostile to India's independence.

Although the British suppressed all uprisings, terrorist outbreaks, and sometimes even propaganda for independence, they made concessions. Indians were given the right to take part in local governments, and posts in the Civil Service were opened to natives who were qualified. In 1909 the India Councils Act, passed by the British Parliament, provided for the election of some members of the legislative councils, both provincial and central, and about the same time one or two Indians were appointed as members of the Viceroy's Executive Council. As a result of agitation during the First World War, the British Parliament passed the Government of India Act (1919). It described the divisions, the offices, and the duties of all branches of the government of India. It reorganized the legislative councils in the provinces and established a two-house legislature for the central government. It did not, however, affect the powers of the native princes. The Act of 1919 did not satisfy the Indian nationalists because under its provisions so many powers were reserved to the native princes and the viceroy. Consequently, they continued their agitations for Indian independence.

In 1919 Gandhi became leader of the Indian nationalists. His followers called him Mahatma (Great Soul). His program for independence was based on the religious idea of non-violence (non-co-operation and non-resistance). He advised his followers not to hold office, not to pay taxes, not to buy British goods, and not to go to British schools. If they should be punished by the British for non-co-operation, they should not resist but should go quietly to prison. He himself was put in protective custody by the British many times.

Gandhi's followers were numerous and they accepted his program so wholeheartedly that the British government was convinced after ten years of Indian resistance that the Government of India Act of 1919 did not meet the desires of the Indians for home rule. After two Round Table conferences (1930, 1931), in one of which Gandhi participated, the British Parliament passed another Government of India Act (1935). This provided for an increase in the number of voters and was intended to bring the native princes into an All-Indian federation. About 32,000 were wealthy enough to vote for members of the upper house and 1,250,000 for members of the lower house of the central legislature. About 36,000,000 could vote for members of the provincial legislatures. This act did not meet the demands of the Indian nationalists. The princes were not willing to join the federation. So the act was never entirely carried out. Gandhi and the Indian Nationalist Congress led by Nehru continued agitation for Indian independence even into the period of the Second World War.

In the spring of 1946 the British government offered the Indians a plan for a unified, independent India. It called for a central government to control defense, foreign affairs, and communications, and for strong regional governments to control economic and social

Ewing Galloway

MAHATMA GANDHI. India's world-famous leader picked this portrait as the most characteristic likeness of himself. It was taken by an Indian photographer in Madras.

developments. To establish this central government the plan called for the viceroy to set up an all-Indian cabinet and for a constituent assembly, representing the provincial assemblies and the princes, to draw up a permanent constitution. Gandhi accepted the plan. The Mohammedans who desired a separate independent state (Pakistan), led by Mohammed Ali Jinnah, hesitated. In July, 1946, they agreed to accept it, but Jinnah announced his determination to work for strong local governments to protect the rights of the Mohammedans. They later withdrew their acceptance and great public disorder followed as Hindus and Mohammedans fought each other.

In spite of the fact that a meeting of the Indian leaders with the British Cabinet in London (December, 1946) was followed by a complete deadlock, Prime Minister Attlee announced (February 20, 1947) the intention of the British government to transfer power to responsible Indian hands not later than June, 1948. This announcement was followed by positive action when the Indian Independence Act received Royal Assent on July 18. This Act which took effect on August 15 provided for a complete revision of the government of India. The King of England ceased to be called Emperor of India. British India was divided into two dominions, India (Hindu) and Pakistan (Moslem). Provision was made for constituent assemblies in each dominion to draw up constitutions. Both dominions are members of the United Nations. In 1949 the prime ministers of the British Commonwealth consented to a declaration by which India might become an independent republic and still stay in the Commonwealth by recognizing the King as the head of the Commonwealth. The native states were given the right to choose between independence and joining one or the other of the two dominions. By far the greater number of them chose to join the Union of India, because most of their peoples were Hindus.

On August 14, Lord Mountbatten for Great Britain formally surrendered British rights and the following day the new dominions were launched. This act, however, was followed by terrible riots between fanatical Hindus and Moslems even in Delhi itself.

On January 30, 1948, Gandhi was murdered by a fanatical Hindu; Jinnah, the Moslem leader, died later the same year.

This problem of Indian unity and independence is complicated not only by the religious difficulties, but also by the social and economic conditions of the country. About 90 per cent of the people are illiterate and earn less than twenty dollars a year. Most of them are peasants. They have little interest in who governs them or how they are being governed.

France possessed a far-flung empire. In 1914, France owned lands in many parts of the world. In the Western Hemisphere, it still owned two small islands off the coast of Newfoundland (St. Pierre and Miquelon), a few islands in the Caribbean Sea, and French Guiana in northeastern South America. Off the coast of French Guiana was Devil's Island, a notorious French penal colony which was abolished by the French Popular Front. In Africa, as we have seen, France owned Tunis, Algeria, the French Congo, French West Africa, and the island of Madagascar off the eastern coast, and held a protectorate in Morocco on the northwestern coast. France possessed also a few trading posts in India, Indo- China, and a few islands in the Pacific.

On the whole, French officials were very successful colonial administrators. The French government established schools, built railways and telegraph lines, and developed the natural resources of their possessions. French traders in the French empire shipped raw materials to France and France exported manufactured goods of many kinds to the different parts of its empire. A few of the colonies were granted representation in the Chamber of Deputies. As a result, French colonials have been for the most part loyal to France. The Senegalese from Africa and the Annamese from Indo-China fought bravely for France in the First World War.

The Dutch built up a very rich empire. Ever since the height of Dutch naval power in the seventeenth century the Dutch have retained possession of an overseas empire many times larger than the mother country. They owned Curacao in the West Indies and Dutch Guiana in northeastern South America. They possessed the Netherlands East Indies, a great empire consisting of the islands of Java, Sumatra, Celebes, a large part of Borneo, and scores of smaller islands in Indonesia. The population of this empire was about 67,000,000. The government of the provinces was conducted by officials appointed by the central government in the Netherlands. From the Netherlands East Indies the Dutch derived great wealth, especially rubber, oil, tin, quinine, and spices.

Other European nations built empires. Belgium obtained great riches from the Belgian Congo. All of Spain's once proud empire was gone except Spanish Morocco in Northwest Africa and the Canaries and Madeira Islands in the Atlantic. Portugal still owned Angola in West Africa, Mozambique in Southeast Africa, and the Azores and Cape Verde Islands in the Atlantic.

By 1914 Germany possessed German East Africa and German Southwest Africa, a few islands in the Pacific, and a lease on an important part of the Shantung peninsula in China. Italy's colonial empire consisted of Tripoli, in North Africa, Eritrea on the west shore of the Red Sea, and Italian Somaliland on the western shore of the Indian Ocean.

The United States became a world power. Although the United States had purchased Alaska from Russia in 1867, it did not acquire a colonial empire until the Spanish-American War in 1898. This war grew out of a revolution by Cubans for independence from Spain. Its chief causes were interference with American economic interests in Cuba and a war fever stirred up by the yellow press over mistreatment of Cubans by the Spanish and the sinking of the battleship *Maine*. This war was fought in the Philippines, in Cuba, and in Puerto Rico. Admiral George Dewey's fleet destroyed a Spanish fleet at the battle of Manila Bay. Land forces, notably Theodore Roosevelt's "Rough Riders," defeated the Spanish in Cuba, while General Miles easily took Puerto Rico. Another Spanish fleet was crushed at the battle of Santiago. The Treaty of Paris (1898) that ended the Spanish-American War ceded to the United States owner-

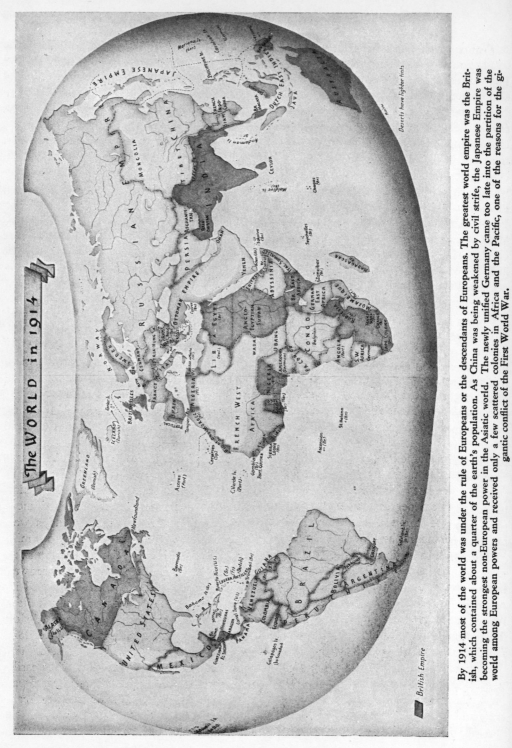

The WORLD in 1914

British Empire

Deserts have lighter tints

By 1914 most of the world was under the rule of Europeans or the descendants of Europeans. The greatest world empire was the British, which contained about a quarter of the earth's population. As China was being weakened by civil strife, the Japanese Empire was becoming the strongest non-European power in the Asiatic world. The newly unified Germany came too late into the partition of the world among European powers and received only a few scattered colonies in Africa and the Pacific, one of the reasons for the gigantic conflict of the First World War.

ship of lands overseas—Puerto Rico in the Caribbean, Guam in the Marianas, and the Philippines in the Far East. In the same year Congress by joint resolution annexed Hawaii and in 1903 the Canal Zone was acquired by treaty with the Republic of Panama. In 1917 the United States purchased the Virgin Islands from Denmark and made its citizens United States citizens. Part of the Samoan Islands, Wake Island, and other widely scattered islands in the Pacific became American possessions.

SUMMARY

In 1914 the vast and far-flung British Empire was larger than any of the other empires. It consisted of dominions, crown colonies, protectorates, and India. Lord Durham's Report (1839) on the government of Canada led to a union of its provinces into the Dominion of Canada (1867). Other dominions were to evolve later on.

The Dominion of Canada has been ably served by four great leaders. Under the leadership of Prime Minister Macdonald, Canada began to expand to the west. The development of the West continued under Prime Minister Laurier; he initiated the policy of Imperial Preference. Since Laurier's time Canada's strength and development have increased while Sir Robert Borden and Mackenzie King were Prime Ministers. Its already friendly relations with the United States have been heightened, and its contributions in two World Wars have demonstrated its loyalty to Great Britain.

In 1900 Australia also became a dominion of the British Empire. Agitation by the people in the several states of Australia for a federal union of these states led to a Constitutional Convention (1897) which drafted a constitution for a federal union. In 1900 the British Parliament approved this constitution and Australia became the second dominion of the British Empire. Like the people of Canada, the people of the Commonwealth of Australia have demonstrated their loyalty to Great Britain by their contributions in two World Wars.

New Zealand became the third dominion (1907). Like the other two dominions, it supported Great Britain loyally in two World Wars.

A few years after the Boer War, representatives from four provinces drew up a constitution for a Union of South Africa and submitted it to the British Parliament. It was approved by the British Parliament and the Union of South Africa became the fourth dominion in the British Empire (1909). General Jan Christian Smuts, a South African, has become one of the foremost statesmen of the world.

Great Britain, after making several attempts to conquer Ireland, finally succeeded (1690) in defeating the Irish armies. The Protestants who governed Ireland did not represent the Irish people, who were overwhelmingly Catholic. In 1801 the British Parliament passed the Act of Union which united Ireland and Great Britain as the Kingdom of Great Britain and Ireland. As the Irish were not satisfied with the government imposed on them, they waged a long struggle for Home Rule. After the First World War, Irish leaders proclaimed Ireland a republic which led to a bitter fight with the British. In recognition of the desires of the Irish for self-government the British Parliament passed an act (1922) which created the Irish Free State. The President of Eire, the successor of the Irish Free State, proclaimed Eire's neutrality in the Second World War.

During the Commercial Revolution the British East India Company, the French East India Company, and the Dutch East India Company established trading posts in India. These companies had private armies. Rivalry for trade in India led to wars between the British and French trading companies. These wars ended in a victory for the British East India Company which continued to govern the British possessions in India until after the Sepoy Mutiny (1857). In 1858 the British government dissolved the British East India Company and established a government over British India which comprised that part of India (almost three fifths) not ruled by native Indian princes.

Under this government, British India was governed by a viceroy, assisted by a council whose members headed departments, and a staff of English officials. From the days of the Commercial Revolution, the British have profited from the natural resources of India. In later times they helped to develop these resources. During all these years they have gained great wealth from India.

Ever since the beginning· of British rule in India, Indians have been dissatisfied by the ways in which it affected them and what they considered to be their rights. In consequence, a movement for political independence developed. From time to time, the British Parliament has recognized the right of Indians for a greater share in government by passing acts to remove the injustices and restrictions of which the Indians complained. In 1947 the Indian Independence Act provided for the setting up of two dominions in India.

The extensive colonial empire of France included Indo-China, scattered islands in the southwest Pacific, islands in the Indian Ocean, large areas in several parts of Africa, small islands off the coast of Newfoundland and in the Caribbean, and French Guiana.

The very rich Dutch empire included the Netherlands East Indies and small possessions in the Western Hemisphere. From the days of the Commercial Revolution, the Dutch have derived great wealth from their empire.

Before 1914 Belgium, Germany, Italy, Japan, and the United States had acquired overseas possessions.

SUMMARY OF PART VIII

Nineteenth century imperialism was the product of a search for markets in which raw materials could be bought, finished products sold, and capital invested, all under the control of the imperialistic nations. It was in large measure a result of the Industrial Revolution. During the course of imperialism large areas of the world were taken over by the imperialistic nations.

Africa was opened up and parcelled out largely after the explorations of Livingstone and Stanley. The nations that participated in this partition were Belgium, Great Britain, France, Germany, Italy, and Spain. In the early years of the twentieth century the only independent-states left in Africa were Liberia and Abyssinia.

In the Far East the doors of both China and Japan were opened up to Western trade and influences. China, though weak, was able to maintain its independence, but was forced to grant many concessions to the imperialistic nations. Japan quickly adopted much of Western civilization. After becoming industrialized and building up an army and a navy, it became imperialistic chiefly at the expense of its neighbor China.

The British Empire, already large at the opening of the nineteenth century, was further expanded and reorganized. Its larger possessions, except for India, became self-governing dominions which in the twentieth century formed the British Commonwealth of Nations. India after much agitation has gained its independence.

Gradually France gained possessions in Africa and Eastern Asia. Germany and Italy, late arrivals in the field, were able to secure less valuable possessions. The Dutch retained possession of a very extensive territory in the East Indies. The United States acquired widely scattered lands including Alaska, Hawaii, Puerto Rico, the Philippines, and the Virgin Islands.

The imperialistic ambitions and rivalries of the great powers resulted in much bitter feeling among them. These rivalries played a major part in plunging the world into the devastations of two world-wide wars, World War I and World War II.

EVENTS THAT TOOK PLACE AT ABOUT THE SAME TIME
1750

	Captain Cook explored east coast of Australia, 1769-1770.
First convict transports arrived in Australia, 1788.	Constitutional Act divided Canada into Upper Canada and Lower Canada, 1791.
Act of Union of Great Britain and Ireland, 1801.	
Catholic Emancipation Act, 1829.	
	Rebellion in Upper and Lower Canada, 1837.
	Lord Durham's Report, 1839.
British sovereignty over New Zealand announced, 1840.	Union Act united Upper and Lower Canada, 1840.
Australia's colonies given self-government, 1850.	
Discovery of gold in Australia, 1851.	
	Newfoundland given self-government, 1855.
Sepoy Mutiny, 1857.	
End of rule of British East India Company, 1858.	
	Dominion of Canada created by the British North America Act, 1867.
Passage of law disestablishing the Anglican Church in Ireland, 1869.	
	Manitoba (1870), British Columbia (1871), Prince Edward Island (1873) made provinces of Dominion of Canada.
Queen Victoria proclaimed Empress of India, 1877.	
	Irish Land Act, 1881.
Beginning of Commonwealth of Australia, 1900.	
	Alberta and Saskatchewan made provinces of Dominion of Canada, 1905.
New Zealand made a dominion, 1907.	
Union of South Africa began, 1910.	Easter Rebellion in Ireland, 1916.
Government of India Act, 1919.	Irish Free State created, 1922.
	British Commonwealth of Nations, 1926.
	Statute of Westminster, 1931.
Government of India Act, 1935.	Newfoundland reverted from a dominion to a crown colony, 1934.
New constitution for Ireland, Eire, 1937.	
Ceylon a dominion, 1948; Burma independent, 1948.	Dominions of India and Pakistan, 1947.
	Newfoundland, a province of Canada, 1949.
Republic of Ireland, 1949.	

1950

EAMON DE VALERA SPEAKS TO A STREET CROWD. De Valera here addresses a throng of Irish Republicans gathered to protest their lack of representation in the Irish Parliament. Photographed in Dublin, 1927.

CHARLES STEWART PARNELL, Protestant leader of the Irish Home Rule party at the time of Gladstone's Home Rule bill. Parnell's mother was American.

DESTRUCTION IN DUBLIN, 1922. Street fighting between opposing factions in the Irish civil war reaches a climax with the rebel republicans barricaded in a hotel.

PREMIER NEHRU. The Indian statesman, philosopher and popular leader is the author of a remarkable world history.

INDIA PRAYS. At right, a ceremony typical of the old India—bathing and prayer in the Ganges.

INDIA FIGHTS. "Passive resistance" to British rule, as practiced by college students in Calcutta, 1938.

PART IX

The Impact of the First World War

After the idea of the Concert of Europe had proved to be a failure as a means of keeping peace, it was abandoned. After the Franco-Prussian War, the major European nations arrayed themselves into one or the other of two armed camps to protect their national interests. Germany, Austria-Hungary, and Italy formed the Triple Alliance; Great Britain, France, and Russia formed another, the Triple Entente.

When the First World War began (1914), Italy was dissatisfied with her prospects and did not take part. After reaching an agreement with Great Britain, France, and Russia that was satisfactory, she withdrew from the Triple Alliance and entered the war (May 23, 1915) on the side of the Triple Entente. After Germany did not make any reply to Japan's demand that it withdraw a German fleet from the Far East and surrender Kiaochow, Japan entered the war (August 23, 1914) on the side of the Allies. On April 7, 1917 the Congress of the United States declared war on Germany and (December 7, 1917) on Austria-Hungary. The United States entered the war on the side of the Triple Entente not as a member of it but as an associated power. Russia fought valiantly for more than three years, but after a revolution a Communistic government signed an armistice (December, 1917) with Germany and withdrew from the war.

After more than four years of bloody and costly warfare, the new German government signed an armistice on November 11, 1918. Now the responsibility for making a lasting peace rested chiefly in the hands of the Allied Powers and the United States.

On January 18, 1919, delegates from the Allied and Associated Powers met in a peace conference in Paris. Most people throughout the world hoped that the treaties drafted by the delegates would be based on justice and therefore likely to result in a lasting peace. They hoped also that a League of Nations would help to prevent wars in the future.

CHAPTER 28

The Breakdown of Peace Among the Major Nations

Peace has been the ideal of men throughout the centuries. The Hebrew prophets dreamed of a happy time when spears would be made into pruning hooks and swords into ploughshares and every man could sit under his own vine and fig tree. Greek poets sang of the blessings of peace and deplored the horrors of war. Nearly all the present day arguments against war and in favor of peace can be found in the plays of Aristophanes and Euripides. Greek leaders tried to prevent wars among the Greek city-states by treaties, arbitration, agreements to enforce peace, and federal leagues, but they never succeeded in establishing a lasting peace. The Roman peace was established by conquest and maintained by force of arms.

During the Middle Ages the Church tried to reduce the horrors of private wars among the feudal nobles by trying to get them to abide by the Truce of God. But it, too, was unsuccessful. After the religious unity of Western Europe had been shattered, secular leaders and thinkers drew up plans for peace. These included Henry IV of France, William Penn, an Englishman who founded the colony of Pennsylvania, and Hugo Grotius, a Dutchman. Hugo Grotius, as we have seen, wrote a book *On the Law of War and Peace* in which he stated laws which, if agreed to by warring nations, would lessen the horrors of war and tend to localize war.

Other men planned various kinds of federations and alliances. Jeremy Bentham, an English reformer, proposed the limitation of armaments, free trade, the abandonment of colonial empires, and a proposal much like the League of Nations. Immanuel Kant proposed the establishment of republican governments in all nations and the formation of a federation of free states in which all would be subject to law just as citizens are in a state.

Metternich planned the Concert of Europe as a means of preserving peace in Europe. The Concert itself failed, but the conferences it held led to other conferences which did much to preserve peace in Europe and to promote the co-operation needed in many other activities of an international character.

In the years before the First World War, national interests were too strong for the forces of peace at work in the world. The great European powers armed themselves and formed alliances. For hundreds of years Great Britain had acted upon the theory that a Balance of Power on the Continent was necessary to protect British national security. British statesmen believed that if Great Britain joined one side of the Balance of Power it would be made so strong that the other side would not be likely to engage in a war of aggression. Before the First World War the threat of German aggression became so great that Great Britain gave up its former theory and joined an alliance with France and Russia.

The assassination of an Austrian archduke at Sarajevo in Bosnia, a province of the Dual Monarchy, brought on the First World War. It was fought with new weapons and new

Bettmann Archive

THE CONGRESS OF BERLIN, 1878. Bismarck, who is shown here welcoming the delegates, said that he acted only as an "honest broker" during the work of the Congress. At the left, Disraeli leans on his cane.

methods, and on many land fronts, and on and under the sea and in the air. In its midst Tsarist Russia was overthrown by a revolution. The United States aided the Allied Powers and together the United States and the Allied Powers defeated the German armies and the German navy.

• • •

The Concert of Europe was a plan for preserving peace in Europe. In 1815 Metternich of Austria and the chief statesmen of Russia, Prussia, and Great Britain planned the Concert of Europe. They hoped it would keep peace among the nations of Europe likely to go to war and put down any revolutions that might endanger the power of the monarchs in Europe. Whenever danger threatened, the Concert was to hold a conference which would agree on all actions necessary to prevent any change in the treaties made at the Congress of Vienna.

In 1820, after a revolution broke out in Naples, the Concert, over the opposition of Great Britain, decided that Austria should suppress it. In 1821, the Concert, again over the opposition of Great Britain, authorized France to suppress a revolution in Spain. Both of these revolutions were suppressed. In 1821 the Greeks revolted against the oppressive Turkish rule under which they had lived for more than three centuries. A third congress which met to deal with this revolution could not agree because of widespread support for Greek liberty. The revolt dragged along for eight years until the Greeks won (1829) their independence. The failure of the members of the Concert of Europe to agree showed that it had not accomplished its purpose.

International conferences led to a great deal of co-operation. Although the Concert of Europe had failed, the idea of holding conferences to settle disputes was made use of again and again down to the eve of the First World War. A congress of European powers met in Paris (1856) to make a treaty of peace after the Crimean War. Another congress met in Berlin (1878) after the Russo-Turkish War to try to arrange peace in the Balkans. In 1884-1885 another congress met in Berlin to adjust the conflicting claims of European countries to lands in Africa. The Algeciras Conference in Spain, at which the United States was represented, ended for a time the dispute between Germany and France over their conflicting claims in Morocco and established an international control over the city of Tangier in Spanish Morocco.

In addition to these conferences which dealt with major international disputes, other international conferences brought about progress in peaceful co-operation in other fields. The International Red Cross was established by an international congress which met in Geneva in 1854. The Telegraph Union (1875), the Postal Union (1878), and the first Berne Convention, which was an international copyright union (1886), were evidences of the willingness of nations to agree on problems of mutual concern. Representatives of learned and scientific societies of many nations met together from time to time to exchange ideas on cultural and scientific subjects. International conferences on missionary work and other religious affairs brought together Christians of different denominations for a discussion of their common problems. When Socialists held their First and Second Internationals, they brought together representatives of workingmen from many nations. Through these international organizations Socialists hoped to make war forever impossible.

The settlement by arbitration of many disputes between the United States and Great Britain including the Alabama Claims, the boundaries of Venezuela, and also those of Alaska and the like encouraged those who were sincere believers in the peaceful settlement of international disputes. The Tsar of Russia was so interested in peace that he called an international peace conference at the Hague in 1899 and another in 1907. The first conference set up a court of arbitration (the Hague Tribunal). The second peace conference at the Hague restated the laws of land and naval warfare, including those dealing with the rights and obligations of neutrals and non-combatants, the treatment of prisoners of war, the laying of mines, and many other questions. Up to July, 1914, many people hoped and some believed that disputes between nations could be settled without war. Unfortunately these peaceful forces were not the only ones that had been at work; the work of others plunged the leading nations of the world into the First World War.

Excessive nationalism played a large part in destroying the hopes of peace-loving peoples. The excessive nationalism of the great European powers had led them to conscript their young men for military training and service in future wars; to invent, perfect, and manufacture new implements of war; to manufacture more highly explosive munitions; to maintain large standing armies and powerful navies; and to hold elaborate maneuvers on land and sea. All these preparations the great powers felt were necessary to provide security against foreign aggression, to strengthen the hand of diplomats in settling disputes, and to enable them to fight for national honor after all other means of protecting it had failed.

Economic nationalism also played a part in destroying the hopes of peace-loving peoples. Nations that desired to become self-sufficient subsidized exporters and their merchant marine. They attempted to protect their manufacturers by placing high tariffs on imports and thereby hindered the flow of goods from one country to another. They competed with one another for commercial concessions and control over different regions of the world. All this led to national rivalries which ended in the national distrust that played so important a part in bringing on the First World War.

The national pride and economic nationalism of Germany, Austria, and Italy on the one hand and of France and Russia on the other played a decisive part in the development of the two hostile alliances which existed in Europe before 1914.

German national pride was based on German national achievements. The national pride of Germany, last of the great European nations to become unified, was based on the accomplishments of the German people. Its scientists made many discoveries, particularly in physics and chemistry, and its mathematicians developed new theories in mathematics. Its inventors devised and its factories produced new industrial machines which its industries used to such an extent that Germany soon ranked high among the industrial nations of the world. Its merchant marine carried its goods and salesmen to all parts of the world. Its university professors achieved world-wide fame and students from many nations thronged to its universities. Likewise the fame of its musicians, particularly Richard Wagner, became world wide and their music was played by many different musicians and orchestras throughout the Western world.

Germany prided itself on the efficiency of its national and city governments and on its social legislation that had promoted the physical and social welfare of workers and many others. It was exceptionally proud of its General Staff and all of its other military and naval officers, of their great traditions, and of the army and navy that they had created. Germany was especially proud of its army because its defeat of Austria (1866) and France (1871) had enabled Bismarck to create the German Empire. German scholars, who were impressed by the great achievements of the Germans, developed the idea that Germans were descended from a peculiarly gifted people *(Aryans)*. Many Germans felt that it was their duty to spread German *Kultur* (the sum-total of their civilization) throughout the world and by force if necessary. To help accomplish its national purposes, the German government decided to build a powerful navy. The favorite German song, *Deutschland ueber alles,* showed that Germans really thought they were a superior people.

The German government endeavored to protect what it considered its national interests. On the west, France was still smarting under the defeat and humiliation of 1870 and the loss of the French provinces of Alsace and Lorraine, and was re-arming in the hope that in a future war it would be able to regain these provinces. On the east was Russia, a colossal nation, whose very size alarmed many German leaders. To prevent a possible alliance of France with Russia and against Germany, Bismarck, the German Chancellor, decided to come to a friendly understanding with Russia. In 1873 he persuaded the Tsar, the Emperor of Austria, and the German Emperor to form the Three Emperors' League. It failed because (1) the Germans and the Russians could not reconcile their conflicting trade interests, and (2) the Austrians and Russians could not reconcile their conflicting interests in the Balkans. Because Germany and Austria had common interests in the Balkans they formed the Dual Alliance (1879) under Bismarck's leadership. After France had occupied Tunis in North Africa, which Italy wanted to colonize, Italy three years later joined Austria and Germany to form the Triple Alliance. By this alliance Italy hoped to secure aid from its other members if the clashing French and Italian interests in the Mediterranean area should lead to war.

The Triple Alliance had a two-fold purpose. The first was to protect its members against either French or Russian attacks or a joint attack by them. The second was to extend German and Austrian influences in the Balkans. For many years Bismarck was firmly convinced that Germany should and could keep British friendship by abstaining from activities that would be apt to lead to colonial and national rivalries. In an effort to carry out his policies he said Germany's future lay in a *Drang nach Osten* (thrust to the East). Germany and Austria, both members of the Triple Alliance, carried out Bismarck's policy consistently. Germans made investments in the Balkans and German princes became rulers in Rumania, Bulgaria, and Albania. Germany helped Austria to annex (1908) the Slavic provinces of Bosnia and Herzegovina, and Rumania in its interests associated itself with the Triple Alliance (1883). Later on Germany loaned money to Turkey and German army officers trained the Turkish army. German capitalists furnished the funds to begin the construction of a railroad from Scutari on the Asiatic side of the Bosporus to Bagdad in Mesopotamia and thus link Berlin and Bagdad.

Germany desired a "place in the sun." The thrust to the East did not satisfy German ambition nor satisfy the German need for markets for the goods produced by its factories. So Germany turned overseas. As we have seen, the German merchant marine had been carrying German goods to all parts of the world where German salesmen sold them. The Germans were particularly successful in increasing the sale of their manufactured products in South America. In spite of this success, however, the Germans were not satisfied. They desired colonies where they could buy and sell with their own money. Many

Germans were emigrating to other countries, especially to the United States and Brazil. So the Germans desired colonies where Germans could settle and remain German citizens. At first Bismarck was opposed to the acquisition of colonies because he wished to avoid colonial rivalry with Great Britain, but after he had changed his mind Germany began to acquire colonies. When the German government found that the best sites for colonies were already occupied, it began to demand a "place in the sun," that is, a colonial empire composed, in part at least, of the colonial possessions of other nations.

Germany challenged the naval supremacy of Great Britain. In 1898 Germany embarked on a large and rapid naval expansion. The emperor, William II, and Alfred von Tirpitz, Secretary of State for Naval Affairs and afterward Admiral, were convinced Germany could not become a great nation without sea power. They are said to have been influenced in part by the writings of an American, Captain Alfred T. Mahan of the United States Navy, who set forth the influence of sea power upon history. After shipping, steel, commercial interests, and German nationalists had succeeded in securing the passage of bills that provided for naval expansion, Germany entered upon a naval race with Great Britain. The German government thought that a powerful navy would serve the interests of Germany more than the friendship of Great Britain. Von Tirpitz wanted to build a "risk navy," that is, one smaller than Britain's but large enough so that Britain would be apt to yield on diplomatic points rather than "risk" war. The British government was alarmed by this challenge to its long naval supremacy. The British reactions to the challenge were well expressed by a leading British statesman who said, "Whatever efforts Germany may make, she must reckon upon our making efforts which will be still greater, because sea power is our life, and in sea power we intend to remain superior."

French national pride was based on French national achievements. The French people were proud of their country and its civilization. French literature, art, and music were admired and studied by many people in other countries. The French were proud of their language which for years had been the language used in diplomacy and spoken by many educated men and women in other countries. They were proud of their army with its sturdy *poilus* (infantrymen) and its military engineers and artillery officers; the latter were said to be the best in the world.

On the other hand, the French were bitter over their defeat in the Franco-Prussian War. They never conceded that the loss of Alsace and Lorraine would become permanent. Many, particularly among the military, were planning a war of revenge and recovery of the lost provinces. Whether that plan was to be fulfilled or not, the proper defense of France against another German invasion remained an ever-present and thorny problem. In an effort to help solve this problem the National Assembly passed (1872) a law which required five years of military training of all young, able-bodied men. The fortresses near Verdun and at other places along the Franco-German frontier were strengthened. The French General Staff studied intensively the problems involved in waging war, including the strategy and tactics employed in large-scale maneuvers.

The national interests of France and Russia led them to form a Dual Alliance. After the failure of the Three Emperors' League and the formation of the Triple Alliance (1882), Bismarck negotiated a three-year treaty with Russia because he wished Germany to remain on as friendly terms with Russia as it had been while the Three Emperors' League was in effect. If France made

war on Germany, then by the terms of the three-year treaty, Russia promised not to aid France. In return, Germany promised to support Russia in the Balkans even though doing so might involve Germany in difficulties with Austria. Before the three-year treaty expired, Bismarck and Russia were willing to renew it, but William II, who had just come to the throne, dismissed Bismarck and took personal charge of the foreign affairs of Germany. The young emperor soon concluded that the Dual Alliance of Germany and Austria-Hungary would serve German national interests better than the three-year treaty with Russia and besides, if continued, it might involve Germany in difficulties with Austria. Consequently, when Russia requested Germany to renew the three-year treaty, William II refused. This refusal helped to drive Russia to the side of France.

In the meantime, French capitalists had helped to industrialize Russia by loaning millions of dollars to the Russian government to build railroads and factories, and also to pay the running expenses of the government. In time, this use of French money strengthened Russia and thereby helped to make it a more powerful ally of France. These relations helped to draw the two countries together, but the most influential factor in doing so was that both feared the ambitions of warlike Germany. As a result, France and Russia formed (1894) a Dual Alliance. France promised to come to the aid of Russia if it were attacked by Germany or by Austria aided by Germany. In return, Russia promised to come to the aid of France if it were attacked by Germany or by Italy aided by Germany.

France and Great Britain settled their conflicting claims in Africa. The French, as we have seen, had acquired a sizable and profitable empire in the Far East and also in Northern Africa. After the interests of France and Britain had collided in the Sudan, these countries agreed (1904) that France was to have a free hand in Morocco. At last these two nations who had for centuries been rivals for colonial empires had ended their rivalry and were about to take the first steps toward greater national security against the growing power of Germany.

Russia had its eyes on Constantinople and the Balkans. Ever since the days of Peter the Great (1689-1725) Russia had struggled to secure a warm water passage to the Mediterranean. It wanted to gain possession of the warm water port of Constantinople. As most of the peoples in the Balkans were, like Russians, Slavs and members of the Greek Orthodox Church, Russia posed as the protector of the Balkan peoples against Turkish tyranny. To help them to secure their freedom from Turkey and to get Constantinople for herself, Russia declared war on Turkey in 1877.

The Russians soon found that Austria and Great Britain were opposed to their getting Constantinople. Austria was opposed because it, too, wanted to penetrate the Balkans. Great Britain was opposed because it thought that if Russia got Constantinople it would soon get into the Mediterranean and that would threaten its life line to the East. Britain sent a fleet to Constantinople toward the close of the Russo-Turkish War (1877-1878) to prevent the Russians from capturing Constantinople, and it succeeded. At the Congress of Berlin, Great Britain, Germany, and Austria united to block Russian expansion. The Russians gained Bessarabian territory from Rumania and also Batum, Kars, and Ardahan from Turkey. The loss of Bessarabian territory aroused enough hostility in Rumania toward Russia to cause Rumania to join the Triple Alliance (1883). The Russians continued to be friendly toward Bulgaria and Serbia, particularly Serbia. Great Britain was satisfied by the agreements made by the Congress of Berlin because Russia had not been able to get Constantinople.

National interests caused Great Britain to join with France and Russia. For many years Great Britain had been proud of its empire and the title "Mistress of the Seas." Its colonial empire was large and the British fleet ruled the seas. British manufacturers, merchants, shippers, and bankers prospered. The alliance of Germany, Austria, and Italy and the alliance of France and Russia seemed to have established a Balance of Power which would keep either alliance from becoming powerful enough to attack the other. The British believed that by intervening on the side of one alliance they would be able to make that alliance so strong that the other alliance would not dare risk a war.

The British were deeply concerned also with the control of the Mediterranean. They feared that if Russia got Constantinople or even free passage through the Bosporus and the Dardanelles for its warships, it would build a huge fleet in the Black Sea and threaten British interests in the Mediterranean. The British and the French by winning the Crimean War (1854-1856) had prevented the Russians from getting Constantinople. In the Russo-Turkish War (1877-1878) Russia tried again to get Constantinople but failed. The British feared Russia in another quarter, because they thought it might advance through Persia and Afghanistan into India. They were soon to learn, however, that the aggressiveness of Germany, not Russia, was the chief threat to their national interests.

The British were aroused when they learned that German salesmen were taking markets away from them, particularly in South America. They became more deeply aroused when Germany began to build a powerful fleet which would help to upset the balance of power in Europe. As both Great Britain and France feared Germany, they ended their colonial rivalry in Africa by agreeing on different spheres of influence, and later on (1904) they reached a friendly agreement known as the *Entente Cordiale* (friendly understanding). It was intended to protect the national interests of both France and Great Britain.

Japan's defeat of Russia (1904-1905) had lessened the fear of Russia's military greatness. Two years later (1907) Great Britain and Russia agreed in the Anglo-Russian Convention to respect the political independence of Persia, but at the same time they divided Persia into three zones, Northern Persia, Central Persia, and Southern Persia. The agreement said that Great Britain would not demand concessions for its subjects in Northern Persia nor would it object to concessions Russia obtained there for its nationals. The opposite was true in Southern Persia. In the central zone both countries were free to obtain concessions. As Russian travelers from Siberia had reached the northern frontier of Afghanistan, British traders had gained a foothold in Afghanistan. In the Anglo-Russian Convention the British agreed not to annex Afghanistan and to grant privileges to Russian traders. Three years before, Britain and France had reconciled their differences and now Britain and Russia had settled theirs. The *Entente Cordiale* and the Anglo-Russian Convention established such friendly relations among Russia, France, and Great Britain that this group of nations was called the Triple Entente. After the outbreak of the First World War, it was changed into a military alliance.

The Triple Alliance and the Triple Entente made every international dispute that involved their members serious even though very minor because it involved all six of the great powers. Germany opposed the advance

International News

ARCHDUKE FRANCIS FERDINAND OF AUSTRIA. The arrow points to the Archduke whose assassination in this automobile at Sarajevo was the event that soon led to the First World War.

of French influence in Morocco in 1905 and again in 1911, but after Great Britain had supported France both times, Germany yielded and an agreement was reached. The Balkan Wars of 1912 and 1913 endangered the peace of Europe because of the conflicting interests of Germany, Austria, and Russia, but they were confined to the Balkans. However, within one year a pistol shot in the Balkans caused a general European war when it was least expected.

The assassination of an Austrian archduke precipitated the First World War. On June 28, 1914, a fanatical Serbian patriot shot and killed Francis Ferdinand, heir to the Austrian throne, at Sarajevo in Bosnia. Four weeks later Austria made such severe and far-reaching demands on Serbia that, if Serbia had accepted them, they would have placed it under the control of Austria. That was Austria's intention. Serbia was the only Balkan state that had remained hostile to German and Austrian expansion into the Balkans. Serbian law made any part of the

Berlin-Bagdad railroad in Serbia the property of Serbia. After Austria had presented an ultimatum to Serbia, Emperor Francis Joseph of Austria wrote the Kaiser that Serbian influence in Balkan politics had to be destroyed. The Kaiser agreed and gave Austria a free hand in Serbia and promised to support Austria in whatever action it took against Serbia. What had happened alarmed Great Britain, and so it asked Germany to agree to a conference of the interested powers to discuss the tense situation. All efforts to preserve peace were in vain. In spite of a conciliatory reply from Serbia, Austria declared war on July 28, 1914.

On July 30, Russia ordered a general mobilization of its armies to keep its treaty obligations to Serbia and so did France to abide by its alliance of 1894 with Russia and to get revenge for 1870. Germany declared war on Russia (August 1) and on France (August 3). At this point the question was: What would Great Britain do? To get into France, Germany invaded Belgium, in spite of a treaty which Prussia had signed. In 1831 and again in 1839, Belgium had been declared a neutralized state by the great powers. Great Britain, Russia, Prussia, Austria, and France had promised by solemn treaty to respect the "perpetual neutrality" of Belgium and the integrity and inviolability of Belgian territory. This pledge had been honored in the Franco-Prussian War. In July, France promised Great Britain it would respect the neutrality of Belgium, but Germany did not agree unless Great Britain would remain neutral. When Germany demanded permission to send its armies through Belgium to invade France, the Belgian cabinet refused and then German armies invaded Belgium. Great Britain believed that German control of Belgium would be dangerous to British interests because Belgium was so near Britain. The German Chancellor Bethmann-Hollweg said that

compared to a war with Great Britain, the treaty that had guaranteed Belgian neutrality was a "scrap of paper." The British thought otherwise and declared war on Germany on August 4.

Within a week Germany, Russia, Belgium, France, and Great Britain had been drawn into the war. Before the war was over it had spread to every continent and ocean and had become the First World War. From 1914 to 1918 there were fifty-two declarations of war. Great Britain, France, Belgium, and their allies were known as the Allies; Germany, Austria-Hungary, Turkey, and Bulgaria were called the Central Powers.

The question of responsibility for the First World War has been hotly debated. From 1914-1918 most people in the allied nations placed the responsibility for the war on Germany. They quoted from German books whose writers claimed that German superiority in culture, intelligence, and military might gave Germany the right to world rule. The actions of the German government during July, 1914, the speed of German mobilization, and the ruthless invasion of Belgium gave substance to the charge of German responsibility. As the war progressed, most people in the allied nations also came to think that it was being fought to keep the world free from German domination—that it was a war for freedom against autocracy and militarism. This interpretation of the war was written into the treaty of Versailles after the German defeat.

After 1918 discussion began on the question of German "war guilt." The Germans, of course, denied sole responsibility and many persons in the allied nations came to agree with them. Careful study of the facts led to the conclusion that Austria's outrageous demands on Serbia placed considerable responsibility on it. The Germans were at fault in promising to support Austria even to the extent of war, in rejecting the British plea for a conference, and in refusing to halt mobilization. Some share of the blame, however, was also placed on Russia and France, particularly for their mobilization before making a declaration of war. Most historians of the 1930's agreed that the basic causes of the war were nationalistic and imperialistic jealousies which led to the formation of rival alliances and also to vast military and naval preparations. The policies and actions of Germany during and after 1939 have caused many to return to the earlier belief in German responsibility for the war.

The warring powers developed new methods of warfare during the First World War. The First World War showed quickly that science and invention were to change the character of warfare. (1) War became an industry which involved whole nations. Men were conscripted without reference to wealth or social status to raise the huge armies which were to be needed. They were given tests and the results of these tests were used to assign them to the different branches of the armed forces. Most skilled workmen who were needed in industry and most scientists were kept at home or assigned to special war services. Farmers were encouraged and even required to raise more foodstuffs than they had before to feed the armed forces. To save food for soldiers, food was rationed in some countries. To the cry, "business as usual," the government replied with restrictions on industry and commerce for the purpose of helping to win the war. Each government took over the control of foreign trade and foreign investments to protect the value of its currency in exchange and to obtain the funds necessary to purchase abroad foods, raw materials, and munitions. The people as a whole in the nations at war were in reality mobilized for war.

(2) Methods of warfare soon underwent great changes. After the first campaigns the war on the western front became trench warfare. Men lived and fought in long, deep trenches and lived in dugouts. Other trenches connected the front lines with the rear. Mud, often water, rats, fleas, and lice plagued the men in the trenches. The land between the trenches of the opposing armies was called "no man's land." Men equipped with periscopes and metal hats stood guard in the trenches to watch the enemy. Barbed wire was stretched in tangles in front to hinder raids. At places where gunfire would be most effective concrete "pill-boxes" contained machine-gunners and sharpshooters. Some distance behind the front line trenches were the secondary lines to which soldiers might retire if the enemy fire was too heavy and where reserves could be hidden for a counter attack.

The artillery behind the trenches had guns powerful enough to shoot large shells many miles and others capable of being fired rapidly at the enemy. Along roads that led from the rear to secondary lines trucks carried supplies, infantrymen, and guns of all kinds; motorcycles carried messages; ambulances carried the wounded to hospitals; and staff cars carried military officers and messengers. In well-protected areas in the rear the headquarters of officers were connected by telephone with every part of the front line under their command, and also with General Headquarters farther to the rear. Aerial photography and observations guided the artillery men and helped to keep headquarters informed of enemy positions and movements. Fighter planes went up to stop enemy observation planes and also to engage in aerial fights with enemy planes, sometimes in fighting squadrons, but more often in desperate duels in the skies.

(3) Many soldiers not at the front shared in the work of the army. The services of eight soldiers were required to sustain one soldier

at the front. Elaborate services of supply were needed to feed, clothe, and arm the fighting forces. Equally detailed hospital corps took care of the sick and the wounded. Religious and charitable organizations provided amusements, religious exercises, and food in a sincere effort to maintain the mental and physical health of soldiers. Women worked as secretaries, nurses, ambulance drivers, hut attendants, and entertainers.

(4) General Headquarters planned the attacks and the General Staff relayed its plans and orders to commanding officers at the front. Scouting patrols crept out at night across "no man's land" to study enemy installations. When an attack was ordered, a signal was given to the artillery to lay down a barrage, that is, gunfire concentrated on the enemy's lines or positions to destroy barbed-wire entanglements and to drive the enemy back. Before the zero-hour (the time for an attack) the men waited by ladders in the trenches for another signal that was to launch the attack and the barrage was moved farther ahead. Then the soldiers climbed out of the trenches and ran across "no man's land" toward the opposing trenches. The enemy meanwhile might have taken refuge in their dug-outs or in trenches in the rear, or elected to stand their ground. As the attack progressed, other soldiers advanced with machine guns. Hand grenades were thrown by soldiers on both sides and bayonets were used at close quarters. A short length of trenches was often won at great cost of human life.

(5) New methods were being devised constantly to break through the enemy lines. The Germans introduced the use of poison gas and thereafter the chemists of both sides vied with each other in producing more deadly gases or better gas masks than the enemy had. The British put armor on a caterpillar tractor and so invented the tank. It was not a great success because the weapon was not efficient enough to be of real service before the war was over.

Artists played their part as they worked out various devices or combinations of color to camouflage positions and to hide them from enemy eyes. They designed weird patterns which were painted on ships in colors so that the ships seemed to be going on courses different from their actual courses to make it difficult for submarines to sink them. Photographers used cameras that were capable of taking pictures of enemy lines and installations from great heights. Submarines capable of staying at sea for longer and longer times were built. As defenses against them, listening devices to detect their approach and depth bombs to sink them were invented. The seas around Europe were filled with deadly mines to blow up ships. Scientific knowledge in mathematics, chemistry, physics, and engineering was used to destroy human life and property. The Industrial Revolution had changed the character of warfare.

(6) From the beginning of the war both sides realized the influence that public opinion had at home and abroad. So propaganda —the spreading of information, true and false, to influence all peoples—became a weapon useful in psychological warfare. Some of it was directed to combat forces to spur on the one side and to discourage the other; some of it to the people at home to keep up their spirits or to encourage revolt in enemy countries; much of it was directed at neutrals to win their sympathy and if possible enlist their support. Propaganda became an important assistant to the sword.

The war was fought on many widely separated fronts. Naval warfare was carried on in the Atlantic, the Pacific, the Indian Ocean, the North Sea, and the Mediterranean. Great armies—French, British, and Belgian—opposed German armies in France and Belgium. The Russians fought against

Germany and Austria-Hungary, in what is now Poland and in East Prussia, and advanced as far as Cracow in Galicia. Italy joined the Allies (1915) and fought the Austrians along the Italo-Austrian frontier. There was fierce fighting in the Balkans, near and in the Dardanelles, in Palestine, and in Mesopotamia. There were minor military campaigns between Allied armies and German armies in Africa and the Japanese took Shantung from the Germans in China. Both sides intrigued and plotted in neutral countries to help gain an advantage over the other. Nearly every part of the world was involved either in the fighting or in furnishing supplies to one side or the other.

Bitter fighting took place at sea. As soon as the war began, the British Navy established a blockade of the Central Powers and began to sweep German shipping from the seas. It accomplished both of its objectives quickly and effectively. Some goods reached Germany by way of neutral countries—Holland, Denmark, Norway, and Sweden—but Britain did not permit these countries to import more than enough to care for their own needs. In this way most German imports, particularly foodstuffs, were prevented from reaching Germany. A few German raiders that roved the seas attacked both Allied and neutral merchant vessels. The British and French navies systematically hunted them down and captured or destroyed them. Some took refuge in neutral ports and were interned there for the rest of the war. The German liner, *Vaterland,* was interned in New York harbor until the United States entered the war and then the United States seized it, changed its name to *Leviathan,* and used it to transport American troops to Great Britain and France.

In January, 1916, Admiral Reinhard Scheer was named to command the German High Seas fleet and on March 14, 1916, Admiral

International News

THE SINKING OF THE *LUSITANIA.* On May 7, 1915, a German submarine torpedoed and sunk the British luxury liner *Lusitania* off the west coast of Ireland. Eleven hundred ninety-eight men, women, and children, including over 128 Americans, lost their lives. This act aroused intense indignation in the United States.

von Tirpitz resigned as Minister of Marine because the Kaiser was unwilling to make unrestricted use of German sea power. On May 31, 1916, Admiral Franz von Hipper in command of a German battle-cruiser squadron ventured out of the heavily mined and strongly fortified naval bases at Cuxhaven, Kiel, and Helgoland and engaged in the battle of Jutland off the coast of Denmark with a British scouting force under command of Admiral Beatty. Before the battle was over the grand fleets of the two powers were involved. In the Battle of Jutland the British lost fourteen ships and the Germans eleven. After an indecisive battle, the German fleet returned home where it remained until it steamed out to surrender in 1918.

German light cruisers slipped through the British blockade, ravaged commerce in the Atlantic, and then slipped through the blockade to their home ports. The German commercial submarine, *Deutschland,* made a trip to Baltimore, Maryland (1916), delivered its cargo, and returned safely with supplies to Germany.

In an attempt to break the blockade, the

Germans resorted to submarine warfare. Submarines ranged far and wide in the Atlantic doing terrific damage to shipping. Both belligerents violated the rights of neutrals. The British stopped neutral merchant ships bound for neutral ports to seize goods and mail whose final destination they charged was Germany. German submarines violated the rules of war by failing to provide for the safety of crews and passengers on belligerent and also on neutral vessels and often by sinking ships without warning. The sinking of the British liner *Lusitania* (May, 1915) with many Americans aboard caused widespread indignation in the United States and thereby increased the already existing hostility to Germany. Unrestricted submarine warfare caused a serious shortage of food in Great Britain and antagonized neutrals. It was one of the many reasons advanced for the declaration of war by the Congress of the United States against Germany on April 6, 1917.

In the same month that the United States entered the war, 875,000 tons of shipping were destroyed, more than half of it British. In an effort to reduce losses in the future, the convoy system was put into effect (May 10, 1917) and it soon proved to be an unqualified success. The British built more destroyers and submarine chasers, developed and used the depth bomb more effectively, scouted for submarines with hydroplanes, and constructed great numbers of merchant ships. As soon as the United States entered the war, it, too, began to build great numbers of merchant ships. By October, 1917, the German submarines had destroyed a total of 8,000,000 tons of shipping but at the cost of fifty submarines. But unrestricted submarine warfare was becoming less and less effective. In the end unrestricted German submarine warfare failed to starve Britain into submission and to prevent the landing of American troops and supplies in Europe.

The destruction of so many German submarines toward the close of the war caused submarine crews to mutiny rather than to go out to sea and to almost certain death. The tightening of the British and American blockade caused great suffering to civilians in Germany chiefly from the lack of certain kinds of foods. This suffering contributed greatly to the breakdown of German civilian morale.

The Allies stopped the German advance on the western front in 1914. More than four years of very bitter fighting took place on the western front in Belgium and northern France. The German plan for winning the war was based on a quick victory over France, then a victorious attack on Russia. France had built forts along the Franco-German border from Switzerland to Luxemburg. To avoid the time, the loss of life, and the use of munitions that would be required to break through these fortifications, Germany requested the Belgian government to permit German troops to cross into France. After Belgium had refused the request, Germany declared war on Belgium and invaded it with powerful armies.

The strong Belgian fortresses withstood the powerful German assaults long enough to allow the French to take up defensive positions in front of the invading German armies and to give the British time to send an expeditionary force under the command of Sir John French to support the French armies. However, the armies of France, Great Britain, and Belgium were not able to hold back the assaults of the German armies. The French and British were driven back to the Marne River and the Belgians toward the English Channel. Victory was almost in the grasp of the German armies, but at a critical moment in the German onslaught, the German High Command ordered several army corps transferred to the eastern front to stem the rapid and unexpected advance of the Russian armies into

International Film

FRENCH RESERVES GETTING INTO BIG BATTLE ON THE MARNE.

East Prussia. Marshal Joffre, the French commander, took advantage of the weakened German forces and ordered French armies to attack the German right flank and center. These attacks were so successful that the German armies were forced to retire to positions which had already been prepared along the Aisne and Somme rivers. There they dug in and settled down to trench warfare that continued almost to the end of the war.

A race to get possession of the ports of Dunkirk, Calais, and Boulogne on the English Channel followed. The Belgians flooded the valley of the Yser River and the heroic resistance of the British in the first battle of Ypres (October-November, 1914) stopped the German drive to capture the Channel ports. Soon trenches dug by both sides reached across France from the English Channel to Switzerland.

In 1915 the French and British made strenuous efforts to drive the Germans from Northern France. In the second battle of Ypres (Apirl 22-May 25), the Germans used (April 22) poison gas (chlorine) for the first time, but they failed to follow up the advantage they had gained when the French abandoned Ypres. From May 9 to June 18 the French launched a terrific assault near Arras which advanced three miles, but at a cost of 400,000 men. In the autumn both the French and British engaged in heavy offensives, but in several weeks of hard fighting they gained but little ground. In the third battle of Artois the British used poison gas for the first time. At the end of 1915 the military situation on the western front was about what it was at the beginning of the year.

Italy joined the Allies in 1915. At the outbreak of the war Italy was interested chiefly in stopping Austrian advances into the Balkans and in gaining possession of lands long inhabited by Italians but still in Austrian possession. The German government tried to get the Dual Monarchy to make enough concessions to Italy to keep it neutral, but Austria would not agree to enough of them to satisfy Italy's demands. By the time Germany had induced it to make these concessions, it was too late because in the meantime the Allies had entered into a treaty with Italy (May, 1915) that granted all of Italy's territorial demands in Europe and also in Africa. In addition, Italy was to get a loan, military aid against Austria, and a share of the war indemnity.

On May 3, 1915, Italy denounced the Triple Alliance and on May 23 declared war on Austria-Hungary. The Italians and Austrians fought along a sixty-mile front north of Trieste. After winning victories (1915-1916), the Italians suffered an overwhelming defeat (1917) at Caporetto where about 300,000 Italians were taken prisoners. The remainder of the Italian armies retreated and rallied on the Piave River to the southwest, and in 1918, with Allied assistance, drove the Austrians back in disorder with the loss of 100,000 men. After the Austrians had appealed for an armistice, the Italians won (October 30, 1918) the battle of Vittorio Veneto in which they captured several hundred thousand Austrian soldiers and the remainder of the defeated Austrian army streamed back home.

The armies of the Central Powers gained great successes in the Balkans. The first Austrian advance into Serbia (1914) was a failure. In 1915 German armies and armies of the Dual Monarchy under the command of August von Mackensen, a German general, overran, crushed, and frightfully punished Serbia. After the dismal failure of Great Britain to force its way to Constantinople in the early part of 1915, Bulgaria joined the Central Powers in the hope of being on the winning side. Rumania joined (1916) the Allies in the hope of annexing a part of Eastern Hungary in which large numbers of Rumanians lived. A strong German army crushed Rumania and secured its wheat and oil, so much needed by Germany. The Allies retaliated by assembling an army at Salonika in Greece and in the last year of the war it advanced northward and broke the lines of the Central Powers in the Balkans.

Turkey joined (1914) the Central Powers. In a secret treaty with France and Great Britain after the outbreak of the war, Russia was promised Constantinople. As Russia's allies needed a sea route to carry much needed supplies to the Russian armies, the British planned an attack on Constantinople at the order of Winston Churchill, First Lord of the Admiralty. A powerful British fleet attempted (February-March, 1915) to steam through the Dardanelles and on to Constantinople, but it failed because of the strength of the forts and mine fields. The military forces which were then landed on the Gallipoli peninsula were unable to capture the forts that guarded the straits.

In the Near East British troops struggled through the marshes along the Shatt-el-Arab and took Bagdad (1917). In October, 1914, Lord Kitchener with a view to future operations against Turkey entered into negotiations with Hussein, an Arab leader in Mecca. As the French were interested in the Near East, they, too, took part in the negotiations. In June, 1916, an Arab revolt against Turkey began with an attack on a Turkish garrison at Medina which resulted in its capture. Thereupon the Turks surrendered the garrison at Mecca and Hussein was proclaimed king of the Arabs. By this time General Edmund Allenby was in command of the British forces. Colonel T. E. Lawrence strengthened the Arab movement against Turkey. After heavy fighting Allenby took Jerusalem (1917). In 1918 he broke through the Turkish lines and with the help of the Arabs, under Lawrence, pushed northward and took Damascus, Beirut, and Aleppo. On October 14, 1918, the Turks appealed to President Wilson for an armistice. The armistice when granted required Turkey to open the straits leading to Constantinople, to release all Allied prisoners, to demobilize its armies, to break off relations with the Central Powers, and to place its territory at the disposal of the Allies for military operations.

In 1916 terrible battles on the western front were fought at Verdun and along the Somme River. From February to June, 1916,

International Film

THE FAMOUS RHEIMS CATHEDRAL AND THE BEAUTIFUL STATUE OF JEAN
D'ARC. Destruction was visited on the cathedral as well as on the buildings nearby as a result
of German shell fire.

the Germans made a terrific drive on the celebrated national fortress of Verdun to weaken the morale of the French and, if successful, open a new way to Paris and to victory. The loss of life on both sides was appalling. The French losses have been estimated at 350,000; the German somewhat less. General Pétain rallied the armies under his command by these stirring words *"Ils ne passeront pas"* (They shall not pass), and they did not.

The Allies retaliated (July-November, 1916) with a futile and costly drive on the positions of the Germans along the Somme River. The British were now under the command of Sir Douglas Haig. In the Somme offensive the British used tanks for the first time, only eighteen in all. British losses in one day were 60,000. The total greatest British advance at any one place was about seven miles. The British lost more than 400,000 and the French nearly 200,000; the Germans lost between 400,000 and 500,000.

In 1917 French and British offensives on the western front failed to drive back the Germans. In December, 1916, General Nivelle succeeded Joffre as Commander-in-Chief of the French armies. He planned a French and British offensive in Northern France which he hoped would drive back the German armies which were now commanded by Field Marshal von Hindenburg with General Ludendorff as quartermaster general. To

Ewing Galloway

The German Kaiser (center), Hindenburg (left), and Ludendorff are shown in general head-quarters in 1917, where they are studying maps of the battle fronts.

strengthen the German line against the attack that he knew was coming, Hindenburg constructed a new, heavily fortified line (Hindenburg Line) and withdrew his armies to this line.

From April 9 to May 4, 1917, British and Canadian forces, after a heavy bombardment and a gas attack, succeeded in advancing about four miles, but they were unable to break through the Hindenburg Line. From April 16 to May 21 the French attacked fiercely, but the Germans had concentrated so many troops in the area under attack that the French offensive was a failure. The French losses were so heavy that they caused mutinies in sixteen army corps. General Nivelle was dismissed and General Henri-Phillipe Pétain,

his successor, decided to stay on the defensive until American troops arrived in numbers large enough to make a successful offensive possible.

In April, 1917, German submarines destroyed more ships than in any other month in the entire war. Many of the submarines were based in Belgian ports. To help curb the submarine menace, Sir Douglas Haig planned an offensive which he hoped would drive back the German armies and enable the British to capture the Belgian ports. Haig's offensive, the third battle of Ypres (July 31-November 10) consisted of eight heavy attacks fought in a driving rain and over muddy ground. The British gained about five miles at the cost of 400,000 men, but were unable to roll back the German right flank. At the end of this offensive British troops were almost as demoralized as the French troops had been after General Nivelle's offensive in April and May.

As a result the outlook for the Allies in December, 1917, was very dark. French and British offensives on the western front had failed, the Italians had suffered a stunning defeat in the Caporetto campaign (October 24-December 26), and the Russians had concluded (December 15) an armistice with the Germans. The war-weary Allies, however, were encouraged by the curbing of the submarine menace and also by the fact that United States troops had arrived in France, and that others would arrive in vast numbers before long.

Inefficiency and corruption helped cause Russian collapse in 1917. At the outbreak of the war the Russian armies quickly advanced like a steam roller into East Prussia. Generals Hindenburg and Ludendorff, who were in command of the German armies on the eastern front, trapped (August 26-30, 1914) a Russian army at Tannenberg in East Prussia and took 100,000 prisoners. The Russian general who commanded the defeated armies shot himself on the field of battle. General von Mackensen defeated another Russian army at the battle of the Masurian Lakes (September 6-15, 1914) and captured 125,-000 Russians.

In the meantime, other Russian armies had penetrated Galicia and had launched attacks in an effort to seize the Carpathian passes that led into Northern Hungary. To relieve the Austrians, von Mackensen advanced on Warsaw while the Austrians were counter-attacking in Galicia. Although these attacks forced the Russians back, they did not succeed in crushing or capturing the Russian armies.

In 1915, after the Russians had taken Przemysl and threatened to break through the Carpathian passes into Northern Hungary, the Austrians and Germans began (May 2) a great offensive in Galicia. The Russians, who were suffering from lack of guns, munitions, and clothing, were driven back and by the end of June the Austro-German armies had driven them out of Galicia. A second great offensive (July-September) was very disastrous to the Russians. By September 16 they had lost all of Russian Poland, Lithuania, Kurland (Courland), and almost 1,000,000 men. The Tsar himself now took the supreme command of the Russian armies.

In 1916 the Austrians withdrew a part of their forces from the Russian front to reinforce their armies that were fighting the Italians. The Italians then appealed to the Russians to attack the Austrians on the eastern front in the hope that they would be forced to call back their forces from the Italian front. In consequence, Russian armies, under General Brusilov, began (June 4) a great offensive in the southern sector of the eastern front. Although they advanced several miles and captured about 500,000 Austrian soldiers, their offensive was stopped by the arrival of heavy German reinforcements before it had accomplished its objectives. Moreover, the Russians had lost about 1,000,000 men in the campaign and their armies were demoralized.

The inefficiency of the Russian service of supply and the unbridled corruption of many of its purchasing agents crippled the Russian armies almost beyond belief. Russian officers sent soldiers into battle without sufficient ammunition and even without guns. The Russian soldier was brave, but he was poorly equipped and poorly fed. Conditions back home were so bad that the people were aflame with discontent. Meanwhile, Rasputin, an evil man, had gained complete control over the Tsarina and through her over the Tsar. In March, 1917, patriotic Russians murdered

Rasputin and in the same month a revolution overthrew the Tsar's government.

After liberals in Russia had made futile efforts to organize a republic and to carry on the war against the Austrians and the Germans, the Bolsheviks overthrew (November 7, 1917) the provisional government and set up a Communist government. On December 15, the Bolsheviks concluded an armistice with Germany and Austria Hungary. In March, 1918, the Treaty of Brest-Litovsk was signed. The year 1917 had brought the Allies to the verge of ruin. But the same year brought them aid from the United States. The withdrawal of Russia from the war gave Germany and Austria-Hungary a great advantage. They could now transfer their armies in the east to the western and Italian fronts where they hoped to win a victory in 1918.

The United States entered the war in 1917. At the outbreak of the war (1914) President Wilson proclaimed the neutrality of the United States and asked all citizens to be "neutral in thought and deed." For a time public opinion in the United States was divided on the question of neutrality.

Many Americans admired the music, literature, and scientific achievements of the Germans. All were impressed by the German victories in the early part of the war. British interference with American mails and trade caused widespread irritation. Many Americans of German and Irish descent openly favored Germany.

On the other hand many Americans favored Great Britain because cultural ties united us with the British people. Our friendship with France which began with Lafayette's help in the American Revolution caused many to sympathize with France. And besides, American factories were turning out large quantities of supplies for the Allies and American investors were loaning them large sums of money. The blockade kept Germany almost entirely out of the American markets and Germany was able to borrow but little money in the United States. Allied propaganda was well handled but the German was not.

Finally, German acts and the influence of Allied propaganda caused the United States to enter the war. The attack on Belgium aroused widespread indignation and the reports of German atrocities in Belgium, some falsified and others greatly exaggerated by British propagandists, increased the mounting hostility to Germany. The sinking of the *Lusitania* and the sinking of other ships, both Allied and neutral, without proper provisions for the safety of their crews aroused more hostility to Germany. Evidence gathered by the United States Secret Service showed that German secret agents were fomenting labor disputes in munitions plants, causing explosions, blowing up bridges, and even negotiating with anti-American groups in Mexico and promising that if Germany won the war the lands that the United States took from Mexico after the Mexican War (1848) would be returned. Gradually most of the people in the United States came to believe that Germany had to be beaten for the preservation of democratic civilization.

In the winter of 1917, the German government, driven desperate by the effects of the Allied blockade, announced another program of unrestricted submarine warfare. In consequence many Allied and some American ships were sunk, and on April 6, 1917, the United States declared war. President Wilson in asking Congress to declare war said:

> The world must be made safe for democracy. Its peace must be planted upon the tested foundations of political liberty. We have no selfish ends to serve. We desire no conquest, no dominion. We seek no indemnities for ourselves, no compensation for the sacrifices we shall freely make. We are but one of the champions of the rights of man-

kind. We shall be satisfied when those rights have been made as secure as the faith and freedom of nations can make them.

The people of the United States entered the war with great enthusiasm. A Selective Service Act was passed by Congress, schools for officers and training camps for soldiers were established, and a Council for National Defense was set up to help put the United States on a war footing.

Under the Selective Service Act more than 24,234,000 men were registered and more than 2,810,296 were drafted into the army. The total of the armed forces of the United States was about 4,355,000. More than 2,-000,000 soldiers were sent to France and of these about 1,390,000 saw active service. The American dead numbered about 130,000 and the wounded about 203,000.

In July, 1917, the War Industries Board, of which Bernard M. Baruch was chairman, began the regulation and expansion of the manufacture of weapons of war. As a result, the industrial capacity of the United States was increased 20 per cent. The Food Administration, under the direction of Herbert C. Hoover, encouraged the production of nine kinds of foodstuffs, and requested everyone to engage in voluntary rationing to avoid

rationing by law. In an effort to secure a much more effective transportation of troops, munitions of war, and all kinds of supplies, the railroads were taken over by the United States government and placed under the direction of Secretary of the Treasury William G. McAdoo. The people, banks, and corporations bought war bonds issued by the United States Treasury in both large and small denominations. Four Liberty Loans and one Victory Loan were oversubscribed. Twenty-one million persons bought Fourth Liberty Loan bonds.

The United States Navy under Admiral William S. Sims played an important part in protecting convoys of troops and supply ships against submarines while crossing the North Atlantic. It assisted the British navy in laying a barrier of mines in the North Sea in an effort to keep German submarines from getting out into the Atlantic.

Soon after the United States declared war on Germany, the French government requested the United States to send an American expeditionary force to France as soon as possible to help bolster up its sagging civilian and military morale. In June, 1917, units of the A.E.F. under General John J. Pershing arrived in England, and shortly afterward

Underwood & Underwood

AMERICAN TROOPS ENCAMPED ON THE AISNE.

they were transferred to France. By March 1918, 300,000 American soldiers were in France, by July more than 1,000,000 were in France, and by November twice as many. These forces were badly needed by the Allies to stem the force of Ludendorff's drives. The Germans, reinforced by armies from the Russian front, were about to begin a terrific assault on the western front for the purpose of ending the war.

In 1918 the Allies and the United States defeated the Germans on the western front. The Germans were disappointed over their submarine campaign. They knew that their allies were war-weary and that the German people were suffering from lack of proper food due largely to the British blockade. In consequence, they decided to make a supreme effort on the western front to gain a victory before the Americans could arrive in great numbers. General Ludendorff planned to attack the British armies on a sixty-mile front south of Arras, break through their lines, defeat their armies, and then drive them westward to the sea. The Germans attacked (March 21, 1918) where the British did not expect an attack and where the British army under General Gough held a long line with few troops. The Germans broke through the British lines and in about two weeks they advanced forty miles. The second great German blow (April 9-29) opened up a wide breach in the British front.

From May 27 to June 6 the third battle of the Aisne took place. The French, too, were taken by surprise and driven back thirteen miles the first day. On May 27 the Germans reached the Marne River at a point only thirty-seven miles from Paris and the French government left Paris for Bordeaux. In April, 1918, the First Division of the United States regular army was put into the battle line, and at Cantigny (May 28) it won the first American military victory in the war. On June 4,

The First World War was a result of extreme national feeling, imperialism, and an armament race among the great powers of Europe. More than three million soldiers were killed in gruelling trench warfare on the western front before the armies of the Allied and Associated Powers broke through the German lines and defeated the German armies.

the Second Division of the United States Army and the French Army halted the German advance at Chateau-Thierry and Belleau Wood. In the second battle of the Marne Ludendorff attacked again east and west of Rheims, but the attack east of Rheims failed. West of Rheims the Germans crossed the Marne, but made little progress against strong American and French forces. General Foch, commander-in-chief of the Allied armies in France, ordered a counter-attack (July 18) which forced the Germans west of Rheims back over the Marne and the French advanced until they took the ground they had just lost.

After the second battle of the Marne, Foch, who had now gained the initiative, kept it from then on. Mobile warfare had replaced trench warfare. American troops smashed the St. Mihiel salient (September 12-13), cleared the Argonne Forest, and broke through the Hindenburg Line while British and French troops broke it farther north. Throughout September and October the Allied drive was continuous. The once invincible German armies along a 250-mile front grew weaker and weaker after their enormous losses. By November 10, the Americans had captured Sedan and the British had penetrated Belgium. Before this the German General Staff knew Germany had lost the war.

Germany's allies in the Balkans collapsed, and then Germany. While the war in the west was going on, the newly reorganized Allied armies defeated Bulgaria (September 29) and it signed an armistice the next day. On October 30, Turkey, who had been beaten, collapsed and signed an armistice. The defeat of the Austrians by Allied armies in October caused Austria to yield on November 4, after having joined Germany on October 4 in an appeal to President Wilson for an armistice. The Germans agreed to the armistice on the promise that the terms of peace would be based on the Fourteen Points which Woodrow Wilson had set forth in January, 1918. These points were:

(1) Open covenants (agreements) openly arrived at.

(2) Freedom of navigation alike in peace and war except as the seas might be closed by international action to enforce international covenants.

(3) The removal, so far as possible, of all economic barriers.

(4) Adequate guarantee that armaments would be reduced to the lowest point consistent with domestic safety.

(5) An impartial adjustment of all colonial claims on the principle that the interests of the population must have equal weight with the claims of the government.

(6) Evacuation of Russian territory and the free determination of its own political and national policy.

(7) Evacuation of troops from Belgium and restoration of its lands.

(8) Evacuation and restoration of French territory and the righting of the wrong done to France in the matter of Alsace-Lorraine.

(9) Readjustment of the frontiers of Italy along clearly recognizable lines of nationality.

(10) Opportunity for self-development of the peoples of Austria-Hungary.

(11) Evacuation and restoration of Rumania, Serbia, and Montenegro, and Serbian access to the sea.

(12) The Turkish parts of the Turkish empire to be given a secure sovereignty, the other peoples in it to be given an opportunity for self-government, and the Dardanelles to be open to the ships of all nations under international guarantee.

(13) An independent Poland to include territories indisputably Polish with free and secure access to the sea.

(14) A general association of nations to be formed to afford mutual guarantees of political independence and territorial integrity to great and small states alike.

On November 3 mutiny broke out in the German fleet at Kiel and it spread to other German ports and to the German armies. On November 9 the abdication of the Kaiser was announced in Berlin, and on the following day he fled to the Netherlands. On November 8 the German armistice commission was received by Foch in his railway car in the Compiegne Forest where the Germans signed an armistice and fighting ceased on the western front at 11 A.M. on November 11. The First World War which had cost the lives of 10,000,000 men was over.

SUMMARY

The Concert of Europe failed to preserve peace in Europe. Nevertheless many other congresses of great powers met and made agreements on questions submitted to them. Many international organizations promoted common action of benefit to all. The first Hague conference established the Hague Tribunal for the adjustment of international disputes by arbitration. The second Hague conference dealt largely with the laws of land and sea warfare and the rights and duties of neutrals.

Excessive national pride and economic nationalism played an important part in arraying the great powers of Europe into two armed camps. German national pride was based on the accomplishments of its scientists, inventors, historians, artists, musicians, and literary men. Germans were proud of their government and of their army and their growing navy.

To protect itself Germany organized the Triple Alliance composed of Germany, Austria-Hungary, and Italy. Another purpose of the Triple Alliance was to extend German and Austrian power and influence throughout the Balkans and even into Turkey and on to Bagdad.

Germany developed an extensive overseas trade, particularly in certain countries in South America. Not satisfied with the success of their overseas trade, the Germans founded colonies in Africa and islands in the Pacific where Germans could settle and remain German citizens. Germany began to build a great navy to protect its overseas trade and colonial empire and as a diplomatic weapon in world affairs.

France was proud of its culture, its language, and its army. It was ashamed of its defeat in 1870 and decided, if possible, to regain Alsace and Lorraine, its lost provinces. It strengthened its army and its fortresses, made an alliance with Russia, and adjusted its colonial differences with Great Britain.

Russia endeavored to secure control of Constantinople and the Balkans. Great Britain took a major part in blocking its endeavor to do so. The British became alarmed at German expansion and sea power and formed with France the *Entente Cordiale*. When Great Britain and France came to terms with Russia, the three of them formed the Triple Entente.

A pistol shot in Bosnia plunged the two armed camps into war. The responsibility for causing this war has been debated ever since; many put the blame on Germany.

The First World War involved almost everybody in the nations at war. Methods of warfare underwent changes. Trenches, heavy artillery, and airplanes made new tactics necessary. Camouflage played its part in the war, and propaganda influenced public opinion both in the warring and in the neutral countries.

Land, sea, and air warfare took place in many parts of the world. The British navy had from the start control of most of the sea lanes and was able to blockade Germany. The German submarines, however, did great damage to allied and neutral shipping.

The Germans won the first battles on the western front but they were prevented from capturing Paris, their chief objective. About four years of indecisive trench warfare ensued. After the United States entered the war the American Expeditionary Force, under the command of General John J. Pershing, helped to break the main line of the German advance.

The Russians were defeated on the eastern front largely because of the inefficiency and corruption of their government. A revolution overthrew the Tsar's government, and later on the Bolsheviks made peace with the Germans.

In the first battles the Italians were defeated by the Austrians, but towards the close of the war the Italian armies, with the help of Great Britain and France, drove the Austrians out of Italy and back into Austria. At the outset of the war the Germans and Austrians conquered their enemies in the Balkans, but in the last year of the war the British defeated the Central Powers in the Balkans.

The United States declared war on Germany (April, 1917). President Wilson declared that one of the aims of the United States in entering the war was "to make the world safe for democracy." The United States conscripted millions of young men for military service, converted its peacetime industries to the production of materials of war, and increased greatly its production of agricultural products. In the autumn of 1918 the Central Powers collapsed and requested an armistice. The fighting came to an end November 11, 1918. It had caused untold suffering, the loss of about 10,000,000 soldiers, the wounding of 20,000,000 others. Its cost has been estimated at about $332,000,000,000.

EVENTS THAT TOOK PLACE AT ABOUT THE SAME TIME
1871

	Three Emperors' League formed, 1873.
Telegraph Union formed, 1875.	
	Russo-Turkish War, 1877-1878.
Postal Union formed, 1878.	Berlin Congress re-made Treaty of San Stefano, 1878.
Dual Alliance—Germany and Austria—1879.	
	France took Tunis, 1881.
Triple Alliance—Germany, Austria, Italy—1882.	
Rumania joined Triple Alliance, 1883.	
	Copyright Union formed, 1886.
William II became emperor of the German Empire, 1888.	
Bismarck dismissed, 1890.	
	Dual Alliance—France and Russia—1893.
	German naval expansion begins, 1898.
First Hague Conference, 1899.	Bagdad railway concession granted to Germans, 1899.
Anglo-Japanese Alliance, 1902.	
Russo-Japanese War, 1904-1905.	Entente Cordiale, 1904.
	Algeciras Conference, 1906.
Second Hague Conference, 1907.	Triple Entente, 1907.
	Austria annexed Bosnia and Herzegovina, 1908.
	Second Moroccan Crisis, 1911.
Assassination of Francis Ferdinand, 1914.	
Outbreak of the First World War, 1914.	
Italy joined the Allies, 1915.	Bulgaria joined the Central Powers, 1915.
Lusitania sunk, 1915.	
Russian Revolution, 1917.	United States entered the First World War, 1917.
Russia and Germany made Treaty of Brest-Litovsk, 1918.	
Woodrow Wilson's Fourteen Points, 1918.	The Armistice, Nov. 11, 1918.

1918

WAR MESSAGE. On April 6, 1917, President Wilson asked Congress to declare war on Germany, "to make the world safe for democracy."

THE GERMAN FLEET SURRENDERS. At right, Admiral Beatty, R.N., Admiral Rodman, U.S.N., King George V, the Prince of Wales (later Edward VIII) and Admiral Sims, U.S.N., witness the surrender of submarines, from the U.S.S. *New York*.

AMERICAN TROOPS IN ACTION. Above, a typical infantry attack of World War I, "somewhere in France."

CANADIANS GO OVER THE TOP. At right, the zero - hour rush from a trench with a soldier (second from right) expressing his contempt for the enemy.

CHAPTER 29

The Paris Peace Conference and the League of Nations

~~~~~~

Hopes were high for a lasting peace when the Peace Conference met at Paris in 1919. Although delegates from thirty-two nations attended, most decisions were made by the representatives of the big powers. A separate treaty was drawn up for each of the defeated powers. The one drawn up for Germany was called the Treaty of Versailles. It inflicted penalties on Germany for its part in the war and contained provisions that were intended to make it impossible for Germany to wage war again. Treaties with the other defeated nations likewise inflicted penalties on them.

The Peace Conference altered the boundaries of most of the older nations on the Continent, created new nations, and fixed their boundaries.

The Peace Conference drew up a Covenant (constitution) for a League of Nations and made it a part of the treaties with each of the defeated powers. The Covenant set up the League of Nations whose purpose was to settle peacefully international disputes which might lead to war. But the Senate of the United States refused to ratify the Treaty of Versailles and the United States did not join the League of Nations.

• • •

The atmosphere and the leaders at the Paris Peace Conference were most unusual. It was composed solely of men who represented the victorious powers because the defeated Central Powers were not permitted to send delegates to negotiate a peace. This conference differed greatly in character from the Congress of Vienna, 105 years before. Gone were monarchs and nobles; missing were grand parties, dinners, and dances which had made the Congress of Vienna so gay; gone, too, were the intrigues of kings and princes to regain lost powers or territories, and also the wiles of Talleyrand and the reactionary Metternich. To be sure there was much intriguing at Paris and the representatives of some countries earnestly desired to regain their lost territories and even to gain new lands. The four most influential men—Wilson, Clemenceau, Lloyd George, and Orlando—were neither monarchs nor nobles. President Wilson had been a college professor and university president; Clemenceau was a journalist; Lloyd George was a lawyer; and Orlando was a professor of constitutional law who had become premier.

The leaders, especially those from Great Britain and the United States, brought with them a large staff of experts in the fields of economics, labor, geography, history, political science, and specialists on regions, nationalities, languages, and also many other subjects. Scarcity of food, crowded hotels, an influenza epidemic, and the serious purpose of many official delegates deprived the occasion of gaiety.

Leaders made the major decisions. Thirty-two Allied and Associated powers were represented at the Conference. The number of

Ewing Galloway

"The Signing of the Treaty of Versailles" in the Hall of Mirrors, 1919, was painted by Sir William Orpen. Wilson, Clemenceau, and Lloyd George, in the center, watch the German delegate sign the treaty.

delegates sent by them was too large to work effectively and also quickly enough to find solutions of the many knotty problems before the peace treaties could be written. For a time decisions were made by a Council of Ten, consisting of the chief representatives of the United States, Great Britain, France, Italy, and Japan, but the Council of Ten worked too slowly and so a smaller Coun-

cil was formed (the Big Four). It consisted of Woodrow Wilson, Clemenceau, Lloyd George, and Orlando. When Orlando withdrew after the other three had refused to agree to Italian claims for territory, the Big Four became the Big Three. The final statement of the peace treaties was written by the Big Three.

The defeated powers were punished be-

Changes after World War I

former Austria-Hungary
" Germany
" Russia
" Bulgaria
Old boundaries
New "

The most important effect of the First World War was the breaking up of the Austro-Hungarian Empire and of a part of Western Russia into small countries. These small countries, extending from Finland to Greece, none of them strong enough to maintain its independence, fell easy prey to Nazi Germany before and during the Second World War.

cause they were held responsible for the war; new national boundaries of older nations were redrawn and new nations were created and their boundaries drawn; the League of Nations was established. Separate treaties were made with each of the defeated powers —Germany, Austria, Hungary, Bulgaria, and Turkey. The Treaty of Versailles, the one the victorious powers made with Germany, had more far-reaching consequences than the treaties made with Austria, Hungary, Bulgaria, and Turkey. For that reason it gave the Big Three the greatest concern. When the German representatives signed the Treaty of Versailles, they acknowledged Germany's sole responsibility for the war. Austria and also Hungary, now separate nations, acknowledged their war guilt, too.

The penalties meted out to the defeated powers, particularly Germany, were designed to punish them, to prevent them from ever waging war again, and to make them pay for the damages they had done during the war. These penalties were territorial, military, naval, and economic.

The territorial penalties meted out (in Europe) to Germany strengthened its neighbors. It was forced to cede Alsace and Lorraine back to France, the towns of Eupen and Malmédy to Belgium, Schleswig back to Denmark, Posen and the Polish Corridor to Poland, and Memel to Lithuania, a new nation whose boundaries were defined in the Treaty of Versailles. All Germany's colonial empire was taken from it. In addition, the Saar Basin, rich in coal deposits, was to be governed under the supervision of the League for fifteen years. During this period France was to have coal from its mines, and at its end (1935) a plebiscite was to be held to determine its future political status in compliance with the terms of the Treaty of Versailles.

The territorial penalties meted out to Germany destroyed its colonial empire. On the continent of Europe certain German lands were ceded to nations of the Allied powers, but the colonial empire was not ceded to victorious powers by the Treaty of Versailles. Instead, German colonies were made mandates of some of these powers under the supervision of the League of Nations. Any nation given a mandate of a former German colony was directed to govern it in the best interests of its inhabitants, to abstain from fortifying it, and to make reports from time to time to the League.

The much larger part of German East Africa and small areas in Togoland and Kamerun, both in West Africa, were mandated to Great Britain. The rest of Togoland and Kamerun were mandated to France, and a small part of German East Africa was mandated to Belgium. German Southwest Africa was mandated to the Union of South Africa. German islands in the Pacific north of the equator (the Marshalls, Pelews, Carolines, and Marianas except Guam) were mandated to Japan and those south of the equator were mandated to New Zealand and Australia.

Military and naval penalties were imposed on Germany. The German army was not to exceed 100,000 men and was not to have any large guns. Compulsory military training was forbidden, the General Staff was to be dissolved, and the use of airplanes for military purposes was prohibited. Many fortresses, including those on Helgoland and in the Rhineland, were ordered dismantled. Germany was forbidden to station troops west of the Rhine or within a belt about thirty miles wide east of the Rhine. The Kiel Canal and German navigable rivers were internationalized. The Kaiser and other offenders against the peace of Europe were to be tried. At the expense of Germany an Allied army of occupation was to hold the left or west bank of the Rhine and bridgeheads on the east bank for fifteen years to see that the terms of the Treaty of Versailles were complied with. The Germans were ordered to surrender their warships to the Allies, and they steamed to Scapa Flow in the Orkney Islands off Scotland where the ships were scuttled by their own crews. Germany was permitted to have a very small navy, but forbidden to build submarines.

Economic penalties were imposed upon Germany. All German merchant ships were to be handed over to the victors and Germany was required to build merchant ships for the

Allies for five years to replace those destroyed during the war. The Allies demanded that Germany pay not only for the civilian property damage it had caused during the war, but also for injuries to the peoples in the countries that Germany occupied. The Treaty of Versailles did not decide upon the amount of these payments (reparations) but left that to be decided by an international commission. After much discussion, it was agreed that Germany should pay only for actual damage to civilian property and in 1921 the amount was fixed at about $33,000,000,000 plus interest and was to be paid in fifty-nine years.

The delegates of the German Republic, the government that had been set up after the flight of the Kaiser, were summoned to the Hall of Mirrors in the Palace of Versailles, where (1871) Bismarck had proclaimed the establishment of the German Empire, and ordered to sign the peace treaty. At first they protested and one of them resigned his official position rather than sign. German delegates protested especially against the war-guilt clause and denied their responsibility for causing the war. They forgot that they had surrendered because they were defeated, and they complained bitterly because Wilson's Fourteen Points had not been carried out completely in the treaty. At length, however, the government of the German Republic authorized its delegates to sign because a refusal might mean invasion and in that event even severer terms.

The Germans kept up a continual agitation against what they called the "Dictate of Versailles," and eventually they refused to abide by its terms. The two problems, reparations and disarmament, which the Peace Conference left for future settlement, were never satisfactorily solved. In twenty years after the ending of the Paris Peace Conference its work was in ruins and most of the nations of the world were at war once more.

The Paris Peace Conference brought an end to the Dual Monarchy of Austria-Hungary. The Hapsburgs were driven from their throne and exiled. Austria, now a small nation, was forbidden to unite with Germany. It had to cede Trentino, a part of the Tyrol, and Trieste to Italy. Bosnia and Herzegovina were made a part of the new state of Yugoslavia, and Bohemia became a part of the newly created republic of Czechoslovakia. In addition to these losses of territory, the Austrian army was severely limited in size, and Austria was ordered to pay reparations.

Peace with Hungary was not made until June, 1920, because of its internal disorders. It lost lands to Czechoslovakia, to Yugoslavia, and to Rumania, in all more than two thirds of its territory and two fifths of its population. The Paris Peace Conference imposed a treaty on Bulgaria by which it was forced to cede territory to Greece and Yugoslavia. Both Hungary and Bulgaria were ordered to pay reparations.

The Turkish Empire was greatly reduced in size. The Treaty of Sèvres with Turkey made by the Paris Peace Conference was considered so harsh by the Turks that they bitterly resented it. It had ceded a part of Turkish possessions in Western Asia Minor to Greece. In the meantime a forceful national leader, Mustafa Kemal, had deposed the Sultan, abolished the Caliphate, and moved the capital from Constantinople to Ankara. When the Greeks attempted to occupy the territory ceded to them in Western Asia Minor, Kemal's army drove them back to the Aegean Sea and compelled them to flee to Greece. After Kemal's victory, a new treaty was made (1923) at Lausanne, Switzerland.

In the Treaty of Lausanne Turkey recognized (1) the independence of a new Arab state, Hedjaz; (2) the establishment of Iraq (Mesopotamia), Palestine, and Transjordania as British mandates, and of Syria as a French mandate; (3) the award of some of its Aegean Islands to Greece and others to Italy; (4) the repatriation of about 3,000,000 Greeks to Greece from Western Asia Minor under the supervision of the League of Nations in exchange for the repatriation of a smaller number of Turks who were living in Greece. Turkey was left in possession of Constantinople, since renamed Istanbul by the Turks.

Poland became an independent nation again. Poland lost its independence when Prussia, Austria, and Russia partitioned it for the third time (1795). Although the Poles had been compelled to live as subjects of one or the other of these three nations, they had kept the patriotism and the culture of their forefathers alive for almost 125 years. Polish patriotism rose to new heights in the First World War. Propaganda for the re-creation of a Polish nation was widespread in Poland and in other countries, particularly in the United States where many persons of Polish ancestry lived. One of the leading propagandists was the famous pianist, Paderewski, who had given many concerts in the United States.

As President Wilson believed in the self-determination of small nations, he included the re-creation of an independent Polish state in his Fourteen Points. Near the close of the war, the Poles set up the Republic of Poland and sent representatives to the Paris Peace Conference at which Poland was recognized as an independent republic. The new Poland was made up for the most part of the lands that had been taken from it in the three partitions. To help free Poland from the economic controls of its powerful neighbors, and to give it access to the Baltic Sea and also about ninety miles of Baltic seacoast, the Paris Peace Conference established the Polish Corridor. It was a strip of land running along

both sides of the lower Vistula River to Danzig on the Baltic Sea. As most of the people living in Danzig were Germans (it had been a member of the Hanseatic League), it was made a free city whose chief executive was to be a commissioner appointed by the League. As the Poles wanted a harbor and naval base entirely under their control, they built a port and naval base at Gdynia on the Baltic.

The Corridor caused constant friction between Poland and Germany because it separated East Prussia, home of the Junkers, from the rest of Germany. Poland itself was faced with internal difficulties because it contained minorities of considerable size—Germans, Jews, Russians, Ruthenians, and Lithuanians. About one third of its inhabitants were not of Polish ancestry and did not speak Polish.

The Republic of Czechoslovakia was created by the Paris Peace Conference. The Czechs (Bohemians) had kept alive Czech nationalism against all the efforts of Austria-Hungary to suppress it. During the First World War the Czechs were forced to fight in the Austrian armies, most of them unwillingly, against the Allied powers. At the same time Masaryk and Benes, great Czech leaders, were working, particularly in the United States, for the right of Czechs to self-determination. At home other Czechs had formed a well-organized underground. In October, 1918, Czechs in Paris proclaimed the birth of the Republic of Czechoslovakia which Wilson recognized because he believed in the self-determination of small nations. Because the Slovaks joined the Czechs in opposition to their former Austrian and Hungarian rulers, the new republic was called Czechoslovakia. When created, it was composed of (1) Bohemia, Moravia, and Austrian Silesia—all had been parts of the former Austrian Empire; and (2) Slovakia, a part of the former kingdom of Hungary. The Paris Peace Conference based the boundaries of Czechoslovakia on historic, national, and strategic considerations. Consequently, Czechoslovakia contained Czechs, Slovaks, and also minorities including Germans, Magyars, Poles, Ruthenians, and Ukrainians. The Czechs, however, outnumbered greatly all the other nationalities in the new Republic.

The Paris Peace Conference created the Kingdom of Yugoslavia. It was made up of Serbia and also Croatia and Slovenia, both formerly parts of Austria-Hungary; Montenegro; and the part of Macedonia that was formerly a part of Bulgaria. The differences in traditions, religions, languages, and nationalities of its peoples kept them from attaining the national unity needed to make the new kingdom a success.

The Paris Peace Conference wrote the Covenant of the League of Nations. Woodrow Wilson thought the greatest achievement of the Paris Peace Conference was the creation of the League of Nations. He hoped it would lead to a lasting peace. Years before 1918 leading men in the United States, Great Britain, and France had discussed and worked for the creation of an international organization for peace. In the United States a League to Enforce Peace had been formed. Several drafts of a constitution for an international organization to promote peace had been made, studied, and revised. This work made it possible for Woodrow Wilson to include as his fourteenth point "a general association of nations must be formed under specific covenants for the purpose of affording mutual guarantees of political independence and territorial integrity to great and small states alike."

At the Paris Peace Conference a League of Nations Commission was appointed to draw up the Covenant (constitution) for the League. It contained specifications for membership in and withdrawal from the League. It described the organization and duties of the

Ewing Galloway

THOMAS G. MASARYK, SCHOLAR, PROFESSOR, STATESMAN, AND FIRST PRESIDENT OF THE REPUBLIC OF CZECHOSLOVAKIA.

agencies which were to carry out its work. It required members to register all treaties with the secretary of the League. It laid down the basic principles on which its officials should act in dealing with mandates, with the Saar and with Danzig, labor, illicit traffic in drugs, diseases, and public health. Altogether it was a most remarkable document.

The League of Nations was to carry on its chief work through four agencies. The original members of the League were to be the United States and those Allied and neutral nations whose governments approved the Covenant. Other nations could become mem-

HOME OF THE LEAGUE OF NATIONS, GENEVA. This 700-room palace of the League
of Nations at Geneva, Switzerland, was completed in 1936 amid the rumblings of war which
the League was created to prevent.

bers by a two-thirds vote of the Assembly. Two years' notice was required for withdrawal. The League of Nations came into existence officially in January, 1920, when the Treaty of Versailles went into effect. The first meeting of the Assembly opened in November of the same year when delegates from forty-two member nations assembled in Geneva. Sixty-three nations were members of the League at one time or another. The agencies through which the League of Nations carried on its work were (1) the Assembly, (2) the Council, (3) the Permanent Secretariat, and (4) the Permanent Court of International Justice.

(1) *The Assembly* was composed of representatives from all member states. Each member nation had one vote and could not have more than three representatives. It elected the non-permanent members of the Council and new members of the League, controlled the budget, and considered any international difficulty that threatened to lead to war. In practice the Assembly was intended to be the agency through which smaller nations could air their grievances to the world and also exert their greatest strength.

(2) *The Council* was composed of permanent and non-permanent members. The permanent members were the United States, Great Britain, France, Italy, and Japan. The non-permanent members (smaller nations) were four member nations elected for a term of three years by the Assembly. The United States refused to join (1920) and later on Japan and Italy withdrew. Germany and the Soviet Union became permanent members of the Council when they joined the League. In 1922 the number of non-permanent members of the Council was increased to six and in 1936 to eleven. The Council could consider any incident that might disturb world peace or peaceful international relations, could investigate and report on disputes between member nations, and could exercise supervision over the work of the League.

(3) *The Permanent Secretariat* was composed of the Secretary-General and his assistants. The League employed them for an indefinite time. The Secretariat kept the minutes of all meetings and the records of the League, registered all treaties, and supervised all activities authorized by the League. Its headquarters were at Berne, the capital of Switzerland, where a palatial building was erected for meetings and other uses of the League.

(4) *The Permanent Court of International Justice* (World Court) was established in 1921 and held its first session (1922) at its seat in The Hague, the capital of the Netherlands. It consisted of fifteen judges chosen for a term of nine years by the Council and Assembly of the League. The World Court was a court of law to hear and to decide cases that had arisen under the provisions of treaties or under the accepted principles of international law.

The Covenant of the League of Nations provided ways of settling international disputes peacefully. In Article XII of the Covenant the member nations of the League agreed to use one of three ways for the peaceful settlement of a dispute: (1) arbitration, (2) judicial settlement by decision of the World Court, (3) mediation by the Council or the Assembly. When a dispute was referred to the Council for settlement, its decisions had to be unanimous except that parties to the dispute were excluded from voting. All members of the League agreed that if they were dissatisfied with an award that had been made by the body to which an international dispute had been referred, they would not go to war until after three months had elapsed. If any member went to war before the three months had elapsed, it was deemed to have made war on all other members of the League. In that event the Covenant provided that the other members would employ sanc-

tions against the offending or aggressor nation. Sanctions meant that the other member nations would stop all financial and trading relations with the offender and that they would regard it as an outlaw among nations.

The Council possessed the power also to recommend to members what military, naval, or air forces each should use to force the offender to come to terms. The League had no armed forces of its own and could not compel its members to act if a war broke out. The Covenant provided three ways of settling disputes which its members solemnly promised to use. Unfortunately, as we shall see, some members refused to use these methods against offenders and their refusal so weakened the League that it was unable to prevent war.

The United States did not join the League of Nations. The Paris peace agreements imposed penalties on the Central Powers, remade the map of Europe and other parts of the Eastern Hemisphere, and made plans for a lasting peace by creating the League of Nations. The Versailles Treaty, which contained the Covenant of the League of Nations, met with immediate opposition when President Wilson submitted it to the United States Senate for ratification. Many Republican Senators, joined by a few Democrats, refused to vote for the Covenant of the League of Nations without reservations or additions that would protect, as they claimed, the Monroe Doctrine and other national interests of the United States. President Wilson refused to accept these reservations to the Covenant and on March 19, 1920, the Senate rejected the Treaty of Versailles. The defeat was due in part to a revival of fear and dislike of foreign entanglements. It was due also to a political attack on President Wilson headed by Henry Cabot Lodge of Massachusetts, chairman of the Senate Foreign Relations Committee. After the Senate had rejected the Treaty of Versailles the

United States made a separate treaty with each of the Central Powers because we were still technically at war with them. The defeat of the Treaty of Versailles meant that the United States would not become a member of the League of Nations. Our absence greatly weakened its strength and influence and contributed to its final failure.

SUMMARY

The Peace Conference met in Paris in 1919. Woodrow Wilson, Clemenceau, and Lloyd George were its leaders. They made most of the major decisions. Separate treaties were made with each of the defeated powers.

Germany was required to acknowledge responsibility for the war. It was forced to cede lands in Europe to victorious European nations. Its colonial empire was taken from it and mandated to one or the other of the allied nations. The size of the Germany army and navy was reduced greatly. The Rhineland was demilitarized and an Allied army of occupation was stationed in Western Germany at German expense. In addition Germany was ordered to pay reparations which the treaty left to a special Reparations Commission which was to fix the amount to be paid.

The Dual Monarchy of Austria-Hungary was completely destroyed and Austria became a small republic. It lost land to Italy and to two new nations, Yugoslavia and Czechoslovakia. It, too, was ordered to pay reparations. Hungary became an independent nation, but it also lost territory to its neighbors and besides it was ordered to pay reparations.

The Turkish Empire refused to accept the terms of the peace treaty which had ceded territory in Western Asia Minor to Greece. A strong nationalist movement, led by Mustafa Kemal, overthrew the Sultan at Constantinople and Kemal's army drove the Greeks out of Western Asia Minor. Afterwards Turkey signed (1923) the Treaty of Lausanne in which it gave up all its former possessions not inhabited by Turks.

The Covenant of the League of Nations was included in the Treaty of Versailles which the Paris Peace Conference made with Germany. The Covenant established an Assembly, a Council, a Permanent Secretariat, and a Permanent Court of International Justice. The Covenant provided ways for the peaceful settlement of international disputes. It was designed to keep peace. The United States Senate refused to ratify the Treaty of Versailles and the United States did not become a member of the League of Nations.

SUMMARY OF PART IX

Many of the efforts that statesmen and diplomats made in the years before the First World War to preserve peace in the world were unsuccessful. An ever-increasing national pride and the growth of economic nationalism among jealous and ambitious nations prevented any united action to keep peace. Each great power thought it could strengthen itself and fulfill its national ambitions by having allies. In time the great powers of Europe were in one or the other of two armed camps, the Triple Alliance and the Triple Entente. A minor incident became thereby of such grave concern to both camps that nearly all Europe was plunged into a war that lasted from August 2, 1914 to November 11, 1918.

Nations not in either of these two armed camps, including the United States and Japan, were drawn into the First World War. It was fought on many fronts in widely separated lands and also on the seven seas. In 1917 Russia collapsed, withdrew, and signed a treaty with Germany that deprived it of much territory. The allied nations and the United States won the war, but at a stupendous cost in lives, suffering, money, materials, and national well-being. Moreover, many serious problems both domestic and foreign followed in the wake of the First World War.

The victorious nations imposed terms of peace on the conquered nations. The losers were forced to cede territory and to agree to pay reparations. Republics replaced monarchies in Germany and Austria. Several other new republics were established in Europe. An enlarged Serbia was called Yugoslavia.

The League of Nations was established as an international political institution to adjust international disputes and thus to preserve peace. Although it was weakened by the refusal of the United States to join it, most men looked upon it as an institution that justified a real hope that war would no longer be employed to settle disputes between nations.

THE BIG FOUR OF THE PEACE CONFERENCE. These statesmen made the important decisions at Paris, in 1918. Left to right, they are Premier Orlando, of Italy; Prime Minister David Lloyd George, of Great Britain, Premier Georges Clemenceau of France; and President Wilson, representing the United States.

"WHITE HOUSE" OF CZECHOSLOVAKIA.
Above, the Castle of Prague seen from the river.
Czech Presidents Masaryk and Benes made the
Castle their official residence.

DR. EDOUARD BENES fo[l]lowed Masaryk as Czech leade[r]

PADEREWSKI of Poland.

ARISTIDE BRIAND, Frenc[h]
premier, worked unsuccessfull[y]
for peace at Locarno and in th[e]
Kellogg pacts.

MUSTAPHA KEMAL ATATURK, above, as Turkey's first president, modernized the state and introduced sweeping reforms. At
left, veiled women of old Turkey walk according to custom, in a
garment-swathed group. Above, girls of modern Turkey step out
in uniform in a celebration at Ankara.

PART X

The Impact of Totalitarianism and Democracy

In President Woodrow Wilson's message (delivered in person) to a joint session of Congress in which he asked Congress to declare war on Germany, he said that one of the purposes for the United States entering the First World War was to make the world safe for democracy. Actually the war and the unsettled conditions that resulted from it subjected all democratic nations to the severest tests and strains. To understand both President Wilson's statement and what actually happened, we must look back a little.

Democracy in the modern sense means the right of the people of a nation to govern themselves through representatives chosen by universal suffrage after free and full discussion of all questions of government that have arisen. Only an intelligent and educated people, competent to judge men and issues, and honest and devoted leaders, who will put the general good above their personal and party interests and prejudices, can make a success of democratic government. It also requires free speech, free press, free and unbiased radio, and uncensored movies. All of these are needed to instruct the voters on public issues and to provide full opportunities for a free public discussion of issues before the voters.

Throughout the nineteenth century the Western world in general seemed to be moving steadily toward a practical realization of the true meaning of democracy and the means for making it a success. Even in countries that were not yet wholly democratic, forms of parliamentary government existed. In these countries the right of the people to vote was limited to the well-to-do, who elected members of different parties to legislative bodies in which the members discussed proposed legislation but did not actually legislate. Imperial Germany had this much democracy and even in tsarist Russia an elected body (the Duma) could discuss proposed legislation and vote on it, though a majority vote did not insure that the legislation would be carried out.

Germany was autocratic because the Kaiser and the Chancellor who was his appointee, could, and often did, disregard or override the will of the Reichstag. President Wilson believed that because the German government was autocratic, German victory in the war would threaten the destruction of the democratic way of life wherever it existed. The democratic countries won the war and afterward the autocratic governments in Germany, both state and national, were overthrown by the German people and a German republic established. Some of the victors, perhaps most of them, confidently but mistakenly thought that German militarism had been destroyed.

After the First World War, democratic government seemed to be on the increase in nearly every country. Woman suffrage increased the number of voters in some countries which were already democratic. In the new nations that were established by the treaties made by the Paris Peace Conference governments were organized on democratic principles. Furthermore the League of Nations was designed to focus world public opinion on any enemy of democracy.

Yet the world was not safe for democracy. The First World War and its aftermath had brought many problems which even the experienced democracies were not able to solve to the satisfaction of their peoples and which the inexperienced democracies, even when they tried in good faith, were not able to solve at all. The warring countries had suffered great loss of life and property. Factories had to be rebuilt in devastated areas and others everywhere reconverted to peacetime production. Coal and iron mines in areas devastated by the war had to be restored to operation. Armies had to be demobilized and that meant former soldiers returned to civilian life and occupations. Government controls over industry, agriculture, and civilian life had to be relaxed and finally abolished in an attempt to bring economic conditions back to normal.

The most competent leadership of the democracies was not able to solve all of their perplexing problems. Perhaps these failures were due in part to the killing or crippling of so many brilliant young men in the war. In some of the new nations it was due to lack of experience of both people and leaders in the democratic way of life. Sometimes it was due to lack of intellectual and moral integrity and at others to a lack of patriotic devotion. These failures on the part of both leaders and peoples in the new nations were to be expected, for many of them lacked experience in democratic government, and some of them had no real desire to see it succeed. The peoples in them were so accustomed to obeying the orders of autocratic governments that they preferred to obey rather than to think for themselves. As a result, they followed a strong political or military leader blindly and devotedly.

The wave of nationalism which swept the world after 1918 made it easy for politically ambitious leaders to arise. Most nations wanted to be self-sufficient. They erected tariffs to protect their manufactures and agriculture. Almost all organized and equipped armies and navies and jealously guarded what they thought were their national rights. Because the peoples in these nations had never fully experienced or appreciated liberty, they were all the more willing to follow a selfish leader who promised them economic security and national glory. In consequence, dictators came to power in some European countries.

CHAPTER 30

Communism in Russia

The first of the new dictatorships was set up (1917) by revolution in Russia. In theory it was a Communist "dictatorship of the proletariat" whose final purpose was to establish a government based on Marxian socialism.

In 1917, after the war-worn Russians revolted against the government of the Tsar, he abdicated. After his abdication, Russia was governed by a provisional government headed by moderates who established a republic, effected some political and economic reforms, and kept Russia in the war against the Central Powers. Opposition to war, however, was so strong among soldiers, peasants, and city workers that the Bolsheviks (Marxian socialists who believed in establishing socialism by revolution) under the vigorous and determined leadership of Lenin, Trotsky, and others overthrew the liberal provisional government in October, 1917.

After the Bolsheviks got control of the government, they made peace with the Central Powers. Their plan to make Russia a communist country was soon interrupted by a civil war (1918-1921) in which foreign powers aided the domestic enemies of the Bolsheviks. After defeating their enemies, the Bolsheviks resumed their communist program under the leadership of Lenin and, after his death, under the leadership of Joseph Stalin.

The Communists have accomplished much of their purpose by carrying out several Five-Year Plans. All land has been seized from private owners for the government (in other words, they have nationalized the land). After the Communists nationalized the land, they divided most of it into rather large tracts and ruthlessly forced peasant families to work it in common. This kind of farming is called collective farming. The Communists have also seized from their private owners and nationalized factories, mines, power plants, railroads, and practically all other kinds of industries and businesses. They have built many schools in which Russian youth are taught to be supporters of the Communist regime. They have brought about many revolutionary changes in the political, economic, and social life of the Russian people.

• • •

The Tsar's conduct of the war led to demands for reform. The Tsar's government failed wretchedly in the management of the war. Tsar Nicholas II himself was weak-willed, lacking in leadership, and under the influence of the Tsarina who was a very superstitious woman. She in turn placed great confidence in an evil man named Rasputin whose advice on the management of the government and the war proved to be very injurious to Russia. The affairs of government under this leadership went from bad to worse. Many office holders and even high ranking army officers were unbelievably corrupt. Large sums of money were wasted or stolen. The army and the navy were most inadequately supplied. The soldiers were often poorly fed, and many were ordered into bat-

611

tle without guns or ammunition. Doctors and nurses were so few and medical supplies were so scarce that thousands upon thousands died from lack of medical care. Workers in the city and peasants, who had obediently believed in and supported the Tsar's government while at home, learned while soldiers in the army how hopelessly inefficient the government of the Tsar really was to wage war successfully.

Conditions on the home front weakened the successful prosecution of the war. Poor working conditions, lack of coal and of food due chiefly to poor transportation, and inefficient distribution of supplies made the life of the workers in the cities unendurable. Strikes and bread riots became common occurrences. The government's demands for food, the oppressions of the landlords and of the village bosses, and the appalling loss of life at the front were much greater than the age-old grievances of the peasants. Russia was ripe for revolt.

The Tsar's only answer to demands for reform was to turn the police and army against those who suggested a change. In 1916, when members of the Duma made suggestions for changes in government, the Tsar dissolved the Duma. Late in 1916 a group of patriotic Russians decided that the influence of Rasputin was so harmful to Russia that one of their number shot him. With Rasputin out of the way the Duma reassembled in March, 1917. The Tsar ordered it dissolved again, and at the same time he ordered strikers in Petrograd to return to work. Both the Duma and the workers refused to obey his orders and most of the army units stationed in Petrograd supported them. On March 11, the president of the Duma sent this telegram to the Tsar:

> Position serious, anarchy in capital, government paralyzed, arrangements for transport, supply, and fuel in complete disorder.

General discontent is increasing. Disorderly firing in the streets. Part of the troops are firing on one another. Essential to entrust some individual who possesses the confidence of the country with the formation of a new government. There must be no delay. Any procrastination fatal. I pray God that in this hour responsibility fall not on the wearer of the crown.

Three days later the Tsar tried to reach Petrograd, but his train had to stop because workmen had pulled up the tracks. At the same time the troops that had been sent to Petrograd joined the revolutionists. On March 15, 1917, after the Tsar had learned that his soldiers were deserting him, his generals convinced him that he should abdicate.

A provisional government tried to carry on the war against the Central Powers. After the Tsar's abdication, a liberal provisional government headed by Prince Lvov gave the press more freedom, freed religious and political prisoners (including Joseph Stalin), recognized the right of workers to unionize and strike, and announced plans for a constituent assembly (constitutional convention) to set up a republic. The leaders of the liberal provisional government thought, however, that the first duty of Russia was to keep its promises to its allies and not to make a separate peace with Germany. In this the leaders met with such opposition from soldiers, workers in the cities, and peasants that Prince Lvov was forced to resign.

Alexander Kerensky, leader of the Social Revolutionary party, who was friendly to the demands of workers and peasants for reform, succeeded Lvov but he, too, wanted to carry on the war against the Central Powers. His lack of united support to carry on the war and the failure of his supporters to agree on a domestic program led to his downfall. A strong leader who had a program that appealed to the masses opposed Kerensky. His name was Ulianov, but he is known as Lenin.

Sovfoto

ARRIVAL OF LENIN (1917) AT THE FINLAND STATION IN PETROGRAD.

Lenin and Trotsky led the Bolshevik Revolution. Lenin (1870-1924) is one of history's ruthless men. He was short and stocky with bulging forehead and sharp, piercing eyes. Endowed with tremendous physical energy, a brilliant mind, and a strong will, he knew what he wanted to do in Russia and how to get it done. These qualities and his dynamic leadership attracted large numbers of soldiers, workers, and peasants to him personally and also to his reform program. Rapidly he became the acknowledged and beloved leader of the Bolsheviks, first in Petrograd and then throughout Russia.

Lenin, the son of a school official, was educated in law at the Universities of Kazan and St. Petersburg. Early in life he joined the revolutionary movement after his elder brother had been hanged for his part in a plot to kill the Tsar. Lenin was an enthusiastic believer in the doctrines of Karl Marx, and because he engaged actively in spreading these doctrines he was sent to imprisonment in Siberia for three years. After he was freed from Siberia he lived in exile (1900-1917), chiefly in Switzerland, where he published a revolutionary newspaper, and wrote pamphlets and books in which he explained the teachings of Marx. In April, 1917, the Germans allowed him to cross Germany and go back to Russia under a safe conduct in the hope, it is claimed, that when in Russia he would increase the great confusion that followed the Tsar's abdication and perhaps cause Russia to withdraw from the war.

Lenin's chief lieutenant was Lev Bronstein, who called himself Leon Trotsky (1879-1940). He was the son of a Jewish farmer. Although he went to school but eight years, his wide reading helped to make him an educated man. Like Lenin, he became a Marxian Socialist early in life. Between 1898 and 1917 he was in prison for four years, was sent to Siberia twice, engaged in revolutionary activities in Germany, Belgium, and France, and edited radical newspapers in London, Vienna, and New York. After the abdication of the Tsar, he returned from New York to Petrograd where he soon took an active part under Lenin in the Bolshevik movement. He was an able orator, adept at arousing the emotions of his hearers, and a military organizer and leader of outstanding ability.

The Bolsheviks seized control of the government and began to make revolutionary changes. Prince Lvov and his supporters believed in establishing a republic. Kerensky and his supporters were members of the Social Revolutionary party. They believed that the land of the nobles should be divided among the peasants. A third party, the Socialist party, was composed of two factions, the Mensheviks and the Bolsheviks. The Mensheviks, like the Fabian Socialists in England, believed socialism should and could be established gradually and by the orderly processes of constitutional government. The Bolsheviks believed socialism should be established by "direct action" (revolution) and maintained by a "dictatorship of the proletariat." Lenin and Trotsky were Bolsheviks.

For some time revolutionary leaders had been busy forming many local soviets (councils) throughout Russia. These soviets were composed chiefly of soldiers, city workers, and peasants. The most powerful soviet was in Petrograd. Soon after the return of Lenin and Trotsky to Petrograd they gained control of this powerful soviet, and thereby control over the soldiers and workers in the capital. In October, 1917, soldiers, under the direction of Lenin and Trotsky, seized the public buildings, arrested government offi-

cials, and took over the control of the city government. The announcement of a program of "peace, bread, and land" by the Bolsheviks won over great numbers of soldiers, workers, and peasants. When Lenin promised rights of "cultural nationalism" (the privilege of a nationality to keep its language and national customs) to the many nationalities living in Russia, he gained a large number of followers among them.

At once the Bolsheviks began to carry out their dictatorial program with tireless energy. The Bolshevik government seized the factories and put them under the control of the workers; Lenin announced that all land was the property of the government. Likewise all banks and all the property of the Russian Orthodox Church were seized by the Bolshevik government. The capital was moved from Petrograd to Moscow and (1924) Petrograd was renamed Leningrad. The Gregorian calendar was adopted and Russia from then on has reckoned time by this calendar which most other nations had been using for many years.

The Bolsheviks made peace with the Central Powers. In March, 1918, the Bolsheviks carried out their promise of peace to the Russian people when they made the Treaty of Brest-Litovsk with the Central Powers. The Germans had Russia at their mercy and made the Russian delegates at Brest-Litovsk fully aware that they were. The peace terms that the Germans dictated to the Russians meant the loss of nearly all of the European lands that had been acquired by Russia since the rule of Peter the Great. Even with Lenin's enormous prestige in the Bolshevik party he found it difficult to get the party to accept the terms of the Treaty of Brest-Litovsk. The humiliation of the rest of the Russian people, who were not members of the Bolshevik party, was far greater than that of the party members. By the Treaty of

Brest-Litovsk the Russians ceded Finland, the Baltic provinces, Russian Poland, and the Ukraine to Germany and Kars and Batum to Turkey.

The Reds defeated the Whites in a civil war. The changes made by the Bolshevik government and the Treaty of Brest-Litovsk met the immediate and determined opposition of nobles, clergy, capitalists, Mensheviks, some army officers, and many other Russians. As a result of this widespread opposition, Russia was soon plunged into the horrors of civil war. The opposing sides were called the Reds (Bolsheviks) and the Whites. The Reds soon organized the Cheka and the Red Army to overcome the opposition of the Whites. The Cheka was a secret police force created to ferret out and imprison all known or suspected enemies of Bolshevism. It did its work effectively and without mercy. Thousands of suspects were caught and executed; other thousands, terrified by its power, fled into exile. The Cheka was succeeded by the OGPU and it by NKVD. Trotsky, who had become War Commissar (head of the war department), organized the Red Army and led it to victory over the armies of the Whites and their allies.

For three years (1918-1921) civil war raged furiously in Russia. The loss of life in the civil war ran into hundreds of thousands. In July, 1918, the Tsar and his family, who had gone to Ekaterinburg in Siberia, were shot on order of the local soviet to prevent anyone from rescuing them and also to prevent any member of the Tsar's immediate family or their descendants from laying claim to the throne of Russia in the future. The Great Powers were alarmed by the Red announcement that they were going to spread Bolshevism into every other nation in the world, and besides they were very anxious to keep supplies that they had furnished Russia from falling into the hands of the Germans. Accordingly, they sent munitions, money, and even armies to support the Whites. This interference by foreigners really aided the Bolsheviks. Many Russians who were not Bolsheviks supported them in their efforts to repel the invaders. Trotsky's remarkable speeches helped greatly to unify the Russian people in their opposition to the invaders.

Gradually the Cheka and the Red Army gained the upper hand. Thereupon the Allies withdrew their support from the Whites, and (1921) the Bolsheviks became masters of Russia.

Lenin tried the New Economic Policy. During the civil war the government had ordered the peasants to give up all grain except that needed for family use and seed. When many peasants refused to do so, the government seized their grain. The peasants retaliated by planting less grain, so that in 1921 it was estimated that agricultural production was about 30 per cent less than before the First World War. A terrible famine resulted (1921) and many foreign agencies, including the American Relief Administration, attempted to feed Russia's starving millions, but, even so, many thousands died of starvation and disease. At the same time factory production had declined by 85 per cent, chiefly because of the inexperience and incompetence of the new managers. For the same reason the distribution of food and goods broke down. To revive industry, agriculture, and trade, Lenin (1921) adopted the New Economic Policy (NEP), a compromise with the Communistic ideal of public ownership of all means of production.

Under NEP peasants were allowed to sell their surplus goods in the public market, but in return for this privilege they agreed to turn over to the government a part of the products they raised instead of paying a tax in money. In cities, small shops privately

MEETING OF LENIN AND STALIN (1905) AT THE FIRST CONFERENCE OF THE
RUSSIAN SOCIAL-DEMOCRATIC WORKERS PARTY IN TAMMERFORS, FINLAND,
THEN A PART OF RUSSIA.

owned were allowed to engage in trade. The
government, however, retained its ownership
of all banks, all large industries, and all public utilities, and control of foreign trade. Under NEP economic conditions began to improve. However, *nepmen* (private capitalists)
began to grow rich. As some peasants *(kulaks)* acquired more land, they hired other
peasants to work for them and thereby became richer. The wealth of these men gave
them great power as money-lenders and village bosses. This slight revival of capitalism
could not long be tolerated by a dictatorial
government bent on controlling everything
and everybody. It was soon ended by Lenin's
successor, Joseph Stalin.

**Stalin became head of the Soviet gov-
ernment.** When Lenin died (1924), Joseph

Stalin, Secretary General of the Communist
party, took his place as head of the Soviet
Union. Stalin, which means *steel,* was the son
of a shoemaker in Georgia in the Caucasus
Mountains, now a republic of the Union of
Soviet Socialist Republics. After he had been
expelled from a theological seminary (1896)
for his socialistic ideas, he devoted himself
solely to the overthrow of the Tsar's government. He traveled all over Russia plotting
and organizing revolutionary groups. As a
result, he obtained a thorough knowledge of
the different nationalities and the natural resources of Russia, and at the same time he
became widely known throughout the country. Although he was an adept at evading
the police, he was caught and imprisoned six
times. He escaped five times. From 1913 to

International News

FAMOUS EXILE IN MEXICAN SANCTUARY. Leon Trotsky, exiled Soviet leader, is pictured here in his home in Mexico City two years before he was murdered.

1917 he was exiled to Siberia within the Arctic Circle. He secured his release as a result of a pardon granted political prisoners during the March revolution in 1917.

During the Civil War Stalin participated in the successful defense of the city of Tsaritsin on the Volga against the White forces. Later its name was changed to Stalingrad, in tribute to Stalin's mythical military genius. Before the Russian Revolution, Stalin had met Lenin in Vienna and Lenin was impressed with the study of nationalities that Stalin was making. Later on Lenin appointed him Commissar of Nationalities, and as Stalin himself was a member of one of the smaller nationalities, he was careful to see that their rights were safeguarded. In 1922, he was elected Secretary General of the Communist party and he held that position until his death.

After the death of Lenin (1924), Stalin and Trotsky were rivals for leadership in the U.S.S.R. Lenin preferred Trotsky over Stalin, saying that Stalin was selfish and unreliable.

Stalin's leadership was bitterly opposed by Trotsky, then War Commissar, and a group of "Old Bolsheviks." Trotsky and his supporters clung to the policy of spreading Communism throughout the world, a policy which Stalin rejected temporarily at least. Stalin proposed to concentrate on the socialization of industry and agriculture and the development of the natural resources of Russia.

Trotsky and his followers continued their opposition to NEP; Stalin and his supporters favored it for the time being. A terrific struggle for power ensued. In 1925, Stalin ousted Trotsky from his position as War Commissar and gradually drove his supporters from office. Trotsky was exiled in 1929 and assassinated (1940) in Mexico City.

In the meantime, Stalin carried out a systematic and terroristic purge of his opponents. Between 1934 and 1938 four great purges wiped out his opposition. Thousands of officials and several prominent generals were given the semblance of trials for treason, found "guilty," and either executed or imprisoned. Some confessed, but their "confessions" in most cases were incredible, and had evidently been forced from them.

From 1924 until his death in March, 1953, Stalin was the acknowledged dictator of the Soviet Union. In physical appearance he was short and stocky with a large head and bushy hair. His enormous power as a dictator was based on a great capacity for work, ruthless extermination of opposition to him through his control over the machinery of government, and a huge outpouring of propaganda.

Upon Stalin's death (March 5, 1953) he was succeeded as Chairman of the Council of Ministers by Giorgi Malenkov, who was at one time Stalin's personal secretary. Malenkov was born in 1902 of middle-class parents. His education was interrupted by the Civil War, in which he participated as a political commissar. From 1922 to 1925 he studied at an engineering school in Moscow. Malenkov joined the Communist party in 1920 and finally rose to be its Secretary. During the Second World War this ruthless man was a member of a committee directing the war and in 1946 was made a member of the Politburo.

Russia carried out the Five-Year Plans. In 1921 Lenin appointed a State Planning Commission (Gosplan) to draw up a Five-Year Plan. Stalin, who had supported NEP as a temporary measure, put the Five-Year Plan (1929-1933), drawn up by the Planning Commission, into operation. Its purpose was to end NEP and make Russia controlled by and for the Communist bureaucracy. The plan contained many proposals for reform including a greater and more rapid development of state-owned heavy industries, electric power plants, and collective farming.

To put the Five-Year Plan into effect, great difficulties had to be overcome. Russian money was worthless in foreign countries. Yet materials and machinery had to be bought in them and competent engineers and successful managers of industrial plants in foreign countries had to be hired at high salaries and brought to Russia. These had to be paid for by the export of goods, chiefly foodstuffs, at a time when foodstuffs were not sufficient to satisfy home needs. Many peasants, especially the *kulaks,* who, with their families numbered about 10,000,000, resisted the formation of collective farms and the seizure of their grain. Their lands were seized, many were killed, and great numbers banished to forced labor in distant regions. While the Five-Year Plan was being put into effect, a serious drought (1931-1932) decreased crop production and as a result nearly 3,000,000 people died of starvation, many of them on farms. The use of unskilled and even forced labor lessened the output of factory goods and slowed down transportation.

In spite of all these difficulties and others, Stalin continued to carry out the Five-Year Plan. In 1928, 3 per cent of the peasants lived on collective farms, but in 1934 the number nad risen to 75 per cent. The government hired engineers from foreign countries and built steel mills, automobile, tractor, and airplane factories. Many great cities grew up around the mills and factories, notably Stalingrad. Industries were established in those parts of Siberia which were rich in raw materials. A huge dam on the Dnepr River provided abundant electric power to the industries in the surrounding region. More trains were operated on old railroads, new railroads were built, and river transportation more highly developed. Government-owned factories doubled the output of tools and machines. At the same time the government put into effect a program for free and compulsory education. Its chief purpose was to wipe out illiteracy and also to indoctrinate the young with Communist views. On the whole the First Five-Year Plan was a success though it was carried out at a terrible cost in human lives and liberty and in a lower standard of living, because the plan emphasized the production of tools and machines rather than goods used by the people.

The Second Five-Year Plan (1933-1938) continued the work already begun under the First Five-Year Plan and called for an increased production of consumer goods to raise the standard of living. At the end of the Second Five-Year Plan, (1) industry was almost entirely socialized, (2) 93 per cent of the peasants lived on collective farms, (3) the standard of living had improved greatly, and (4) 33,000,000 children were enrolled in the elementary and secondary schools and 1,000,000 in higher institutions of learning.

A Third Five-Year Plan, begun in 1938, laid still more emphasis on raising the standard of living. It was interrupted the next year by the outbreak of the Second World War. Then the necessity of defending their homeland compelled the Russians to shift to a great extent from the Third Five-Year Plan and to concentrate on the production of arms and implements of war.

Preparation for war had been one of the motives underlying the Five-Year Plans from the beginning. Stalin had gained control over the armed forces after his expulsion of Trotsky. He then placed officers loyal to him in all the important positions. By means of the Five-Year Plans Stalin planned to modernize and mechanize the armed forces. During the Second Five-Year Plan the budget of the armed forces was increased about twenty times over that in 1932. Moreover the size of the standing army was constantly increased during the 1930's. The industrialization under the Five-Year Plans greatly aided the Red Army for the task that it was soon to face in World War Two.

Before the older industrial cities of Western Russia were overrun by the Germans much of the machinery in their factories was transported eastward to the factories in new cities that had been built and to others that were being built east of the Urals. But even so Stalin said at a banquet in Teheran attended by Roosevelt, Churchill, and other dignitaries of the United Nations that without American production the war would have been lost.

The Soviet Union is governed under a constitution adopted in 1936. The first constitution of the U.S.S.R. was in effect from 1923 to 1936 when it was succeeded by a new constitution written by a commission headed by Stalin. It was, of course, adopted by the All-Union Congress of Soviets at the very time when Stalin was engaged in purging the opposition to him in the Communist party. Because Stalin is said to have written many parts of the constitution himself, this document is frequently called "Stalin's Constitution."

The official name of Russia is The Union of Soviet Socialist Republics. One article in the constitution states that the Soviet Union is a federal union. Today this union is composed of sixteen Union Republics in somewhat the same way that the United States is composed of forty-eight states. The word Soviet means council; it is used in the official name of Russia because much of the work of the government, both in the central government of the Soviet Union and in the sixteen Union Republics, is done by Soviets.

Article 1 of the constitution says that "The Union of Soviet Socialist Republics is a so

THE GOVERNMENT OF
THE SOVIET UNION

THE ORGANIZATION OF
THE COMMUNIST PARTY

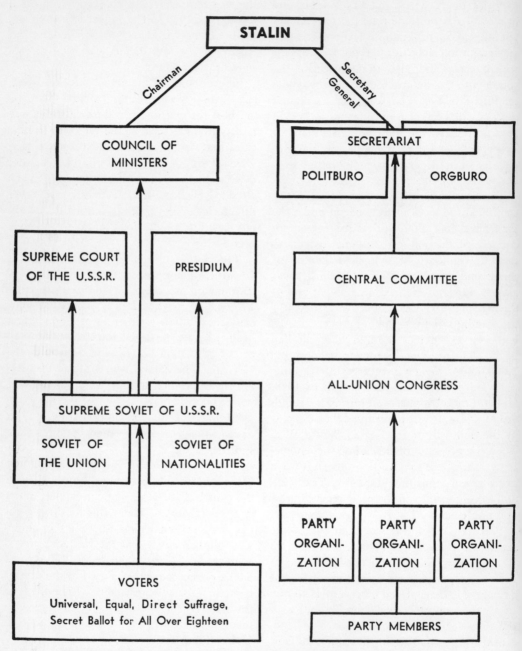

STALIN

Chairman

Secretary General

COUNCIL OF
MINISTERS

SECRETARIAT

POLITBURO   ORGBURO

SUPREME COURT
OF THE U.S.S.R.

PRESIDIUM

CENTRAL COMMITTEE

ALL-UNION CONGRESS

SUPREME SOVIET OF U.S.S.R.

SOVIET OF
THE UNION

SOVIET OF
NATIONALITIES

PARTY
ORGANI-
ZATION

PARTY
ORGANI-
ZATION

PARTY
ORGANI-
ZATION

VOTERS

Universal, Equal, Direct Suffrage,
Secret Ballot for All Over Eighteen

PARTY MEMBERS

CHART OF THE GOVERNMENT OF THE SOVIET UNION UNDER STALIN.

cialist state of workers and peasants." It is socialist because the chief means of producing wealth are "owned" by the people, and the government is to manage all of them for the benefit, in theory, of all the people. The accompanying diagram pictures the Soviet government as it was under Stalin. Recent changes have eliminated the Secretary-General, the Politburo, and the Orgburo, as explained later.

The Supreme Soviet of the U.S.S.R. has two chambers. Under the constitution (1936) the voters elect the Supreme Soviet. Under the first constitution men who had been aristocrats, priests, businessmen, and employers of labor under the Tsar's regime were not permitted to vote. Under the constitution of 1936 all men and women over eighteen years of age, excepting criminals and mentally deficient, are qualified to vote by secret ballot for candidates for the Supreme Soviet. All candidates for the Supreme Soviet are nominated by the Communist party. It is the only party permitted and usually nominates but one candidate for an elective office.

The Supreme Soviet consists of two houses: *The Soviet of the Union* and *The Soviet of Nationalities.* Together they contain nearly 1300 members elected for a term of four years. Thus the Supreme Soviet is more than twice as large as the Congress of the United States. *The Soviet of the Union* is composed of more than 650 members chosen from electoral districts on the basis of one member for every 300,000 people. *The Soviet of Nationalities* consists of about 650 members. Each, of the sixteen republics has the same number of representatives in the Soviet of Nationalities, and each member represents one district. Each Union Republic has twenty-five representatives and the remaining representatives (about 300) are allotted to regional districts and nationality groups. Just as the Senate of the United States was designed to protect the rights of individual states, so the Soviet of Nationalities was designed to protect the rights and interests of the many nationalities of the Soviet Union—on paper, at any rate.

In actual practice the Supreme Soviet is in direct contrast to the democratic legislative bodies of the United States and Great Britain. A member of the Supreme Soviet is hand-picked by the Communist party, the only party permitted to exist. He is not responsible to the voters at all. He votes as he is told to vote by his Communist chieftain. No dissent or freedom of action is tolerated. As the Supreme Soviet meets for only a few days twice a year, there is not time enough for free debate even if it was permitted. Measures approved by the Central Committee of the Communist party are introduced by a member of the Council of Ministers, also hand-picked. A few approved speeches are made and the bill is passed by a unanimous vote. This is dictatorship with only a mock-show of democracy.

The Presidium and the Council of Ministers possess executive powers. The Presidium consists of thirty-three members elected by a joint session of the two houses of the Supreme Soviet. The Presidium is accountable only in theory to the Supreme Soviet as its membership is dictated by the leadership of the Communist party. Actually the powers of these thirty-three men are greater than those of the Supreme Soviet because they have the authority to interpret laws and to issue decrees.

The Presidium possesses extensive executive powers. The chairman of the Presidium is sometimes called the president of the Soviet Union because certain of his duties are much like those of our president, such as receiving foreign diplomats and distinguished visitors, but the Soviet Union really does not have a president. The Presidium can convene and also dissolve a session of the Supreme Soviet, declare war (if the Supreme Soviet is not in session), mobilize the armed forces, appoint their commanders, award decorations, ratify treaties, and perform many other executive functions. Three examples illustrate its power: it declared war on Germany when Russia was attacked in 1941; it created a State Defense Committee with Stalin as chairman to conduct the war; and in 1945 it made the Soviet Union a member of the United Nations by ratifying the United Nations Charter.

The highest executive agency of the Soviet Union is the Council of Ministers. Like the Presidium, the choice of its membership is dictated by the leadership of the Communist party. Like the Presidium also, it is accountable only in theory to the Supreme Soviet. The Council of Ministers is not really responsible to the legislative branch as are the cabinets of France and Great Britain, where an adverse vote of the legislature overthrows a cabinet.

Each member of the Council of Ministers is the head of an important government department just as a member of the President's Cabinet in the United States is secretary or head of a department. Thus there is a Minister of Defense, of Foreign Affairs, of the Coal Industry, of Railways, and others. The members of the Council of Ministers have other duties which they perform as a body. Acting together they co-ordinate the work of the various departments, supervise economic planning, make plans for the defense of their homeland, and initiate, direct, and carry out foreign policy.

The members of the soviet of each republic, each national unit, each region, each district, each city, and each village are elected by the voters living in them. A Council of Ministers directs the governmental activities in each republic.

The Supreme Court of the U.S.S.R. is the highest court in the Soviet Union. Its members are chosen by the Supreme Soviet for a term of five years. It can give advisory opinions on the meaning of laws, but cannot declare a law unconstitutional as the Supreme Court of the United States can. It hears cases appealed from the courts of the republics and tries cases involving officials of the central government of the Soviet Union. Each republic and each region has its court whose judges are likewise elected for five-year terms. Three fourths of all cases at law are tried in the People's Courts, the lowest courts in the Soviet system. A People's Court consists of a judge and two citizen associates; all three are elected for a term of three years by the voters within the jurisdiction of the court. Each citizen associate has the same power as a judge in deciding cases. There are no juries in Soviet courts; trials are not necessarily public; and the secret police have almost unlimited power of arrest, examination, and imprisonment.

The Communist party controls the government of the Soviet Union. The Constitution of 1936 states that the Communist party is "the vanguard of the working people in their struggle to strengthen and develop the socialist system." It is the only political party permitted throughout the U.S.S.R. It is most unusual for a candidate not approved by the party to be elected to office. The Communist party is at the helm of the Russian ship of state, setting and steering the course. The Central Committee of the party captains the ship of state; the other officers and members of the crew are all members of the Communist party.

It is not easy to become a member of the Communist party, and to remain a member and in good standing a Communist has to work hard. To gain membership, an applicant has to pass a year's course of instruction in the theories, practices, and history

Sovfoto

RED SQUARE AND LENIN MAUSOLEUM IN MOSCOW. At the end of the square is the Cathedral of St. Basil, to the right is one of the towers of the Kremlin Wall, part of which can be seen. In the foreground, right, is the mausoleum where the body of Lenin is on view in a glass case. From the roof of Lenin's tomb the leaders of the Soviet Union review parades.

of the Communist party. A party member thus is forced to spend countless hours after his working day doing party work. Much of this time is spent in adult education courses, which are nothing except hours of boring propaganda. He must be willing to go wherever he is sent and do efficiently whatever task the party assigns to him. Failure to do any of these and failure to set an example of good conduct may result in expulsion from the party. Moreover, a member's achievements and conduct are subject to examination from time to time. As the life of the party member is hard, so the rewards may be great. The highest positions in the government, the best jobs, the best living conditions, greater opportunities for education, and other benefits are given to party members. Partly be-

cause of the demands made of a Communist, the party membership is small. Out of an estimated population of about 200,000,000 only approximately 7,000,000 are party members. Most of these have been educated since 1917. Thus they are the products of Communist education and philosophy.

The Communist party controls the government of the Soviet Union chiefly through the Presidium of the Central Committee of the Communist party. The Politburo and the Orgburo were abolished in 1952. They were replaced by the Presidium, which, since March, 1953, has consisted of ten members and four alternates.

In reality, the Presidium holds the supreme power in the government of the Soviet Union. It determines who shall hold influential positions in the government and decides on policies and programs which the government is to carry out. As Communist parties in other countries take their orders from Moscow, the Presidium is thus also the directing center of world Communism. No records of its proceedings are made public. Probably its members discuss policies, but once a decision on a policy has been reached it must be followed without change and with complete obedience. Automatically the decision of the Presidium of the Communist party of today becomes the Soviet law of tomorrow. Likewise its decisions become the "party line" of Communist parties in other countries, which parrot them throughout the world.

Civil liberty is denied in the Soviet Union. Although the Soviet constitution proclaims equality of all citizens before the law, freedom of speech and press, these civil rights are enjoyed only by those who support the Communist regime. Freedom of speech and press "must be in conformity with the interest of the toilers in order to strengthen the socialist system." This severe limitation actually denies real freedom.

Ever since the Communists seized power, the secret police (Cheka, OGPU, and later NKVD and MVD) have terrorized the Russian people to maintain the power of the Communist party. The Ministry for Internal Affairs, which controls the secret police, has unlimited powers of imprisonment and death over Soviet citizens. It supervises concentration camps and compulsory labor projects to which untold millions of offenders against the Communist regime have been sent.

Freedom of religious worship, though proclaimed, is subject to very severe restrictions. As the Russian Orthodox Church had supported and been supported by the Tsarist regime, its property was seized and made the property of the state. Its clergy and also the clergy of all other religious denominations were denied the right to vote. As the government's suppression of the Orthodox Church did not destroy the people's religious faith, a League of Militant Atheists was organized (1925) to carry on anti-religious propaganda. A law (1929) permitted the formation of religious societies which could lease church buildings from the government, but they could not carry on educational, recreational, or charitable work, all of which are the sole concern of the government.

After the outbreak of the Second World War some of the religious prohibitions were relaxed. Theological seminaries were, and still are, permitted to carry on their work and religious education in the homes is allowed, but organized religious instruction of youth under fifteen is still forbidden. In 1943 a congress of bishops of the Russian Orthodox Church was permitted to reorganize the Holy Synod (a council to govern the Church) and to re-establish the Patriarchate (the office of the head of the Church), but the government promotes, as it always has, antireligious education in the schools.

Perhaps the most unusual and farseeing of the liberties listed in the new constitution of the Soviet Union are those that grant liberties to the many nationalities in the Soviet Union. Stalin himself was a Georgian (a minor nationality) so he was interested personally in seeing that minor nationalities enjoyed cultural freedom—in Soviet style. The Tsarist regime tried to "Russify" all its nationalities, but the Soviet Union has not. They granted all of them the right to take part in the political life of the Union and to enjoy and develop their own cultures. But, no nationality is permitted to exalt its nationalism above that of the Soviet Union and nationalism must be "socialist in content." Severe punishment has been inflicted on members of nationalities who have violated these restrictions, especially on Ukrainians and Jews.

The government of the U.S.S.R. plans the production of all manufactured goods and all agricultural products. A government planning commission (Gosplan) plans the production of goods in each large industry and a Council for each of them sees that the plans for its production are carried out. The chief Minister of this Council is a member of the Council of Ministers. Light or local industries belong to the government of the republics or self-governing regions and are managed in the same way as the large industries.

All managers of industries are appointed by the Ministers and are strictly controlled by them. Wages are set by the government. After an unsatisfactory attempt to establish uniform wages, regardless of ability or quantity of work done, the government established a piece-work system which required a certain amount of work in a given time. It gave bonuses to those who did more than the requirement or to those who devised improvements in methods. Every workman belongs to a trade union. Since wages are set by the government, the unions concern themselves with social insurance, recreational and health facilities, technical and trade education, the publication of trade and factory newspapers, and other activities affecting the welfare of the workers.

Workers receive special premiums and rewards for inventions which become the property of the government. Housing facilities for the workers and nurseries for the children are provided by the government. By hard or skillful work the worker can increase his income and improve his standard of living. The Communists claim the worker has gained security and an economic status much higher than he had in Tsarist Russia, but this claim is seriously questioned today.

Today there are three types of farms in the Soviet Union: (1) collective farms, (2)

Sovfoto

Machines have been used in threshing and other agricultural operations on Ukrainian collective farms for a long time. This threshing crew is at work on a collective farm in the Kiev Region.

state farms, and (3) small farms managed by individual farmers. The most important of the three are the collective farms because they contain about four fifths of all the farming land in the Soviet Union. Lately many small collective farms have been merged to increase the regime's control of the peasants and to get maximum production. The families on a collective farm are members of a co-operative society which, in theory but not in fact, owns the buildings, owns or rents the tractors, combines, and other machinery. The workers on a collective farm are required to work together in the fields, barns, and dairies. Each has to do a certain amount of work called a work day. Energetic and skillful farmers are able to get in as many as 600 such work days in a single year.

After all expenses of a collective farm are paid, including a fixed amount of produce to the government and an agricultural tax paid in cash, the remainder of the farm income and the produce is divided among the workers on the basis of the kind of work each has done and the number of work days he has to his credit. Each family owns its own house and domestic animals, and enjoys the free use of land for a garden. Most, however, are poor by comparison with Western standards.

The spare time of the members of the family may be spent cultivating its garden. However, workers who neglect to work the required minimum number of hours on the collective farm may be deprived of their garden plots and be expelled from the collective.

The government of the U.S.S.R. controls all education and culture. School attendance is compulsory for children from eight to fourteen. After this age a few, primarily the more talented children of parents who have attained a higher social or party position, finish secondary school and go on to institutions of higher learning. Moreover, in 1940 the government began to charge tuition for the last three years of secondary schools and for higher education. This forced many students out of school. One expert states that nineteen out of twenty students have to leave school before the tenth grade. Also, since 1940 about a million youths between fourteen and seventeen have been drafted annually into the State Labor Reserves for service in factory schools for three years and in an industry for four years. This is nothing less than forced labor.

In the first flush of revolution the leaders tried to break completely with the education of the past because they thought it to be capitalistic. In consequence, workers and peasants who were not qualified were admitted to colleges and universities, textbooks were used but little, students were granted a large measure of self-government and allowed to plan their own studies. It was soon discovered, however, that students educated under this system did not obtain a sufficient amount of basic knowledge. As a result, textbooks are used more, lectures are given, required readings are assigned, examinations are given, and marks are recorded.

Political propaganda runs through the whole curriculum. All textbooks are carefully prepared under government supervision to conform to Communist party teachings. Teachers are required to instill in the minds of children a high sense of devotion to Soviet authority. Much time is devoted to teaching Communist doctrines, to pointing out the alleged benefits enjoyed under Soviet rule, and to criticizing capitalist countries. The subject of history is especially distorted to glorify Russia.

Medicine is almost entirely socialized under the direction of the Minister of Health. All physicians are employed by the government and many of them are women. Medical care is free, but a patient may pay for treatment by a particular specialist. Physicians may carry on a private practice in addition to their government work, but income from such practice is heavily taxed.

In the Soviet Union the work of artists— painters, sculptors, musicians, writers—is subject to strict supervision. These artists must not produce any work which would in any way violate the teachings of the Communist party regarding their art. On the contrary, artists must glorify Russia. Their themes must be concerned with teaching "party truths." Freedom of artistic expression simply does not exist under totalitarianism.

Books are printed by publishing houses owned and financed by the government. Newspapers belong to the government, the Communist party, or to trade unions. *Izvestia* (News) is owned by the government and *Pravda* (Truth) by the Communist party. All articles printed in them are censored to see that they contain nothing that could be considered harmful to the Soviet government. Radio and television are owned, directed, and censored by the government.

The government is financed by income from taxation and from other sources. The turnover tax is a tax paid to the Soviet Treasury by all government-owned businesses. It yields about 60 per cent of all income received by the Soviet Treasury. The rate of the turnover tax on any product is a fixed per cent of the selling price of that product. For example, in 1936 the selling price of a kilogram (about 2.2 pounds) of sugar was 4.20 rubles. Of this amount 3.57 rubles were paid to the Soviet Treasury by the government-owned sugar refinery. Thus the rate of the turnover tax on sugar was 85 per cent. The remainder, 0.63 of a ruble, was kept by the management of the sugar refinery to pay the cost of production.

Other sources of government revenue are income and inheritance taxes, social insurance premiums, and proceeds from the sale of government bonds. All banks are state owned, but they pay interest to individual depositors. Foreign trade is conducted entirely by the government of the Soviet Union. Since the Second World War it has made a number of trade agreements with the countries of eastern and northern Europe by which goods are bartered at fixed prices.

The Soviet Union played an important part in world affairs. For some years after the Bolshevik Revolution many nations did not recognize the Soviet Union, partly because it was a Communist government and partly because it had refused to pay the debts the Tsarist government owed to foreigners.

Karl Marx had said, "The proletarians have nothing to lose but their chains; they have the whole world to win. Workingmen of all countries, unite!" Therefore Communism in its beginning was intended to be internationalistic. In London in 1864 Marx founded the International Workingmen's Association, known as the First International, whose aim was the enrollment of workers in socialist parties. It held congresses; but dissension among its members led to its break-down in 1876. The Second International was organized in 1889. It maintained a central office and held congresses until 1914 when the socialist parties, particularly in Germany and France, supported the First World War waged by their respective governments and thereby they abandoned internationalism. In general, the Second International was controlled by moderates who favored the extension of socialism by peaceful means.

In 1919 the Third International (Comintern) was organized by Communists in Moscow. It was devoted to the spread of Communism in other countries by violent means if necessary and eventually most of the Communist parties in other countries joined the Comintern. The Communist parties in these countries (including the United States) got their orders and financial support from the Comintern in Moscow. As a result, many governments considered the Comintern a menace to their internal peace and national safety. The Soviet government maintained it had no direct connection with the Comintern, but the Communist party of the Soviet Union, of which Stalin was Secretary, was the largest and most powerful supporting member of the Comintern. During the Second World War Stalin dissolved the Comintern, perhaps as a temporary strategic move to calm the fears of his allies.

In spite of the activities of the Comintern, the Soviet Union gained the recognition of foreign countries. The German Republic recognized the Soviet Union (1922) and Great Britain did likewise (1924). Other countries followed including the United States (1934). In 1934, the year after Japan and Germany withdrew from the League of Nations, the Soviet Union joined the League and signed non-aggression pacts with most of its neighbors, the last one with Germany (1939).

SUMMARY

The men who got control of the government of Russia by revolution (October, 1917) believed in the communistic theories of Karl Marx. After they had made the peace of Brest-Litovsk with the Central Powers (1918) and become masters of Russia (1921), they put their communistic theories into practice. Soon, however, opposition to these practices was so great that Lenin was forced to depart to some extent from the communistic theory that the government should own and operate all means of the production and distribution of goods. Under the New Economic Policy (NEP), peasants and owners of small businesses were permitted to sell their surplus goods to make money, and small concerns were permitted to manufacture and sell their goods. The government, however, kept the ownership and control of all other means of producing and distributing goods.

Stalin, who succeeded Lenin (1924), considered the New Economic Policy a temporary policy. In 1929 under his direction the Soviet government put the First Five-Year Plan into effect. Under this plan the government built steel mills, automobile, tractor, and airplane factories, electric power plants, and railroads and improved water transportation. To meet the need for more metals, iron and other kinds of mines were opened. The Second Five-Year Plan increased the production of goods which the people needed—clothing, shoes, household furnishings, and many other kinds of goods. Under both plans the government increased the number of collective farms, educated many teachers, and built many schools in which an ever-increasing number of children obtained an elementary education. The outbreak of the Second World War forced the Russians to depart from the Third Five-Year Plan and to concentrate on the production of arms and implements of war.

In 1936 the Russians adopted a new constitution. Under it Russia is a federal union of sixteen republics. A Supreme Soviet composed of two houses elected by universal suffrage is the law-making body. The Presidium and the Council of Ministers execute the laws. The largest number of cases at law are tried in the lowest courts, People's Courts. Trial by jury is unknown in Soviet courts and trials are not necessarily public, but the constitution states that a person accused of a crime has the right to a defense. The control of the government of the Soviet Union is entirely in the hands of the Communist party which consists of about 7,000,000 well-disciplined and hard-working members. Nominations of candidates for offices are entirely in the hands of the Communist party. Seldom is a non-party member nominated and generally only one candidate for an office is nominated. The Presidium is today composed of fourteen members; it directs all the activities of the Communist party.

The Communists have had control of the government of Russia since 1917. By nationalizing all land, all banks, all industries, all public utilities, and all the businesses they have destroyed completely the capitalistic system that once prevailed in Russia. The Communist government has provided more education for the people and claims it has raised their standard of living far above what it was under the Tsars. However, some informed writers believe that if the industrialization begun under the Tsars had continued the Russian people would have a higher standard of living today than they now have under Communism. Nevertheless the might of the Soviet armies stemmed the tide of Nazi aggression in the Second World War. However, Soviet imperialism since the war has aroused fear in the minds of the peoples of the democratic countries.

EVENTS THAT TOOK PLACE AT ABOUT THE SAME TIME
1917

	Abdication of Tsar, March, 1917.
Bolshevik Revolution, October, 1917.	Provisional government, March to October, 1917.
	Treaty of Brest-Litovsk, 1918.
	Comintern founded, 1919.
Civil War, 1918-1921.	New Economic Policy begun, 1921.
	First constitution of the Soviet Union, 1923.
Death of Lenin, 1924.	
	Stalin succeeded Lenin and struggled with Trotsky, 1924-1929.
	First Five-Year Plan, 1928-1933.
Trotsky exiled, 1929.	
Severe famine, 1932-1933.	
	Second Five-Year Plan, 1933-1938.
	United States recognized the Soviet Union, 1934.
	Soviet Union joined League of Nations, 1934.
	Constitution of 1936.
Trotsky assassinated, 1940.	Third Five-Year Plan, 1938.

THREE MAJOR REVOLUTIONISTS. Left to right, Trotsky, Lenin, Kamenev, in the early days of the Soviet Union. Lenin is enshrined as a hero but Trotsky was exiled, Kamenev executed.

NICHOLAS II AND HIS FAMILY. The last official photograph of the Romanoff rulers before their execution by Bolsheviks.

GREGORY RASPUTIN, the illiterate "monk" who was the evil genius of the Romanoffs.

RUSSIAN REVOLUTION, left. Police fire on revolutionists during the street fighting in Moscow, 1917.

LENIN SPEAKS, below. Red banners wave over Petrograd after the Bolshevik victory, as Lenin addresses a hopeful and curious crowd.

MAY DAY IN MOS-
COW. In 1939, with Rus-
sian power a new, un-
known factor in Europe,
tanks and other mecha-
nized forces of the Red
Army paraded through
Red Square, before Len-
in's tomb and under huge
pictures of Lenin and of
Stalin.

HAPPY DICTATOR.
Stalin smiles as he ac-
knowledges applause from
a May Day crowd.

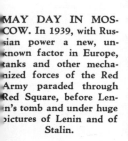

CHAPTER 31

Fascism in Italy and Nazism in Germany

While the Russians were endeavoring to solve their postwar problems through Communism, the Italians led by Mussolini turned to Fascism. After a brief period under a republic the Germans led by Hitler and the Nazi party established the Third Reich. Authoritarianism as expressed in the theory and practices of Fascism and Nazism ended constitutional government in Italy and Germany. In Italy the weak central government was unable to cope with the grave political and social disorders that followed the First World War. The spirit of lawlessness and disunity provided the opportunity for the politically ambitious Mussolini to head a movement that fastened Fascism on Italy. In Germany, the Weimar Republic survived the attacks of the militarists and monarchists, but its weakness provided Hitler with the opportunity to gain control over the government and put into effect the principles of National Socialism.

• • •

Fascism controls completely the lives of individuals. In the confusion and disorder that prevailed in most phases of Italian life in the postwar period the constitutional government was transformed into a dictatorship, a fascist state. The basic idea of Fascism is authoritarianism, which means that the nation has supreme power over the individual. In other words individuals live only to serve the nation as civilians or soldiers, and consequently the leader of a fascist nation must make clear to them what they should do.

Because Fascism requires complete obedience, the nation has to be directed by a leader who possesses dictatorial powers; no opposition or even criticism is allowed. This means the end of civil liberties. All of the older virtues such as mercy and charity and the practice of the Golden Rule, Fascists regard as signs of weakness. In practice a fascist nation is a military nation; its citizens are organized, drilled, and commanded as though an army, and their highest aim is military glory.

Political unrest and social disorders in postwar Italy paved the way for Fascism. After the end of the First World War, Italy entered upon a period of dire economic distress. It had a huge public debt, its money had sunk to one fourth of its pre-war value in other countries, prices rose, and unemployment increased. Low wages and poor working conditions in factories resulted in many strikes in the industrial cities in Northern Italy. In 1920 workers seized and attempted to operate more than 600 factories employing over half a million workers. The workers were unsuccessful in their attempt to run the factories and soon gave them back to their owners; but the seizure of factories had greatly alarmed industrialists. Peasants as well as city workers also resorted to violence. They demanded that the estates of their landlords be divided. Some peasants even killed landlords, burned their houses, and seized their lands. Thus landlords as well as industrialists desired a strong government that could and would protect their lives and property.

The Socialists profited by the economic discontent and the social and political disunity in Italy. In the election of 1919 they won 156 seats in the Chamber of Deputies. The Socialist members hissed the name of the king and cheered the name of Lenin. Some veterans, industrialists, landlords, and all others who feared revolution were willing to support a strong leader. At the same time thousands of soldiers were returning to civilian life and were demanding jobs which they thought should be given them in part payment for their services to their country. The government did nothing for them and, worst of all, little for those soldiers who had been disabled. Many of the soldiers, therefore, came to feel that they had fought in vain and especially so because Italy's demands for territory were not all granted by the Paris Peace Conference.

Amidst this confusion and disorder, political leadership was ineffective and the government's business was poorly administered. There were over twenty parties in the Chamber of Deputies, many of them representing purely local interests.

At this time the Italian fondness for clubs showed itself. There had been clubs in ancient Italy such as those formed to secure Roman citizenship for the Italians and those which Julius Caesar used in his rise to power. Their modern successors were the Carbonari, who fought for Italian freedom after 1815, the criminal Mafia and Black Hand societies, and Mazzini's patriotic Young Italy, which tried to establish an Italian republic in 1848. Some of the clubs which were formed in postwar Italy were Communist. However, atheistic Communism secured little following among Catholic Italians. Other clubs were Socialist. The strongest of the clubs proved to be those made up mostly of young men who wore black shirts and called themselves *fascisti*. They had accepted the ideas of Fascism. The word Fascism seems to have been derived from the Italian word *fascio* which means bank or club. Mussolini called his organization *Fascio de Combattimento*. As its symbol he used the ancient Roman *fasces,* the bundle of rods and ax which was carried by attendants upon the magistrates of Rome as a symbol of their power. Fascist ideas of authority appealed to those who wanted order restored. Fascist glorification of the nation appealed to many patriotic young Italians. The hostility of the Fascists to Communism won them the support of those industrialists and aristocrats who were frightened by the threat of Communism. The religious part of the Fascist program attracted many. They passed a rule, which later became law in all Italy, forbidding swearing in public places. Their methods attracted the adventurous. Fascist leaders organized their followers into private armed bands and sent them out with guns and clubs to fight the members of the Communist and Socialist clubs. Above everything else, their founder, Benito Mussolini, caught the imagination of great numbers of Italians and gained their support.

Mussolini (1883-1945) founded Fascism. His father was a blacksmith and a Socialist and his mother was a school teacher. He attended normal school and became a school teacher. After saving a little money, he went to Switzerland where he attended the Universities of Lausanne and Geneva, working to pay his expenses. He was expelled from Switzerland for his writings in a radical newspaper and later from Austria for the same reason. Returning to Italy he became the editor of *Avanti* (Forward), the official newspaper of the Socialist party. As editor of *Avanti,* Mussolini first opposed Italian entrance into the First World War, but soon he changed his mind and began to advocate intervention. For this he was expelled from the Socialist party.

He then founded a newspaper *Il Popolo d'Italia,* in which he urged Italy to join the Allies. After Italy entered the war (1915), Mussolini fought in the Italian army against the Austrians, was wounded, and honorably discharged from the army. Upon his return to Milan he began to develop his political program in *Il Popolo d'Italia.* In 1919 he organized his first *fascio* in Milan and soon many Fascist clubs were formed in other cities. They adopted the *fasces* as their emblem and gave their founder, Il Duce, the old Roman salute, the outstretched hand.

Mussolini was short and stocky; he had a protruding lower jaw which he liked to jut out to give himself a commanding appearance. He fancied he bore a resemblance to Napoleon and he delighted in Napoleonic poses. He was physically strong and vigorous and made a cult of athletics and physical fitness. He was a skillful actor, adept at making dramatic appearances and swaying crowds by his emotional speeches. He had a knack for pithy statements. To the youth of Italy he said, "Believe! Obey! Fight!" To his Fascist followers he said, "Live dangerously! If I advance, follow me; if I retreat, kill me; if I die, avenge me," and "Better a day like a lion than a hundred years like a sheep."

The Fascists marched on Rome and Mussolini became premier. The Fascist movement, supported by money from people who feared revolution, grew rapidly. Fascists (Black Shirts, because a black shirt was a part of their uniform) openly attacked Socialists, Communists, and organizations of peasants and workingmen. The police and the army, because they contained many Fascist sympathizers, offered no resistance to these attacks.

In October, 1922, at a great Fascist congress in Naples, Mussolini demanded the admission of Fascists to the cabinet. After Premier Facta refused, the Fascists began their armed march on Rome seizing railroads and telegraph lines on the way. Then the king, fearing the Fascists less than he feared civil strife, refused to authorize Facta to use the army against them and the Fascists entered Rome. Facta resigned and the king made Mussolini premier. Mussolini came to Rome from Milan in a sleeping car to accept the office.

Mussolini became dictator of Italy. Gradually Mussolini brought the Italian government under his sway and filled its offices with his Fascist supporters. In November, 1922, parliament granted him dictatorial powers for one year during which he was to restore order and bring about reforms. In 1923 he secured the passage of a law which would give the party which won a majority in an election two thirds of the seats in the Chamber of Deputies. Then he held an election and saw to it that the Fascists won. In 1926 he became "His Excellency the Chevalier President Benito Mussolino, Head of Government, Prime Minister, Secretary of State for Foreign Affairs, for War, for the Navy, and for Aviation." All opposition to these high-handed changes by those who were losing their democratic rights was ruthlessly suppressed. All secret societies were forbidden and their leaders mistreated, some even killed. The outstanding example of this ruthlessness was the murder by Fascists of Matteotti, a Socialist member of the Chamber of Deputies, who had written a book, *The Fascists Exposed.* This brutal deed caused a crisis which Mussolini weathered with some difficulty. It convinced anti-Fascists that it was not safe to combat Fascism openly.

In 1928 a new election law was passed. It reduced the election of members of the Chamber of Deputies to a farce. By this law, the Grand Council of the Fascist party, under the thumb of Mussolini, was to submit to the voters a slate of 400 candidates. The voters

Ewing Galloway

BENITO MUSSOLINI AND FASCIST LEADERS

were to vote "yes" or "no" on the whole slate. No other candidates could run and of course no other party was permitted. Furthermore the right to vote was strictly limited to those owning property or paying fees to certain government organizations. This law reduced the number of voters from nearly 10,000,000 to about 3,000,000. Needless to say the Fascist candidates always won. In 1938 the Grand Council abolished the Chamber of Deputies and replaced it with a Chamber of Fasces and Corporations. The last trace of the old constitutional government of Italy which had been won at such cost had been wiped out.

The Fascists brought the economic life of Italy under their control. To accomplish this, Mussolini organized what he called the Corporate State. Thirteen national corporations were created, one for employers and another for workers in each of the six main divisions of national economic life, and one for the professions. A National Council of Corporations, headed by a cabinet member responsible to Il Duce, supervised these corporations. Each was composed of local unions (syndicates). The syndicate of workers and the syndicate of employers made agreements regarding hours and conditions of work, wages, and prices. Lockouts and strikes were forbidden and any dispute which workers and employers could not settle through their syndicates would be settled by a labor court composed of judges appointed by Il Duce himself. Both labor and capital were brought under the close supervision of the government. Labor lost both its right to form independent unions and to strike. Businessmen were told whom to hire, what and how much to produce, and what profits they were permitted to make. Economic freedom thus disappeared along with political freedom.

International News

ITALY'S BALILLA CELEBRATE TENTH ANNIVERSARY. Members of the motorcycle corps of the Balilla, or youth organization, parade outside the ruins of the Coliseum. To help win the support of youth for Fascism, Mussolini formed this organization which was composed of youngsters between the ages of fourteen and eighteen.

For a time Mussolini met with apparent success. Public order was restored, the budget was balanced, money was stabilized in value, trains ran on time, and production in factories and on farms increased. The unemployed were given jobs on public works including the building of great highways and the excavation of the ruins of imperial Rome. In a vain endeavor to free Italy from dependence on imported coal, the abundant Italian water power was used for the production of electricity. Industries were protected by high tariffs. Shipping companies received large subsidies from the government in an attempt to expand Italian trade, especially throughout the Mediterranean and with the United States. Special rates on Italian ships and railroads were offered to attract foreign tourists because they would spend money in Italy and thus give the Italian government more credit to use abroad.

The most rigorous efforts to make Italy self-sufficient were made in what is called the "Battle of Wheat." To achieve this, marshes were drained, waste land was plowed and sown to crops, and methods of farming were improved. At the same time Mussolini tried to persuade the people to vary their diet and eat less macaroni, that favorite Italian dish which required much wheat. Despite his efforts Mussolini never succeeded in making Italy independent of imports of coal, machinery, and food.

Mussolini indoctrinated the youth of Italy with Fascism. To make Italy a strong nation, Mussolini thought that there should be a more rapid increase in population. He therefore forbade emigration and did all he could to encourage large families. There was some increase in population but not enough to meet his desires. To make the new generation loyal Fascists, Mussolini took charge of education. Textbooks were written which contained propaganda highly favorable to Fascism and were intended to make Fascists out of students. Anti-Fascist teachers and professors were removed and all teaching was carefully supervised by Fascists. Fascist youth organizations of a military nature took the place of the Boy Scouts. Girls belonged to clubs which laid emphasis on housekeeping and the rearing of children.

Mussolini made a Concordat with the Pope. Unlike the Communists in Russia and the Nazis in Germany, Mussolini did not quarrel with the Church. On the contrary, he took steps to bring an end to the long standing dispute between the Papacy and the Italian government which began (1870) with the Italian seizure of Rome. At that time the Pope had declared himself a "prisoner in the Vatican" and forbade Catholics to take part in the Italian government. However, many did take part.

After Mussolini came to power, Pope Pius XI came to believe that if the antagonism between the Papacy and the Italian government could be replaced by a friendly understanding between himself and the Fascist government, Italy would benefit. Consequently, the Pope and Mussolini signed a concordat (1929) called the Lateran Accord in which Vatican City, consisting of 108 acres around the Vatican and St. Peter's Church, was established as an independent nation. The powers of the Pope as the ruler of Vatican City included the power to send and to receive ambassadors, coin money, issue postage stamps, and maintain a radio station. The Italian government paid $100,000,000 to the Papacy for the Papal states confiscated during the unification of Italy. Mussolini recognized the Catholic Church as the state church and the teaching of the Catholic religion was made compulsory in all schools.

Loss of freedom was the price Italians paid for Mussolini's rule. Travelers in Italy (1930) who saw the surface improvements which Fascism had brought about sometimes talked about how much good Mussolini had done. This was a superficial view for it did not include the price the Italians had paid for these improvements. This price was the loss of freedom in their lives and businesses. All publications were strictly censored. Freedom of teaching and of speech disappeared. Correspondents of foreign newspapers who criticized Mussolini or his party were expelled from Italy. It was not safe for even a tourist to mention Mussolini's name in public. Employers, workers, and farmers were strictly regulated. Wages of city workers were low, employer's profits were set by the government, and heavy taxation absorbed much of them. The standard of living of most Italians had been lowered with the exception of favored Fascists and wealthy aristocrats. Life had become a serious matter for the once gay and pleasure-loving Italians.

Economic conditions grew steadily worse during the world economic d e p r e s s i o n. Italian foreign trade fell off and the national debt grew larger. The number of unemployed increased. As they had to be cared for at public expense, taxes were increased still more. The competition of large numbers of unemployed for available jobs caused wages to go down; the work day was made longer. Consequently, the workers made hardly enough to live on. As early as 1928, a former prime minister of Italy predicted what would happen when a dictator got his ship of state on the rocks. He wrote, "Several centuries before Christ, Plato, the greatest of

Greek philosophers, wrote that dictatorship always ended in war, saying that when the dictator himself lost he made war. There is no example in modern history of a dictatorship that has not ended in war, revolution, or both."

Imperialism caused Mussolini's downfall. To take the minds of the people from their desperate plight, Mussolini launched them on a campaign of imperialism which brought about his own downfall and the ruin of Italy. Mussolini held aloft "the grandeur that was Rome" before the eyes of the Italians to awaken dreams of a new Roman Empire. He called the Mediterranean, *mare nostrum,* our sea. In 1927 he established a protectorate over Albania on the eastern shore of the Adriatic and (1939) he sent his army to Albania and annexed it to Italy. His armies conquered Ethiopia in 1935 in defiance of the League of Nations. He interfered constantly in the affairs of Greece. He sent Italian troops (1936) to the aid of Franco in his struggle to become dictator of Spain. He encouraged his followers to claim Tunis and Algeria, French possessions in Africa. Finally he and Hitler formed the Rome-Berlin Axis and later on he took Italy into the Second World War on the side of Germany (1940).

His armies were defeated in Greece and in North Africa and had to be aided by German troops sent by Hitler. His aircraft and navy were unable to break British control in the Mediterranean. He followed Japan and Germany into war against the United States (1941) and two years later he saw his country invaded by American and British troops. In 1944 he was forced out of office by vote of his own Grand Council. A fugitive, he was shot by Italian partisans near Milan on April 28, 1945. His Fascist state had proved a complete failure. The forces of democracy, which he had despised and condemned, overran Italy, and his own country-men assassinated him for the wrong he had done his own country.

The Germans established a republic under great difficulties. In 1914 most Social Democrats had joined with all other Germans, except a few Socialists who held fast to socialist principles, in supporting the war. In the summer of 1918 after the Social Democratic party became convinced that Germany had lost the war, it demanded the ousting of the Kaiser because President Wilson had said that was the first condition on which peace could be negotiated. At first the Kaiser refused to abdicate. However, the German General Staff decided that the war was lost and that the remaining German strength should be conserved for the next war. Disorders broke out in Germany, particularly revolts of sailors in Kiel and Hamburg. Then the Kaiser yielded. On November 10, 1918 he fled in despair from Germany, took refuge in neutral Holland, and on November 28 he abdicated. He lived in ease and comfort on an estate in Doorn, until his death during the Second World War. Uprisings of the people in the German states caused their kings, princes, and dukes to renounce their titles and privileges.

From November, 1918 until February, 1919, Germany was ruled by a Council of People's Commissars headed by Friedrich Ebert, a Social Democrat. The chief enemies of the new republic were from the extreme left, the German Communists. Karl Liebknecht, their leader, called himself *Spartacus* after the gladiator who had tried to free the slaves in Southern Italy. He and his chief assistant, Rosa Luxembourg, hoped to establish a German Communist state modeled on that of Russia. In the last of many Communist uprisings (January, 1919) Liebknecht attempted to seize control of the central government in Berlin. He failed to gain enough popular support to overthrow the provisional government and establish a Communist government; both he and Rosa Luxembourg were arrested and on their way to prison they were killed. After their deaths the Communists did not make any more attempts to gain control of the government.

While the Council of People's Commissars was in power it made provisions for the election of members to a constitutional assembly. At this election all adult men and women could vote. In February, 1919, the constitutional assembly met at Weimar in Saxony. It drew up a constitution and elected Ebert president.

The Weimar constitution determined the form of government of the new German Republic. It provided for the election of a president by popular vote for a term of seven years. Like the president of France, he was not to have much power except in a time of emergency, when he could set aside the constitution and rule by decree. The legislative branch of the government was to consist of two houses, the Reichsrat and the Reichstag. The members of the Reichsrat were to be appointed by the heads of the new German states. The members of the Reichstag were to be elected by German men and women over twenty years of age. The number of members of each political party in the Reichstag was to be in proportion to the per cent of the total vote that it received. The President was to appoint the Chancellor who in turn was to choose the cabinet, all of whom were to be responsible directly to the Reichstag. The German Republic was to be a federation of all the German states. It was to have charge of foreign affairs, national defense, finance, all railway, river, and ocean transportation, and all social legislation. Church and private schools were to be abolished and all schools placed under government control.' The constitution contained also a bill of rights guaranteeing the people personal liberty, freedom of speech, press, and religion. Constitutions guaranteeing these rights were also adopted by the new German states.

The German Republic struggled to maintain public order. Throughout the life of the republic it met with the determined opposition of the extreme right which was composed of monarchists and all others who were opposed to a republic. They accused the leaders of the republic of having betrayed the nation in the last days of the war and therefore of having been a cause of German defeat. The German people as a whole never accepted the fact that they had lost the war because they said their armies had not been defeated in battle. The leaders of the republic were accused of having ruined Germany by signing the Versailles Treaty which most German people resented. The majority of the German people seemed to have preferred monarchy and a militaristic program for the German nation. Later events led many people to conclude that the majority of the German people never respected or supported the republican leadership.

Soon the extreme nationalists and monarchists made attempts to overthrow the government. They were led by army officers and supported by bands of veterans of the First World War who joined either one or the other of two organizations, Steel Helmets and Free Corps. They murdered two able republicans, Erzberger and Rathenau. They tried twice by an uprising (*putsch*) to seize power. The first was led by Kapp in Berlin (1920), and the second by General Ludendorff in Munich in 1923. The latter was the celebrated "beer hall putsch" in which Adolf Hitler took a leading part. Both failed because army leaders were not yet ready to support the overthrow of the republic. However, (1925) these leaders indicated their future policy by supporting the royalist Field Marshal Hindenburg for president.

Inflation in Germany wiped out all debts and savings. To carry on the First World War, the government sold great quantities of bonds to Germans and at the same time printed a great deal of paper money. After the peace treaty had been signed, the government owed a large sum of money for reparations. In January, 1923, after the Germans claimed that they were unable to make full reparations payments, the French seized the Ruhr. Instead of meeting the country's financial difficulties by higher taxes and control of prices, the government printed more and more paper money. The faster this money was printed, the less the mark (the unit of currency) was worth.

In prewar times the mark was worth about twenty-four cents in American money. An American professor in Germany in the summer of 1922 found that the retail price of a hat was 600 marks or $1.50 when an American dollar was worth 400 marks. The next day he bought the same hat for $.75, because that day a dollar was worth 800 marks. Germans who had paper money rushed to buy goods and real estate or exchanged their money for the money of foreign countries. In the summer of 1923 a United States dollar was worth 1,000,000 marks and the decline of the mark still continued. When this inflation was at its height, a week's wages would not buy a loaf of bread the day after the wages were received. German money was wholly worthless, but the German government and great industrial and commercial corporations paid off their bonds with this worthless money. Those Germans who owned real property or foreign investments were in good shape. People living on fixed salaries or on fixed incomes from rents and investments in bonds were ruined. Savings in banks were wiped out and millions of Germans were impoverished. Foreign investors in German bonds lost the money they had invested.

In 1923 the government took action to provide Germany with a sound currency. New marks (Rentenmarks) were printed and the security for these new marks was a government mortgage on land and industry in Germany. The old marks were redeemed with the new money at the rate of one trillion marks for one Rentenmark, worth about twenty-four cents in American money. In 1924 the government replaced Rentenmarks by Reichsmarks secured by $200,000,000 in gold borrowed abroad, much of it in the United States. At the same time the government tried to make its income balance its expenses by increasing taxes and cutting government spending. Hjalmar Schacht was the financial leader who re-established German credit at home and abroad.

After the Reichsmark had been issued, German business and industry revived. The owners of German industries organized large trusts (cartels) to control the quantity and the price of goods and to monopolize the markets where they were to be sold. Industries whose goods were produced in large quantities, particularly the coal and steel industries in the Ruhr and the great chemical works, became very active. The increase in production in German industries helped to restore prosperity to the railroads.

The German Republic entered into friendly relations with its neighbors. From 1925 to 1929 Germany's relations with other countries improved under the guidance of its foreign minister, Gustave Stresemann. It recognized Soviet Russia (1922) and the two countries began trade relations. In 1925 the French withdrew from the Ruhr, and Germany for about six years made its reparations payments regularly. In 1925 the Locarno Pact was signed by Germany, France, Great Britain, Italy, and Belgium. The

Treaty of Versailles had defined the boundary between Germany and France and also the boundary between Germany and Belgium. The nations that signed the Locarno Pact promised to respect these boundaries. The same powers, which included Germany, also agreed that all German territory west of a line drawn about fifty miles east of the Rhine should not be fortified. In 1926 the Allied governments began to withdraw their troops from Germany. In the same year Germany was admitted to the League of Nations. Germany signed arbitration and non-aggression treaties with a number of its neighbors, and also with other nations who had signed the Paris Peace Pact which renounced war as an instrument of national policy except in case of self-defense.

German military leaders planned for the next war. Secretly, under the leadership of General von Seeckt, German military leaders went to work as soon as the First World War was over. A military commission examined the ways in which the war had been conducted to discover what mistakes Germany had made. German scientists were making and testing new weapons of war and designing new types of aircraft and submarines. German diplomatic agents were reporting on the preparations other nations were making for war. Men were being trained to be soldiers in spite of the provisions of the Treaty of Versailles which limited the size of the German army to 100,000 men. German military leaders were preparing for a new war.

Hitler (1889-1945) became the leader of the National Socialist Party. Meanwhile Adolf Hitler was developing and expanding the National Socialist (Nazi) party. It was called national because its leaders said it would defend the national interests of Germany against outside powers and socialist because it would place the interests of the

poor above the interests of the rich. Hitler was born April 20, 1889 in Austria. A social misfit as a boy, he studied art but he failed as an artist and became a house painter. He grew up with a fierce hatred of socialists and Jews whom he blamed for his own lot in life. In 1912 he migrated from Vienna to Munich and there he enlisted (1914) in the German army. He became a corporal, was wounded and gassed, and was awarded the Iron Cross, a medal of honor in the German army. His admiration for everything German was unlimited. He had a contempt for the masses of the people and hated everything liberal and democratic, indeed everything which in his opinion did not or could not contribute to the greatness of Germany.

After the war he joined a few other men who were dissatisfied with the conditions in Germany and who had founded the National Socialist party. After gaining the support of powerful leaders, including General Ludendorff, he took a leading part in the Munich beer hall putsch (1923) which was a complete failure. For his part in this revolt Hitler was sentenced to five years in prison, but within less than a year he was released. While in prison he wrote *Mein Kampf* (My Struggle), the "Bible" of all Nazis. It became the platform of the Nazi party. The theories in *Mein Kampf,* later elaborated by Nazi leaders, include these points: (1) the Germans have been since remote antiquity, by virtue of their Blood and Soil, a *Herrenvolk* (Master Race); (2) the Communists and the Jews are the chief internal enemies of Germany because they caused her to lose the First World War; (3) France is Germany's eternal enemy and must be crushed; (4) Russia and Russian Communism are the immediate enemy; (5) democracy is weak; the masses are incompetent, easily led by propagandists and must be controlled by a dictatorial government; (6) the individual exists only to serve the nation; he must subordinate himself to it completely and he must find his greatest joy in its service; (7) not only democracy, but also all the Christian virtues must be stamped out as un-German weaknesses; (8) the German nation must be supreme in the world.

The Nazis talked of three German empires. The first was the Holy Roman Empire of the Middle Ages. The second was the empire of the Hohenzollerns. The third, called the Third Reich, was to be the empire created by Hitler and his Nazi followers and in their opinion it was destined to be much greater than either of the other two. The Third Reich, needing *lebensraum* (living space), would seek it throughout the world, but especially in the Ukraine, a rich agricultural land in Western Russia. The Fatherland must awake, throw off its chains, and expand. The program of propaganda, war, and expansion laid down in *Mein Kampf* was followed by Hitler after he became Chancellor of Germany. It was most unfortunate for the world that this book was not read more widely and, when read, better understood and taken seriously by statesmen in other countries.

Hitler toiled (1925-1933) to increase the number of his Nazi followers. The swastika (hooked cross) was adopted as the party emblem. Party meetings were held with tremendous fanfare at which Hitler delivered fiery and emotional orations amid the display of many banners. Armed bands of Brown Shirts *(SA)* and storm troopers publicly attacked Jews and Communists on the streets. Elite Body Guards *(SS)* protected Nazi leaders wherever they went in Germany. The Republic, faithful to its democratic principles, did not suppress these acts of violence.

In addition to the use of propaganda and physical violence, Adolf Hitler was helped to become Chancellor by (1) the world economic depression, and (2) the German political system. The depression brought great hardship to Germany as it did to all other countries. Banks failed, factories shut down, businesses went bankrupt, farmers lost markets for their crops, and workers lost their jobs. By 1932, 6,000,000 Germans were unemployed. Both the Nazi and the Communist parties gained additional supporters from the discontented and suffering.

Germany, unlike the United States and Great Britain, had several political parties. Because of this, no one party ever had a majority in the Reichstag. As a result, a party leader who wanted to become Chancellor had to form a coalition of parties as did the premier in France. When the Chancellor lost the support of some members of his coalition, it was broken up and he was forced to form a new one or step aside and give another party leader a chance to form a new coalition. In 1930 the Chancellor was Dr. Heinrich Bruening, the leader of the Center (Catholic) party, who headed a coalition of moderates loyal to the Republic. In 1932 Bruening resigned because he was unable to get the co-operation of the Reichstag and President von Hindenburg for measures dealing with Germany's depression. He was followed by Franz von Papen, a conservative and a member of the Center Party. In an election (July, 1932) for members of the Reichstag the Nazis secured 230 seats and the Communists eighty-nine. The Nazi party was now the largest in the Reichstag, but it did not have a majority.

At this juncture a place in the cabinet was offered Hitler, but he refused it because he was not offered the Chancellorship. He wanted "all or nothing." He was determined to rule or ruin. Government in Germany was at a standstill. Von Papen and his successor, von Schleicher, were utterly unable to do anything in the face of Nazi and Communist opposition. Finally on January 30, 1933, Hindenburg, who had been re-elected president, appointed Adolf Hitler Chancellor of Germany. Hitler was the leader of the largest party in the Reichstag, but even now the Nazis still did not have a majority. In the hope of securing a majority in the Reichstag it was dissolved and a new election held.

Hitler gained control of the German government. A fiery and violent campaign followed. The Nazis denounced the Socialists and Communists, condemned the Treaty of Versailles, and promised to create a more powerful and greater Germany in which all would have jobs. A few days before the voting was to take place, the Reichstag building was gutted by fire. The Nazis charged that the Communists had set the fire, but we now know that the Nazis themselves set it for the purpose of winning votes in the election by blaming the fire on the Communists. This charge, the prevention and breaking-up of Communist meetings, and the arrest of Communist leaders were effective in helping the Nazis win the election. The Nazis and the Nationalists together won a majority of the seats in the Reichstag which soon granted Hitler dictatorial powers for four years. The Nationalist party then dissolved itself and merged with the Nazis. After the Reichstag outlawed the other political parties, there remained only one party and one leader. On March 12, 1933, the black, red, and gold flag of the Republic was replaced by the black, white, and red flag of the German Empire with a swastika, emblem of National Socialism, in its center. On April 1, Hitler's Reichstag, by voting dictatorial powers to him, established the Third German Empire (Third Reich) which Hitler proclaimed would last for more than a thousand years. The overwhelming majority of German people rallied around their new leader, *Der Fuehrer,* and committed themselves without reserve to Nazism.

Many factors contributed to Hitler's victory. Most Germans took pride in the firm belief that they belonged to a master race. The workers in the industries, many of whom had been Socialists, were won over by the socialist principles in National Socialism because it promised them jobs. The middle class, depressed by defeat in the war and the loss of their wealth by inflation, thought they saw in Hitler's Third Reich an opportunity to secure greater national glory for Germany and also to regain their lost wealth. Many young men and women, even university graduates, were unable to get jobs because of the depression. After Hitler promised that he would provide jobs, they eagerly turned to him. A university student, who by hard study and competitive examinations had won a scholarship that was to pay his expenses for three years at a university, remarked in 1922 in the midst of the inflation that if he had all his scholarship money in his hand he could not pay his living expenses for one day. Such a student was an easy prey in the future for Hitler's propaganda.

Hitler's idea of a master race was not a new idea in German history. From the seventeenth century, German leaders had taught the Germans that they should submit willingly to authority, that their government would take care of them, and that military service should be their highest glory. They had been told for generations that the Germans were superior to other peoples. The historian Treitschke, a professor at the University of Berlin (1874-1896) wrote "Our age is the age of iron; and if the strong vanquish the weak, it is the law of life." A Nazi historian wrote a book in which he endeavored to prove that the ancient Germans were superior to the Romans when the Roman Empire was at its height.

Hitler's Master Race theory was but a simplification and an exaggeration of the teachings of German university professors. These professors had taught that the great civilizations of history had been created by the Indo-European peoples whom they called Indo-Germans, or Aryans. The Germans, the professors said, were the purest of these Indo-Germans, and as such it was the duty of the German people to rule the world.

Hitler gained complete mastery over Germany. He was not a German but an Austrian; not an officer in the German army in the First World War, but a corporal. Of medium height and not impressive in appearance, he was nevertheless an orator able to sway great crowds of his ardent supporters. He influenced very many Germans to become loyal followers, even many who were intelligent and well-educated. The German victories in the beginning of the Second World War made him appear to be a military genius who had a remarkable sense of timing. His later mistakes and defeats destroyed his reputation as a military leader.

Some of Hitler's successes were due to the ability of his chief lieutenants. The most important of these were Himmler, Goebbels, and Goering. Heinrich Himmler, a country school teacher, became head of the *SS* during the rise of Hitler and of the Gestapo after Hitler became *Der Fuehrer*. As the merciless and brutally ruthless head of the Gestapo he was the most feared and hated man in Germany. Goebbels, of peasant stock and club-footed, was a graduate of the University of Heidelberg. Hitler made him Minister of Popular Enlightenment and Propaganda. Goering was an army officer, orator, and air ace of the First World War. He liked to strut proudly in public in one or the other of his many uniforms bedecked with medals. When the Nazis conquered other countries, he took objects of art in great numbers from their owners. Hitler made him head of the reborn German air force (*Luftwaffe*). Hitler's chief lieutenant, Hess, was moody and self-effacing. Rosenberg was the so-called

philosopher of the Nazi movement. Ley was Minister of Labor and Streicher was editor of *Der Stürmer* and chief Jew-baiter.

All of these men were entirely lacking in that honor which would cause them to keep their word. In addition to this lack of honor, they possessed a supreme and cynical contempt even for the great masses of Germans. Hitler himself gave expression to this lack of honor when he said:

> I am willing to sign anything. I will do anything to facilitate the success of my policy. I am prepared to guarantee all frontiers and to make non-aggression pacts and friendly alliances with anybody. . . . Why should I not make an agreement in good faith today and unhesitatingly break it tomorrow if the future of the German people demands it?

He expressed his attitude toward the common people when in *Mein Kampf* he wrote:

> The power which put in motion the great religious and political avalanches of history, from the beginning of time, was the power of the spoken word. The broad masses of the people will submit, always and only, to the force of speech. . . . The perception of the great masses is only very limited, their understanding is small, but their forgetfulness is great.

Hitler crushed all opposition to him within the party by a purge. His only dangerous opponents after he had gained dictatorial powers were Nazis themselves. These men felt that Hitler had gone over to big business and thereby had betrayed the socialist principles in National Socialism. The *SA* (storm troopers), who had borne the brunt of the violent struggles to establish National Socialism, thought that they were being pushed aside and neglected. Their commander, Roehm, was one of the moving spirits in a plot which Hitler thought was a threat to his power. Roehm may have been aided by General von Schleicher of the General Staff and Franz von Papen, ex-Chancellor and aristocrat. The plot was discovered and Hitler ordered (June 30, 1934) a blood purge. Several hundred of the plotters including von Schleicher, his wife, and Roehm were murdered. Von Papen was not killed because President Hindenburg ordered the regular army to protect him from the Nazis.

After the death of Hindenburg (August 2, 1934) the last trace of the Republic disappeared. Although a plebiscite voted Hitler the title and powers of President, he preferred to be *Der Fuehrer,* leader of the German nation.

Hitler established and organized a new government. Hitler's program for Germany may be summed up in two words—autarchy (self-sufficiency) and rearmament. By self-sufficiency Hitler meant that Germany should produce at home and bring under German control abroad all the necessities of life and the needs of total war. His program required the regimentation of every person and the control of every thing in the German nation under the sole direction of *Der Fuehrer.*

To achieve autarchy, all government activities were centralized in Hitler and the ministers whom he had appointed. The Reichstag met only to hear his fiery and boastful speeches. The Reichsrat, which represented the German states, was abolished. Their legislatures were also abolished, their powers were taken over by the central Nazi government, and over each state Hitler placed a Nazi leader responsible only to him, and thereby the German states lost all their political powers. Several national plebiscites were held to prove to the world that the Nazi regime had the approval of the German people. The voters were carefully watched by the Nazis; only a few dared vote "No." But supervision of the plebiscites was hardly necessary because Hitler always had the solid backing of an overwhelming majority of Germans anyway.

The Nazi government rigidly controlled all economic activities. Two Four-Year Plans, which included all kinds of German production, were adopted to make Germany independent of the outside world. The peasants did not secure the division of the land for which they had hoped because great estates can be run more easily than small farms by the decrees of a central government. Farmers were told what to plant and when to plant it. Measures were taken to improve the productivity of the soil and thus to increase the production of foodstuffs. Hitler said he was determined that Germans should never again suffer starvation because of a naval blockade as they had in the First World War.

The output and prices of German industries were also regulated. Many industrialists who had backed Hitler's rise to power regretted having done so when they found that they were completely under his orders. They were heavily taxed. They saw much of their wealth pass into the possession of Hitler's followers, some of whom became enormously rich.

Labor unions were abolished, their funds, buildings, and records were seized, and many of their leaders thrown into concentration camps. The Trustees of Labor under the Minister of Economic Affairs regulated wages, hours, and conditions of labor. Union activities and control over recreation and social affairs were placed under the control of a Labor Front directed by Robert Ley. Strikes and lockouts were strictly forbidden. The government compensated in small part for low wages by controlling prices and rents, by providing better housing, and by setting low rates for travel on holidays and reducing prices for admission to sporting events and theaters.

Foreign trade was wholly in the hands of the government. Before a German could buy anything abroad he had to have a license. If

BURNING BOOKS. Young Nazis cheer as they salute their leaders in Berlin's Opera Plaza during a book-burning orgy in which 20,000 volumes, some of them by writers of international fame, were reduced to ashes as a part of a program to rid the country of "Un-German" literature.

a foreigner wished to buy goods in Germany, he had to purchase marks at prices fixed by the government and pay for the desired goods with these marks. Germany bought necessities from foreign countries on a barter basis devised by Hjalmar Schacht. For example, Germany bargained with the Balkan nations to secure their entire surplus of grain, meat, and oil in exchange for the products of German factories, many kinds of which the peoples of the Balkan countries did not want. In many barter agreements the Germans dealt in promises and did not keep their side of the bargain.

The Nazis made education serve their purposes. Education underwent a thorough revision to make it an effective agency of Nazi propaganda among the youth. All teachers in lower schools who were suspected of anti-Nazi sentiment were discharged and Nazis, whether qualified or not, took their places. Textbooks for these schools were rewritten to further the Nazification of German youth. The Youth Movement, estab-

lished under the Weimar Republic, was taken over by the Nazis and changed into the Hitler Youth. Boys and girls were taught Nazi principles until they became fanatical Nazis and completely loyal to Hitler. Boys who took part in athletics were given military training. Girls were taught that their greatest aim in life should be to bear children. Boys and girls were sent during vacations to work on farms and help produce foodstuffs.

The universities were taken over completely by the Nazis. All professors who wished to maintain their integrity as scholars possessed of independent judgment escaped into exile or were sent to concentration camps and their places taken by men who had to be, first of all, loyal Nazis. The high reputation which the German universities had built up over hundreds of years was completely lost.

A Reich Culture Chamber, headed by Goebbels, took charge of literature, journalism, radio, moving pictures, painting, the theater, music, and sculpture. All books which the Culture Chamber considered anti-

Nazi were banned or burned. Germany's newspapers which did not fall into step with Hitler were suppressed or taken over by the Nazis.

Hitler taught that loyalty to country was the highest loyalty. This teaching meant that loyalty to a church and to God had to occupy a place in men's minds below loyalty to country. Some of the more extreme Nazis who despised Christian virtues wanted to abolish Christianity and re-establish the worship of Woden and the other gods of German paganism because these gods were believed to glory in war. Other Nazis wished to establish a national church to which all should belong. These rejected the *Old Testament* and parts of the *New Testament* because they claimed they were Jewish. They denied that Christ was a Jew and endeavored to draw up a religious creed suitable for the people who lived under the Third Reich.

By government decree all Protestant churches were combined into one German Church under the direction of Pastor Ludwig Mueller, an army chaplain. Standing in Martin Luther's pulpit in the church on whose door Luther had posted his ninety-five theses, Mueller announced a program to make the German Church the servant of National Socialism. A small group of Lutheran pastors led by Martin Niemoeller, a submarine commander in the First World War, resisted but unsuccessfully all Nazi attempts to control Lutheranism. They were suppressed and Niemoeller was finally confined in a concentration camp (1938) until he was freed by American troops in 1945.

Hitler had trouble with the Catholics in Germany. In a Concordat with the Papacy (1933) the Church agreed not to engage in political activity and Hitler promised not to interfere with the Catholic Church. But leaders of the Church, particularly Cardinal Faulhaber in Munich, objected to the control which the government exercised over the education of Catholic youth and criticized Nazi anti-Semitism and many of its atrocious deeds. *Heil Hitler* took the place of the traditional *Grüss Gott,* a German greeting.

Nazis persecuted Jews. Anti-Semitism, dislike or hatred for Jews, had been widespread in Germany during the Middle Ages as it had been in other countries of Europe. In the course of centuries it had died down and in most countries Jews had become prominent in business, music, art, science, and literature. German Jews had served Germany loyally in the First World War. In postwar Germany some had profited during the inflation and so had other Germans. Many German Jews had become successful business and professional men. Their success aroused the jealousy of those Germans who had been less successful.

To gain the support of Germans who disliked Jews, Hitler and his leading Nazis carried on a bitter anti-Semitic campaign. In spite of convincing evidence to the contrary, they insisted that the Jews were internationalists and Communists bent on world domination, that they were responsible for the loss of the First World War, and that they were profiteers, cheaters, and members of an inferior race.

After Hitler became Chancellor, he was determined to exterminate the 600,000 Jews in Germany. A civil law (1933) expelled nearly all "non-Aryans" from government employ. At first any person having a Jewish grandparent was considered non-Aryan. In 1935 the Nuremberg Laws deprived Jews of citizenship, even including persons who were one-quarter Jewish, and forbade the marriage of a Jew and a German. Other laws excluded Jews from the professions and limited the number of Jewish children in public schools to 1.5 per cent of the total enrollment. Many renowned Jewish scholars were dismissed from their positions by the Nazis, and others

Ewing Galloway

NAZI TROOPS MARCHING.

fled voluntarily. Perhaps the best known of these is Albert Einstein, a mathematician and physicist of international reputation, who found refuge in the United States, where he became an American citizen. Businesses owned by Jews were confiscated; Jews were required to take distinctive names, wear garments bearing J (mark of a Jew), and live in specified areas (ghettos) in cities. Great numbers were thrown into concentration camps and during the Second World War untold numbers were murdered with fiendish brutality.

After a Polish Jew had shot an official in the German Embassy in Paris (1938), Nazi leaders incited the German people to destroy Jewish property and synagogues and to kill Jews. The German Jews were assessed a collective fine of about $250,000,000. Books written by Jews were burned, music composed by Jews was banned, and Jewish works of art destroyed. The poetry of Heine might not be read nor the music of Mendelssohn played. As many Jews as could escaped from Germany with their lives but many without much property.

Hitler rearmed Germany to conquer the world. Even before Germany was completely regimented, an attempt was made to complete its autarchy by accumulating extensive stock piles of goods, including metals, rubber, oil, and foodstuffs. The building up of stock piles was really a part of the rearmament program, for Hitler was preparing for total war. The military part of rearmament was speeded up by the manufacture of weapons and the training of soldiers.

The Treaty of Versailles had limited the German army to 100,000 soldiers, but to get around this limitation every soldier in it was trained to be an officer, sergeant, or corporal so that a sufficient number of officers would be available to train the large army that was soon to be raised. The Free Corps, *SA*, and *SS* were well-drilled private armies. Youth received military training in the guise of athletic exercises. Because powered aircraft were forbidden by the Treaty of Versailles, young

Germans who studied aviation were trained in gliders.

After the Reichstag voted Hitler dictatorial powers (1933) he made a speech declaring Germany's peaceful intentions, but in the same year, after he withdrew Germany from a Disarmament Conference then in session and later in the same year from the League of Nations, his true intentions became known. Strengthened in natural resources by the recovery of the Saar Basin after the plebiscite (January, 1935), he announced on March 15 following that Germany repudiated the military limitations of the Versailles Treaty and that conscription would be renewed. By a naval agreement in the summer of 1935 Great Britain, with curious blindness, consented to an increase in the German navy up to 35 per cent of Britain's surface craft and 45 per cent of its submarines. The factories in Germany hummed night and day with activity. The unemployed were quickly absorbed in the rearmament program. When a few Germans complained of the shortage of consumer goods, Goering replied for the government that the German people preferred "cannon before butter." He was right. Wages sank, the number of working hours was increased, and taxes went up. Most of the people bore their burdens without complaint.

The Germans had one great advantage over the other nations in rearmament. They had no equipment left after the First World War and so were able to build anew, making use of the experience they had gained in that war. Their generals, having lost the First World War, were ready to discard the traditional methods of strategy and tactics and create new ones suited to the new weapons. Stock piles of all kinds of goods, including foodstuffs and oil, were gathered, the army was equipped and trained, and the General Staff, in drawing its plans made a wise use of the lessons learned from its investigations of the First World War. By 1939 Germany was ready for total war.

SUMMARY

Political unrest and social disorders in Italy after the First World War helped ambitious men to fasten Fascism on Italy and to overthrow its constitutional government. The workers in factories and peasants on great estates were so dissatisfied that they took over factories and estates. In this grave crisis, the central government was weak and political leadership ineffective. Before this time many Italians had become Socialists; even Mussolini had been a Socialist. Mussolini organized Fascist clubs to combat political unrest and social disorders. The Fascists marched on Rome (1922) and with the approval of King Victor Emmanuel, Mussolini became premier and soon dictator. He organized the government along Fascist lines. His destruction of constitutional government wiped out all political and other freedoms.

Mussolini brought the economic life of Italy under his control by organizing thirteen corporations, six of employers, six of workers, and one of professional men. He regulated wages, prices, and the production of goods. The loss of political freedom was soon followed by the loss of economic freedom. His economic changes seemed for a time to have brought about a measure of prosperity at a great cost to the workers and small businessmen.

Mussolini's control of education and of the clubs which he established for boys and girls made most of them ardent Fascists who were willing to do whatever Mussolini wanted. He came to an agreement with the Pope which ended the almost sixty years of strife between the government of Italy and the Papacy.

As economic conditions in Italy grew worse during the world depression, Mussolini attempted to take the attention of the people away from conditions at home by interesting them in a war to gain an empire in Africa. In the Second World War, he failed to keep American and British troops from capturing his country, and his own countrymen killed him.

At the close of the First World War, Germany became a republic which endeavored to maintain public order. It met with opposition from Communists and reactionary monarchists, both of which it succeeded in overcoming. Inflation wiped out the German national debt, but it ruined many Germans. Loans of money from foreign countries, much of it from the United States, enabled Germany to restore its credit and to put its money on a sound basis.

During its lifetime the German republic engaged in friendly relations with its neighbors. It signed the Locarno Pact. The Allied armies of occupation were withdrawn and Germany joined the League of Nations. Nevertheless, the military were secretly at work to overthrow the Republic and to rearm.

A new party, the National Socialist party, was formed and in time Adolf Hitler became its dictatorial leader. While he was in prison for taking part in an unsuccessful revolt against the republic, he wrote *Mein Kampf* in which he set forth his Nazi program. After his release, he worked to increase the numbers and influence of the Nazi party. The widespread suffering caused by the severe world economic depression caused many to join his party. In January, 1933, President Hindenburg appointed him Chancellor of Germany. In March, 1933, he became *Der Fuehrer,* dictator of the Third Reich. He was supported by many workers, many middle class people, most wealthy people, and by military leaders.

Hitler crushed Nazis who opposed his rule by a purge (1934). He overthrew the German government, established and organized a new government on Nazi principles, and regimented the lives of all Germans. He controlled all economic activities, regulated labor, and regimented foreign trade. He caused youth to support Nazism, and he gave them military training. All cultural activities were strictly supervised in the interest of National Socialism. The Nazis brought a large number of Lutherans under their control, but they did not succeed so well with the Catholics. They persecuted the Jews. Hitler withdrew Germany from the Disarmament Conference and from the League of Nations and announced that Germany would renew conscription. He made a naval treaty with Great Britain that was highly favorable to Germany. He began his rearmament program; he assembled huge stock piles of all kinds of materials needed by civilians and armed forces in a total war.

EVENTS THAT TOOK PLACE AT ABOUT THE SAME TIME

ITALY	1917	GERMANY
		Abdication of Kaiser, 1918.
		Armistice, November 11, 1918.
Mussolini founded first *fascio,* 1919.		Communist uprisings, 1919.
		Constitutional Assembly, Weimar, 1919.
		Kapp *putsch,* 1920.
Fascists marched on Rome and Mussolini made premier, 1922.		
New electoral law, 1923.		Hitler's "beer hall putsch," 1923.
Murder of Matteotti, 1924.		*Mein Kampf* published, 1924.

EVENTS THAT TOOK PLACE AT ABOUT THE SAME TIME (Cont.)

ITALY	1917	GERMANY
		French withdrew from Ruhr, 1925.
		Hindenburg elected president, 1925.
		Locarno Pact, 1925.
Confederations of employees and employers begun, 1926.		Germany joined League of Nations, 1926.
Protectorate over Albania established, 1927.		
Electoral Law of 1928.		
Economic depression began, 1929.		
Battle of Wheat.		The depression became severe, 1931.
		Nazi party largest in Reichstag by 1932.
		Hitler appointed Chancellor, 1933.
		Reichstag fire, 1933.
		Germany withdrew from the League of Nations, 1933.
		"Blood Purge," 1934.
Conquest of Ethiopia, 1935.		Hitler announced rearming of Germany, 1935.
		Nuremberg Laws, 1935.
Rome-Berlin Axis formed, 1936.		German troops occupied the Rhineland, 1936.
Mussolini intervened in Spanish Civil War, 1936.		Hitler intervened in Spanish Civil War, 1936.
Chamber of Deputies abolished, 1938.		

NAZIS ON THE MARCH. In the annual Nazi celebration of the "Beer Cellar Putsch" of 1923, Hitler and Goering, in center, march with the elite through swastika-decorated streets.

HITLER IN ROME. Der Fuehrer and Il Duce met in mutual accord when Hitler paid a visit to Rome in 1938.

MY GOOD FRIEND FRANCO. In Berlin, in 1940, Hitler and the flattered Franco end a friendly war-time conference with a hand-clasp.

BOMBING OF BARCELONA. Franco's bombers have just released the bomb which burst in the center of the Loyalist-occupied city. More than a thousand civilians were killed in the air raids on the city.

SPANISH VOLUNTEERS. Above, Spanish Loyalists, without uniforms, fire from a roof.

LOYALIST TROOPS, right, reconnoitre and fire at Fascists still hidden in the houses of a newly-occupied village. Civilian casualties and the destruction of ancient landmarks were characteristic of the three years of civil war.

CHAPTER 32

Democracy in Great Britain and France

After the First World War democracy was very much alive in Great Britain and France although dictators ruled in many other European countries. Democracy was strong in Great Britain where it had begun centuries ago and also in France where Liberty, Equality, and Fraternity still greatly influenced the thinking of most Frenchmen. The British Parliament granted the right to vote to more people than ever before and the British continued to hold free elections for members of Parliament and other officers. The Labor party grew in numbers until it became the second largest party in Parliament. Ministries changed from time to time as they always had. Depression caused serious economic problems and labor unrest, but a general strike failed because it was not supported by the public. The British cabinet handled successfully a most unusual crisis in regard to the crown. Even though grave problems faced the British they clung to their democratic way of free and full public discussion, free elections, and Parliamentary action, which usually resulted in compromises.

The Third French Republic faced many serious governmental problems which it endeavored to solve in a democratic way through legislative action by its Chamber of Deputies and Senate. The most difficult of all these problems was the national debt and the unbalanced budget. In spite of strenuous efforts the French government failed to find a solution of this problem that would be acceptable to the majority of the French. The many political parties in the French Parliament made decisive action impossible. Ministries changed rapidly. France seemed strong and prosperous, but in reality it was weak and in the grave crisis that lay ahead the badly divided government failed to protect vital French national interests.

• • •

The British continued to strengthen democracy after the war. Great Britain had been led to victory in the First World War by a coalition government composed of both Liberals and Conservatives headed by Lloyd George, a Liberal. At the moment of victory democracy was strengthened in Great Britain by removing (1918) all property qualifications for voting and by granting women over thirty the right to vote. As early as 1869 John Stuart Mill had advocated equal rights for women in a book entitled *Subjection of Women*. For many years before the First World War a militant band of women (suffragettes) led by Mrs. Pankhurst and her daughters had campaigned for woman suffrage. They made speeches and picketed Parliament, and after they were arrested they went on hunger strikes in jail, all to no avail. The participation of many women in the war effort brought partial victory to their cause. In 1918 with many soldiers out of the country, lest the votes of women overwhelm the votes of men, the vote was granted only to women over thirty. The Reform Bill (1918) extended the right to vote to about 8,000,000

International News

BRITISH SUFFRAGETTE LEADER. Miss Sylvia Pankhurst, militant and fiery leader of the woman suffrage movement in Great Britain, is shown here being carried from the suffragette headquarters in Bow Street, London. The suffragettes made use of this and other sensational incidents in their campaign to get the right to vote on the same terms as men.

men and women. The Reform Bill of 1928 permitted women to vote on the same terms as men.

The British government dealt with postwar economic problems. The 1918 election (the khaki election) gave overwhelming support to the coalition government. For two years all went well. Then in 1921-1922 a postwar economic depression set in. A large part of British prewar trade had been taken over during the war by the United States and Japan. Demand for British ships, for British textiles, and British coal declined and the decline caused much unemployment in ship-

building, textile manufacturing, and coal mining. In 1922 more than 2,000,000 people were unemployed. In 1912 Parliament had passed a National Insurance Act which provided a small sum (dole) to be paid to men and women who had lost their jobs. Because this sum proved inadequate for the unemployed, it was increased by the coalition government which was still headed by Lloyd George. The increase added greatly to the taxes which the government had levied owing to the war.

Although the Conservative members of the coalition in the Commons had voted for the

Ewing Galloway

J. RAMSAY MACDONALD, FIRST MEMBER OF
THE LABOR PARTY TO BECOME PRIME MIN-
ISTER OF GREAT BRITAIN.

increase in taxation, they were dissatisfied and withdrew from the coalition, and that lost Lloyd George his majority in the Commons. His loss of a majority forced an election (1922) which the Conservatives won. It marked an important change in British politics. The election led to a split in the Liberal party caused by a personal break between its two leaders, Asquith and Lloyd George. Moreover, neither leader had a program for a solution of the nation's problems. As a result, the Liberal party declined in numbers.

The Labor party gradually rose to power in Great Britain. The place of the Liberal party as a rival of the Conservative party was taken by the Labor party. This party which developed out of the Trade Union movement, had been slowly increasing in numbers since 1900. In 1906 it took the name Labor party. It made little progress before 1914, but after the war its social and economic program attracted many to its ranks. It proposed government ownership of railroads, other public utilities, and coal mines. It urged the government to provide low-priced but livable houses for the poor and also financial aid to the unemployed. When the Conservatives proposed the adoption of tariffs to protect British industry, the Labor party declared in favor of free trade.

In January, 1924, after another election, the Labor and Liberal parties combined had more members in the House of Commons than the Conservatives. They formed a coalition and the leader of the Labor party, J. Ramsay MacDonald, became Prime Minister. He was the son of a Scottish coal miner and had worked in the mines himself. He was self-educated, a journalist, and a pacifist. Philip Snowden, his Chancellor of the Exchequer, who had been a clerk, proved to be a very able financier. Arthur Henderson, Home Secretary, had been an ironworker. Partly because they depended on Liberal co-operation for their majority in the House of Commons and partly because their leaders had been trained by experience in Parliament in the traditional British way of doing things, the Labor government did not attempt any radical reforms. It increased the dole to the unemployed and with government aid built several thousand inexpensive houses. It recognized the Soviet Union (1924). At that time the Bolsheviks were unpopular in Great Britain because they were thought to be anti-religious and besides they had refused to pay the debts the Tsar's government owed to Great Britain. Because the Labor party recognized the Soviet Union, the Liberals withdrew their support. A new election was ordered in Oct., 1924, and the Conservatives won.

The Conservatives failed to solve Britain's pressing economic problems. From 1924-1929 Great Britain was governed by the Conservative party headed by Stanley Baldwin, a cautious but determined businessman. He succeeded in restoring British credit abroad, but failed to solve the problem of unemployment. In an effort to increase employment the Baldwin government passed tariffs to protect British manufactured goods from the competition of foreign goods. In an effort to improve conditions in coal mining, it appointed a Royal Commission to study and report on conditions in the coal mining industry. These conditions were due to many factors. The increased use of fuel oil and of electricity developed by water power had caused a decline in the demand for coal. The cost of mining had increased and in many coal mines the best veins had been exhausted and consequently the quality of coal had declined. In some mines near Newcastle on the North Sea the veins had been mined until the workings extended under the sea. Even with low wages many mines failed to pay expenses and in order to keep them in operation the government granted subsidies to the owners. Some were closed down. The result was unemployment for many and deplorable living conditions for most mine workers and their families.

In these conditions labor unrest among miners was inevitable. A coal strike (1921) failed when the railway and transport workers union refused to support it with a sympathetic strike. Trouble again rose in 1926 when a Royal Commission recommended the end of subsidies, the closing of some mines, and drastic wage reductions. The miners replied, "Not a penny off the pay, not a minute on the day," and went on strike. On May 4, 1926, a general strike was declared by the Trade Union Council, the organization of all trade unions in Great Britain, to support the

miners' union. Although it lasted nine days it was a complete failure, because the public was not ready to uphold such revolutionary methods. On the contrary, it supported the government while it suppressed the strike. Its failure was a blow not only to the miners' union but to all other British labor unions. In an effort to prevent general strikes, Parliament passed the Trades Disputes Act (1927). It declared illegal all sympathetic strikes and all strikes and lockouts called for political purposes. By it, unions were forbidden to collect money from their members for political purposes without the written consent of each member given in advance.

The world economic depression created new problems. An improvement in world economic conditions generally and a brief freedom from labor difficulties brought some measure of prosperity (1927) to Great Britain which lasted until 1929, the beginning of the world economic depression. A general election (1929) gave the Labor party a majority in the House of Commons. Its leader was Ramsay MacDonald who became Prime Minister again just before the world economic depression began. As in the United States, so in Great Britain, much money invested in stocks of corporations was lost and businesses failed. The number of unemployed rose to over 2,000,000. As the Labor government was unable to improve economic conditions, it was succeeded by a coalition government (1931), called a National Government with Ramsay MacDonald as Prime Minister. Although the National Government contained Liberal and Labor members, most of its members were Conservatives and consequently its policies were for the most part Conservative.

The National Government passed acts designed to help solve economic problems caused by the world depression. On September 21, 1931, Great Britain went off the gold

International News

STANLEY BALDWIN. The Prime Minister is pictured here just after his Conservative party won a majority in the election of 1935. In 1937 he retired from public life and was made the Earl of Bewdley by George VI.

standard. In other words, it ceased redeeming its paper money in gold. The pound sterling sank in value from almost five dollars to a little less than four. This shrinkage made it easier for foreign countries to buy from Great Britain because they could now buy more British pounds with their money than before, and thus the foreign demand for British goods increased.

In 1932 a tariff was passed which gave protection to English manufacturers against imported goods and set quotas on imports of foodstuffs and thereby aided British farmers. A Wheat Act set a standard price for wheat and provided subsidies to farmers if the world price fell below the standard price set.

The sale of potatoes and milk, the production of sugar beets, and cattle raising were brought under government regulation and support. The Coal Act (1938) provided for the government purchase of coal mines from their private owners. The dole provided by the National Insurance Act was increased. Except for a small outlay for building houses, the government failed to adopt a general plan of public works or other public activities to create employment. Great Britain "muddled through" the depression years. Small Communist and Fascist groups arose, but gained few followers. As always before, English public opinion supported traditional ways.

The British monarchy survived a crisis. In June, 1935, Ramsay MacDonald resigned because of ill health and Stanley Baldwin became Prime Minister again. A most unusual event took place while he was Prime Minister, the abdication of Edward VIII. For many years while he was Prince of Wales he had traveled throughout the British Empire and many foreign countries as an ambassador of good will and of course as the future king of Great Britain. At forty-five years of age he was still a bachelor. Shortly after he became king, but before his coronation, it was learned that he intended to marry an American, Mrs. Wallis Simpson, as soon as she received a divorce from her second husband. Marriage to a divorcee was contrary to the canon law of the Anglican Church of which he was the head. The king's intention shocked the Archbishop of Canterbury and many other people in Great Britain. As he was determined to marry Mrs. Simpson, he had to abdicate as king. On December 12, 1936, his brother succeeded to the throne as George VI, and granted Edward the title Duke of Windsor. The widespread acclaim which greeted the new king proved the loyalty of the people throughout the British Empire to the monarchy.

International News

CORONATION PICTURE OF GREAT BRITAIN'S ROYAL FAMILY, 1936: King George VI and his wife, with Princesses Elizabeth (later Queen Elizabeth II) and Margaret.

In 1937 Baldwin retired and Sir Neville Chamberlain became Prime Minister. By far the most important events while he was Prime Minister were in the field of foreign affairs and will be studied later. By 1939 economic conditions had improved again. The British monarchy and the British form of democracy were thoroughly entrenched in the hearts of the people.

The Third French Republic faced difficult governmental problems after the First World War. The Third Republic had played a large part in a victorious war, and French democracy seemed (1918) to be firmly entrenched. Its large army of experienced soldiers, its re-acquisition of Alsace and Lorraine, and its treaties with Poland, Czechoslovakia, and Yugoslavia made France appear to be the strongest military power in Europe. There were, to be sure, some dark clouds. France had lost over 1,400,000 men in the war (about one tenth of its male population) and another tenth had been crippled. Some of its industrial and mining areas in the North had been devastated by the warring armies and others were sabotaged by the Germans just before the German armies were driven out of France. The cost of the war had been paid for, not wholly by taxes, but by loans and the issue of paper money. Loans and the circulation of paper money caused inflation and thereby the purchasing power of the franc declined. Before the war the franc was worth about twenty cents in United States money. At the end of the war it was worth approximately eight cents and later on it was worth even less. The decline in the value of the franc had far-reaching effects on the economic life of France.

The problems of reconstruction and defense received serious attention. The devastated areas were restored and mines and factories were speedily reopened and put into operation. French leaders were deeply disturbed because the Treaty of Versailles had not made the Rhine the eastern frontier of France. On this frontier both leaders and people thought their safety from any future German aggression depended. In 1930 the Maginot Line, composed of a series of strong defensive fortifications, was built to protect France from another German invasion.

The financial problems were difficult to solve primarily because a solution depended on agreement among many political parties. In 1925 Great Britain had two major political parties, but France had nine large parties and several smaller parties. Ministers were, therefore, dependent on coalitions made up of several political parties. Any reform measure which would increase taxes or cut down government expenditures by releasing some of the unnecessarily large number of government employees was bound to meet with the disapproval of some of the political parties. When this took place, their members who made up the coalition withdrew and thereby caused the downfall of the cabinet.

The political history of France from 1919-1930 is well summed up in the phrase "the Battle of the Budget." In 1919 the coalition of political parties that had governed France during the war broke into two groups (blocs), a conservative bloc and a liberal bloc and the conservative bloc won the election. Clemenceau retired and his place as leader of the conservatives was taken by Poincaré who was premier from 1922 to 1924. He hoped to improve French finances by France's share of the reparations Germany was to pay. In 1923 when Germany failed to make its payments, France joined by Belgium occupied the Ruhr, the great industrial center of Germany. This move was unpopular abroad and besides it failed to cause Germany to resume her reparations payments.

An election in 1924 resulted in a majority for the group of liberal parties called the "radical bloc" led by Herriot. It failed so completely that in 1926 Poincaré became premier again. He succeeded in raising taxes enough and in reducing government expenditures enough to balance the budget temporarily. A balanced budget restored the credit of France, and a stabilized franc at about five cents (about two cents higher than its lowest value) helped to improve economic conditions. But even so he failed to solve the basic problems which faced the Third French Republic.

Factions hindered the Third Republic from solving its problems. In the years that followed, a ministry that represented the right followed rapidly one that represented the left in bewildering succession. Gradually the political groups became more clearly defined. The conservatives (the right) were businessmen and peasants. They were united by their fear of Communism and opposed all reforms. Some conservatives, who had become distrustful of democracy, organized Fascist leagues and did not hesitate to stage riots in the streets of Paris. Some of these conservatives wanted to restore the monarchy, others wanted to establish an authoritarian state like that in Germany or Italy. The propaganda of Otto Abetz, a German in Paris, influenced many conservatives to admire Germany and to believe in the principles of the Nazi government. Abetz posed as a friend of France who wanted to bring France and Germany together against Communism, but his real object was to weaken France and thereby to make it an easy prey for Germany. Many prominent leaders, notably Pierre Laval, and some officers in the army sympathized with these anti-democratic groups even though they did not join them.

International News

LEON BLUM INTERVIEWED BY REPORTERS. He had just succeeded in forming a cabinet in March, 1938. For two days France had been virtually without a government, and it was at this time that Hitler annexed Austria.

The radicals (the left) were composed of three parties, Radical Socialists, who were members of the liberal and anti-clerical middle class, Socialists, and Communists. After an election (1936), these parties formed a coalition government known as the Popular Front which made Léon Blum premier. This government made the Bank of France a government bank, put the forty-hour week into effect in French industries, strengthened collective bargaining, and made the manufacture of munitions and implements of war a function of the government. In spite of these efforts to improve the condition of the workers, the Popular Front was unable to cope successfully with an epidemic of sit-down strikes in French factories, and it failed completely to balance the budget. After the election that followed, the conservative coalition headed by Daladier, did away with most of the work of the Popular Front.

In spite of the government's failure to solve economic problems, France remained fairly prosperous. Agriculture—always the basis of French economy—prospered, particularly after the Popular Front had established a Wheat Office which brought wheat from farms to markets where it was needed. The luxury trades, including silks, high-priced gowns, hats, and perfumes, were little affected by the depression. In fact, there was relatively little unemployment in France during the world depression in comparison with the unemployment in Germany, Italy, Great Britain, and the United States.

In 1939 France appeared strong. Its army was believed to be the best in the world. The Maginot Line was thought by the French to be impregnable. No one questioned the devotion of the majority of the French people to democracy, liberty, equality, and fraternity. Nevertheless, France was so hopelessly divided by political parties that its ministries swung from left to right and from right to left time and time again. The instability of a ministry made fruitless the efforts of leaders who tried to improve conditions. Although France appeared strong, the oncoming war with Germany proved her to be weak. In 1940 France fell rapidly before the onslaughts of the German invader and the Third Republic came to an end.

SUMMARY

The British parliamentary system continued to strengthen democracy by removing all property qualifications for voting, by granting women the right to vote on the same terms as men, and by extending aid to the unemployed. The Labor party when it was in power (1924) increased the dole and recognized the Soviet Union. Labor unrest led to a general strike, which was a failure. To help prevent another general strike the Trades Disputes Act (1927) was passed by Parliament under Conservative leadership. It greatly restricted the activities of organized labor unions.

The world economic depression created new problems. Unemployment increased greatly. Great Britain went off the gold standard. A tariff act, a wheat act, and other laws helped industry and agriculture through the depression years. In spite of all its difficulties British democracy survived them and remained thoroughly entrenched in the hearts of the people.

After the First World War the Third French Republic faced difficult problems. The devastation that was wrought by the war was largely overcome. The measures taken to combat inflation and solve financial problems were for the most part ineffectual.

Factionalism led to the formation of many parties and these made the central government weak and unstable. Some Frenchmen favored a monarchy, some an authoritarian form of government; the supporters of the republic were divided into many parties. Governments changed frequently. France appeared to be prosperous and strong. Events proved that the Third French Republic was too weak to survive its greatest crisis, and in 1940 it came to an end.

SUMMARY OF PART X

The future of democracy seemed bright at the close of the First World War. The Germans had done away with their autocratic empire and had established a republic. The new nations established by the peace treaties had all adopted democratic constitutions. Russia, to be sure, had exchanged the Tsarist autocracy for the totalitarian regime of its Communist dictatorship. This rule was no closer to democracy than the rule of the Tsars had ever been. Events proved that the hope of a bright future for democracy was not to come to pass. The Italians followed Mussolini who overthrew the constitution of Italy and made it a Fascist state. Hitler overthrew the German Republic and became the dictator of the Third Reich. The British and French people continued to support democracy even amid great economic difficulties. French national strength, however, was greatly weakened by deep-seated factional and party strife. By 1939 the democratic nations stood side by side against the totalitarian powers, Germany and Italy, and a second world war was required to preserve the democratic way of life.

EVENTS THAT TOOK PLACE AT ABOUT THE SAME TIME

GREAT BRITAIN	1918	FRANCE
Coalition government, Lloyd George, Prime Minister, 1918.		
		Battle of the Budget, 1919-1930.
Coal strike, 1921.		Coalition government dissolved, 1919.
Two million workers out of work, 1922,		Conservatives won election, 1919.
A. Bonar Law, Prime Minister, 1922-1923.		Poincaré, Premier, 1922-1924.
Stanley Baldwin, Prime Minister, 1923-24.		
Labor party (formed 1906) opposition party.		France and Belgium occupied Ruhr, 1923.
Ramsay MacDonald, Prime Minister, first Labor party cabinet, 1924.		
Recognition of Soviet Union, 1924.		"Radical bloc" won election, 1924.
Conservatives won election, 1924.		Edouard Herriot, Premier, 1924-1925.
Stanley Baldwin, Prime Minister, 1924-1929.		
Conservatives passed protective tariff, 1924.		
General strike called and failed, 1926.		Briand, Premier, 1925-1926.
Trades Disputes Act, 1927.		Poincaré, Premier, 1926-1929; balanced the budget, 1926.
Labor party won election, 1929; Ramsay MacDonald, Prime Minister, 1929-1931.		Twenty ministries, 1929-1936.
World economic depression, 1929.		
Labor government succeeded by National government, 1931.		
Ramsay MacDonald, Prime Minister, 1931-1935.		
Great Britain went off gold standard, 1931.		
Another protective tariff act passed, 1932.		
World Economic Conference in London, 1933.		
Ramsay MacDonald resigned; Stanley Baldwin, Prime Minister, 1935-1937.		
Death of George V, 1936.		
Abdication of Edward VIII, 1936.		Popular Front formed, 1936; Léon Blum, Premier.
George VI became king, 1936.		Bank of France and munitions industry nationalized, 1936.
Neville Chamberlain, Prime Minister, 1937.		
		Second Popular Front, Léon Blum, Premier, 1938.
		Edouard Daladier succeeded Blum, 1938.

THE DUKE AND
DUCHESS OF WIND-
SOR. The world-famou[...]
bride and groom afte[...]
their marriage in France[...]
which followed shortl[...]
after Edward's abdication[...]

DAVID LLOYD GEORGE. This
brilliant Welshman sponsored a
program of social reform, became
Britain's Prime Minister during
World War I, and represented
Britain at the Peace Conference in
Paris. (British Information Serv-
ice.)

PART XI

The Impact of the Second World War

The Second World War began September 1, 1939, a little less than twenty-one years after the First World War ended. The bright hopes of future peace which many men held in 1918 failed of realization. The League of Nations accomplished many good things in the broad fields of international co-operation in social and humanitarian projects, particularly in matters of health and sanitation. It settled many minor disputes between great nations and some major disputes between small nations. Nevertheless in its chief aim, the establishment of collective security and the prevention of war, it failed. In spite of the investigations and reports of its agents, the Japanese continued unchecked in their imperialistic career in the Far East. The League could not or did not thwart the imperialistic ambitions of Mussolini in Africa. It did not prevent the intervention of nations in the Spanish Civil War that made it the testing ground of weapons for the Second World War. Hitler moved almost unchallenged in his program for German rearmament and expansion. Whatever the causes, the fine attempt at collective security failed and the world was plunged into war.

Nearly all countries in the world participated in the Second World War and none escaped its effects. Within those at war nearly all people had a share in one way or another in the war effort. The war was fought on a scientific level that far out-distanced all previous wars. The final victory over Japan came with the triumph of the scientists, the invention of the atom bomb.

The authoritarian powers won many great victories in the first three years of the war. They rushed on almost unchecked in Western and Northern Europe, and in the Balkans. Hitler's armies advanced almost to Moscow, reached the Volga at Stalingrad, and penetrated the Caucasus. In North Africa the Axis forces gained the frontier of Egypt and threatened the British life line. France was crushed and for a time Great Britain stood alone.

The Japanese attack on Pearl Harbor brought the United States into the war. They also gained great initial success by sweeping through the Philippines, Malaya, and Burma to the frontiers of India, and along the islands until from New Guinea they threatened Australia.

The democratic powers with Russia formed the United Nations, girded themselves, and began the march to victory. With great toil at home and prodigious deeds of valor on land and sea they pushed the forces of their enemies back until in the spring and summer of 1945 they won a total victory.

CHAPTER 33

The Breakdown of Collective Security

Collective security, the idea that a group of nations could preserve peace by united action against an aggressor, was the aim of the victorious nations in the peace settlement signed (1919) at Versailles. Germany was to be so weakened that it would not again be a menace to the peace of the world. It was hoped that republics, which most men thought would be peace-loving, would take the place of forms of governments that had been warlike. The League of Nations was to help to settle international disputes and thereby preserve peace. The twenty years that followed the Paris Peace Conference were filled with international disputes. In nearly every one of them war was being waged somewhere. These years of tension ended in a greater and more terrible war than had ever been waged before; it destroyed the plans for collective security made by the founders of the League of Nations.

● ● ●

The League of Nations' accomplishments were many. About forty international disputes were referred to the League. Those which involved smaller nations were adjusted for the time being. The League was less successful in adjusting disputes between larger nations. In these disputes the Assembly of the League provided an aggrieved nation with an opportunity to present its case to the members of the League and to public opinion throughout the world.

After Turkey had defeated Greece in a war in Asia Minor and forced the Greeks to flee from Asia Minor back to Greece, a League of Nations Commission helped Greek refugees to settle in Greece and carried on relief work among them. The League rendered financial aid to Austria, Hungary, and the Balkan countries to aid them in reconstruction. Its health service sent doctors, nurses, and medicines to the Balkans and stamped out a typhus epidemic in Poland. The League promoted scientific studies to prevent epidemics. It made strenuous efforts to break up international traffic in opium. Its International Labor Organization compiled vast quantities of statistics and made many recommendations to the members of the League for labor legislation, but only a few were accepted.

The Permanent Court of International Justice settled many cases at law between nations. Its members included, at different times, Charles Evans Hughes, Frank B. Kellogg, Manley O. Hudson, distinguished American jurists and scholars.

The League of Nations failed to accomplish its main purpose. Although the League accomplished much, as we have just seen, it failed in its main purpose, which was to insure a lasting peace. Its failure was not due to the League's activities, but to the failure of the members of the League to support its activities. The absence of the United States weakened the power and prestige of the League, but did not cause its failure. It failed chiefly because (1) the Great Powers did not make as much use of it as they could have made. When their international disputes were referred to the League, most of them were not decided by the League but by older methods, conferences of ambassadors or heads of nations. (2) When the League did make decisions on disputes that had been referred to it, the powers failed at critical times to carry them out. At times differences between Great Britain and France made it impossible for them to work together in an effort to settle disputes and to make decisions vital to their national welfare and that of other nations. (3) The extreme nationalism of Japan, Germany, and Italy and their eventual withdrawal from the League made it impossible for the League to prevent war.

Germany finally succeeded in getting the amount of reparations reduced. The two most thorny problems which the Paris Peace Conference left unsolved were (1) the amount of German reparations, and (2) a program for general disarmament.

The Conference left the amount of German reparations to be decided by the special Reparations Commission provided for in the Treaty of Versailles. In 1921 this Commission, after hearing the claims of the Allied Powers and after requesting Germany in vain to make an offer, agreed that the amount of reparations to be paid by Germany was about $33,-000,000,000 plus interest. The Reparations Commission decided that Germany should pay slightly more than $500,000,000 a year in money and goods on the installment plan and that these installments were to be distributed among the Allied Powers. The German government claimed that it could not make these payments because (1) Germany had to buy large quantities of raw materials and foodstuffs abroad, and to pay for these imports and to pay the reparations installments would require the export either of gold or of manufactured goods or both. (2) Germany's supplies of gold were low. (3) High tariffs levied by other countries to protect home industries would prevent the export of sufficient manufactured goods to enable Germany to pay for imports and also reparations.

In 1922 Germany asked for a postponement of payments, but the request was refused. In 1923, after the Germans stopped paying reparations, the French and Belgians occupied the rich industrial region of the Ruhr to break Germany's will to resist the payment of reparations. The British, who desired the restoration of trade with Germany, objected to the French and Belgian occupation of the Ruhr. In general, public opinion was against France. The Germans in the Ruhr refused to work the mines and factories. Thereupon the Reparations Commission appointed a committee of experts headed by Charles G. Dawes, an American, to decide what should be done about reparations.

The Dawes Plan (1924) did not alter the total amount due the victors, but it provided for a loan to Germany to assist it to restore the pre-war value of the mark and to make fixed annual reparations payments which were to be financed out of special taxes in Germany. When the Dawes Plan was accepted by the nations involved, the French and Belgians withdrew from the Ruhr. German economic life improved and the reparations payments were met, sometimes by special taxes, but often with money obtained from American and British banks. Under the Dawes Plan American and British banks loaned the Germans more money than the total reparations due.

Nevertheless, the Germans continued their agitation for a decrease in the amount of reparations, and so in 1929 another committee headed by Owen D. Young, an American, drew up the Young Plan. It fixed the total amount of reparations at about $8,000,-000 which was to be paid in fifty-eight years. The Germans had been successful in securing a decrease in reparations. Within

Ewing Galloway

HUGE CROWD IN PROTEST MEETING ON THE KONIGSPLATZ, MUNICH. A gathering of non-Socialist parties to protest French occupation of the Ruhr. Students with flags and soldiers in foreground.

three years, however, the world economic depression brought an end to all reparations payments.

A program for disarmament posed a problem too difficult for statesmen to solve. It appeared for a time as if something had been accomplished in the limitation of navies, but time was to prove this appearance false. Under President Harding, the United States took the lead in the effort to limit navies. After the United States Senate had surveyed the naval situation throughout the world, it concluded that a naval race among the leading naval powers was very apt to take place. In an attempt to prevent any naval race it called a conference to consider the possibility of limiting the size of navies and also to discuss relations in the Pacific. This conference included representatives from Great Britain,

Japan, France, and Italy. It met in Washington (1921-1922) under the chairmanship of Secretary of State Charles Evans Hughes. In the Five-Power treaty the Washington Conference arrived at a formula known as the 5:5:3:1.67:1.67 ratio to be applied to large warships of 10,000 tons and over. The ratio 5:5 meant that Great Britain and the United States were to have equal tonnage in large warships; the ratio 5:3 meant that Japan was to have three fifths of the tonnage of Great Britain and the United States. Italy and France were placed on an equal footing with each other at 1.67:1.67. This agreement required great sacrifices by the United States and Great Britain. Great Britain's naval goal had been a navy equal to any two other navies combined. The treaty which was signed by the five powers that attended the Conference required the United States to scrap some battleships already in the process of construction, to the great harm of its navy in the future. Great Britain also scrapped battleships. As Japan resented having a lesser navy than the United States and Great Britain, it sought naval equality with them.

The Washington Conference also made the Four-Power and Nine-Power treaties. In the Four-Power Treaty, the United States, Great Britain, France, and Japan agreed to respect one another's island possessions in the Pacific and to consult with one another if an international dispute should arise. In the Nine-Power Treaty the signers (including the United States, Great Britain, and Japan) pledged that they would respect the independence of China, its territorial integrity, and the continuation of the Open Door Policy of the United States which gave all nations the right to trade with China on equal terms.

After the Washington Conference, the nations that took part in it discussed the size of cruisers, the number of submarines, and other perplexing naval problems. To settle these controversial questions another conference was held in London in 1930. Great Britain, the United States, and Japan reached an agreement in regard to smaller craft. The new ratio was 10:10:7 and equality for submarines, but France and Italy refused to sign the agreement. In 1934 Japan broke up a conference when its demand for naval equality with the United States and Great Britain was refused. At this time it gave the required two years' notice of its repudiation of the Washington Five-Power Treaty. The following year (1935) Great Britain signed a naval agreement with Germany in which the latter was allowed to increase its fleet up to 35 per cent of Britain's surface craft and 45 per cent of its submarines. By this time Hitler's rearmament of Germany had so altered the

world situation that the limitation of navies was not even a subject for discussion. The naval race that the United States Senate feared and tried to prevent was on.

Efforts to limit the size and equipment of armies met with failure. In 1921 the Council of the League appointed a special commission to draw up proposals for the limitation of the size and equipment of armies for the consideration of the members of the League. The report of the commission was approved by the Assembly of the League (1924), but failed to be ratified by a single power. The same year on motion of Ramsay MacDonald, Prime Minister of Great Britain, and of Herriot, Premier of France, the Assembly adopted the Geneva Protocol. This ambitious document condemned aggressive war as an international crime, defined an aggressor as any nation which refused to submit to arbitration, provided for economic boycotts of aggressor nations by order of the Council, and called for an international conference on military disarmament. By the time this document reached London, MacDonald was out of office and Stanley Baldwin, his conservative successor, would have none of it, and the British Dominions rejected it.

The discussions of military disarmament each year in the Assembly led to the appointment of a new commission to make another study of military disarmament. At a meeting of this commission (1928) Litvinoff, the Soviet representative, proposed complete and immediate disarmament. His motion was not even seconded. In 1932 another Disarmament Conference met in Geneva; about sixty nations were represented. During two years of meetings and discussions it accomplished nothing. France demanded security; Germany demanded equality in armaments; every nation found serious fault with each plan to disarm. In October, 1933, Hitler, who intended to rearm, withdrew Germany from the Conference and very shortly from the League. Two years later, as we have seen, he secured Great Britain's permission to increase the size of his navy. In May, 1934, the Geneva Disarmament Conference disbanded. The total failure of the Geneva Disarmament Conference meant that the large nations in Europe were committed to rearmament on a colossal scale.

The nations of Europe put their faith in peace pacts. Pacts were made with almost startling rapidity, and in the end they proved worse than futile. All these pacts seemed to indicate a lack of confidence in the League which was established to make such pacts unnecessary. The diplomats could not or would not change their accustomed patterns of thought. France sought allies as a protection against Germany. To this end it made an alliance with Belgium (1920). To secure the friendship of Poland, France aided Poland (1920) in its war against the Soviet Union and made an alliance with it (1924). Meanwhile, by the Treaty of Rapallo (1922) Germany recognized the Soviet Union and entered into diplomatic relations with it. France also made pacts with Czechoslovakia (1924), Rumania (1926), and Yugoslavia (1927). These three nations had (1920-1921) united for mutual protection in what was called the *Little Entente.* To keep the other European powers from uniting against it, the Soviet Union made treaties of non-aggression and neutrality (between 1925 and 1933) with a number of nations in Europe and others in Asia. Italy also was busy making pacts with most of the other nations in Europe. Mussolini was not yet ready to become an aggressor.

Two of these pacts, the Locarno Pact and the Pact of Paris, were large scale attempts to provide collective security. At the suggestion of Stresemann of Germany and Briand of France, a meeting was held (1925) in Locarno, Switzerland. Germany, France,

Great Britain, Italy, Belgium, Poland, and Czechoslovakia sent delegates. Several treaties were made. Together they comprised the Locarno Pact. The seven nations that signed the Locarno Pact agreed to accept as final the provisions of the Versailles Treaty that defined the western boundary of Germany and provided for an area fifty kilometers east of the Rhine in which Germany was not to station troops. They agreed also that they would not make war upon one another except in self-defense or in case of violation of the pact or the League Covenant. All controversial questions which arose among them were to be settled by peaceful means. After the Locarno Pact had been signed, Germany was admitted to the League of Nations (1926).

The spirit of friendliness which grew out of the Locarno meeting prompted Briand to propose to Secretary of State Kellogg of the United States a joint conference to outlaw war between their nations. Kellogg, who had already negotiated a number of arbitration treaties for the United States, agreed and suggested that other nations be asked to outlaw war. In 1928 delegates from fifteen nations adopted the Pact of Paris (Kellogg-Briand Peace Pact). Within a short time thirty more nations signed it. By this Pact, forty-five nations agreed to renounce war as a means of achieving their national policies except when necessary to defend national security. Aggression was condemned and an agreement was made that all disputes should be settled by peaceful means. The Pact of Paris did not contain any provision for its enforcement.

The world-wide economic depression brought new problems. In the autumn of 1929 prices on the New York stock market collapsed. This collapse was the first sign, but not the cause, of a world-wide depression. In the United States wild speculation in real estate and in markets where stocks and other goods were sold had caused a rise in prices much higher than values warranted. When prices fell, the speculators who had borrowed money from banks were unable to pay their loans and many banks failed. The closing of factories caused unemployment everywhere and brought great misery to millions of people. For a time the United States Steel Corporation worked at only 10 per cent of its capacity because of the small demand for steel products. Many of the unemployed did not have any money with which to buy goods and so more factories closed down. The increase in unemployment that followed caused a still further decline in purchasing power.

Most of the European nations were spending more than they were collecting in taxes. They made up the difference by borrowing. When the French government called its loans to the Bank of Austria, that bank could not pay them and closed its doors. Great Britain was paying out so much gold that it was unable to maintain sufficient gold reserves to protect its paper money. It went off the gold standard, that is, it refused to pay any more gold to the holders of paper money. Other nations went off the gold standard, including the United States (1933).

Trade among nations had been badly hampered by the tariffs which most of them had passed after the First World War. The abandonment of the gold standard lessened trade among nations still more because the values of national currencies changed from day to day. As a result, a buyer of goods in a foreign country could not tell what his purchases would cost when the time came to pay for them. After going off the gold standard, many nations increased their tariffs in an attempt to protect their home industries.

The governments who were unable to pay their international debts found their financial burdens greatly increased. Political parties in every country had different solutions

International News

EFFECT OF THE WORLD-WIDE ECONOMIC DEPRESSION. Police in New York City are shown holding back some of the 10,000 men on relief rolls who stormed the offices of WPA to apply for jobs on projects financed by the federal government to relieve unemployment.

for the difficulties, and leaders found it hard to secure majorities for any measures intended to improve economic conditions. Consequently, political unrest was rife in many countries. The suffering of Germans and the weakness of the German Republic contributed greatly to the rise of the Nazi party. French ministries changed constantly and bitter feeling developed between conservatives generally and the Popular Front. Even Great Britain found it necessary to suspend its customary parliamentary government and to establish a national government composed of all three political parties, Liberal, Conservative and Labor. The New Deal in the United States carried the Federal government into new areas of economic and social life.

The depression caused complications among the nations who could not pay their international debts. In 1931 President Hoover proposed a general moratorium (suspension of payment) of German reparations and international debts for a year. The following year at Lausanne an agreement was reached for a further reduction of reparations, but it never took effect because the European Allies, being unable to get a satisfactory settlement of their debts to the United States, never ratified it. After 1933 Germany, now controlled by Nazis, refused to pay any more reparations, and among the European nations only Finland paid on its debt to the United States.

During the First World War and immediately after it the United States government loaned huge sums to the Allied nations, including Great Britain, France, Italy, Belgium, and others, and to the new nations created by the Paris Peace Conference. Most of the debtor nations said that the money we had loaned them was an American contribution to victory and that the debts should be cancelled. Much discussion of the debt question followed in the United States. The United States government agreed to a reduction of these debts, but it refused to cancel them. Much of the money which the Germans paid other nations in reparations was borrowed from American and British banks. Some of the money obtained from reparations payments by European nations was used by them to pay their debts to the United States. In 1934 Congress passed the Johnson Act which forbade any person or organization in the United States to loan money to nations which had not paid their debts to the United States.

A World Economic Conference, which met in London (1933) to consider war debts, reparations, tariffs, and commodity prices, failed when President Roosevelt withdrew his support because he wanted to bring about a rise in commodity prices in the United States before entering into any international agreement. All of these perplexities which arose out of the abandonment of the gold standard, the increase in tariffs, the severe decline in international trade, and the refusal of debtor nations to pay their international debts caused a tension among the nations that made it increasingly difficult for them to work together in an attempt to solve their economic problems.

The nations prepared for the Second World War, 1931-1939. In 1931, two years before the World Economic Conference, the period of peace pacts and outward good will came to an end. During the next eight years the nations of the world moved steadily toward war. One after another of the nations that had signed peace pacts violated their pledges. The violators of these pacts trained men for war, manufactured huge armaments and built great fleets of airplanes and new and heavily armed warships. The momentous decisions that led to the Second World War were: (1) the Japanese decision to make themselves masters of the Far East, (2) Mussolini's decision to carry out imperialistic policies, (3) Franco's decision to overthrow the Spanish Republic, and finally (4) Hitler's decision to renew aggressive militarism and imperialism.

Japanese nationalists and imperialists attempted to master East Asia. Economic conditions, national pride, and the military traditions of the Japanese led them to attempt to master East Asia. Japan needed more food for its people, more raw materials for its industries, and greater overseas markets for its goods. Japan proper was overcrowded. Although it is about the same size as California, its population was estimated (1940) to be about 73,000,000. Only a bountiful supply of fish kept many Japanese from actual starvation. Great numbers of workers were employed at very low wages in factories. Japan had to import basic raw materials, including coal, iron, oil, rubber, and cotton, to supply the needs of factories for the manufacture of goods, much of which were exported. To pay for these imports, manufactured goods had to be sold abroad. Great quantities of inferior goods at low prices were exported, particularly to the United States, Latin America, the Philippines, and China. To secure foodstuffs and raw materials and also markets for their manufactured goods, the Japanese thought they had to control the resources and markets of East Asia.

National pride and military tradition made them feel that they were entitled to be masters of East Asia. Many Japanese believed their emperor to be a god, descended from the Sun Goddess, and that they were superior to all other peoples. The Samurai tradition of the more aristocratic officers of the army made it their duty and their pride to fight for the glory and power of the emperor. The Japanese victory over Russia (1904-1905) gave them confidence in their ability to gain mastery over East Asia.

Racial antagonisms also urged them on. They resented the law of the United States that excluded them from the United States and also the presence, possessions, and power of white men in East Asia. They hoped to drive all white men out of East Asia. They called their program "Asia for the Asiatics," and later the "Co-Prosperity Sphere for East Asia."

The Japanese planned a vast territorial expansion in East Asia. After the modernization of Japan began in 1868, the Japanese made plans for territorial expansion which they enlarged from time to time. They planned: (1) to add to the four main islands of Japan other islands near Japan, (2) to get possession of Korea and at least economic control of China, and (3) to extend their new empire to include the Philippines, Indo-China, Siam, the Malay Peninsula, and the numerous islands in the Southwest Pacific. In 1874 the Japanese occupied the Bonin Islands, south of Japan. After a successful war with China (1895), Japan annexed Formosa and the Pescadores (islands between Formosa and China) and gained a free hand in Korea. After Japan's victory over Russia it annexed the Liaotung peninsula and the southern half of Sakhalin island, valuable for its minerals and fisheries.

In 1910 Japan annexed Korea without opposition by the United States and the European powers that had interests in the Far East. During the First World War, while the nations of the Western world were unable to interfere, Japan made Twenty-One Demands on China. These demands involved special economic and political privileges which, if granted, would have brought China under Japanese control. After the United States had protested, Japan did not insist on its most far-reaching demands. However, Japan did gain economic control over Manchuria and Inner Mongolia, both parts of China. The Paris Peace Settlement (1919) mandated to Japan all of the Caroline, Marshall, and Mariana islands except Guam, which had belonged to Germany before the First World War. The Shantung Peninsula, which Japan had taken from Germany in the First World War, was later given back to China because of pressure from the United States.

From 1919 to 1931 Japan appeared on the surface to be peaceful and willing to cooperate with other nations. It joined the League of Nations, and it occupied a permanent seat on the Council of the League. At the Washington Conference (1921-1922) Japan accepted the naval ratio agreed upon; it signed the Four-Power Treaty to respect the possessions of the United States, Great Britain, and France in the Pacific; and also signed the Nine-Power Treaty which guaranteed the political independence and territorial integrity of China and the Open Door

Policy. In 1928 Japan signed the Kellogg-Briand Pact to outlaw war as an instrument of national policy. This co-operation of Japan with the other nations of the world was due to the policies of political liberals and leading industrialists of Japan, but they were contrary to the national policies of the Japanese nationalists and militarists.

Japanese nationalists and militarists gained control of the government. Extreme nationalists, chiefly army officers, resented bitterly all of this co-operation with Western powers, which they considered concessions injurious to Japan's national interests. They fought vigorously against the policies of the political liberals and industrialists. Their power in the government grew rapidly after Hirohito became emperor (1926). The sufferings of the Japanese which resulted from the collapse of foreign trade in the world depression and from a Chinese boycott of Japanese goods strengthened the hands of the nationalists and militarists. After a liberal premier was murdered (May 15, 1932) the nationalists and militarists secured control of the government. Liberal leaders were forced into retirement. Several were murdered in 1936. With this overthrow of liberalism, Japan was committed to a military and naval expansion which the nationalists and militarists thought would make Japan master of East Asia.

Japanese aggressors seized Manchuria, a part of China. The first stage in territorial aggression was the seizure and occupation of Manchuria. On September 18, 1931, the Japanese themselves set off an explosion which damaged very slightly the Japanese-owned railway near Mukden, capital of Manchuria, and blamed it on the Chinese. The Japanese army, acting apparently without orders from the government, seized all the strategic centers in Manchuria and thereby gained military control over it. Manchuria was then set up (1932) as a puppet nation (Manchukuo) with Henry Pu-Yi, ex-emperor of China, as emperor under the protection and control of the Japanese army.

United States Secretary of State, Henry L. Stimson, sent a protest (1932) to the Japanese government. His protest, known as the Stimson Doctrine, stated that the Japanese had violated the Nine-Power Treaty and the Kellogg-Briand Pact and announced that the United States would not recognize the acquisition of territory made by armed force in violation of treaty agreements. The League of Nations then met its first great test in handling a case involving a major power. The League appointed a commission under Lord Lytton to investigate and report. The report condemned Japan and recommended the restoration of Manchuria to China. The Council and the Assembly, while accepting the Stimson Doctrine and the Lytton report, did not take any action to force Japan out of Manchuria. The member nations of the League and also the United States were apparently not willing to act together against Japan. Angered by the report, Matsuoka, the chairman of the Japanese delegation to the League, announced (1933) Japan's withdrawal from the League. The cause of world peace had suffered a telling blow.

The Japanese War against China began in 1931. The Japanese army was not content with the seizure of Manchuria. In 1933 it invaded the Chinese province of Jehol and annexed it to their puppet nation Manchukuo. In 1934 the Japanese government proclaimed Manchukuo an independent nation and declared that Japan assumed exclusive responsibility for maintaining peace in the Far East. The army also penetrated into Inner Mongolia and into some of the provinces of North China. It even established a garrison of troops near Peiping. After the Chinese retaliated with a boycott of Japanese goods, war between the two nations was certain. In July, 1937, a clash between Japanese troops and Chinese troops at the Marco Polo Bridge near Peiping was used by Japanese leaders as an excuse for a full-fledged invasion of China but without any declaration of war. The everywhere-victorious Japanese expected a quick victory over the poorly equipped Chinese. Peiping and Tientsin were taken in one month. The Japanese navy attempted to take Shanghai but had to call on the army for help. Shanghai fell in November, 1937. The horrible Japanese atrocities which followed the fall of Nanking (December, 1937) shocked the civilized world. The United States and the League of Nations protested but did little else.

The Japanese established a puppet state at Nanking under a Chinese president. The advance of the Japanese armies continued and Canton fell (1938). Yet all of these military successes did not bring the quick and decisive victory which the Japanese had expected, because the Chinese continued to resist the Japanese advance.

The Japanese invaders could not break the Chinese will to continue the war. Though the Chinese suffered greatly, they continued to fight. More Chinese cities were bombed and pillaged by the Japanese. Many of the Chinese in the occupied area were enslaved. The Chinese government printed paper money to pay its expenses, now greatly increased by war, and that caused a serious inflation which raised prices so high that most people were unable to purchase goods that they needed badly. The Japanese armies continued to defeat the Chinese armies and overran large sections of Eastern China including many seaports. The Japanese occupation of these seaports cut off all communication by sea with the Western powers, and thus they were unable to send any supplies to Chinese ports. Until a few months before the Japanese

attacked Pearl Harbor (December 7, 1941) they were able to buy oil, scrap iron, munitions, cotton, and anything else they wanted in the United States for use against the Chinese.

The Chinese leader, Chiang Kai-shek, kept his armies intact and withdrew them before the superior armament of the enemy. He moved his capital from Nanking to Chungking behind the mountains in Western China. He secured loans from the United States and also Great Britain who sent military supplies to him over the Burma Road, the road from Lashio in Burma to Chungking. Trucks loaded with war supplies moved slowly over this dangerous road to help China continue the war. To appease the Japanese, the British closed the Burma Road for three months in 1940 rather than risk trouble in the Far East, while fighting the Battle of Britain to save the home islands from German invasion. In 1940 an American aviator, General Claire Chennault, organized the Flying Tigers, a force of volunteer American aviators who fought courageously and devastatingly against the Japanese armies and their military installations.

The Chinese people continued to bear their sufferings, defeats, and bombings with heroism and fortitude. Before the Japanese had conquered much of Eastern China, the Chinese dismantled the machinery in factories and carried it laboriously to the west where they set it up again and began to produce goods. As the Japanese conquered more of Eastern China, the Chinese dismantled more machinery and carried it to the west. Schools and colleges were moved to the west where they continued their work. Relatively few of the Chinese who remained in the conquered areas collaborated with the Japanese. Small bands of Chinese guerillas wiped out small bands of Japanese soldiers, tore up railroads, and destroyed supplies. In some areas the Japanese controlled only the railroad lines and the towns and cities on them. The torture and execution of guerillas and the destruction of cities and villages did not break the Chinese will to resist the hated invader. After their first successes, the Japanese made no attempt to take Chungking. The Chinese could not drive them out of the provinces they had conquered. The war seemed to have come to a stalemate.

Japan and the U.S.S.R., though at peace, did not trust each other. To guard against Japanese attack, the Soviet Union organized a strong army and stationed it along the international boundary between Siberia and the Chinese province of Manchuria which had been under the control of Japan since 1931. The Soviet army got its provisions and military supplies chiefly from farms and factories in Siberia. The Japanese were always afraid that this army might attack them while they were busy fighting elsewhere. To guard against such a Soviet attack, they stationed an army on their side of the international boundary. In 1936 they signed the Anti-Comintern Pact with Hitler. This pact was made, so the signers said, to prevent the spread of Communism by the Third International (Comintern). The signing of the pact did not disrupt the outwardly friendly relations between the Soviet Union and Japan even though the pact was really an alliance against the U.S.S.R. Although the Soviet Union did not make war directly upon Japan it aided China by sending war supplies overland. However, the tension between the U.S.S.R. and Japan led to a number of battles along the border of Manchuria and Siberia. One of these battles (1938) was a large battle which the Soviet Union won. In 1945, shortly before Germany's surrender to the United Nations, the Soviet Union announced that the neutrality treaty which it had made with Japan (1941) for five years would lapse in one year. In August, 1945, before the treaty had lapsed, the U.S.S.R. declared war on Japan and swiftly invaded Manchuria with overwhelming power.

The Japanese planned to drive the United States, France, Great Britain, and the Netherlands out of the East. Though the Japanese had not been able to conquer China, they were planning aggressions elsewhere. For years Japanese spies had been busy collecting military information in Alaska, along the west coast of the United States, in Hawaii, in the Philippines, and also in the Dutch and British possessions which they were planning to seize. In 1934 Japan repudiated the Five-Power Treaty which it had signed at the Washington Conference (1921-1922) and the naval agreement which it had signed at the London Conference (1930), both of which had limited the Japanese navy, and began to build warships with feverish haste. It increased its air force and trained its armies for island and jungle warfare. On December 7, 1941, the air arm of a Japanese fleet attacked Pearl Harbor, the American naval base in Hawaii, and a few hours later an air attack was made on Manila. The Japanese had begun in earnest to execute their plan to drive the United States, France, Great Britain, and the Netherlands out of the East.

Mussolini's decision to carry out imperialistic policies threatened the peace of the world. The Japanese struck the first blow at world peace and the League of Nations when they invaded Manchuria (1931). Mussolini struck the second in 1935 when he attacked Ethiopia. As he thought himself a modern Caesar, he had grandiose plans for a new Italian empire. In 1912, Italy in a successful war with Turkey gained possession of Tripoli (Libya) and the Dodecanese Islands in the Mediterranean Sea close to Turkey. Though Mussolini never stated his imperialistic program explicitly, he is said to have desired to gain a controlling influence over Greece and ownership of Corsica, Tunisia, Algeria, and other French possessions in Africa. Control over them would give Italy control over the Mediterranean Sea which he hopefully called *mare nostrum* (our sea), as the ancient Romans termed it.

Mussolini's first step was to gain control of the Adriatic Sea. In 1923 he bombarded and seized Corfu, an island west of Greece (ancient Corcyra), as he said, to punish the Greeks for killing Italians in Albania, a small weak kingdom across the Adriatic from Italy. The Greek government appealed to the League of Nations to force Mussolini to evacuate Corfu. At first he defied the League, but later on he yielded to pressure from Great Britain and France and withdrew his troops from Corfu. In 1927 he secured a protectorate over Albania which gave him a foothold in the Balkan peninsula north of Greece, and in 1939 he conquered Albania and annexed it to Italy. This gave him a port (Durazzo) near the entrance to the Adriatic Sea from which he could launch a land attack on Greece.

Mussolini's second step was his aggression against Ethiopia. In 1935 he attacked the kingdom of Ethiopia, formerly called Abyssinia. It lay between the Sudan on the west and Somaliland and Italian Eritrea on the east. It was the only country in Africa except Liberia that was not a possession of a European nation. Many of its people are Coptic Christians and its rulers have claimed to be descendants of King Solomon. The Italians had tried to conquer Ethiopia (1896) but had been disastrously defeated at Adowa. Haile Selassie, who became king (1930), had started to modernize his kingdom. He granted it a constitution modeled after the English constitution, founded a national bank, established public schools, built railroads, and joined the League of Nations. Mussolini planned the conquest of Ethiopia to avenge

the Italian defeat at Adowa, to gain lands for Italy's surplus population, and to give Italian capitalists an opportunity to invest their surplus capital.

The League of Nations failed in its efforts to restrain Mussolini. After Mussolini had begun the invasion that led to the conquest of Ethiopia (1935), Haile Selassie appealed to the League of Nations for protection. The French and British were both opposed to Mussolini's action; the French because he had designs on their possessions in Africa; the British because Italian control of Ethiopia would threaten British control of the Red Sea and the British life line to India. Their efforts to restrain Mussolini were a failure. The Commission appointed by the Council of the League failed also in its efforts and Mussolini began his invasion of Ethiopia. Thereupon the Council of the League declared Italy an aggressor, and a vote of the Assembly ordered the League members to apply economic sanctions against Italy, that is, to refuse to sell food, ammunition, and raw materials to Italy and also not to permit imports from Italy. But sanctions were not placed on oil, Italy's greatest need, as Britain and France did not want to risk war with Italy because they were unprepared. As the United States was not a League member it continued to sell oil and other commodities that Italy needed.

The Italian army and air force with the use of poison gas won an easy victory over the poorly equipped Ethiopians. Before the Italians entered Addis Ababa, the capital of Ethiopia, Haile Selassie fled to Great Britain. On May 9, 1936, Mussolini announced that Ethiopia had been annexed to Italy and that King Victor Emmanuel was to assume the title Emperor of Ethiopia. In a little more than a month afterward and in spite of the protests of Haile Selassie, the League Council voted to end the sanctions which had never

International News

Residents of Addis Ababa, capital of Ethiopia, are boarding a train on the French-owned railway that runs to Djibouti, French Somaliland, after Italian planes had bombed and laid waste Adowa and Adigrat.

been enforced anyway. The League of Nations had failed completely because its members would not co-operate in carrying out the League's order. British leaders felt that Great Britain's failure to check Mussolini was due to its unpreparedness for war. Consequently (1937), the British government appropriated some $7,000,000,000 to strengthen the army and navy in the next five years.

Mussolini and Hitler joined hands. After his defiance of Great Britain, France, and the League of Nations, and his conquest of Ethiopia, Mussolini and Hitler agreed (1936) that their countries would act together in foreign affairs; and thereby they established the Rome-Berlin Axis. In 1937 Mussolini made Italy a partner with Germany and Japan in the Anti-Comintern Pact. In May, 1939, the Rome-Berlin Axis was strengthened by a military alliance of Italy and Germany. Mussolini's conquest of Ethiopia, his part in forming the Rome-Berlin Axis, his joining the Anti-Comintern Pact, and his military alliance with Hitler made his position clear. To aid Franco to overthrow the government of the Spanish Republic, Mussolini (1936) sent soldiers who were said to be volunteers and also military equipment, and Hitler sent airplanes, pilots, and technicians. In 1937 he withdrew Italy from the League of Nations, four years after Hitler had withdrawn Germany from the League. He reluctantly accepted the German occupation of Austria (1938) and the seizure of Czechoslovakia (1939). He encouraged the Italians to shout loudly in great mass meetings for the possession of the French island of Corsica and for Tunisia in North Africa which also belonged to France, but he did not act to fulfill their desires. In the first months of the Second World War he remained neutral, but on June 10, 1940, while France was reeling under the blows of the Germans, he declared war on France and Great Britain and ordered his armies to invade Southern France. The agreement of Hitler and Mussolini to act together in foreign affairs had been put into effect, first in Spain and now in France.

Hard times in Spain led to serious internal conflicts. During the First World War neutral Spain became fairly prosperous because the warring nations bought its iron, munitions, and other goods. After the fighting was over, the foreign demand for Spanish goods decreased greatly, unemployment increased, and war-time prosperity declined rapidly. In these hard times the conservatives struggled to hold their power and privileges and the liberals struggled to take them away.

The conservatives were composed chiefly of the royal family, the churchmen, and the nobility. They owned most of the land which was worked by poor peasants, many of whom could neither read nor write. A few large and politically powerful corporations controlled most of the industries. They paid low wages and working conditions were bad. Small businessmen who had to pay heavy taxes were dissatisfied because the nobles and the Church didn't pay any. Army officers and conservatives controlled the government. The monarch, Alphonso XIII, and his ministers did not have the support of the masses of the people who demanded reforms which were not granted.

During the First World War manufacturing had increased rapidly in the province of Catalonia, especially in Barcelona, Spain's largest and most prosperous seaport. At this time democratic ideas had captured the imagination of large numbers of city workers and peasants. The Catalonians and Basques demanded political independence. As these internal conflicts and many others were raging, the army suffered serious defeats and heavy losses in its attempts to suppress a revolt against Spanish rule in Morocco in Northwest Africa. After a battle in which more than 12,000 men were killed, the commanding general committed suicide. Army officers were accused of inefficiency and corruption; the Spanish government faced a serious political crisis. After a garrison at Barcelona had mutinied and a separatist movement had broken out, Primo de Rivera, with the approval of the king, took Barcelona and established a military dictatorship (1923).

Rivera's program was "country, monarchy, and religion." He set aside the constitution, proclaimed martial law, dissolved the Cortes (parliament), suspended jury trial, suppressed freedom of speech, censored the press, imprisoned some liberal opponents, and harried others out of the land. He closed the University of Madrid and others to remove the opposition of students and intellectuals. His denial of the constitutional rights of the people aroused such a widespread and ever-increasing popular discontent against his dictatorship and also the monarchy that he ended his dictatorship and became prime minister. He did restore order in Spain and peace in Morocco, but he was unable to remove the causes of internal conflicts. Discouraged and in ill health he resigned (1930). After Rivera's resignation, King Alphonso announced the restoration of the constitution and set a date for the election of candidates for the Cortes. The government then called for municipal and provincial elections and promised the election of a constituent assembly which would draw up a constitution.

Spanish liberals established a republic. The municipal elections (April 12, 1931) resulted in an overwhelming victory for the republicans. Zamora, the republican leader, called for the abdication of the king. There-upon Alphonso fled to France (April 16) without abdicating. Zamora set up a provi-sional government with himself as president. The election of members to the constituent assembly gave the republicans a huge ma-jority. A committee of the assembly declared Alphonso guilty of high treason, forbade his return to Spain, and confiscated all royal property. Spain was then declared a republic.

In December, 1931, a new constitution was adopted. It provided for universal suffrage, a Cortes of one house, and a president to be elected for a term of six years. Army officers and clergymen were not eligible to be elected president.

The republican government separated the Church from the state, nationalized church property but left it in the custody of the clergy, dissolved the Jesuit order and confis-cated its property, and forbade members of religious orders to engage in business. Spain was to have complete religious liberty. Mar-riage and divorce were to be under govern-ment control. Public utilities were national-ized. The government confiscated the lands of the Church and the estates of large land-owners and divided the confiscated lands among peasants who did not have enough land to make a living. Church schools were abolished and the education of youth was placed under the control of the government. Nearly all of these reforms had been accom-plished by the French Revolution 150 years before.

The reforms of the republican govern-ment led to civil war. These reforms aroused the hostility of those who had been deprived of their ancient powers and privileges. To offset the work of the republicans, a group of army officers organized the Phalange, a so-ciety with Fascist principles. In 1936 an elec-tion of candidates for the Cortes was held in which the Left parties (Republicans, Social-ists, Syndicalists, Communists) combined in a *Popular Front* and won a decisive victory. They planned to make more reforms, dis-missed army officers suspected of disloyalty to the republic, and assigned others to the com-mand of armies overseas.

The Spanish Civil War began with a revolt of army chiefs in Spanish Morocco and spread rapidly to garrison towns in Spain. In Madrid and Barcelona the government held its own against the revolt. The leaders of the revolt were Generals Franco and Mola, who had the support of most of the army and air force and large Moorish contingents. The Loyalists, that is, the government party, though poorly equipped, fought with great bravery.

The Spanish Civil War affected interna-tional affairs. Because Franco planned a Fascist government for Spain, Italy and Ger-many were willing to help him. In addition they hoped that by gaining influence in Spain they would also gain influence in Latin America where Spanish influence was thought to be strong. Mussolini hoped to secure badly needed supplies of metals which were abun-dant in Spain. He sent soldiers and war equip-ment to Franco and Germany sent him air-planes, pilots, and technicians. Because some of the supporters of the government were Communists, the Soviet Union sent advisers, aviators, planes, and other supplies to the Loyalists. Many thousands of volunteers went from France, England, and the United States to fight on the side of the Loyalists.

Great Britain and France adopted a pol-icy of non-intervention. The governments of Great Britain and France refused to inter-vene directly in the fighting in Spain. How-ever, they did place an embargo on the ship-ment of war materials to either Franco or the Loyalists. In 1936 twenty-seven nations, led by Great Britain and France, signed a non-intervention agreement. British and French policy was due largely to a decided difference of opinions in each of these countries on the reasons for the Spanish Civil War, to a fear of Communism, and in greater measure perhaps to fear that intervention would result in a general European war which they hoped to be able to prevent. Even though Germany and Italy joined in the non-intervention agreement they managed in one way and another to aid Franco. The non-intervention policy sealed the fate of the duly elected Spanish government because it could not buy supplies to equip its army while Franco continued to get all he needed from Germany and Italy. On January 6, 1937, the Congress of the United States passed a joint resolution forbidding the export of munitions "for use of either of the opposing forces in Spain." The Spanish republican government appealed to the League of Nations against the armed intervention of Germany and Italy, but the League did not act. The Spanish Civil War widened the breach between Great Britain and France on one side, and Germany and Italy on the other. It served also as a testing ground for new military equipment of Italy, Germany, and the Soviet Union.

The Spanish Civil War continued to drag on for almost three years. Many cities were destroyed by bombing and the countryside was devastated. On January 26, 1939, Barcelona was captured by Franco with the aid of Italian troops. Two hundred thousand Loyalist soldiers crossed into France where they were disarmed and interned by the French government. The war came to an end with the surrender of Madrid (March 28, 1939) and in less than a month Franco announced Spain's adherence to the German-Japanese-Italian Anti-Comintern Pact. The Spanish Civil War took a terrible toll of human lives; 700,000 had been killed in battle, 30,000 executed, and 15,000 killed in air raids. After twenty years of bitter political struggles and a frightful civil war, the government ended

Acme

General Franco salutes troops in Madrid victory parade after Franco's forces, aided by German and Italian soldiers, money, and equipment, had won the Spanish Civil War.

in a dictatorship that denied the people democratic rights and maintained close relations with the dictators of Germany and Italy.

Hitler decided to renew aggressive militarism and imperialism. After the First World War many a German questioned about the future replied, *"Das kommt,"* meaning "The day of victory will come." The German General Staff made its plans for the next war in secret and the German youth were given the physical training necessary to make them good soldiers when the time came. Hitler brought German militarism out into the open, speeded rearmament, and revived German imperialism until it became more aggressive than it had ever been. In 1933 he withdrew Germany from the Disarmament Conference at Geneva and also from the League of Nations. In 1935 he announced that Germany repudiated the Versailles Treaty and was going to renew universal military conscription. Great Britain, France, and Italy joined in a protest against Germany's policy. France replied to Hitler's repudiation of the Treaty of Versailles by making a military alliance with the Soviet Union (1935) which pledged each country to help the other in case of unprovoked aggression. The League of Nations condemned Germany, but did nothing. Indeed, within three months after Hitler's repudiation of the Versailles Treaty, Great Britain, as we have seen, signed a naval agreement which permitted Germany to build its navy up to 35 per cent of Britain's surface craft and 45 per cent of her submarines.

In 1936, while Great Britain and France were deeply concerned with Mussolini's invasion of Ethiopia, Hitler denounced the Locarno Pact, sent his armies across the Rhine into the Rhineland, and began its refortification. He used the Franco-Russian military alliance as an excuse for doing so, claiming falsely that it was a violation of the Locarno Pact. It seemed so certain that France could stop re-occupation of the Rhineland that some German generals advised against it, but when Hitler did invade the Rhineland the French government failed to act. Again European powers and the League protested to the German government. Some members of the French cabinet wanted to use French armies to drive Hitler out of the Rhineland, but others did not. Because of this disunity and Britain's unwillingness to take part in driving Hitler out, nothing was done. While Hitler's troops were marching across the Rhine, he declared before the Reichstag that Germany had "no territorial demands to make in Europe."

In spite of what he had just said, Hitler and the General Staff speeded up Germany's rearmament and made plans for a war that was to engulf nearly all of the world. The Germans tested their new airplanes and tanks in the Spanish Civil War to see what improvements should be made. The formation of the Rome-Berlin Axis gave added strength to Hitler's pronouncements on foreign policies. He tried to use the Anti-Comintern Pact with Japan and Italy to show that he was the real defender of European civilization against Communism.

The first victim of Hitler's aggressive militarism and imperialism was Austria. Before the First World War Vienna had been the capital and center of the trade, politics, and culture of the Dual Monarchy. At the Paris Peace Conference, the Dual Monarchy was dismembered and a part of it, Austria, became a small republic. Because of the great loss of territory and the disruption of trade by tariff walls, the Austrians found it difficult to make a living. Although the Austrians were almost ruined economically, they made a valiant effort, under the leadership of their Marxian socialist government, to revive the economic life of their country. The socialist housing program in Vienna attracted widespread attention even in the United States. The anti-clericalism of the Marxian Socialists involved them in trouble with the Christian Socialists when they came into power. Under Chancellor Engelbert Dollfuss (1932) the Christian Socialists established a dictatorship (1934) that suppressed rigorously the Marxian Socialists. On July 25, 1934, those Austrians who had succumbed to Nazi propaganda revolted and murdered Dollfuss. Their failure to gain control over the Austrian government was due in part to the opposition of Mussolini who did not see eye to eye with Hitler until the Rome-Berlin Axis was formed (1936). Kurt Schuschnigg succeeded Dollfuss as chancellor and the Christian Socialist government lasted until 1938 when it was overthrown by Hitler.

The Christian Socialist government under Chancellor Schuschnigg had imprisoned many Austrian Nazis. In February, 1938, Hitler invited Schuschnigg to Berchtesgaden in Germany, and while he was there the most ruthless pressure forced him to promise to release the Austrian Nazis and to take certain Nazis whom Hitler named into his cabinet. After Hitler made a speech (February, 1938) in which he promised to protect all German minorities outside Germany, Schuschnigg announced that Austria would remain independent and that a plebiscite would be held on the question of Austrian independence. Thereupon Hitler demanded the postponement of the plebiscite and the resignation of Schuschnigg. Schuschnigg resigned and the Austrian Nazi who became chancellor of Austria asked Hitler to intervene to restore order. The Austrians knew they were not strong enough to resist and so in March, 1938, a German army marched into Austria and Hitler announced the annexation of Austria to Germany.

Mussolini, who had protected Austria from Nazi seizure in 1934, was now silent because he and Hitler had agreed (1936) to act together on foreign affairs. The other European powers were silent, too. The so-called plebiscite that was held in Austria a while later and under Nazi auspices appeared to show the approval of the Austrian people for Hitler's annexation of their country. However, the plebiscite did not show how many were opposed because nearly all who were opposed did not dare to vote no.

The second victim of Hitler's aggressive militarism and imperialism was Czechoslovakia. Under the wise guidance of President Masaryk and Prime Minister Benes the Republic of Czechoslovakia had become strong and prosperous. Agriculture and industry thrived, particularly the Skoda iron works which manufactured steel and armaments. Like many other nations in Europe, the Czechs were plagued by the baffling problems raised by minorities. One of these minorities, the agricultural and somewhat backward Slovakians in the eastern part of the republic, claimed that they did not have their rightful share in the government of Czechoslovakia. Their complaints were recognized and remedied in part and perhaps could have been wholly remedied in time.

A much greater and more difficult minority problem was raised by the Germans who lived in the northern fringe of Czechoslovakia (Sudetenland). It was almost entirely German. The ancestors of some of them had settled in the Sudetenland to escape the ravages of the Thirty Years' War. The Sudeten Germans, while professing loyalty to the Republic of Czechoslovakia, claimed that they were being discriminated against by the government and by the schools. Czech leaders tried to satisfy their claims, but without much success. The Sudetens, who were definitely pro-German and highly receptive to Nazi propaganda, created eventually the crisis which led to the destruction of the Republic of Czechoslovakia.

After Hitler became Chancellor of Germany (1933), a Nazi party led by Konrad Henlein was formed among the Sudetens. In February, 1938, Hitler promised protection to German minorities outside Germany including, of course, the Sudetens. Within a few days the government of Czechoslovakia stated that it would defend itself against interference by a foreign power. In April, 1938, Henlein demanded that the Czechoslovakian government grant Sudeten Germans the rights enjoyed by the Czechs, meaning self-government for the Sudetens and also entire freedom to adopt the Nazi program. After the Czechoslovakian government had rejected his demand, he appealed to Hitler who said that the Sudetens should be given the right to determine their own government. Hitler's answer brought on a crisis in the international affairs of Europe. France and the Soviet Union were bound by treaties to go to the aid of Czechoslovakia if Germany invaded it. Chamberlain, Prime Minister of Great Britain, met Hitler at Berchtesgaden to try to reach a peaceful settlement of the Sudeten problem. They agreed that Czechoslovakia should cede to Germany the part of Sudeten-

International News

THE PRIME MINISTER AND THE DICTATOR. Prime Minister Neville Chamberlain and
Il Duce chat before attending the secret session of the Four-Power Conference at Munich. At right
is Count Ciano, Italian Foreign Minister and son-in-law of Mussolini.

land in which the inhabitants were almost all Germans.

Chamberlain then returned to Britain. A few days later Hitler demanded the cession of all Sudetenland by October 1 or he would order his armies to march into Czechoslovakia. Chamberlain then asked for another conference and President Roosevelt wrote both Hitler and Mussolini urging them to attend a conference. The Soviet Union requested that it be permitted to send a representative to the conference, but the request was denied by the powers involved even though the Soviet Union was bound by

a treaty with Czechoslovakia to go to the aid of that country if it were attacked. A conference was held at Munich (September 29, 1938). It was attended by Chamberlain, Hitler, Mussolini, and Daladier, Premier of France. At this conference Chamberlain and Daladier deserted the republic their governments had helped to create and promised to support, and advised it to yield to Hitler's demands.

Partly in exchange for his promise that he would never make any more demands for territory in Europe, Chamberlain and Daladier yielded to all of Hitler's demands on

International News

HITLER REVIEWING HIS GUARD IN PRAGUE. Chancellor Adolph Hitler is here shown inspecting his honor guard in front of Hradcany Castle in March, 1939, just after his troops had occupied the capital of the Republic of Czechoslovakia, the second victim of Hitler's imperialism.

Czechoslovakia. Chamberlain returned to London and announced that he had brought "peace in our time." Daladier, returning to Paris with the realization that France had violated a solemn pledge, was received by a cheering crowd. In the words of the time Hitler had been appeased again. Czechoslovakia had erected strong fortifications near the border between itself and Germany. It had a well-trained army and at Skoda one of the most modern munitions plants in Europe. But it yielded to the advice of Chamberlain and Daladier because it believed it could not defend itself alone against Hitler's armies. Hitler showed that appeasement meant little to him and that he considered his own promises of no value when he helped Slovakia gain its independence and also when on March 15, 1939, he sent German troops to march into Prague and thereby brought the Republic of Czechoslovakia to an end.

Almost without firing a gun Hitler had occupied and re-fortified the Rhineland, and annexed Austria and most of Czechoslovakia. All the Austrians and Czechs and the natural resources of their countries were now his to help carry on his aggressive militaristic and imperialistic program. Hitler's destruction of the Republic of Czechoslovakia changed the foreign policy of Great Britain and France. Both hastened to make a treaty with Poland in which they made a promise to aid Poland with all their forces if Poland decided to resist German aggression by force of arms.

The third victim of Hitler's aggressive militarism and imperialism was Poland. After the Paris Peace Conference Poland faced the most difficult tasks of any of the new nations that had been created by it. The area of Poland was about 150,000 square miles and its population was about 28,000,-000 composed of several jealous nationalities including Germans. The majority of the Poles were very poor and they had but little, if any, experience in self-government. From the establishment of the Polish Republic (1919) up to 1939 the Polish government was controlled most of the time by General Josef Pilsudski, a military dictator. In 1934 Hitler made a pact with Pilsudski.

Acme

SIGNING OF NON-AGGRESSION PACT BE-
TWEEN GERMANY AND THE SOVIET UNION
IN AUGUST, 1939. Left to right are shown: German
Foreign Minister von Ribbentrop, German Under-
States Secretary Gaus, Marshal Stalin, and Soviet For-
eign Minister Molotov.

The Paris Peace Conference had created
the Polish Corridor, a strip of land which separated East Prussia (part of Germany) from
the rest of Germany to give the Republic of
Poland an outlet to the Baltic Sea. It had also
made Danzig on the Baltic a free city under
the supervision of the League of Nations.
After several years of Hitler propaganda to
make Danzig a part of Germany, he demanded (October 24, 1938) the return of
Danzig to Germany and a rail and motor road
for German use across the Polish Corridor
to East Prussia. These demands created a new
crisis and, to make matters worse, Hitler repudiated the non-aggression pact that he had
made with Poland in 1934. Great Britain and
France assured Poland that they would
comply with the terms of the treaty each had
made with her and both made active preparations for the war they were now sure
would come. While each of them was trying
to reach an understanding with the Soviet
Union, they and the world were startled by
the announcement (August 23, 1939) that
Germany and the Soviet Union had signed a
non-aggression pact. As Hitler now thought
that he was secure from a Russian attack in

the East, he hesitated no longer to carry out
his military aggression and imperialism
against Poland. On September 1, 1939, without a declaration of war, German armies invaded Poland. On September 3, Great Britain
and France declared war on Germany. The
Second World War had begun in a little less
than twenty-one years after the First World
War had ended.

**Great Britain and France failed to agree
on united action.** The failure of Great
Britain and France to work together harmoni-
ously, continuously, and effectively after the
end of the First World War and even during
the first years of Hitler's rule enabled Germany
to rearm and to begin its well-planned military aggression and imperialism. British and
French leaders thought they could keep peace
by a policy of appeasement (making concessions to Hitler's demands) in hope that he
would not ask for anything more. Frequent
political changes in the government of France
caused it to lack a consistent policy in foreign
affairs and caused it to be difficult to make
decisions at certain times and impossible at
others. The peoples of the world in general
underestimated the fanaticism of Hitler and
the willingness of the German people to obey
his orders.

Although Great Britain and France had co-
operated as faithful allies in the First World
War, they found it very difficult to continue
that co-operation after the war was over
chiefly because their national interests were
different. Great Britain was interested primarily in the restoration of normal conditions
on the Continent that would lead to a revival
of trade. The British desired a prosperous but
peaceful Germany. For a long time many of
them thought Communism in Russia was a
greater menace to the peace and security of
the world than German militarism had been.
France was interested primarily in national
security. Many living Frenchmen remembered

ll too well the havoc wrought by two German invasions of their country. The French were determined to use every means possible to prevent another German invasion. They were unalterably and irrevocably opposed to any changes in the Treaty of Versailles. They demanded a strict enforcement of all of its provisions. They demanded Germany pay reparations in full to help pay their debts to other countries, and also to defray the cost of restoring the areas in France devastated by the war.

The rift between Great Britain and France came out into the open when Great Britain did not approve the French and Belgian invasion of the Ruhr (1923). After the invasion of the Ruhr the British would not sign any international agreement (except the Locarno Pact) intended to give France the national security which the French people so greatly desired. The difference of opinion between the statesmen of these two nations reached its climax when the British refused to assist the French, who were themselves not in entire agreement, in driving Hitler out of the Rhineland (1936). The Anglo-German Naval Agreement (1935) alarmed and frightened French leaders. Although the British denounced Hitler's invasion of the Rhineland, they were unwilling to support those leaders in France who wanted to use force to drive him and his troops out of the Rhineland. The British and French failed to act together when Hitler annexed Austria, destroyed the Republic of Czechoslovakia and annexed the richer part of it, and helped Slovakia gain its independence.

The British tried to appease Hitler. The British decided not to act when Hitler invaded, occupied, and re-fortified the Rhineland, annexed Austria, and destroyed the Republic of Czechoslovakia because the leaders of the Conservative government thought British interests would be served better by making concessions to Hitler rather than by refusing his demands and thereby run the risk of a general European war. Many circumstances seemed to favor this policy of appeasement. Although a number of Liberals and Laborites opposed appeasement, most Conservatives favored it. One notable exception was Winston Churchill who denounced appeasement bitterly and, with almost prophetic insight, told the British what Hitler had in store for them. The people, for the most part, approved appeasement. Although the huge wave of pacifism that had swept over Great Britain after the First World War had died down, many still felt that peace at any price was better than war.

Some British leaders in government, business, and society still thought a strong Germany would be a bulwark against Communistic Russia. Many of these thought they "could do business with Hitler." Wrongly, as events proved, they believed that Hitler could be relied upon to keep his word. Only when this belief had been proven false by his destruction of the Republic of Czechoslovakia did Great Britain abandon its appeasement policy and redouble its efforts to arm.

Britain was not ready for war. British energies and British money had been used in an effort to solve the many perplexing economic and social problems that weighed heavily on millions of British people. The British army had at this time become what it was before the First World War, a small professional army. The British did not consider a large and costly standing army and air force necessary for the protection of their national interests. The navy, they thought, was sufficient for the protection of the Empire, but even that had been limited by the Washington and London naval agreements. In the present circumstances war on the Continent might be disastrous to Great Britain. German superiority in the air, which was well known by British leaders, seemed to clinch the reasons for appeasement that might keep the peace.

Germany was not the only country that was rearming. In 1930 Mussolini began to appropriate huge sums of money for the Italian army and navy, including the building of a large number of submarines. Italy's naval expansion was of great concern to Great Britain chiefly because of its life line in the Mediterranean. When Mussolini defied Great Britain, and France also, at the time of the Ethiopian crisis he knew that Great Britain had appropriated but small sums to strengthen its navy. Great Britain's failure to take any action against Mussolini was due largely to its fear to risk a naval war with him. As he knew that Great Britain was weak, he went ahead with his plans to conquer Ethiopia. As we have seen, after Mussolini had conquered Ethiopia, Great Britain appropriated (1937) $7,000,000,000 to strengthen its army and navy.

Disunity in France made the government helpless at times. From 1919 until the Germans invaded France in 1940, the French army had been considered the strongest in Europe. To guard against another invasion, the French had constructed a line of strong fortifications that connected underground (known from its builder as the Maginot Line) from Switzerland almost to Sedan. From there to the Belgian border the fortifications were known as the Little Maginot Line.

In 1931, when Austria proposed a customs union with Germany, France, Italy, and Czechoslovakia protested on the grounds that such a union would be contrary to the treaty obligations assumed at the Paris Peace Conference. In consequence, Austria and Germany announced abandonment of a customs union. When Hitler's invasion of Austria took place (1938), France, in the midst of a cabinet crisis, was without a government that could act. At Munich (1938) Daladier joined with Chamberlain in appeasing Hitler. The weakness of the French government at this time seems to have been due primarily, if not entirely, to political and economic disunity in France.

Frenchmen, as we have seen, were divided into many political parties and schools of political and economic opinion. Some wanted a monarchy; others wanted Fascism. Some wanted friendly relations with Nazi Germany. Most were interested only in the solution of internal economic and social problems but they differed greatly in the ways to solve them. All of these opinions were reflected in politics. French cabinets changed rapidly. Coalition followed coalition so rapidly that a Premier and a Foreign Minister did not remain in office long enough to develop a consistent foreign policy and therefore little was done by France to check Hitler. Some French military leaders believed that the French army and the Maginot Line were strong enough to hold the German army at bay. They desired only to defend France against another German invasion. In the main, the French people, like the British, wanted peace. The French workingmen, unlike the German workingmen, preferred butter to cannon. The internal weaknesses that continued to manifest themselves in France after the outbreak of the Second World War were contributing causes to the swift defeat of the French armies and thereby to the swift downfall of the Third French Republic.

The people in many nations underestimated Hitler and Hitlerite Germany. After Hitler came to power, he and other German leaders were exceedingly skillful in their propaganda both at home and abroad. They secured admirers, even adherents, in every nation including our own by setting forth what they claimed were the virtues of the

Nazi system. The Nazis gained some of their support abroad by posing as Italy did as a "have not" nation which was trying to get only what it claimed was its share of the world's wealth from the "haves." Hitler's propaganda minister, Goebbels, tried to make people everywhere believe that it would be all right to unite all Germans in Europe into one nation. A great many thought that the kind of government the Germans had was not the concern of anyone else, if the German people were satisfied. The seizure of Prague and the attack on Poland awakened almost everybody, but too late for their safety, to the aggressive militarism and imperialism of Hitlerite Germany.

Hitler had a keen sense of timing. He occupied (1936) the Rhineland while England and France were deeply concerned (1935-1936) over Mussolini's success in Ethiopia. He invaded Austria (1938) while France

was in the midst of a cabinet crisis. He seized Prague (1939) at the time when France was weakened by a wave of strikes. These acts showed that he knew he would not be interfered with because the nations which might object were deeply involved in troubles at home.

For years before the outbreak of the Second World War Hitler's power to bend the Germans to his will was much greater than almost everyone in other countries realized. They followed him obediently and willingly, while they endured patiently all the deprivations and hardships needed to prepare Germany for total war. After the outbreak of the war they continued to follow Hitler even more faithfully than ever and to meet every demand he made upon them. He had made them believe that they were a master race and that the other peoples in Europe and elsewhere should be their slaves.

SUMMARY

From 1919-1931 the League of Nations accomplished much in adjusting peacefully the international disputes of weak nations, but it failed utterly in adjusting peacefully the international disputes that involved the strong powers—Japan, China, Italy, Great Britain, France, and Germany.

The Paris Peace Conference decided that Germany should pay reparations, but it left the amount that Germany would be ordered to pay to be determined by an international Reparations Commission appointed by the League of Nations. Germany accepted reluctantly the amount set (about $33,000,000,000 plus interest) by the Commission, but in 1923 it did not pay its annual installment. Thereupon France and Belgium occupied the Ruhr for the purpose of forcing Germany to continue making payments.

In an effort to settle the amount to be paid by Germany, the Reparations Commission appointed a committee headed by Charles G. Dawes. The Dawes Plan (1924) did not reduce the amount to be paid, but it provided a plan whereby Germany could pay. Germany continued to agitate for a reduction. The Young Plan (1929) reduced the amount of reparations to $8,000,000,000. The world-wide economic depression which began in 1929 led President Hoover to declare a suspension of payments on international debts and also on reparations for one year. At the end of that time all payments on international debts and reparations ceased, except by Finland.

The Washington Conference (1921-1922) set limits to the size of the navies of the major naval powers. Eventually these powers discarded the limitations. Disarmament conferences failed to limit the size and equipment of armies. While efforts to limit armaments were being made, many nations thought that non-aggression pacts, neutrality pacts, and alliances would help to preserve peace, but all failed. The Locarno Pact (1925) was intended to settle the major questions at issue between its signers and pledged them not to make war on one another. In the Pact of Paris (1928) forty-five nations agreed to renounce war as a means of carrying out their national policies except in self-defense. At the Washington Conference the nations that signed the Four-Power and Nine-Power treaties attempted to promote peaceful international relations in the Pacific and to guarantee the political independence and territorial integrity of China.

During the World Depression which began in 1929, many nations went off the gold standard and then trade between them became even more difficult than it had been under high tariffs. Many nations could not pay their debts to other nations. The World Economic Conference (1933) which met in London to try to improve trade among nations was a complete failure partly because President Roosevelt withdrew his support.

A series of events (1931-1939) led to the Second World War. After Japan's modernization had begun (1868) the Japanese began to think of acquiring more territory. They gained possession of a number of islands near Japan and also the large island of Formosa off the east coast of China. After Japan's victory over Russia in the Russo-Japanese War (1904-1905), Russia ceded Japan Port Arthur and the southern half of Sakhalin Island. Japan annexed Korea (1910). While the First World War was going on, Japan seized the German possessions in the Shantung peninsula and the Treaty of Versailles awarded them to Japan. After the war was over, the United States induced Japan to give up its holdings in the Shantung peninsula to China. In 1919 the Paris Peace Conference mandated all the German-owned islands in the Pacific north of the equator to Japan. Japan joined the League of Nations, signed (1921-1922) the treaties made at the Washington Conference, and signed (1928) the Pact of Paris.

In 1931-1932 Japan seized Manchuria in violation of the Nine-Power Treaty and the Pact of Paris and continued its attempts to master the Far East. After the Council and the Assembly of the League condemned Japan for seizing Manchuria and recommended the restoration of Chinese rule over Manchuria, Japan withdrew (1933) from the League. Thereafter Japan ignored the League and penetrated North China and Inner Mongolia and southward almost to the gates of Peiping. The Japanese began (1937) a war against China and before the Second World War had ended Japan had succeeded in conquering a large part of Eastern China. In 1936 Japan signed the Anti-Comintern Pact with Germany. The Japanese plan to master East Asia included attacks on the United States, the Philippines, and on British possessions in Southeast Asia and on the Netherlands East Indies.

Mussolini's imperialistic policy included the establishment of an empire in Northern and Eastern Africa. He secured control of the Adriatic Sea. He conquered Ethiopia (1935-1936) and Albania (1939). Great Britain, France, and also the League failed in their efforts to restrain him. He and Hitler (1936) established the Rome-Berlin Axis and he signed the Anti-Comintern Pact which had been agreed upon by Hitler and Japan. In June, 1940, he led Italy into the Second World War on the side of Hitlerite Germany.

The Spanish Civil War brought on another international crisis. After the dictatorship of Rivera had failed to improve conditions in Spain, a political coalition abolished the monarchy and established a republic. General Franco attacked the republican government. Mussolini and Hitler aided Franco and the Soviet Union aided the republican government (the Loyalists). The non-intervention agreement signed by Great Britain, France, Germany, Italy, and other nations and the hands-off policy of the United States helped Franco overthrow the Spanish Republic and establish a dictatorship.

Hitler rearmed Germany, withdrew Germany from the League, denounced the Locarno Pact, and refortified the Rhineland. Austria (1938) was the first victim of his military aggression and imperialism. In a conference at Munich (1938) Chamberlain and Daladier yielded to Hitler's demands for the Sudetenland and Mussolini supported him. The German army marched into Czechoslovakia (1939) and annexed the western and richer part to Germany. The eastern part, Slovakia, became a puppet state of Germany. Poland was the third victim of Hitler's military aggression and imperialism (1939). Great Britain and France then declared war on Germany, as they had agreed in treaties with Poland, with the full realization that a long and costly war lay ahead of them.

The coming of this war was due in part to the failure of Great Britain and France to agree on united action against Germany before Hitler became too strong. Both the British and the French underestimated the power of the forces behind Hitler, and disunity in France prevented its government from taking a strong stand against Hitler's aggressions. Moreover, the skillful propaganda of Goebbels won Germany many supporters in other lands.

EVENTS THAT TOOK PLACE AT ABOUT THE SAME TIME

	GERMANY	ITALY	JAPAN	LEAGUE OF NATIONS AND INTERNATIONAL AGREEMENTS
1919 to 1929	Weimar Republic established, 1919. Recognized the Soviet Union, 1922. Stopped paying reparations, 1922. Ruhr occupied by France and Belgium, 1923.	Mussolini made premier, 1922. Mussolini seized Corfu, 1923. Mussolini established protectorate over Albania, 1927.	Given mandate over Carolines, Pelews, Marianas (except Guam) by Paris Peace Conference, 1919. Signed Five, Four, and Nine-Power treaties, 1922. Gave Shantung back to China, 1922. Hirohito became emperor, 1926. Signed Pact of Paris, 1928.	Reparations Commission fixed amount of German reparations, 1921. Washington Conference made the Five, Four, and Nine-Power Treaties, 1921-1922. Little Entente established, 1921-1922. France made alliance with Belgium (1920), Poland (1924), Czechoslovakia (1924), Rumania (1926), and Yugoslavia (1927). Geneva Protocol, 1924. Dawes Plan, 1924. Locarno Pact, 1925. Pact of Paris, 1928. Young Plan, 1929. Beginning of world economic depression, 1929.

EVENTS THAT TOOK PLACE AT ABOUT THE SAME TIME (Cont.)

	GERMANY	ITALY	JAPAN	LEAGUE OF NATIONS AND INTERNATIONAL AGREEMENTS
1929 to 1935	Hitler became Chancellor, 1933. Hitler withdrew Germany from Geneva Disarmament Conference and from the League of Nations, 1933. Hitler made a non-aggression pact with Poland, 1934. Hitler announced repudiation of Treaty of Versailles and the renewal of conscription, 1935. Great Britain and France protested but took no action, 1935. Hitler made naval treaty with Great Britain, 1935.	Mussolini attacked Ethiopia, 1935.	Seized Manchuria, 1931-1932. Report of Lytton Commission, 1932. Announced withdrawal from League of Nations, 1933. Annexed Jehol to Manchuria, 1933. Broke up London Naval Conference, 1934.	London Naval Conference, 1930. Hoover moratorium, 1931. Geneva Disarmament Conference, 1932. World Economic Conference in London, 1933. Geneva Disarmament Conference disbanded, 1934. Soviet Union joined League of Nations, 1934. France made military alliance with Russia, 1935. Council of League voted to impose sanctions on Italy, 1935. France made military alliance with the Soviet Union, 1935.
1935 to 1939	Hitler reoccupied and refortified Rhineland, 1936. Rome-Berlin Axis, 1936.	Mussolini annexed Ethiopia and announced that the king of Italy had become emperor of Ethiopia, 1936. Rome-Berlin Axis, 1936.	Signed Anti-Comintern Pact with Germany, 1936.	League of Nations voted to end sanctions against Italy, 1936. Non-Intervention Agreement in regard to Spanish Civil War signed by twenty-seven nations, 1936.

EVENTS THAT TOOK PLACE AT ABOUT THE SAME TIME (Cont.)

	GERMANY	ITALY	JAPAN	LEAGUE OF NATIONS AND INTERNATIONAL AGREEMENTS
	Hitler sent soldiers to Spain, 1937.	Mussolini sent soldiers to Spain, 1937.	Began war on China, 1937.	
		Mussolini signed the Anti-Comintern Pact, 1937.	Captured Shanghai and Nanking, 1937, Canton, 1938.	
		Mussolini withdrew Italy from League of Nations, 1937.		
1935 to 1939 (cont.)	Hitler seized Austria, 1938. Hitler annexed Sudetenland by Munich Agreement, 1938. Hitler demanded return of Danzig; repudiated non-aggression pact with Poland, 1938. Hitler smashed the Republic of Czechoslovakia, 1939. Hitler and Stalin made non-aggression pact, August, 1939. Hitler's armies invaded Poland, September 1, 1939.			

UNEMPLOYED. In 1932, bread lines like this one before the Municipal Lodging House in New York kept all eyes in the United States on pressing domestic problems.

"BREAD!" "WORK!" Hunger marchers reaching Paris, in 1930, carried banners and placards with the universal demand. This photograph made in 1930 shows a French crisis which came between the Washington bonus march, left, and the demonstrations in London two years later. (See below.)

BONUS MARCHERS, here shown in front of the Washington Monument, so alarmed the nation's capital that troops were used to oust them.

HUNGER MARCHERS. From the "depressed areas" of Britain, the unemployed marched on London with petitions for relief. Here, in 1932, they enter Hyde Park.

LAST HOPE. Haile Selassie, in 1936, is here shown making his last vain appeal to the League of Nations to save Ethiopia —and the structure of collective security.

BOMBED BABY. When Japanese bombs fell on Shanghai, this child photographed in the ruins of the railway station won world sympathy. The bombings continued for thirteen years of war.

BUSINESS BOOMED AT ESSEN. While collective security collapsed, chimneys smoked at the Krupp armament works in Germany. (Below.)

CHAPTER 34

The Mighty Onrush of the Axis Powers

The Second World War was fought on land, in the air, on the seven seas, and under the sea in nearly all parts of the world with many new and highly destructive weapons. Its cost was enormous. At its close many of the victorious nations were almost bankrupt and the vanquished entirely so. The aggressor nations—Germany, Italy, and Japan—were totally defeated and acknowledged total defeat by surrendering unconditionally. Their cities and factories were almost entirely destroyed and hundreds of thousands of people were left destitute.

• • •

The Second World War engulfed most of the people in nearly all the nations of the world. It began in Europe with the German attack on Poland September 1, 1939, and the fighting in Europe ended May 7, 1945, with Germany's unconditional surrender to the United Nations. It began in the Pacific with the Japanese attack on Pearl Harbor December 7, 1941, and the fighting ended August 14, 1945, with Japan's unconditional surrender to the United Nations. The Second World War was the most terrible war in all history. Millions of lives were lost and hundreds of billions of dollars were spent. The weapons used were the most destructive that the mind of man could devise. The war brought death and suffering to untold millions on the battlefields and anxiety, anguish, and sorrow to homes throughout the world. It was fought on land, in the air, on the sea, and under the

sea. It was fought on farms, in factories, in cities, towns and villages, and homes in nearly every civilized country. It was fought also in research laboratories manned by scientists. It was total war and global war.

In the major countries involved men were drafted and trained to serve in the army, air force, or navy. New weapons and devices and new tactics on land, on the sea and under the sea, and in the air required that most soldiers be given long periods of training, that many acquire new skills, and that some attain a high degree of skill in the use of special weapons. The foregoing was true not only of the special services, but even in the infantry and artillery where soldiers were grouped according to the weapons they used.

Women served as nurses, secretaries, mechanicians, and technicians. In Great Britain where the need of women in war services was greater than in the United States, they were drafted. In the Soviet army women fought in the ranks on the ground and also in the air.

In the United States and Great Britain men who remained at home and who could be of service to the war effort came under regulation. They were "frozen" in their jobs on farms or in factories. Many went or were sent to places where their labor was most needed. Efforts were made to prevent strikes either by law or by mutual agreement between management and labor. Many women and girls worked in factories or on farms to replace men who had gone to war. Women and girls worked in victory gardens, sewed and rolled bandages for the Red Cross, helped in hospitals, and took part in civilian defense. The government sent entertainers all over the world and movies were shown to help keep up the morale of the fighting forces.

In countries occupied by the Germans many men, women, and even children belonged to the "underground," a secret organization that worked for the liberation of their homelands from their enemies. Its members fought as guerillas, destroyed enemy supplies and communications, harassed small bodies of troops, rescued friendly fliers who had parachuted to earth, and gave the proper authorities information about enemy installations, activities, troop concentrations, supplies, and other useful facts.

Governments stimulated the production of foodstuffs and war material needed to win victory. Farmers were urged and assisted to increase agricultural production. Many peacetime industries were converted to the manufacture of implements of war and soon their peacetime goods disappeared from the markets. Materials needed for the war were allotted by the governments on priority, that is, on the basis of war needs. Many foods and manufactured products were rationed for the purpose of securing fair distribution of scarce goods. Travel was restricted. Prices and wages were regulated in an effort to prevent inflation. Governments increased taxes to levels previously unknown, and the people, corporations, and municipalities bought billions of dollars worth of bonds. A few unscrupulous persons profited from "black markets," where goods were bought and sold illegally, contrary to rationing regulations and at prices above those fixed by the government.

The restrictions and the burdens in countries other than the United States were in general greater and more severe because the shortages were greater. But in all the countries engaged in this war and even in those which succeeded in remaining neutral, scarcely a person escaped from the burdens of war.

Assembly lines in factories aided greatly in producing the goods that helped win the war. So great was the demand for nearly all kinds of materials of war that nearly all of them, from large ships to the most delicate electrical devices, were put together on assembly lines. The different parts of these materials were standardized, made in different factories, and later assembled in factories into the finished product. Often the workers in the factories that produced these different parts did not know to what use they were to be put. The American system of manufacture resulted in a speeding up of production. The assembly line, however, had its drawbacks. For example, after a design for a plane had been accepted and the manufacture started in different factories, any major changes would slow down production. Some kinds of planes, tanks, and other war materials became obsolete before they were off the assembly line because of later inventions and improvements. American experience with assembly line production and American ingenuity in rapid adaptation of improvements to war equipment furnished the armed forces of the United States with all the war materials they needed, and also a part of the war materials needed by our allies.

New and highly destructive weapons were employed in the Second World War. New weapons were invented, improved, and manufactured in tremendous quantities. Infantrymen were no longer soldiers competent to use only a rifle and bayonet. They were experts in the use of a tommy-gun (an automatic rifle), a bazooka (a small jet-propelled anti-tank gun), and a hand grenade, and their comrades in arms supported them with greatly improved machine guns, mortars, tanks, and airplanes. Rapid firing motorized artillery was supported by huge cannons capable of firing giant shells for many miles. These shells had enough penetrating power to pierce heavy steel armor and to explode with very devastating effects.

Tanks were high powered weapons. The huge and heavily armored tanks that broke through strongly fortified lines were soon followed by lighter and swifter tanks that ranged behind the enemy lines in much the same way that the cavalry had in former times. Soldiers were transported in trucks, not only to battle lines, but through them. The defense against tank attacks was anti-tank guns, grenades, tank traps, and steel and concrete road blocks. Land mines were laid to explode under the advancing tanks and under the feet of infantrymen. The Germans specialized in booby-traps, mines set to explode when a door was opened, a window raised, a souvenir unwarily picked up, and even when a wounded soldier or a dead body was moved. Highly trained technicians hunted for booby-traps and rendered them harmless. Mine detectors operated by specially trained soldiers cleared land mines from roads and other places before advancing soldiers. One weapon of the first war was happily missing from combat use. Neither side used poison gas.

Small planes buzzed over and behind battle lines, radioed directions to artillerymen, and reported troop movements or the evacuation of tank concentrations. Dive bombers and light bombers aided the infantry by tactical bombing of troops, fortified places in the lines, and supply dumps and bridges behind the lines.

While the American armies were advancing in France, they employed planes to protect their flanks from enemy attacks. Bombers flew from bases in the rear of the battle lines to bomb industrial and communication centers, railway trains, munition and synthetic oil plants, gasoline refineries, and storage tanks far behind the enemy lines, in an effort to destroy the enemy's capacity to make war. Fighter planes on both sides shot down enemy bombers and protected their own bombers by engaging the fighter planes sent up to destroy them. Toward the end of the war the Germans developed robot bombs which, driven by rockets or jet-propelled, flew on their deadly missions without a pilot. Huge balloons in great numbers that held up wire nets (balloon barrages) were sent up and "anchored" around cities and fleets to make bombing planes fly high and thus to make it more difficult for them to hit their targets. Anti-aircraft guns shot explosive shells into the air to destroy attacking planes.

New methods of warfare were employed in the Second World War. The Germans devised *Blitzkrieg* (lightning war) and the Americans, British, and Russians improved on it. In *Blitzkrieg* bombers endeavored to isolate battlefields by destroying roads and bridges over which the enemy might bring up supplies and reinforcements. Dive bombers and artillery fire attacked enemy lines. Then tanks supported by troops brought up in trucks advanced to break the enemy lines. Behind them other troops advanced and the artillery moved up near enough to enable it to help hold the breach made by the tanks. Later on in the war, soldiers (paratroopers) were flown to the rear of enemy battle lines with their equipment in huge transport planes and dropped by parachute; others were transported in gliders and in glider "trains" which glided to earth. These tactics resulted in great mobility in warfare and created confusion not only where paratroopers landed, but also in the front line among enemy troops whose supplies they cut off.

Naval warfare was likewise transformed. Submarines which had a much greater cruising range and which had heavier armaments than those of the First World War wrought deadly havoc on all kinds of ships. Often they

Acme

NAVY LST'S DISGORGE THEIR CARGOES ON THE BEACH OF LEYTE ISLAND.

traveled in packs. Merchant ships, as in the First World War, sailed in convoys guarded by fast destroyers which attacked submarines on the surface with shells or under water with depth bombs.

The airplane brought about the greatest change in warfare at sea. Land-based bombers and blimps patrolled coastal waters to watch for submarines or to bomb convoys of merchant ships. Planes from aircraft carriers, that accompanied convoys, guarded troop ships and other ships in a convoy from attacks by air and patrolled the sea lanes looking for submarines which either singly or in packs lay in wait for their prey.

Large and small aircraft carriers sailed with fleets across oceans. Aircraft put an

"umbrella" over fleets to protect them from enemy attacks. They bombed shore installations of the enemy to enable troops to land with the fewest possible number of casualties. They attacked enemy convoys with bombs, machine guns, and rockets. They bombed enemy airfields from which the enemy might send land-based bombers against the fleets that they were protecting. They bombed faraway enemy military, naval, and supply bases and cities. Huge battleships still played their part and enormous aircraft carriers became effective fighting units of fleets.

The requirements of naval warfare over such vast areas as existed in the Pacific led to the creation of task forces. Each of these consisted of a complete fleet in itself—aircraft carriers, battleships, cruisers, destroyers, supply ships, and lesser craft. Task forces raided enemy strong points and destroyed enemy warships and merchant ships. Naval battles were fought in which warships did not fire at each other because all the attacks were made by airplanes. All ships, even merchantmen, bristled with anti-aircraft guns. The United States Navy dispatched oil tankers, ships loaded with medical supplies, food, and clothing, hospital ships, repair ships to repair planes, and even floating drydocks to repair ships at sea in the Pacific.

Destroyers, destroyer escorts, and PT boats did magnificent work in patrolling convoys and fleets. They co-operated with huge battleships, battle cruisers, cruisers, and aircraft carriers in destroying enemy warships, transports, and merchant shipping, and in protecting the larger naval units and also fighting forces that had landed on enemy shores.

To facilitate landing operations on hostile shores, boats were invented which could carry troops and their equipment and supplies close or even to dry land. Amphibious warfare (war on both land and sea) was employed by Americans and British in the landings on the coasts of North Africa and Europe, and by Americans on islands in the Pacific.

The war was fought by specialists at home and in the front lines. Some of these specialists were radar men, radio men, supply officers, snipers, and men trained to use special weapons. Others were employed in and by the Office of Strategic Services (OSS) and the Office of War Information (OWI). The army and navy gave qualified civilians special training in languages to act as interpreters, to handle prisoners of war, and to engage in espionage (spying) and counter-espionage (spying on the enemy's spies). Other men were trained in military government that they might be able to set up military governments in countries we were determined to conquer.

Still others engaged in psychological warfare. They made radio broadcasts or wrote leaflets to be distributed by shells or planes over enemy countries to weaken the morale of the peoples.

The engineering sciences played an amazing part in the war. A Defense Research Board in the United States, composed of scientists under the leadership of Dr. Vannevar Bush, directed and supported scientific research of many kinds to help win the war. Each of the products of this research was thoroughly tested before the Board authorized its use in the war effort. Engineers designed new and larger planes and developed engines of tremendous horsepower to drive aircraft through the air. The turbo-supercharger provided the engines with sufficient oxygen to enable them to run at high altitudes where there was not enough oxygen in the air to afford proper combustion. Oxygen tanks, electrically heated clothing, and pressurized chambers in airplanes made it possible for crews who wore oxygen masks to live in the rarefied air of the stratosphere. Engineers invented the robot bomb and jet-propelled plane capable of a speed of 600 miles or more per hour.

To aid in land warfare a British engineer invented the Bailey bridge, a light but strong bridge which could be thrown across rivers—even the Rhine—very quickly. Engineers developed automatic devices that aimed guns and navigated planes and ships accurately. Soldiers in the Signal Corps strung telephone wires, but when they had to be strung long distances quickly the Signal Corps used airplanes. Scientists had earlier developed communication by radio that enabled men in planes or tanks to talk to each other and to their commanders and to receive orders from them. Front line troops equipped with walkie-talkies could talk with their officers, give them information, and hear their orders at short distances. Ships were equipped with devices capable of recording sounds which the human ear could not hear and magnifying them so that they could be heard. These devices, when installed on ships, enabled naval personnel to detect submarines in motion under water.

At first radar was used for defense, but later it was developed until it was used for offense. A radar machine sends out pulses of radio energy, some of which meet an object, and from it the pulses are reflected back to the radar machine which gives an interpretation of the object and its position. It was used at first to detect the approach of planes and later on to detect the location of ships, submarines, channel markers, and shore lines. When attached to an anti-aircraft gun it directed the gun's fire with great accuracy. Night fighters used it to locate enemy planes at night. It saved Great Britain from much bombing by planes in the early part of the war and from bombing by robot bombs in the last months of the war. It made possible precision bombing of targets at night and through clouds and fog. Because it could be used to distinguish between land and water, it was of great value in landing attacks, particularly in the dropping of parachute troops on islands and coastal areas. It was used to guide planes back to their bases when their missions were over. So many of the best scientists worked to improve it that many radar machines were already surpassed by new ones before the older ones could be put in use. Americans, under Dr. Vannevar Bush, developed a shell that had a proximity fuse (a fuse that caused a shell to explode as it neared an object at which it had been aimed.)

At last, after years of work and the expenditure of more than two billion dollars, the best scientific and mathematical minds of the United States, Great Britain, and Canada produced the atom bomb. It was made by "splitting atoms" and therewith releasing tremendous atomic energies. Two atom bombs dropped on Japan helped bring the war against the Japanese to a sudden end and thereby saved the lives of incalculable numbers of Americans in the armed forces in the Pacific.

Medical science saved the lives of a large percentage of the wounded. Men went into battle equipped with the basic needs of first aid, particularly sulfa powder, which, when sprinkled on a wound, prevented infection. Devoted medical corpsmen, including conscientious objectors, gave morphine and often, at the risk of their own lives, carried the wounded to doctors and nurses behind the lines, where plasma was injected into their veins to reduce the effect of shock. From there they were carried, often in planes, to base hospitals and from there back to their home countries. Sulfa, plasma, whole blood, and penicillin were great life savers, but the skill of surgeons and nurses saved the lives of many others who in the First World War would have died. New vaccines prevented the spread of infectious diseases such as typhus and cholera. Insecticides, including DDT, sprayed by airplanes on infested localities and applied to individuals, killed mosquitoes and lice which are carriers of diseases. Thus the health of the armed forces was guarded.

The war became truly global. Portugal, Spain, Switzerland, and Sweden were the only nations in Europe which remained neutral throughout the war. Most of the peoples of Africa and the Near East felt its deadly impact. Soviet, British, and American troops were stationed in Iran. India was involved also. After Japan and the United States entered the war, it spread all over the Far East and over many islands in the Pacific. Every one of the twenty Latin American Republics declared war on one or more of the Axis powers. Brazil sent a military force to Italy and Mexico sent a military force to the Southwest Pacific.

At first the strength of the Axis powers, who were well prepared for the struggle, seemed irresistible. The Germans won a quick and easy victory over Poland. They had the largest air force in the world. Their army was well-trained and equipped with the latest weapons. The technique of the *Blitzkrieg* had been developed. The German-Soviet non-aggression pact (August 23, 1939) freed the Germans from the immediate danger of a war on two fronts, a situation which they deemed extremely hazardous to their national security.

On September 1, 1939, German armies invaded Poland without a declaration of war. On September 3, Great Britain and France declared war on Germany as they were bound to do by their treaties with Poland. The Polish war was very short. Two great German army groups, one in the north composed of two armies and another in the south of three, made sudden and swift attacks while two air fleets dropped bombs on Polish cities and towns, airfields, and railroads. The destruction of the railroads made it impossible for the Poles to bring their reserves up to the battle lines. German tanks, aided by dive-bombing planes, broke the Polish lines and infantry carried by trucks and on motorcycles poured through the gaps. Two German armies, one from the north and the other from the south, met in Central Poland and completely surrounded and captured the main Polish army. Another northern army swept east of Warsaw to unite with the southern armies and complete the envelopment of the Polish troops.

The Poles were unable to stop the German attack. Great Britain and France were unable to send them aid because they had no direct contact with Poland. On September 17, 1939, a Soviet army entered Poland from the east

without opposition. The *Luftwaffe* (German Air Force) bombed Warsaw fearfully and needlessly to show the world what havoc their bombers could cause a city. Warsaw fell to the Germans on September 27. Poland was partitioned for the fifth time. The Germans got the western part which was industrial; the Russians got the eastern part which was largely agricultural. Central Poland was set up as a Polish state under German protection. Some of the leaders of Poland fled to London where they formed a government in exile. In the course of the war, the Germans put hundreds of thousands of Poles to death. Over a million were taken forcibly to Germany and compelled to work as slaves for their conquerors. Polish Jews were executed in mass murders. Nevertheless, a strong underground movement developed which the Germans were never able to suppress.

The warring powers spent the winter of 1939-1940 in feverish preparations. A German army was stationed in the Siegfried Line, a complicated system of fortifications in depth west of the Rhine, to prevent an invasion of Germany. The French manned and strengthened the Maginot Line. The British sent an army of 158,000 men, under Lord Gort, to France. Planes of each side flew over each other's territory on exploratory missions but few bombs were dropped. So little action was there that newspapers called the war in the west a "phony war."

All the member countries of the British Commonwealth of Nations, except Eire, supported Great Britain by promptly declaring war on Germany. Prime Minister De Valera of Eire proclaimed its neutrality. Belgium, hoping to avoid war, had given up its alliance with France before the war and declared itself neutral. The Soviet Union, as if fearful of future events, and in spite of its non-aggression pact with Germany, proceeded to strengthen its western frontier zone of defense.

The Soviet Union attacked Finland to protect its northwestern frontier. The Russians were fearful of a German attack even though both nations had just signed (1939) a non-aggression pact. To protect the Soviet Union from a German invasion across the Finnish border, which was only sixteen miles from Leningrad, the Russians demanded that Finland cede land near Leningrad and in Northern Finland on the Arctic Ocean to the Soviet Union and grant it military and naval bases in other parts of Finland. When Finland refused, the Soviet Union declared war. The Finns put up an heroic defense, which aroused much admiration in Western Europe and the United States. Nevertheless Soviet military power crushed the Finnish army. On March 12, 1940, Finland surrendered and yielded to Soviet demands. In the spring of 1940 the Baltic States—Latvia, Estonia, and Lithuania—were occupied by the Soviet army and incorporated as republics into the Soviet Union. Before this time the Hitler government had asked Germans in the Baltic States (Balts) to return to Germany and what was left of them now were withdrawn by Hitler and given farms in Western Poland of which their owners were dispossessed.

The British fleet rapidly gained control of the seas and established a blockade of Germany. German merchant shipping was driven from the seas except in the Baltic. The Germans retaliated with submarines, mines, and airplanes. Many British ships were sunk. In addition, German pocket battleships and cruisers succeeded in running the blockade and doing damage to British shipping. On December 13, 1939, the *Graf Spee,* a German pocket battleship, was so badly damaged by three British cruisers off the coast of neutral Uruguay that she fled into the harbor of Montevideo. As Uruguay was bound to enforce the laws of neutrality, it would allow the *Graf Spee* to remain in port only four days

or be interned. The captain on orders from Hitler sailed out of the harbor and scuttled his ship.

The Germans conquered Denmark and Norway. The war on land in the West began in earnest in the spring of 1940. To protect their northern flank and to gain bases on the Atlantic for submarines, the Germans on April 9 occupied Denmark and invaded Norway. On that morning when the Danes woke up, they found their country occupied by the Germans. Relatively few Danes collaborated with them. The king stayed in Copenhagen and became the center of Danish resistance.

Before the invasion many Germans had gone into Norway in the guise of tourists. At a signal they appeared in uniform fully equipped; other German troops landed from transport planes and from ships. German boys who had been befriended by the Norwegians after the First World War returned during the invasion as guides to the German troops.

Before the Germans invaded Norway a Norwegian Nazi party had been formed. Its leader was Vidkun Quisling, whose name has since been used as a synonym for traitor. To aid the Norwegians who were putting up a gallant fight, the British landed troops on the Norwegian coast, but the distance from their bases made it difficult to supply them, and impossible for them to maintain themselves unless supported by airplanes. France sent troops also. The stronger German armed forces and German superiority in the air soon forced the British and French to withdraw from Norway. On June 9, 1940, the Norwegian army surrendered and King Haakon fled to Great Britain. The Norwegian government ordered all its merchant ships which were out of home ports (1024 in number) to render service to the nations at war with Germany. During the rest of the war the greater part of the Norwegian people did all they could

The German people were serious in their belief that Germany was so much superior to other
countries that it would be able to conquer the entire world. Germany might have succeeded but
for the alertness and sacrifices of the British Air Forces, the valiant resistance of the Soviet armies,
and the military might and industrial power of the United States.

to resist the Quisling government and to sabotage the German war effort.

By the conquest of Denmark and Norway, the Germans gained a long seacoast containing many fine harbors which they could use as bases for ships and submarines. They secured also airfields from which they could attack the northern supply routes to Great Britain and later on to Russia. They also got fish, timber, and other supplies that otherwise would have gone to Great Britain. They won the rich agricultural products of Denmark, most of which formerly had gone to feed Britain. Everything that Germany gained by conquering Denmark and Norway meant serious losses to Great Britain.

The British defeat in Norway aroused the British people. A vote of censure of Chamberlain's conduct of the war failed by only a few votes. A short time later the *Blitzkrieg* struck the Low Countries and Chamberlain resigned. On May 10, 1940, King George VI appointed Winston Churchill Prime Minister.

The Germans conquered the Netherlands, Luxemburg, Belgium, and France. This time the Germans planned the conquest of France more thoroughly than they had in 1914. The Maginot Line made a frontal assault on France most difficult.

They planned an assault on the Netherlands and Belgium that was designed to gain possession of them and at the same time to cause the French and British armies to go northward to the aid of the Low Countries. While this was going on they planned a drive through the Ardennes Forest just beyond the northern end of the Maginot Line. The German armies, after getting through the Ardennes Forest, were to drive straight to the coast thus splitting the allied armies in the north from the larger French armies in the south. They could then join the German armies in the north and together capture and destroy the allied armies in Belgium. If

successful they could then turn south, envelop the French armies farther south, and take the Maginot Line from the rear. Their plans were in large part successfully carried out. Only British courage and a supreme effort by British aviators, civilians, and seamen prevented their entire success.

On the eve of the assaults on the Netherlands and Belgium, Hitler said to his armies:

"The hour has come for the decisive battle for the future of the German nation. For 300 years the rulers of England and France have made it their aim to prevent any real consolidation of Europe and above all to keep Germany weak and helpless. With this your hour has come. The fight which begins today will decide the destiny of the German people for 1000 years. Now do your duty."

On May 10, German armies invaded the Netherlands and Belgium with the assistance of fifth columnists. The Netherlands was conquered in six days. Parachute troops seized airfields, bridges, and highways. Rotterdam was frightfully bombed by German planes to show again, as they had at Warsaw, what awful havoc German bombers could cause. Queen Wilhelmina and the royal family escaped to Great Britain and formed a Dutch government in exile. The Dutch surrendered on May 15, 1940.

The Belgians resisted heroically, but their forts and defense lines could not withstand the German assaults. Brussels fell within a week. The Belgian army was still in the field and the British army and a large French army had come up from the south to its support.

On May 10, German armies began to advance through the Ardennes Forest which the French had thought impassable for an army. When they reached the weak extension of the Maginot Line along the Meuse, north of Sedan, tank columns aided by dive bombers cut a gap fifty miles wide in the French defenses. The German infantry poured through·and

Acme

German conquerors of France are shown marching along Champs Elysees in 1940.

two columns of German tanks then drove in parallel lines to the channel coast. The infantry went between them. The Belgian, British, and French armies north of the German armies were effectively cut off from the main French army to the south. All efforts from both north and south to break this German corridor to the coast failed.

On May 28, King Leopold of Belgium surrendered the Belgian army because his troops were almost out of supplies and he was convinced that the situation was hopeless. The French and British armies were trapped. Protected by brilliant and heroic rear-guard fighting they fell back to the beaches at Dunkirk. While British planes gained mastery of the air, the British put into use every kind of boat that could cross the Channel. The rescue and evacuation (May 26-June 3, 1940) of more than 335,000 British, French, and Belgian soldiers to England was unparalleled in history. However, they were compelled to leave most of their equipment behind them.

German armies then turned south to conquer France. All France was in almost utter confusion. The roads over which French armies retreated southward were so cluttered with refugees going in the same direction that few supplies and reinforcements from the south ever reached them. German dive bombers wrought frightful havoc along these crowded roads. Though individual units of

the French army fought bravely, the government and most of the army commanders lacked the determination to put up a strong resistance to the German invasion.

The desperate plight of France was made more so when Mussolini declared war (June 10, 1940) on both France and Great Britain and quickly invaded Southeastern France. To save Paris from the fate of Warsaw and Rotterdam, the French government declared it an open city (one that will not be defended). On June 14, the Germans entered Paris triumphantly. Before the fall of Paris the French cabinet had fled to Tours and then to Bordeaux.

In support of those French ministers who wished to carry on the war, Churchill flew to Bordeaux and proposed that the French and British empires form an indissoluble union with a joint constitution, one cabinet, one parliament, and a common citizenship. The British offer was rejected. Some of the French ministers led by Reynaud wished to retire to French North Africa and to continue the war from there in alliance with Great Britain. Others were convinced that further fighting would be in vain. Premier Reynaud resigned and Marshal Petain formed a new cabinet. He moved the seat of government to Vichy and asked the Germans for terms of peace.

On June 22, 1940, in the same railroad car in the same place in the Forest of Compiegne where the armistice ending the First World War had been signed, a French delegation sent by Petain's government signed Hitler's armistice terms. Hitler danced with glee. Three days later the French signed an armistice with Mussolini. Under the terms of the armistice with Germany, the German army was to occupy the northern half of France and the entire French coast on the Atlantic and the English Channel. The occupying forces were to have control of all factories, mines, and transportation facilities. The

French were to pay the cost of the German occupation. Germany was to hold all French prisoners of war until peace was made and all Axis prisoners were to be released at once. If, in the opinion of the Germans, the French did not fulfill all the terms of the armistice, the Germans had the right to declare the armistice at an end.

In the unoccupied area, the remnants of the French parliament established the Vichy government, fascist in type, with Marshal Petain as Chief of the French State. Later on Pierre Laval, who had been premier of France, became the chief minister in the Vichy government.

Petain abolished the Third French Republic and suppressed all political parties and labor unions. He endeavored to substitute "Work, Family, and Fatherland" for "Liberty, Equality, and Fraternity" which had been the watchwords of France since the French Revolution.

Patriotic Frenchmen and women did not agree with Petain's policies and many of them joined the underground forces which became known near the close of the war as the French Forces of the Interior. The Vichy government and also the Germans inflicted severe and brutal punishments on them but in the summer before the final liberation of France they played a particularly effective part.

The Third French Republic came to an end with a swiftness that astounded the world. Its fall was due in part to the strategy of the German General Staff and to the speed and might of the German attacks. In part it was due to disunity in France. Many Frenchmen, particularly monarchists, had never been in favor of the Third French Republic. They feared the socialist tendencies of the Popular Front and admired the Nazi political system. The ideas of these men infected ministers and army officers and thereby greatly weakened their will to defend France. The French min-

Acme

Hitler is shown doing the victory jig after signing the armistice with France in 1940.

isters may be blamed because they had done nothing to stop Hitler's reoccupation of the Rhineland and to prepare France for the war which they all thought was bound to come. The weakness of the French political system, which could function only by a coalition of parties, was also a cause of the downfall of France. The French General Staff was at fault. It placed more reliance than it should have on the defensive strength of the Maginot Line because it could be outflanked on the north and was by the Germans. It did not heed the writings of Colonel Charles de Gaulle who, before the war, had foretold the military effectiveness of mechanized equipment in warfare. It failed to provide an air force adequate to defend France.

Colonel de Gaulle, who had been Undersecretary for War, escaped to London where he announced the establishment of a Free French government in these words on October 27, 1940: "As long as the French government and the representatives of the French people do not exist normally and independently of the enemy, the powers formerly performed by the Chief of State and by the Council of Ministers will be exercised by the leader of the Free French forces assisted by a Council of Defense." He recruited an army composed of loyal Frenchmen who had escaped from France and French soldiers who had escaped from Dunkirk. The Petain government sentenced Colonel de Gaulle *in absentia* to death for treason.

The Germans failed to conquer Great Britain. Nazi Germany had triumphed in Western Europe. Only Great Britain challenged Hitler's power as it had challenged that of Napoleon more than a century earlier. The British situation in July, 1940, was desperate. Most of its army had been rescued from Dunkirk, but it had to leave behind nearly all of its equipment. The British air force was small in comparison with the German. Submarines were sinking great numbers of British ships loaded with desperately needed supplies. The United States was neutral. Great Britain stood alone with its back to the wall. Only the English Channel and the British fleet stood guard against a probable *Blitzkrieg*. However, Great Britain had a superb leader and an indomitable and heroic people.

Winston Churchill proved himself to be one of the greatest war leaders in history. For centuries his family had been prominent in Great Britain; his mother was an American. He had been educated to be a soldier. During the Boer War he was a war correspondent, had been captured, and had escaped. Returning home, he entered politics and served several terms in Parliament, at times a Liberal, at others a Conservative. In the First World War he was First Lord of the Admiralty until the failure of the expedition he sent against the Dardanelles discredited him. During Hitler's rise to power, Churchill more than once gave stern warning in Parliament of the impending danger to Great Britain and to the world, but his warnings were unheeded. At its moment of greatest danger, the nation turned to him. He has a strong resonant voice and the ability to express his thoughts and ideas clearly, forcefully, and eloquently. His choice of words is unsurpassed. Above all he had the indomitable courage and stoical fortitude needed by a great war leader. In his first address to Parliament as Prime Minister he said: "I would say to the House, as I said to those (the Ministers) who have joined this government; I have nothing to offer but blood, toil, tears, and sweat." On the day after the fall of Dunkirk, June 4, 1940, he declared:

> We shall go on to the end, we shall fight in France, we shall fight on the sea and oceans, we shall fight with growing confidence and growing strength in the air. We shall defend our Island, whatever the cost may be, we shall fight on the beaches, we shall fight on the landing grounds, we shall fight in the fields and in the streets, we shall fight in the hills; we shall never surrender, and even if, which I do not for a moment believe, this Island or a large part of it were subjugated and starving, then our Empire beyond the seas, armed and guarded by the British fleet, would carry on the struggle, until, in God's good time, the New World, with all its power and might, steps forth to the rescue and the liberation of the Old.

The people of Great Britain were worthy of their matchless leader. All Great Britain was put into a state of defense. Men were drafted into the armed forces and women worked on farms and in factories making war equipment. Older men became members of Home Defense units to help repel an invasion if and when it occurred. They served in whatever capacity they were able. They even removed road signs so that if England were invaded, the invaders would be hindered in their advances. Never during the war did the courage of the British people lag or their determination falter.

The invasion never came. The Germans collected thousands of barges in the Channel ports on the Continent, attempted to secure

Acme

LONDON AFTER GERMAN AIR RAID.

control over the English Channel itself, to destroy the towns on the British coasts by bombing, and at the same time to destroy the Royal Air Force. Their failure in these attempts and the loss of great numbers of their own planes were perhaps the chief reasons why the Germans did not invade England. On July 19, about three weeks before the Germans launched their terrific air assaults on Great Britain, Hitler offered peace and threatened the destruction of the British Empire if his offer was not accepted. He said:

". . . for once believe me when I predict a great empire will be destroyed, an empire that was never my intention to destroy or even to harm. I do realize that this struggle, if it continues, can end only with the complete annihilation of one or the other of the two adversaries. Mr. Churchill may believe this will be Germany. I know it will be Britain."

The British government spurned with firmness Hitler's offer of peace. It was not intimi-

dated by his dire threat of destroying the British Empire.

The Germans began their bombing on August 8, 1940. In ten days the Royal Air Force destroyed 697 German planes and lost 153. From August 24 to September 5, Goering tried to destroy British airfields and thus ground British fighters. While the Germans were bombing the British airfields, the British destroyed 562 German planes, losing 219 themselves, but from these 219 Royal Air Force planes 132 pilots parachuted safely to earth and later on re-entered the Battle of Britain. From September 6 to October 5, the Germans concentrated their attacks on London. They raided by night and by day. London suffered terribly and so did the industrial cities in the midlands—Birmingham, Manchester, Liverpool, and Sheffield. Probably the most devastating air attack was the night long bombing of Coventry on November 14, 1940. But the British people never wavered and the British Spitfires and Hurricanes continued to take a heavier toll of German airplanes than the German Air Force could afford to lose. In day raids during the Battle of Britain the Germans lost 2375 planes and their crews. Night raids continued until the end of December and thereafter fleets of bombers flew to visit death and destruction on many British cities. But the Battle of Britain had been won by the British.

The British victory in this battle was due first of all to the airmen who manned the fighting planes known as the Spitfires and Hurricanes. "Never," said Churchill, "in the field of human conflict was so much owed by so many to so few." Balloon barrages and anti-aircraft fire helped. The newly invented radar enabled the British watchers to detect the approach of German planes and to direct fighter pilots where to fly their planes to engage the German planes in combat. After the Germans found daylight bombing too costly, they turned to night bombings and then Britain speedily trained night fighters who flew in planes equipped with radar to attack and destroy the German night bombers.

Amid fearful devastation, terrible suffering, and many deaths due to bombings, the British people never lost their courage nor even their sense of humor. The government enforced a blackout and built air-raid shelters. Air-raid wardens, first aid squads, ambulance units, and fire brigades rendered valiant service. Most of their members were volunteers who served without pay. Some became expert in removing time fuses that had failed to explode bombs. The fighting spirit and the grim determination of the British improved as they "carried on." By the end of 1940 the Germans knew that Great Britain could not be bombed into submission. The British army had by this time grown strong enough to resist a German invasion. Hitler's failure to invade England or to bomb it into submission caused him to turn his attention early in 1941 to the conquest of the Balkan countries and the Soviet Union, even though he and the Soviet Union had signed a non-aggression pact.

The German conquest of France and the Battle of Britain made many Americans realize that a German victory would endanger our national security. After the Senate had rejected the Treaty of Versailles and refused to join the World Court, a majority of the American people became isolationists, that is, they were determined to stay out of European entanglements and future wars. The bickerings of European nations and the failure of all debtor nations, except Finland, to pay their debts to the United States convinced many Americans that our participation in the First World War had been a mistake. A Senate Committee, headed by Senator Gerald P. Nye, revealed that munitions makers had made huge profits during the war. These revelations helped lead many to the belief that the United States should do everything possible to stay out of future wars.

In general, public opinion in the United States supported the Five-Power Treaty and the Pact of Paris. Congress reduced the appropriations asked by the Army and Navy to a minimum. The majority of the people became convinced that the United States must remain at peace and to do so must avoid all entanglements in European affairs. Accordingly, in the midst of the crisis over Ethiopia in 1935, Congress passed a Neutrality Act. It prohibited the export of arms, munitions, and implements of war to countries at war. It prohibited vessels flying the United States flag from transporting them for the use of countries at war. It required the registration and licensing of persons engaged in manufacturing, exporting, or importing war materials. It prohibited American citizens from sailing on ships of countries engaged in war unless they had the permission of the United States Department of State. This provision was intended to prevent such a threat to peace as that caused by the loss of American lives when the *Lusitania,* a British ship, was sunk by a German submarine in the First World War.

In the same year that the Neutrality Act was passed (1935) President Roosevelt sent a special message to Mussolini asking him to refrain from making war on Ethiopia. The Neutrality Act was later strengthened by amendments intended to help keep the United States neutral. Japan got around American neutrality laws by not declaring war on China.

President Roosevelt made efforts to bring about peaceful solutions of the German controversies with Czechoslovakia and Poland, but in vain. The United States was still isolationist when the Second World War broke out on September 1, 1939. Two days later the

President issued a proclamation declaring the United States a neutral country.

On November 4, the Neutrality Act was amended; the new provisions were known as "cash and carry." Any belligerent nation could buy what it needed in the United States provided it paid cash (loans and credits were forbidden) and carried its purchases in its own ships. The Neutrality Act compelled the President to specify combat areas which all American citizens, vessels, and planes were forbidden to enter. The vast majority of the people of the United States were determined that their country should not be drawn again into a war in Europe.

To help keep the war away from our shores, an Inter-American Conference, held in Panama (1939), declared that belligerent vessels were forbidden to come closer than 300 miles to the shores of Latin America and the United States. Despite this declaration, British cruisers and the *Graf Spee* fought a naval battle on December 13, 1939, off the coast of Uruguay.

The fall of France in June, 1940, caused great concern to many people in the United States. After France fell, a Gallup poll showed that 36 per cent of the American people believed in helping Great Britain at the risk of war while 64 per cent believed that the United States should stay out of the war. In January, 1941, 68 per cent believed the United States should help Great Britain while 32 per cent believed we should stay out of war.

The danger of a British collapse also alarmed many others. They feared that if Britain collapsed the United States would find itself without strong allies in a world that might soon be dominated by Nazi Germany. Although public opinion was at first divided on the wisdom of participating for a second time in a war in Europe, it was united on the necessity of placing the United States in a state of preparedness. In an effort to create greater unity in the country, President Roosevelt appointed two prominent Republicans to his cabinet, Henry L. Stimson, Secretary of War, and Frank Knox, Secretary of the Navy.

Congress established a National Defense Advisory Board which was replaced by the Office of Production Management. Some factories engaged in peace-time production began to manufacture guns, tanks, planes, and munitions of war. On the President's recommendation, Congress provided for the construction of a "two-ocean navy," one fleet for the Atlantic, the other for the Pacific. On September 1, 1940, the National Guard was called to arms. In the same month Congress passed the Selective Service Act which provided for one year of military training for modern warfare. It was the first use of conscription in peace time in the history of the United States. The United States and Canada set up the Joint Defense Board to lay plans for their common defense. After the fall of the Netherlands and France, an Inter-American Conference was held in Havana (July 30, 1940). It adopted the Act of Havana which provided that a joint trusteeship for each of the French and Dutch colonies in the Western Hemisphere could be set up if necessary to prevent their seizure by Germany.

The United States became the arsenal of democracy. After the British had lost their equipment at Dunkirk, Great Britain was almost defenseless. President Roosevelt then took steps to aid Great Britain. We sent a supply of arms which the British could use in repelling an invasion. Soon thereafter (September, 1940) President Roosevelt and Prime Minister Churchill entered into an agreement whereby the United States gave Great Britain fifty destroyers built during the First World War and in return Great Britain granted the United States ninety-nine year leases on naval bases in Jamaica, St. Lucia, Trinidad, Antigua, and British Guiana and also a gift of bases in Bermuda and Newfoundland.

As public opinion became aroused by the military successes of Germany, many Americans came to believe that the United States should give to Great Britain "all aid short of war." On December 29, 1940, President Roosevelt said over the radio, "We must be the great arsenal of democracy."

In his annual message to Congress on January 6, 1941, President Roosevelt proclaimed the Four Freedoms as the ideal of the United States—Freedom of Speech, Freedom of Religion, Freedom from Want, and Freedom from Fear. In the same message the President asked Congress "for authority and for funds sufficient to manufacture additional munitions and war supplies of many kinds, to be turned over to those nations which are now in actual war with aggressive nations." "The time is near," he said, "when they will not be able to pay for them all in ready cash. We cannot, and we will not, tell them that they must surrender, merely because of present inability to pay for the weapons which we know they must have."

Shortly after this message a bill to carry out the President's recommendation was introduced into the House of Representatives. After two months of discussion, Congress passed (March, 1941) the bill which then became known as the Lend-Lease Act. It empowered the President to sell, lease, or exchange any arms or goods to any country "whose defense the President deems vital to the defense of the United States." Under Lend-Lease over $50,000,000,000 worth of goods were in time delivered to foreign countries, most of whom were engaged in the war. The United States received in return commodities scarce in the United States, the use of bases in friendly countries, food, services of various kinds, and repayment in money according to the financial ability of the countries that received Lend-Lease.

To help insure the safe transportation of Lend-Lease materials across the North Atlantic, Greenland, valuable chiefly for weather forecasting stations, was occupied in April, 1941, by agreement with the Danish Ambassador in Washington. Some of the Nazis there were captured; others escaped. Iceland, first occupied by Great Britain, was taken over by the United States in July, 1941. The sinking of many merchant ships during the spring and summer and of the destroyer *Reuben H. James* on convoy duty out of Iceland in October led to the repeal of the Neutrality Act and to the arming and convoying of American merchant vessels with orders from President Roosevelt "to shoot at sight" any Axis war vessel. The United States was close to war.

President Roosevelt and Prime Minister Churchill drew up the Atlantic Charter. In August, 1941, President Roosevelt and Prime Minister Churchill conferred on *H.M.S. Prince of Wales* off the coast of Newfoundland. Both were accompanied by a military and naval staff, other officials, and economic experts. At the end of the conference the President and Prime Minister Churchill issued a joint declaration called the Atlantic Charter which stated the aims of the two powers as follows:

The President of the United States of America and the Prime Minister, Mr. Churchill, representing his Majesty's Government in the United Kingdom, being met together, deem it right to make known certain common principles in the national policies of their respective countries on which they base their hopes for a better future for the world.

FIRST: Their countries seek no aggrandizement, territorial or other;

SECOND: They desire to see no territorial changes that do not accord with the freely expressed wishes of the peoples concerned;

THIRD: They respect the right of all peoples to choose the form of government under which they will live; and they wish to see sovereign rights and self-government restored to those who have been forcibly deprived of them;

FOURTH: They will endeavor, with due respect for their existing obligations, to further the enjoyment by all States, great and small, victor or vanquished of access, on equal terms, to the trade and to the raw materials of the world which are needed for their economic prosperity;

FIFTH: They desire to bring about the fullest collaboration between all nations in the economic field with the object of securing for all, improved labor standards, economic adjustment and social security;

SIXTH: After the final destruction of the Nazi tyranny, they hope to see established a peace which will afford to all nations the means of dwelling in safety within their own boundaries, and which will afford assurance that all the men in all the lands may live out their lives in freedom from fear and want;

SEVENTH: Such a peace should enable all men to traverse the high seas and oceans without hindrance;

EIGHTH: They believe that all of the nations of the world, for realistic as well as spiritual reasons, must come to the abandonment of the use of force. Since no future peace can be maintained if land, sea, or air armaments continue to be employed by nations which threaten, or may threaten, aggression outside of their frontiers, they believe, pending the establishment of a wider and permanent system of general security, that the disarmament of such nations is essential. They will likewise aid and encourage all other practicable measures which will lighten for peace loving peoples the crushing burden of armaments.

Almost a year before the Atlantic Charter was drawn up, Mussolini was attempting to carry out his imperialistic policies. He planned to conquer Egypt, to gain control of the Suez Canal, and thereby to cut the "lifeline" of the British Empire. In September, 1940, a few months after Italy had invaded France, an Italian army under General Graziani advanced from its base in Tripoli eastward until it was about sixty miles inside the northwestern frontier of Egypt. The British under General Wavell struck back and with the aid of the Free French forces from French Equatorial Africa drove the Italians all the way back to Tripoli. The Italians had also planned to invade Egypt from Ethiopia, but a British force liberated Ethiopia from the Italians and (May, 1941) Hailie Selassie regained his throne.

While the Petain government was at Bordeaux, it assured the British that the French fleet would never be allowed to fall into the hands of either Germany or Italy. In July, 1940, after the French had signed an armistice with Hitler, the British seized all French ships in British harbors and ordered the French fleet at Alexandria not to leave and later the British immobilized it. Another unit of the French fleet was at Oran and still others were at Toulon, Dakar, and Madagascar. The British gave (July 3, 1941) the commander of the French fleet at Oran three choices. He could join the British, turn over his ships to the British, or sail his ships to some port in the West Indies where they could be demobilized. When the French commander refused to accept any of these choices, the British fired upon the French ships and damaged them severely.

The French fleet, based at Toulon, remained in the hands of the Vichy government until November, 1942. When the Germans attempted to seize it, most of the ships were blown up or scuttled by their crews. The French fleet at Alexandria, which had been immobilized by the British, joined later on in the war against the Axis powers. Afterwards the British fleet had to deal only with the Italian fleet in the Mediterranean. From

Malta and from aircraft carriers British planes bombed objectives in Italy and Italian warships. One squadron of planes even bombed the Italian naval base at Taranto and sank half the Italian battle fleet. In March, 1941, the British Mediterranean fleet sighted an Italian fleet off Cape Matapan, southwest of Crete. In a night battle the British inflicted a crushing defeat on the Italian fleet. After the bombing of the Italian fleet at Taranto and the defeat in the Battle of Cape Matapan, the Italian navy was inactive except for submarines which continued to sink British ships in the Mediterranean.

After the Germans saw that the British were defeating the Italians in North Africa they sent aid. Italian and German planes bombed the British island of Malta more than 3200 times and attacked the British merchant ships so fiercely that supplies for the British army in North Africa had to go all the way around Africa to Egypt. General Rommel, the German commander of the Axis forces in North Africa, advanced eastward for another attack on Egypt, but the British under Wavell drove him back to Tripoli. Here he was reinforced and with considerable skill he defeated the British and drove them back toward Egypt. In July, 1942, Rommel's army reached El Alamein in Egypt, seventy miles west of Alexandria. Here British forces resisted the attacks of Axis armies so stoutly that they could not advance any further. Both armies then settled down to await reinforcements and supplies before renewing the battle.

Mussolini's imperialism led him to attempt to conquer Greece. After the Greek army had been defeated in a short war with Turkey (1921-1922), the Greek monarchy was overthrown (1923) by a revolution and a republic established under the leadership of Venizelos, a Cretan, who had been Prime Minister during the First World War. The

continual conflict between the monarchists and the republicans caused political unrest and public disorder. In 1935, General Metaxas, a forceful military leader, restored the monarchy. In October, 1940, Germany and Italy demanded that Greece grant territory to Italy and Bulgaria, and air bases to Germany and Italy, and that Greece reorganize its government. Before the time set for a reply from Greece, Mussolini ordered his army in Albania to invade Greece from the northwest.

The Greek armies, under Metaxas, fought Mussolini's invading armies with a heroism and determination worthy of their brave ancestors in ancient times. The Italian armies were driven out of Greece and across Albania almost to the Adriatic Sea. They were saved from utter defeat when Hitler's forces came to their rescue.

Hitler conquered the Balkan countries. After the First World War, a Communist uprising in Hungary, under Bela Kun, had been suppressed (1919), and a regency was established under Admiral Horthy, who ruled the country with an iron hand until Hitler forced him to join the Axis (November 20, 1940).

Rumania was easily drawn into the Axis. For years it had been torn by almost open warfare between the Peasant party and the Iron Guard, whose members were violent Fascists. In 1940 King Carol, who was unpopular because of his personal life, was easily expelled by the Iron Guard. It established a fascist rule in the name of Carol's young son, Michael. The Soviet Union forced Rumania to cede a part of Bessarabia to it. Germany and Italy forced Rumania to cede about a half of Transylvania to Hungary, to permit German troops to enter the country, and to join the Axis (November 23, 1940).

The third victim of Hitler was Bulgaria. It was ruled by King Boris much the same way that Horthy ruled Hungary. Although an internal crisis caused Bulgaria to reject Hitler's first request to join the Axis, it finally joined (March 1, 1941).

The fourth victim of Hitler was Yugoslavia. It had been under the autocratic rule of King Alexander and a group of Serb army officers. But after Alexander was assassinated in France (1931) Prince Paul who became regent continued Alexander's policies. The failure of Prince Paul to satisfy the demands of the Croats for a greater share in the government led to grave public disorder and eventually to the destruction of the monarchy. The disunited country was an easy prey for Hitler who demanded (February 14, 1941) that Yugoslavia adhere to an Axis pact, permit the passage of troops and munitions, grant economic co-operation with Germany, and accept without resistance the German occupation of Bulgaria.

On March 25, 1941, the Yugoslav government adhered to the Axis pact. On March 27, an anti-Nazi *coup d'etat* ousted Prince Paul, and King Peter II took charge of the government. He formed a government of national union representing the views of the Serb, Croat, and Slovene peoples and on April 3, Yugoslavia mobilized its armed forces. On April 5, Yugoslavia and the Soviet Union signed a treaty of friendship and non-aggression. On April 6, Germany, Italy, and Bulgaria attacked Yugoslavia and on April 10 Hungary also attacked it. Mechanized armies from Rumania, Bulgaria, and Hungary that poured across the frontiers scattered the Yugoslav forces and cut the country into pieces. Although Belgrade, the capital of Yugoslavia, had been declared an open city by the Yugoslavs, it was cruelly demolished by German bombs and then occupied by the Germans. In eleven days the war was all over and Yugoslavia was divided up among its Fascist neighbors.

The successes of the Nazis in Hungary, Rumania, Bulgaria, and Yugoslavia opened the way for German armies to advance into Greece. The British sent 60,000 veterans, many of them Australians and New Zealanders, from Wavell's already weak forces in Africa to aid the Greeks. However, the British were not able to send forces in sufficient numbers to cope with the larger German armies that were pouring into Greece. The British forces were almost without arms and air support so they were unable to stem the Nazi advance. German armies from Bulgaria and Yugoslavia swooped down upon Greece. The brilliant defense of the Pass of Thermopylae by New Zealand troops held back the Germans advancing toward Athens and helped the British to perform wonders in evacuating most of their troops from Athens to Crete, but they had to leave 15,000 behind. On April 21, three days after the fall of Yugoslavia, German armies captured Athens and raised the swastika on the Acropolis. On April 23, Greece surrendered to Germany and Italy.

If the Germans were to conquer North Africa and control the Near East, they had to capture Crete. On May 20, 1941, they launched the first airborne invasion in history. Parachute shock troops seized airfields in Crete, and fleets of gliders carrying troops brought in thousands of troops equipped for mechanized warfare. The *Luftwaffe* punished the British navy cruelly. By the end of May the Germans had control of Crete and the British, leaving half their forces dead or prisoners, had to go through another Dunkirk, this time to Egypt. Hitler had now gained bases from which he hoped to launch an attack on Syria and the Middle East in conjunction with Rommel's forces in North Africa.

Great Britain and the Free French prevented the Germans from getting control of the Near East. German conquest of the countries of the Near East would have been a severe blow to the British. It would have enabled the Germans to gain possession of the Suez Canal and of the Mosul oil fields in Iraq from which pipe lines ran to Haifa in Palestine to supply oil to the British fleet and planes in the eastern Mediterranean. It would also have endangered British control of India and, after Germany attacked the Soviet Union, prevented Lend-Lease and other supplies from reaching the Soviet armies by way of Iran.

After the fall of France, the government of Syria (a French mandate) carried out the Vichy government's policy of co-operating with the Nazis. The kingdom of Iraq had made a treaty with Great Britain which gave the British the right to intervene in Iraq in case of war. For some time German and Italian agents had been stirring up opposition to the British in Iraq, and on April 4, 1941, Iraqi who favored the Axis revolted and seized control of the pro-British government. The British acted promptly. They sent forces into Iraq from Basra on the Persian Gulf and others across the desert from Palestine. They were aided by Free French troops from Palestine. The planes Hitler sent the rebels from air bases in Syria did not prevent the British and Free French from putting down the pro-Axis revolt. By June 1, 1941, the pro-British government was restored. The Axis agents fled to Iran.

After Hitler attacked the Soviet Union, Great Britain and the Soviet Union asked the government of Iran to expel the Axis agents, but it did not. Consequently, on August 25, 1941, Soviet and British troops occupied Iran. A few days later the parliament of Iran gave up the Axis agents and allowed Soviet and British troops to remain in Iran to protect their oil supplies and the lines of transportation of Lend-Lease and other war supplies through Iran to the Soviet armies.

To prevent German forces in Crete from crossing into Syria, British and Free French forces from Palestine and Iraq invaded (June 8, 1941) it and by July 14 Syria was in their hands. Hitler now gave up whatever plans he may have had for the immediate conquest of the Near East and struck with tremendous force at the Soviet Union.

Hitler decided to invade the Soviet Union. He reached this decision because (1) he needed the rich grain fields of the Ukraine, the industrial output of factories in the Soviet Union, and the labor of its millions; (2) he had complete confidence in the ability of his armies to destroy the Soviet armies which had seemed to be inefficient in the first part of the Finnish War; (3) he posed as the champion of Western civilization against Communism and now he was going to destroy Communism. He may have been influenced by the thought that Great Britain would cease its war upon him and join him in an attack on the Soviet Union to destroy Communism.

On June 22, 1941, German mechanized armies (about 180 divisions) attacked the Soviet Union without a declaration of war and in violation of the non-aggression pact that Hitler had signed (1939) with the Soviet Union. Italy (June 22), Rumania (June 22), Finland (June 26), and Hungary (June 27) declared war on the Soviet Union. Indeed, before long Hitler, like Napoleon, was using troops from nearly all the countries in Europe.

On the very day that Hitler attacked the Soviet Union, whatever hope he may have had that Great Britain would join him was dashed by Winston Churchill, who spoke these ever-memorable words:

Can you doubt what our policy will be? We have but one aim, and one single, irrevocable purpose. We are resolved to destroy Hitler and every vestige of the Nazi regime;

from this nothing will turn us—nothing. We will never parley. We will never negotiate with Hitler or any of his men. We shall fight him by land, we shall fight him by sea, we shall fight him in the air, until, with God's help, we have rid the earth of his shadow and liberated its peoples from his yoke.

Any man or state who fights against Nazidom will have our aid. Any man or state who marches with Hitler is our foe. This applies not only to organized states, but to all representatives of that vile race of Quislings who make themselves the tools and agents of the Nazi regime against their fellow countrymen and against the lands of their birth. These Quislings, like the Nazi leaders themselves, if not disposed of by their fellow countrymen, which would save trouble, will be delivered by us on the morrow of victory to the justice of the allied tribunals.

That is our policy and that is our declaration. It follows, therefore, that we shall give whatever help we can to Russia and to the Russian people. We shall appeal to all our friends and allies in every part of the world to take the same course and pursue it as we shall, faithfully and steadfastly.

On June 24, President Roosevelt promised aid to the Soviet Union, but the United States was not able to send much Lend-Lease material until March, 1942, because of its commitments to the British who were in desperate need in Egypt.

Three German army groups invaded the Soviet Union. The northern group, under von Leeb, was to drive through the Baltic States and capture Leningrad. The central and largest group, under von Bock, had Moscow as its objective. The southern group, under von Rundstedt, was to sweep through Southern Poland and the Ukraine to the Black Sea. As these army groups advanced, they planned to envelop and destroy the Soviet armies in their paths.

On a front about 2000 miles long, the Germans employed the same *Blitzkrieg* tactics that they had so successfully used in Poland, the Low Countries, France, and the Balkans.

Acme

SOVIET "SCORCHED EARTH" POLICY IN RETREAT FROM GERMANS. This policy deprived the Germans of much of the fruit of their military successes.

Within a few days the Germans occupied the buffer lands (the Baltic States, Eastern Poland, and Bessarabia) which the Soviet Union had taken (1939-1940). The Russians have always had to retire in the face of a sudden aggression because they lack a sea frontier and easily defended natural boundaries. The Soviet armies now withdrew before the German onslaughts, but as they did so, they carried out the "scorched earth" policy which Stalin ordered (July 3, 1941).

The scorched earth policy, patriotism, and sound strategy saved the Soviet armies. The Russians burned their crops, villages, and farm buildings. They dismantled machines in factories and moved them east of the Ural Mountains. They blew up the huge dam and the power installations on the Dnepr River. Many of the men, women, boys, and girls who remained in the conquered areas concealed themselves in the woods and engaged in skillfull guerilla fighting as their ancestors had during Napoleon's invasion.

The Nazi attack
on Poland and
Russia
1939 – 1942

10 million Poles and Ukrainians killed.
The greatest mass murder in history

After the First World War Russia became a communistic dictatorship. After great political and social turmoil and a civil war, the country was organized along communistic lines and it had become relatively productive before the German invasion (1941) upset all the progress that had been made. The great Ukrainian industrial plants were bodily moved to Siberia and the Soviet armies gradually withdrew eastward almost to Moscow before they were able to halt and strike back successfully.

No fifth column aided the invaders. The patriotic Russians fought for Mother Russia with amazing courage and grim determination. The Russian generals let German tank forces through their lines, closed the gaps behind them, and then encircled and proceeded to destroy the tank forces. When the Soviet armies were attacked by stronger German forces, they retired to prevent being encircled, captured, or slain. When Soviet forces found themselves surrounded, they did not surrender but when possible forced their way out of the trap by fierce fighting. The German armies advanced, but in spite of their claims they did not succeed in destroying the Soviet armies which was their main objective.

Marshals Voroshilov, Timoshenko, Budenny, and Zhukov proved themselves masterful strategists. As the area of the Soviet Union is so great, the Soviet generals could afford to retire farther and farther into the interior to gain the time needed to obtain more supplies and to train new armies. As was often repeated, they were trading space for time. Hitler found, as Napoleon had before him, that the vast area of the Soviet Union and the bitter winters together with the courage of the Soviet peoples were unconquerable foes.

The northern army group failed to capture Leningrad. It advanced rapidly through Lithuania, Latvia, and Estonia to join the Finns in an attack on Leningrad. Finland soon regained the territory which the Russians had taken from it in 1940. By August the Germans under von Leeb had reached the outskirts of Leningrad while a Finnish army commanded by Baron von Mannerheim attacked the city from the northwest.

Between August and November the Germans tried desperately to capture Leningrad. They cut the railroad to Moscow, and they and the Finns cut the railroad to Murmansk. Leningrad was bombed by the *Luftwaffe,* shelled by heavy German artillery, stormed by hundreds of tanks, and attacked by about 600,000 soldiers. Russian forces under Marshal Voroshilov, aided by civilian defenders, heroically resisted the invaders. Air and artillery attacks demolished a large part of the city and the din of battle could be heard in the streets, but the invaders were not able to take the city. In November, 1941, the Germans and Finns laid siege to it in the hope that its defending armies and citizens would be starved into submission. Although it was besieged for more than two years, it was still in the hands of the Russians when they launched a great counter-offensive in the winter of 1943.

The central army group failed to capture Moscow. It advanced eastward in two columns through Poland and to the north of the Pripet marshes and drove back the Soviet forces under the command of Marshal Timoshenko. The Germans enveloped Minsk (July 10) and falsely claimed the encirclement and destruction of a huge Soviet army. After the Soviet forces held the invaders at bay for several days on the Beresina River, another advance brought the Germans to Smolensk where a fierce battle raged from July 12 to August 11. Again by the use of encircling tactics the Germans took the ruined city which was all on fire. There the Germans halted to regroup their forces for a terrific assault on Moscow.

During September heavy rains made mechanized warfare on a large scale impossible, but by the first of October the ground was frozen. On October 2, the Germans launched their great offensive to capture Moscow. "Today," Hitler told his troops, "begins the great decisive battle of the year."

The Germans brought troops from both north and south to join their central army group and then they launched a three-pronged attack on Moscow. The northern prong struck northeast from Smolensk toward Kalinin which it captured (October 23) thus threatening to envelop Moscow from the north. At one point on this northern sector the Germans were within five miles of Moscow. The southern prong struck southeastward through Bryansk and Orel toward Tula which it nearly surrounded but failed to capture. It was to envelop Moscow from the south. The central prong advanced eastward through Viazma to take Moscow by frontal assault. At the point of farthest advance it was within twenty-five miles of Moscow.

During October the fighting raged on three

fronts around Moscow. On October 15 the Soviet government began a mass evacuation from Moscow of civilians not needed in its defense. On October 19, the Soviet government declared Moscow in a state of siege, moved the seat of government eastward to Kuibyshev on the Volga, and announced that Marshal Zhukov had been appointed to command the central front. He replaced Timoshenko who had been sent to command the Soviet armies in the southeastern Ukraine where the Germans were pressing forward relentlessly toward Rostov.

On November 16, the Germans launched a new attack which they thought would enable them to take Moscow. The Russians, soldiers and civilians alike, fought back savagely and heroically. Thousands of women dug trenches and anti-tank ditches in front of their capital. By December Moscow was two-thirds surrounded and seven of the railroads that led to the city and also the Moscow-Volga canal were cut.

When the fury of the German assault had spent itself, Zhukov threw reserves, which he had held out of battle, at the flanks of the German army (December 6, 1941). This attack began a Soviet counter-offensive that lasted until March 8, 1942. It was fought in the bitter cold and in the deep snow of a particularly severe winter for which Hitler had failed to supply his soldiers with the winter clothing they so sorely needed. Moreover, the Germans had to abandon much motorized equipment when the oil in the engines "froze." The Soviet winter offensive drove the German front back at distances varying from 50 to 240 miles. The losses on both sides were very heavy; the Soviet army admitted losses of 434,000 killed and wounded and the German losses were more than twice as large. The central army group had failed to crush the Soviet armies and to capture Moscow. Never again were they to be so near

the Soviet capital as they were at the high tide of their power in December, 1941.

The southern army group advanced through the Ukraine to Rostov. Its objectives were the fertile grain producing lands and industrial cities of the Ukraine and the mineral wealth of the Donetz basin. Marshal von Rundstedt commanded the southern group while Budenny commanded the Soviet forces until Marshal Timoshenko replaced him.

German and Rumanian forces invaded that part of Bessarabia which the Soviet Union had forced Rumania to cede to it (1940), entered the Ukraine, and began a drive to capture Odessa, the greatest port on the Black Sea. After a siege that lasted about two months, it was captured (October 16). Before the Russians evacuated the city they carried away everything of value that they could and destroyed the rest.

In the meantime, German and Hungarian armies drove through Southern Poland into the Ukraine. All the country west of the Dnepr River was overrun and the retreating Soviet forces dynamited (August 24) their great dam and power plant at Dnepropetrovsk on the Dnepr to prevent them from falling into the hands of the onrushing Germans. The industrial city of Kiev, the 1000 year old capital of the Ukraine and a city of almost a million inhabitants, was the next objective of the Germans. It resisted the German assaults for nearly two months. After tremendous encircling movement during which Budenny's forces east of Kiev were badly mauled, the Germans captured the ruined city (September 20) after desperate street-to-street fighting. Kharkov, another industrial city of almost a million, was captured (October 27) and the Soviets retreated toward Rostov at the mouth of the Don which the Germans captured (November 23).

Meanwhile, German and Rumanian forces

in the south, after the fall of Odessa, plunged across the Dnepr and invaded the Crimean peninsula. Their chief objective was the naval base at Sevastopol on the tip of the peninsula. By December all of the peninsula except Sevastopol was in the hands of the enemy who now laid siege to it.

On November 7, 1941, the twenty-fourth anniversary of the Communist Revolution of 1917, Stalin spoke these words to the Russian people:

> The enemy has seized the greater part of the Ukraine, White Russia, Moldavia, Lithuania, Latvia, Estonia, and a number of other regions. He has penetrated to the Don, hangs like a dark cloud over Leningrad, and our glorious capital, Moscow. . . . But the price he paid is enormous. The German invaders wish to have a war of extermination. If this is the German wish, they will get it.

As Stalin spoke these words, the Soviet armies were about to open a winter offensive on a vast scale.

Late in November, just before the Soviet counter-attacks on the Moscow and Leningrad fronts began, Marshal Timoshenko launched a counter-offensive in the south. Rostov was recaptured (November 30), and during the winter of 1941-1942 Soviet armies drove the Germans back to a line extending roughly north from Rostov through Kharkov to Kursk. Other Soviet forces took the Kerch peninsula at the eastern tip of the Crimea, recaptured a part of the eastern Crimea and relieved the German pressure on Sevastopol.

The southern army group failed to capture Stalingrad. In the summer of 1942 the Germans launched (June 13, 1942) a second great offensive against the Soviet Union which lasted until November 10. This offensive had to succeed or the Germans would be doomed to defeat. The United States was now in the war against Germany, Lend-Lease supplies were pouring into the Soviet Union in

ever-increasing quantities, the R.A.F. was carrying out more air raids on German industries, and the production of war supplies was being stepped up in Soviet factories east of the Ural Mountains.

Hitler now turned his attention away from the capture of Moscow and concentrated it on the southern front. He hoped to seize the lower Volga to capture the Caucasus and its rich oil fields and to shut off Lend-Lease supplies to the Soviet Union by way of Iran. If these objectives were accomplished during the summer, the Germans could strike north and take Moscow from the east before the Russian winter set in.

Before they began their general offensive the Germans drove the Russians out of the Kerch peninsula (May, 1942). Then they carried out a terrific assault on Sevastopol which they had been besieging for about seven months. In taking the city German planes in one month made 25,000 flights and dropped 125,000 bombs while their heavy artillery fired 30,000 tons of shells. After this bombardment had destroyed the defenses and made a shambles of the city, massed assaults of infantry took it (July 3) street-by-street. Only a few Soviet soldiers escaped by sea.

While the Germans were taking Sevastopol, other German armies attacked the Soviet armies farther north. One army which advanced eastward from Kursk captured (July 7) Voronezh and cut the railroad from Moscow to Rostov, but was unable to advance any farther eastward. Three other German armies moved southeastward across the Donetz River. Two of them drove toward Stalingrad on the Volga while the third attacked Rostov. After fierce air attacks, Rostov fell (July 25) to the Germans for a second time.

After the capture of Rostov, the Germans plunged forward relentlessly into the Caucasus. Their objectives were the rich food-producing regions and the oil fields at Maikop, Grozny, and Baku. In a few days all railroads running into the Caucasus from the north were in German hands. The Soviet forces in the Caucasus were now cut off from Soviet forces to the north. Moreover, the Soviets withdrew most of their tank forces to the east shortly after the fall of Rostov because they needed them to defend Stalingrad and the Caspian oil fields. Infantry, artillery, and Cossack cavalry now faced heavy attacks by German mechanized armies and the ever present *Luftwaffe*.

On August 8, the Germans captured the oil fields at Maikop, but they benefited little, if any, thereby. In September, German and Rumanian armies under air cover crossed the Kerch Strait and joined the German armies that had swept down from Rostov. On September 11, Soviet forces evacuated the naval base at Novorossisk on the northeast shore of the Black Sea.

As the Germans and Rumanians fought their way south through passes in the Caucasus Mountains, Soviet resistance stiffened. It slowed the advance of the enemy by effective use of anti-tank guns and stopped the invaders about fifty miles north of Grozny. The German campaign in the Caucasus had failed to capture the oil fields at Grozny and Baku and to keep Lend-Lease supplies from reaching the Soviet Union by way of Iran.

While the Germans were penetrating the Caucasus, two other German armies crossed the Donetz River. The Soviets, outnumbered in men, planes, and tanks, put up a stubborn resistance, but were gradually driven back to the Don. By the middle of August, 1942, both German armies had crossed the Don and were ready to launch an attack on Stalingrad, now only forty miles away.

Stalingrad (formerly Tsaritsyn), which stretched for about twenty miles along the west bank of the Volga, was a modern industrial city of about 600,000 inhabitants. It had been built up as a part of the first Five-Year Plan and in 1942 was a vital cog in the war machine because it produced steel, tanks, munitions, and armaments. Its capture would deprive the Soviet Union of these war materials and also of oil, wheat, and Lend-Lease supplies from Iran which were transported up the Volga, the greatest artery of transportation in the Soviet Union. The Russians knew that Stalingrad would be difficult to defend because it was situated in rather flat country. In consequence, they had constructed a defense system about twenty miles in depth west of the city. It consisted of strong concrete pill-boxes, tank traps, minefields, and heavy artillery emplacements.

Von Bock, the German commander, launched a three-pronged attack on Stalingrad as he had on Moscow the previous year. One prong attacked from the north, another from the south, and still another from the west. The real battle for the capture of Stalingrad began on August 23, 1942, when German forces under General von Paulus reached the Volga north of the city. The actual assaults began September 14 and lasted for sixty-six days. The Germans assaulted the city with everything they had at their command: 1000 planes, scores of tanks, heavy artillery, and waves of infantry. Bombs from planes and shells from heavy artillery made a shambles of the city. The Russians, who used the rubble and wrecked buildings for defense, fought desperately for every street, every building, and even every room in some buildings. After the German air force had destroyed the bridges across the Volga, the Russians built a bridge two feet under water over which civilians and soldiers carried supplies at night.

Although the Germans reached the Volga both north and south of Stalingrad and captured most of the city, they could not take

Sovfoto

LAST BATTLE AT STALINGRAD. At the factory where the thunder of battle had roared an unusual silence now fell. The last shot had been fired; the epic Battle of Stalingrad was over.

all of it. By November 19, they had driven the Russians back to a high bluff along the Volga, but could not drive them across the river. The Germans had failed to capture Stalingrad, to take the oil fields of the Caucasus, and to destroy the Soviet armies. Moreover, a new threat to the Germans had arisen in the West because on November 7-8, while they were trying desperately to capture Stalingrad, American and British forces had landed in North Africa.

In the autumn of 1942 the Germans had reached the summit of their power. They were masters of most of Europe. Rommel's army and the Italian army were at El Alamein in northwestern Egypt. Other German armies had occupied the richest agricultural and industrial regions of the Soviet Union. They had reached the Volga and had penetrated the Caucasus. German submarines were causing great destruction of Allied shipping in the Atlantic and were threatening to cut Great Britain off from supplies.

The Germans made use of the human and material resources of the countries they conquered. They stripped the conquered countries of everything they thought would help Germany win the war. Thou-

sands of men and women were taken forcibly from France, Belgium, the Netherlands, Poland, Czechoslovakia, the Balkan countries, and the Soviet Union to Germany where their German masters made them slave laborers in factories, in mines, and on farms. Many Russian women and girls were forced to do work in German households. Foodstuffs taken from the conquered lands enabled the Germans to live well while their slave laborers and millions of people in the captured lands starved. German factories manned by forced labor poured out munitions. Slave labor made it possible to install some industries underground where they would be safe from Allied bombings.

The Germans wreaked savage and inhuman vengeance on the peoples in the conquered countries. After Reinhard Heydrich, the Nazi governor of Czechoslovakia, was killed near the village of Lidice, it was wiped out (June 10, 1942). Jews, Poles, Russians, and other conquered peoples were exterminated brutally by the hundreds of thousands. Many more, including Germans who were hostile to Nazi ideas, suffered untold horrors in concentration camps. In the autumn of 1942 the world seemed to lie at the feet of Hitlerite Germany and the Nazis thought they were destined to be its rulers.

The United States refused to accept Japan's proposals for a New Order in East Asia. The Chino-Japanese war had been raging for a little more than two years before the war in Europe began. By the close of the year 1938 the Japanese had captured most of the cities of Eastern and Southeastern China. The United States government held that Japanese aggression in China violated the Nine-Power Treaty and the Pact of Paris.

Early in 1939 the continuing Japanese aggression alarmed the United States, Great Britain, France, and the Netherlands, all of whom had vital interests in the Far East. In

February, 1939, Japanese forces occupied the Chinese island of Hainan and the next month they seized the Spratly Islands. Both of these lie in the South China Sea and could be used as bases for military operations against French Indo-China, the Philippines, Singapore, and the Netherlands East Indies. To protect its vital interests, in April the United States transferred strong naval forces from the Atlantic to the Pacific.

After the Japanese invaded China, they destroyed the properties of Americans, violated their rights, and mistreated them. The United States tried in vain to reach an agreement on these problems with Japan. In consequence, the United States gave (July, 1939) the six-month notice that was necessary to bring to an end the commercial treaty with Japan that had existed since 1911. After the treaty had expired, the United States could legally put an embargo on the shipment of materials to Japan.

After the fall of the Netherlands and France in 1940, the Japanese militarists and imperialists became increasingly bolder. At the request of the Japanese government, Great Britain (now engaged in a life and death struggle with Hitler) closed (July 18, 1939) the Burma Road for three months, thus cutting the flow of supplies to China. When the Japanese government threatened to use force against French Indo-China, the Vichy government made a military agreement with Japan. It gave the Japanese the right to use three airfields in Indo-China and to transport troops across it to fight the Chinese. In spite of this agreement, Japanese forces attacked Northern Indo-China and occupied several strategic places. Secretary of State Cordell Hull said that the United States disapproved what the Japanese had done. On September 26, 1940, President Roosevelt placed an embargo on the export of all scrap steel and iron except to the countries of the Western Hemisphere and to Great Britain. This meant that Japan could no longer buy these materials from the United States to supply the needs of its army and navy.

On the day after the President's announcement of this embargo, Japan, Germany, and Italy signed a ten-year military alliance which was aimed directly at the United States. Each member of the alliance agreed to assist any other member with all political, economic, and military means when it was attacked by a power not involved in either the European or the Chino-Japanese conflict. The treaty stated also that Japan recognized and respected the leadership of Germany and Italy in the establishment of a New Order in Europe and that Germany and Italy recognized and respected the leadership of Japan in the establishment of a New Order in Greater East Asia. The government of the United States now considered the situation in the Far East so dangerous that the State Department warned (October 8, 1940) Americans to get out of China, Japan, Manchuria, Hong Kong, and French Indo-China. At the same time Great Britain announced that the Burma Road would be reopened (October 18) when the three-month period expired. The situation in the Far East was very critical, but war was not to break out for more than a year.

During the summer and autumn of 1941, the relations of the United States, Great Britain, and the Netherlands East Indies with Japan became more and more strained. Japan was determined to defeat China and establish a New Order in Greater East Asia. The United States, Great Britain, and the Netherlands East Indies were equally determined to stop further Japanese aggression.

Japan continued to exert pressure on Vichy France and forced it to make (July 26, 1941) another treaty very favorable to Japan and very menacing to American, British, and Dutch interests in the Far East. In this treaty

Japan got the right to maintain troops and to establish military bases in Southern Indo-China. Thereupon both the United States and Great Britain froze Japanese assets. This meant that these assets could not be used to buy any goods in those countries. On August 1, 1941, President Roosevelt placed an embargo on the export of aviation oil and gasoline which made it impossible for the Japanese to get these vital war supplies from the United States.

Shortly afterwards the United States promised Lend-Lease aid to China and announced that it planned to send a military mission to Chungking. In October, representatives of the United States, Breat Britain, the Netherlands East Indies, Australia, and China held a joint military conference to discuss joint defense plans. In the same month Great Britain sent the battleship *Prince of Wales* and the battle-cruiser *Repulse* to the Far East. Moreover, the Netherlands East Indies suspended its trade treaty with Japan and by doing so cut off Japan from oil supplies in the Indies.

As the powers took a firm attitude toward Japanese aggression, an important change took place in the Japanese government. On October 16, 1941, the civilian premier of Japan resigned and was succeeded by General Tojo who formed a cabinet composed mostly of military officers. The Japanese parliament was now called into session to appropriate huge sums of money for the army and navy. Early in November the cabinet sent special envoy, Saburo Kurusu, to Washington to aid Ambassador Nomura in his negotiations with Secretary of State Hull. Before the arrival of Kurusu, Hull warned President Roosevelt and his colleagues in the Cabinet that relations with Japan were very critical. At this time Prime Minister Churchill promised that Great Britain would declare war on Japan if Japan attacked the United States.

Acme

SECRETARY OF STATE HULL WITH NOMURA AND KURUSU. The Japanese presented proposals which were unacceptable to the government of the United States.

On November 20, Nomura and Kurusu presented a set of new proposals to Secretary Hull. They proposed that the United States stop giving aid to China, resume trade with Japan, and supply Japan with "a required quantity of oil." If the United States would accept these proposals, then Japan would not make further armed advances into Southeastern Asia and the southern Pacific, would withdraw to Northern Indo-China the armed forces it had in Southern Indo-China, and also withdraw all its forces from Northern Indo-China after peace had been restored between Japan and China. In plain language, the Japanese wanted the United States to help Japan win its war against China.

On November 26, 1941, Hull presented Nomura and Kurusu with new American proposals. He proposed that Japan "withdraw all military, naval, air, and police forces" from China and Indo-China and rec-

Acme

THE TWISTED HULK OF THE *U.S.S. ARIZONA*
AT PEARL HARBOR.

ognize the government of Chiang Kai-shek. If the Japanese government would do this, the United States would make a trade treaty with Japan and free Japanese assets in the United States.

While the Japanese government was considering the American proposals, it was increasing its armed forces in Indo-China. On December 6, 1941, President Roosevelt sent a personal message to Emperor Hirohito asking him to withdraw them from Indo-China. On Sunday, December 7, 1941, at 7:50 A.M. Honolulu time (1:20 P.M. Washington time), Japanese planes flying from carriers, bombed the United States naval and military base at Pearl Harbor in Hawaii. One hour after that attack had begun, and even while Japanese planes were sowing death and destruction in Hawaii, Nomura and Kurusu called on Secretary Hull at the State Department and handed him a reply to the American proposals of November 26. After he had read the reply, Secretary Hull said to the Japanese representatives:

> I have never seen a document that was more crowded with infamous falsehoods and distortions—infamous falsehoods and dis-

tortions on a scale so huge that I never imagined until today that any government on this planet was capable of uttering them.

The attack on Pearl Harbor without a declaration of war aroused the indignation of the people of the United States and united them, as nothing else had been able to do, in defense of their country. The following day the Congress of the United States declared war on Japan. On December 11, 1941, Germany and Italy who had made a military alliance with Japan declared war on the United States; on the same day the United States declared war on them.

The Japanese attack on Pearl Harbor was the first blow in a well-planned campaign. This campaign was designed to gain possession of the entire eastern coast of Asia and the islands that lay along it. It was well-timed. The United States, unprepared for war, was straining every sinew to send war equipment to Great Britain and the Soviet Union who were fighting a life and death struggle against Hitler and Mussolini. German armies were threatening the capture of Moscow and Leningrad. A large part of the American fleet in the Pacific had been ordered into the Atlantic.

To help make their New Order in Greater East Asia safe, it was necessary to put the United States fleet in the Pacific out of action. The Japanese planned their campaigns skillfully. The preparations for the attack on Pearl Harbor were painstakingly and secretly rehearsed. It caught the American defenders unawares and resulted in the greatest naval disaster known to American history. Admiral King in his *Report* summed up the damage it caused in these words:

> Of the eight battleships in the harbor, the *Arizona* was wrecked, the *Oklahoma* capsized and three other battleships were so badly damaged that they were resting on the bottom. The damages to the other three were

comparatively minor in character. A total of 19 ships was hit, including three light cruisers which were not seriously damaged. Three destroyers were hit and damaged (all three were later restored to service). Of the 202 Navy planes ready for use on that morning only 52 were able to take the air after the raid.

Personnel casualties were in proportion to the material damage. The Navy and Marine Corps suffered a loss of 2117 officers and men killed and 960 missing.

The Japanese losses were about 60 planes, attributable mainly to anti-aircraft fire . . .

On the same day that the Japanese attacked Pearl Harbor, they attacked Wake, Midway, and Guam (American islands in the Pacific), Hong Kong, the Philippines, and Singapore. The very next day they invaded Thailand (Siam) which gave up immediately. Guam fell on December 12. The Marines on Wake Island, after an heroic defense under Major James P. S. Devereux, surrendered on December 23. Midway was successfully defended and remained a strategic American naval base throughout the war. Hong Kong was bombed into submission after its water supply on the mainland had been cut off. The British surrendered on December 25.

The Japanese captured the Philippines. A sudden air attack on the airfields near Manila on December 7 destroyed the greater part of the American Air Force in the Philippines. On December 10, a Japanese air force bombed the naval base at Cavite crippling the power plant and other installations. On the same day Japanese forces landed at two points on the northern coast of Luzon, but an attempt to land strong forces on Lingayen Gulf was turned back by the defending forces who wiped out the Japanese invaders. By December 24, however, the Japanese had succeeded in landing armies both north and south of Manila which was now the objective of a pincer's attack.

The army defending Manila consisted of United States regulars; National Guard Units from New Mexico, California, Kentucky, Ohio, and Illinois; air force personnel; a regiment of Marines; about 1000 sailors; 12,000 Filipino scouts; and 60,000 other Filipinos whom General Douglas MacArthur had been engaged in training for the Philippine government. General MacArthur declared Manila an open city to prevent damage to it and then withdrew his army into the Bataan Peninsula. The Japanese bombed Manila twice (December 27 and 28) and occupied it (January 2, 1942).

Japanese control of the seas around the Philippines and also of the air made impossible all attempts to supply, reinforce, or evacuate American troops. Two out of every three ships which attempted to run the Japanese blockade were destroyed. The American and Filipino troops fought gallantly though conditions were hopeless. They were worn out by constant fighting and short rations and at least 20,000 soldiers were ill with malaria. In these circumstances, further defense on Bataan was impossible and President Roosevelt ordered (February 22, 1942) General MacArthur to leave for Australia. On his arrival there he said, "I shall return."

On April 9, 1942, General Jonathan Wainwright was forced to surrender the 36,000 troops left on Bataan. The island fortress of Corregidor, after a fearful bombing and a terrific pounding from artillery on land and from heavy guns on ships, fell on May 6 after the Japanese succeeded in landing on the island. When General MacArthur was informed of the fall of Corregidor he paid his respects to its intrepid defenders in these ever-memorable words:

Corregidor needs no comment from me. It has sounded its own story at the mouth of its guns. It has scrolled its own epitaph on enemy tablets. But through the bloody haze

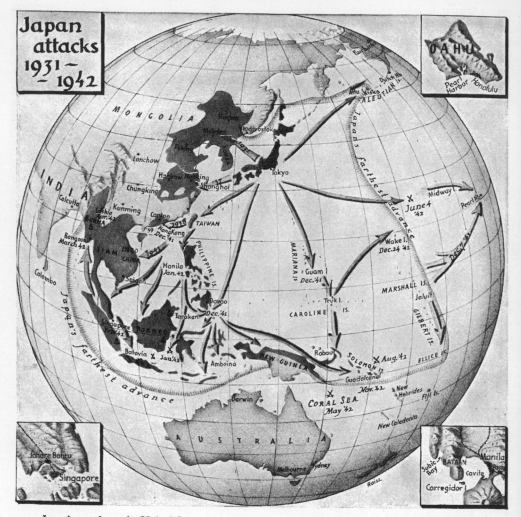

Japan's attack on the United States came as a surprise to many Americans. Overestimating their own power, the Japanese launched their surprise attack (December 7, 1941) on Pearl Harbor. Initial successes seemed to justify the ambitions of the imperialistic military leaders of Tokyo because, within a half year, the flag of the Rising Sun was waving over rich lands from Burma and the Philippines to the Gilbert Islands.

of its last reverberating shot I shall always seem to see a vision of grim, gaunt, ghostly men still unafraid.

The exhausted American and Filipino troops were subjected by their conquerors to such brutal and humiliating treatment in the long march to a prisoner-of-war camp without food or water that many died on the march. It was called "the death march of Bataan." The American troops on the other islands were overcome more quickly. Prisoners of war, along with civilians, were confined in Japanese prison camps, where they were so inhumanly treated that many of them died and many who survived suffered brutal treatment.

Acme

MALAYAN MOTHER AT SINGAPORE MOURNING THE LOSS OF HER LITTLE
CHILD

The Japanese captured Malaya and Singapore. At the same time that the Japanese were invading the Philippines, other Japanese forces, numbering about 200,000, were launching an attack on the Malay Peninsula. Their objectives were the capture of Malaya, which produced nearly half of the world's raw rubber and more than one fourth of its tin, and Singapore, the great British naval base on an island at the tip of the peninsula. Singapore was a city of about 600,000 inhabitants.

At the beginning of the Japanese invasion of Malaya, the British suffered a stunning naval loss. On December 7, 1941, the British battleship *Prince of Wales* and the battle cruiser *Repulse* under command of Admiral Phillips steamed north from Singapore without air protection to intercept a Japanese convoy on its way to the east coast of the Malay Peninsula. On December 10, they were attacked, bombed, torpedoed, and sunk off the southeast coast of Malaya by Japanese planes. "In my whole experience," said Winston Churchill, "I do not remember any naval blow so painful as the sinking of the *Prince of Wales* and the *Repulse*." The loss of these powerful ships left the British with only weak naval forces in the East to oppose the powerful Japanese navy.

While Japanese planes from bases in Thailand and Indo-China bombed British airfields in Northern Malaya, their troops landed on its northeast coast, cut across a very narrow part of the peninsula to the west coast, and by so doing cut communications between Malaya and Burma. Then the Japanese began a drive southward down the west and also down the east coast. Training in jungle fighting enabled the Japanese soldiers to work through the British lines, to encircle British strong points, and to drive the defending armies, composed of British, Australian, and Indian units, back toward Singapore.

Acme

GENERAL STILWELL RETREATING IN BURMA.

On January 30, 1942, the defenders evacuated Johore Bahru, crossed the half-mile causeway across Johore Strait to Singapore and then blew up the causeway. Singapore had been built for defense against an attack from the sea and consequently its guns pointed seaward. Moreover, its water supply came from the mainland. After a siege of about two weeks during which Singapore was almost continually bombed and mercilessly pounded by Japanese artillery, the Japanese crossed Johore Strait and captured the two water reservoirs in the city. Further resistance was futile, escape was impossible, and so the British garrison of about 70,000 troops surrendered unconditionally on February 15, 1942. The fall of Singapore was, in the words of Winston Churchill, "the greatest disaster to British arms which history records." It gave the Japanese control over the passage between the Indian and Pacific Oceans through the Straits of Malacca; it made easier the Japanese conquest of Sumatra and Java; and it released Japanese forces for the campaign now going on in Burma.

The Japanese capture of Burma cut the Burma Road. The objectives of the Burma campaign were: (1) to capture Rangoon, the main port of Burma; (2) to cut the Burma Road; and (3) to secure control of the Burmese oil fields and tin mines. Ever since the Japanese had gained possession of China's ports, war supplies for China from the outside world had been transported by sea to Rangoon. From Rangoon they were transported by railroad to Lashio, the western end of the Burma Road. From Lashio they were carried by trucks over the Burma Road through Kunming to Chungking, China's wartime capital. The capture of Rangoon and the cutting of the Burma Road would strike a serious blow to the Chinese by depriving them of desperately needed war equipment.

While the Malaya campaign was going on, Japanese forces, aided by a puppet army from Thailand and by Burmese who were very discontented with British rule, invaded (January 5, 1942) Southern Burma from Thailand. Just before this invasion began and all during it, Rangoon was heavily bombed by Japanese air forces. The British forces defending Rangoon under General Wavell had some air support from the R.A.F. and from the American Volunteer Group (Flying Tigers), but the Japanese had a greater number of planes. Using the same jungle fighting tactics that they were using in Malaya, the Japanese drove slowly but surely westward toward Rangoon which they captured (March 9, 1942). The garrison at Rangoon, however, escaped capture and marched north to join other forces in resisting further Japanese advances while Chinese forces under General Joseph Stilwell, an American, moved southward to defend against the Japanese advance.

As the Japanese drove northward from Rangoon up the valleys of the Irrawaddy, Sittang, and Salween Rivers, another Japanese army from Thailand invaded Northern Burma. It defeated Chinese forces, captured Lashio, and outflanked the British and Chinese forces to the south. Leaving their heavy war equipment behind, the British retreated westward into India. A small tired group of Chinese, British, Americans, and Burmese, led by General Stilwell, also beat a painful but hasty retreat through the jungles to India.

By May 13, 1942, the Japanese had control over most of Burma. China was cut off from war supplies from the west except for those that could be flown in over the Himalayas from India. Moreover, the Japanese could now invade China from the west along the Burma Road and also invade India from the east. Indeed on April 5, 1942, a naval force steamed into the Bay of Bengal, bombed Colombo on the island of Ceylon, and sank three British warships and several merchant vessels. To defend against an amphibious attack on India and to protect their sea lanes in the Indian Ocean, the British rushed strong naval forces from the Atlantic and seized the island of Madagascar (May 7, 1942) from its Vichy government.

The Japanese captured the Netherlands East Indies. Japan's plan to establish a New Order in Greater East Asia included the conquest of the Netherlands East Indies, a vast archipelago consisting of four large islands (Sumatra, Java, Borneo, Celebes) and a host of smaller islands. They are inhabited by about 70,000,000 people and are, as they have been for centuries, a rich storehouse of agricultural and mineral resources. Here are produced most of the world's quinine, three fourths of its raw rubber, almost half of its tin, three fourths of the oil produced in the Far East, and many other products, including spices, sugar, tobacco, coconuts, and tea. Possession of these islands would enable Japan to obtain strategic raw materials and foodstuffs which it did not have in its home land.

While the Japanese were conquering the Philippines, Malaya, and Burma, they were also conquering the Netherlands East Indies. The first step was the landing (December 17, 1941) on Sarawak, a British protectorate on the northwest coast of Borneo which produced oil. On December 20, the Japanese captured the port of Davao on the large island of Mindanao in the southern Philippines which they used as a naval and air base for assaults on the islands of Borneo, Celebes, Amboina, and Dutch New Guinea. By January 21, 1942, their occupation of bases on the eastern coast of Borneo and the western coast of Celebes planted them firmly on both sides of Macassar Strait, the waterway between the island of Borneo and the island of Celebes.

On January 23, a fleet of about 100 Japanese warships and transports steamed south through Macassar Strait toward Java. From January 23-29 this fleet was attacked in the Battle of Macassar Strait by Dutch and American planes, submarines, destroyers, and cruisers which sank sixteen ships, badly damaged twenty-two others, and forced the Japanese fleet to turn back. However, the conquest of the East Indies was not long delayed.

On January 30, Japanese landed on Amboina and by February 4 they controlled it, including its naval base and airfields. After the fall of Singapore, the Japanese bombed airfields on Sumatra and landed on it in spite of heavy losses. Soon Sumatra was in their possession. At about the same time they conquered Timor and Bali east of Java and then sent a convoy escorted by a powerful fleet into the Java Sea. American, Dutch, British, and Australian naval forces engaged the Japanese in the Battle of the Java Sea (February 27-28, 1942). The superior Japanese fleet inflicted a crushing defeat on the weak naval forces of the Allies. Only four American destroyers escaped destruction.

After the Battle of the Java Sea, Java was doomed. The Japanese landed at three places on Java, captured Batavia, its capital, and Surabaya, a naval base. On March 9, 1942, the Dutch surrendered 98,000 soldiers. All the Netherlands East Indies with their enormous resources were in the possession of the Japanese who now menaced Australia.

The Japanese prepared the way for an assault on Australia. In the Central Pacific, the Japanese held at the outset of the war the Mariana, Caroline, and Marshall Islands which had been mandated to them by the Paris Peace Conference after the end of the First World War. In violation of the terms of the mandate, the Japanese had fortified them and refused to allow other nations to inspect these fortifications.

Immediately after Pearl Harbor, the Japanese moved from the Marshall Islands into the Gilbert Islands, British possessions. From their strongly fortified base at Truk in the Carolines and from their newly acquired bases in the Philippines and the East Indies the Japanese also drove south and east into the islands of New Guinea, New Britain, and the Solomons. They captured Rabaul on New Britain (January 27, 1942) and Bougainville on one of the Solomons (January 29). From these bases they moved on during the spring to Tulagi and Guadalcanal, other islands in the Solomons, where they began to build airfields. During the spring of 1942, they seized several ports on the northern coast of New Guinea and began an advance over the mountains to Port Moresby on the southern coast opposite Port Darwin in Northern Australia.

These campaigns were designed to open the path and provide bases for an attack on Australia and to cut the direct route for the shipment of supplies from the United States to Australia.

United States forces were on the defensive. The destruction of ships and planes at Pearl Harbor, the loss of the Philippines, and the unpreparedness of the United States forced American forces in the Pacific to be on the defensive. Their strategy was to check the Japanese wherever possible, to hold them back as long as they could, and to do all the damage they could to Japanese installations. The Battles of Macassar Strait and the Java Sea were essentially defensive actions fought to check the advance of the Japanese as long as possible. On February 1, 1942, an American task force raided Japanese installations on the Marshall and Gilbert Islands. This raid was followed shortly by raids on New Britain, Wake, and Marcus Islands and on Japanese bases on New Guinea. On April 18,

1942, sixteen army bombers, under the command of Major James H. Doolittle, took off from the carrier *Hornet,* bombed Tokyo and other cities, and then flew on to China. Most of the crews reached safety with the aid of the Chinese, but the Japanese captured eight men and executed three in violation of the rules of war.

The Battle of the Coral Sea (May 4-8, 1942) was fought by the United States Navy in an attempt to stop Japanese advance southward, probably to New Caledonia and to Australia. In this battle the two fleets never sighted each other; all attacks were made by planes from American and Japanese carriers. Both sides suffered losses, but Japan's were the more serious in the long run because we could replace our losses more quickly than the Japanese. Our heaviest loss was the aircraft carrier *Lexington.* The battle was an American victory because it checked Japanese advances southward.

A United States task force defeated a powerful Japanese fleet at the Battle of Midway. On June 3, 1942, an American patrol plane sighted a great armada of at least eighty-eight ships (battleships, carriers, cruisers, destroyers, supply vessels, transports, and smaller craft) which the Japanese had sent into the Central Pacific to attack Midway and probably Hawaii. In anticipation of such an attack, a large portion of the American fleet had been recalled from the South Pacific. Before this time American experts had broken the Japanese code for radio messages, so our officers knew the Japanese were on their way before they were sighted.

Heroic attacks by American planes from carriers and by Flying Fortresses based on Midway (June 3-6) resulted in the destruction of four carriers, one heavy cruiser and three destroyers; three battleships, three heavy cruisers, one light cruiser, and several destroyers were damaged. The enemy lost at least 275 airplanes and 4800 men. The Americans lost the carrier *Yorktown,* a destroyer, about 150 planes, and 307 men. In the words of Admiral King this defeat was the "first decisive defeat suffered by the Japanese navy in 350 years."

The American victory at Midway made another Japanese advance in the Central Pacific impossible. It ended all danger to Hawaii, brought the United States and Japanese navies in the Pacific nearer to equality, ruined the Japanese carrier fleet, and caused the death of the best of the Japanese pilots. For these reasons it was one of the decisive battles of the Second World War.

While the main Japanese fleet was advancing on Midway, a secondary fleet launched an attack on Dutch Harbor, an American naval and air base in the Aleutian Islands. American planes attacked it and compelled it to retreat. On their retreat the Japanese seized Kiska and Attu, two small islands in the western Aleutians. From there they threatened Dutch Harbor and the northwestern supply route from the United States to Soviet Siberia. They were also a potential threat to the northwestern states of the United States.

In the autumn of 1942 the onrush of the Japanese had reached its climax. The Japanese had overrun much of Eastern and Southeastern Asia, the Philippines, the Netherlands East Indies, and many other islands in the Pacific. They were poised for an invasion of India and Australia. Despite their loss at Midway, they still occupied positions that made them exceedingly dangerous enemies of the United States. The outlook at this critical time seemed dark indeed for Great Britain, the United States, and the nations allied with them.

SUMMARY

In the Second World War almost the entire populations of the warring countries were involved either as civilians or as members of the armed forces.

In a few weeks Germany overran and conquered Poland and enslaved very many of the Polish people. After Finland refused Soviet demands for lands and bases, war resulted in the defeat of the Finns and they granted Soviet demands. The Soviets occupied the Baltic States, made them republics, and incorporated them in the Soviet Union.

In the spring of 1940, Germany invaded and conquered in succession Denmark, Norway, Luxemburg, the Netherlands, Belgium, and a large part of France, including its Atlantic coast and Paris. Germany's frightful bombing of Great Britain ended in failure because it did not cause the valiant British to submit to Hitler's demands.

After the First World War, the majority of Americans believed that the United States should keep out of European wars. Consequently, Congress passed (1935) a Neutrality Act to help accomplish this purpose. It was amended (1939) to permit warring nations to buy war materials in the United States on a cash and carry basis. As the war in Europe continued, the United States took other measures to strengthen our national security by establishing the National Defense Advisory Board, and the Office of Production Management, and also by passing the Selective Service Act. The Lend-Lease Act empowered the President to sell or lease to, or exchange goods with, nations whose defense he thought vital to the United States. In the Atlantic Charter President Roosevelt and Prime Minister Churchill, meeting on a battleship at sea, stated what they thought were the common aims of the United States and Great Britain for the future.

After failing to conquer Great Britain, Hitler turned (1941) in fury upon the Balkan States. He forced Hungary, Rumania, and Bulgaria to join the Axis and overran and subjugated Yugoslavia and Greece, which Mussolini had failed to conquer. Using Greece as a base, he conquered the island of Crete.

As the Third French Republic was about to fall, Mussolini invaded Southeastern France and a few months later (September, 1940) he ordered his army in Libya to capture Egypt and the Suez Canal and thereby cut the life line of Great Britain to India. He failed here as he had in Greece. After Mussolini had failed in both Greece and North Africa, Hitler took over in both theaters because he, too, wanted to inflict serious damage on British interests. The Germans succeeded in Greece, and in North Africa they advanced into Egypt.

The execution of Hitler's vast and comprehensive plans for the conquest of the Soviet Union wreaked terrible havoc on the Soviet peoples, their homes, farms, and villages. It resulted in the destruction of cities, factories, and mines, but it did not lead to the capture of Leningrad and Moscow, two of its chief objectives.

A Soviet counter-offensive in the winter of 1941-1942 drove the Germans back on all battle fronts. In 1942 Hitler's armies attempted to capture the lower Volga region, the Caucasus with its rich oil fields, and to shut off Lend-Lease supplies from Iran. The Germans penetrated the Caucasus, but they failed to capture Stalingrad.

In the autumn of 1942 the Germans reached the summit of their power and from then on they were on the defensive. From all the conquered countries the Germans took everything of value they could and shipped it back home. They took hundreds of thousands of people in the conquered countries by force to Germany where they compelled them to work as slave laborers on farms, in factories, and in mines and homes.

The Chino-Japanese War was still raging when war broke out in Europe and Hitler's successes there prevented Great Britain, France, and the Netherlands, the countries in Europe most affected by Japanese aggression, from taking action of any kind. Consequently, the

Japanese militarists and imperialists became increasingly bolder in their expansion southward until it alarmed the United States which sent a strong naval force from the Atlantic to our great naval base at Pearl Harbor.

Owing to a lack of any military opposition, Japan occupied Hainan, the Spratly Islands, and Indo-China. In September, 1940, Japan, Germany, and Italy made a military alliance. After Japan and the United States failed to agree on their differences in the Far East, Japan attacked Pearl Harbor, the Philippines, Hong Kong, and other places.

By the end of 1942, the Japanese had conquered the Philippines, Hong Kong, Malaya, Singapore, Burma, and the Netherlands East Indies, and were poised for an assault on Australia. The United States Navy finally became strong enough to check the Japanese in the Battle of the Coral Sea and to defeat a powerful Japanese fleet in the Battle of Midway. In the autumn of 1942, the Japanese had reached the summit of their power and began to decline while the might and power of the United States rapidly increased largely because of our great productive capacity.

EVENTS THAT TOOK PLACE AT ABOUT THE SAME TIME

YEAR	EUROPE	AFRICA	FAR EAST	UNITED STATES
1939	Sept. 1, Germany invaded Poland. Sept. 3, Great Britain, France, India, Australia, New Zealand declared war on Germany. Sept. 10, Canada declared war on Germany. Sept. 17, Soviet troops occupied Eastern Poland. Sept. 26, Germany and Soviet Union partitioned Poland. Nov. 30, Soviet Union invaded Finland.	Sept. 6, Union of South Africa declared war on Germany.	1937-1939, Japan attacked China, July 7, 1937. By 1939 Peiping, Tientsin, Shanghai, Nanking, Hangchow, Canton, and other cities in Japanese hands. Puppet Chinese government installed in Nanking.	July 26, United States announced termination of commercial treaty with Japan. Sept. 5, United States proclaimed neutrality in the European war. Nov. 4, United States repealed the arms embargo (cash and carry).

EVENTS THAT TOOK PLACE AT ABOUT THE SAME TIME (Cont.)

YEAR	EUROPE	AFRICA	FAR EAST	UNITED STATES
1940	Mar. 12, Soviet-Finnish peace treaty signed. April 9, Germany invaded Denmark and Norway. May 10, Germany invaded Belgium, Luxemburg, and the Netherlands. May 29-June 4, Battle of Dunkirk. June 10, Italy declared war on France and Britain. June 13, Fall of Paris. June 22, France signed armistice with Germany. June 24, France signed armistice with Italy.			
		July 3, Battle of Oran.		
			July 8, Great Britain closed Burma Road.	
				July 30, Act of Havana.
		Aug. 4, Italians attacked British Somaliland.		
	Aug. 11, Blitz on England began.			Sept. 2, United States and Great Britain conclude deal for exchange of fifty destroyers for lease of naval and air bases.
		Sept. 15, Italy invaded Egypt from Libya.		
				Sept. 16, Congress passed first Selective Service Act.

EVENTS THAT TOOK PLACE AT ABOUT THE SAME TIME (Cont.)

Year	Europe	Africa	Far East	United States
1940 *cont.*			Sept. 22, Japanese troops began occupation of French Indo-China.	
				Sept. 26, President Roosevelt embargoed export of scrap iron and steel.
	Sept. 27, Germany, Italy, Japan signed 10-year military-economic alliance.		Sept. 27, Japan, Germany, Italy signed 10-year military alliance.	
			Oct. 18, Great Britain re-opened the Burma Road.	
	Oct. 28, Italy attacked Greece.			
				Nov. 6, President Roosevelt elected for a third term.
	Nov. 20-24, Hungary, Rumania, Slovakia joined the Axis.			
		Dec. 15, British drove Italians out of Egypt.		
				Dec. 17, President Roosevelt proposed Lend-Lease materials to Great Britain.
1941				Jan. 6, President Roosevelt recommended Lend-Lease to Congress and stated the Four Freedoms.
	March 1, Bulgaria joined the Axis.			
				March 11, President Roosevelt signed Lend-Lease Act.

EVENTS THAT TOOK PLACE AT ABOUT THE SAME TIME (Cont.)

YEAR	EUROPE	AFRICA	FAR EAST	UNITED STATES
1941 cont.	April 6, Germany, Italy, Bulgaria attacked Yugoslavia and Greece.			
				April 9, United States took over protection of Greenland.
			April 16, Japan-Soviet Union signed five-year neutrality pact.	
	April 17, Yugoslav army surrendered. April 23, Greece surrendered to Germany and Italy.			
		May 6, Haile Selassie regained Ethiopian throne.		
				May 27, President Roosevelt proclaimed unlimited national emergency.
	June 22, Germany invaded the Soviet Union. Soviet Union attacked Finland.			
				July 7, United States occupied Iceland.
			July 25, United States froze Japanese assets.	
				Aug. 14, Roosevelt and Churchill announced the Atlantic Charter. Sept. 11, Roosevelt announced shoot-on-sight order to U. S. Navy.
	Sept. 20, Germans captured Kiev. Oct. 17, Germans captured Odessa. Oct. 27, Germans captured Kharkov.			

EVENTS THAT TOOK PLACE AT ABOUT THE SAME TIME (Cont.)

Year	Europe	Africa	Far East	United States
1941 cont.				Oct. 31, *Reuben James* torpedoed and sunk by Germans.
	Nov. 23, Germans captured Rostov. Nov. 30, Russians recaptured Rostov.			
			Dec. 7, Japan attacked Pearl Harbor. Dec. 8, United States and Great Britain declared war on Japan. Dec. 10, *Prince of Wales* and *Repulse* sunk.	
				Dec. 11, Germany and Italy declared war on United States.
			Dec. 25, Hong Kong captured by Japanese.	
1942				Jan. 1, Declaration of the United Nations signed.
			Jan. 23, Battle of Macassar Strait.	
		Jan. 29, Axis forces occupied Bengasi.		
			Feb. 15, Japanese captured Singapore. Apr. 8, Fall of Bataan. May 4-8, Battle of the Coral Sea. May 7, Fall of Corregidor. June 3-6, Battle of Midway.	
	June 10, Nazis destroyed Lidice.			

EVENTS THAT TOOK PLACE AT ABOUT THE SAME TIME (Cont.)

YEAR	EUROPE	AFRICA	FAR EAST	UNITED STATES
1942 cont.	July 3, Germans captured Sevastopol. July 28, Germans captured Rostov. Nov. 22, Russians began offensive in Stalingrad.	June 20-21, Germans captured Tobruk. Nov. 2, British defeated Axis at El Alamein. Nov. 7, American armies landed in North Africa. Nov. 14, British captured Tobruk. Nov. 20, British captured Bengasi.	June 12-21, Japanese occupied Attu and Kiska. Aug. 7-10, Americans invaded Solomon Islands.	

EVACUATION FROM DUNKIRK. British and French soldiers wait on the Dunkirk dunes for the ships from England.

FALL OF FRANCE. As the flags of fallen France were carried through Marseilles on their way to Africa, the people in the streets watched weeping—and were not ashamed of their tears.

BLIND JUSTICE. In Washington, Secretary of War Stimson, wearing blindfold, draws No. 3485—the first number of the 1942 levy. The fishbowl is the one used in the first World War.

NURSERY SCHOOL BLITZED. Children whose mothers are making munitions enter an air raid shelter in England.

V FOR VICTORY. Above, Britain's war premier, Winston Churchill, makes the sign for resistance.

LONDON IN FLAMES. At right, fires started by night bombing illuminate the dome of St. Paul's Cathedral.

CHAPTER 35

The Total Victory of the United Nations
Over the Axis Powers

On January 1, 1942, less than one month after the Japanese bombing assault on Pearl Harbor, twenty-six nations formed the United Nations to help bring about the abject and unconditional surrender of the Axis powers. It took them more than three and one-half years to achieve this colossal task. During these years they fought their enemies on land and in the air on three continents—Europe, Africa, and Asia—and also waged war relentlessly over the broad expanses of the Atlantic and Pacific. The Axis powers were crushed chiefly by the United States, The Soviet Union, and the British Commonwealth of Nations. China helped to the best of its ability.

While American, British, and Free French forces were conquering the German and Italian forces in North Africa, the Soviet armies were driving the Germans and their allies back westward in the Soviet Union. As the Soviet armies continued their drive westward, the United States and Great Britain invaded Italy and forced the Italian government to surrender unconditionally. Italy was the first of the Axis powers to be defeated.

As the Soviet armies advanced westward on several fronts, American, British and Canadian armies invaded and liberated France, and also Belgium, the Netherlands, and Luxemburg, and then drove eastward into Western Germany. By May, 1945, the German armies, hopelessly defeated and hemmed in on all sides, surrendered in the hundreds of thousands and those who spoke for Germany surrendered unconditionally to the representatives of the United States, the Soviet Union, Great Britain, and France. Germany was the second and most powerful of the Axis powers to be defeated.

In the meantime, armed forces of the United States and the British Commonwealth of Nations, aided by China, were waging offensive war against the Japanese on widely separated fronts in the Pacific and the Far East. In the closing days of the war they were aided by the Soviet Union. On August 14, 1945, after atom bombs had wrought fearful destruction of property and terrible loss of lives in two Japanese cities, the government of Japan surrendered unconditionally. The remaining Axis power had been defeated and the most destructive, costly, and bloody war in all history had ended in the total victory of the United Nations over the Axis powers.

• • •

The United Nations promised to work together to defeat their Axis enemies. After the United States entered the war, President Roosevelt and leaders of the other nations at war with the Axis powers deemed that the first step toward victory was the creation of a united front. In this movement President Roosevelt took the lead in the establishment of the United Nations. On January 1, 1942, he and the representatives of twenty-five other nations which had declared war on one or more of the Axis powers signed the Declaration by the United Nations. In the Declaration each government accepted the principles set forth in the Atlantic Charter, pledged that it would employ its full resources against the Axis powers with which it was at war, promised to co-operate with all other members of the United Nations, and promised also not to make a separate peace with its Axis enemies.

To secure hemispheric solidarity for common defense and to prevent as far as possible subversive activities of Axis agents throughout Latin America, a conference was called to meet (January 15, 1942) at Rio de Janeiro. As a result of this conference, all the Latin American republics, except Chile and Argentina, broke off diplomatic relations with the Axis and most of those who had not already done so declared war.

To promote unity in the war effort, Roosevelt and Churchill agreed after conferences in Washington to create a Combined Chiefs of Staff which would include high-ranking military officers of their countries. The War Department declared (February 6, 1942) that its purpose was "to insure complete co-ordination of the war effort of Great Britain and the United States, including the production and distribution of their war supplies and to provide for full British and American collaboration with the United Nations."

The leaders of the great powers among the United Nations realized that they must co-operate to bring about the defeat of the Axis powers. Consequently, they drew up and signed a number of agreements. The United States and Great Britain signed (February 23, 1942) a mutual aid agreement in which they promised to provide each other with war supplies, services, and i n f o r m a t i o n needed to help win the war. Great Britain and the Soviet Union signed (May 26, 1942)

a twenty-year mutual assistance treaty in which they promised to fight together against Germany, to make peace only by mutual agreement, and to co-operate for peace after the war was won. The United States and the Soviet Union signed (June 11, 1942) a mutual aid agreement in which the United States agreed to furnish more Lend-Lease supplies. However, before the United States could act effectively, it had to make preparations to play its part in the war.

The United States girded itself for war. Fortunately, the United States had already begun to prepare for war. On October 16, 1940, draft boards had registered 16,000,000 men between the ages of twenty-one and thirty-six for one year of military service in the Western Hemisphere and the possessions of the United States. In August, 1941, Congress extended the length of service of all army men to eighteen months. Huge military camps were built to house these soldiers. By the fall of 1941 about 1,500,000 men, including Regulars and National Guard troops, were serving in the Army and about 425,000 in the Navy, Marine Corps, and Coast Guard. After the United States entered the war, Congress removed the restrictions on the use of troops only in the Western Hemisphere, extended the period of military service to six months after the end of hostilities, and required the registration of all men between eighteen and sixty-four. Quotas from the draft boards were increased until all men able to fight and not excused for essential work as civilians had been drafted into the armed forces. During 1942 the number was increased to 7,000,000 and by the end of 1944 nearly 11,500,000 were in arms, approximately 3,000,000 of whom were in the Navy.

Congress made provisions for the voluntary enlistment of women to do clerical work and many other kinds of duties in the Army, Navy, Marines, and Coast Guard. All the drafted men and the enlisted women were given tests to determine in which branches of the armed forces they could serve most effectively. After these men and women had been taken into the services, they were given basic training to help them serve more efficiently in the branches of the service to which they were assigned. Each branch of the armed services had its own training program.

Tests were given men to help determine which of them possessed the capacity to become officers and those chosen were given special training. The War Department planned to give every man at least three months basic training and at least nine months more which would include army maneuvers under simulated war conditions before he was prepared to be sent to a war zone. Soldiers were chosen for special units which were given special training to prepare them for desert or mountain fighting or for amphibious warfare. The purpose of this training was to make our soldiers wary and skillful in actual combat.

Tests were given soldiers to determine whether they possessed the ability to become flyers. Those who passed the tests were given highly specialized training to enable them to be pilots, navigators, bombers, or gunners. Lessons learned in actual combat were quickly reported and taught to men in training. Two years after Pearl Harbor, the Army had over 100,000 pilots and more than 500,000 highly trained technicians who serviced the different kinds of planes.

The Army had in all 610 special services in which soldiers and enlisted women received training to enable them to perform specialized tasks. The tasks included chaplains, doctors, dentists, nurses, lawyers, accountants, teachers of special subjects, shopkeepers, clerks, mechanics, cooks, military police, signal men, and soldiers skilled in chemical warfare.

The Navy, Marine Corps, and Coast Guard also had special schools for the training of their officers, their air forces, and their enlisted men. The Navy established special schools at a number of colleges and universities in which cadets were given physical and mental training to help make them expert pilots. After a pilot had learned to take off, fly and land at a flying field, he then learned how to take off and land from an aircraft carrier. The Marine Corps trained marines in amphibious warfare and in jungle fighting. The Coast Guard trained coast guardsmen to assist the Navy in landing troops on enemy shores. The Navy organized Construction Battalions (Seabees) to build army and navy bases, to construct and repair airfields, to do many other kinds of work needed overseas, and to take part in amphibious warfare. Admiral King said of them:

The accomplishments of the Seabees have been one of the outstanding features of the war. In the Pacific, where distances are great and the expeditious construction of bases is frequently of vital importance, the construction accomplished by the Seabees has been of invaluable assistance. Furthermore, the Seabees have participated in practically every amphibious operation undertaken . . ., landing with the first waves of assault troops to bring equipment ashore and set up temporary bases of operation. Other specialized services performed by the Seabees included the handling of pontoon gear, the repair of motor vehicles, loading and unloading of cargo vessels, and in fact every kind of construction job that has to be done.

A group of highly skilled men were brought together into the Office of Strategic Service to provide specialized information and to assist the military in learning and interpreting enemy secrets.

Even though a great number of men and women served in the armed forces, those who remained at home won the battle of production. In his annual message to Congress on January 6, 1942, President Roosevelt asked management and labor to produce in 1942 60,000 planes, 45,000 tanks, 20,000 anti-aircraft guns, and 8,000,000 tons of merchant ships. To pay for these war materials and other war costs, he asked Congress to authorize the expenditure of $56,000,000,000. Management and labor more than met the goals of production set by the President. Moreover, farmers added more than 5,000,-000 acres to the land already under cultivation and increased the supply of foodstuffs about 12 per cent. To replace the ships sunk by the Germans, our shipyards in 1943 averaged three ships a day. Some of the smaller ones were built in less than forty days and in all about 19,000,000 tons of merchant ships and 2,500,000 tons of naval vessels were launched in 1943.

Between July 1, 1940, and September 30, 1944, our factories turned out 70,000 tanks, more than 230,000 airplanes of many different kinds, and also the guns and ammunition needed by them.

Management and labor co-operated to produce war materials on a vast scale. Manufacturers and industrialists exchanged patents and blueprints. Scientists pooled their knowledge to improve the older weapons of war and to invent and develop new ones. Labor organizations gave the government pledges that their members would not strike and management pledged that lockouts would not occur. The speed and efficiency with which untrained men and women learned to do the highly specialized types of work needed in the production of war materials was astounding to all.

The United States became, in fact, the arsenal of democracy. It trained, equipped, transported, and supplied its own vast armed forces and shipped supplies of all kinds to its allies.

Franklin Delano Roosevelt (1882-1945) was an inspiring war leader. During the First World War, he had been Assistant Secretary of the Navy under Josephus Daniels. In this position he had shown marked ability. In 1920 he was candidate for Vice President on the Democratic ticket. In 1921 he was stricken with infantile paralysis which seriously impaired his ability to walk. Despite this handicap, he re-entered politics and embarked on a political career unique in United States history. He was elected governor of New York in 1928 and re-elected in 1930. He was elected President of the United States in 1932 and was re-elected three times. In his first inaugural address, delivered in the midst of a world-wide economic depression, he said: "We have nothing to fear but fear itself." This optimistic statement helped to raise the hopes of the discouraged people. In the early years of his first administration, he developed the New Deal as a program for relieving the distress caused by the economic depression that had begun in 1929. Many Americans did not favor the New Deal, but after Pearl Harbor nearly all were united for the prosecution of the war.

President Roosevelt was a handsome man. His personality, his courageous leadership, his sense of humor, and his official acts won him millions of supporters. His voice, which carried particularly well over radio, helped to give him his great hold over people. He had a fine command of the English language. He made effective use of such phrases as "the forgotten man," "the arsenal of democracy," and "the Four Freedoms." More than any other leader he was responsible for maintaining good will and unity of action among the leaders of the nations fighting the Axis powers.

Roosevelt and Churchill decided to conquer Germany and Italy first. After the Japanese attack on Pearl Harbor, Roosevelt,

Churchill, and their military, naval, and economic advisers met in Washington late in December, 1941. They decided to concentrate their combined forces against the forces of Hitler and Mussolini and to wage a defensive war on Japan. At that time the military might of the Nazis and Fascists seemed to be a more dangerous threat to the national security of the United States and Great Britain than the Japanese. Once the Nazis and Fascists were defeated and put out of the war, the combined forces of the United States and Great Britain could then concentrate on Japan. This plan was modified, however, as the war went on because the United States was able to produce sufficient war supplies, merchant ships, and warships and to train millions of men in the armed services to meet our promises in the war against the Nazis and Fascists and to wage war on a vast scale against the Japanese.

The United States and Great Britain won the Battle of the Atlantic. From September, 1939, to March, 1940, more than 200 British and 200 neutral merchant ships had been sunk by German and Italian submarines, by German and Italian planes, and by magnetic mines sown by planes. The greatest menace to shipping was the German submarines which hunted their prey both singly and in packs. The British were greatly hampered in their war on the submarines by the lack of bases in Eire which had been available to them and the Americans in the First World War. Moreover, the Germans had submarine bases in Denmark, Norway, and France which they did not have in the First World War.

At first the British made little headway against the submarine menace because they did not have enough naval vessels to patrol the vast expanse of the seas and oceans through which their ships sailed. The fifty destroyers they received from the United States (1940) were of some assistance. The bombing of German submarine bases and the use on ships of devices against magnetic mines reduced the sinkings a little.

After the passage of the Lend-Lease Act (March, 1941), the United States government became alarmed because the high rate of sinkings was preventing much Lend-Lease material from reaching the British. In May, 1941, President Roosevelt revealed that at that time German submarines and surface raiders were sinking merchant ships at a rate three times greater than British shipyards could produce them and more than twice the combined British and American production.

To help prevent the sinking of merchant ships, the United States Navy put into effect the neutrality patrol system. Under this system, American warships and planes in the western Atlantic warned merchant ships of the presence of German submarines and surface raiders. After the United States had occupied Greenland (April, 1941) and Iceland (June, 1941), the neutrality patrol, from bases on them, extended its operations farther into the North Atlantic. At about the same time it was extended also into the South Atlantic. In September, 1941, after a German submarine had attacked the American destroyer *Greer* while on patrol duty, President Roosevelt ordered the United States naval and air patrol to protect all merchant ships in the Atlantic and to shoot on sight enemy war vessels.

Despite all that the British and Americans were doing to curb the German submarine menace, the Germans in 1941 sank 3,700,000 tons of merchant shipping, nearly twice the tonnage produced in British and American shipyards that year. Moreover, because American merchant ships were forbidden by the Neutrality Act to carry cargoes to ports of countries at war, Lend-Lease materials could not be delivered to Britain and the Soviet Union in quantities sufficient to meet their

Acme

Coast Guardsmen watch the explosion of a depth charge which blew a Nazi sub to the surface.

war needs. Consequently, at the request of President Roosevelt, Congress in November, 1941, repealed certain sections of the Neutrality Act to permit the arming of American merchant ships and to authorize them to carry war supplies to ports of countries fighting Germany and Italy.

In the meantime, the British Navy won a great naval victory. In May, 1941, the *Bismarck,* Germany's newest and most powerful battleship, and the *Prinz Eugen* set out from a Norwegian port to raid British shipping on the North Atlantic. Their sailing had been observed by a British plane and so the British sent the battleship *Prince of Wales* and the battle cruiser *Hood* to do battle with them. On May 24, 1941, in the Denmark Strait between Greenland and Iceland, the *Bismarck* sank the *Hood* when a shell from it hit the *Hood's* magazine, and also succeeded in damaging the *Prince of Wales*. On May 26 a British airplane sighted the *Bismarck* about 550 miles off the southwestern coast of England. At once battleships, cruisers, destroyers, and planes took after it. After severe bombing and shelling, they sank the *Bismarck* (May 27) with almost its entire crew. The cruiser *Prinz Eugen* escaped to Brest where it joined the *Gneisenau* and the *Scharnhorst*. In February, 1942, these three warships took advantage of a heavy fog and of German interfer-

ence with British radar to escape through the English Channel and the North Sea to their home ports.

By the time the United States had entered the war, the Battle of the Atlantic had reached its most critical stage. Bombers and submarines based on Norway attacked convoys bound for Murmansk with supplies for the Soviet Union and did great damage. In 1942, they sank one fourth of all the merchant ships sailing on this route. German submarines lurked off American ports, sank coastal shipping, and drove coastal oil tankers from the sea. Between January and November, 1942, they sank 498 merchant ships, 201 of them American.

The United States government took extraordinary measures to combat the submarine menace. All lights along the Atlantic coast were dimmed or blacked out and coastal shipping was convoyed. Coast Guard ships patrolled the waters of the western Atlantic; Army, Navy, and Coast Guard planes and blimps and planes from the Civil Air Patrol (unarmed civilians flying their own planes) hunted the submarines. Escorts and escort carriers (baby flat-tops) convoyed ships across the Atlantic. Long range bombers from bases in Newfoundland, Labrador, Greenland, Iceland, and the British Isles took a heavy toll of German submarines while new devices and techniques used by the British and United States navies enabled surface ships to destroy many submarines. In May, 1943, the United States and Great Britain sank more than thirty submarines and for several months thereafter they averaged about one submarine a day. In September, 1943, Churchill announced that the Germans had not been able to sink a single ship in the North Atlantic for four months. Moreover, by this time tonnage of ships constructed was more than the losses by about 3,000,000 tons. By the autumn of 1943 the United States and

Great Britain had the submarine menace well under control.

On December 26, 1943, the *Scharnhorst* sailed from a Norwegian port to attack a British convoy to the Soviet Union. In a battle in which the British used skillful naval tactics, they overtook and sunk it. The German battleship *Von Tirpitz* was sunk in a Norwegian fjord by British bombers (November 1, 1944).

By the middle of 1944 over 500 German submarines had been destroyed. During the war German submarines sank 2770 ships. Another 2000 were destroyed by mines, German aircraft, the attacks of surface ships, accidents, and other causes. Nevertheless, of the 4,500,000 troops sent overseas to the African and European campaigns only 3604 were reported lost at sea. The United States and Great Britain by united efforts won the battle of the Atlantic.

The Combined Chiefs of Staff planned the conquest of North Africa. Roosevelt, Churchill, and their combined Chiefs of Staff met again in Washington (June, 1942) and drew up a well-organized plan for the conquest of North Africa. It included a British drive westward from Egypt and combined American and British landings at Oran and Algiers in Algeria and an American landing at Casablanca in French Morocco. The forces in the West were to move eastward into Tunisia and the forces in the East were to move westward through Libya and Tripoli to hold the Axis armies between them in a vise-like grip and crush them.

To help carry these plans into effect the British sent more troops and supplies to Egypt. The United States sent tanks, trucks, guns, and service forces around Africa and landed them on the west shore of the Red Sea. American aviators flew planes to Brazil and thence across the Atlantic and across Africa to the British forces in Egypt. In August, 1942, the British government removed General Sir Claude Auchinleck from command of the British forces in the Middle East and replaced him with General Sir Harold Alexander. The command of the British Eighth Army in Egypt which was composed of British, Australian, New Zealand, South African, and Indian divisions was given to General Sir Bernard Law Montgomery.

Montgomery's forces defeated Rommel's forces in Egypt and drove them across Libya. By October, 1942, the British Eighth Army had more guns, tanks, and planes than Rommel's Axis armies. On the night of October 23, Montgomery launched a vast offensive which was intended to drive the Axis armies out of Egypt into Libya. His planes bombed the enemy's supply dumps and troop concentrations. A tremendous artillery barrage softened up the enemy lines while sappers under the protection of aircraft cleared the way through German minefields for tanks and artillery. Strong tank attacks then turned the German left flank along the Mediterranean coast. Rommel did not have the reserves needed to stem the tide of the British forces surging westward. In the twelve-day battle of El Alamein he lost 500 tanks, 1000 guns, and 600 planes. The Axis casualties were reported to be 59,000 of whom 34,000 were Germans. All danger to the Suez Canal was past and all fear of the Germans penetrating the Near East was ended.

Rommel conducted a skillful retreat westward across Libya strewing mines in the way of the British army. He escaped all the attempts of the British and Free French, who had marched northward from the oases of the Sahara, to trap him. He retreated about 1600 miles westward from El Alamein until he reached (February, 1943) the shelter of the Mareth Line, which the French had built years before to protect Tunisia, before he halted his armies.

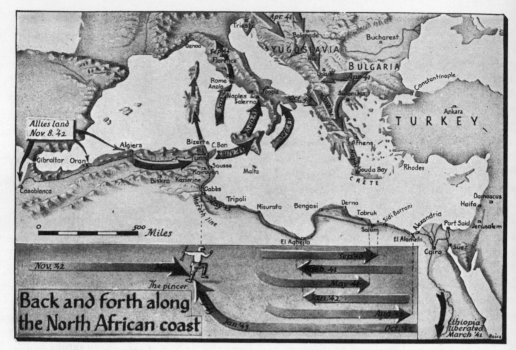

Along a single highway in North Africa the most fantastic battles of the Second World War were waged. Attacks and counterattacks carried the contesting armies back and forth until, in August, 1942, the Nazis reached El Alamein, inside Egypt and about sixty miles from Alexandria. Finally, in 1943, American, British, and French forces crushed the Axis armies in Tunisia.

American and British forces, under General Eisenhower, invaded North Africa. In the meantime, the western phase of the general campaign had been progressing under General Dwight D. Eisenhower, commander-in-chief of the American and British forces which had invaded North Africa. General Eisenhower proved himself to be a great strategist. He possessed the ability to choose officers capable of doing the work assigned to them and was a master at getting high-ranking officers of different nations to work together in harmony.

In late October, 1942, a vast convoy sailed directly from the United States to North Africa while two convoys sailed from Great Britain. These convoys were made up of over 500 transport and supply ships protected by about 350 warships of all kinds. Preparations

for the landings in North Africa had been made by negotiations carried on with French officials favorable to the invasion by Lieutenant General Mark Clark and other American officers who landed in French North Africa from a British submarine. As a result, most of the French forces did not resist the landings.

On November 8, 1942, British and American forces landed at Oran and Algiers on the Mediterranean coast of Algeria while American forces landed at Casablanca on the Atlantic coast of French Morocco. At the same time airborne troops were flown from Great Britain to seize the airfield at Oran. The forces that landed at Algiers did not encounter much opposition and Algiers surrendered that day. The resistance of the French at Oran was stiffer, but it, too, was in the hands of the Americans and British on

November 10. The French at Casablanca put up the stiffest resistance of all. A French naval force consisting of the battleship *Jean Bart,* cruisers, and destroyers opened fire on the American fleet. After a two-day battle, American warships and dive bombers crushed the French naval forces. In the meantime, tank forces assaulted Casablanca which surrendered (November 10). On November 11, at Algiers, Admiral Darlan, head of the French administration in North Africa, signed an armistice and ordered all French forces in North Africa to stop fighting and to join the Americans and British. Admiral Darlan's surrender gave the Allies undisputed sway over Algeria, French Morocco, and French West Africa.

American, British, and Free French forces won the Battle of Tunisia. General Eisenhower now ordered American and British troops to advance eastward through Algeria into Tunisia to seize the ports of Bizerte and Tunis in Northern Tunisia before the Germans could occupy them. However, the Germans were able to get there first. From Sicily, Italy, and Southern France, which the Germans had occupied when the Allies landed in North Africa, the Germans sent thousands of German and Italian troops into Bizerte and Tunis. These Axis forces in Northern Tunisia were under the command of General von Arnim. Field Marshal Rommel, now behind the Mareth Line, commanded the Axis forces in Southern Tunisia.

On February 14, 1943, Rommel launched one of his Panzer divisions westward against inexperienced American troops. He succeeded in driving them through the Kasserine Pass (February 20) and thereby endangered the whole American position. However, reinforcements from Oran, powerful tank attacks, and heavy air assaults drove the Germans back through the pass after several days of hard fighting.

Between March 21 and 27 Montgomery's

Acme

In the Allied invasion of North Africa in November, 1942, more than 850 ships of all kinds took part.

army outflanked the Mareth Line and pursued the Germans northward along the eastern coast of Tunisia. As the British, aided by the French, advanced from the south, American and other British and French forces drove eastward toward Bizerte and Tunis. In April, Hitler ordered Rommel to return to Germany and placed all the Axis forces in Tunisia under the command of von Arnim. On May 7, British forces captured Tunis and on the same day American forces captured Bizerte. On May 12, 1943, General von Arnim surrendered about 225,000 troops. Secretary of War Stimson reported that in the whole Tunisian campaign the Allies captured 226,600, killed 30,000, and wounded 26,400 Axis soldiers. It was a brilliant victory.

The victory in Tunisia liberated North Africa from the Axis. It enabled the Allies to gain air bases to help protect Allied shipping in the Mediterranean which British and American sea power now controlled. It won for the United States and Great Britain the support of thousands of French soldiers. It provided air bases from which air attacks could be made on Axis-held islands in the Mediterranean and on Italy itself. Moreover, it provided a spring-board in North Africa from which the Allies could launch the inva-

Acme

YANK BOMBERS BLASTING PLOESTI OIL
FIELDS IN RUMANIA.

sion of Sicily agreed upon at the Casablanca
conference.

**Roosevelt and Churchill drew up plans
for the conduct of the war at Casablanca
and Washington.** From January 14-26, 1943,
four months before the North African campaign came to an end, the two great leaders
and their combined Chiefs of Staff met at
Casablanca to make plans for the defeat and
destruction of the Axis powers. General
Charles de Gaulle, commander of the Fighting French, and General Henri Giraud, who
had been made High Commissioner of French
Africa after the assassination of Admiral
Darlan, took part in the conference. Although Premier Stalin and Generalissimo
Chiang Kai-shek were unable to attend, they
were sent the plans decided upon by the conference. These plans provided for an invasion
of Sicily and Italy and for a more active
prosecution of the war against Japan. At this
conference President Roosevelt stated that
the ultimate object of the United Nations was
the unconditional surrender of the Axis
powers.

In May, 1943, as the Axis forces were surrendering in Tunisia, Roosevelt, Churchill,
and the Combined Chiefs of Staff met in
Washington. This conference, designated the
Trident Conference, drew up plans for the
use of American and British land, sea, and air
forces against the Germans and Italians in
Europe and the Japanese in the Pacific and
Far East. It decided to knock Italy out of the
war and to strike Germany a serious blow by
bombing the oil fields of Ploesti in Rumania
from which the Germans were obtaining
3,000,000 tons of oil a year. The first air raid
on these oil fields was carried out (August,
1943) by a force of 178 B-24 heavy bombers
from North Africa. This attack and those
which followed it deprived Germany of much
badly needed oil. The Trident Conference decided also to launch an attack from Great
Britain on the German armies in France and
set the spring of 1944 as the date for the attack. The Conference agreed to speed up the
attack on the Japanese by driving them from
the Aleutians, the Marshalls, and other
islands on the outer rim of Japanese defenses
and by flying more war materials from India
over the Himalayas to China.

**American, British, and Canadian forces
conquered Sicily in thirty-nine days.** On
July 10-11, 1943, American, British, and
Canadian forces, under the command of General Sir Harold Alexander, began landing in
Sicily. They consisted of an American army
under Lieutenant General Patton, a British
army under General Montgomery, and a
Canadian division. 3,266 vessels carried 160,-
000 men, 1,008 guns, and 600 tanks from
North Africa to Sicily. Airborne troops also
landed in advance of the ground invaders.
The Americans landed in Southern Sicily and
the British and Canadians at its southeastern
tip. The plans for the campaign provided that
the Americans were to conquer Western Sicily
and then advance eastward along its northern coast while the British were to advance

northward along the eastern coast. Then these forces were to trap the Axis armies in the northeastern corner of Sicily and prevent them from escaping across the narrow Strait of Messina to the Italian mainland.

A part of the American forces advanced with great speed, conquered Western Sicily, took Palermo, and then drove eastward along the northern coastal road from Palermo to Messina. Twice American forces, with the assistance of the Navy, landed behind the Axis forces in Northern Sicily. Another part of the American forces drove through central Sicily toward Messina. Meantime, the British were driving up the east coast of Sicily, but before the American and British forces reached Messina the Germans succeeded in evacuating 88,000 troops to the mainland.

In the Sicilian campaign, about 100,000 Axis soldiers were taken prisoners and about 12,000 were killed and wounded. The conquest of Sicily made the Mediterranean safer for Allied shipping. It provided bases for the invasion of the mainland of Italy and its effects on the minds of the people of Italy, including members of the Fascist party, hastened Italy's surrender.

Italy surrendered unconditionally on September 3, 1943. While the Sicilian campaign was going on, dire events were taking place in Italy. The loss of the Italian empire in Africa, the destruction of many ships of the Italian fleet, the bombing of Italian cities including Rome, and the onrush of the Allies in Sicily made the Italian people war-weary and convinced them that they were standing on the brink of military disaster. In these distressing circumstances, Mussolini appealed to Hitler for help. In answer to this appeal, Hitler told Mussolini to abandon Southern Italy and to defend only the industrial north. When Mussolini presented this proposition to the Fascist Grand Council (July 24, 1943), nineteen of the twenty-five members voted it

down and asked King Victor Emmanuel to take over the leadership of the nation. The next day Mussolini was summoned to the palace and dismissed by the king who had him arrested and thrown in prison from which he was rescued by Nazi parachute troops (September 12, 1943). The king then appointed Marshal Badoglio, conqueror of Ethiopia, Prime Minister of Italy. Badoglio dissolved the Fascist party.

Shortly after Badoglio was made Prime Minister of Italy, the Germans sent many troops into Italy because they realized that Italy would surrender soon. After prolonged negotiations, the Italian government surrendered unconditionally (September 3, 1943) on terms approved by the United States, Great Britain, and the Soviet Union. General Eisenhower did not announce the surrender over radio from Algiers until September 8 to forestall the Germans from taking over Italian coastal defenses before Allied troops could land on the Italian mainland through the Gulf of Salerno. The terms of the armistice with Italy required the Italian government to surrender its navy and air force, to turn over to the Allies any merchant ships they demanded, to withdraw its soldiers from all fronts, and to give up its airfields to the Allies. The Italian navy, except for the ships destroyed by the Germans, steamed to Malta where it surrendered to the British—six battleships, eight cruisers, twenty-seven destroyers, and nineteen submarines.

The surrender of Italy knocked one partner of the Axis out of the war. It completely freed the Mediterranean Sea and thereby released British and American naval forces to fight Japan. However, the unconditional surrender of Italy did not deliver the Italian mainland into Allied hands because the German armies in Italy disarmed the Italian soldiers and brought Italy under German control. More than a year and a half of hard fighting was necessary to wrest Italy from the Germans.

American and British forces invaded Italy and captured Foggia and Naples. The invasion of Italy was undertaken chiefly for these reasons. It would compel Hitler to use forces in Italy which he would otherwise be able to employ against the Soviet armies and later on against the Allies after they invaded France. It would provide airfields from which industries in Germany and in the German-held Balkans could be bombed from a much shorter range.

On September 3, 1943, the British Eighth Army under General Montgomery crossed the narrow Strait of Messina under cover of heavy artillery bombardment and air protection, landed at the toe of Italy's boot, and advanced northward. On September 9, British airborne troops captured the Italian naval base at Taranto and then drove northward. On the same day, the United States Fifth Army, composed of American and British divisions under Lieutenant General Mark W. Clark, landed at Salerno about forty miles southeast of Naples.

After the Italian government had surrendered, the German High Command thought that the Allies would make an amphibious landing near Naples. Consequently, it had sent strong forces to the Naples area who now resisted the landings fiercely. After six days of bitter and costly fighting, during which the Fifth Army was aided by naval gunfire and bombings by the air forces, it established a beachhead. On September 17, the Fifth Army made a contact with the British Eighth Army which had advanced rapidly from the south. General Clark's forces then drove northward toward Naples while the Eighth Army struck northeastward and captured the airfields at Foggia (September 27). Possession of these airfields enabled heavy bombers to bomb German air bases in Austria, factories in Southern Germany, and industrial and transportation centers in the Balkans.

On October 1, 1943, the Fifth Army occupied Naples which the Germans had evacuated after demolishing the port installations, disrupting the water system, and mining many buildings. After army engineers had repaired the port installations, Allied ships landed war supplies at Naples from which they were transported to the Fifth Army for use in the battles along the Volturno River.

The American Fifth Army liberated Rome. After the Fifth Army captured Naples, the German forces under Field Marshal Albert Kesselring retreated northward and took up positions along the Volturno River. On October 13, 1943, the Fifth Army crossed the Volturno and the Germans withdrew to the Gustav Line which stretched across Italy about seventy-five miles southeast of Rome. Fierce battles followed in this mountainous country where the Romans and Samnites once fought. The key position in the Gustav Line was the village of Cassino and a nearby hill on which stood the famous Benedictine monastery.

On January 22, 1944, forces of the Fifth Army established a beachhead near Anzio about twenty-five miles south of Rome. It was hoped that these troops would disrupt communications in the rear of the German forces at Cassino, force them to withdraw northward and thus open a path to Rome. These hopes were not realized. The Germans threw in additional troops and hemmed the Americans in. From their positions in the hills above Anzio, the Germans shelled and bombed the American lines continuously. They did not succeed, however, in driving them out or in keeping supplies from being brought in to them.

In the meantime, some of the bitterest fighting of the whole war was raging at Cassino. From their position on Monte Cassino,

Acme

THE RUINS OF CASSINO, ITALY.

the Germans could observe Allied movements and direct the fire of their guns against advancing soldiers. After two attacks in early February, 1944, had failed to capture Monte Cassino, a heavy artillery and air bombardment almost completely destroyed the celebrated monastery. Another assault on the hill on February 18 and still another in March failed to capture it. The Allies then regrouped their forces on all fronts for a tremendous offensive to capture Cassino, break through the Gustav Line, and capture Rome.

On May 11, 1944, a general advance began in which the forces around Cassino, the troops at Anzio, and the British Eighth Army all took part. French, Poles, New Zealanders, and American troops of Japanese descent played an important role in this advance. The Gustav Line was breached, Monte Cassino was captured (May 17 1944) and the Ger-

mans were forced to retreat northward towards Rome. As the Allies captured stronghold after stronghold, the Germans decided not to defend Rome, which Kesselring declared an open city. Thus historic Rome was saved from the destruction that had been visited upon the capitals of some of the other nations of Europe. On June 14, 1944, the Fifth Army entered Rome, the first capital to be liberated from German control.

The Soviet armies defeated and captured the German army at Stalingrad. In the autumn of 1942 German armies, as we have seen, were in the Caucasus. They were on the banks of the Volga north and south of Stalingrad though they had not captured all of that city. In the north they held a position at Rzhev, west of Moscow. They were still besieging Leningrad. The Soviet armies had lost over 4,000,000 men. In November,

Acme

LIBERATED ROMAN CITIZENS GREETING AL-
LIED TROOPS IN JUNE, 1944.

1942, the Soviet armies started an offensive to drive the Germans out of the Soviet Union which did not stop until it had accomplished its purpose.

To make this offensive possible, the Soviet government had raised and trained 4,500,000 men for its armies. Soviet factories behind the Urals poured out war supplies. The United States and Great Britain sent tanks, guns, trucks, and planes in huge quantities. Some were convoyed to Murmansk, a Soviet port on the Arctic Sea, others to Archangel on the White Sea, and still others to Basra on the Persian Gulf from which they were transported through Iran to the Soviet Union. The United States shipped still more supplies across the North Pacific to Vladivostok in Siberia. Soviet pilots flew planes from Fairbanks, Alaska, to bases in Siberia. From October, 1941, to January, 1944, the United States exported to the Soviet Union 7800 planes, 4700 tanks and tank destroyers, 170,000 trucks, 6,000,000 pairs of military boots, more than 200,000 field telephones, and 700,000 tons of explosives, 740,000 tons of aviation gasoline, 1,350,000 tons of steel, and

2,250,000 tons of food. Altogether the United States sent the Soviet Union Lend-Lease aid to the value of $11,000,000,000. After these war supplies had been assembled, the huge Soviet armies employed a masterful strategy and superb tactics for the use of them. Low-flying Stormovik planes bombed enemy lines and supply routes to disrupt enemy communications.

Side by side they concentrated their heavy guns whose tremendous fire power made breaches in enemy lines through which armored tanks and infantry poured. Wherever Soviet armies fought, they employed the same tactics.

On November 19, 1942, a Soviet army broke through the northern flank of the German army assaulting Stalingrad. Another Soviet army outflanked the German army in the south. These Soviet armies cut the railroads used to supply the German lines and on November 23 joined forces behind the German army. The Germans were overwhelmed by superior Soviet forces and fire power. The German forces sent to reinforce the German army were also defeated. Ordered by Hitler to resist, the Germans fought as long as they could. For a time they were supplied by air, but the Soviet air force shot the German planes down in such numbers that only meagre supplies reached the soldiers. Defeated, encircled, cold, and hungry the Germans were forced to surrender (February 2, 1943).

The Soviet army reported the capture of more than 200,000 German troops (including Field Marshal von Paulus and fifteen generals), 60,000 trucks, 6700 guns, and 1500 tanks. Hitler decreed that the German people should carry out a period of national mourning for the loss of so great an army. On the other hand, the Soviet peoples rejoiced at the astounding victory their armies had won over the Germans.

The Russian
Counterattack
1943-'45

It took two years of war and incredible sacrifices of the people until the Russians were able to turn the tide and drive the Nazis back into Germany. For almost two years the Soviet armies alone took the full impact of Nazi land power, but from November, 1942, on they were aided by the second front opened by the British and Americans in Africa and later on in Europe.

During the winter offensive of 1943 the Soviet armies advanced all along a front from Leningrad to the Black Sea. While the deliverance of Stalingrad from the Germans was taking place, another Soviet army forced the Germans to withdraw from the northern Caucasus to Rostov which the Soviets recaptured (February 17, 1943). Other German forces in the Caucasus retreated across the

Kerch Strait into the Crimea, but managed to keep control of a small area on the eastern side of the strait near Novorossisk.

Between Stalingrad and Voronezh the Soviet armies launched two offensives that inflicted heavy losses on the German armies, drove them back from the Don to positions west of the Donetz, and recaptured Kursk and Kharkov. In March, 1943, however, the

Sovfoto

Hitlerite soldiers are shown here laying down their guns and helmets as they surrender to Red Army troops on the southwestern front.

Germans launched a counteroffensive which resulted in the recapture of Kharkov before the spring mud put an end to the fighting.

On the Moscow front Marshal Zhukov mounted an offensive which resulted in the capture of Rzhev and thereby wiped out all danger to Moscow. In this offensive the Soviet forces advanced 169 miles westward and cleared the way for an attack on Smolensk which the Germans had fortified strongly. In the meantime, other Soviet forces attacked in the area of Leningrad, which had been under siege since the summer of 1941. Employing a terrific artillery barrage from 200 guns per mile on a ten-mile front, the Soviet forces were able to cross the Neva and thereby establish rail communication to Leningrad. At the end of March, 1943, Stalin reported that these winter offensives had freed 185,000 square miles of Soviet territory from German domination. He claimed also the death and capture of more than 1,000,000 Axis soldiers.

Between the spring of 1943 and the spring of 1944 the Soviet armies drove the Axis armies back into Rumania and Poland. At about the same time that the Americans, British, and Canadians were invading Sicily, the Germans launched (July 5, 1943) an offensive on the Orel-Belgorod front which was designed to retake Kursk. They were able to advance a few miles, but on July 12 the Soviet forces, under cover of the heaviest artillery

barrage in all history, began an advance that led to the capture of both Orel and Belgorod (August 5, 1943). Other Soviet forces retook Kharkov (August 23) and the Germans in full retreat all along the line fell back to positions along the Dnepr. There they endeavored to make a stand, but the Soviet forces pressed forward relentlessly. They crossed the Dnepr (October 1) and Kiev fell to them (November 6, 1943).

Meanwhile, farther south Soviet forces drove westward from Rostov while other forces drove the remaining Germans from the area around Novorossisk. By the end of October, 1943, the northern coast of the Sea of Azov and most of the lower Dnepr were in Soviet hands and the Axis forces in the Crimea were isolated.

While these victories were being won in the south, Soviet armies west and southwest of Moscow drove forward. They captured Bryansk (September 17), Smolensk (September 25), and Gomel (November 11). During the summer and autumn of 1943 the Soviet armies had driven the Germans out of a vast area between the Donetz and Dnepr Rivers, thus gaining control over most of the Ukraine with its rich agricultural and mineral resources. Stalin reported that during the summer and autumn of 1943 the Soviet armies had killed 900,000 Axis soldiers and freed 135,000 square miles of territory from German domination.

During the winter of 1944 the Soviet armies continued their onslaughts against the Axis forces. In the north, a Soviet offensive which drove the Germans westward to the border of Estonia opened direct railroad communication between Leningrad and Moscow and freed the inhabitants of Leningrad from fearful artillery bombardments which they had suffered for about two and a half years. This offensive cleared the way for Soviet forces to invade and re-take the Baltic states.

In the winter fighting, the Soviet armies made their greatest gains along the southern front. Between December 29, 1943, and April 10, 1944, they swept some Axis forces back into Southeastern Poland and others into Rumania. The German and Rumanian forces in the Crimea were attacked in April in an offensive that led to their utter defeat and the recapture of Sevastopol (May 10, 1944). These victories in the south placed the Soviet armies in a position to invade the Balkans and to defeat Hitler's satellite nations—Rumania, Bulgaria, and Hungary. By May, 1944, almost all of the Soviet Union had been liberated from the control of Axis invaders. The Soviets in Eastern Europe and the Americans and British in Western Europe were now ready to crush the Axis armies between the jaws of a powerful vise according to plans drawn up by the leaders of the great powers at the Teheran Conference.

Leaders of the great powers among the United Nations met in conferences to draw up plans for the defeat of the Axis powers. In August, 1943, as the campaign in Italy was drawing to a close, Roosevelt, Churchill, and the Combined Chiefs of Staff held the Quadrant Conference in Quebec. This conference decided that an invasion of the Toulon-Marseille area in Southern France should be undertaken at the same time that Normandy was invaded. Moreover, it agreed to recognize the French Committee of National Liberation, which was headed by General de Gaulle, as the representative of the Free French who were fighting the Axis powers. The war against Japan, however, was the chief concern of the Quadrant Conference at which Generalissimo Chiang Kai-shek was represented by Mr. T. V. Soong. After surveying the situation in the Far East, the conference decided to launch an offensive against the Japanese in Northern Burma, to fly 20,000 tons of war supplies a month over the

Himalayas to China, and to subject Japan itself to devastating air bombardments.

In October, 1943, Cordell Hull, Secretary of State of the United States, Anthony Eden, Secretary of State for Foreign Affairs in Great Britain, and Vyacheslav Molotov, Soviet Minister for Foreign Affairs, held conferences in Moscow to consider problems arising out of the war. On November 1, they released the Moscow Pact which pledged the countries its signers represented to establish an international organization to help maintain peace and security, to destroy Fascism in Italy, and to give the Italian people every opportunity to establish a government based on democratic principles. The Moscow Pact also pledged its signers to free Austria from German domination, to permit its people to set up a free and independent nation, and to punish those Germans who were guilty of atrocities.

At Cairo, Egypt, from November 22-26, 1943, Roosevelt, Churchill, and the Combined Chiefs of Staff conferred for the first time with Generalissimo Chiang Kai-shek to discuss military operations against Japan and also what punishment should be meted out to Japan after it was defeated. They agreed (1) to fight together until they forced Japan to surrender unconditionally; (2) to strip Japan of all islands in the Pacific that it had seized since the beginning of the First World War; (3) to restore Formosa, the Pescadores, and Manchuria to China; (4) to make Korea eventually an independent nation.

After conferring with Chiang Kai-shek at Cairo, Roosevelt, Churchill, and the Combined Chiefs of Staff journeyed to Teheran in Iran for their first meeting (November 28-December 1, 1943) with Premier Stalin. At this conference plans were perfected for the destruction of the Axis forces. While the Soviet armies attacked from the East, American and British armies were to invade Nor-

Sovfoto

Seated on the portico of the Russian Embassy at Teheran, Iran, during their conference (November 28 to December 1, 1943) are: Joseph Stalin, Franklin D. Roosevelt, and Winston Churchill. Those whose faces are visible in the background are members of their advisory staffs.

mandy and Southern France. In a declaration issued at the end of the conference, Roosevelt, Churchill, and Stalin said, "No power on earth can prevent our destroying the German armies by land, their U-Boats by sea, and their war plants from the air. Our attack will be relentless and increasing." They agreed also "to make a peace which will command the goodwill of the overwhelming mass of the peoples of the world and banish the scourge and terror of war for many generations." The great offensives for which plans were made at Teheran began June, 1944, and ended with the complete defeat of Finland, Rumania, Bulgaria, Hungary, and Germany.

The British and Americans carried out ever-increasing air attacks against Germany. The British opened an air offensive against Germany even before the Battle of Britain was over. British planes attacked German ships, laid mines in coastal waters, and attacked submarine bases. In November, 1941, 400 planes made a night raid on Berlin. From that time on the pace was speeded up.

Acme

AMERICAN BOMBERS ATTACKING FOCKE-WULF AIRCRAFT FACTORY, GERMANY.

Raids were made on industrial cities and rail centers. The British learned that by massing their bombers they could make what was known as saturation attacks, that is, attacks which would wipe out a given objective. On May 30, 1942, 1000 bombers dropped 3000 tons of bombs on Cologne in ninety minutes. A similar raid the next night did great damage to industrial plants in Essen.

In the summer of 1942, the United States Eighth Air Force under the command of General Carl Spaatz began its raids from Great Britain on Germany. It engaged in precision bombing during the day time. The first day time raids resulted in the loss of many American bombers, but the fighting strength of the Fortresses and the development of fighter planes with a greater cruising radius which could fly with the bombers to protect them cut losses greatly.

In the summer of 1943, the British and Americans began to bomb Germany twenty-four hours a day. To cut down losses of planes on long, round-trip bombing missions on which aircraft were exposed to almost constant attack, the United States and British air forces put in operation (August, 1943) a system of shuttle-bombing between bases in Great Britain and North Africa. After bases in Italy had been captured, shuttle-bombing flights were carried on between Great Britain and Italy and later on between Italy and the Soviet Union.

The bombings did great damage to German war industries, particularly airplane factories, munition works, synthetic oil plants, railroad centers, and steel works. On August 17, 1943, United States Flying Fortresses bombed ball-bearing works at Schweinfurt near Nuremberg. The destruction caused by this raid seriously hampered the use of mechanized war equipment. The Germans concentrated their anti-aircraft guns to shoot down the bombers and increased the number of their fighter planes to stop the American and British bombers, but with little success. From the first bombings by American planes to the end of 1943, American and British planes dropped 330,000 tons of bombs on Germany. Berlin became a special target because of its importance as the capital of Germany and also as an industrial city. On one mission March 8, 1944, more than 2000 American planes dropped 350,000 incendiary and 10,000 demolition bombs on Berlin. Although bombings did great damage to the cities and military resources of Germany, the Combined Chiefs of Staff concluded that Germany could not be bombed into submission. The only road to victory was the defeat of the German armies and this, they felt, could be accomplished only by an invasion of the Continent.

The Americans and British prepared for the invasion of France. As early as April, 1942, the Combined Chiefs of Staff began to make plans for such an invasion and in June, 1942, General Eisenhower was sent to England to begin preparations for United States preparation in the invasion. This military operation which was given the name ROUND-UP was scheduled for the summer of 1943. Such an invasion would require so great a concentration of soldiers and war materials that proper preparations would be long and difficult. Moreover, by July, 1942, German armies were advancing rapidly on the southeastern front in the Soviet Union and Rommel's forces stood before El Alamein in Egypt. These advances were such dire threats

to the Allied cause that the Combined Chiefs of Staff thought action must be taken as soon as possible to relieve the pressure on the Soviet armies and on the British forces in Egypt. For these and other reasons it was decided to invade North Africa where the enemy was weakest but at the same time to continue preparations for the invasion of France.

On August 19, 1942, an exploratory raid of about 7,000 Canadian, British, and American troops on Dieppe showed clearly what the invasion problems were and what terrible dangers had to be faced. About half of the invading forces were lost.

At the Trident Conference (May, 1943), it was agreed to change the code name ROUNDUP to OVERLORD and the spring of 1944 was designated as the target date. At the Quadrant Conference in Quebec (August, 1943), Roosevelt and Churchill approved the preliminary plans drawn up by the Combined Chiefs of Staff. These plans called for the invasion to take place early in May on the beaches of Normandy, but a shortage of landing craft forced a postponement. When Roosevelt, Churchill, and Stalin met in Teheran (December, 1943) the plans were discussed, the date set for the end of May or the first week in June, 1944, and Stalin agreed to start an offensive at about the same time. On December 24, 1943, Roosevelt and Churchill appointed General Eisenhower Supreme Allied Commander of the British and United States Expeditionary Forces. He was ordered to proceed from Algiers to London where he set up his headquarters and went to work with his vast staff on the final plans for the invasion of Normandy.

Troops were rushed in such numbers to Great Britain from the United States that by June, 1944, 1,562,000 American troops were stationed in Great Britain. A stockpile of about 2,500,000 tons of war supplies had been assembled for the invasion alone. All military, naval, and air personnel were given special training to fit them for their momentous tasks. General Marshall, Chief of Staff of the United States Army, reported:

The units arriving in the United Kingdom from America were well trained, especially in fast-moving corps and army operations over large areas; those coming from the Mediterranean were battle-tested. Nevertheless, everything possible was done during their staging period in the United Kingdom to increase their combat efficiency despite the limited terrain available in a densely populated and cultivated countryside. The troops which were to make the assault landings maneuvered realistically on beaches and ground which approximated the target areas. In the early spring of 1944, joint exercises of the ground, sea, and air forces which were to make the attack were held along the southern coast of England. It was a full-dress rehearsal.

In the spring of 1944, American and British air forces began to prepare directly for the invasion of Normandy by bombing key bridges, railroad centers, airfields, radar installations, and coastal guns. General Eisenhower later reported: "Our D-day experience was to convince us that the carefully laid plans of the German High Command to oppose OVERLORD with an efficient air force in great strength were completely frustrated by strategic bombing operations." The bombings destroyed seventy-four bridges and tunnels leading to the invasion area and so many locomotives and cars that the Germans could not bring up reinforcements in time to stop the invasion.

The invasion of Normandy was a complete success. The Combined Chiefs of Staff decided that the invasion should take place on the coast of Normandy between the mouth of the Seine River and the Cotentin peninsula in Brittany. This region was chosen because "the defenses were relatively light and the beaches were of high capacity and sheltered from prevailing winds. The terrain, more-

Acme

GENERAL EISENHOWER IN NORMANDY.

over, was suitable for airfield development and the consolidation and ultimate expansion of the beachhead." To take the place of a badly needed port, two artificial harbors were constructed in England and towed to the invasion coast. One was wrecked by a·heavy gale, but the other withstood it and was used very effectively for the landing of men and supplies.

On D-day, June 6, 1944, shortly after midnight, the air forces began dropping bombs on the coastal defenses. As it grew light, they attacked targets along the shore and artillery positions inland. British and American warships threw heavy shells into the enemy positions. Three airborne divisions, one British and two American, were dropped behind the Atlantic Wall to seize bridges and strong points for the purpose of helping to protect the landings on the beaches.

Hitler's vaunted Atlantic Wall was an intricate and formidable system of defenses along the northern coast of France designed to make an invasion impossible. General Marshall thus describes these defenses on the beaches of Normandy:

They consisted first of bands of underwater obstacles designed to break up formations of landing craft; mines were freely used to make these obstacles more lethal. The beaches themselves were heavily mined and strung with wire. Concrete pill-boxes and gun emplacements were sited to deliver withering cross-fire along beaches. All exits leading inland from the beaches were blocked by antitank walls and ditches, mine fields, and barbed wire. Further inland, mortars and artillery were sited to deliver indirect fire on the beaches. Open fields were blocked against glider landings by patterns of heavy stakes.

Nevertheless, a detailed knowledge of these defenses obtained by the intelligence services helped to enable the Allied forces to breach them.

American, Canadian, and British forces sailed from ports on the south coast of England in the greatest armada in history consisting of over 4000 ships protected by more than 800 warships. The Channel in that area had been swept clear of mines. Destroyers and patrol boats prevented even one submarine from penetrating the armada. An umbrella of more than 10,000 planes protected it from air attacks. Before the landings were made demolition crews removed obstacles and, in spite of rough water, all kinds of landing craft discharged soldiers, guns, tanks, food, and ammunition on the shore.

The invaders who were under the over-all command of Field Marshal Montgomery landed on five beaches, the British and Canadians on the left, the Americans on the right. Boats and planes which were equipped with devices to jam German radar sets had made feints which convinced the Germans that the attack would come in the Calais area. Even

after the landings had been made, the Germans thought they were merely preliminary and held a large force at Calais where they thought a landing was sure to come.

The fiercest fighting took place at the central beachhead. Once a beachhead had been made secure, troops and supplies began pouring in from the ships. By the night of D-day all of the divisions had established themselves firmly. During the first six days of the landing operations, 326,547 men, 54,186 vehicles, and 104,428 tons of stores were brought ashore. The landing forces joined the beachheads and then pushed inland and formed a continuous line. The Germans, unable to bring up their troops quickly because Allied bombers had wreaked such havoc on bridges and railroads, failed to counterattack before the Allied forces outnumbered the Germans opposing them.

American forces captured Cherbourg. After the Allied forces had established their beachheads, American forces on the right advanced west and then north to capture the port of Cherbourg, badly needed for the handling of men and supplies. After bitter and costly fighting, it fell to the Americans (June 26, 1944). However, the Germans had so wrecked its port installations that supplies had to be brought in over the beaches until they could be repaired. American engineers set to work at a feverish pace to repair them. By July 19 some supplies could be unloaded at Cherbourg, by the end of August 10,000 tons a day were being unloaded, and by the end of October the port facilities were completely restored, a great achievement of the American engineers.

The British captured Caen. As the Americans were taking Cherbourg, the British began an attack on Caen which was designed to break through the German lines which had been strengthened by soldiers rushed south from Calais. One of the reasons for the stiff

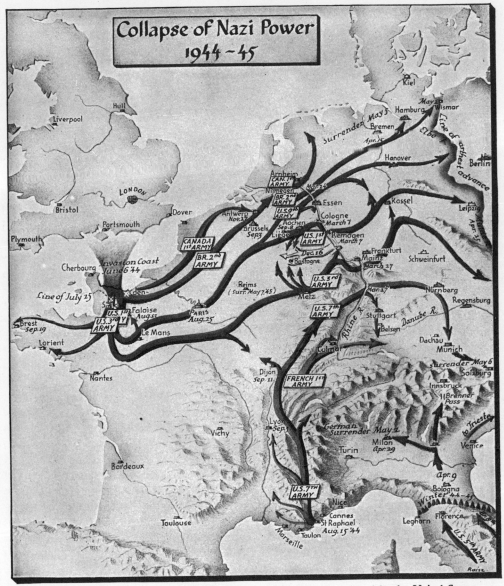

Collapse of Nazi Power 1944–45

The battles of the Second World War which will be long remembered in the United States started with the invasion of "Fortress Europe" (June 6, 1944) and led to the unconditional surrender of Germany on May 7, 1945.

resistance to the British at Caen was the determination of the Germans to keep possession of the stations along the northern coast of France from which the V-1 robot (buzz) bombs were launched.

These bombs, which were jet-propelled and carried a ton of high explosives, flew at a speed of about 400 miles an hour. At about the time the Allies were landing on the beaches of Normandy, the Germans began launching V-1's, chiefly on London, where they caused great destruction of property and inflicted more than 21,000 casualties by the first of September, 1944. About a million women and children were evacuated from London as the buzz bombs began falling.

The measures which the British and Americans took to curb this "secret" weapon of Hitler included heavier balloon barrages, intensive anti-aircraft fire, bombing attacks on launching sites, and very speedy planes to shoot down the bombs. These measures were so effective that they stopped the V-1 attacks by September, 1944, but immediately the Germans began to use the V-2, a rocket-bomb which was shot into the stratosphere and fell so speedily that no defense against it was possible. Although it was not so destructive as the V-1 the Germans continued to use the V-2 until the last of the bases from which it was shot was captured in the spring of 1945.

On July 8, 1944, Field Marshal Montgomery launched a heavy assault on Caen in defense of which the Germans employed 700 of the 900 tanks they had available in this area. Caen fell (July 9), but the British were not able to break through the German lines. However, Montgomery's offensive did result in destroying most of the German tank forces in this sector and in pinning down large numbers of German forces, which aided greatly the American forces who were attacking St. Lô. During the heavy fighting near Caen, the Germans suffered a heavy blow when Field Marshal Rommel, one of their great military leaders, was fatally wounded (July 17).

The Americans broke through the German lines at St. Lô. After the German defenses were softened up by artillery fire and terrific bombing by planes, American forces under General Omar Bradley launched an attack which resulted in the capture of St. Lô (July 18), and in breaking the German line of defense. Through this break the mechan-

ized American Third Army under General George S. Patton, Jr., poured with great speed. A part of his army turned east to Le Mans and another continued south to clear the Germans out of Brittany and out of the great ports of Brest, Lorient, and St. Nazaire because they were needed as receiving depots for American men and supplies. By the middle of August all of Brittany was in American hands except for the ports which were enemy strongholds.

As the Americans were breaking through the German lines at St. Lô, the world was startled by the announcement of an attempt to assassinate Hitler which had taken place July 20, 1944. When a bomb exploded in his headquarters, Hitler received slight injuries, but some of the military leaders who were conferring with him were killed. Some of those who had plotted to take the Fuehrer's life were army officers. Consequently, they were hunted down and executed and Hitler made Himmler, the Gestapo chief, the head of the Home Army.

After Patton's Third Army poured through the corridor made by the break through the German lines, the Germans launched heavy attacks in the desperate hope of driving a wedge through the corridor to the sea and thus cutting off General Patton's forces from the other American forces to the north. By doing so the Germans put themselves into a trap. Their advance was stopped and they found themselves almost encircled by the British and Canadians, the First Army, and part of the Third Army. The battle which followed was called the Battle of the Pocket (August 18-23, 1944). Desperate German resistance kept open a narrow corridor through which some German forces escaped, but the Allied armies captured 100,000 and killed and wounded thousands more. The German Seventh Army to which had been entrusted the defense of Normandy had been destroyed as an effective fighting force. The remnants of this army now beat a hasty retreat eastward across the Seine, but as they did so they were raked by Allied artillery and heavily bombed by the air forces.

American, British, and French forces invaded Southern France. While the Allied and German armies were locked in fierce combat in Normandy, other Allied forces invaded Southern France. The invasion was preceded by four days of intensive air bombing and shelling from naval vessels off the shore. A vast armada of more than 1500 ships transported the United States Seventh Army under the command of Lieutenant General Alexander W. Patch and the First French Army under General Jean de Tassigny from ports in Corsica and Italy to beaches in Southern France between Cannes and Toulon.

On the night before the invasion, American, British, and French airborne troops seized important points. On August 15 the Seventh Army landed on the coast southwest of Cannes and was followed immediately by the First French Army. Aided by the French Forces of the Interior (Maquis), both armies advanced rapidly against weak resistance. The Seventh Army drove 140 miles in eight days. The French captured the badly needed ports of Marseille (August 23) and Toulon (August 26) and then struck northward up the Rhone valley and joined the forces of the Seventh Army that had pushed westward to the Rhone. Lyon was captured (September 3) and then the Allied forces advanced rapidly northward toward the Belfort Gap which led into Germany between the Jura and Vosges mountains.

Allied armies liberated France, Belgium, and Luxemburg. After the Battle of the Pocket, the Third Army under General Patton advanced eastward with great speed. As it approached Paris, 50,000 members of the French Forces of the Interior and the Paris

Acme

GENERAL DE GAULLE LEADING THE LIBERATION OF PARIS PARADE.

police rose up (August 19, 1944) against their Nazi overlords and in four days of street fighting gained possession of a large part of the city. On August 25, the French 2nd Armored Division under General Jacques-Phillipe Leclerc entered Paris and American forces soon followed them. The soldiers of this division had begun their march from Lake Chad in French Equatorial Africa. They had taken part in the fighting in Tunisia and then had been transported to England from which they invaded Normandy as a unit in General Patton's Third Army. They climaxed their struggle by completing the liberation of their capital city. On August 26, 1944, General Charles de Gaulle entered Paris and, with the support of the French Forces of the Interior, became head of the French Provisional Government. A few days later this government abolished all the laws which had been passed by the Vichy government.

General Patton's army continued its rapid advance through Chateau-Thierry and Verdun (September 3) until it reached the line of the Moselle from Nancy to the vicinity of Metz. On September 11, at Dijon, units of the Third Army met units of the Seventh Army which had driven up the Rhone valley. By this time the task of supplying the rapidly advancing Third Army had become enormous. Although trucks and airplanes had

Ewing Galloway

American troops march through the Arc de Triomphe in a parade to celebrate the liberation of Paris from Nazi occupation, as Parisians line the streets and cheer them.

rushed supplies to the advanced units, they were not able to supply the mechanized units with all the gasoline they needed. Consequently, the speed of the advance had to be cut down until additional supplies could be brought up.

In the meantime, to get badly needed ports where war supplies could be landed and then transported to the fighting forces, the Canadian First Army advanced northeastward along the northern coast of France. By September 30, it had captured the ports of Le Havre, Dieppe, Boulogne, and Calais and also had in its grip some of the sites from which V bombs had been launched on English cities. Although the Germans had wrecked the port installations in these ports,

they were soon repaired and supplies began moving through them.

After the Battle of the Pocket, the British Second Army advanced rapidly eastward on the right of the Canadian First Army. It crossed the lower Seine, drove 195 miles in four days to capture Brussels (September 3) and the port of Antwerp (September 4), crossed the Albert Canal and entered the Netherlands (September 12). Although Antwerp fell before the Germans could wreck its port installations, they still had strong garrisons on islands at the mouth of the Schelde and also on both sides of the Schelde estuary. The Germans had to be driven from these positions before the Allies could use the port of Antwerp. After several weeks of bitter and

Acme

Followed by jeering townspeople, a French woman collaborator is led back to her home after having her hair shaved off.

costly fighting which included amphibious operations, Canadian and British forces cleared the Germans from the mouth of the Schelde (November 9). By November 27, the port of Antwerp was in use but under heavy attacks by V bombs which caused thousands of military and civilian casualties. Despite these bombs, 25,000 tons of war supplies were handled daily at Antwerp and the Allied armies were kept supplied with the military stores made necessary by their rapid advances.

After the defeat of the Germans in the Battle of the Pocket, the United States First Army under General Courtney H. Hodges crossed the Seine and then drove northward through Soissons and St. Quentin, scenes of bitter fighting in the First World War. At Mons it trapped five retreating German divisions, killed and wounded thousands, and captured 20,000 prisoners. Continuing its rapid advance through Sedan, the First Army crossed the Belgian frontier (September 2), captured Liége (September 8), drove through Luxemburg and stood on German soil (September 11). In the middle of September, 1944, almost all of Northern France and substantial parts of Belgium and Luxemburg were in Allied hands, and Allied armies had penetrated the Netherlands and Western Germany.

General Eisenhower directed the grand assault on Germany. He ordered a general advance of all the armies under his command

Acme

U S. Infantrymen of the 9th Division are shown here as they break through the Siegfried line (the Westwall).

to the Rhine for the purpose of destroying any and all German armies that resisted them. He decided to concentrate his strongest forces in the north to force a crossing of the Lower Rhine beyond the main fortifications of the Westwall (Siegfried Line). If this plan were successful, his forces could outflank the northern end of the Westwall and enter the north German plain which, with its good roads, was more suitable for rapid advance than the mountainous and wooded lands to the south.

To carry out his plan he sent (September 17, 1944) three airborne divisions consisting of 35,000 American, British, and Polish troops to capture bridges across the Maas, Waal, and Lower Rhine Rivers and to establish bridgeheads on their eastern banks. This airborne invasion, which was the largest ever attempted, required the use of 2800 planes and more than 1600 gliders on the first two days. After the airborne troops had secured the bridges, the British Second Army under Field Marshal Montgomery was to advance across the bridges through the Netherlands and thus cut off the German troops in Western Holland. The American airborne troops that landed near Eindhoven seized bridges over the Maas and Waal rivers which the Second Army crossed. The British airborne troops that landed farther east at Arnhem met such fierce German resistance that they were forced to withdraw to the left bank of the Lower Rhine after suffering very heavy losses (September 25).

To the south of the British Second Army, the American Ninth Army under Lieutenant General William H. Simpson advanced to the Roer River. To the south of the Ninth Army, the American First Army under General Hodges took the famous German city of Aachen (October 21) after shelling and bombing had reduced it to rubble. In November and early December, General Hodges advanced eastward and began an attack to gain possession of the dams which controlled the flooding of the Roer Valley, but before his mission could be accomplished the Germans launched their Ardennes counteroffensive.

The American Third Army under General Patton whose advance had been slowed up near Metz for lack of supplies resumed its advance to the Moselle and captured Nancy (September 15). The Germans in the fortifications at Metz resisted stoutly because Metz was the entrance to the Saar Basin, important for its coal mines. The city of Metz was captured (November 22), but soldiers in seven of its forts continued to resist until they were forced to surrender on December 13.

In the meantime, on the southern front General Patch's Seventh Army and the French First Army under General de Tassigny were conducting offensives. The French First Army breached the German line at the Belfort Gap (November 18), reached the Rhine and captured Mulhouse on November 22. Farther north the Seventh Army advanced through Strassbourg and by the middle of December had crossed the German frontier and penetrated the defenses of the Westwall. The Allied armies had advanced all along the line from Switzerland to the Netherlands and now the Germans launched their last great offensive in a supreme effort to stave off impending defeat.

The Germans launched the Ardennes counteroffensive, but were defeated in the Battle of the Bulge. On direct orders from Hitler, Field Marshal von Rundstedt formed an army of twenty-four divisions of the best German troops in the heavily wooded area east of the Ardennes Forest. Hitler hoped that von Rundstedt's army would be able to break through the lightly held American lines, to capture Liége, the supply base for the northern armies, and then be able to push on and capture Antwerp. If the break-through were successful, the Allied armies in the north would be cut off from those in the south. If Antwerp were captured, it would be very difficult to supply the northern armies.

The attack was very well planned. The thick forests and several days of cloudy weather enabled the Germans to conceal their forces from the eyes of watchful Allied aviators. Moreover, General Eisenhower had concentrated his seasoned troops north and south of this part of the front which was lightly held by four American divisions.

On December 16 the Luftwaffe began the attack by bombing Allied airfields, and German paratroopers, some in British and American uniforms, were dropped behind the American lines. Eight of the best mechanized divisions of the German army in the West attacked on a forty-mile front. The Americans resisted heroically. They held St. Vith until December 22 even though the Germans planned to take it five days before. Allied headquarters ordered an airborne division commanded by Brigadier General Anthony C. McAuliffe to reinforce the American defenders at Bastogne. When the Germans had surrounded this garrison and demanded its surrender (December 22, 1944), General McAuliffe answered "Aw, nuts."

The Germans advanced about fifty miles until they were stopped by stubborn resistance in the center and by attacks on the flanks.

During this advance the weather had been so bad that the Allied air forces could do little to assist the infantry, but it cleared on Christmas Day. On December 19, General Eisenhower had put all the northern forces under the command of Montgomery because telephone communications between the forces commanded by General Bradley had been seriously disrupted. Montgomery ordered Allied forces to attack the northern flank of the German armies to prevent them from widening the bulge while General Patton's troops attacked the southern flank with the same purpose. Elements of the 5th Division of the Third Army which were fighting in the Saar on the morning of December 20 moved sixty-nine miles during the day and attacked the southern edge of the bulge before nightfall. By December 26 Bastogne had been relieved and the Germans began to retreat under terrific pressure from the south, west, and north. By January 28 the bulge had been flattened out and the plans of the Germans were thwarted. They lost 220,000 men, including 110,000 prisoners, and more than 1400 tanks and assault guns. Their defeat in the Battle of the Bulge seriously weakened their army reserves and their morale suffered a blow from which it never entirely recovered. In the West the Allies were now poised for the Battle of Germany. Meanwhile, in the East the Soviet armies had been carrying on an offensive which led to the surrender of Hitler's satellite states.

Soviet armies in the summer of 1944 knocked Finland out of the war. At the Teheran Conference Premier Stalin promised to launch a vast offensive on the eastern front at about the same time that the Allies invaded Normandy. To keep this promise, the Soviet armies launched attacks along a 1300-mile front which extended from the Gulf of Finland to the Black Sea.

On June 10, four days after Allied armies landed on the Normandy beaches, a Soviet army mounted an offensive in Finland which breached the Mannerheim Line and resulted in the capture of Viborg (June 20). Another Soviet army advanced more than 150 miles north of Lake Ladoga and still another offensive enabled the Soviets to gain possession of the ship canal from Leningrad to the White Sea. The Germans were now so heavily engaged on other fighting fronts in the East and also in Italy and France that they could not send any reinforcements to Finland. Consequently, the Finnish government asked (September 4) the Soviet Union for an armistice which was signed (September 19, 1944). By the terms of the armistice the Soviet Union guaranteed the political independence of Finland; Finland ceded the region of Petsamo to the Soviet Union; and Finland agreed to pay reparations in commodities to the value of $300,000,000.

Soviet armies drove the Germans out of the Baltic states and invaded Poland. While the fighting in Finland was going on, three Soviet armies invaded the Baltic states, Estonia, Latvia, and Lithuania. The objectives of these invasions were to destroy the German forces in these states and to protect the northern flank of the Soviet armies that were invading Poland. Vilna, the capital of Lithuania, fell to Soviet forces (July 13), and so did Tallinin, the capital of Estonia (September 23), and Riga, the capital of Latvia (October 13). On October 19, 1944, spearheads of one Soviet army entered East Prussia, and by the end of the year 1944 all of Latvia and almost all of Lithuania and Estonia were in Soviet hands.

In the meantime, other powerful Soviet armies whose objective was Warsaw drove westward on the central front. They took Vitebsk (June 24), Minsk (July 3), and drove forward into Poland. The southern forces reached the Vistula River south of

Warsaw while the northern forces reached the outskirts of the city. By July 23, the Soviet armies had advanced westward 200 miles and at this time they reported that 381,410 German soldiers had been killed and 150,231 captured in these offensives.

As the Soviet armies converged on Warsaw, a Polish underground force in Warsaw known as the Polish Home Army under the command of General Bor, rose (August 1, 1944) in revolt against their hated Nazi oppressors. Although they received some war supplies that were dropped from American and British planes, they were not strong enough to overcome the Germans. Moreover, the Soviet forces did not choose to cross the Vistula and take Warsaw and so General Bor had to surrender his forces to the Germans (October 2, 1944). By this time the Soviet armies had advanced so far that they had to slow down their advance until lines of communication could be strengthened and supplies transported to the fighting forces. The battle front before Warsaw remained relatively quiet, therefore, until the Soviet armies launched a great and powerful winter offensive in January, 1945.

Soviet armies defeated Rumania. As the offensive against Warsaw slowed down, partly because of German resistance and partly because of the necessity of bringing up supplies, another offensive started in the south. Two Soviet armies began a campaign against Rumania (August 20) that was designed to knock it out of the war. They soon reached the Danube River and captured Constanta, the Black Sea port at the mouth of the Danube (August 29).

In the meantime, as Soviet forces were driving on Constanta, King Michael of Rumania ordered (August 23) the Rumanian forces to stop fighting the Soviet armies. He commanded them to join the Soviet forces in ousting the Germans from Rumania, and

to attack Hungary, Hitler's ally, for the purpose of regaining that part of Transylvania which Hitler had taken from Rumania and given to Hungary.

By August 31, 1944, the Soviet forces had captured the Ploesti oil fields (severely damaged by Allied bombings) and entered Bucharest, the capital of Rumania. After several days of negotiations, the Rumanian government agreed (September 13, 1944) to the terms of an armistice which had been drawn up by representatives of the Soviet Union, the United States, and Great Britain. By the terms of the armistice (1) Rumania agreed to the restoration of the boundary between the Soviet Union and Rumania which had existed before Rumania entered the war; (2) Rumania promised to pay the Soviet Union reparations in commodities to the value of $300,000,000; and (3) the Soviet Union, the United States, and Great Britain agreed that Hitler's grant of a part of Transylvania to Hungary was no longer in effect. Another one of Hitler's tottering satellite states had been brought to its knees in defeat.

Soviet armies defeated Bulgaria. While the Soviet forces were plunging into Rumania, the Bulgarian government considered it advisable to sever its ties with Germany. Bulgaria was a signer of both the Tripartite Pact and the Anti-Comintern Pact and had declared war on the United States and Great Britain but not on the Soviet Union. German troops were stationed in Bulgaria. On August 26, 1944, the Bulgarian government announced that it had withdrawn from the war, but this action did not satisfy the Soviet government because the Bulgarian government might still permit the German troops to stay in Bulgaria. Consequently, the Soviet Union declared war (September 5) on Bulgaria and the next day Bulgaria asked the Soviet Union for an armistice and declared war on Germany. By the terms of the armistice, Bulgaria had to withdraw all its armed forces from Yugoslavia and Greece.

Greece, Albania, and Yugoslavia were freed from Nazi domination. After Rumania and Bulgaria declared war on Germany, their armies joined the Soviet forces in an attack on German forces in Yugoslavia which forced the Germans to begin to withdraw their troops from the Aegean islands and Greece. British troops landed in Greece and in co-operation with Greek underground forces pursued the fleeing Germans northward until by the middle of November, 1944, all German forces had been driven from Greece. British forces from Italy also landed in Albania to help liberate it from Axis control. This mission was accomplished by the end of 1944.

The Germans had never been able to establish control over all of Yugoslavia. Guerilla forces, first the Chetniks, and later the Partisans led by Marshal Tito, held positions in the hills and mountains from which they could not be expelled by the Germans, who employed about 125,000 troops against them. After Bulgaria declared war on Germany, Soviet and Bulgarian forces advanced westward into Yugoslavia to assist Tito in driving the Germans from his country. The British forces that had landed in Albania also co-operated in this task. On October 20, 1944, Belgrade was captured by Soviet forces and by the end of the year almost all of the German forces had been driven from Yugoslavia. The Balkan peninsula was now liberated from German domination and Germany was open to invasion through Hungary and Austria.

Soviet and Rumanian armies forced Hungary out of the war. While Soviet and Bulgarian forces were pushing into Yugoslavia, other Soviet armies together with Rumanian forces drove speedily into Hungary. As these forces advanced over the Hungarian plain, Admiral Horthy tried to take Hungary out of the war. He asked the Soviet Union for an armistice (October 15, 1944), but Hungarian Fascists who were aided by the Germans denounced Horthy's request. By early November Soviet forces had reached the outskirts of Budapest and laid siege to the capital. The German forces resisted so bitterly that the Soviet forces were not able to capture Budapest until February 13, 1945, after costly fighting street by street.

In the meantime, however, Hungarians in the areas of Hungary that had been liberated formed a provisional government that made an armistice with the Allies. On December 30, 1944, this government declared war on Germany and asked for an armistice which was drawn up by representatives of the Soviet Union, the United States, and Great Britain and signed on January 20, 1945. By the terms of the armistice Hungary had to withdraw all its forces from Czechoslovakia, Rumania, and Yugoslavia, pay reparations in commodities to the Soviet Union, Czechoslovakia, and Yugoslavia, and give up the territory which Hitler had given it. The last of Hitler's satellite nations had been knocked out of the war. Now the Germans had to fight for their very lives on their own soil.

The leaders of the United States, the Soviet Union, and Great Britain laid plans for the utter defeat of Germany. Up to January, 1945, there had been but little co-operation between the Allied armies in the West and the Soviet armies in the East. To secure the necessary co-operation, President Roosevelt, at the request of General Eisenhower, persuaded Premier Stalin to agree to confer with representatives from General Eisenhower. At the conference, which was held in January, 1945, General Eisenhower's representatives explained to Stalin the plans which had been drawn up for the destruction of the German armies on the western front. At the same time, Premier Stalin explained the

Acme

Stettinius, Molotov, Stalin, Roosevelt, and Churchill dine at Livadia Palace during Crimea conference.

Soviet plans for a vast offensive to crush the German armies on the eastern front. As the Allied armies advanced from the West and the Soviet armies from the East, Germany was to be battered into abject defeat.

As these offensives were launched, Roosevelt, Churchill, and Stalin and their military and diplomatic advisers held their second conference at Yalta in the Crimea (February 4-11, 1945). The Report of the Crimea Conference summed up the general plan for the defeat of Germany in these words:

The military staffs of the three Allied nations have met in daily meetings throughout the Conference. . . . The fullest information has been interchanged. The timing, scope, and co-ordination of new and even more powerful blows to be launched by our armies and air forces into the heart of Germany from the East, West, North, and South have been fully agreed upon and planned in detail . . . Nazi Germany is doomed. The German people will only make the cost of their defeat heavier to themselves by attempting to continue a hopeless resistance. . . . It is our inflexible purpose to destroy German militarism and Nazism and to ensure that Germany will never again be able to disturb the peace of the world.

From this time on to the unconditional surrender of Germany, the heads of the American and British armies in the West exchanged information with the heads of the Soviet armies in the East almost every day.

United States First Army forces crossed the Rhine at Remagen. After the Allies had stopped the German counteroffensive in the Ardennes Forest and won the Battle of the Bulge, their next task was to smash the German forces west of the Rhine. After this mission had been accomplished, they were to establish bridgeheads across the Rhine, destroy the German armies east of the Rhine, and then advance into the heart of Germany. By February, 1945, the strength of the German air force had been very greatly weakened by the bombing of airplane and ball-bearing factories and synthetic oil plants. Moreover, the Soviet armies had captured the Ploesti oil fields. By this time it was estimated that the production of oil in Germany was only 20 per cent of what it had been before the destructive air raids on German oil plants. Superiority in the air was to be a great aid to the Allies as they drove into Germany.

General Eisenhower planned to have his northern forces cross the Rhine on to the north German plain where mechanized warfare would enable his armies to advance rapidly. After the Canadian First Army had cleared the Germans out of the lower Schelde, it advanced (February 8, 1945) eastward to drive the remaining Germans out of the Netherlands. While this was going on the British Second Army advanced to Cleves on the Rhine (February 12). After the American First Army under General Hodges had captured the Roer River dams (February 10), the Ninth Army under General Simpson crossed the Roer and reached the Rhine at Wesel.

After the capture of the Roer River dams, the First Army drove toward Cologne which fell (March 7) and the retreating Germans demolished the bridges over the Rhine at Cologne. A part of the First Army had turned south along the west bank of the Rhine. On March 7, elements of its Ninth Armored Division found to their surprise that the Ludendorff Bridge at Remagen was intact. Quickly cutting the wires that led to charges of dynamite placed on the piers of the bridge, daring American soldiers prevented the Germans from destroying it. Tanks and infantry immediately poured across the bridge and soon established a small bridgehead on the east bank of the Rhine. General Bradley immediately began to take advantage of this piece of good fortune by building up the bridgehead until by March 9 American forces had penetrated three miles into Germany on the east bank of the Rhine.

The Germans now made a desperate attempt to destroy the bridge by artillery fire and air bombings, but American air forces established an umbrella over it. However, on March 17, the central span, which had been weakened by a last-minute attempt of the Germans to destroy it and by the terrific strain to which it had been subjected, collapsed into the river. But by that time American engineers had built floating bridges across the Rhine. By March 24 the bridgehead held by the First Army at Remagen was twenty-five miles long and ten miles deep, and within it three army corps were poised ready to strike another blow at the Germans.

The American Third and Seventh Armies encircled the German forces in the Saar. The Saar Basin was one of Germany's rich industrial districts where quantities of coal, iron, and steel were produced. As the Soviet forces were already in Silesia, another rich industrial district, the loss of the Saar would still further cripple the German war machine.

The Third Army drove down the Moselle valley to Coblenz (March 16, 1945) on the Rhine and then a part of it turned south and began an encirclement of the German forces in the Saar. Farther south the Seventh Army, which drove eastward and then turned north, made a junction with forces of the Third Army thereby encircling most of the German forces in the Saar. In the meantime, the First French Army, aided by Americans, cleared the Germans out of Alsace. By March 25, the Saar was in American hands, thousands of German soldiers had been captured and all resistance west of the Rhine had been crushed. The Allied armies in the West were now ready to drive into the very heart of Germany to meet the Soviet armies who were conducting an offensive in Eastern Germany on a vast scale.

The Soviet armies crushed the German armies on the eastern front. As the Battle of the Bulge was being won by the Allied armies on the western front, the Soviet armies began

Ewing Galloway

AMERICAN INFANTRYMEN PATROLLING A STREET IN RUINS IN SAARLAU-
TERN, GERMANY.

their winter offensive (January 12, 1945). On the central front in Poland the Soviet armies advanced rapidly. They captured Warsaw (January 17), and Cracow (January 19), and by the end of the month had entered the great industrial region of Silesia. In the north other armies advanced toward Königsberg in East Prussia, but met with determined resistance. Most of East Prussia was in Soviet hands by the first of February, but Königsberg did not fall until April 9. In the meantime, Soviet forces drove westward and captured Danzig (March 29). In the south, after Budapest had been captured (February 13), the Germans tried unsuccessfully to recapture it. The Soviet forces then advanced speedily along the Danube and captured Vienna (April 13).

The Germans made their last desperate stand along the Oder River east of Berlin where a terrific battle was fought April 15-20, 1945. Marshal Zhukov reported that the Germans had massed about 500,000 soldiers to prevent the Soviet armies from breaking through the battle line. To soften up the German defenses, the Soviet command opened up a devastating artillery barrage from about 22,000 guns while 5000 airplanes bombed the German defenses. From April 15-20, the Soviet armies inflicted a decisive defeat on the Germans and captured about 350,000 prisoners. The road to Berlin was now open and fighting began in its suburbs (April 22). By this time Allied forces had reached the Elbe west of Berlin.

General Eisenhower's armies dealt the German armies in the West knockout blows. After the Remagen bridgehead had been established and all German forces west of the Rhine defeated, General Eisenhower's armies were ready for great assaults all along a battle line which extended roughly from the Netherlands along the Rhine to the Swiss border. By this time the forces under his command numbered 4,000,000 men.

The American and British air forces began the attack by bombing rail centers, airfields, factories, gun emplacements, and concentrations of army troops. General Eisenhower reported that during four days (March 21-24, 1945) American and British air forces based in Great Britain, Western Europe, and Italy

Acme

**RUINS OF REICHSTAG BUILDING AFTER THE
BATTLE OF BERLIN**

flew over 42,000 sorties against Germany.

On March 22, the Third Army crossed the Rhine south of Mainz and then drove eastward to capture Frankfurt (March 29). On the evening of March 23 shells from heavy artillery hit the German defenses east of the Rhine in the Wesel area on the northern front. After this barrage, the British Second Army began crossing the Rhine north of Wesel. The next morning the main attack was launched as more soldiers of the Second Army built up the bridgehead and the American Ninth Army crossed the Rhine south of Wesel. At the same time, two divisions of airborne troops carried in almost 3000 transport planes, and gliders, protected by about 3000 fighter planes, landed on the east bank of the Rhine. Only forty-six planes were shot down by German anti-aircraft fire and not a single transport was attacked by the German air force because the Allied air forces were so numerous and so strong. While General Eisenhower and Prime Minister Churchill looked on, other troops of the Ninth Army crossed the Rhine in naval landing craft which had been brought overland from the northern coast of France. Within two days seven bridges had been built across the Rhine in the Wesel area and the troops had driven eastward from the river to a depth of six miles.

The First Canadian Army crossed the Rhine north of Wesel and then drove into the Netherlands to capture the remaining German forces in the northern and eastern parts of that country.

On the southern front both the American Seventh and the First French armies crossed the Rhine during the last week in March. All of the Allied armies were now across the Rhine and ready to wipe up the crumbling German forces. Hitler now replaced Field Marshal von Rundstedt with Field Marshal Albert Kesselring whom he ordered from Italy to assume the hopeless task of trying to stem the mighty onrush of the Allied armies.

After the Ninth Army crossed the Rhine south of Wesel and drove eastward, a part of it swung south. After the First Army crossed the Rhine at Remagen and drove eastward, it swung north. On April 1, 1945, these two forces met west of Kassel and thereby completely enveloped the German armies in the Ruhr, Germany's richest industrial district. By April 18, the American forces which mopped up the German forces in the Ruhr pocket had taken more than 325,000 prisoners. With the Saar and the Ruhr in American hands and Silesia in possession of the Soviet forces, the German armies could not be supplied with the necessary war equipment. They now faced utter collapse.

As the armies of the United States and its Allies swept forward to victory, the world was stunned on April 2, 1945, by the announcement over the radio that President Franklin D. Roosevelt had died at Warm Springs, Georgia. Worn out by his unceasing labors, the President died before he could rejoice in the victory over Germany which he had worked so hard to achieve. In the House of Commons, Prime Minister Churchill paid tribute to him in these words: "There died the greatest American friend we have ever known and the greatest champion of human freedom who has ever brought help and comfort from the New World to the Old."

After the British Second Army crossed the Rhine, it drove eastward toward the Baltic. The Germans resisted stoutly at Bremen which was not captured until April 26. In the meantime the British captured Hamburg (April 20) and by May 2 were in Wismar on the Baltic. On May 5 Admiral von Friedeburg surrendered all German land, naval, and air forces in the Netherlands, Northwestern Germany, and Denmark to Field Marshal Montgomery.

After the envelopment of the Ruhr, part of the Ninth Army pushed eastward through Hanover to the Elbe (April 11) and the First Army drove to the Mulde valley capturing Leipzig (April 20). General Eisenhower ordered the First and Ninth Armies to stop at the Elbe and Mulde Rivers, as required by the Yalta agreement.

The advances of the Third and Seventh Armies farther south were just as spectacular. After the Third Army captured Frankfurt it took Kassel and then drove eastward into Czechoslovakia (April 18). Some divisions of the Third Army moved south to the Danube (April 22) and then drove eastward along its northern bank into Austria to make a junction with the Soviet forces.

After the Seventh Army crossed the Rhine, it too drove rapidly eastward. It captured Nuremberg (April 20), scene of many Nazi party congresses and Munich (April 29), birthplace of the Nazi party. On April 29 patrols of the Seventh Army met patrols of the Fifth Army which had advanced northward from Italy through the Brenner Pass. On May 4, 1945, troops of the Seventh Army seized Berchtesgaden, Hitler's mountain refuge.

After the First French Army crossed the Rhine, it advanced eastward and then turned south to capture the German forces in the Black Forest. By the first of May it had driven along the Swiss border and had entered Western Austria. In the meantime, the Germans in Italy had surrendered.

After months of the hardest kind of fighting in Northern Italy, the Allies compelled the Axis forces to surrender unconditionally. After General Mark Clark's Fifth Army captured Rome (June 4, 1944), two days before the invasion of Normandy, it and the British Eighth Army struck northward. The Fifth Army drove up along the coast of the Tyrrhenian Sea, captured the important seaport of Leghorn (July 19) and laid siege to Pisa which fell (September 2). In the meantime, Polish forces in the Eighth Army had advanced fifty miles up the Adriatic coast. After very heavy fighting, British troops in the Fifth Army entered Florence (August 4), but it took them and the Eighth Army about two weeks to capture the entire city.

After the fall of Pisa and Florence, the Germans withdrew north of the Arno to the Gothic Line. It was an elaborate defense system which ran across the Italian peninsula from the Ligurian Sea just north of Pisa along the Apennines to a point north of Rimini on the Adriatic. It was designed to help keep the Allies from entering the rich industrial Po Valley.

On September 10, 1944, the Allies launched an offensive which, after three months of bitter fighting, broke through the Gothic Line. The British Eighth Army captured Rimini (September 21), but neither it nor the Fifth Army was able to advance through the Apennines into the Po valley during the adverse weather conditions of the winter.

On April 9, 1945, the American Fifth and the British Eighth Armies, now under the over-all command of General Mark Clark, launched their spring drive. Opposing them were the Germans and several Italian divisions of the Italian Socialist Republic which Mussolini had established in Northern Italy under German protection. After unusually heavy fighting, Fifth and Eighth Army forces captured Bologna (April 21) and then burst with full force into the Po Valley. At the same time Fifth Army forces captured the naval base of La Spezia on the Ligurian coast and drove on to Turin.

After the Fifth and Eighth Armies burst into the Po Valley, a part of the Fifth Army drove northward into the foothills of the Alps while another part drove up the Po Valley and reached the populous city of Milan (April 29). The Eighth Army drove northward and then eastward and made a junction with Marshal Tito's Yugoslavian forces north of Trieste. The Allied armies, capturing German and Italian troops by the thousands, were aided by Italian partisans who rose against Mussolini and his German protectors.

On April 28, 1945, Italian partisans caught Mussolini near Como, tried him, and then shot him. They took his body to Milan where it was hung up by the heels and spat upon by those who detested him. Thus did the life of the vain, boastful, and dictatorial Duce come to an inglorious end.

On April 26, General von Vietinhoff-Scheel, who realized that further resistance was senseless, began negotiations for the surrender of the German and Italian forces in Northern Italy. On April 29, 1945, he surrendered unconditionally to General Mark Clark about 1,000,000 German and Italian soldiers. The long and costly campaign which started when the toe of Italy's boot was invaded in September, 1943, had now ended in total victory for the Allied forces over their Axis enemies. Moreover, the end of the war in Germany was not far off.

Germany surrendered unconditionally on May 7, 1945. By the end of April the Allied forces in the West had reached the line agreed upon at Yalta and many divisions halted. By this time German soldiers who knew that Germany had lost the war were surrendering by the thousands. On April 25, American patrols met Soviet patrols on the Elbe River, and on the same day the Soviet armies completely surrounded Berlin.

On May 1, 1945, when the Soviet forces had almost all Berlin in their possession, Hitler's death was announced over the radio. His body has never been found because it is now established beyond reasonable doubt that after he committed suicide by shooting himself his body was burned. Goebbels committed suicide; Himmler was captured and committed suicide by taking poison (May 23, 1945); Goering was captured, tried as a war criminal, and sentenced to death, but committed suicide by taking poison before the sentence could be executed.

Before he committed suicide, Hitler had appointed Grand Admiral Karl Doenitz to succeed him. Doenitz made one last effort to divide the United Nations by offering to surrender to the United States and Great Britain thus hoping to cause friction between them and the Soviet Union. General Eisenhower told Colonel General Alfred Jodl, Doenitz's representative, that if Germany did not surrender unconditionally within forty-eight hours on both fronts at the same time he would seal the western front and prevent any further movement westward of German soldiers and civilians.

General Eisenhower's ultimatum compelled Doenitz to yield. On May 7, 1945, in General Eisenhower's headquarters at Rheims, Jodl, who acted in behalf of the German High Command, surrendered unconditionally all German land, sea, and air forces to General Eisenhower and simultaneously to the Soviet High Command. Lieutenant Walter Bedell Smith, Chief of Staff, signed for General Eisenhower; General Ivan Susloparoff

Acme

GERMANS PREPARING TO SIGN SURRENDER DOCUMENT AT RHEIMS, FRANCE.

for the Soviet High Command; and General F. Sevez for the French. On May 8, 1945, in Berlin, Field Marshal Wilhelm Keitel, Chief of the German High Command, signed a formal ratification of the surrender. Air Chief Marshal Sir Arthur Tedder signed for General Eisenhower and Marshal Gregory Zhukov for the Soviet High Command.

The second member of the Axis had now gone down in total defeat, but said President Truman, "Our victory is but half won. The West is free but the East is still in bondage." Victory over Japan was not to be delayed for long, however, because now the United States and Great Britain could transfer land, sea, and air forces from Europe to crush the Japanese in the Far East and force them, too, into unconditional surrender.

The war against the Japanese involved the greatest problem of transportation. It had to be fought thousands of miles from the United States. Kiska and Attu in the Aleu-tians, which the Japanese had seized, were nearly 3000 air miles from Seattle. Our bases in Australia were about 7000 miles from San Francisco and therefore it took nearly a month for convoys to sail there. Moreover, troops, planes, and war supplies had to be shipped half way around the world to India where they were needed to assist the British in defending India and to furnish war supplies to China.

Before the United States could counterattack Japan it had to establish and equip strong bases thousands of miles from the United States. Before attacks could be launched against Japanese strongholds on the Pacific these bases had to be supplied with great quantities of war supplies of all kinds and great numbers of soldiers had to be stationed in them. The transportation of men and supplies required the construction of many merchant ships.

The demands of the war against Japan

placed a heavy burden on the United States Navy. It had to guard convoys, to protect men and supplies while they were being landed, and to protect them from attacks after they had landed. Once this was accomplished the Navy could turn its chief attention to its major function of destroying the Japanese navy and transporting the armed forces of the United States nearer and nearer to the Japanese homeland. For these purposes the construction of all kinds of warships, navy planes, and landing craft was rushed.

The demands of the European war fronts which had been given priority had to be met first. Nevertheless, American soldiers were transported to Australia to strengthen its forces which were under the command of General Douglas MacArthur.

United States forces began offensive warfare on Guadalcanal. On August 7, 1942, Marines landed on the Florida, Tulagi, and Guadalcanal islands in the Solomons. At first the fighting was fiercer on Florida and Tulagi than on Guadalcanal, but later on when the Japanese fought desperately to recover the airfield which the Marines captured on Guadalcanal, the fighting on Guadalcanal was fiercer. On August 9 in a night attack near Savo Island, Japanese warships surprised United States and Australian warships that were protecting the Marines and sank three American and one Australian cruisers and damaged other warships.

After their naval success, Japanese planes from Rabaul on New Britain began to bomb the American position on Guadalcanal and Japanese destroyers landed soldiers to reinforce the troops that were trying to drive the Marines from the airfield they had captured. Indeed Japanese destroyers made nightly runs with such regularity through the Slot, a passageway between the islands from Bougainville to Guadalcanal, that the Americans called them the "Tokyo Express."

American engineers repaired the airfield and it was re-named Henderson Field. A United States fighter squadron that landed on Henderson Field put up a strong resistance to the Japanese bombers. From August 23-25, planes from Henderson Field and from aircraft carriers did serious damage to the Japanese fleet. In October army troops landed on Guadalcanal to reinforce the Marines. The Japanese kept attacking fiercely, but the Americans repelled all attacks. The Americans gained control of the air and the Navy won a decisive victory over the Japanese off Guadalcanal (November 13-15). Gradually the Japanese on Guadalcanal were wiped out and by February 9, 1943, Guadalcanal was entirely in American hands. The victory on Guadalcanal removed all threats of cutting American supply lines to Australia.

American and Australian forces drove the Japanese out of southeastern New Guinea. In their sweep toward Australia, the Japanese had advanced through southeastern New Guinea and had established bases at Gona and Buna. From these bases they planned to advance over the Owen Stanley mountains to take Port Moresby. Shortly after General MacArthur took over the command of the Allied forces in the Southwest Pacific, he established a base at Port Moresby and an airfield at Milne Bay.

On August 26, 1942, while heavy fighting was taking place on Guadalcanal, the Japanese carried out an amphibious assault on the base at Milne Bay, but American and Australian forces decisively defeated them. In the meantime, other Japanese forces who advanced over the Owen Stanley mountains got within about thirty-two miles of Port Moresby before the Australians stopped them (September 17).

The Australians then advanced over the Owen Stanley mountains driving the Japanese before them while the United States

Ewing Galloway

GUADALCANAL. A bivouac area and supply dump the day after the Japanese retreated on Guadalcanal. Shell and bomb craters are used as fox-holes by the troops. Native carriers help the soldiers move rations and supplies.

Fifth Air Force bombed Japanese supply lines and the bases at Gona and Buna. American forces and their supplies were flown over the mountains to aid in the attacks on Gona and Buna. After exceptionally heavy jungle fighting, American and Australian forces captured Gona (December 9) and Buna (December 13). By January 23, 1943, all the Japanese positions in southeastern New Guinea had been taken and the Japanese had been driven back northward to their bases at Lae and Salamaua. The victories on Guadalcanal and in southeastern New Guinea saved Australia from invasion. Now General MacArthur's forces were ready to launch new attacks to drive the Japanese still farther northward.

United States forces recaptured Attu and Kiska. As we have already seen, the Jap- anese captured Attu and Kiska in June, 1942. To defend Alaska against this threat from the Aleutians, the United States strengthened its defenses at Dutch Harbor, Kodiak, and other Alaskan bases and built the Alaska Highway from Dawson Creek, a railroad terminal in Canada, to Fairbanks, Alaska. The United States also built air bases on Adak and Amchitka islands in the Aleutians from which bombers pounded the Japanese positions on Attu and Kiska.

On May 11, 1943, American forces landed on Attu. After heavy fighting in the bitter cold and fog in which all Japanese soldiers were either killed or committed suicide, Attu was recaptured (May 30, 1943). When American and Canadian forces landed on Kiska in August, 1943, they found that the

The superior naval, military, and air power of the United States turned the tide against the Japanese. With the strategy of "island hopping," the American army and navy in two parallel lines of air, sea, and land assaults brought the war close to the Japanese homeland and subjected it to heavy aerial attacks. Japan quickly surrendered under the added impact of the atom bombs dropped on Hiroshima and Nagasaki in August, 1945.

Japanese had abandoned their base under cover of heavy fogs. Apparently they concluded that the capture of Attu about 100 miles to the westward had made it impossible for them to hold their base on Kiska. Thereafter to the end of the war American air forces based in the Aleutians bombed Japanese positions in the Kurile Islands north of the main islands of Japan.

Americans and Australians conquered New Guinea. The Japanese still held strong bases in Salamaua and Lae in southeastern New Guinea. When the Japanese endeavored to reinforce their troops at these bases, American planes attacked their convoys in the Battle of the Bismarck Sea (March 1-3, 1943). At the cost of one bomber, three pursuit planes, and thirteen casualties, American planes destroyed twenty-two ships, sixty-one planes, and about 15,000 troops being carried on transports. General MacArthur later declared that this was the decisive battle in the New Guinea campaign.

At the Trident Conference in Washington (May, 1943), General MacArthur was directed to seize the rest of New Guinea, the remainder of the Solomons, and the Bismarck archipelago. Consequently, he was sent reinforcements and more war supplies. In July, 1943, after General MacArthur had been appointed by the United States Chiefs of Staff over-all commander of all army, navy, and air forces in the South Pacific, he began an advance in New Guinea. American and Australian troops were convoyed by sea or flown over the jungle to attack Salamaua and Lae. Lieutenant General George C. Kenny commanded the air force; Admiral William E. Barbey the fleet, and Lieutenant General Walter Krueger the ground forces. Salamaua fell September 11, 1943, and Lae September 16, and by February, 1944, all of southeastern New Guinea had been wrested from the Japanese.

General MacArthur's next advance was to Hollandia, more than 400 miles westward, where the Japanese had three excellent airfields. His forces were convoyed along the northern coast of New Guinea by transports protected by aircraft carriers and other naval craft. A part of these American forces landed at Aitape, east of Hollandia, and others near Hollandia. By April 30, 1944, Hollandia was in American hands and in September MacArthur moved his headquarters from Brisbane, Australia, to Hollandia. This advance from eastern New Guinea to Hollandia cut off more than 50,000 Japanese

troops from their bases of supplies and left them useless and hopeless in the jungles. In June, Biak Island was captured and by the end of July, 1944, General MacArthur's forces had reached the western tip of the Island of New Guinea.

American and New Zealand forces conquered the rest of the Solomons. After the capture of Guadalcanal American and New Zealand forces supported by the South Pacific fleet under the command of Admiral William F. Halsey began the conquest of the rest of the Solomons. After six weeks of hard fighting, American soldiers captured the airstrip at Munda on New Georgia Island (August 5, 1943). The Seabees repaired the airstrip which the Japanese had damaged severely before they abandoned it to the Americans.

One after another the islands fell. New Zealand troops occupied two islands in the Treasury group late in October. In November, Marines under the command of Lieutenant General A. A. Vandegrift landed in Empress Augusta Bay on Bougainville Island. Here they established a naval base and three airfields from which the key Japanese air base at Rabaul on New Britain Island was bombed. By this time the Americans had secured control of the sea by defeating all Japanese naval and air forces sent against them and by causing serious losses to the Japanese navy. They were, therefore, able to cut the enemy supply lines to Bougainville and isolate the troops on it just as MacArthur had isolated the troops on New Guinea. The Americans by-passed Rabaul on northern New Britain also and occupied positions in southern New Britain and the Admiralty Islands (February, 1944). From these bases they cut the Japanese at Rabaul off from supplies and American air forces bombed Rabaul so mercilessly that they destroyed it as a Japanese base.

Acme

UNITED STATES CRUISER BOMBARDING JAP-
ANESE ON WAKE ISLAND.

By the end of July, 1944, the Allied forces in the Southwest Pacific had advanced 1300 miles from Guadalcanal and had put 135,000 Japanese troops out of the war. All of these advances in New Guinea and through the Solomons had been made under the most adverse climatic conditions. The weather was fearfully hot and rainy. The dense jungles that covered most of the islands were diffi-cult for our soldiers to go through and roads were almost entirely lacking. Small groups of soldiers had to wipe out the Jap-anese in hand to hand fighting. Malaria and other tropical diseases caused our soldiers great suffering until preventives and specifics were furnished in sufficient quantities either to prevent or to cure these diseases.

American forces in the Central Pacific under the command of Admiral Chester W. Nimitz captured the Gilbert and Mar-shall Islands. By the summer of 1943 Ameri-can production of war materials and ships and the increase in the number of men trained for military and naval service made it possible for the United States to conduct offensive warfare in the Pacific as well as in Sicily and Italy. By this time the severe losses which the Americans had inflicted on the

Japanese at Midway and in the Southwest Pacific had given them naval and air superi-ority over the Japanese in the Pacific.

Admiral Nimitz was now prepared to launch a general assault at the Japanese in the Central Pacific. Each attack in the gen-eral assault was made for the purpose of securing bases and airstrips from which other attacks could be made even nearer to Japan. The immediate objective was to capture the Gilbert and Marshall Islands in the Central Pacific. After this was accomplished, Ameri-can forces could strike at the great Japanese naval base at Truk in the Carolines and then invade the Mariana Islands. After all this had been achieved, the Navy would be able to support General MacArthur in his return to the Philippines and to secure the islands nearer and nearer Japan from which its in-dustries and cities could be bombed more effectively.

After a terrific naval and air bombardment, Marines and army forces invaded (November 21, 1943) the islands of Makin and Tarawa in the Gilberts. The capture of Makin was not so difficult as Tarawa and it fell on No-bember 22. The Japanese had converted Ta-rawa into a strong fortress with concrete bunkers and blockhouses reinforced with steel and covered with sand and coral. Al-though they were bombed heavily, the bombs did them little damage. The Marines landing at Tarawa were hampered by enemy gun fire and also by high reefs on which some of the landing boats were stranded. Once ashore they assaulted the Japanese fortifications with hand grenades and flame-throwers. Aft-er four days of terrible and costly fighting, the determined heroism of the Marines wiped out the last of the Japanese defenders.

The second assault was upon the Japanese base at Kwajalein in the Marshalls, northwest of the Gilberts (January 31, 1944). Marines and Army forces, after fierce fighting, secured possession of it (February 8, 1944). The utter devastation which American fire-power visited on Kwajalein is typical of that visited on other Japanese-held possessions. Lieutenant General Robert C. Richardson, Jr., commander of the Army in the Central Pacific, described it in these words:

As a result of the air, naval, and artillery bombardment, the scene at Kwajalein was one of great devastation. The destruction was complete. . . . With the exception of rubble left by concrete structures, there were no buildings standing. All those which had been made of any other material except concrete had been completely burned or destroyed. The result was that there were practically no stores left except a few packages of rice and a little clothing and ammunition scattered here and there.

Between February 19-22, Marine and Army forces captured Eniwetok, another island in the Marshalls, which had a good air base from which the Japanese naval base at Truk could be bombed. Already powerful naval task forces under the command of Admiral Raymond A. Spruance had raided Truk (February 17-18, 1944). The Japanese fleet based on Truk had already fled to avoid being trapped by the American task force whose planes destroyed 201 Japanese planes and twenty-three ships. The next American advance westward rendered it useless to the Japanese. This advance led to the conquest of the islands of Saipan, Tinian, and Guam in the Marianas.

The conquest of the Marianas led to the invasion of the Philippines and a more intense bombing of Japan. Saipan was the first island in the Marianas to be attacked. From June 11-14, 1944, planes from United States task forces (carriers, battleships, cruisers, destroyers, and other vessels) under the general command of Admiral Spruance bombed Saipan, Tinian, and Guam. At the same time a Japanese fleet steamed eastward from its base in Philippine waters and sent up its planes to counterattack the American planes. In the great aerial battle which followed (June 19, 1944), the Japanese lost 420 aircraft, the Americans twenty-seven. The loss of so many carrier-based planes compelled the Japanese fleet to flee back to its base, but as it did so it was pursued by planes from the American fleet. The American planes sank three Japanese carriers and a tanker and damaged eleven other warships; three American ships were damaged. The American planes returned to their carriers in the darkness. Like the Battle of the Coral Sea, the First Battle of the Philippine Sea was fought entirely by planes. The warships of the two opposing fleets did not come close enough to exchange shots.

In the meantime, Marines and Army forces had already begun (June 15, 1944) the invasion of Saipan. The island was strongly fortified and honeycombed with many caves. The enemy resisted stubbornly until on July 7 those who had not been wiped out made a Banzai charge, a suicidal counterattack in which soldiers rushed to certain death at the hands of the victorious Americans.

Tinian fell to the Americans (August 1). The Japanese fought bitterly to retain possession of Guam which had been an American possession from the time of the Spanish-American War down to its capture by the Japanese in 1941. After a terrific pounding for seventeen days by carrier-based planes and naval guns, Marine and Army forces landed on Guam (July 20). After twenty days of savage fighting, it was securely in the hands of Americans. Battle statistics indicate that the Japanese fought to the bitter end. More than 14,000 Japanese were killed on Guam while the American loss was 1226 killed. On August 13, 1944, Admiral Nimitz reported that in the battles in the Central Pacific from Makin to Guam 52,323 Japanese had been killed and 3022 taken prisoner while the loss of American lives was reported to be 5903.

After the capture of Saipan, Tinian, and Guam the Seabees quickly constructed great airstrips on them. From these strips planes flew to bomb Truk and Iwo Jima from time to time and giant B-29 Superfortresses flew to Japan to bomb factories, shipyards, air and naval bases. The success of the forces under Admiral Nimitz enabled him to establish advance headquarters on Guam (January, 1945) to bring him much closer to the scene of operations. His forces were now able to assist General MacArthur and his troops in the return to the Philippines.

General MacArthur's forces landed on the island of Leyte in the Central Philippines. Before the Philippines could be invaded, Japanese bases in the Palau Islands and on Morotai had to be occupied. To weaken Japanese air forces which could be used to oppose landings on these islands, planes from carriers ranged far and wide to attack Japanese air bases on them and also in the Southern and Central Philippines. On September 15, 1944, American forces landed on Morotai and on Peleliu in the Palaus. Morotai was soon in American hands and by October 13 all opposition on Peleliu and other islands in the Palau group had been overcome. The Americans had won vital air and naval bases along the route to the Philippines.

American air forces then carried out extensive bombings in preparation for the landings on Leyte in the Philippines. From the latter part of September until the middle of October carrier task forces carried out a number of bold raids on Japanese airfields, naval and military bases, and coastal shipping in Formosa, the Philippines, and the Ryukyu Islands. Task Force 58 under Vice Admiral Marc A. Mitscher in raids on the Philippines and Formosa destroyed or damaged almost

900 enemy planes and more than 200 ships. After American forces had captured the Philippines, General George C. Kenney, commander of the Far East Air Force, reported that wrecks of nearly 3000 Japanese planes were found strewn on the airfields of the Philippines.

On October 19, 1944, a vast armada of about 650 ships of all kinds approached the eastern coast of the island of Leyte in the Central Philippines. The invasion which was two months ahead of its original schedule was under the over-all command of General MacArthur. The Seventh Fleet under Vice Admiral Thomas C. Kinkaid transported and protected the landings (October 20) of the Sixth Army under General Walter Krueger. The Third Fleet under Admiral Halsey stood out to sea east of Leyte to engage any Japanese warships that might offer opposition. The landings which were only lightly opposed by the Japanese were completely successful and within a few days the beachhead was securely established. As it was being established, however, Japanese naval forces steamed forth to challenge the American naval forces that were protecting the Leyte invasion. They hoped to wipe out the American naval forces, destroy the troopships, and thereby isolate the American troops on Leyte.

The United States Navy and its air arm crushed the Japanese navy in the Battle for Leyte Gulf. From October 23-26, 1944, American naval units fought almost simultaneously three decisive naval engagements known collectively as the Battle for Leyte Gulf (Second Battle of the Philippine Sea). Three Japanese naval forces, a Southern Force, a Central Force, and a Northern Force advanced eastward to attack American naval units.

The Southern Force, consisting of seven warships which were headed for Leyte Gulf, entered the Surigao Strait (October 24). On

October 25, units of the Seventh Fleet under Rear Admiral Jesse B. Oldendorf utterly defeated it in the Battle of Surigao Strait by employing skillfully naval tactics known as "crossing the T."

The Central Force, consisting of twenty-six ships, had been observed by submarines on October 23 and was headed for San Bernardino Strait. Before it got there, it was attacked by carrier-based planes and submarines from the Third Fleet which inflicted such heavy damage on it that some ships were forced to turn back. However, the remainder sailed through San Bernardino Strait and turned southward along the eastern coast of the island of Samar where they attacked (October 25) a vastly weaker escort carrier force of the Seventh Fleet under the command of Rear Admiral C. A. F. Sprague. In the Battle of Samar the lighter American force fought so valiantly and fiercely that the Japanese broke off the engagement and retired toward San Bernardino Strait. As it did so and while it was passing through the Strait, carrier-based planes from the Third Fleet inflicted very heavy losses on it. The Northern Force, consisting of seventeen warships, approached the Philippines probably from Japan. Units of the Third Fleet under Admiral Halsey attacked it (October 25) in the Battle off Cape Engano (northeastern tip of Luzon Island). Three Japanese carriers, a cruiser, and a destroyer were sunk and heavy damage was inflicted on two battleships and on other warships. The Third Fleet lost the carrier *Princeton*.

In these three decisive naval battles the United States Navy had inflicted such crushing blows on the Japanese navy that Japan was practically eliminated as a sea power. From this time on to the end of the war the remnants of the once powerful Japanese navy were so weak that they could not oppose American amphibious operations.

The Americans defeated the Japanese forces on Leyte. After General MacArthur's forces had established beachheads on Leyte, the Japanese made desperate attempts to reinforce their troops. They were now commanded by General Tomoyoki Yamashita, the conqueror of Singapore and Bataan. The Japanese were unable to land many reinforcements on Leyte because General Kenney's land-based planes and Admiral Halsey's carrier-based planes destroyed many transports and the destroyers that were trying to protect them. The sinking of these transports cost the Japanese the lives of many troops that otherwise would have reinforced General Yamashita's army.

The campaign for Leyte during November and December, 1944, was fought under the most trying weather conditions brought about by violent storms of the rainy season. Despite these adverse weather conditions and the bitter opposition of the best and most numerous Japanese troops that the Americans had yet faced, General Krueger's forces drove steadily forward. On December 25, General MacArthur announced that all organized resistance on Leyte had ended. The Americans were now ready for the next great step in the conquest of the Philippines, the capture of the island of Luzon.

The Americans won the battle of Luzon and recaptured Manila and Corregidor. On December 15, 1944, while the fighting on Leyte was still going on, American troops who had been convoyed from Leyte Gulf landed on the southwest coast of the island of Mindoro which is very near the southern coast of Luzon. Within two days they won possession of a strategic air base on Mindoro and thereby seriously threatened Japan's shipping lanes through the South China Sea to the Southern Philippines, the Netherlands East Indies, and Malaya. Moreover, the occupation of Mindoro led the Japanese to be-

Acme

DESTRUCTION OF MANILA BY THE JAPANESE.

lieve that General MacArthur's forces would land on Southern Luzon.

On January 9, 1945, an American convoy, well protected by the United States Navy and its air arm, made it appear that it was headed for the southern coast of Luzon. However, it sailed north and landed Sixth Army troops on beaches in Lingayen Gulf about 100 miles north of Manila where the Japanese had landed in 1941. The troops that landed there and other troops that landed about three weeks later on the western coast of Luzon and south of Manila began a three-pronged drive on the Philippine capital. By February 4, American troops had reached the outskirts of Manila. General MacArthur requested General Yamashita to declare Manila an open city to prevent its destruction, but he refused. Consequently, in the bitter fighting that followed, much of the city was destroyed. On February 23, 1945, General MacArthur an-

nounced that organized resistance had ended in the city of Manila and four days later he turned over the government of the Philippines to President Sergio Osmena.

While Manila was being taken street by street, American naval and air forces pounded Corregidor heavily. On February 16, parachute troops and an amphibious force landed on Corregidor which fell to them after the Japanese had continued a suicidal resistance for two weeks.

After the fall of Manila the Japanese continued resistance in the mountainous regions of Luzon until July. The smaller islands in the Philippines fell to the Americans in quick succession. The Japanese, however, put up stiff resistance on the large island of Mindanao. Americans landed there (March 10, 1945) and began its conquest. Davao, the chief city of Mindanao, fell to them (May 4, 1945). Although General MacArthur announced the liberation of the Philippines (July 5, 1945), isolated forces of Japanese were still fighting bitterly at the end of the war a few weeks later.

The Allies drove the Japanese out of Burma. While the forces of MacArthur and Nimitz were advancing steadily from the east, British, American, Indian, and Chinese troops were driving the Japanese out of Burma. In 1943 the Combined Chiefs of Staff created the Southeast Asia Command and made Admiral Lord Louis Mountbatten its supreme commander with Lieutenant General Joseph W. Stilwell as his deputy. The task which their forces faced was threefold. Their first task was to prevent a successful Japanese invasion of India; the second was to reopen land communications with China; the third was to defeat the Japanese and drive them out of Burma.

The Japanese actually crossed the frontier between Burma and India into Eastern India (March 13, 1944). They cut off Imphal, capital of Manipur, in an effort to sever the Assam-Bengal railroad. This railroad was the chief supply line for the Chinese and American forces to the north. Not until June 30, 1944, did the British and Indian armies succeed in repelling this serious threat and accomplish their first task.

Meantime, the Allies had proceeded with their second task. Since the closing of the Burma Road (February, 1942), American planes had been carrying supplies over the "Hump" into China, that is, over the Himalaya Mountains, 19,000 feet high, which separate India and China. By January, 1945, about 44,000 tons of supplies a month were being flown to the Chinese over the "Hump." However, these flights were costly in men and planes and could not supply the Chinese with all the war supplies they needed. Many planes and crews were lost because of bad weather. Native tribesmen helped many of

the men to return to their bases. Air rescue squads flew over the jungle and dropped by parachutes food, medical supplies, medical corpsmen, and guides to help the crews of other lost planes to get back to their bases.

The need for direct land communication between bases in eastern India and China was evident. To accomplish this a Chinese army trained and led by General Stilwell advanced from Ledo into Northern Burma (February 1, 1944). Airborne troops were used to assist in their advance. The preceding year General Orde C. Wingate had begun harassing the Japanese by leading British airborne troops on raids behind the Japanese lines. His raiders were joined by a force of jungle-trained Americans commanded by Brigadier General Frank D. Merrill and known as Merrill's Marauders. They were flown into the jungle (March 5, 1944) in planes and gliders. They prepared air strips, and began attacks on the Japanese supply lines.

As the Chinese and American troops advanced, engineers supervised the building of a road from Ledo at the head of the rail line in India to Myitkina in northern Burma and thence to Bhamo where it joined the old Burma Road. Chinese troops cleared the Burma Road from Kunming in China south toward Bhamo. On January 28, 1945, the road was completed and the first American truck convoy under Brigadier General Lewis A. Pick, who built the Ledo Road, rolled into China. Generalissimo Chiang Kai-shek renamed the Ledo Road the Stilwell Road in honor of General Stilwell.

The British began their third task in December, 1944, after they had successfully resisted the Japanese invasion of India. They invaded Burma and drove toward Mandalay and Rangoon. The Japanese, harassed by the raiders, and defeated by the advancing British and Indian troops fell back before them. Mandalay was taken (March 22, 1945) and

Acme

THE RAISING OF THE FLAG BY THE MA-
RINES ON IWO JIMA.

Rangoon, chief Burmese port, on May 4, 1945. British and Indian troops were ready for an invasion of Thailand and also for the liberation of Singapore when the war came to an end.

The Chinese resisted doggedly. During the war the Japanese captured a large part of Eastern China including all the sea ports thus cutting the Chinese off from the coast. They made advances from time to time into the "rice bowl," the rice growing area of China along the Yangtze River. They bombed Chungking, wartime capital of China, merci-lessly. Although the Chinese people suffered terribly from inflation and from devastation caused by the war, they continued to fight the Japanese to the best of their ability.

At first they were assisted by the Flying Tigers, an air force of American volunteers under Major General Claire Chennault. When the United States entered the war, the Flying Tigers were absorbed into the Four-teenth Air Force of the United States Army. These men fought brilliantly, at first with

few planes and scant supplies. As their power increased, they built more airfields in South-ern China with Chinese assistance and even raided Japanese shipping off the Chinese coast. In 1944, however, the Japanese staged an offensive which forced the Fourteenth Air Force to destroy and evacuate several impor-tant airfields in Southeastern China.

In the spring of 1945 the Chinese armies were ready to assume the offensive. They as-sisted, as we have seen, in the recapture of the Burma Road. They began an advance into Southeastern China to recapture the airfields that had been abandoned and to win a port for an American landing if that should prove necessary. They gained considerable success, reaching Foochow (May 13, 1945) on the coast, though they could not hold it. The end of the war made a further advance unneces-sary by the Chinese armies.

American submarines and task forces in-flicted very heavy losses on the Japanese merchant marine. As the American forces in the Pacific prepared for the final blows against the Japanese islands, American naval victories had almost isolated them. Through-out the war American submarines had been operating in Japanese waters. By the sum-mer of 1944 they had sunk 687 Japanese ves-sels and damaged many more, over one third of Japanese prewar merchant shipping. The Japanese were compelled to convoy their sup-ply ships and to use small boats along the Chinese coast. The submarine war made it difficult for them to get the much needed sup-ply of oil and rubber from Malaya and the islands of the East Indies.

As the American fleet grew in power and acquired bases on Guam, Saipan, Tinian, and the Philippines, task forces ranged the east-ern waters doing great damage to Japanese shipping. By the end of the war the Japanese merchant marine had declined from 7,000,-000 to 1,500,000 tons. The submarines had sunk 167 warships and 1089 merchant vessels and damaged or probably sunk 300 more.

To get air bases nearer to Japan, the Americans captured Iwo Jima and Okinawa. The bombers from Guam, Saipan, and Tinian began their task of reducing Japanese industrial power (November 24, 1944). For these raids huge Superfortresses, B-29 bombers, were used. The distance from Saipan to Tokyo was more than 1500 miles. Fighter planes could not accompany the bombers for this distance, and bombers which became disabled or ran out of fuel were unable to return to their bases. In addition, Japanese air forces on Iwo Jima attacked the bombers on their flights to and from Japan and also raided our bases in the Marianas.

Admiral Nimitz, therefore, determined on the conquest of Iwo Jima in the Volcano Islands, about 640 miles from Tokyo. It is a small island about one and one-half miles wide. It is composed of volcanic rock and had been heavily fortified by the Japanese. Because Iwo Jima was so small and contained only two landing beaches, it was impossible for the Americans to make a surprise landing. Consequently, the most painstaking preparation had to be made to keep the loss of lives as low as possible. For seven months previous to the landing, Iwo Jima was bombed off and on from the air and bombarded by ships at sea. During the three days previous to the landing, Iwo Jima was furiously bombed.

On February 19, 1945, two Marine divisions landed on the southeast shore of Iwo Jima and by the time Iwo Jima was in American hands a naval force of more than 800 ships had landed 60,000 Marines on the island. The American advance was rigorously resisted by about 20,000 Japanese well protected in an interlocking system of caves, pillboxes, and blockhouses. Moreover, artillery on Mt. Suribachi and other high points poured a deadly fire on the landing beaches.

Acme

An American soldier shares his rations with Japanese children on Okinawa.

After terrific fighting, the Marines succeeded in taking Mt. Suribachi and in capturing the airfields. The conquest of Iwo Jima which was completed March 16 cost the lives of more than 4000 Marines and also the wounding of 13,000. Almost all of the Japanese garrison of about 20,000 troops was wiped out. However, the B-29's could use it for distress landings and it is estimated that possession of Iwo Jima saved the lives of more than 9000 American airmen. Fighter planes that used it as a base flew with bombers to protect them in other attacks against Japan.

American army and naval forces were then sent against Okinawa, largest of the Ryukyu Islands, which is about sixty-five miles long and about 350 miles southwest of Japan. Possession of this island would give the Americans more airfields closer to Japan, several excellent harbors, and would provide a base for the ultimate invasion of Japan itself. Okinawa was strongly defended by about 120,000 Japanese.

On April 1 Tenth Army forces and Marines under Lieutenant General Simon B. Buckner landed on the southwest coast of Okinawa. The landing was almost unopposed. However, fierce fighting soon devel-

Acme

Atom bomb explodes over Nagasaki.

oped on the southern end of the island. The fleet, which stood guard, shelled enemy shore installations and sent its planes to assist the land forces. In a counsel of despair the Japanese resorted to suicide bombing. A corps of young aviators was enlisted who were willing to crash rocket-accelerated aircraft carrying more than a ton of high explosives on American warships. Their attacks were called *Kamikaze* (divine wind) after the typhoon which had saved Japan from the invading forces of Kublai Khan. Most of the planes in the Kamikaze attacks were shot down before they hit American warships, but before Okinawa had been captured about 250 vessels of all kinds had been hit, most of them by suicide crashes. The battle on land was pushed to its conclusion. The northern part of the island fell quickly. In the south, however, the Japanese fought fiercely. Marine and army units pressed upon them steadily, and gradually annihilated them. General Buckner was killed by a Japanese shell while observing

operations (June 18) and was succeeded by Major General Roy S. Geiger of the United States Marine Corps. The capture of Okinawa was completed June 21. The conquest of Okinawa had cost the Americans 11,260 killed and 33,769 wounded; the Japanese losses were more than 109,000 killed and about 8000 prisoners.

The Americans closed in on Japan. While plans were being completed for the invasion of Japan, American air forces and fleets closed in on the home islands. Bombers from all the American bases on islands within range and those from China rained storms of high explosives and incendiary bombs on Japanese cities. They almost completely destroyed Japanese production of steel and planes and wiped out oil refineries. They reduced large parts of the major cities of Japan to ruins.

The task forces of the fleet ranged around Japan and sent their carrier-based planes on devastating raids against Japanese airfields and naval installations. They so reduced the Japanese fleet that by the end of July the Japanese had not a single battleship fit for operations. American warships sailed in close enough to Japan to pour their gunfire into the industrial plants along the coast. Bombers also dropped leaflets informing the Japanese people of the dire straits to which their military and imperialistic leaders had brought them. These pamphlets helped to prepare the people for surrender.

Two atom bombs dropped on Japan led the Japanese government to surrender unconditionally. On July 26 President Truman and Prime Minister Attlee at the Potsdam Conference issued the Potsdam Declaration which said:

> The time has come for Japan to decide whether she will continue to be controlled by those self-willed militaristic advisers whose unintelligent calculations have brought

Acme

General MacArthur signs Japanese surrender document on board
the *Missouri* anchored in Tokyo Bay.

the Empire of Japan to the threshold of annihilation, or whether she will follow the path of reason. . . . We call upon the government of Japan to proclaim now the unconditional surrender of all Japanese armed forces, and to provide proper and adequate assurances of their good faith in such action. The alternative for Japan is prompt and utter destruction.

The Japanese rejected this appeal and by doing so brought down upon the people of two Japanese cities the most awful military blow in the history of the world.

While President Truman and Prime Minister Attlee were conferring at Potsdam, a new and terribly destructive atom bomb was taken to a desert area in New Mexico where it was detonated (July 16). The observers of this experiment were awed by the devastating effects of the first atom bomb ever to be exploded. A report on the experiment in New

Mexico was immediately sent to the President at Potsdam, who decided, on advice from experts, to use an atom bomb against Japan to shorten the war and save American lives.

On August 6, 1945, a B-29 dropped one bomb on the city of Hiroshima, a Japanese military base, and a city of about 343,000 inhabitants. This bomb, which had the destructive force of 20,000 tons of TNT, destroyed about 60 per cent of the city of Hiroshima. In February, 1946, Supreme Allied Headquarters announced that the casualties in Hiroshima as a result of the atom bomb were: dead, 78,150; still missing, 13,983; seriously wounded, 9,428; slightly injured, 27,997. President Truman again asked the Japanese government to surrender and again it refused. On August 8, the Soviet Union, in accordance with an agreement made at Yalta, declared war on Japan, and its armies invaded Manchuria the next day. On August 9, a second atom bomb, more powerful than the first, was dropped on the industrial city of Nagasaki, which was also a naval base. The smoke from this bomb rose 50,000 feet in the air and was visible for more than 175 miles.

On Friday, August 10, President Truman told the Japanese government that more atom bombs would be dropped if it did not surrender unconditionally at once. On the same day the Japanese government offered to surrender if the emperor's authority was not impaired. President Truman replied that in case of surrender the emperor would be subject to the orders of General MacArthur. On Tuesday, August 14, at 7:00 P.M. Eastern War Time, President Truman announced that the Japanese had surrendered unconditionally. On Saturday, September 1 our time (September 2, Japanese time), formal signing of the documents of surrender took place in Tokyo Harbor on the battleship *Missouri* in the presence of General MacArthur, Admiral Nimitz, General Wainwright, released from prison camp, and high ranking military and naval officers of powers allied with the United States. General MacArthur signed as Supreme Commander for the Allied Powers and Admiral Nimitz signed for the United States. Five days later General MacArthur entered Tokyo where his troops raised the United States Flag over the American Embassy. This flag was the one which had flown over the Capitol in Washington, D. C., on December 7, 1941, when the Japanese attacked Pearl Harbor. It had flown over Rome and Berlin after their capture and also over the *Missouri* while the terms of surrender were being signed. With the total defeat and unconditional surrender of Japan, the greatest war in history had come to an end four months after the surrender of Germany.

SUMMARY

The United Nations was formed on January 1, 1942, and more than three and a half years elapsed before its members compelled the last of the Axis powers to surrender unconditionally. During these years the United States fought a total and global war on widely separated fronts on land, on and under the sea, and in the air.

After the United States entered the war, it stepped up its war preparations feverishly. Millions of men were trained in camps, schools, and colleges to help make them capable of performing the tasks assigned to them. Women also were enlisted to do many kinds of war work for the Army, Navy, Marines, and Coast Guard. American factories turned out vast quantities of all kinds of war supplies for the armed forces of the United States and its Allies. American shipyards built ships faster than the German submarines could destroy them and American farmers produced foodstuffs to feed our people and to help feed those in countries allied with us. Indeed the efficiency of American methods of mass production and the productivity of American farmers and workers were a most powerful factor in bringing about the total defeat of the Axis powers.

When Roosevelt and Churchill decided (December, 1941) to wage offensive warfare on Italy and Germany and defensive warfare on Japan, German submarines were sinking merchant ships twice as fast as they could be built in American and British shipyards. In 1942 and 1943 the United States and British navies and airplanes waged such relentless warfare on the German submarines that by the autumn of 1943 they had the submarine menace well under control.

German and Italian armies suffered their first great defeat in North Africa as they were crushed between Montgomery's forces and Eisenhower's American, British, and Free French Forces. The Allied forces invaded Sicily and while they were defeating the German and

Italian armies there, Mussolini was overthrown and the Italian government surrendered unconditionally. However, the Germans still had to be driven from Italy and so it was invaded by the Allies (September, 1943). After eight months of hard fighting they captured Rome (June, 1944) and drove the Germans northward into the Po Valley, where, after almost a year of hard fighting, they surrendered unconditionally in May, 1945.

In November, 1942, Soviet armies launched an offensive at Stalingrad which resulted in the capture of a large German army. This offensive began the long drive westward which did not stop until Berlin was in Soviet hands. During the winter offensive of 1943 the Soviet armies advanced along a front which extended from Leningrad to the Black Sea. Between the spring of 1943 and the spring of 1944 they drove the Axis armies back into Poland and Rumania. During the summer and autumn of 1944 the Soviet armies knocked Finland and Rumania out of the war, overran Bulgaria, helped free Greece, Albania, and Yugoslavia from Nazi domination, and captured much of Hungary.

While the Soviet armies were advancing on Germany from the East, American, British, and Canadian forces invaded Normandy (June 6, 1944) and later on other Allied forces invaded Southern France (August 15, 1944). These forces defeated the German armies and liberated France, Belgium, and Luxemburg from the Nazi yoke. The Ardennes counteroffensive failed to stem the advance of the Allied armies who crossed the Rhine, captured the Saar and the Ruhr, liberated the Netherlands, and plunged into the very heart of Germany to make a junction with the Soviet armies advancing from the East. By May, 1945, the German armies were utterly defeated, Berlin was in Soviet hands, and many German cities were largely in ruins as a result of terrific air bombings. On May 7, 1945, Admiral Doenitz, who had come to power after Hitler's suicide, authorized the German High Command to surrender unconditionally to General Eisenhower and the Soviet High Command. The most powerful of the Axis powers had been totally defeated.

In the meantime, two vast offensives against the Japanese were being fought in the Southwest Pacific and in the Central Pacific. As General MacArthur's forces fought their way through the Solomons and New Guinea, other forces under Admiral Nimitz conducted an offensive across the Central Pacific from the Marshall and Gilbert Islands to the Marianas and the Carolines. Then the forces under MacArthur and Nimitz co-operated in the invasion the capture of the Philippines. Iwo Jima and Okinawa were captured and from air bases on them Japanese cities were bombed with devastating effects. A third great offensive drove the Japanese out of Burma and re-opened the Burma Road to China.

After two atom bombs had been dropped on Hiroshima and Nagasaki and after the Soviet Union had declared war on Japan and invaded Manchuria, the Japanese government surrendered unconditionally (August 14, 1945). The Second World War which began September 1, 1939 had ended in the total victory of the United Nations over the Axis powers.

SUMMARY OF PART XI

The League of Nations was established to provide collective security for the nations of the world and was designed to prevent war. It settled some minor disputes and it accomplished many good things to the great benefit of the peoples of the world. It failed, however, in its major purpose. The League's most powerful members would not use its machinery or support its decisions. In spite of the existence of the League diplomats made use of the time-honored method of conferences at which they made pacts. These, too, failed when ambitious rulers violated them. Japan, Italy, and Germany, in turn, launched programs of military aggression in defiance both of the League and of the pacts which they had signed. The policy of appeasement used by Great Britain and France proved a dismal failure and on September 1, 1939, the Second World War began.

The Second World War, beginning in Europe as a war of Great Britain and France as allies against Germany, spread until it engulfed nearly all the nations of the world. Science and invention made this war the most deadly and destructive war in world history. During the first three years of the war the totalitarian powers were everywhere victorious. Norway, the Netherlands, Belgium, and France were swallowed up and the Third French Republic, badly beaten, was brought to an inglorious end. Hitler's armies overran the Balkans and then drove into the Soviet Union. By the summer of 1942 they had driven nearly to Moscow, reached the Volga at Stalingrad, conquered the Crimea, and penetrated the region of the Caucasus Mountains. Germans and Italians together after some setbacks had penetrated Egypt.

In the Far East Japan, entering the war with an attack on Pearl Harbor that brought the United States into the conflict, rapidly overran the shores of Southeastern Asia to Singapore, and conquered Burma to the border of India. The Japanese gained possession of the Philippines and the British and Dutch islands to the south, (Borneo, Java, Sumatra, and many others). They landed on the northern shores of New Guinea whence they threatened Australia and by starting to establish bases and airfields in the Solomons they menaced the supply line between the United States and Australia. At this point they were checked both on the sea and on land, chiefly by American forces.

The nations opposed to the Axis powers, acting together in the United Nations, gradually mustered their strength. Prodigies of production in Great Britain and the Soviet Union, but especially in the United States, furnished them the sinews of war. They struck back with vigor and determination. Germans and Italians in Egypt were rolled back while an American and British army was landed on the western end of the North African coast. In succession North Africa, Sicily, and most of Italy fell to their prowess. Italy surrendered unconditionally on September 3, 1943, shortly before the allied invasion of the Italian mainland. In June, 1944, American and British troops landed in Normandy and started to drive the Germans back to the Rhine. The Russians, rallying magnificently, trapped the German army at Stalingrad and steadily pushed the Germans out of the Soviet Union. In the spring of 1945 the Americans and British crossed the Rhine, the Russians invaded Germany and Austria, and on May 7, 1945, at Rheims (May 8, in Berlin) the Germans surrendered unconditionally to the United Nations.

In the late summer of 1942 the forces of the United States and Australia took the offensive against Japan. The Marines landed on Guadalcanal, and the Solomons were regained step by step. MacArthur's forces crossed New Guinea and leapfrogged along its northern coast. In the far north the United States Army regained Attu and Kiska from the Japanese. The forces of the United States hopped from island to island in the Central Pacific in terrific battles. At last the stage was set for MacArthur's return to the Philippines. This he did on October 21, 1944, under the strong protection of the United States Navy. This Navy won a great victory over the Japanese in the waters of the Philippines and shortly afterwards Manila and Corregidor were recaptured. From the newly-regained base at Guam, American flyers began the bombing of Japan while the fleets cleared the eastern waters of Japanese shipping. Iwo Jima was taken to protect American planes from Japanese attacks and to provide a landing base. As a step toward the invasion of Japan itself American forces were landed on Okinawa. Finally, two atom bombs were dropped on Japanese cities and the Soviet Union declared war on Japan. On August 14, 1945, the Japanese also yielded in unconditional surrender. The Second World War had come to an end. It had cost the lives of millions of people, the expenditure of billions of dollars, intense suffering, and untold anguish.

EVENTS THAT TOOK PLACE AT ABOUT THE SAME TIME

Year	Europe	Africa	Pacific and the Far East
1942			Aug. 7, Americans invaded the Solomons. Sept. 17, Japanese defeated near Port Moresby.
		Oct. 23-Nov. 2, British defeated Rommel's forces at El Alamein. Nov. 8, British and American forces landed in North Africa.	
	Nov. 22, Soviet forces began offensive in Stalingrad.		Dec. 9, Fall of Gona. Dec. 13, Fall of Buna.
1943		Jan. 14-26, Casablanca Conference. Jan. 23, British entered Tripoli.	
	Feb. 2, German Army at Stalingrad surrendered. Feb. 17, Soviet forces recaptured Rostov.	Feb. 22, Americans occupied Kassarine Pass.	
		Mar. 29, British breached Mareth line in Tunisia. May 12, Axis forces surrendered in Tunisia.	Mar. 1-3, Battle of the Bismarck Sea. May 11, Americans invaded Attu.
	July 10, Allies began invasion of Sicily. July 24, Mussolini ousted as Italian premier.		
	Sept. 8, Italy's unconditional surrender announced. Sept. 9, Allies landed at Salerno.		Aug. 15, American and Canadian forces occupied Kiska.

EVENTS THAT TOOK PLACE AT ABOUT THE SAME TIME (Cont.)

YEAR	EUROPE	AFRICA	PACIFIC AND THE FAR EAST
1943 cont.	Oct. 1, Capture of Naples. Nov. 6, Soviet forces captured Kiev.		Sept. 11, Fall of Salamana. Sept. 16, Fall of Lae.
		Nov. 22-26, Cairo Conference.	Nov. 22, Americans captured Makin. Nov. 25, Americans captured Tarawa.
		Nov. 28-Dec. 1, Teheran Conference.	
1944	Jan. 20, End of siege of Leningrad. Jan. 22, Allied forces made landing at Anzio.		
	Mar. 15, Monte Cassino destroyed by air attack. Apr. 10, Russians captured Odessa.		Feb. 8, Americans captured Kwajalein.
			Apr. 30, Hollandia in American hands.
	May 10, Soviet forces took Sevastopol. June 4, Rome captured by Americans. June 6, D-day, Allied invasion of Normandy. June 26, Americans captured Cherbourg. July 20, Attempted assassination of Hitler. Aug. 4, Allies entered Florence. Aug. 15, Allied armies invaded Southern France. Aug. 25, Paris taken by Allies. British captured Antwerp. Sept. 13, Rumania signed armistice with Soviet Union. Sept. 19, Finland signed Armistice with Soviet Union.		June 15, Americans invaded Saipan. June 19, United States naval forces defeated Japanese in First Battle of the Philippine Sea. July 20, Americans landed on Guam.

EVENTS THAT TOOK PLACE AT ABOUT THE SAME TIME (Cont.)

Year	Europe	Africa	Pacific and the Far East
1944 cont.			Sept. 15, Americans landed on Morotai and on Peleliu.
	Oct. 20, Soviet forces captured Belgrade. Oct. 21, Americans captured Aachen.		Oct. 20, Invasion of Leyte begun.
			Oct. 23-26, Battle for Leyte Gulf.
	Nov. 12, British planes sank the *Tirpitz*.		Dec. 15, Americans invaded Mindoro.
	Dec. 18, Germans began the Ardennes counteroffensive.		Dec. 25, Leyte in American hands.
1945	Jan. 17, Soviet forces captured Warsaw. Jan. 28, Battle of the Bulge ended. Feb. 4-12, Yalta Conference. Feb. 13, Soviet forces captured Budapest.		Jan. 9, Americans landed at Lingayen Gulf. Jan. 28, Ledo Road completed.
	Mar. 7, Americans captured Remagen Bridge and crossed the Rhine.		Feb. 19, Americans landed on Iwo Jima. Feb. 23, Japanese resistance in Manila ended.
	Mar. 25, The Saar in American hands.		Mar. 22, British captured Mandalay. Apr. 1, Americans invaded Okinawa.
	Apr. 13, Soviet forces captured Vienna. Apr. 18, German resistance in Ruhr ended. Apr. 21, Americans captured Nuremberg. Apr. 28, Mussolini shot by partisans. Apr. 29, Axis forces surrendered in Italy. May 1, Hitler's death announced.		

EVENTS THAT TOOK PLACE AT ABOUT THE SAME TIME (Cont.)

YEAR	EUROPE	AFRICA	PACIFIC AND THE FAR EAST
1945 *cont.*	May 2, Berlin in hands of Soviet forces. May 7-8, Germans signed acts of surrender.		May 4, British captured Rangoon. July 5, Gen. MacArthur announced Philippine Islands liberated. July 26, Potsdam ultimatum delivered to Japan. Aug. 6, First atom bomb dropped on Hiroshima. Aug. 8, Russia declared war on Japan. Aug. 9, Second atom bomb dropped on Nagasaki. Aug. 14, Japanese surrender announced. Sept. 2, Japanese signed act of surrender on *U.S.S. Missouri.*

D-DAY, JUNE 1944. American invasion forces land on a beachhead in the north of France. Smoke in the background is from supporting fire by the Navy.

MARSHAL TITO. Below, the Premier of Jugoslavia in his summer home at Bled. After Tito's partisan troops proved effective against the Nazis, his control of the country made him a key figure in the "cold war" between the U.S.S.R. and the Western powers.

Belgian Government Information Center

BATTLE OF THE BULGE. Above, Americans in Belgium during the battle which cost many lives.

ZUKOV AND EISENHOWER, below. Zukov headed the Russian assault on Germany from the east, while Eisenhower was supreme commander of U.S. and British forces in the west.

British Information Service

SWORD OF STALINGRAD. Presented at Teheran; inscribed "To the steelhearted citizens of Stalingrad. The gift of King George VI, in token of the homage of the British people."

GOERING UNDER GUARD. Above, the Reich Marshal is permitted to sit for a photograph, in the witness box at the Nuremburg trials.

QUISLING IN THE DOCK. Vidkun Quisling, pale-faced, faces an accusing world during his trial in 1945. The Norwegian whose name became a synonym for treason was executed.

PIERRE LAVAL ON TRIAL. Above, the former premier consults his lawyer during the trial which resulted in a death sentence.

PETAIN IN COURT, still wearing his seven stars as Marshal of France. Henri Philippe Petain, head of the Nazi-dominated Vichy government, was given a death sentence which was commuted to life imprisonment.

PART XII

The Quest for a Lasting Peace

With the ending of the Second World War the victorious nations began the quest for a lasting peace. In a great international conference at San Francisco a charter was drawn up and adopted for the United Nations. This gave it an organization and powers which all hoped would make it succeed where the League of Nations had failed. Steps were taken also to assist in the economic rebuilding of the distressed nations and to promote good cultural relations among all men.

The postwar world faced many difficulties. The conquered nations presented serious problems for the victors. Peace treaties had to be drawn up, boundaries settled, and reparations provided for. The political and economic life of these nations had to be rebuilt, completely in the case of Germany. Their power to make war again had to be effectively destroyed. The principles of democracy had to be instilled into the Germans and the Japanese. The victorious nations had also to set their own houses in order, demobilize their troops, restore agriculture, and rebuild trade and industry on a peacetime basis. Above all, the United Nations had to be made a going concern.

These problems were all complicated by acute shortages of materials, inflation, black markets and political and social tensions which were increased in intensity by the spread of Communism.

All of these problems the victorious nations set themselves valiantly to solve. All the machinery of peace at home and abroad was put into operation. The organs of the United Nations began to meet and deal with pressing international questions. The growing tension between the Soviet Union on the one hand and the United States and Great Britain, often joined by France on the other hand, has made it difficult for the United Nations to accomplish much. Yet it has attained some success and perhaps will do more in the future. Inside the nations, in spite of much suffering and many conflicts, many solid advances have been achieved. Much still remains to be done, however, if the people of the world are to enjoy the blessings of the democratic way of life under a sure and lasting peace.

CHAPTER 36

The Establishment of the United Nations

While the armed forces of the United Nations were fighting and winning the terrible war that we have just described, statesmen were planning an international organization to prevent future wars. In 1943 the United States House of Representatives adopted a resolution which pledged its approval of the entrance of the United States into an international organization to prevent war. Soon after, the United States Senate adopted a similar resolution. In 1944 representatives of the United States, Great Britain, the Soviet Union, and China drew up the Dumbarton Oaks Proposals. In February, 1945, President Roosevelt, Prime Minister Churchill, and Premier Stalin called the San Francisco Conference. This conference, which made use of the Dumbarton Oaks Proposals, drew up the United Nations Charter. The chief purpose of the United Nations is to preserve a lasting peace.

Other conferences were held during the Second World War. The Bretton Woods Conference drew up plans for an International Monetary Fund and also for an International Bank. The Quebec Conference set up the Food and Agricultural Organization. A conference in Washington, D. C., adjourned to Atlantic City, N. J., where it established the United Nations Relief and Rehabilitation Administration to help distressed peoples in war-torn countries. A conference in London drew up the constitution of the United Nations Educational, Scientific, and Cultural Organization (UNESCO).

• • •

The United Nations planned for peace during the Second World War. In August, 1941, four months before Pearl Harbor, President Roosevelt and Prime Minister Churchill met on a warship in the North Atlantic and wrote the Atlantic Charter. In this charter they called the attention of the world to the supreme need for "a peace which will afford to all nations the means of dwelling in safety within their own boundaries" and for the "establishment of a wider and permanent system of general security."

By the middle of 1943 when it had become evident that the United Nations would eventually subdue their Axis enemies, public opinion in the United Nations began to call for an organization intended to maintain a lasting peace. In September, 1943, the United States House of Representatives adopted the Fulbright Resolution which pledged the House to support the participation of the United States in an organization to "establish and to maintain a just and lasting peace." A few weeks later the adoption of Senator Connally's Resolution pledged the United States Senate to support the creation of an international organization for peace.

In October, 1943, President Roosevelt sent Secretary of State Cordell Hull to Moscow to

Official United Nations

United Nations Conference on International Organization, met in San Francisco, May, 1945. This conference drafted the Charter of the United Nations.

meet with the foreign ministers of the Soviet Union, Great Britain, and China to explore the possibilities of carrying on the war more effectively and the means of maintaining a lasting peace after the war. These four statesmen drew up and signed the Moscow Declaration. It stated that the four great powers believed it was necessary to establish as soon as possible an international organization which would be open to all peace-loving countries both large and small.

The Moscow Declaration's emphasis on creating a world security organization at the earliest possible moment speeded the work already begun in the United States. In 1941 the United States Department of State had set up an Advisory Committee on Postwar Foreign Policies. It consisted of high officials in the State Department, leading members of the Senate and of the House of Representatives, and distinguished experts in many different fields who did not hold positions in the government. This committee made a very elaborate and careful study of postwar problems. Using the material compiled and the report made by the Advisory Committee, an-

other committee was set up in the State Department to draft a concrete proposal for an international peace and security organization. In July, 1944, the American proposal was submitted to the British, Soviet, and Chinese governments. Shortly thereafter, each of these governments submitted a draft of its proposals to the government of the United States. On invitation of Secretary of State Hull, representatives of the United States, Great Britain, the Soviet Union, and China met (August, 1944) at Dumbarton Oaks, Washington, D. C., to make a final draft. This conference, after seven weeks of discussion, issued the Dumbarton Oaks Proposals, a plan for an international security organization which had been worked out from the drafts made by the four powers.

The next step toward the goal of international security was taken by the Big Three— Roosevelt, Churchill, and Stalin—at the Yalta Conference in the Crimea in February, 1945. The Crimea Declaration announced that a conference of the United Nations would meet on April 25, 1945, at San Francisco to draw up a charter for the United Nations based on the Dumbarton Oaks Proposals. Between the publication of the Dumbarton Oaks Proposals and the opening of the San Francisco Conference a tremendous amount of public discussion took place. The Department of State distributed nearly 2,000,000 copies of the Dumbarton Oaks Proposals, furnished speakers for 250 speaking engagements, and assisted in the preparation of a motion picture film and of a radio series explaining the proposals. It is interesting to note that the Department of State received weekly as many as 20,000 letters relating to them.

The San Francisco Conference drew up the Charter of the United Nations. The San Francisco Conference met on April 25, 1945, and was in session until June 26. Two hundred eighty-two delegates from fifty governments assisted by about 5,000 advisers took part. More than 2,500 representatives of the press, radio, and newsreels reported the activities of the Conference. The services of 120 interpreters and translators were required. The cost of the Conference, which amounted to nearly $2,000,000, was paid by the United States.

The most notable delegates were the chairmen of the delegations of the five great powers; the chairmanship of the sessions of the Conference rotated among them. These chairmen were Edward R. Stettinius (United States); Vyacheslav M. Molotov (Soviet Union); Anthony Eden (Great Britain); T. V. Soong (China); and Georges Bidault

GENERAL JAN C. SMUTS IN HIS LIBRARY AT PRETORIA, SOUTH AFRICA. He played a noteworthy part in drafting the Covenant of the League of Nations and also the Charter of the United Nations.

The Honorable Dr. Herbert Vere Evatt, when Attorney General of Australia and Minister for External Affairs, figured prominently in the early conferences of the United Nations, where he expressed the viewpoints of the smaller nations.

(France). Mention should also be made of General Jan Christian Smuts of the Union of South Africa, who had shared in drafting the Covenant of the League of Nations, and of Dr. Herbert Evatt of Australia, the eloquent spokesman of the small nations. The United States delegation appointed by President Roosevelt consisted of Chairman Edward R. Stettinius; Secretary of State Cordell Hull, Senior Advisor; Senator Tom Connally; Senator Arthur H. Vandenberg; Representative Sol Bloom; Representative Charles A. Eaton; Commander Harold E. Stassen, USNR; and Virginia C. Gildersleeve, Dean of Barnard College, Columbia University.

At the opening of the Conference a number of committees were appointed to consider specific sections of the Dumbarton Oaks Proposals. After weeks of hard work the United Nations Charter was completed. On June 26,

Acme

SIGNING OF THE UNITED NATIONS CHARTER AT SAN FRANCISCO, 1945. Representatives of fifty nations signed the Charter which is printed in five official languages: English, Russian, French, Chinese, and Spanish.

1945, the day on which the Charter was signed, the dream of Woodrow Wilson, Franklin Delano Roosevelt, and of all peace loving peoples throughout the world for a lasting peace seemed closer to realization. Under the glare of spotlights and with newsreel and newspaper cameramen recording the historic event, the delegates signed the United Nations Charter which was printed in the five languages officially agreed upon by the members of the Conference.

Addressing the delegates at the final session of the United Nations Conference, President Truman said:

> Oh, what a great day this can be in history. . . . Upon all of us, in all of our countries, is now laid the duty of transforming into action these words which you have written. Upon our decisive action rests the hope of those who have fallen, those now living, and those yet unborn—the hope for a world of free countries—with decent standards of living—which will work and co-operate in a friendly, civilized community of nations. .

The Charter provided that after the five great powers (the United States, the Union of Soviet Socialist Republics, Great Britain, China, and France) and a majority of all other signers ratified the Charter, the United Nations would set up an organization to carry on its work. By October, 1945, the required number of nations had ratified the Charter and plans were then begun to build the new international organization.

The fifty nations represented at the San Francisco Conference and Poland became *original* members of the United Nations by ratifying the Charter. Any other "peaceloving" nation may be admitted by a two-thirds vote of the General Assembly of the United Nations upon recommendation of the Security Council. Also upon recommendation of the Security Council, the General Assembly may suspend a member nation and thereby prevent it from exercising its rights and privileges as a member. The Security Council may restore a suspended member to its rights and privileges. A member who persistently violates the principles of the Charter may be expelled from the organization by the General Assembly on the recommendation of the Security Council. The Charter does not contain any provision that specifically permits or prohibits the withdrawal of a member.

The United Nations pledged themselves to accomplish the noble purposes set forth in the Charter. These noble purposes are (1) to prevent war, (2) to settle international disputes by peaceful means, (3) to develop friendly relations among nations based on respect for the principle of equal rights and self-determination of peoples, and (4) to improve economic and social conditions throughout the world. To achieve these purposes each member nation made four solemn promises: (1) to settle peacefully its disputes with other nations, (2) to refrain from using force contrary to the provisions of the Charter, (3) to support the United Nations in carrying out the provisions of the Charter and to refrain from giving help to any nation against which the United Nations is taking action, and (4) to co-operate in raising standards of living and in solving health, educational, and racial problems.

Six principal organs do the work of the United Nations. These organs are (1) the General Assembly, (2) the Security Council, (3) the Economic and Social Council, (4) the Trusteeship Council, (5) the International Court of Justice, (6) the Secretariat.

The General Assembly. All members of the United Nations are represented in the General Assembly. Each member nation has one vote but can send as many as five representatives. Thus all nations are equal in the General Assembly. A two-thirds vote is required to decide a major question; a majority vote decides all other questions. The General Assembly meets annually, but it may hold special sessions at the request of the Security Council or of a majority of the United Nations.

The General Assembly has the power:

(1) to discuss any question affecting peace and security;

(2) to make recommendations for the settlement of any dispute unless the Security Council is already dealing with it;

(3) to study other subjects stated in the Charter and make recommendations regarding them;

(4) to admit new members, to suspend the rights and privileges of a member, and to expel a member;

(5) to elect the six non-permanent members of the Security Council, the eighteen members of the Economic and Social Council, and all members of the Trusteeship Council except the five permanent members;

(6) to elect a Secretary-General on recommendation of the Security Council, and with the Security Council to choose the members of the International Court of Justice;

(7) to control the budget.

The General Assembly is a forum in which any member has the right to present the views of his country and to promote its interests. In November, 1947, the General Assembly set up a committee composed of one representative from each member nation. This Little Assembly considers dangerous situations if the General Assembly is not in session.

The Security Council. It consists of eleven members, five permanent and six non-permanent. The five permanent members are the United States, the Union of Soviet Socialist Republics, Great Britain, China, and France. The six non-permanent members are elected by the General Assembly for two-year terms. To insure rotation among the non-permanent members, they are not eligible for re-election at the expiration of their terms.

The rules governing voting in the Security Council were formulated by the Big Three in the Yalta Conference and later written into the Charter at the San Francisco Conference.

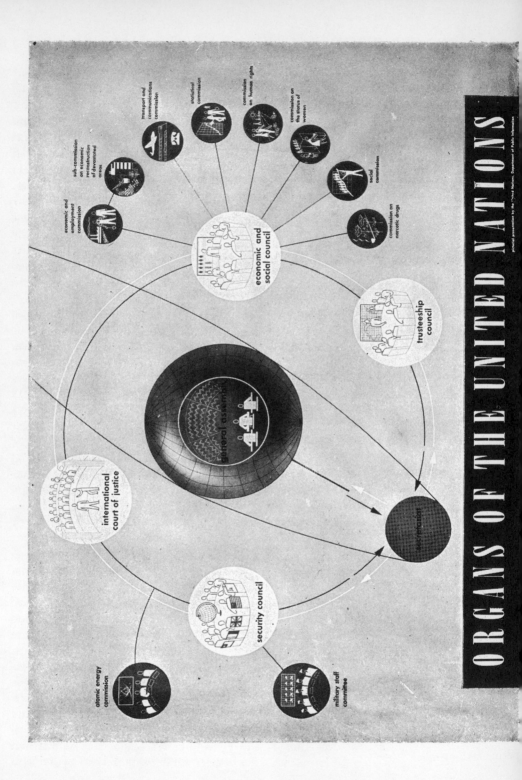

ORGANS OF THE UNITED NATIONS

pictorial presentation by the United Nations, Department of Public Information

economic and employment commission

sub-commission on economic reconstruction of devastated areas

transport and communications commission

statistical commission

commission on human rights

commission on the status of women

social commission

commission on narcotic drugs

economic and social council

trusteeship council

general assembly

international court of justice

security council

secretariat

atomic energy commission

military staff committee

Each of the eleven members of the Security Council has one vote. When the question under consideration is one of procedure, that is, what subjects shall be considered, the votes of *any seven members* decide the question. On all other questions, including recommendations and proposals for action by the United Nations, the votes of seven members *including the votes of all the permanent members decide the question.* However, in a decision with respect to the peaceful settlement of a dispute a party or parties to that dispute must abstain from voting. This means that if Great Britain and France were engaged in a dispute, they would have to abstain from voting when the Security Council proposed a solution of the dispute. The Security Council holds meetings from time to time and *is so organized that it is able to function continuously.*

The major purpose of the Security Council is to maintain international peace and security and to see to it, if possible, that nations settle their disputes peacefully. Every member of the United Nations promises to settle a dispute with another member by peaceful methods—negotiation, mediation, arbitration, or judicial settlement by the International Court of Justice.

Let us suppose that Nation A and Nation B fail to make use of these methods even when called upon to do so by the Security Council. Then the Security Council may decide to look into the dispute, or the General Assembly, or any member of the United Nations, or one of the parties to the dispute may ask the Security Council to look into it. Then the Council can take the following steps to settle the dispute:

(1) By vote of any seven members, the Council can decide to discuss the dispute.

(2) After the dispute is discussed, an investigation can be ordered by the affirmative vote of seven members, including all the permanent members.

(3) After investigation, the Security Council can recommend to Nation A and Nation B a peaceful method of settlement.

(4) If Nation A refuses to accept this peaceful settlement, the Security Council can "get tough" with Nation A. It can now call upon the members of the United Nations to use against A any or all of these drastic measures short of war: breaking off diplomatic relations, partial or complete stoppage of commercial and financial relations, and the suspension of communication by rail, sea, air, wire, radio, and any other means of communication. If the other members of the United Nations stand together, Nation A will certainly hesitate before bringing such effective measures down on its head.

(5) If Nation A still persists in refusing a peaceful settlement, the Security Council has a powerful weapon left. It can use air, land, and naval forces against Nation A. For this purpose each member of the United Nations agrees to have immediately available air forces and to furnish its quota of land and sea forces necessary to maintain peace and security. A Military Staff Committee, consisting of the Chiefs of Staff of the permanent members of the Council or their representatives, will be responsible for the strategic direction of the armed forces placed at the disposal of the Council.

The Economic and Social Council. One purpose of this Council is to improve standards of living and to promote economic and social progress. It consists of eighteen members of the United Nations elected by the General Assembly for a term of three years. A retiring member is not eligible for re-election at the expiration of its term. Each of the eighteen member nations is allowed one vote.

The chief purpose of the Economic and Social Council is to secure international cooperation in economic and social matters. It is charged with the responsibility of trying to

Official United Nations

This is a photograph of the first Military Staff Committee of the United Nations. This committee advises the Security Council on military matters.

get nations to co-operate to increase trade and thereby to improve standards of living, to promote a greater respect for human rights, to provide education for more people, to control more effectively epidemic diseases, and to protect and to improve the health of peoples everywhere in the world.

To carry out its responsibility, the Economic and Social Council is given the power: (1) to make studies of international economic and social problems, (2) to make reports and recommendations based on these studies to the General Assembly, (3) to call international conferences, (4) to co-ordinate the work of special agencies such as the International Labor Organization, the United Nations Educational, Scientific, and Cultural Organization, and others. In his report to the President, former Secretary of State Edward R. Stettinius said of the Economic and Social Council, "The battle for peace has to be fought on two fronts. The first is the security front where victory spells freedom from fear. The second is the economic and social front where victory means freedom from want. Only victory on both fronts can assure the world of an enduring peace." The Economic and Social Council is dedicated to the task of achieving freedom from want.

The Trusteeship Council. It was created to insure the political, economic, social, and educational advancement of dependent peoples

Official United Nations

Mrs. Franklin D. Roosevelt listens intently at a meeting of the Commission on Human Rights of the United Nations Economic and Social Council, of which she was chairman.

The Charter itself does not place any territories under the supervision of the Trusteeship Council. It simply provides that agreements may be made by nations governing such territories to place them under the *supervision* of the Trusteeship Council. Three classes of territories are mentioned in the Charter: 1) territories placed under a mandate of the League of Nations after the First World War, (2) territories taken from enemy nations as a result of the Second World War, 3) territories that may be placed voluntarily under trusteeship by nations now governing them.

Membership in the Trusteeship Council is divided equally between those members of the United Nations who administer trust territories and those who do not, but it must include the five permanent members of the Security Council. The General Assembly elects all except the five permanent members. The Charter gives the Trusteeship Council

power to see to it that nations who administer trust territories govern them in the best interests of their inhabitants and even assist them to become self-governing and eventually independent. It can require annual reports from the nation governing a trust territory, visit a trust territory to see whether it is well-governed, consider petitions from the people, and even govern a trust territory. Thus it is hoped that people living in a trust territory will be governed justly and fairly rather than exploited as has so often happened in the past.

The International Court of Justice. This Court consists of fifteen judges no two of whom may be citizens of the same country. They are elected by the General Assembly and the Security Council for a term of nine years, and a judge is eligible for re-election at the expiration of his term. The Court is to sit at The Hague in the Netherlands, but may sit elsewhere whenever the Court considers it

Official United Nations

First United Nations Secretary-General, Trygve Lie of Norway, seals agreement on narcotic drugs.

advisable. All decisions are made by a major-ity vote. Every member of the United Nations becomes a member of the International Court of Justice when it ratifies the United Nations Charter. A nation that is not a member of the United Nations can become a member of the Court upon recommendation of the Se-curity Council on conditions determined by the General Assembly.

Only nations may be parties in a case tried by the International Court of Justice. It has the power to decide only those legal disputes involving international law that are volun-tarily submitted to it. The Court must render advisory opinions on questions of interna-

tional law or the interpretation of a treat when so requested by the Security Council o the General Assembly. Just as nations provid courts in which their citizens may have thei legal disputes decided, so the United Nation now provides a court, the International Cour of Justice, in which nations may have their in ternational legal disputes decided.

The Secretariat. The Secretariat consist of the Secretary-General and his staff. Th Secretary-General is the chief administrativ officer of the United Nations. He is electe by the General Assembly upon recommenda tion of the Security Council. He chooses hi own staff with due consideration for compe tence and distribution by nations. The Secretary-General has one power which the Secretary-General of the League of Nations did not have. He can bring to the attention of the Security Council any international question which he believes may lead to war. The Secretary-General and his staff do the routine work of the United Nations. They conduct its correspondence, make preparations for its meetings, register treaties, prepare an annual report to the General Assembly, and perform other duties assigned to the Secretariat by the other principal organs of the United Nations.

The United Nations Charter can be amended. Two steps must be taken before it can be amended. First, the proposed amendment must be adopted by a two-thirds vote of the members of the General Assembly. Second, the proposed amendment must then be ratified by the governments of two thirds of the members, *including all five permanent members.* Thus the United Nations Charter cannot be amended without the consent of two thirds of the United States Senate. A conference to consider revision of the Charter may be called by a two-thirds vote of the General Assembly and a majority of the Security Council. If a conference has not been called to consider revision of the Charter, then the tenth annual session of the Assembly will decide whether to call such a meeting.

The Bretton Woods Conference drew up plans for international financial co-operation. In July, 1944, delegates from forty-four countries met at Bretton Woods, New Hampshire, to draw up plans (1) to help revive and expand international trade, and (2) to make loans of money at a low rate of interest and on long terms available to countries whose industries and agriculture were damaged during the Second World War. Loans on the same terms are to be made to countries that need money to develop industries. To accomplish these purposes, the delegates drew up plans for the International Monetary Fund and the International Bank for Reconstruction and Development. The United Nations Charter gives the Economic and Social Council power to make agreements between these two financial agencies and the United Nations.

The chief purpose of the International Monetary Fund is to help increase trade among nations. The delegates at Bretton Woods believed that if they could do something to increase trade, industrial and agricultural production would be increased and employment would rise. They provided two principal ways to help increase international trade. (1) The nations that contribute to the International Monetary Fund state the value of their own currency in relation to the currency of other countries. These values must be stated in terms of gold, or in terms of American dollars. Thereafter the value of the currency of each country may go up or down only 1 per cent. This nearly constant value of the currency of a country prevents an importer in London engaged in the business of selling American automobiles from going bankrupt because a sudden rise in the exchange value of the American dollar forces him to pay out a greater number of British pounds to buy automobiles than the number of pounds that he has agreed to sell them for to his customers in Britain.

(2) The capital of the International Monetary Fund is about $8,000,000,000, contributed by the members according to their economic strength. Because the economic strength of the United States is very great, it has paid the largest amount ($2,750,000,-000). Although the Soviet Union participated in the Bretton Woods Conference, it did not join the Fund.

When the value of the goods a country imports from another country is greater than the value of the goods it exports to that country, we say it has an unfavorable balance of trade. The balance has to be paid in gold or in the money of the country from which the goods were imported. If the country with the unfavorable balance of trade does not have any gold, it can deposit some of its own money in the International Monetary Fund and get in return the money of the country from which the goods were imported. For example, if Great Britain needed American dollars to pay for an unfavorable balance of trade, it would deposit British pounds in the Fund and get American dollars to pay its unfavorable trade balance. British importers would thus be able to pay for goods they bought from American producers and American producers would have a market for their goods in Great Britain.

A Board of Governors consisting of one Governor appointed by each member nation determines the policies that govern the use of the International Monetary Fund, but a smaller board carries out these policies. The more money a country has contributed to the Fund, the more votes it has. The United States has about 27 per cent of the votes because it is the largest contributor. A member nation may withdraw from the Fund any time it chooses to do so.

The International Bank makes loans to countries and to private companies. The delegates at Bretton Woods assumed that countries whose industries and agriculture had been devastated in the Second World War would need to borrow money for reconstruction. This need was the principal reason for setting up the International Bank. It has an authorized capital of $10,000,000,000 from which it can make loans. Capital is provided by the nations who are members of the Bank. The share of the United States is $3,175,000,000. As the Soviet Union is not a member of the Fund, it cannot belong to the Bank. The Bank makes its loans direct to countries and to private businesses and guarantees loans made by private banks.

The International Bank will not loan money to countries and private companies so long as they can get loans for productive purposes from private banks anywhere on reasonable terms. Two examples illustrate the kind of loans made by the International Bank. In 1947 the Bank loaned the government of France $250,000,000 to assist it in financing the reconstruction and development of French economic life disrupted by the war. The government of Chile has negotiated two loans to finance the development of hydro-electric power and the purchase of agricultural machinery. The terms of loans vary according to the type of the loans. The French loan was for twenty years.

The International Bank also guarantees loans made by private banks for which it charges a commission.

A Board of Governors consisting of one Governor appointed by each member nation determines the policies of the International Bank, but a smaller board of directors carries out these policies. The United States has a little more than 38 per cent of the votes.

The Food and Agriculture Organization was formed to help achieve "freedom from want." In 1943 representatives from forty-four countries met in a conference at Hot Springs, Virginia, to consider world food and agriculture problems. The members of the conference agreed that the first task of the United Nations was to win the war and then to free millions of people from hunger. They agreed also that during the period of critical food shortages certain to occur immediately after the war all nations should co-operate to increase the production of foodstuffs and to distribute as much as they could spare to peoples in want. The Hot Springs Conference hoped that the nations of the world would take measures which would lead to greater production and better distribution of the products of farms, fisheries, and forests.

The Hot Springs Conference drew up a declaration which contained broad recommendations to increase world agricultural production and to improve distribution and chose a temporary commission to make a constitution for a permanent organization. In 1945 at Quebec a second conference set up the Food and Agriculture Organization of the United Nations (FAO). By 1946, forty-two nations had become members of FAO.

The aim of FAO is "to make good nutrition, good health, and good standards of living for everyone the goal of world policies in agriculture, forestry, and fisheries." To accomplish this aim FAO (1) promotes scientific research in nutrition, agriculture, conservation of natural resources, marketing, and other related subjects; (2) collects and sends out to governments information on food and agriculture; (3) recommends national and international action on problems relating to food and agriculture; and (4) furnishes technical assistance to governments on request.

The members of FAO hold conferences to decide policies and at these conferences each member has one vote. An Executive Committee carries out the policies decided upon by the conference.

The United Nations Relief and Rehabilitation Administration (UNRRA) helped distressed people in liberated countries in Europe and the Far East. During the Second World War Axis armies overran thirty-five countries in Europe and Asia. In Europe the number of "displaced persons" was estimated to be more than 12,000,000. In China they were estimated to be 40,000,000. Displaced persons consisted of prisoners of war who worked for the enemy, persons who were taken forcibly from their homes in occupied countries and compelled to work for the enemy, and many others who had fled from their homes to escape the ravages of war.

To cope with this gigantic problem, representatives from forty-four nations in 1943 in Washington, D. C., signed an agreement which established UNRRA. Then the representatives went to Atlantic City, New Jersey, to decide in conference what should and could be done to get relief to suffering peoples in Europe and Asia. The Atlantic City Conference decided that UNRRA should (1) furnish needy peoples with food, clothing, fuel, medicines, household supplies, seeds, fertilizers, and other materials; (2) provide health and welfare services; (3) help displaced persons to return to their homes; and (4) furnish machinery needed to increase agricultural production, the boats and equipment needed to increase the catch of fish, and the machinery needed to restore public utilities. When UNRRA was disbanded (1949), its final report disclosed an expenditure of nearly $4,000,000,000, 73 per cent given by the United States.

The United Nations Educational, Scientific, and Cultural Organizations (UNESCO) was formed to promote international co-operation in education, science, and culture. In November, 1945, delegates from forty-three nations who met in London drew up the Constitution of the United Nations Educational, Scientific, and Cultural Organization.

The purposes of the members of UNESCO are (1) to co-operate in the work of helping the peoples of the different nations to know more about one another so that there may be better understanding among them; (2) to help spread popular education; and (3) to maintain, increase, and spread knowledge by protecting the world's inheritance of books and works of art, by exchanging teachers and others active in the field of education, and by making publications widely available.

UNESCO has sponsored international meetings of teachers to develop methods and materials for increasing understanding among peoples. It has sent educational missions to several countries and has projected the translation of the world's great books into many languages. The headquarters of UNESCO are in Paris, France. The Soviet Union is the only great power that is not a member of UNESCO. In the United States, UNESCO's program is carried out by a National Commission of distinguished leaders in many fields.

The UN has enjoyed successes and experienced failures. Like the League of Nations, the UN has perhaps enjoyed its greatest successes in carrying out projects through its specialized agencies to promote human welfare. During its existence of about five years the International Refugee Organization resettled more than a million displaced persons and returned about 73,000 to their native countries. The International Children's Emergency Fund vaccinated more than 14,000,000 children in various countries. At one time it was feeding more than four million children in Europe. It has taken measures in all Asian countries to improve the care of children and to control their diseases. The World Health Organization has done much to combat tuberculosis, malaria, typhus, and certain tropical diseases. A Universal Declaration of Human Rights and a Convention on Genocide have been drawn up. However, no measures have yet been devised to make them effective and perhaps they never can be made so, as they involve deep questions of national sovereignty. Nevertheless, a reading of them might tend to prick the conscience of mankind.

Like the League of Nations again, the UN has been able to settle conflicts in which major powers were not seriously involved. Some of these will be discussed later in this volume. The UN has not been able to settle conflicts involving major powers. It could not prevent the Korean War nor would UN military action have been possible if the Soviet Union had been represented in the Security Council and thus able to use its veto. The Indo-China War was not made a matter for UN action even though its implications were international. No solution has been reached on the international control of atomic energy or on disarmament, but, of course, these are very knotty problems which will require a very long time to solve. At any rate the UN provides an international forum where viewpoints can be expressed and grievances voiced. Through discussion solutions are sometimes reached.

SUMMARY

We have traced the development of the idea that peace-loving nations should form an organization to establish and maintain a just and lasting peace. The Atlantic Charter, the Moscow Declaration, the Dumbarton Oaks Proposals, and the Crimea Declaration prepared the ground for the San Francisco Conference where representatives from fifty nations wrote the United Nations Charter.

The United Nations Charter set forth the framework of the United Nations. Six principal organs do the work of this international organization. The General Assembly provides a forum where all members can present their views. The Security Council is chiefly responsible for the peaceful settlement of international disputes and is authorized to take economic and military action against an aggressor. The Economic and Social Council is intended to promote economic and social progress; the Trusteeship Council to help insure fair treatment of dependent peoples. The International

Court of Justice hears and decides international disputes legal in nature. The Secretariat does the routine work of the United Nations.

While the Second World War was going on, the United Nations held other conferences which created international organizations to deal with problems that concerned the peoples of the world. The Bretton Woods Conference created the International Monetary Fund and the International Bank. The Hot Springs and Quebec Conferences established the Food and Agriculture Organization to help the people of the world produce more foodstuffs to the end that they may be better fed. The Washington and Atlantic City Conferences set up UNRRA to feed and care for millions of people in countries devastated by war. The first General Conference of UNESCO in Paris laid out more than 100 projects for this international organization to carry out.

These international conferences show that men from all over the world, speaking different languages and differing in race and religion, can get together around a conference table and create organizations to help solve world problems and work for enduring peace.

French Press and Information Service.

U. S. DELEGATION. At the Conference of Foreign Ministers held in Paris in April, 1946, the United States was represented by a delegation headed by Secretary of State James F. Byrnes, center. At Byrnes' right sits Senator Tom Connally of Texas, chairman of the Foreign Affairs Committee of the Senate. Senator Vandenberg, Republican collaborator in the "bi-partisan foreign policy," is seen in profile at the extreme right. (Photographed at the Luxembourg Palace.)

CHINESE "REDS" ATTACK. Above, Communist forces machine-gun a Nationalist stronghold. According to the Russian photographer, the gun is American-made—i.e., was captured from Nationalists using U. S. arms.

MAO TSE-TUNG. Leader both in the Chinese civil war and in the formation of the Central People's government, Mao Tse-tung, left, is still a young man.

HO CHI MINH, left, below, leads the leftwing movement in French Indochina. His position, recognized by the Soviet Union, parallels that of Mao Tse-tung in China.

CANTON PARADE. Below, crowds greet Communist victors, given flowers as they march in triumph through Canton.

CHAPTER 37

National Developments Since the Second World War

The Second World War left the Axis Nations in a state of utter collapse, several of the United Nations heavily devastated, and nearly all of them greatly weakened. The postwar years have been full of political and economic stresses and strains. For most peoples the problems of reconstruction and recovery have overshadowed all others. But nearly everywhere the work of reconstruction and recovery has been hampered by acute shortages of fuel, industrial and agricultural equipment, manpower, and various kinds of consumer goods. Inflation has been a besetting difficulty, black markets have flourished, and prices have been very high. At the same time, conflicting political ideals have produced tensions and political instability on a wide front, and in some countries, especially China, they have rendered united governmental action impossible.

• • •

Great Britain faced grave domestic problems. When the Germans surrendered unconditionally (May, 1945), a general election was long overdue in Great Britain. Prime Minister Churchill conferred immediately with Clement Attlee, leader of the Labor Party, and asked him to continue the all-party coalition government until the unconditional surrender of Japan, but Attlee refused. Consequently, Parliament was dissolved in June and a general election was held (July 5, 1945) in which the Labor party won a clear majority of seats in the new House. Attlee then became Prime Minister and formed a Labor government which took office (August 5, 1945). Nine days later Japan surrendered and the Labor party was able to turn its attention to the grave domestic problems which resulted from almost six years of warfare.

These problems were perhaps the most baffling the British government had ever faced. The Second World War had exerted a terrific strain on the government and people of Great Britain. It had left the government financially weak and the people tired. Moreover, India, Burma, Palestine, and other parts of the Empire were restless. The long all-out war effort had cost the British much of their foreign trade, forced them to sell about $5,000,000,000 worth of bonds and stocks which they had owned in foreign countries, and added about $14,000,000,000 to the foreign debt. It had also raised taxes to levels never reached before, reduced the British merchant marine by more than 30 per cent, left British industry in need of large quantities of new equipment, and many homes, stores, and factories in ruins. Moreover, a low birth rate over several decades and the loss of hundreds of thousands of men in the war reduced the labor supply. All these dire consequences boded ill for the economic reconstruction of Great Britain.

The economic life of the British people is based primarily on manufacturing and world-wide commerce. To live, the British must import large quantities of food and, to manufacture, they must import many industrial

Acme

Clement Attlee and his wife are cheered after the sweeping Labor party victory which made him Prime Minister.

raw materials. These imports must be paid for largely through exports of manufactures. Consequently, British economic life cannot recover without an expanding export trade. This fact goes far to explain why British statesmen have worked so hard at the meetings of the United Nations and at the conferences of the Council of Foreign Ministers to open and to expand the channels of world trade.

On February 21, 1947, the Labor government issued a White Paper under the title *Economic Survey for 1947*. This document called attention to the fact that enormous difficulties faced the nation. It stated that the British should sell abroad as many prod-

ucts as they could to get money with which to buy foodstuffs and raw materials. It insisted that there would have to be a great deal of toil and sweat if the British people were to overcome their economic difficulties.

Coal production, the very basis of British economic life, was in 1946 almost 40,000,000 tons less than it was in the year before the war began. Production in nearly every industry was hampered by want of coal. This crippling shortage was due primarily to the use of inadequate and out-of-date machinery and to severe depletion of some of the best mines. Since 1947 the British have been able to increase their production of this vital resource. Coal production for 1953 approached that of the last year before the war began. In general, the British have also been able to increase production in other fields and likewise their exports. The value in pounds sterling of British exports in 1953 was more than double that of 1938, a gain that was truly impressive.

During the years immediately after the war, the Labor government under Prime Minister Atlee (1945-1951) began to carry out its program of socialism. It purchased certain businesses and industries from their private owners. By the winter of 1950 the government had nationalized the Bank of England, the coal mines, overseas communications, railways, trucking, canal, and air systems, and health services. The iron and steel industries were nationalized in 1951.

This trend toward more and more socialism was severely criticized by the Conservatives. In October, 1951, they defeated their Labor opponents in the general election. Winston Churchill then became prime minister for the second time. One of the early acts of Churchill was to denationalize the steel and trucking industries. On February 6, 1952 George VI died and was succeeded by his daughter Elizabeth II. The new Queen honored Churchill with knighthood and thus he became Sir Winston Churchill in April, 1953.

Great Britain faced pressing imperial problems, especially in Palestine. Soon after the end of the Second World War, the Labor government began a careful re-examination of Britain's commitments in various parts of the Empire. In 1946 the British government agreed to withdraw all troops from Egypt and to grant Burma independence. In February, 1947, the Labor government announced that Britain would grant India its independence and withdraw its soldiers and officials from India in favor of responsible Indian authorities by June, 1948. India became a self-

The Royal Family is seen talking to some of the people of South Africa during its tour in 1947.

governing dominion in 1947. Burmese in favor of independence were in a majority in the election (1947) and Burma became an independent republic in 1948, the year that Ceylon attained the status of a self-governing dominion.

In many ways Palestine has been Britain's most trying imperial problem during the postwar period. Palestine is a small agricultural land (about as large as the state of Vermont) lying between the River Jordan and the Mediterranean Sea. Of its population of less than 2,000,000 about 600,000 are Jews and about 1,100,000 Arabs. Friction between Arab and Jew is old and deepseated. After the collapse of the Turkish Empire in the First World War, the Holy Land passed into British hands and in 1917 Lord Balfour urged that it be made into a Jewish Homeland. In 1923 Britain assumed control of Palestine under a mandate granted by the League of Nations. Since then the Holy Land has been a source of trouble to British leaders. Between 1921 and 1947 eight committees studied the Palestinian problem in an effort to arrive at a workable arrangement. The Arabs bitterly resisted every British attempt to develop Palestine into a National Homeland for the Jews.

After the Second World War, Britain's

The Zulus dance before the Royal Family during its visit to South Africa in 1947. The war dance is the favorite form of recreation among the Zulus and many other tribes.

Labor government invited the United States to help it work out a solution of the Palestinian problem. An Anglo-American Committee of Inquiry studied the problem and made a rather lengthy report in April, 1946. This report recommended that the government of Palestine remain under the mandate until it could become a trustee territory under the United Nations, and that Palestine ultimately "become a State which guards the rights and interests of Moslems, Jews, and Christians alike." This compromise proposal was rejected by both Jews and Arabs. In the autumn of 1946 and winter of 1946-47, the British government, with civil strife and terrorism widespread in the Holy Land, tried to persuade Arabs and Jews to agree to a division of the country into separate Jewish and Arab provinces under the broad supervision of Britain. Neither the Jews nor the Arabs were willing to accept this arrangement. The Jews continued to insist on a single independent Jewish Homeland, and the Arabs, strongly supported by Arabs in nearby countries of the Middle East, held out for a single state under Arab control. In the face of this division of opinion between Jew and Arab, Britain announced in February, 1947, that she would submit the problem of the Holy Land to the United Nations and ask it to recommend a settlement. On November 29, 1947, the General Assembly of the United Nations voted to partition Palestine into three parts: an Arab state, a Jewish state, and Jerusalem, a trusteeship of the United Nations. On May 14, 1948, Britain withdrew her forces from Palestine and the Jewish National Council proclaimed the Republic of Israel. Severe fighting between Jews and Arabs lasted until both sides in January, 1949, accepted the Security Council's cease-fire order. By the spring of 1949 Israel and the Arab states had concluded armistices. In May, 1949, Israel was admitted to membership in the United Nations. A United Nations Palestine Conciliation Commission was set up to help settle differences between Israel and the Arab states. Ralph Bunche, United Nations Mediator after the assassination of Count Bernadotte, did much to bring about the armistices.

The Fourth French Republic was born after the liberation of France. After the Allied conquest of North Africa in the spring of 1943, a Provisional Consultative Assembly was set up in Algeria to draft plans for the government of France as soon as the Allies liberated it. This Assembly created a Committee of National Liberation, under the leadership of General Charles de Gaulle, to function as the provisional government. After Allied forces occupied Paris on August 25, 1944, this Committee took over the powers of civil government in those regions of France which had been liberated. In the course of the next few months, as the Allied armies drove the Germans out of France, it extended its control over all France, and began to struggle with the perplexing social and economic problems which resulted from the war.

On October 25, 1945, a National Constituent Assembly was elected to draft a new constitution, and to govern France until a government had been set up under this constitution. The vast majority of the seats in the Assembly were shared almost equally by three political parties—the *Movement Républican Populaire* (M.R.P.), the Socialists, and the Communists. The powerful M.R.P. party was a product of the Second World War, and claimed to represent the best elements of the Resistance forces. It is basically a progressive Catholic party calling for the spiritual rebirth of the nation and an economic system in which the French government will exercise strict control over business, industry, and agriculture, but still leave them largely under private ownership.

As party struggles quickly developed, it was soon clear that the war had done little to heal the great cleavages in French political life. De Gaulle, who had many supporters from the Center and Right, advocated a strong executive branch of government. Maurice Thorez, the leader of the Communist party, who had also many Socialist supporters, urged an all-powerful legislature of one house. On January 20, 1946, de Gaulle resigned as head of the government. Three days later, the National Constituent Assembly elected Felix Gouin, a Socialist, to take his place. On May 5, 1946, the Assembly's new Constitution, which contained many provisions sponsored by the Communists, was rejected by the French voters by about a million votes.

It was now necessary to start all over. On June 2, 1946, another National Constituent Assembly was elected. Again the M.R.P., the Socialists, and Communists emerged with the bulk of the seats. The new Assembly went to work immediately, and on September 29 it announced that the new revised Constitution was finished. Two weeks later the French voters approved the new Constitution by a sizable margin.

The Constitution of the Fourth French Republic is a compromise between the advocates of a strong executive branch of government and the advocates of a powerful legislature of one house. Full legislative power is vested in a National Assembly whose members are elected by universal suffrage for a term of five years. The second house, the Council of the Republic, is elected indirectly by communal and departmental units. It acts in an advisory capacity to the Assembly. A newly-elected Assembly cannot be dissolved during the first eighteen months of its life, and then only after two successive votes of no-confidence. This should give added stability to the French Cabinet system because it prevents a minority from overthrowing a Cabinet as was the case under the Third French Republic.

Though the powers of the President are slightly broader than under the Third Republic, the President cannot dissolve the National Assembly. He is elected by joint session of the National Assembly and the Council of the Republic for a term of seven years, and is eligible for re-election. He heads the French Union, a new imperial council which supervises the overseas possessions. Cabinet ministers are appointed by the President, but, of course, are responsible to the Assembly.

On October 28, 1946, the Constitution of the Fourth French Republic went into effect and a few days later elections were held for the National Assembly. The M.R.P. and the Communists emerged with more than half of the seats. On January 16, 1947, Vincent Auriol, a Socialist, was elected first President of the Fourth French Republic. He was succeeded in 1954 by René Coty. In the elections in 1951 both the Communists and the M.R.P. lost heavily, the Communists suffering a reduction of nearly half their membership in the National Assembly. The constitution of the Fourth French Republic has not brought political stability to France. French government, as in the past, has witnessed a rapid succession of premiers and cabinets, bewildering to France and to the world.

French economic life is recovering from the ill effects of the war. Although most of France's factories and farms were not gravely damaged by the Second World War, its transportation system, merchant marine, port facilities, and mines were hard hit. Its recovery, though in no sense spectacular, has been reasonably good. It was able to borrow about $2,000,000,000 from Great Britain and the United States within a year after the end of the war, and by 1947 France was producing a little more than 80 per cent of what it had produced before the war. Like most other countries, it has been materially hampered by inadequate coal supplies, inflation, and the black market. Inflation has been a singularly stubborn and besetting problem. Moreover, from the end of the Second World War to the signing of the truce in July, 1954, France faced the necessity of spending large

sums of money waging war in her colony of Indo-China against Communist forces led by Ho Chi Minh.

On January 10, 1947, the Monnet Plan was published. The primary aim of this Plan is the rapid modernization and mechanization of French industry and agriculture. On March 27, 1947, an agreement was signed with Italy for the transfer of 200,000 Italian workers to France during 1947. Above all, France needs more workers, stabilized prices, and a measure of political unity if she is to get on a firm footing. A program of nationalization has been cautiously pressed forward.

Belgians disagreed on the restoration of King Leopold, but united to restore the economic life of their country. On September 21, 1944, shortly after the Allied armies had freed Belgium from Nazi domination, the Belgian Parliament elected Prince Charles to serve as regent until it could be decided whether or not King Leopold should be permitted to regain the throne. The prewar Christian Social (Catholic), Liberal, and Socialist parties continued to dominate the political picture. The most powerful of the parties, the Christian Social, favored King Leopold's return to the throne and judicious and mild treatment for those charged with having collaborated with the Germans. The Liberal and Socialist parties, supported by the Communists, opposed King Leopold's return and asked that no mercy be shown to collaborators. Throughout 1945 there was considerable agitation for a referendum to determine whether Belgium should remain a liberal monarchy or become a republic. However, the supporters of limited monarchy held the upper hand, and on January 20, 1946, the Premier announced that there was no thought of allowing the principle of monarchy to become the "subject of electoral strife."

On February 17, 1946, the first postwar general election was held. Nearly half of the seats in both houses of Parliament went to the Liberal and Socialist parties. The powerful Christian Social party said that it would not participate in the government unless King Leopold were restored to the throne. The Liberal, Socialist, and Communist parties, who firmly believed that Leopold should not be restored to the throne, formed a coalition to run the government, but they had a very narrow majority. In July, 1951, King Leopold abdicated and was succeeded by his son, the Crown Prince Baudouin.

Fortunately for the Belgian people there have been no such differences of opinion concerning economic policies. Almost from the day of liberation the major parties have worked together to restore the transportation system, to increase coal production, to expand the export trade, and to control inflation. As a result of these efforts, Belgium has increased its production greatly since the day of liberation from the Germans. Like France, Belgium has encouraged the immigration of Italian workers to replace the German prisoners of war.

The Netherlands have recovered rapidly. The Netherlands suffered greater damage during the Second World War than any other country in Western Europe. At the time of liberation its railroads were largely in ruins, about 60 per cent of its prewar merchant marine had been destroyed; several of its ports were badly damaged; and over 200,000 acres of its land inundated. The Dutch people tackled their problems with energy and intelligence, and by the spring of 1947 they had made great headway toward the restoration of their roads, railroads, and canals, monetary system, and agriculture. Recovery would have been faster if the economy had not been tied up with Germany's.

Because Queen Wilhelmina, although in exile, was able to retain the loyalty of her subjects during the German occupation, the postwar political scene has been comparatively peaceful. The Catholic People's party and the Labor party, which secured the bulk of the seats in Parliament as a result of the general election of May 17, 1946, have concentrated their efforts pretty heavily on the empire. Unrest in the Netherlands East Indies led to the Malevo Conference (July, 1946). At that Conference the Netherlands government advanced proposals for the formation of a United States of Indonesia, embracing Borneo, Java, Sumatra, and the other islands in the Netherlands East Indies. An agreement between the Netherlands and the newly-formed Indonesian Republic was reached in 1947. Differences of opinion on carrying out this agreement led to warfare between Dutch and Indonesian armed forces. The United Nations intervened, got the fighting stopped, and assisted the contestants in reaching an agreement. In December, 1949, the Netherlands recognized the independence of the United States of Indonesia, a federation of 16 states. The only link between the federation and the Netherlands is that both are members of a Dutch-Indonesian Union of which the Dutch monarch is the symbolic head.

Italy became a republic. On June 5, 1944, the day after Allied forces captured Rome, King Victor Emmanuel turned over his powers to the Crown Prince, though he himself did not officially abdicate. Shortly thereafter Ivanoe Bonomi succeeded Marshal Badoglio as head of the government. The monarchical issue, which had been openly discussed since the fall of Mussolini, now became the most warmly debated political question. Opinions were sharply divided especially in the southern regions of the country where sentiment in favor of retaining the monarchy was strongest. The Committees of National Liberation, which were formed in 1943 to oppose Fascism, generally excluded those who favored monarchy. On June

22, 1944, the Bonomi government announced that the Italians would not be given an opportunity to decide whether they wanted a monarchy or a republic until the war was ended and a Constituent Assembly elected.

After the liberation of Northern Italy in the spring of 1945, republican opinion gained ground because so many workers in the industrial cities in the north favored a republic. Consequently, the struggle between monarchical and republican groups grew sharper. On May 9, 1946, King Victor Emmanuel abdicated and was succeeded by his son Humberto, who promised a liberal constitutional monarchy. On June 2, 1946, the referendum on the monarchy and elections to the Constituent Assembly were held at the same time. The vote went against the monarchy, and on June 10 the Constituent Assembly proclaimed Italy a republic.

In the Constituent Assembly the chief parties were the Christian Democrats (the progressive Catholic group) with 207 members, the Socialists with 115 members, and the Communists with 104 members. The Assembly met on June 25, 1946, and proceeded to the tasks of drafting a constitution and governing Italy until the constitution was made and accepted. Signor Enrico de Nicola was named by the Assembly Provisional President of the Republic. Alcide de Gasperi, Christian Democrat, formed a coalition cabinet and tackled the pressing economic problems that faced the country.

Italy's new constitution went into effect in January, 1948. The first election was held in April amidst great excitement and with the eyes of the world focused on the result. This election was generally regarded as a contest between the non-Communist parties, favored by the Western powers, and the Communists and their allies, favored by Russia. The United States undoubtedly exerted some influence on the election by passing the European Recovery Plan, by giving Italy twenty-nine merchant vessels, and by agreeing with Britain and France that Trieste should be restored to Italy. The election resulted in a substantial increase in seats won by the Christian Democrats, but the Communists and their allies had nearly as many seats as they had in the Constituent Assembly.

The nominal head of republican Italy under the Constitution of 1948 is a president elected for a term of seven years by the National Assembly. It elected Luigi Einaudi in May, 1948. The real executive power is in the hands of the prime minister and his cabinet, responsible to the National Assembly. Laws are made by the National Assembly, which consists of a popularly elected Chamber of Representatives and the Senate.

The Allies divided Germany into zones of occupation. After the Allied Armies had fought their way to the very heart of the Reich, Hitler authorized Grand Admiral Karl Doenitz to assume control of the government. Doenitz surrendered the remaining German forces, and on May 23, 1945, the Allies abolished his government and arrested its leading members. The Allies issued a series of orders which divided Germany into zones of occupation, each under the control of one of the victorious powers, the United States, the Soviet Union, Great Britain, and France. The cities of Berlin and Vienna were placed under joint Allied control. The victors created also an Allied Control Council (composed of the commanders-in-chief of the Big Four Powers) to sit in Berlin and act for the whole of Germany. On July 11, 1945, the Allied Control Council took over the administration of Berlin, and the plans for occupation gradually went into operation.

At the Potsdam Conference (July 17-August 2, 1945) the Big Three—Truman, Stalin, and Churchill (succeeded by Attlee) —drafted a set of plans for the control of

Acme

Stalin, Truman, and Churchill met at Potsdam, Germany, where they discussed the problems of governing defeated Germany and also the conduct of the war against Japan.

Germany during the period of occupation. Among the major points set forth in the Potsdam Declaration were (1) the disarmament and demilitarization of Germany; (2) the uprooting of Nazi institutions and the direction of German education so as to promote a democratic way of life; (3) the trial of leading Nazi war criminals; (4) the control of German industry so as to restrict the output of "metals, chemicals, machinery, and other items directly necessary to a war economy"; (5) the collection of reparations from Germany; and (6) the surrender of the territory east of the Oder and Niesse rivers to Poland and the Soviet Union until the boundaries of Eastern Germany were definitely fixed by treaty.

Germany had fought on until it was ut-terly crushed, and the situation inside the country bordered on chaos. Its whole economic and political life was completely disrupted, and over wide areas factories, mines, railroad yards, bridges, power systems, and the like were in ruins. The administration of government also collapsed during the final days of the war as hundreds of thousands of officials fled, burning or hiding their records. At the same time several million displaced persons—mostly foreign slave laborers and prisoners of war—roamed the country and added to the confusion. The problem of the restoration of order was complicated by the fact that nearly all of the ablest administrators, industrialists, and technicians were Nazis. Nearly every European country was desperately in need of goods and, to eliminate the Nazis from industry and transportation, would mean a great loss in efficiency and output. Consequently there would be fewer goods not only for Germany but for Europe as a whole. Another serious problem arose from the scarcity of able-bodied German men and the heavy preponderance of old men, cripples, women, and young children.

The United States, after a series of elections in its zone in 1946, took the initiative in handing over to the Germans the bulk of executive authority over local matters. In January, 1947, civilian courts replaced military government courts in the British zone. But in the French and Russian zones the Occupation Authorities still maintained a firm control.

The United States, Great Britain, France and the Soviet Union failed to reach an agreement on the economic and political unity of Germany. Throughout 1946 the major difficulty in the way of the execution of the Potsdam Plan was the failure of the Big Four to agree. Despite the fact that the Plan was modified considerably, there were sharp differences of opinion on practically every point. Perhaps the most spectacular and persistent point of discord was the matter of economic relations among the four zones. For various reasons Britain and the United States became anxious early in 1946 to establish full trade among all the zones of occupation as the first step toward the economic unity of the zones. The Soviet Union opposed such a move. Its zone was fairly well balanced between manufacturing and farming and the Soviet Union wanted to tie the trade of its zone to the countries of Central Europe. France, who feared above all things that a powerful Germany might rise again, tended almost instinctively to oppose trade among all the zones of occupation because it might hasten German revival. Unable to get Soviet co-operation, Britain and the United States took concrete steps in October, 1946, to abolish the trade barriers between their zones, and in 1947, put the zones under joint control.

During 1947 the Western powers and the Soviet Union drew farther and farther apart on the question of creating a united Germany. It was clear that the Soviet Union aimed to dominate any future united Germany.

In January, 1948, Secretary Bevin of Great Britain proposed that a state be set up in Western Germany composed of the areas controlled by the United States, Great Britain, and France. Accordingly, a Six-Power Conference consisting of these countries and the three Benelux states agreed, in the spring of 1948, to establish a state in Western Germany comprised of the three western zones. The Soviet Union, which had previously walked out of the Allied Control Council, replied by clamping a blockade on all ground communications between the western zones and Berlin. To supply their Berlin zones, the Western powers maintained an airlift at great expense for about a year.

In the meantime, a Parliamentary Council, composed of representatives from the states in the Western zones, framed a constitution for a federation in Western Germany. The German Federal Republic, with its capital at Bonn, began its existence in September, 1949. At this time civilian Allied Commissioners replaced the military. Eastern Germany remained under Soviet domination.

The Nuremberg War Crimes Trial was a unique event. From November 20, 1945, to October 1, 1946, twenty-two top-ranking German war leaders, along with six Nazi organizations, were tried for planning and waging offensive war and committing acts of murder and enslavement against neighboring peoples. The trial was conducted by an Allied Military Tribunal in accordance with a charter drafted by the United Nations War Crimes Commission. Many people believed that this trial would help to curb aggression

Acme

THE TRIAL OF TWENTY-ONE HIGH-RANKING NAZIS AT NUREMBERG, GER-MANY. Eleven were given death sentences; seven were sentenced to prison; three were acquitted. Goering committed suicide by taking poison before he could be executed.

in the future by holding aggressors individually responsible for acts contrary to accepted principles of international law.

The trial opened on November 20, 1945, in Nuremberg with Sir Geoffrey Lawrence of Great Britain presiding. Robert H. Jackson, Associate Justice of the Supreme Court of the United States, was the chief American prosecutor. By the beginning of March, 1946, the Prosecution had completed its case. The Counsel for the indicted Nazi leaders then opened their case. The argument used most frequently by the defendants was that they were merely tools in Hitler's hands. Field Marshal Keitel declared in the course of his defense that Hitler had ordered the murder

of all Allied fliers who fell over Germany, but that he had refused to execute the order. On July 4, 1946, the Defense finished its case. Then the six indicted Nazi organizations were tried for guilt in the murder of hundreds of thousands of people.

The verdict, containing about 100,000 words, was read on September 30 and October 1, 1946. The verdict stated: "To initiate war is not only an international crime, it is the supreme crime." Of the individual defendants, all except Hjalmar Schacht, Franz von Papen, and Hans Fritsche were found guilty on one or more charges. The sentences ranged from hanging to periods of imprisonment. Verdicts of guilty were returned

Sovfoto

ALEXIUS, THE PATRIARCH OF MOSCOW AND
OF ALL RUSSIA, IN HIS STUDY.

against the Nazi Leadership Corps, the *SS,*
the Gestapo, and *SD* (Security Agency).

**The Soviet Union turned from war to
peace.** The Second World War left a deep
imprint on the Soviet Union. It gave an enormous impulse to agricultural and industrial
expansion in its vast Eastern regions and
also produced many changes in government.
Several of the prewar autonomous Soviet
Socialist Republics were abolished. The
names of many towns, especially those bearing German names, were changed. Since the
end of the war, the Supreme Soviet has
changed the name of the Council of People's
Commissars to Council of Ministers, and has
created more than a dozen new ministries.
Although most of the new ministries are economic in character, ministries have been set
up for Higher Education and Motion Pictures. Moreover, regional ministries have
made their appearance. For the production of
coal and oil separate ministries have been

created for Western and Eastern regions.

At the same time there were significant developments in the social, religious, and educational fields. In 1944 the Presidium issued an
important decree concerning marriage, moth-
erhood, and divorce. It was designed primarily to strengthen the family and to increase the birth rate. Among other things it
provided special decorations and increased
financial aid for mothers of large families,
extended the network of child medical centers and nurseries, and made divorce a fairly
difficult and expensive procedure.

In the religious field marked improvement
occurred in the relations between the Orthodox Church and the Soviet government. From
the first the Orthodox Church gave whole-
hearted support to the war effort, and in the
autumn of 1943 Stalin authorized the creation of a Holy Synod as a ruling body for
the Church. Metropolitan Sergei of Moscow
was enthroned as Patriarch of all Russia. The
Church was granted the right to publish religious literature, to perform marriages, and
give religious instruction to children in their
homes. In February, 1946, the Russian Socialist Federated Soviet Republic, the most populous of the republics in the Soviet Union,
issued a decree exempting monasteries and
their lands from taxes. Whether this new official attitude toward religious denominations
will become permanent, no one can say.

**The goals of the Fourth Five-Year Plan
were the development of industry and agriculture and the restoration of war-torn
areas.** About the time that Japan was defeated in 1945, the Soviet authorities announced the inauguration of a Fourth Five-
Year Plan to run until 1950. This Plan was
at first officially called the First Post-War
Five-Year Plan, but the Soviet press soon began to speak of it as the Fourth Five-Year
Plan, and this title is used now. Its broad objectives were the complete restoration of the

areas devastated during the war and the "further development of the entire Soviet economy." As the months passed, details concerning the new Plan slowly came to light. In the spring and summer of 1946 the Supreme Soviet released additional information and published numerous control figures for the Fourth Five-Year Plan in many branches of industry. In such basic industries as iron, steel, coal, oil, and electric power, the production goals set for 1950 ranged from about 20 to 70 per cent above the 1940 levels. Priority was given to heavy industry, and industrial and technical schools designed to give more workers "factory-plant education" turned out new workers and technicians at maximum speed.

The new factories and plants were built in widely separated places but the Urals will remain the great hub of Russian industry, especially of the metal industries. The Soviet government has planned a great expansion of the production of chemicals, oil, and non-ferrous metals in the Urals and plans have been drawn also for bringing adequate supplies of coal from the mines near Karaganda and Kuznetsk. The industrial centers scattered across central Asia, Siberia, and the Far East were to be greatly expanded. Approximately seventy-five new power stations, most of them hydro-electric, were to be completed or begun by 1950. Perhaps the most imposing was under construction on the Angara River at Irkutsk. Soviet authorities say that it will be larger than the T.V.A. in our country. The Fourth Five-Year Plan called for the installation of 1,500,000 kw. of new power capacity in the Eastern regions alone. The tractor and automotive industry was to be greatly expanded and will remain concentrated in the regions of Gorky, Moscow, Kharkov, and Stalingrad.

The Communists defeated the Nationalists in China. After the close of the Second World War the conflict between Chiang Kai-shek's Nationalist government and the Russian-supported Chinese Communists developed into a full-scale civil war. In spite of American aid to the Nationalists, the Communist armies relentlessly advanced. By October, 1948, Manchuria was in their hands and during the next year they captured Nanking, Shanghai, Hankow, and Canton. Chiang-Kai-shek and his government fled to Formosa. In October, 1949, the Communists proclaimed the Chinese People's Republic, with its capital at Peiping, as the government of China. In February, 1950, Communist China and the Soviet Union signed a thirty-year agreement for mutual military aid.

Communist China entered the Korean conflict. After the Second World War the United States could not get the Soviet Union to agree on the creation of an independent Korean government. As a result, two governments were set up, a Communist "people's republic" north of the 38th parallel and the Republic of Korea, south of it. The latter was recognized as the legal government of Korea by the United States and the United Nations. The United States withdrew its occupation forces from southern Korea a few months later. The Soviet Union said it had withdrawn its forces from northern Korea, but the North Korean government would not permit a United Nations commission to verify it.

On June 25, 1950, North Korean forces trained and armed by the Soviet Union, without warning, crossed the 38th parallel and launched an invasion of the Republic of Korea. An emergency session of the Security Council of the United Nations held this invasion a breach of the peace and asked that it be stopped and North Korean forces withdrawn. President Truman at once ordered United States forces under General MacArthur to help carry out the Security Council's resolution by going to the aid of the South Koreans. As the conflict continued in Korea, many other nations contributed armed forces and supplies, but by far the most were American. The conflict became a United Nations conflict and General MacArthur was appointed commander of its forces.

As the South Korean and UN forces were greatly inferior in numbers and arms, they were driven southward by the North Koreans, until in August they held only a small beachhead in southeast Korea. The arrival of reinforcements enabled the UN forces in September to counterattack and to launch an amphibious attack at Inchon behind the North Korean lines. At the end of October the UN forces were completely victorious and had driven to the Korea-Manchuria border. Now a new foe entered the conflict. Communist China threw as many as 400,000 troops into North Korea from Manchuria. Suffering terrible losses at the hands of the withdrawing UN forces, the Communists drove southward and took Seoul, capital of the Republic of Korea. On March 15, 1951, however, UN troops reoccupied Seoul and later stood roughly along the 38th parallel where Communist drives in April and May failed.

While this terrible fighting was going on, Communist China rejected a UN proposal for a cease-fire arrangement made in November, 1950, and spurned a truce offered by General MacArthur in March, 1951, shortly before President Truman removed him from all his commands. On June 23, 1951, the Soviet Union proposed a cease-fire and on July 5th the UN and the Communists agreed to begin cease-fire talks at Kaesong. The spokesmen for both sides met off and on during the summer, but reached no agreement.

An armistice ended the Korean War. Shortly after the death of Stalin the truce negotiations, which had been broken off months before, were resumed at Panmunjom in April, 1953. Evidently, Malenkov, in the interest of consolidating the new Soviet regime, was now anxious to end what Stalin had instigated. An armistice was finally signed on July 27 (Tokyo time). It ended a terrible three-years' war which killed about 500,000 military personnel and civilians on the South Korean-UN side and many more on the Communist side.

In brief, the armistice made the actual battle line, almost entirely north of the 38th parallel, the dividing line between South Korea and North Korea. A demilitarized zone was set up between them. Prisoners of war were given the right to choose either to return to their original countries or to seek political refuge in the country of their choice. Although the UN forces did not win a decisive victory, they did stop North Korean aggression and thus preserved South Korean independence. They inflicted terrible losses on North Korea and her ally, Communist China. However, the problem of creating a unified Korea still remains.

SUMMARY

The postwar years have been extremely hard for most of the peoples of Europe and Asia. Efforts at recovery have been hampered by acute shortages of fuel, industrial and agricultural machinery, consumer goods, and by inflation and conflicting political aims. Great Britain, France, Belgium, the Netherlands, and Italy have all made substantial progress, though of varying degrees, toward the reparation of war damages and the restoration of production.

China, Germany, and Japan have made a start on the road to reconstruction, and the Soviet Union, with its Fourth Five-Year Plan placing primary emphasis on the restoration of its western regions, has made considerable headway. In nearly all countries much attention has been given to the further mechanization of industry, agriculture, and transportation, and to the expansion of export trade in order to pay for badly needed imports. A rather pronounced trend toward greater government regulation in industry and agriculture has been widespread.

At the same time many significant political developments have taken place. France has drafted a new constitution and created a Fourth Republic, Italy has proclaimed itself a republic, the Soviet Union has abolished some of its autonomous Republics and made important alterations in its administrative and governmental machinery. In June, 1950, North Korea backed and supplied by Soviet Russia attacked the South Korean Republic. Responding to this first test of collective security, the UN, chiefly with American forces, waged war for three years and checked this aggression.

EVENTS THAT TOOK PLACE AT ABOUT THE SAME TIME

YEAR		EVENTS
1945	May 23,	Allies abolished Doenitz government in Germany.
	July 5,	General election held in Great Britain.
	July 17-August 2,	Potsdam Conference of the Big Three.
	August 5,	British Labor Government took office.
	November 20, 1945- October 2, 1946,	Nuremberg War Crimes Trials.
1946	March 7,	Japan's provisional government proclaimed new constitution.
	March 18,	Supreme Soviet adopted the Fourth Five-Year Plan.
	May 9,	King Victor Emmanuel abdicated.
	June 2,	French voters elected second National Constituent Assembly.
	June 2,	Italian voters chose a republican form of government.
	October 13,	French voters accepted constitution of the Fourth French Republic.
	December 20,	Great Britain promised Burma independence.
1947	January 1,	United States and Great Britain merged their zones of occupation in Germany.
	February 18,	Great Britain submitted problem of Palestine to the UN.
1948	January 1,	Italy's republican constitution went into effect.
1949	May 11,	Israel admitted to the United Nations.
	September 12,	German Federal Republic began.
	October 1,	Communists proclaimed Chinese People's Republic.
1950	February 14,	Thirty-year agreement of Soviet Union and China.
	June 25,	Korean War began.
1951	July 16,	Leopold III of Belgium abdicated.
1952	February 6,	Succession of Queen Elizabeth II.
1953	July 27,	Korean armistice signed.
1954	July 21,	Indo-China armistice signed.

GUNS AT THEIR SHOULDERS. Above, girl members of Haganah hoe their crop while keeping themselves armed to resist Arab attack. This combination of farm work with guard duty became common practice in the Galilee area of the state of Israel.

ROUTING SNIPERS, HAIFA. Jewish fighters below are shown driving the last Arab forces from Haifa. A mass evacuation followed.

PREMIER DAVID BEN-GURION, right, under a portrait of Theodore Hertzl, the founder of Zionism announces the birth of the state of Israel.

CHAPTER 38

The Quest for Peace

From the attack on Pearl Harbor on December 7, 1941, to the surrender of Japan, August 14, 1945, there was substantial agreement among the United States, Great Britain, the Soviet Union, and China. During this period the Big Four co-operated in the joint task of destroying the military might of their Axis enemies. The goal was clear and its attainment was a matter of life and death. The essential requirements for unity and co-operation were thus present. Moreover, the military might of the Big Four was so great that the smaller powers did not question their right to make the main decisions. But with the collapse of the Axis powers the great bond which had held the Big Four in substantial unity was gone, and they were free to pursue their own policies without reference to a united war effort. As everyone with even a modest acquaintance with history expected, great differences soon arose among them.

• • •

The United States and Great Britain struggled against the Soviet Union for influence in Poland, Central Europe, and the Balkans. The collapse of German power in the region from Poland to Greece paved the way for a contest among the Great Powers for influence in this area. The struggle for power across Central Europe soon became the focal point of relations between Russia and the Western nations, and it produced the severest strain on their co-operation. For example, this rivalry was at the bottom of the

long and heated disputes over Trieste and the Italo-Yugoslav boundary, democratic governments and free elections in the liberated countries of Central Europe and the Balkans, and the control of the Danube and the Straits. The Soviet Union, rich in raw materials and inclined toward rigidly controlled foreign trade, concentrated its efforts on the extension of the areas over which it could maintain almost exclusive economic control. Britain, on the contrary, dependent on the outside world for food and raw materials, wished to open and enlarge trade lanes. This economic difference added much friction to Anglo-Soviet relations.

The Report issued at the end of the Yalta Conference contained a Declaration on Liberated Europe. The Declaration called for the establishment of provisional governments in the liberated states (Poland, Czechoslovakia, Yugoslavia, Greece) and former Axis satellites (Rumania, Bulgaria, Hungary) which would be broadly representative of all democratic elements in the population. After a provisional government was established in each of these countries, it was to hold free elections in which the voters could choose a government responsive to the will of the people. But the political situation in these countries was extremely complicated and the Soviet Union was bent on the creation and maintenance of governments that would remain completely loyal to it. Free elections, upon which Britain and the United States insisted, were almost certain to reduce the influence of the Communist elements. The Report also promised that Marshal Tito's regime in Yugoslavia would be broadened and that the Russian-supported Lublin Government of Poland would be reorganized to include democratic leaders from Poland itself and from the Polish Government-in-Exile in London. It would then be called the Polish Provisional Government of National Unity.

All through the spring of 1945 the United States and Great Britain pressed the Soviet Union to live up to the Yalta Agreement and broaden the base of the Lublin government in Poland. Sharp words were exchanged in May, 1945, when the fact came to light that the Soviet government had arrested sixteen Polish political leaders on the charge of "preparing diversionary acts in the rear of the Red Army." However, in June the Lublin regime was broadened to give some representation to the democratic groups in Poland and to the Polish Government-in-Exile in London. Shortly thereafter, Great Britain, the United States, and China recognized the new Polish Provisional government. On January 19, 1947, the Polish election was held and the Communist bloc won as was to be expected. Mikolajczyk, leader of the Peasant party, declared that the parties under Soviet influence had terrorized the opposition. The United States and Great Britain protested to the Polish government that the election obviously was not "free and unfettered." After its victory in the election, the Communist bloc stamped out all opposition from the Peasant party and Mikolajczyk fled to London.

Conditions in the other liberated states, except Greece, and in the former Axis satellite states roughly follow a pattern, although it took longer to complete the pattern in some of them. The pattern was: Soviet military occupation during the advance to Germany, Soviet backing for Communist parties, Communist acquisition of key posts in the cabinets —police, justice, defense—elimination of opposition leaders, control of the government, and the framing of new constitutions, modeled on that of the Soviet Union.

In 1946 in both Bulgaria and Rumania the Communist bloc won elections. In both the monarchy was abolished and replaced by a "people's republic." In 1948 the Communists won decisive victories in the elections in each country, and in Bulgaria the Communist Fatherland Front has been declared the only official party. Both countries have nationalized all business of any size and have redistributed land. On February 24, 1950, the United States froze the assets of Bulgarian and Rumanian citizens in the United States and broke off diplomatic relations with Bulgaria. In Yugoslavia Marshal Tito's Communist regime had Russian support from the beginning. However, on June 28, 1948, the Yugoslav Communist party was expelled from the Cominform because the Marshal held that the peasants are the bulwark of the Yugoslav state.

In Czechoslovakia and Hungary conditions were different for a short time. A broad coalition of parties governed in each state. In Czechoslovakia the coalition was under Klement Gottwald, a Communist. However, in February, 1948, the Communists carried out a coup d'état and in June proclaimed a Soviet-type constitution. The election in Hungary in 1945 gave the moderate parties a majority with the Smallholders party far in the lead. The Communists began to gain strength and in the spring of 1947 they forced the resignation of Premier Nagy. In the election which followed the Communists replaced the Smallholders as the chief party. Finally, in the spring of 1949 the Communists secured complete control and adopted a constitution for a "people's republic." In the meantime, Cardinal Mindszenty, for opposing the Communist regime, was arrested, "tried", and sentenced to life imprisonment.

Greece, hard hit by the German occupation, has been torn by civil strife between the Communists and Right Wing groups. Greece's strategic position with relation to the Straits, the Middle East, and the Mediterranean, has made it one of the focal points of Anglo-Soviet rivalry. Turkey's position has been about as difficult. Fear of the Soviet Union has led Turkey to retain its large military establishment so as not to be caught off guard. This is a heavy drain on its finances as well as its manpower and productive capacity. In the spring of 1947 the situation in Greece and Turkey became so critical that the government of the United States decided to give them substantial financial assistance in an effort to strengthen their hands in the face of Soviet pressure.

The first meeting of the Council of Foreign Ministers in London ended in a stalemate. At the Potsdam Conference (July 17-August 2, 1945) it was agreed that a Council of Foreign Ministers representing the United States, Great Britain, the Soviet Union, France, and China should be created to begin work on treaties of peace for Italy, Bulgaria, Rumania, Hungary, and Finland. From September 11 to October 2, 1945, the first meeting of the Council of Foreign Ministers was held in London. As the Foreign Ministers discussed the making of treaties, they discovered, as they had feared, that there were snags and bogs at every turn. The Soviet foreign minister, V. M. Molotov, was irked by the unwillingness of the Western powers to recognize the governments of Rumania and Bulgaria and was bent on bringing the region from the Baltic to the Mediterranean Sea into the Soviet zone of power. Consequently, he maneuvered stubbornly to strengthen the bargaining position of his country. Byrnes, Bevin, and Georges Bidault, the French foreign minister, hoping to check the flow of Soviet power westward, refused to give ground. Various issues were raised but the

clashes of opinion were so sharp that no headway could be made.

The matter which brought a complete stalemate, and apparently ended the conference, was Molotov's contention that neither France nor China should participate in the framing of these five treaties. Byrnes and Bevin finally agreed to limit the preliminary drafts of the treaties largely to the Big Three powers provided a general peace conference were held without delay in which all the nations that had fought the European Axis were represented. Molotov said that his government had not made up its mind about a general peace conference, and that he could not agree to it. With this deadlock concerning procedure unbroken, the meeting adjourned on October 2.

But the stalemate at London was a step forward in the sense that it enabled the Foreign Ministers to feel out one another and discover the major points of difference. They were then in a position to consider intelligently ways and means of reconciling in some fashion those differences. Through the autumn and early winter their deputies labored in London in an effort to eliminate difficulties in procedure and to loosen, at least, some of the other knots.

The second meeting of the Council of Foreign Ministers in Moscow (December 16-26, 1945) made important decisions. This meeting was, in general, harmonious. Bevin and Byrnes were prepared to make important concessions to Molotov, and the latter was willing to retreat slightly from the line that he had defended at London. At the very beginning of the meeting the Foreign Ministers agreed on the procedure for drafting the treaties with Germany's former satellites. China would not participate in the drafting of any of these treaties; France's participation would be limited to the treaty with Italy; and the treaty with Finland would

Official United Nations

UNITED NATIONS GENERAL ASSEMBLY IN LONDON. James F. Byrnes, Secretary of State and chairman of the United States delegation to the United Nations General Assembly, is shown addressing a plenary session.

be drawn by Great Britain and the Soviet Union alone. All the drafts would then be presented to a general peace conference to be called not later than May 1, 1946. The final wording of the treaties would be in the hands of the nations responsible for the tentative drafts.

The Moscow Conference also produced certain other important decisions. The Big Three powers agreed to establish a Far Eastern Commission and Allied Control Council for Japan; to recognize the governments of Bulgaria and Rumania as soon as they were made a little more representative of all the major political groups; and to recommend to the United Nations the creation of a Commission for the control of atomic energy. Thus the Moscow Conference pretty well cleared the ground for the real work of peace making. The Foreign Ministers' deputies began to grapple with the real problems just as the General Assembly of the United Nations met in London for its first session.

The first session of the United Nations **set up the machinery required by the Charter.** The Charter of the United Nations came into force on October 24, 1945. Toward the end of November the Preparatory Commission of the United Nations assembled in London to draft plans for the first session. The Commission had among its members several veterans of the League of Nations, and their experience with, and knowledge of, the rules for international bodies helped it to do its work well.

On January 10, 1946, the General Assembly of the United Nations opened its first session in London. The delegates of fifty-one nations were present, many of them among the world's outstanding political figures. In an address of welcome, Prime Minister Attlee declared that the United Nations should become the decisive factor in the domain of foreign policy, and that its ultimate goal should be world security and freedom based on justice and the moral law. The Assembly then elected Henri Spaak of Belgium president and turned to the work before it.

The main purpose of the first session was to set up the machinery provided for in the Charter, so that the whole United Nations organization could begin to function. This was a big task, but when the session ended, most of the machinery had been set up. After creating a General (Steering) Committee, the General Assembly tackled the job of bringing into existence the United Nations' most powerful organ, the Security Council. With a minimum of delay, the General Assembly elected Brazil, Egypt, Mexico, Poland, the Netherlands, and Australia as the six non-permanent members, and by the end of the first week the Security Council was ready to go to work. During the next month the Assembly, with the assistance of the Security Council, elected fifteen judges to the International Court of Justice, set up the Economic and Social Council and various specialized committees and agencies, approved the establishment of an Atomic Energy Commission, and elected Trygve Lie of Norway Secretary-General (he was succeeded in 1953 by Dag Hammarskjöld of Sweden). But it was not the birth of the United Nations' main agencies that caught world attention during the first general meeting. It was a series of explosions in the Security Council.

British and Soviet delegates in the Security Council clashed over the questions of Iran, Greece, and Indonesia. On January 19 the Iranian delegation charged the Soviet Union with undue interference in the internal affairs of its country and requested that the Security Council investigate the situation. Led by Andrei Vishinsky, deputy foreign minister, the Soviet delegation maneuvered brilliantly. Immediately the Ukrainian delegation charged that British forces in Indonesia created a "threat to the maintenance of international peace and security," and the Soviet delegation made a similar charge with regard to the presence of British soldiers in Greece. Ernest

Bevin heatedly denied that British forces in Greece and Indonesia in any way menaced international peace. He invited the Council to investigate and see for itself. On January 25 the Iranian, Greek, and Indonesian cases were placed on the Security Council's agenda. It was now obvious that stormy days lay ahead, and that the rivalry between the Soviet Union on one hand and the United States and Great Britain on the other hand would be reflected in the deliberations of the Security Council. This rivalry continued as a constant source of trouble.

The majority of the members of the Security Council apparently felt that the Soviet's introduction of the Greek and Indonesian questions into the discussion was an attempt to divert attention from the Iranian issue. The latter question was in a different class from the other two because the Iranian government brought the charge and continued to push it. Andrei Gromyko, Soviet delegate to the Security Council, and Vishinsky tried desperately to get Iran's complaint removed from the agenda. They failed in this, but on January 30, after three days of tense discussion, the Council agreed to postpone consideration of the Iranian complaint while the Soviet Union and Iran negotiated. However, the Council retained the right to ask for information at any time on the progress of negotiations and to return to the matter if negotiations failed to produce a satisfactory solution.

The questions of Greece and Indonesia occupied much of the Council's time until the close of the London session on February 17, 1946. On several occasions Bevin and Vishinsky clashed head on. Vishinsky accused Bevin of gross exaggeration and carelessness with facts, and Bevin told Vishinsky that his accusation was only more Moscow propaganda. The majority of the delegates agreed that there were no real grounds for action against

Britain, and the cases of Greece and Indonesia were soon dropped.

In New York the Security Council took up the Iranian and Spanish questions. When the Security Council reassembled (March 25, 1946) at Hunter College, New York, it immediately returned to the Iranian case. The chief point at issue now was the failure of the Soviet Union to withdraw its troops from Iran, in accordance with the terms of the Anglo-Soviet-Iranian treaty of June 29, 1942. Gromyko, speaking for the Soviet Union, asked that the case be stricken from the agenda. He said that negotiations were proceeding smoothly and that Soviet troops were withdrawing and would be out of Iranian territory in five or six weeks. But the Council voted nine to two to keep the case on the agenda. Gromyko then sought to get all discussion of the case deferred for a short time. Defeated again, Gromyko, amidst great tension, gathered his papers and strode from the Council room.

On April 8, a flood of light was thrown on the whole matter when the Iranian government published the text of an oil agreement with the Soviet Union. The agreement provided for the creation of a Russo-Persian oil company with the Soviet Union owning fifty-one per cent of the stock, the lease to run for fifty years. On May 24, 1946, the Iranian government announced that Soviet forces had evacuated Iranian soil, and this virtually ended the affair.

Meantime, Oscar Lange, the Polish representative, brought before the Security Council a question destined to trouble it for many months. On April 17 he made a long and detailed indictment of the Franco regime in Spain and declared that its activities were a menace to world peace. He said that, in view of this fact, the members of the United Nations should sever diplomatic relations with Franco. The Soviet, French, and Mexican delegates supported the Polish position, but the delegates of the other nations expressed the belief that Franco's government was not a menace to world peace and thus was not within the scope of the Charter. The matter was warmly debated, and a few days later a committee was set up to "determine whether the situation in Spain has led to international friction and does endanger international peace and security." A few weeks later this Committee reported its findings, but they were indecisive and the debate proceeded. No action, however, was taken. Several of the delegates pointed out that intervention in the internal affairs of a state was a grave matter, and that drastic action against Franco might precipitate a new civil war in Spain.

The third meeting of the Council of Foreign Ministers discussed problems involved in making peace treaties with former Axis satellite states. While the United Nations held its first meeting, the deputies of the Big Four Foreign Ministers worked on the treaties in London. On April 25, 1946, the Council of Foreign Ministers met in Paris for its third meeting. It opened in an atmosphere of cordiality, but when the ministers attempted to get at the heart of the questions on the agenda sharp cleavages appeared. Undaunted, they kept pressing forward, and when the meeting ended on May 16, 1946, they had discussed all the questions and had reached agreement on some points.

The sharpest disagreements were over the disposition of Trieste, the Julian March (the region lying north of Trieste), Italy's colonies, and reparations. Molotov immediately asked for the inclusion of the whole of Trieste and the Julian March in Yugoslavia, the Soviet Union's satellite, and insisted that the Soviet Union should hold the trusteeship over Tripolitania and have military bases in the Dodecanese Islands. These demands met determined opposition from Great Britain, the United States, and France. However, it was generally felt that Molotov was using the old diplomatic device of asking for far more than he expected to get in the hope of getting as much as he could.

There was a rather extended discussion of Italy's colonies and various conflicting proposals were made. Molotov soon announced that the Soviet Union would not press for the trusteeship over Tripolitania. He then proposed a rather complicated joint Big Four trusteeship for Italy's African territories with the Soviet Union holding the upper hand in the trusteeship for Tripolitania. But Molotov's counterproposal was firmly opposed by the other three Foreign Ministers and the deadlock on this issue remained to the end of the conference. Bidault, who played the role of mediator between the Soviet Union and the United States and Great Britain, insisted that Italy should hold the trusteeships under the United Nations.

On the question of reparations Molotov insisted that Italy should pay $300,000,000, two thirds of which was to go to Yugoslavia, Albania, and Greece. Byrnes called for a committee of experts to study Italy's capacity to pay. It was pointed out that the United States, Great Britain, and Canada had sent approximately a billion dollars in goods and direct aid to Italy since the armistice, and that, if the eastern powers collected reparations, Great Britain and the United States would in large measure pay them. It was finally agreed that Italy was to pay reparations, but there was no agreement on how they were to be paid. Moreover, it was decided to divide the bulk of Italy's fleet among the Allies, leaving Italy four cruisers and some smaller craft.

But the bitterest struggle of all revolved around the Italo-Yugoslav boundary. This was to be expected because for centuries nations had fought over the Julian area. Here the Adriatic reaches out toward Austria, Hungary, and the Middle Danube, and it contains two excellent ports—Trieste and Fiume. Across this key region successive waves of Italians, Teutons, and Slavs have clashed. Whether viewed from a political, economic, or racial angle, it presents extremely complex problems. For example, the bulk of the population of Trieste is Italian but its hinterland is predominantly Slav; it was built into a great city and port by Austria with a generous expenditure of capital, engineering skill, and labor. The Soviet Union fought hard to put Trieste into the hands of Yugoslavia, because of its importance to the trade and business of the whole Danubian basin which it hopes to dominate. The Four-Power Commission set up to report on the Italo-Yugoslav boundary failed to reach an agreement and drew four different boundary lines. This problem was debated off and on until the end of the Conference, but no decision was reached.

Meanwhile, many other problems were raised at the Conference. Byrnes and Bevin repeatedly tried to get Austria on the agenda, and on May 15, Byrnes called for the creation of a committee to study the more basic problems relative to Germany and to report at the next conference of Foreign Ministers. Byrnes also continued to press for a full peace conference at an early date. Bidault presented the French plan for the Ruhr and the Rhineland. It called for the Ruhr as a separate political area under international supervision with a large measure of self-government for the population. It asked for the inclusion of the Saar within the French economic system and for the permanent demilitarization of the Left Bank of the Rhine. When the Council of Foreign Ministers recessed on May 16, it had reached agreement on four issues: (1) the return of Transylvania to Rumania; (2) the inclusion of southern Dobruja in Bulgaria; (3) the alteration of the Italian armistice so as to give Italy control over her internal affairs; and (4) the principle that Italy was to pay reparations.

The fourth meeting of the Council of Foreign Ministers agreed on a peace conference and on the Italo-Yugoslav boundary. At the fourth meeting of the Council of Foreign Ministers in Paris (June 15-July 12, 1946) the range of discussion was extended. But despite the fact that the discussion was on a broader base than at any previous conference, the great debate revolved largely around two issues: the calling of a twenty-one nation peace conference and the Italo-Yugoslav boundary. From the very beginning of the meeting Byrnes and Bevin pressed for an early peace conference. Molotov insisted, but less vigorously than formerly, that there should be no peace conference until all important issues involved in the five treaties were settled.

Early in July, a tentative agreement on the Italo-Yugoslav boundary loomed, and Great Britain, the United States, and France agreed to $100,000,000 from Italy in goods and reparations for the Soviet Union. Molotov then consented to an early peace conference provided certain general rules of procedure were laid down by the Big Four. After bitter debate, it was agreed that general rules of procedure should be worked out as recommendations to the Conference. On July 9 the French government sent invitations to the twenty-one nations who had actively waged war against the Axis powers in Europe to send delegates to Paris for a general Peace Conference to open on July 29, 1946.

Meantime, the long deadlock over the Italo-Yugoslav boundary was broken largely by the compromise effort of the French. On June 29, Bidault submitted a proposal for the solution of the Trieste problems. The heart of this proposal was the international-

ization of Trieste and the adjoining territory for a period of years, to be administered by the Big Four, Italy, and Yugoslavia under the supervision of the Security Council. With slight modifications this plan was accepted. At the same time it was tentatively agreed that about six sevenths of the Julian March was to go to Yugoslavia and about one seventh to Italy. From a strictly ethnic point of view this was not too far from right. Among the other issues settled at this meeting of the Foreign Ministers were the transfer of the Dodecanese Islands to Greece, Italy's retention of the south Tyrol to the Brenner Pass; and the cession of the tiny area of Briga-Tenda (above Nice) to France.

The Paris Peace Conference considered the draft treaties with Italy and the four Axis satellite states. The Peace Conference which sat at Paris from July 29-October 15, 1946, to consider the draft treaties of peace with Italy, Hungary, Rumania, Bulgaria, and Finland was unique among gatherings of this sort because all it could do was discuss the draft treaties and recommend changes. The Council of Foreign Ministers still had the final word. But that did not mean that the influence of the Peace Conference was negligible. When the majority of the twenty-one nations represented at Paris approved an item, it had a much better chance of standing in the final text of the treaty.

At the opening session of the Peace Conference on July 29, Bidault, Foreign Minister of France, was elected President. As was expected, the twenty-one nations struggled for several days over matters of procedure. At the insistence of Molotov the Council of Foreign Ministers had recommended that a two-thirds majority be required to pass recommendations involving changes in the text of the draft treaties. The small nations made a desperate attempt to extend the authority of the Conference and thus prevent the great powers from controlling everything. Herbert Evatt of Australia, with the backing of the delegates from most of the smaller states, led the fight for a simple majority vote on all issues, and for representation of each nation on each of the main committees which were to be created to work on the chief problems. After several days of heated discussion, Bevin, with Byrnes' support, proposed that all recommendations which got a majority vote be submitted to the Council of Foreign Ministers. Though the Soviet bloc opposed this proposal, the Rules Committee approved it on August 8.

In a plenary session on August 9 the main rules for procedure were settled. It was agreed that the chairmanship of the Conference was to rotate among the Big Four; that the chairmen of the nine working committees (a Political Committee for each of the five treaties, an Italian Economic Committee, a Balkan Economic Committee, a Military Committee, and a Drafting Committee) were to be from the smaller nations; and that all recommendations passed by a simple majority go to the Council of Foreign Ministers for its consideration.

After matters of procedure had been settled, the Peace Conference turned its attention to the texts of the treaties. As the great controversial issues arose, the Conference became a sort of sounding board for world opinion and a mirror of the struggle between the Soviet Union and its satellites on the one side and the Western powers on the other. The nervous, wiry Byrnes and the formal, stubborn Molotov clashed repeatedly. Molotov denounced American capitalism and imperialism and charged that Great Britain and the United States were sponsoring the principle of equality because it fitted into their scheme to use their money to subjugate and strangle the smaller nations. Byrnes and Bevin pointed out that they were not asking for territory or reparations and that the Soviet Union had already incorporated several small nations into the Soviet Union and seemed bent on permanently subjugating several others. Such accusations as these, often irrelevant and designed to influence world opinion, not only slowed the work of the Conference but heightened tensions between the Eastern and Western groups of powers. But it was all part of the great struggle for position. Sometimes it went beyond the realm of debate. The Soviet Union gave material assistance to the Communist elements in Greece and put pressure on Turkey in the hope of getting concessions with regard to the Dardanelles, while the United States sent naval vessels into the Aegean.

During the course of the Peace Conference nearly every article of the draft treaties came up for general discussion. Several hundred amendments were offered, and often there were several amendments to a single clause. Of the score and more of major points which were warmly discussed, the ones that caused the most trouble were the Italo-Yugoslav boundary, the quantity and distribution of reparations, the Italian colonies, the control of commerce on the Danube, the Greco-Bulgarian boundary, and the control of the Straits. It will be noted that all these issues involved in one way or another the balancing of interests between East and West, and that, of course, is the reason why they were the big questions.

Though the Peace Conference was unable to resolve all the issues connected with Trieste and the Julian March, it succeeded in narrowing the area of disagreement. Various draft laws for the government of the Free Territory of Trieste were presented and discussed at length. It was immediately discovered that there were wide differences of opinion concerning the authority to be conferred upon the governor, who was to be appointed by the Security Council and responsible to it. The Soviet and Yugoslav drafts reduced the powers of the governor to a minimum and attempted to create a government in Trieste that would insure Yugoslav domination of it. The British, French, and United States drafts attempted to insure firm international control by giving wide powers, including the control of the police, to the governor. The details of the proposed plans for the government of the Free Territory were debated repeatedly over a period of about two months. An attempt on the part of the Italian and Yugoslav governments to solve the problem by direct negotiation failed. Finally, on October 3, the Italian Political Committee sat all night and adopted section by section the French draft of the laws for the government of the Free Territory. The vote on the controversial points was nearly always fourteen to six with the Soviets and their neighbors voting negatively. Near the end of the year 1946, the Council of Foreign Ministers completed the details of the government of the Free Territory of Trieste at their meeting in New York.

While the question of navigation on the Danube remained unsettled in detail, the Peace Conference broke a long standing deadlock on October 11 when it adopted by a two-thirds vote the French proposal for freedom of navigation under a system of international control. The Peace Conference also registered its opposition to the effort of the Soviet Union to give Bulgaria a port on the Aegean and to leave the control of the Straits to powers bordering on the Black Sea.

When the Council of Foreign Ministers met in New York in November, 1946, to put the five treaties in final form, it was clear that the Peace Conference had carried forward the work of peace making. Few issues were successfully reopened that were approved by a majority vote at Paris. But progress was painfully slow until Molotov and Byrnes loosened most of the remaining log-jams by means of a series of private talks. Though some issues were left to be settled later by commissions, the Foreign Ministers had the five treaties in well-nigh final shape by mid-December, 1946. These treaties were signed at Paris on February 10, 1947.

Italy and the satellite states lost territory and have to pay reparations. Italy ceded four small areas, including the Tenda and Briga districts to France, the Dodecanese islands to Greece, and the bulk of the Julian March and some small Adriatic islands to Yugoslavia, and renounced, pending a final settlement, all claims to her former African territories. The Free Territory of Trieste, with a free port within the city, was placed under the control of the Security Council to be administered in accordance with a Statute framed by the Four Foreign Ministers. The governor of the Free Territory was appointed by the Security Council and was responsible for the independence of the Free Territory.

Later the disputed Trieste area was divided into two zones. Zone A, occupied by British and American troops, included the city of Trieste and the northern sector. Zone B, occupied by Yugoslavian troops, was the southern sector. In 1954 an agreement was reached by which Italy got Zone A and Yugoslavia Zone B. This settlement supposedly strengthened the North Atlantic Treaty Organization. It did this by making possible military cooperation between Italy and the Balkan alliance of Yugoslavia, Greece, and Turkey. Yugoslavia has received economic aid from the United States.

In the Balkan treaties the territorial clauses followed pretty closely the arrangements made after the First World War. Transylvania was taken from Hungary and restored to Rumania. Bessarabia and Bukovina were transferred from Rumania to the Soviet Union. The Southern Dobruja went to Bulgaria.

Finland returned to the boundaries created in March, 1940, except that it ceded the Petsamo area to Russia, giving the latter a common border with Norway.

Reparations payments were imposed on each of the five countries. Italy was assessed $360,000,000, Finland, Hungary, and Rumania $300,000,000 each, and Bulgaria $70,-000,000. The Soviet Union got the bulk ($900,000,000) of these reparations payments. This served to give it a head start in its effort to become the dominant commercial power of this whole region.

The General Assembly of the United Nations has toiled in the interests of world peace. In 1954 the membership of the United Nations was 60. It was increased by the admission of these new members: Sweden, Iceland, Thailand, and Afghanistan (all in 1946); Yemen and Pakistan (1947); Burma (1948); Israel (1949); and Indonesia (1950). Since 1950 the cold war has prevented the admission of any more members. Soviet vetoes denied Italy and Japan membership in 1952. A Russian proposal to admit a block of 14 nations failed to pass.

Over the troublesome years since its creation, the General Assembly has worked hard to achieve beneficial results in three main fields: (1) the settlement of political controversies, (2) the improvement of UN methods, and (3) the creation of better social and economic conditions for mankind.

The first significant political dispute was referred to the General Assembly by the United States in the autumn of 1947. It resulted from the failure of the United States and the Soviet Union to agree on the creation of an independent Korean government. The General Assembly voted that an election should be held for a National Assembly to establish a Korean government, and sent a commission to observe the election. The Soviet-dominated northern zone denied the

Official United Nations

Afghanistan, Iceland, and Sweden are admitted to membership in the United Nations. United States Marines salute the flags of Sweden (left), Iceland (center), and Afghanistan which were raised for the first time on the grounds of the General Assembly's temporary headquarters at Flushing Meadows as representatives of the three new Member States of the United Nations took their places on the floor of the meeting hall.

commission admission and so the election could be held only in the southern zone. The elected National Assembly adopted a constitution setting up the new Republic of Korea in the southern zone. In 1948 the government was recognized by the United States and the General Assembly as the legal government of Korea. In the same year a "people's republic" was set up in North Korea, which contains about one-third of the country's people and a little more than one-half its area.

Another political dispute in which both the General Assembly and the Security Council took action was the controversy over aid rendered Communists in Greece by Albania, Bulgaria, and Yugoslavia. The General Assembly appointed a Balkan Commission to investigate charges that these three nations had aided Greek guerrilla forces. In 1948, on the basis of reports by the Commission, the Assembly concluded that aid had been rendered. The Assembly's action focused world

GENERAL ASSEMBLY OF THE UNITED NATIONS. This shows the New York City Building, at the old World's Fair grounds, Flushing Meadows, where the General Assembly of the United Nations convened on October 23, 1946.

attention on the Balkan situation. In the meantime, the Greek government outlawed the Communist party and arrested Communist leaders. In the election on March 5, 1950, the moderate parties of the center gained ground.

To help increase the effectiveness of the United Nations, the General Assembly in 1947 created an Interim Committee ("Little Assembly") to function when the larger body is not in session. All member nations are entitled to membership on it. It proved its value and was continued by the Third (1948) and Fourth (1949) Sessions of the Assembly.

It is well known that the veto power pos-

sessed by the permanent members of the Security Council has prevented action many times, especially on the admission of new members to the United Nations. In fact, the Soviet Union up to the winter of 1950 had used the veto more than 50 times. To facilitate action in the Council, the Assembly at its Third Session in Paris in 1948 made several recommendations on the use of the veto. It adopted a resolution, over Soviet objection, asking that the Security Council consider 35 different kinds of decisions as procedural matters and therefore not subject to veto. It recommended also that the veto not apply to the

GENERAL ASSEMBLY OF THE UNITED NATIONS. This view shows the meeting hall at the opening of the second part of the first session of the United Nations General Assembly.

admission of new members and to the peaceful settlement of disputes.

The General Assembly, working chiefly through the specialized agencies of the United Nations, has taken action to help better mankind's social and economic conditions. It approved the establishment of the International Refugee Organization, which in 1948 helped resettle 200,000 displaced persons. In the same year the World Health Organization vaccinated millions of children in Europe and Asia.

In 1948 the Assembly approved the Universal Declaration of Human Rights, a statement of rights which all peoples in all nations should enjoy. It also submitted to the member states a Convention on Genocide designed to help prevent deliberate mass killings of people on racial or religious grounds. The Fourth Session (1949) approved a program for technical assistance to underdeveloped areas. President Truman earlier in that year had stated his famous Point Four. The sum and substance of Point Four is that the United States must "embark on a bold new program for making the benefits of our scientific advances and industrial progress available for the improvement and growth of underdeveloped areas."

The United Nations Atomic Energy

Commission made recommendations for international control of atomic energy. On the day that the first atom bomb fell on Japan, President Truman declared that the bomb was "too dangerous to be let loose in a lawless world" and ways and means would have to be found for the international control of this new power. Since that day the question of the control of atomic power has been debated far and wide. The Atomic Energy Commission was created in January, 1946, by the United Nations, and on June 14 of that year it held its first meeting. Bernard Baruch, United States delegate on the Atomic Energy Commission, told the Commission that the United States would dispose of all of its atom bombs and share atomic secrets provided adequate safeguards against the use of the bomb in war were set up. The only hope, he insisted, in achieving this goal lay in the establishment of an international Atomic Authority "within the framework of the United Nations." He said that it should have complete control over the manufacture and use of atomic energy, be wholly free from any right of veto by any power in any circumstances, and be authorized to inflict severe punishment upon any nation found guilty of violating any agreement made for the control of atomic energy. Soviet statesmen did not like the system of international control set forth in Baruch's Plan. Shortly thereafter, the Soviet delegate on the Atomic Energy Commission presented a plan to the Commission which would place the system of international control "within the framework of the Security Council" and thus make it subject to veto.

After its creation in 1946 the United Nations Atomic Energy Committee (UNAEC) held hundreds of meetings. Two basic plans for international control of atomic energy were the subjects for discussion at these meetings. On November 4, 1948, the Third Session of the General Assembly approved the plan developed and supported by the majority of the UNAEC. The other plan was that developed and supported by the Soviet Union and its satellites. The United Nations reached a deadlock over these two plans, as a plan cannot be adopted without the approval of the Security Council, in which the veto can be used.

The plan approved by the majority of the General Assembly was based on proposals made by the United States to the UNAEC. It proposed: (1) the creation of an international control agency by the United Nations to own, operate, and manage all dangerous facilities for the production of atomic energy; (2) the control agency should have the unimpeded right to make inspections within the borders of any member nation; (3) the outlawry of the atomic bomb after the control agency was set up; (4) the use of the veto power on questions involving atomic energy should be banned.

The plan supported by the minority in the General Assembly and developed by the Soviet Union proposed: (1) the signing of two treaties at the same time; (2) the outlawry of the atomic bomb and the destruction of existing bombs by one treaty; (3) the setting up of an international control agency by the other treaty; (4) ownership and operation of all atomic facilities by individual nations with limited rights of inspection; (5) the right to use the veto power in the Security Council on questions involving atomic energy.

Because of the deadlock over these two plans, the UNAEC decided on July 29, 1949, to suspend further discussion until there was reasonable hope that an agreement could be reached. The UNAEC three years later was combined with another commission to form the Disarmaments Commission. This new commission has discussed all kinds of armaments including such devices as atomic and germ warfare. It has failed to reach any

The Atomic Energy Commission of the United Nations recommended in its First Report that an international authority be created to see to it that atomic energy be used only for peaceful purposes.

solutions, nor does it seem likely that any can be reached in a divided world beset with fear and tensions caused by Communist imperialism.

An atomic race developed. In September, 1949, President Truman said that he possessed evidence that an atomic explosion had taken place in the Soviet Union. A few months later the President ordered work on the production of the H-bomb, or hydrogen bomb, to proceed. At this time leading American physicists estimated that a hydrogen bomb would be so powerful that one bomb could destroy the largest city in the world. Malenkov, Stalin's successor, claimed in August, 1953, that Russian scientists had produced a hydrogen bomb. The United States Atomic Energy Commission had previously stated that experiments favorable to hydrogen bomb research had been conducted by it at Eniwetok Atoll in the Pacific. At the same time research in the development of guided missiles was being carried on in the United States and the Soviet Union. It has even been predicted that within ten years a guided missile loaded with a hydrogen warhead can be launched accurately on a target a distance of 5,000 miles away. After a million years on this earth man now faced the problem of controlling man-made forces that could destroy him and all he had created down through the centuries.

On the other hand, atomic power can be used for peaceful purposes. Atomic energy might be used to replace coal, oil, and water power. The use of atomic materials in medicine could prove to be a boon to mankind. President Eisenhower had these uses in mind in the winter of 1954 when he addressed the General Assembly of the United Nations. He asked other nations possessing atomic materials to release some of them into an international pool to be used for the benefit of mankind. He promised that the United States would contribute if other nations would do so. But other countries were slow to come forward and help to carry out his suggestion. To help safeguard the atomic materials and secrets of the United States, Congress had already (1946) passed the Atomic Energy Act. It provided the death penalty for anyone convicted of dealing in atomic weapons or atomic secrets with intent to harm the United States.

The United States financed the Marshall Plan. During the spring of 1947 American leaders debated the advisability of giving financial assistance to Greece and Turkey, partly in an effort to check Soviet power in those regions. On May 22, 1947, President Truman signed a bill which Congress had passed providing for $400,000,000 for aid to Greece and Turkey by July, 1948.

During the early summer of 1947 the so-called Marshall Plan became the chief focus of the struggle between the Eastern and Western groups of powers. On June 5, George C. Marshall, the Secretary of State of the United States, outlined a plan to promote European recovery. The Plan called upon the states of Europe to work out balance sheets of their resources and their needs, and tell the United States how it could best help Europe to help itself. The reaction of the nations of Western Europe to the Marshall Plan was overwhelmingly favorable, but the Soviet Union and its satellite states were cautious and critical. Molotov held that the Marshall Plan would involve too much interference in the internal affairs of other nations, and that the U.S.S.R. could not agree to it.

The governments of France and Great Britain then invited all the nations of Europe except the Soviet Union, Germany, and Spain to participate in a European confer-

ence. Sixteen nations immediately accepted the invitation, but eight nations, under the influence of the U.S.S.R., refused to participate. The Conference opened on July 12, 1947, and set up a series of committees to study and report on Europe's needs.

In September the Conference reported that it needed $19,300,000,000 in goods and money to carry out its four-year European Recovery Plan (ERP). In November President Truman asked a special session of Congress to authorize the spending over a four-year period of $17,000,000,000 to help carry out ERP. In December Congress appropriated nearly $600,000,000 for winter relief to France, Italy, and Austria and continued the discussion of the President's request into the regular session which began January 3, 1948. In April, 1948, Congress created an Economic Co-operative Administration and voted $5,-300,000,000 to finance ERP for the first year.

As Russia's answer to the Marshall Plan, Molotov continued his efforts to bind the states of Central and Eastern Europe closer to the Soviet Union. On October 5, 1947, representatives of the Communist parties of nine countries (the Soviet Union, its six satellites in Central and Eastern Europe, France, and Italy) at a conference in Warsaw announced the formation of the Communist Information Bureau (Cominform). Its declared purpose is the exchange of information among the Communist parties and co-ordination of their activities. However, many believe the Cominform is really a revival of the Comintern because its fundamental aim is world revolution and the destruction of the capitalist system.

The Marshall Plan continued until the end of 1951. During this time it spent about $12,-500,000. Its successor, the Mutual Security Agency, was given the duty of administering all foreign aid operations. Unquestionably, the foreign aid program assisted the economic recovery of the Western European nations. As their economic conditions improved, their peoples were disinclined to turn to Communism, and the Communist parties lost ground. In addition, American production and employment were stimulated as the United States government bought these billions of dollars' worth of goods for shipment abroad. American critics of the foreign aid program pointed out its high cost and complained that the recipients of the aid did not at times seem to be strong supporters of the United States.

The North Atlantic Treaty made the United States a member of a military alliance. Immediately after the Communist *coup d'état* in Czechoslovakia in February, 1948, representatives from the governments of Great Britain, France, Belgium, the Netherlands, and Luxemburg reached an agreement at Brussels. The chief object of the meeting at Brussels was to see what action could be taken to provide greater security for these nations. On March 17, 1948, these five nations signed the Brussels Pact. This treaty provided for a fifty-year military alliance. If any member of the alliance is attacked, the others are bound to come to its defense. Subsequently, the five powers, now known as the Western Union, made arrangements for military and naval co-operation.

Shortly after the signing of the Brussels Pact the United States and Canada entered into negotiations with Great Britain, France, Belgium, the Netherlands, and Luxemburg for the purpose of extending collective security to nations in the North Atlantic area. Iceland, Norway, Denmark, Portugal, and Italy were invited to participate in the negotiations. The discussions resulted in the drafting of the North Atlantic Treaty, which was signed in Washington on April 4, 1949. Later Greece and Turkey signed.

The North Atlantic Treaty created a twen-ty-year military alliance among its members. By its terms "an armed attack against one or more of them in Europe or North America shall be considered an attack against them all." Each member is pledged to come to the aid of any member that is attacked. The ratification of the North Atlantic Treaty by the United States Senate marked an historic departure from traditional American foreign policy. It was the first time in its history that the United States had entered into a treaty of alliance with foreign countries.

NATO and EDC were formed against Communist aggression. Preparations to enable the signers of the North Atlantic Treaty to back it up soon got under way as the North Atlantic Treaty Organization (NATO) was created. Its directing bodies were the North Atlantic Council, composed of the foreign ministers of the member nations, a defense committee, and a military committee. In 1949 Congress passed the Mutual Defense Assistance Act, which appropriated $1,000,000,000 to be spent in providing military equipment for member nations in need of it. Much larger sums were later made available. Other NATO members also increased their defense budgets.

In 1950 the North Atlantic Council decided to put all NATO forces under a supreme commander. General Dwight D. Eisenhower was appointed to the position and set up the Supreme Headquarters Allied Powers in Europe (SHAPE) near Paris in 1951. He commanded NATO forces for only about a year, when he resigned to engage in his successful campaign for President. Standardization of certain weapons for NATO forces was decided upon in 1952, the first year extensive maneuvers were carried out.

On May 27, 1952, a second step was taken to bolster the defense of Western Europe. A treaty was drawn up which laid the foundations of the European Defense Community

(EDC). EDC was to consist of France, West Germany, Italy, Belgium, the Netherlands, and Luxembourg. In 1954 France and Italy had not yet ratified the treaty, but the settlement of the Trieste problem and the Indo-China War raised hopes that they would.

Besides the strengthening of Western European defenses, the treaty had two other purposes. It allowed the rearmament of West Germany and was designed to help allay the fears of France and other nations over this rearmament. EDC was to have a European army which would be under the general command of NATO. The West German forces were limited to a peacetime strength of 410,000 men and the nation was forbidden to make aircraft, large warships, atomic and biological weapons.

Opposition to EDC arose in several countries. The Soviet Union protested. France dreaded a militarized Germany. In autumn, 1954, France, having refused to support EDC, agreed to participate in a Western European Union (an extension of the Brussels Pact) including West Germany and Italy. Britain was to maintain troops on the Continent, thus allaying French fears of the new German army.

The Japanese peace treaty is signed. After Japan had been defeated in the Second World War, it passed under military occupation. General MacArthur, Supreme Commander of the Allied Powers in the Pacific, commanded the occupation. Through his orders Japan was swiftly shorn of its imperial military system and its autocratic government. In March, 1946, a new democratic constitution was adopted, providing for parliamentary rule and universal suffrage. In 1947 the Security Council of the United Nations assigned the United States a trusteeship over the Carolines, Marshalls, and Marianas (except Guam).

On September 8, 1951, delegates from 49 nations at a conference in San Francisco signed a treaty of peace with Japan. The Treaty was largely the work of John Foster Dulles, who later became Secretary of State in the Eisenhower government. The Soviet Union, Poland, and Czechoslovakia refused to sign. The treaty (1) limits Japan to rule over her four main islands, (2) provides that the Ryukyu and Bonin islands are to be placed under UN trusteeships and that Japan give up title to Formosa, the Kurile Islands, and South Sakhalin, (3) states that Japan should pay reparations and that Japan will apply for membership in the UN.

At the same time the United States and Japan concluded a security treaty. The United States assumed the responsibility of maintaining armed forces in Japan to deter attack on that country. A mutual defense treaty was also made with the Republic of the Philippines and one with Australia and New Zealand known as ANZUS. These agreements along with the North Atlantic and Rio de Janeiro treaties commit the United States to the defense of widely separated countries all over the globe. They are the results of the position of world leadership and responsibility to which the United States has come since it entered on the path of world power after the Spanish-American War of 1898.

A peace contract with West Germany was signed. In Bonn, on May 26, 1952, the Allied powers of the West—Great Britain, France, the United States—and the Federal Republic of Germany (West Germany) signed a contract to end the state of war and remove the controls set up by the Occupation.

It was agreed that Allied troops could be retained in West Germany to protect that nation's security. Moreover, the Western Powers were free to bring in troops without consultation with the Federal Republic. The Allied Land Commissions and High Commission were abolished, and the occupation statute was repealed The Federal Republic was to become a partner in the European Community and to join EDC.

Among the terms of this agreement were the following: (1) Industries that had a great concentration of economic power and were considered a menace to peace were to be decentralized; (2) property removed from foreign countries by the Nazis was to be restored; (3) persons victimized by the Nazi regime were to receive compensation. It was agreed that Germany, of which the eastern part remained in the grip of the Soviet Union, was to be reunited by peaceful means. This last aim, however, was obviously a distant one. Conflicting ideologies and the power conflicts of great nations had wrought a breach that could be healed only by great concessions by several nations unless they chose to settle the problem by war.

A long war was waged in Indo-China. Indo-China is an area about the size of New England and with a population of about 27,000,000 in 1950. Its mineral resources include tin, tungsten, manganese, zinc, iron, and coal. It is rich in rice and rubber. During the last half of the nineteenth century the French got possession of this large area in Southeastern Asia. During the Second World War the Japanese occupied this part of the French colonial empire.

During and immediately after the Second World War, the forces of nationalism already aroused by French misrule and stimulated by anti-colonial voices throughout Asia, grew stronger. The French tried to resume their former control after the Japanese left. They then found they had to deal with nationalist groups that had come into existence.

One of these in northern Vietnam was led by Ho Chi Minh, tutored in Moscow and founder of the Indochinese Communist party. In 1946 Ho led an attack on the French at Hanoi, thus beginning a war which lasted for more than seven years. Vietnam was divided into two parts. Northern Vietnam became known as Vietminh under the leadership of Ho, supported by Communist China and the Soviet Union. The remainder was recognized by the French as the State of Vietnam with Bao Dai, who spent most of his time on the French Riviera in pleasure, as titular head. France recognized native governments in Laos and Cambodia, which, with Vietnam, comprised the Associated States of Indo-China in the French Union. This arrangement did not completely satisfy these three states, who wanted their independence.

The French with great difficulty tried to combat Ho's guerrilla tactics and sent some of their best troops to Indo-China. Beginning in 1951 the United States furnished war supplies to the French which finally amounted to a value of about $2,000,000,000. Secretary of State Dulles tried to get support for collective action in behalf of the hard-pressed French. He was unable to succeed. The French people were getting weary of the war, the free countries of Asia favored an independent Indo-China, the British looked toward a truce, and many Americans feared taking any action which might embroil American troops again in a war on the mainland of Asia, after the bloodshed in Korea.

On May 7, 1954, Ho's Vietminh forces, aided by heavy artillery supplied by Communist China, captured the French stronghold of Dienbienphu and its defenders. The rich Red River delta leading to the cities of Hanoi and Haiphong were now open to the Communists. The French cabinet fell and a new one pledged to ending the Indo-China War was formed with Pierre Mendès-France as premier.

At Geneva on July 21, 1954, truce agreements worked out by Mendès-France; Molotov, foreign minister of the Soviet Union; and Chou En-lai, foreign minister of Communist China, were signed. The United States did not sign the truce agreements with France, the Associated States, Vietminh, the Soviet Union, Communist China, and Great Britain. Instead it issued a separate document in which it said, in effect, that the United States accepted the terms without approving them.

The terms of the truce were a victory for Ho Chi Minh and his Chinese and Russian supporters. Vietminh got all of what had been Vietnam north of the 17th parallel, an easily defended area containing about 12,-000,000 people. This region contains the cities of Hanoi and Haiphong, a major commercial port. It raises sufficient foodstuffs to feed this population with a surplus for export, and it mines abundant mineral resources. The Communists also stood a good chance of gaining control of all of Vietnam by winning the election, which, within two years, would determine the central government of Vietnam.

What the future holds for the rest of Southeast Asia cannot be predicted with any certainty. At any rate for the first time in twenty-three years the world was free of a fighting war, even though the cold war would doubtless continue. Sir Winston Churchill had already spoken of a "real good try" for "peaceful co-existence." President Eisenhower said that he was "glad that agreement had been reached at Geneva to stop bloodshed in Indo-China," but "any renewal of Communist aggression would be viewed by us as a matter of grave concern." The United States had previously proposed the formation of a Southeast Asia Treaty Organization (SATO) to resist further Communist aggression in that region.

SUMMARY

The quest for peace in the postwar years has made headway despite the conflicting aims of the great powers. Early in 1946 nearly all of the basic organs of the United Nations began functioning. Since then the General Assembly and Security Council have discussed some of the most crucial issues of the time, including the control of atomic energy, the reduction and regulation of armaments, the Franco regime in Spain, and the fate of Palestine. But to date the United Nations' accomplishments are meager and it has yet to prove itself equal to its great task.

In the autumn of 1945 the Council of Foreign Ministers tackled the problem of treaties of peace with Italy, Finland, Hungary, Bulgaria, and Rumania. After approximately sixteen months of work the Council of Foreign Ministers completed these treaties and they were signed in Paris on February 10, 1947.

From March 10 to April 24, 1947, the Council of Foreign Ministers worked in Moscow on the German and Austrian treaties. However they reached few agreements.

The rivalry between the Soviet Union on one hand and the United States on the other continues unabated. The Marshall Plan, NATO, and EDC resulted from this rivalry and fear. The Korean War and Communist aggression in Indo-China were Soviet-sponsored. But it must be remembered that our world is made up of many peoples with deep-seated rivalries, varying modes of conduct, and differing forms of government. In the domain of international life we must take the long view and not expect too much too soon. Generations of patient and intelligent effort will be required to build a world in which men can have full confidence in the force of law.

SUMMARY OF PART XII

As the devasting Second World War was drawing to a close, the nations that were about to emerge victorious took up the age-old quest for peace. At the San Francisco Conference in 1945 they launched the United Nations, on which rests the hopes of mankind for peace in the future. Other conferences during and after the war created organizations for international economic and cultural co-operation and for the relief of distressed peoples.

After the war ended, the nations that had been engaged in it attempted to straighten out the political, economic, and social chaos which the war had caused. To enable the peoples to return to normal life, tremendous political and economic problems had to be solved. Several changes in government have been made. In Great Britain the Labor party displaced the Conservative party and was later displaced in its turn; in France the Fourth French Republic was created; in Italy a republican government has replaced the monarchy. Germany and Austria have been divided into zones of occupation by the United States, the Soviet Union, Great Britain, and France. Economic recovery in all the war-torn countries of Europe has been severely hindered by lack of machinery, shortages of materials, inflation, and black markets. In China civil war between Nationalists and Communists resulted in a Communist victory.

The relations between nations have been beset with grave difficulties. The organs of the United Nations have been set up and they have made some achievements. However, the United Nations has not been able to make a plan for the control of atomic energy which would be acceptable to the United States and the Soviet Union. Furthermore, the United Nations has become more and more an arena for diplomatic struggles between the Soviet Union and its satellites on one side, and the United States, Great Britain, and their supporters on the other. Peace treaties have been made with Finland, Italy, Japan, and the defeated Balkan countries, but the baffling and perplexing problems involved in making peace with Germany and Austria have not been solved at the present writing. Great Britain has granted independence to India, but the attainment of independence has been marked by pillage and massacre. Spain is still under the control of Franco and his totalitarian system. But in Japan, with American aid, democracy seems to be gaining.

A view of the world today, therefore, discloses that many nations face complex internal problems as they attempt to recover from the effects of the war. The problems involved in the relations among nations are even more complex and difficult to solve. Everywhere an enlightened public opinion is needed for their successful solution. On their solution depends the peace, prosperity, and happiness of all mankind.

EVENTS THAT TOOK PLACE AT ABOUT THE SAME TIME (Cont.)

Year		Events
1945	September 11-October 2,	First meeting of the Council of Foreign Ministers in London.
	October 24,	Charter of United Nations ratified by required number of nations.
	December 16-26,	Second meeting of the Council of Foreign Ministers held in Moscow.
1946	January 10-February 17,	United Nations General Assembly held its first session in London.
	January 17-February 17,	Security Council held its first session in London.
	March 25,	Security Council began second session at Hunter College, New York.
	April 25-May 16,	Third meeting of the Council of Foreign Ministers held in Paris.
	May 24,	Government of Iran announced that Soviet forces had withdrawn from Iran.
	June 15-July 12,	Fourth meeting of the Council of Foreign Ministers held in Paris.
	July 29-October 15,	Paris Peace Conference discussed peace treaties with Italy and the Axis satellite states.
	October 23-December 16,	United Nations General Assembly in session at Lake Success, New York.
	November 4-December 12,	Fifth meeting of the Council of Foreign Ministers held in New York.
1947	February 10,	Treaties with Italy and the Axis satellite states signed in Paris.
	March 4,	Treaty providing for an Anglo-French alliance signed by Bevin and Bidault.
	May 22,	President Truman signed bill providing $400,000,000 to aid Greece and Turkey.
	September 16,	European Economic Conference asks for $19,300,000,-000 to help carry out ERP.
1948	February 23,	Communists completed *coup d'état* in Czechoslovakia.
	March 17,	Brussels Pact signed by twelve nations.
	June 28,	Cominform expelled Yugoslav Communist party.
1949	February 8,	Cardinal Mindszenty given life sentence.
	April 4,	North Atlantic Treaty signed.
	September 23,	President Truman announced atomic explosion in Soviet Union.
	September 28,	Congress voted military aid to European members of North Atlantic Pact.
1950	January 31,	President Truman said United States would work on production of an H-bomb.
	June 25,	South Korea invaded by North Korean troops.

EVENTS THAT TOOK PLACE AT ABOUT THE SAME TIME (Cont.)

YEAR		EVENTS
1951	July 23,	NATO headquarters officially opened.
	September 8,	Japanese peace treaty signed.
1952	April 29,	ANZUS founded.
	May 26,	Peace contract signed with West Germany.
	May 27,	European Defense Community founded.
	November 2,	Eisenhower elected President.
1953	March 5,	Malenkov succeeded Stalin.
	July 27,	Korean War truce signed.
1954	July 21,	Indo-China truce signed.
1955	April 6,	Anthony Eden became British Prime Minister on retirement of Winston Churchill.
	April 15,	29 Asian and African nations opened Bandung Conference.
	April 18,	Albert Einstein died.
	May 5,	West Germany achieved sovereignty with NATO membership as Paris Treaties took effect.
	May 15,	Sovereignty was restored to Austria.
	August 8,	United Nations World Conference on Atomic Energy opened in Geneva.
	September 19,	Péron rule in Argentina ended by military revolt.
1956	July 26,	Egypt seized Suez Canal.
	August 23,	18 nations agreed on approach on internationalizing Suez Canal.
	September 9,	Egypt rejected international control of Suez Canal.
	October 26,	82 nations signed charter for "atoms-for-peace" organization.
	October 29,	Israel launched major attack into Egypt's Sinai peninsula.
	October 31,	Britain and France attacked Egypt by air preliminary to invasion.
	November 1,	Hungary renounced Warsaw Pact with Russia and asked United Nations protection for neutrality.
	November 4,	Britain and France invaded Egypt. Soviet Russia opened all-out attack to crush Hungarian revolt.
	November 6,	Britain and France ordered cease-fire in Egypt. Dwight D. Eisenhower re-elected President of United States.
	November 15,	First contingents of United Nations Emergency Force arrived in Suez area.
	December 22,	British and French troops began complete withdrawal from Egypt.

EVENTS THAT TOOK PLACE AT ABOUT THE SAME TIME (Cont.)

YEAR		EVENTS
1957	March 12,	United Nations Emergency Force began final take-over in Egyptian areas seized by Israel.
	March 29,	Suez Canal reopened to traffic under Egyptian control.
	July 1,	International Geophysical Year for study of earth began.
	October 4,	Russia launched the first earth satellite called Sputnik I—184 pound sphere.
	November 3,	Russia launched second earth satellite (carrying a dog) called Sputnik II—1120 pound cylinder.
1958	January 22,	Pérez Jiménez government in Venezuela overthrown.
	January 31,	United States launched successfully its first earth satellite, called Explorer—30.8 pound cylinder.
	February 5,	Union of Egypt and Syria ratified—called United Arab Republic.
	February 14,	Proclamation of new union of Iraq and Jordan—called Arab Federation.

INDEX

(All references to pages 1-422 are in Volume I)